DISTRIBUTED DATABASE MANAGEMENT SYSTEMS

T0335496

Press Operating Committee

Chair
Linda Shafer
former Director, Software Quality Institute
The University of Texas at Austin

Editor-in-Chief
Alan Clements
Professor
University of Teesside

Board Members

Mark J. Christensen, *Independent Consultant*
James W. Cortada, *IBM Institute for Business Value*
Richard E. (Dick) Fairley, *Founder and Principal Associate, Software Engineering Management Associates (SEMA)*
Phillip Laplante, *Professor of Software Engineering, Penn State University*
Evan Butterfield, *Director of Products and Services*
Kate Guillemette, *Product Development Editor, CS Press*

IEEE Computer Society Publications
The world-renowned IEEE Computer Society publishes, promotes, and distributes a wide variety of
authoritative computer science and engineering texts. These books are available from most retail outlets.
Visit the CS Store at *http://computer.org/store* for a list of products.

IEEE Computer Society / Wiley Partnership
The IEEE Computer Society and Wiley partnership allows the CS Press authored book program to
produce a number of exciting new titles in areas of computer science, computing and networking with a
special focus on software engineering. IEEE Computer Society members continue to receive a 15%
discount on these titles when purchased through Wiley or at wiley.com/ieeecs.

To submit questions about the program or send proposals please e-mail kguillemette@computer.org or
write to Books, IEEE Computer Society, 10662 Los Vaqueros Circle, Los Alamitos, CA 90720-1314.
Telephone +1-714-816-2169.

Additional information regarding the Computer Society authored book program can also be
accessed from our web site at *http://computer.org/cspress.*

DISTRIBUTED DATABASE MANAGEMENT SYSTEMS

A Practical Approach

SAEED K. RAHIMI
University of St. Thomas

FRANK S. HAUG
University of St. Thomas

A JOHN WILEY & SONS, INC., PUBLICATION

All marks are the properties of their respective owners.

IBM® and DB2® are registered trademarks of IBM.

JBoss®, Red Hat®, and all JBoss-based trademarks are trademarks or registered trademarks of Red Hat, Inc. in the United States and other countries.

Linux® is a registered trademark of Linus Torvalds.

Access®, ActiveX®, Excel®, MS®, Microsoft®, MS-DOS®, Microsoft Windows®, SQL Server®, Visual Basic®, Visual C#®, Visual C++®, Visual Studio®, Windows 2000®, Windows NT®, Windows Server®, Windows Vista®, Windows XP®, Windows 7, and Windows® are either registered trademarks or trademarks of Microsoft Corporation in the United States and/or other countries.

Oracle® is a registered trademark of Oracle Corporation.

Sun®, Java®, and all Java-based marks are trademarks or registered trademarks of Sun Microsystems, Inc. in the United States and other countries.

Sybase® is a registered trademark of Sybase, Inc.

UNIX® is a registered trademark of The Open Group.

Copyright © 2010 by IEEE Computer Society. All rights reserved.

Published by John Wiley & Sons, Inc., Hoboken, New Jersey.
Published simultaneously in Canada.

No part of this publication may be reproduced, stored in a retrieval system, or transmitted in any form or by any means, electronic, mechanical, photocopying, recording, scanning, or otherwise, except as permitted under Section 107 or 108 of the 1976 United States Copyright Act, without either the prior written permission of the Publisher, or authorization through payment of the appropriate per-copy fee to the Copyright Clearance Center, Inc., 222 Rosewood Drive, Danvers, MA 01923, 978-750-8400, fax 978-646-8600, or on the web at www.copyright.com. Requests to the Publisher for permission should be addressed to the Permissions Department, John Wiley & Sons, Inc., 111 River Street, Hoboken, NJ 07030, (201) 748-6011, fax (201) 748-6008.

Limit of Liability/Disclaimer of Warranty: While the publisher and author have used their best efforts in preparing this book, they make no representations or warranties with respect to the accuracy or completeness of the contents of this book and specifically disclaim any implied warranties of merchantability or fitness for a particular purpose. No warranty may be created or extended by sales representatives or written sales materials. The advice and strategies contained herein may not be suitable for your situation. You should consult with a professional where appropriate. Neither the publisher nor author shall be liable for any loss of profit or any other commercial damages, including but not limited to special, incidental, consequential, or other damages.

For general information on our other products and services please contact our Customer Care Department within the U.S. at 877-762-2974, outside the U.S. at 317-572-3993 or fax 317-572-4002.

Wiley also publishes its books in a variety of electronic formats. Some content that appears in print, however, may not be available in electronic format.

Library of Congress Cataloging-in-Publication Data is available.

ISBN 978-0-470-40745-5

10 9 8 7 6 5 4 3 2 1

To my mother, Behjat, and my father, Mohammad—though they were not given the opportunity to attend or finish school, they did everything they could to make sure that all of their seven children obtained college degrees.
S. K. R.

To my mother who taught me to love reading, learning, and books; my father who taught me to love mathematics, science, and computers; and the rest of my family who put up with me while we wrote this book —this would not have been possible without you.
F. S. H.

CONTENTS

9 DDBE Security   **357**

By Bradley S. Rubin

10 Data Modeling Overview   **383**

PREFACE

A centralized **database management system (DBMS)** is a complex software program that allows an enterprise to control its data on a single machine. In the past two decades, there have been many mergers and acquisitions, which have resulted in organizations owning more than one DBMS. Not all of these systems came from the same vendor. For example, it is common for an enterprise to own a mainframe database that is controlled by IBM DB2 and a few other smaller workgroup (or departmental) databases controlled by Oracle, Microsoft SQL Server, Sybase, or other vendors. Most of the time, users need to access their own workgroup database. Yet, sometimes, users need to access data in some other workgroup's database, or even in the larger, enterprise-level database. The need to share data that is dispersed across an enterprise cannot be satisfied by centralized DBMS software. To address this requirement, a new breed of software to manage dispersed (or distributed data) called a **distributed database management system (DDBMS)** is required.

A DDBMS maintains and manages data across multiple computers. A DDBMS can be thought of as a collection of multiple, separate DBMSs, each running on a separate computer, and utilizing some communication facility to coordinate their activities in providing shared access to the enterprise data. The fact that data is dispersed across different computers and controlled by different DBMS products is completely hidden from the users. Users of such a system will access and use data as if the data were locally available and controlled by a single DBMS.

This book addresses the issues in design and development of a DDBMS. In the chapters that follow we will address the issues involved in developing such a system and outline different approaches for solving these problems. We will also present two Java-based frameworks and one Microsoft .NET-based framework that provide the underlying structure needed to develop a DDBMS.

ACCOMPANYING WEBSITE

The official website for this book (www.computer.org/Rahimi_Haug) contains important information for the book, such as links to the starter kit software bundles for all three starter kits (JMS-SKIT, J2EE-SKIT, and DNET-SKIT), error corrections from the text, and any updates to the source code, book content, or starter kits.

STRUCTURE OF THE BOOK

This book has been organized into 3 distinct units. Unit 1 addresses distributed database theory. These chapters explore the issues with various aspects of a distributed database system and discuss the various techniques and mechanisms that are available to address these issues. Unit 2 (Chapters 10 through 14) focuses on the "state of the practice" for distributed databases. The initial chapters in this unit present a general data modeling overview and discuss several data modeling alternatives. The later chapters focus on the architectural requirements and present architectural alternatives including the traditional, top–down design of a homogenous distributed database, the bottom–up design of a heterogeneous federated database, and two new, nontraditional architectural approaches that focus on environments with more dynamic deployment characteristics. Unit 3 (Chapters 15 through 19) focuses on distributed database implementation. The chapters in this unit examine three platforms suitable for distributed database development. Three starter kits are discussed, along with the platforms on which they are built. The platforms discussed include the Java Message Service (JMS), the Java 2 Enterprise Edition (J2EE), and the Microsoft .NET Framework.

Unit 1: Theory

In order to design and ultimately build a DDBMS, we must first understand what a distributed database is, what a DDBMS does, and the issues it must overcome. First, this unit provides an overview of the DDBMS and its required functionality. Then, it examines each major subset in detail. By examining both the "big picture" and the "little details," this unit lays the theoretical foundation for understanding the internal processing of the DDBMS.

Unit 2: State of the Practice

Because most practitioners will probably not have the luxury of designing a distributed database environment (DDBE) completely from scratch, this unit examines the architectural alternatives (and issues) that a practitioner will likely encounter in the real world. First, we review the differences between conceptual, logical, and physical data models. Then, this unit focuses on several logical data modeling alternatives (along with some practical physical considerations) used "in practice" in the real world today. In order to address the "state of the practice," this unit explores four (two traditional and two alternative) DDBE architectures that are designed to be used in an environment with existing DBMS implementations. Then the general requirements for any platform capable of implementing a DDBE architectural alternative (including those that are yet-to-be-invented by the reader) are explored.

Unit 3: Implementation

Because architectures are large, complicated designs, even the "little details" discussed in them can seem "miles above the ground" compared to the more "down to earth" considerations that need to be addressed when attempting to create an actual implementation. Recent advances in software development have made it much easier to implement complex, distributed applications. In fact, there are multiple alternatives to choose from when selecting the platform, development, and deployment details. These alternatives all have various facilities to support distributed application development and deployment. In order for a practitioner to become proficient in any particular alternative, they need to make a substantial investment of time, effort, and perhaps money as well. Therefore, in the real world there are several alternatives to choose from, but there are also strong pressures to use a particular general approach, or even a particular, specific alternative. Having said that, we must recognize that there are no alternatives specifically targeted at DDBE implementation. This unit attempts to alleviate some of the confusion and provide a concrete place to start development of a real DDBE. This unit examines three implementation alternatives in detail and then for each of the three alternatives, this unit provides a detailed overview and an extensible framework, called a starter kit (SKIT). Each SKIT is discussed in detail. An example extension is presented to demonstrate how the SKIT can be used as the starting point for a real DDBE project implementation.

CHAPTERS OF THE BOOK

This book consists of 19 chapters as outlined below.

Chapter 1: Introduction

There are two fundamental types of architecture suitable for implementing a database management system (DBMS). The most well-known and ubiquitous architectural type is called the Centralized DBMS architecture. It is very well defined, very mature, and so common that, when the "Centralized" part of the name is omitted and the term "DBMS architecture" is used, this architecture is assumed by default. The other architectural type is not as common, not as mature, and not as well defined; it is called the Distributed DBMS (DDBMS) architecture. In this introductory chapter, we describe both architectural types and then compare and contrast them. Chapter 1 discusses the strengths and weaknesses of each and motivates the reader to understand which architecture is most appropriate for his/her situation. This chapter also examines different implementation alternatives for distributed query execution, and analyzes master–slave and triangular distributed execution control mechanisms. How to calculate the communication costs for each execution alternative using two examples is also explained.

Chapter 2: Data Distribution Alternatives

This chapter studies and compares different data distribution design alternatives for a distributed database management system. We analyze fragmentation alternatives—specifically, horizontal, vertical, and hybrid fragmentation. We discuss the impact of supporting data replication and consider data placement issues. The correctness criteria for each of these approaches will also be outlined. We explain how a DDBMS provides fragmentation, location, and distribution transparencies and also discuss how to design a global data dictionary to support these transparencies. We present some examples of different distribution designs and use them to illustrate the impact of different data distribution transparencies on user queries.

Chapter 3: Database Control

This chapter focuses on the issues related to security and semantic integrity control of centralized and distributed database systems. If not controlled, the integrity of a database is jeopardized when the database is exposed to concurrent transactions. One of the most fundamental reasons for using transactions is to preserve the integrity of the data; therefore, both centralized and distributed semantic integrity issues are presented and discussed. We consider how to leverage the semantic integrity control mechanisms in our local (centralized) database management systems when implementing distributed integrity control and discuss the impact of data distribution on the distributed and local enforcement implementation. We examine four implementation alternatives for implementing semantic integrity enforcement and evaluate the advantages and disadvantages of each and present a mechanism for analyzing the costs associated with enforcing semantic integrity in a distributed system by focusing on the number of messages required for different implementation alternatives.

Chapter 4: Query Optimization

In a centralized system query optimization is either rule-based or cost-based. Regardless of the approach to optimization in a centralized system, the main object of the query optimizer is to minimize response time for the query. The cost components of query optimization are CPU time and disk access time. It turns out that disk access time is the dominant factor in the cost of the query. As such, most query optimizers focus on minimizing the number of disk I/Os and therefore minimizing the disk access time. This chapter will focus on processing queries in a distributed database management system. We extend the concept of query processing in a centralized system to incorporate distribution. In a distributed database management system, the cost components of a query processing time are local CPU time, local disk access time for all servers involved in the query, and the communication cost required for synchronization of these servers activities. Because the communication cost is the dominant cost factor in a distributed query, distributed query optimization needs to focus on minimizing this cost. We discuss optimization alternatives for distributed queries that focus on reducing the number of messages required to execute a query in a distributed system. To minimize the communication cost, one needs to make sure that the system has an optimized distribution design and that the proper allocation of information to different database servers has been made. It has been shown that to solve this problem considering all factors involved is an NP-hard problem. Therefore, the goal is to solve the problem not in an optimal fashion but close to it.

Chapter 5: Controlling Concurrency

This chapter covers the concurrency issues in a distributed database management system. We start by defining what a transaction is and the properties that a transaction must satisfy in a database management system and then review concurrency control alternatives for a centralized database management system and outline two classes of concurrency control algorithms (pessimistic and optimistic). We analyze how these alternatives are changed to accommodate the needs of a distributed database management system concurrency control. Because each class of algorithms can be implemented using either locks or timestamps, we will evaluate the advantages and disadvantages for both locking-based and timestamp-based implementations of concurrency control algorithms. Most concurrency control approaches use locking as the main mechanism for providing isolation.

Chapter 6: Deadlock Handling

When locks are used, transactions that concurrently run in the system may get into a deadlocked state. A deadlock is defined as a state of the system where two or more transactions are stuck in an infinite waiting cycle. This means that each transaction in the cycle is holding one or more locks and waiting to obtain another lock that is currently being held by one of the other transactions in the cycle. Because each transaction does not release the locks it is holding, all transactions will wait indefinitely. This chapter discusses the three classical approaches for dealing with the deadlock problems in a centralized system: namely, deadlock prevention, deadlock avoidance, and deadlock detection and how these approaches can be used within a distributed database management system, as well as the advantages and disadvantages of each approach. It explains the use of preacquisition of all locks for deadlock prevention approaches and discusses how the wait–die and wound–wait algorithms provide for deadlock avoidance. A centralized and a distributed deadlock detection and removal approach is also presented.

Chapter 7: Replication Control

Replicating a table or fragment can improve the availability, reliability, and resiliency of our data (as discussed in Chapter 2) and can greatly improve the performance of our system (especially with respect to query optimization as discussed in Chapter 4). Unfortunately, environments with replication also have more complicated modification issues. This chapter discusses the effect of replication in a distributed database management system. We focus on replication control, which is the techniques we use to ensure mutual consistency and synchronization across all replicated tables and table fragments. Controlling replication is an issue specific to distributed database management systems. There are many alternatives to controlling replication in a DDBMS environment, which we categorize as asynchronous or synchronous replication control algorithms. We discuss the Unanimous, Primary-Copy, Distributed, Voting-Based, Quorum-Based, and Token-Passing-Based replication control algorithms.

Chapter 8: Failure and Commit Protocols

A DBMS must guarantee that the contents of a database are maintained consistent even when failures are present in the system. This chapter discusses fault tolerance in a DBMS, which deals with transaction failures, power failures, and computer hardware failures. We examine the commit protocols that are used by a DDBMS to provide for such a guarantee discuss how the DDBMS determines whether a particular transaction is safe to commit or not. Also examineed is how the DBMS fault tolerance mechanism aborts the transaction when it is unsafe, and how the system commits the transaction when all modifications of a transaction have been successfully written to the log. In a centralized system, the log manager is responsible for working with the transaction manager to correctly implement the commit protocols. In a distributed system, on the other hand, multiple DBMS servers need to coordinate their activities to make sure that a global transaction can successfully commit or abort at all DBMS sites where the transaction has made some changes. Therefore, we discuss how the DDBMS implements distributed commit protocols examine alternative distributed commit protocols such as two-phase and three-phase commits. One of the most difficult failures in a distributed system is network partitioning (when a set of computers are networked together but they are isolated from another set of computers that are interconnected). When network partitioning happens, there is a danger that computers in each partition unilaterally decide to commit or abort the transaction. If the two partitions do not decide on the same action (either both committing or both aborting the transaction), the integrity of the database will be lost. Therefore, we also examine a quorum-based commit protocol that deals with network partitioning.

Chapter 9: DDBE Security

This chapter discusses the security issues, including authentication, authorization, encryption, and programming techniques for improving data privacy and security in a distributed database environment (DDBE). Since communication is the basis for cooperating database servers in a DDBE, we have to make sure that server communication and user access to data are secure; therefore, we examine private-key and public-key security approaches discuss Secure Sockets Layer (SSL) and Transport Layer Security (TLS) and explain how certificates of authority are used in a distributed database system for components and applications (including web-based applications). We also consider "tunneling" approaches including Virtual Private Network (VPN) and Secure Shell (SSH) and discuss their potential role in a distributed database system.

Chapter 10: Data Modeling Overview

This chapter provides an overview of data modeling concepts and techniques, examines data modeling, and discusses its purpose. We consider different ways to create and categorize data models and data modeling languages and next, focus on conceptual data modeling and present three different languages for creating conceptual data models and diagrams. We explore entity relationship modeling in detail and consider some other conceptual modeling techniques. We briefly discuss logical data modeling and how its purpose is different from conceptual data modeling. Similarly, we discuss physical data modeling and how its purpose is different from both conceptual and logical data modeling and then briefly consider some of the nomenclature and notations used in capturing these various types of data models. Finally, we examine how these different types of data modeling coexist within a heterogeneous database environment.

Chapter 11: Logical Data Models

This chapter examines four logical data modeling languages used by databases in the real world. The relational data model is the first modeling language considered because it is the foundation of many centralized DBMSs. It is also the most-likely logical modeling language for a DDBE and we examine this language in detail. The hierarchical data model and the network data model are two logical modeling languages that are both found in some legacy database systems, particularly on the mainframe. Therefore, we also look at these languages. Object-oriented programming (OOP) has become the de facto standard for many organizations. While OOP applications can access data stored in any format, the most natural format is the format found in an object-oriented DBMS (OODBMS). This format is also found in so-called object persistence engines. Object-oriented databases use an object-oriented modeling language that is fundamentally different from the other modeling languages discussed in this chapter. Some similarities exist between the languages however, and these are discussed. For each modeling language, we discuss the notation and nomenclature, and the rules that need to be followed when converting a conceptual data model into a data model created using one of these logical modeling languages. We briefly compare and contrast the four languages and consider some of the issues that need to be addressed when forward and reverse engineering data models use these languages.

Chapter 12: Traditional DDBE Architectures

In the real world, several different architectural alternatives can be used instead of the traditional, homogeneous DDBMS, which is designed top–down. Federated databases or multidatabases are integrated existing database servers that are built from the bottom up. In a federated database management system, the data that an organization needs already exists in multiple database servers. These databases may or may not all be of the same type (same data model and/or data modeling language). This heterogeneous set of databases needs to be integrated to provide for uniform and relational based interface for the users of the federated database system. Issues involved in such an integration are data model translation to relational data model and integration of a set of relational data models into a federated view.

Chapter 13: New DDBE Architectures

Traditionally, a component or subsystem in a DDBE architecture is not an independent process. This chapter explores the architecture of distributed database environments. Most components in a traditional architecture are controlled by one or more subsystems, and most subsystems are themselves designed with a "chain of command" defined for the components inside them. Therefore, the first new architecture presented is one where the components and subsystems work in cooperation with each other rather than working under the control of each other. Another traditional characteristic found in most architectures is the simple fact that the subsystems within a DDBE architecture are not "all created equal." Certain subsystems in the architecture are designed to be more important, more authoritative, or simply larger and more sophisticated than others. This also means that the architecture is somewhat rigid, even when the development and deployment environments provide dynamic deployment and configuration services. Therefore, this chapter also presents another new architecture where the subsystems are closer to being equal peers. This also allows the environment to be more dynamic and allow the peer systems to join and leave the environment with relative ease and flexibility.

Chapter 14: DDBE Platform Requirements

A distributed database environment (DDBE) runs on top of a network of computers. Each of these computers has its own operating system and perhaps other systems, such as a local DBMS, that need to be incorporated into the DDBE architecture. Although each individual computer has its own operating system, there is no such thing as a completely distributed operating system environment. This means that we must write a layer of software to sit on top of existing software deployed at each individual computer. We call this layer of software the DDBE Platform. This layer can be architected (and implemented) in many different ways. Rather than focusing on a specific implementation, this chapter focuses on the architectural issues and general DDBE Platform Requirements, in particular, how our DDBE Platform needs to deal with communication, component naming, architectural security, deployment, distributed transaction, and general portability/interoperability issues. This chapter also briefly explores some of the implementations that are capable of providing some (or possibly all) of the DDBE Platform requirements. We examine RPC and RMI mechanisms for Remote Calls, the Java Message Service (JMS) implementation for Remote Messaging. We also present a high-level overview of XML Web Services, which is a relatively new technique for implementing service providers in a cross-platform fashion.

Chapter 15: The JMS Starter Kit

This chapter considers how to develop a distributed database management system called a DDBE that can be used to integrate databases from Oracle, Microsoft, IBM, Sybase, and others. We provide a DDBE starter kit, which serves as a starting point for developing our own DDBE components and subsystems and includes a framework and an example extension. It is implemented using Java 2 Standard Edition (J2SE) augmented by an implementation of the Java Message Service (JMS). We can use the framework as a base to get a jumpstart in building a heterogeneous distributed database management system using Java without the additional complexity (or power) of a full J2EE Application Server. We discuss how to use this framework and how to create new extensions in order to implement any additional functionality not currently provided by the framework. Finally, we present the example extension (written using the starter kit) that uses three databases and discuss the steps required to set up and run the example.

Chapter 16: The J2EE Platform

This chapter discusses the J2EE platform by presenting a brief overview of the platform and looking at the specific implementation details for various DDBE Platform Services. In particular, we identify the J2EE Services defined in the J2EE Specification that satisfy the requirements we identified in Chapter 14. We also consider the different implementations to choose from at this time, including Apache Geronimo and JBoss and examine the remote-ability support provided by Enterprise Java Beans (EJB) and discuss how other J2EE facilities can be used for DDBE projects. Facilities discussed include the Java Naming and Directory Interface (JNDI), XML Web Services, and RMI, as well as an overview of the Security, Deployment, and Transaction Management facilities that J2EE provides.

Chapter 17: The J2EE Starter Kit

Another DDBE starter kit is presented here similar to the one we presented in Chapter 15. However, this starter kit is implemented using the J2EE platform and is capable of being ported to several J2EE implementation alternatives with minimal modifications. We can use this framework as a base to get a jumpstart in building a heterogeneous distributed database management system using J2EE and the full power of the subsystems it provides. In particular, the remote-ability and distributed transaction management facilities make this a more powerful (and more complicated) implementation than the JMS/J2SE approach we used in Chapter 15. The starter kit includes a framework and an example extension. We discuss how to use this framework and how to create new extensions in order to implement any additional functionality not currently provided by the framework. Finally, we present a simple example extension (written using the starter kit) that uses three databases and discuss its design.

Chapter 18: The Microsoft .NET Platform

This chapter uses the Microsoft .NET Framework as a potential DDBE development platform by presenting a brief overview of the platform and looking at the specific implementation details for various DDBE Platform Requirements previously identified in Chapter 14. In particular, we examine the TCP/IP Remoting and HTTP Remoting implementations for Remote-Code Execution and also explore the general messaging facilities and support for XML Web Services. We discuss how the Microsoft .NET Framework-based DDBE platform can provide Directory Services, and by presenting also examine how the platform supports Security, Deployment, and Transaction Management.

Chapter 19: The DNET Starter Kit

This chapter presents another DDBE starter kit, similar to the one in Chapter 17. However, this starter kit is implemented using the Microsoft .NET Framework. Therefore, we can use this framework as a base to get a jumpstart in building our own heterogeneous distributed database management system using any of the Microsoft .NET Framework supported programming languages (Visual C#, Visual C++, or Visual Basic). The starter kit leverages the facilities available in the Microsoft .NET Framework-based platform, and we discuss how the facilities identified in Chapter 18 can be used to build our own DDBE projects. The starter kit includes a framework and an example extension we discuss how to use this framework and how to create new extensions in order to implement any additional functionality not currently provided by the framework. Finally, a simple example extension (written using the starter kit) that uses three databases and discuss its design is presented.

USING THIS BOOK EFFECTIVELY

The following describes different paths or "tracks" through the book:

- When this book is used in a classroom environment, it is recommended that Unit 1 be used in its entirety and in the order presented. Depending on the scope of the class, selected information from Unit 2 should also be included based on the degree of heterogeneity discussed in the class. This track would most likely include all of Unit 1 (Chapters 1–9) and at least some parts of Chapters 10 and 11.
- If the class includes any implementation activities or implementation considerations, then once again we recommend that Unit 1 be included, but now Chapters 10, 11, and 14 also have a significant contribution to make. This track should also include the appropriate chapters from Unit 3 based on the implementation platform chosen. In other words, it should include either the J2EE chapters (Chapters 16 and 17), Microsoft .NET Framework-based chapters (Chapters 18 and 19), or the JMS chapter (Chapter 15).
- For readers planning to design their own DDBMS architecture in the real world, Chapter 1 and the chapters in Unit 2 (Chapters 10–14) provide the necessary background to understand the architectural requirements of the system. Once again, the appropriate chapters from Unit 3 can be selected based on the development platform(s) selected for the reader's implementation.
- Readers working with an existing DDBMS architecture can use Unit 1 as a reference for the theoretical underpinnings behind the component and subsystem designs in their implementation. Unit 2 can be used to understand the architectural issues or perhaps to consider changes to their architecture. Unit 3 can be selected based on the existing development environments or perhaps to implement prototypes in an alternative development environment.

ACKNOWLEDGMENTS

Our special thanks go to the following people: Dr. Brad Rubin from the University of St. Thomas, Graduate Programs in Software, for contributing the chapter on security; Dyanne Haug and Patricia Rahimi for their valuable feedback and review of the first draft of this book: we greatly appreciate their time and patience; Dr. Khalid Albarrak from IBM, for helping us with acquiring the InfoSphere Federation Server software and installing and debugging it, and for providing feedback on our test setup and test results; and Saladin Cerimagic from the University of St. Thomas, Graduate Programs in Software, for his help with and discussions about concurrency.

SAEED K. RAHIMI
FRANK S. HAUG

1

INTRODUCTION

Distributed: (adjective)   of, relating to, or being a computer network in which at least some of the processing is done by the individual workstations and information is shared by and often stored at the workstations.

— Merriam Webster's 11th Collegiate Dictionary

Database (noun)   a [sic] usually large collection of data organized especially for rapid search and retrieval (as by a computer).

—Merriam-Webster's 11th Collegiate Dictionary

Informally speaking, a **database (DB)** is simply a collection of data stored on a computer, and the term **distributed** simply means that more than one computer might cooperate in order to perform some task. Most people working with distributed databases would accept both of the preceding definitions without any reservations or complaints. Unfortunately, achieving this same level of consensus is not as easy for any of the other concepts involved with **distributed databases (DDBs)**. A DDB is not simply "more than one computer cooperating to store a collection of data"—this definition would include situations that are not really distributed databases, such as any machine that contains a DB and also mounts a remote file system from another machine. Similarly, this would be a bad definition because it would not apply to any scenario where we deploy a DDB on a single computer. Even when a DDB is deployed using only one computer, it remains a DDB because it is still **possible to deploy it across multiple computers**. Often, in order to discuss a particular approach for implementing a DB, we need to use more restrictive and specific definitions. This means that the same terms might have conflicting definitions when we consider more than one DB implementation alternative. This can be very confusing when researching DBs in general and especially confusing when focusing on DDBs. Therefore, in this chapter, we

Distributed Database Management Systems by Saeed K. Rahimi and Frank S. Haug
Copyright © 2010 the IEEE Computer Society

will present some definitions and archetypical examples along with a new taxonomy. We hope that these will help to minimize the confusion and make it easier to discuss multiple implementation alternatives throughout the rest of the book.

1.1 DATABASE CONCEPTS

Whenever we use the term "DB" in this book, we are always contemplating a collection of **persistent** data. This means that we "save" the data to some form of **secondary storage** (the data usually written to some form of hard disk). As long as we shut things down in an orderly fashion (following the correct procedures as opposed to experiencing a power failure or hardware failure), all the data written to secondary storage should still exist when the system comes back online. We can usually think of the data in a DB as being stored in one or more files, possibly spanning several partitions, or even several hard disk drives—even if the data is actually being stored in something more sophisticated than a simple file.

1.1.1 Data Models

Every DB captures data in two interdependent respects; it captures both the **data structure** and the **data content**. The term "data content" refers to the values actually stored in the DB, and usually this is what we are referring to when we simply say "data." The term "data structure" refers to all the necessary details that describe how the data is stored. This includes things like the format, length, location details for the data, and further details that identify how the data's internal parts and pieces are interconnected. When we want to talk about the structure of data, we usually refer to it as the **data model (DM)** (also called the **DB's schema**, or simply the **schema**). Often, we will use a special language or programmatic facility to create and modify the DM. When describing this language or facility, authors sometimes refer to the facility or language as "the data model" as well, but if we want to be more precise, this is actually the **data modeling language (ML)**—even when there is no textual language. The DM captures many details about the data being stored, but the DM does not include the actual data content. We call all of these details in the DM **metadata**, which is informally defined as "data about data" or "everything about data except the content itself." We will revisit data models and data modeling languages in Chapters 10 and 11.

1.1.2 Database Operations

Usually, we want to perform several different kinds of operations on DBs. Every DB must at least support the ability to "create" new data content (store new data values in the DB) and the ability to retrieve existing data content. After all, if we could not create new data, then the DB would always be empty! Similarly, if we could not retrieve the data, then the data would serve no purpose. However, these operations do not need to support the same kind of interface; for example, perhaps the data creation facility runs as a batch process but the retrieval facility might support interactive requests from a program or user. We usually expect newer DB software to support much more sophisticated operations than minimum requirements dictate. In particular, we usually want the ability to update and delete existing data content. We call this set of operations **CRUD** (which stands for "create, retrieve, update, and delete"). Most modern DBs also support similar operations involving the data structures and their constituent parts. Even when the DBs support these additional "schema CRUD" operations, complicated restrictions that are dependent on the ML and sometimes dependent on very idiosyncratic deployment details can prevent some schema operations from succeeding.

Some DBs support operations that are even more powerful than schema and data CRUD operations. For example, many DBs support the concept of a **query**, which we will define as "a request to retrieve a collection of data that can potentially use complex criteria to broaden or limit the collection of data involved." Likewise, many DBs support the concept of a **command**, which we will define as "a request to create new data, to update existing data, or to delete existing data—potentially using complex criteria similar to a query." Most modern DBs that support both queries and commands even allow us to use separate queries (called **subqueries**) to specify the complex criteria for these operations.

Any DB that supports CRUD operations must consider **concurrent access** and **conflicting operations**. Anytime two or more requests (any combination of queries and commands) attempt to access overlapping collections of data, we have concurrent access. If all of the operations are only retrieving data (no creation, update, or deletion), then the DB can implement the correct behavior without needing any sophisticated logic. If any one of the operations needs to perform a write (create, update, or delete), then we have conflicting operations on overlapping data. Whenever this happens, there are potential problems if the DB allows all of the operations to execute, then the execution order might potentially change the results seen by the programs or users making the requests. In Chapters 5, 6, and 8, we will discuss the techniques that a DB might use to control these situations.

1.1.3   Database Management

When DBs are used to capture large amounts of data content, or complex data structures, the potential for errors becomes an important concern—especially when the size and complexity make it difficult for human verification. In order to address these potential errors and other issues (like the conflicting operation scenario that we mentioned earlier), we need to use some specialized software. The DB vendor can deploy this specialized software as a library, as a separate program, or as a collection of separate programs and libraries. Regardless of the deployment, we call this specialized software a **database management system (DBMS)**. Vendors usually deploy a DBMS as a collection of separate programs and libraries.

1.1.4   DB Clients, Servers, and Environments

There is no real standard definition for a DBMS, but when a DBMS is deployed using one or more programs, this collection of programs is usually referred to as the **DB-Server**. Any application program that needs to connect to a DB is usually referred to as the **DB-Client**. Some authors consider the DB-Server and the DBMS to be equivalent—if there is no DB-Server, then there is no DBMS; so the terms **DBMS-Server** and **DBMS-Client** are also very common. However, even when there is no DB-Server, the application using the DB is still usually called the DB-Client. Different

DBMS implementations have different restrictions. For example, some DBMSs can manage more than one DB, while other implementations require a separate DBMS for each DB.

Because of these differences (and many more that we will not discuss here), it is sometimes difficult to compare different implementations and deployments. Simply using the term "DBMS" can suggest certain features or restrictions in the mind of the reader that the author did not intend. For example, we expect most modern DBMSs to provide certain facilities, such as some mechanism for defining and enforcing integrity constraints—but these facilities are not necessarily required for all situations. If we were to use the term "DBMS" in one of these situations where these "expected" facilities were not required, the reader might incorrectly assume that the "extra" facilities (or restrictions) were a required part of the discussion. Therefore, we introduce a new term, **database environment (DBE)**, which simply means one or more DBs along with any software providing at least the minimum set of required data operations and management facilities. In other words, a DBE focuses on the DB and the desired functionality—it can include a DBMS if that is part of the deployment, but does not have to include a DBMS as long as the necessary functionality is present. Similarly, the term DBE can be applied to DBs deployed on a single host, as well as DBs deployed over a distributed set of machines. By using this new term, we can ignore the architectural and deployment details when they are not relevant. While this might seem unnecessary, it will prevent the awkward phrasing we would have to use otherwise. (If you prefer, you can substitute a phrase like "one or more DB instances with the optional DBMS applications, libraries, or services needed to implement the expected data operations and management facilities required for this context" whenever you see the term "DBE.") There are times when we will explicitly use the term DBMS; in those instances, we are emphasizing the use of a traditional DBMS rather than some other facility with more or less capabilities or limitations. For example, we would use the term DBMS when we want to imply that an actual DBMS product such as Oracle, DB2, and so on is being used. If we use the term DBE, we could still be referring to one of these products, but we could also be referring to any other combination of software with greater, lesser, or equal levels of functionality. As we shall see, the term "DBE" can even refer to a larger system containing several other DBs, DBMSs, and DBEs within it!

1.2 DBE ARCHITECTURAL CONCEPTS

When considering the architecture of a complicated system, such as a DBE, there are several different ways we can view the details. In this section, we will provide a very brief and high-level view useful for discussing the archetypical DBE architectures used later in the chapter and later in the book. We will revisit architectural concerns in Chapters 12 to 15. For our purposes here, we will merely consider **services, components, subsystems**, and **sites**.

1.2.1 Services

Regardless of the deployment details, we can create logical collections of related functionality called **services**. For example, we mentioned earlier that many DBs support queries; we can call the logical grouping of the software that implements this functionality the **query service**. We can define services like this for both publicly visible functions (such as query) and internal functions (such as query optimization). Services are merely logical collections, which means that they do not necessarily have corresponding structure duplicated in the actual implementation or deployment details. We call any piece of software that uses a service a **service consumer**, while any piece of software implementing the service is called a **service provider**. Implicitly, each service has at least one **interface** (similar to a contractual agreement that defines the inputs, outputs, and protocols used by the service consumers and providers). These interfaces can be very abstract (merely specifying an order of steps to be taken) or they can describe very tangible details such as data types or even textual syntax. Most of these interface details are usually only present in lower-level design diagrams—not the high-level architectural or deployment diagrams.

The same piece of software can be both a service consumer and a service provider and can even consume or provide several different services using many different interfaces—but it is usually better to limit the number of services involved for an individual piece of code. Although we can talk about the services as part of the overall architecture or deployment (like interfaces), we usually do not see them directly represented in architectural or deployment diagrams. Instead, we usually see the **components** and **subsystems** (which we will discuss further in the next section) implementing the services in these diagrams. We will discuss services further in Chapter 14.

1.2.2 Components and Subsystems

For our purposes, a **component** is simply a deployable bundle that provides a reasonably cohesive set of functionality, and a **subsystem** is a collection of one or more components that work together toward a common goal. Whenever we want to use the two terms interchangeably, we will use the term **COS (component or subsystem)**. Unlike a service, which is merely a logical grouping, a COS is a physical grouping, which means that it does have a corresponding structure in the implementation. Frequently, we name these COSs after the primary service that they **provide**. There can be multiple instances of the same COS deployed within the system. These instances are often referred to as **servers**, although we can also use other terminology. For example, we might see a Query COS defined in the architecture, and several Query Servers (instances of the Query COS) deployed within the environment. Alternatively, we might refer to these COSs or their deployed instances as Query Managers, Query Processors, Query Controllers, or even some other name. Different instances of the same COS can have different implementation and configuration details, as long as the instances still provide all the necessary services using the correct protocols and interfaces. We usually represent a COS in an architectural diagram as a box or oval with its name written inside. Deployment diagrams show each COS instance similarly, but usually the instance name includes some additional hint (such as a number, abbreviation, or other deployment detail) to help differentiate the instances from each other.

1.2.3 Sites

The term **site** represents a logical location in an architectural diagram or a deployment diagram—typically, this is a real, physical machine, but that is not necessarily true.

For example, we might have a deployment using two sites (named Site-A and Site-B). This means that those two sites could be any two machines as long as all of the necessary requirements are satisfied for the machines and their network connections. In certain circumstances, we could also deploy all of the subsystems located at Site-A and Site-B on the same machine. Remember, a DDB deployed on a single machine is still a DDB. In other words, as long as the deployment plan does not explicitly forbid deploying all the COS instances for that DDB on a single machine, we can deploy them this way and still consider it a DDB. Architectural and deployment diagrams depict sites as container objects (usually with the site name and the deployed COS instances included inside them) when there is more than one site involved; otherwise it is assumed that everything in the diagram is located in a single site, which may or may not be named in the diagram.

1.3 ARCHETYPICAL DBE ARCHITECTURES

As we have already discussed, when considering a DBE, there are some bare minimum requirements that need to be present—namely, the ability to add new data content and retrieve existing content. Most real-world DBEs provide more than just this minimal level of functionality. In particular, the update and delete operations for data are usually provided. We might see some more sophisticated facilities such as the query service and other services supporting schema operations. In this section, we will briefly consider the typical services we would expect to see in a DBE. Then, we will consider some archetypical DBE architectures.

1.3.1 Required Services

Figure 1.1 shows a simplistic architectural diagram for a minimal DBE. The architecture shown is somewhat unrealistic. In this architecture, there is a separate subsystem for each service discussed in this section, and each subsystem is named the same as the service that it provides. These subsystems are contained within a larger subsystem,

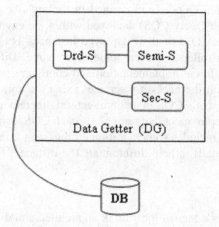

Figure 1.1 DBE architectural diagram emphasizing the minimum required services.

which we call the **Data Getter (DG)**. This DBE provides (at least) three services—they are named Drd-S, Sec-S, and Semi-S. When reading this diagram, we should recall that it is a DBE and, therefore, the services shown should be considered vitally important, or at least expected—but there might be additional services provided by the environment that are not shown here. For example, this diagram does not show any service providers for query or command operations but that does **not necessarily** mean we cannot use this diagram to discuss a DBE with those facilities—instead, it merely means that any DBE without those unmentioned facilities is still **potentially** represented by this diagram.

Whenever we use an architectural or deployment diagram for a DBE, we are usually highlighting some requirement or feature of the environment within a specific context; in this case, we are merely showing what a "bare minimum" DBE must provide, and the four services shown here satisfy those minimum requirements. Every DBE must include a service providing the ability to retrieve data from the DB. We will call this the **Data Read Service (Drd-S)**. Since most DBEs also have at least a basic level of privacy or confidentiality, there should always be some form of **Security Service (Sec-S)**. In an effort to be inclusive, we can consider DBEs with "no security" to be implementing a Sec-S that "permits everyone to do everything." Any real-world DBE should have a Sec-S providing both authentication and authorization, which we will discuss further in Chapter 9. The Drd-S uses the Sec-S to ensure that private data remains unseen by those without proper permissions. There is usually another service providing at least some minimal level of integrity checking or enforcement. This other service is responsible for preventing semantic errors (e.g., data content representing a salary must be greater than zero, otherwise it is a semantic error). Similar to the Sec-S, this service can be less than perfect, or perhaps even implemented using an "allow all modifications" policy if explicit constraints are not defined. We call this service the **Semantic Integrity Service (Semi-S)**, and we will discuss it further in Chapter 3. This service can be used by several services, including the Drd-S, which can use it to provide default values for the content it retrieves (among other possibilities).

1.3.2 Basic Services

In Section 1.1.2, we said that every DB must provide **some mechanism** for populating data (otherwise the DB would always be empty), but we also said that each DB might support different interfaces for the mechanisms they use. Therefore, the ability to write data is **not always** implemented as a service, or in the very least, it is not always implemented in a way that we can incorporate into our DBE architecture. For example, if the only data population mechanism provided by a particular DBE was a program that only supported interactive user input (text screens or graphical dialog boxes) then we could not use that program as a service provider in any meaningful sense. However, if the DBE does provide a "program-friendly" mechanism to write data, we can call this the **Data Write Service (Dwr-S)**. Although it is not a required service, and it is not present in all DBEs, it is typically present in most traditional DBMS products, and in many other DBEs we will consider. If there is a Dwr-S, then it uses the Sec-S (to prevent unauthorized data content additions, modifications, and removals) and the Semi-S (to prevent causing any semantic errors when it adds, modifies, or removes any data content). Once again, unless we specify the requirements more explicitly, it is possible for the Sec-S and Semi-S in a particular DBE to provide varying degrees of

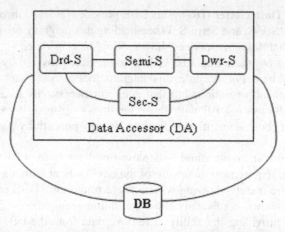

Figure 1.2 DBE architectural diagram emphasizing the basic services.

functionality for these services. Figure 1.2 shows the architectural diagram for a DBE providing the basic services we just discussed. Here, we show all the services used to access the data for read or write operations as a single subsystem called the **Data Accessor (DA)**. We could also have shown the Data Getter subsystem in place of the Drd-S. However, we did not include it here because the Semi-S and Sec-S are used by both the read and the write operations. Similarly, we could consider the combination of the Dwr-S, Semi-S, and Sec-S to be a "Data Setter" subsystem, but these details do not usually add much value to our diagram. In other words, the DA **always** implicitly includes a DG as part of it and the services shown in Figure 1.2.

1.3.3 Expected Services

Every DBE must supply the functionality contained in the DG, and many DBEs will provide the functionality contained in the DA, but often we expect a DBE to be more powerful than these minimal or basic scenarios. In particular, we mentioned the query service earlier, and here we will call it the **Query Request Service (Qreq-S)**. Most modern DBMSs should provide this as well as some form of **Query Optimization Service (Qopt-S)**, but neither of these services is a requirement for all DBEs. Typically, the Qreq-S forms a plan for a query and then passes the plan on to the Qopt-S. The Qopt-S optimizes the plan and then uses the Drd-S to retrieve the data matching the query criteria. We will discuss the Qreq-S and Qopt-S further in Chapter 4. We also mentioned that some DBEs have the ability to execute commands (create, update, and delete operations with potentially complex criteria). Therefore, in most DBEs providing DA operations, we would also expect to see an **Execution Service (Exec-S)** and **Execution Optimization Service (Eopt-S)** to encapsulate these command operations. Again, these are present in most DBMSs, but not necessarily present in all DBEs. Chapter 3 will explore these services further. Often, there is a "nonprogrammatic" interface provided to users. In particular, many relational DBMSs support a special language (called the SQL) and provide batch and/or interactive facilities that users can employ to pass queries and commands to the DB. We will call the service providing this function the **User Interface Service (UI-S)**. This service is not always present in

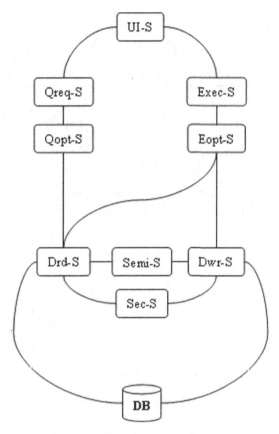

Figure 1.3   DBE architectural diagram emphasizing the expected services.

a DBE and is usually implemented differently, including different syntax, features, and restrictions for the queries and commands. However, we would expect most modern DBMSs (including nonrelational ones) to provide some sort of UI-S. Figure 1.3 shows an example of a typical DBE providing these expected services.

1.3.4   Expected Subsystems

Figure 1.4 shows a reasonably realistic DBE set of subsystems for the architecture we looked at in Figure 1.3; it contains all the same services, but we have bundled the services into four subsystems: the **application processor (AP)**, the **query processor (QP)**, the **command processor (CP)**, and the **data accessor (DA)**. Two of the subsystems (QP and CP) are contained within one of the others (AP), while the other two subsystems (AP and DA) are shown as independent packages. Each component has been allocated to one of the subsystems, and the communication links shown only connect subsystems rather than the components inside them. Although the communication links are not quite as detailed, there is no real loss of information when we do this in a diagram. We have placed the Qreq-S and Qopt-S inside the QP. Similarly, we have placed the Exec-S and Eopt-S inside the CP. The AP subsystem contains the combination of

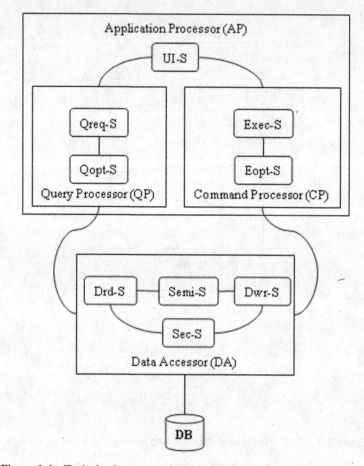

Figure 1.4   Typical subsystems of simple DBE with the expected services.

the UI-S, QP, and CP subsystems. All the remaining service components have been allocated to the DA, which we discussed in Section 1.3.2.

1.3.5   Typical DBMS Services

There can be many other services and subsystems in a DBE, but often these additional services and subsystems are highly dependent on other details, specific to the particular DBE being considered. This is especially true when the particular DBE being focused upon is a DBMS. For example, in a DBE with a Dwr-S, we might include one or more services to handle conflicting operations. Such a DBE might use one or more of the following: a **Transaction Management Service (Tran-S)**, a **Locking Service (Lock-S)**, a **Timestamping Service (Time-S)**, or a **Deadlock Handling Service (Dead-S)**—all of which will be discussed in Chapters 5 and 6. Similarly, most modern relational DBMSs have a **Fallback and Recovery Service (Rec-S)**, which we will discuss in Chapter 8. The architectural diagram for a DBE like this is shown in Figure 1.5; notice that the services shown are implemented as components inside a single subsystem, called "DBMS" in this diagram. If the DBE is for a DDB, we might

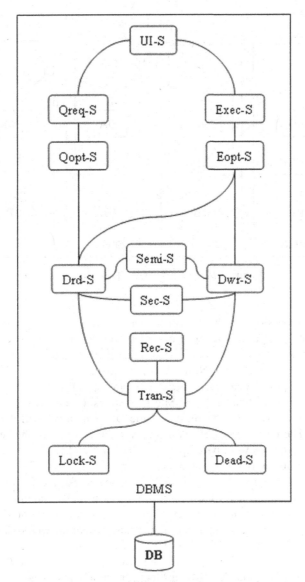

Figure 1.5   DBE architectural diagram for a typical DBMS.

even have a **Replication Service (Repl-S)**, which is not shown in Figure 1.5 (because that architecture is not for a distributed DB). We will discuss the Repl-S in Chapter 7.

1.3.6   Summary Level Diagrams

If we wanted to show the high-level architectural details for an environment containing all of the DBEs just discussed (from Fig. 1.1, 1.2, 1.4, and 1.5) in the same diagram, only the "most visible" subsystem packages would probably be shown (we would not see the components or smaller contained subsystems in this diagram). We can always

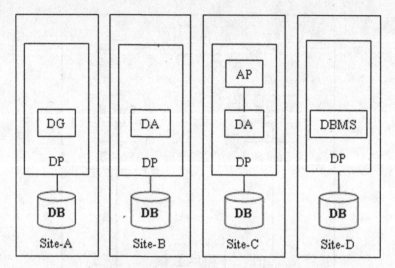

Figure 1.6 Summary level DBE diagrams.

create separate, more detailed diagrams for each subsystem as needed (similar to those shown previously), but at this level of consideration those details would probably not add much value. Figure 1.6 is a more reasonable diagram to use when considering the system at this (or a higher) level. Notice that the site on the left of the diagram (Site-A) contains the DBE from Figure 1.1. Site-B contains the DBE from Figure 1.2, Site-C contains the DBE from Figure 1.4, and Site-D contains the DBE from Figure 1.5. Each DBE consists of a single subsystem, called the DP (which we will discuss further in Section 1.6.2). The DP contains all the necessary subsystems for the centralized DBE at each site. If these sites were participating in a distributed DBE, we might only show the DP box with no internal subsystems displayed.

Although these pictures are useful, they are not a substitute for the actual design and deployment details (most of which are not shown). The diagrams cannot convey many subtle details. For example, suppose the DBE at Site-C did not have a QP; this diagram would still look the same, and the detailed diagram would still look similar to Figure 1.4, except that the QP would be missing. In this scenario, all data retrieval would need to use the DA directly. In other words, the DA's client would need to iterate over all the data and use program logic in the client to discard unwanted data values. Similarly, if the CP at Site-C in this scenario did not support subqueries for its criteria, then the DB-Client might need to iterate over the data values using the DA and use either the CP or the DA to create, modify, or delete data values in the DB. The functionality inside the service components (such as the Semi-S or Sec-S) can also vary greatly between different DBEs: even when the diagram shows these components, we cannot determine how similar or different the implementation details really are by merely looking at the pictures. In fact, since most DBMSs have all of the functionality required by the AP, DA, and DG subsystems, it is also possible for every DBE in the diagram (including those at Site-A, Site-B, and Site-C) to be a DBMS—if this were the case, then we would be providing much more than the minimum requirements for Site-A, Site-B, and Site-C. The opposite is not true, however: Site D must contain a DBMS, with the expected level of functionality required, and not merely a DG, DA, or

AP/DA combination. Once again, all of the specific requirements are not shown in these diagrams and must therefore be found within other diagrams and design documentation.

All of the figures we have looked at so far are architectural diagrams, not deployment diagrams. This means that the components and subsystems listed in the diagram could be bundled into several different possible deployment packages. For example, all of these services could be deployed as a single program, with a single instance installed on a single machine, which we could then call a DBE or DBMS. An alternate deployment of this same architecture could have several instances of this single DBE/DBMS program installed on one or more machines. Even though we have only shown a single DB in the diagram, there might be several DBs deployed—this diagram does not tell us if we can use the same DBE/DBMS for all of these DBs or if there must be a separate instance for each one.

1.4   A NEW TAXONOMY

We mentioned earlier that "DBE" is a new term representing several different possible implementations for similar functionality. Because a DBE considers the system at such an abstract level, it can be used to refer to a wide variety of possible architectures and deployments. In this section, we will present a new taxonomy to be used for classifying all the possible DBE alternatives that we might consider when exploring DB and DDB issues. For our purposes, we will consider a new taxonomy with four levels, presented in order from most abstract to most specific. We hope that this arrangement will reduce the complexity for each successive level and simplify the taxonomic groups (the taxa) containing the environments that we ultimately want to discuss. Like most taxonomies, the extreme cases are most useful for understanding the categorical differences between the taxa, but most real-world DBEs will most likely fall somewhere between the extremes.

The four levels of categorizations (from most abstract to most specific) are:

- COS distribution and deployment (COS-DAD)
- COS closedness or openness (COS-COO)
- Schema and data visibility (SAD-VIS)
- Schema and data control (SAD-CON)

1.4.1   COS Distribution and Deployment

The first level in our taxonomy is the **COS distribution and deployment (COS-DAD)** level. This is perhaps the easiest level to understand, and usually this is the first classification that we want to make when evaluating a particular DBE. The two extreme cases that define this level are the completely **centralized DBE (CDBE)** and the fully **distributed DBE (DDBE)**.

In a completely CDBE, we must deploy all the DBs, and COS instances on a single machine. In other words, placing any of the COS instances or DB instances on a second, separate machine is strictly forbidden. This case includes the initial releases of most traditional DBMSs (such as Oracle, Sybase, Informix, etc.) and many other early DBs that did not have a DBMS-Server (such as dBase, Paradox, Clipper, FoxPro, Microsoft Access, etc.). Most modern releases of DBMSs and DBs have moved away from this extreme scenario slightly, since we can often deploy the DB-Clients on a separate machine for many of these systems. Similarly, some modern DBMSs have some ability to distribute their DBs (using techniques such as mirroring, etc.), but they are still essentially a CDBE since the "almost distributed DBs" are not really a "true DB" in the same sense as the original DB that they attempt to duplicate.

If each COS instance and each DB instance is deployed on a separate machine, then we have the other extreme (the fully DDBE). Of course, in the real world, we would probably not go to this extreme—in the very least, it is usually not necessary to separate components within the same subsystem from each other, and also not necessary to separate the lowest-level subsystems (such as the DAs) from the DBs (i.e., the files containing the data structure and content) that they access. Typically, the DDBE will consist of one or more "coordinating" server instances (providing services across the entire DDBE) and a set of DBEs that combine to make the DDBE work. We call each of these DBEs a **Sub-DBE (S-DBE)**, because they combine to form the DDBE in a way that is similar to how subsystems combine to form a system. Each S-DBE is a DBE in its own right, which means that each of them is also subject to categorization too using this taxonomy—in particular, each S-DBE can be either a centralized DBE or another distributed DBE. Most S-DBEs are centralized environments, especially for traditional architectures such as the ones we will discuss in Chapter 12. In this book, we are mostly interested in DDBEs and really only consider the CDBEs when we want to evaluate some type of DDBE or examine the S-DBE inside a larger DDBE.

1.4.2   COS Closedness or Openness

The second level in our taxonomy is the **COS closedness or openness (COS-COO)** level. This level considers the software implementation and integration issues for the major subsystems, components, and the DB storage itself. Although we will introduce the two extreme cases for this level (**completely open** and **completely closed**), the COSs in most DBEs will occupy a strata (a series of gradations) within this level rather than either extreme scenario.

There is no such thing as a commercial off-the-shelf (COTS) DDBE that we can simply buy and install. Even if there were such a product, we would still probably want to integrate some of our existing COS instances into the DDBE architecture. Conversely, if our goal was to create our own DDBE "from the ground up," it is doubtful that we would write absolutely everything (including the operating systems, file systems, etc.) completely from scratch. Therefore, every DDBE needs to integrate multiple COS instances, some of which we did not write ourselves, regardless of which architectural alternative we choose to implement. When attempting to integrate all of these COS instances, we need to consider the public interface exposed by each COS. Since most of these COSs were not designed with a DDBE specifically in mind, it is quite possible that the interfaces they expose will not provide everything we need. Simply put, there are several DDBE algorithms and services that can only be implemented when we have complete access to the underlying implementation for the COS instances involved—this is especially true if we want to perform our own DDBE research. For example, suppose we wanted to develop a new mechanism for distributed deadlock handling based on a new variation of locking. Obviously, we could only do this if we were able to see (and perhaps even modify) the underlying locking implementation details for each Sub-DBE in the environment.

Subsystems that provide either "unrestrained access" or at least "sufficient access" to the underlying state and implementation details are **open** to us, while systems that do not are **closed** to us. While most real subsystems provide some level of access, determining the degree to which a particular subsystem is open or closed depends on the actual interfaces it exposes and the type of functionality we are trying to implement. If all the COS instances are open to us, then we have the first extreme case (completely open). If all the COS instances are closed to us, then we have the other extreme case (completely closed).

A completely open DDBE can occur in any of these three scenarios:

- If we write all of the components or service instances ourselves (from scratch)
- If we use free and open source software (FOSS) for all the COS instances that we do not write ourselves
- If we obtain some sort of agreement or arrangement with the COS vendors (for all the COS instances that we do not write ourselves) allowing us the open access we need

The first two scenarios are possible, but in order to satisfy either one, we must completely avoid any non-FOSS, COTS products. Many organizations will be reluctant or unable to do this. The third scenario is also somewhat unusual, since it would most likely involve legal contracts and perhaps additional licensing fees. This means that a completely open DDBE is a very rare situation. A completely closed DDBE can only occur if we do not have sufficient access to the implementation details for any of the COS instances in the DDBE: in other words, only if each COS instance in the DDBE were a black box whose inner mechanisms completely prevented our attempts to understand or integrate. This is a very common situation for the components inside a COTS centralized DBE, where we have no access to the inner workings of the algorithms (such as locking). However, since we cannot buy a COTS distributed DBE, this extreme scenario is impossible for a DDBE.

Each DDBE can be a slightly different situation, but typically, the COS instances become "more open" the further removed they are from the DB. This is because there are many COTS products (such as DBMSs) that we might choose to use in the lower levels of the architecture (closer to the DB), but the higher-level COS software does not exist, which means that we need to write the higher-level COS software ourselves. Remember that any software we write ourselves is always open to us (regardless of whether we give this access to others).

1.4.3   Schema and Data Visibility

The third level in our taxonomy is the schema and data visibility (SAD-VIS) level. In this level, we are considering the DB schema and all the data content stored in each DB in the environment. For a CDBE, this is not very interesting because, typically, there is only a single DB to consider or all the DBs use the same ML. However, a DDBE can be a much more complicated consideration. In a DDBE, each DB is actually under S-DBE, which is a DBE in its own right (usually a CDBE). Different DBEs can potentially have different MLs, which means that the ML for the DDBE and the ML for each S-DBE it contains could theoretically be different. In reality, there are not that many different MLs, so it is not likely that there would be that many different ones used in the same environment; but the simple fact that there might be different MLs within the same DDBE is important to consider. We will discuss this further in Chapters 2 and 12.

Assuming that there is an appropriate way to combine the different MLs into a single (perhaps different) ML, we can now consider the "combined schema" for all the DBs in the DDBE. If the "most powerful user in the DDBE," which we will call the **DDB administrator (DDBA)**, can see all of the data structure across all the DBs, then we have **total schema visibility (TSV)**. In other words, TSV means that there are no hidden data structures and there is no structure missing from the combined schema but present in one of the S-DBE schemas. Similarly, we can consider the data content for the combined schema and compare it to the data content in each S-DBE. If every data value present in the S-DBE DBs is visible to the DDBA in the DDBE, then we have **total data visibility (TDV)**. In other words, TDV means that there is no hidden data content; there is no data value missing from the DDBE but present in one of the CDBE DBs. When we have both total schema visibility and total data visibility, we have the first extreme case for this level, namely, **total visibility (TV)**. TV can happen in the real world, and in fact, it is a requirement for some particular DDBE architectures, some of which we will discuss in Chapter 12.

It should be obvious that the other extreme case is not possible—if the combined schema was empty and all the data content were hidden, then the DDBE would be completely worthless! If we have some hidden schema, then we have **partial schema visibility (PSV)**. If we have some hidden data, then we have **partial data visibility (PDV)**. Having either PSV, PDV, or both PSV and PDV is referred to as **partial visibility (PV)**. PV is a common occurrence and even a requirement for some particular DDBE architectures. We will also discuss some of these architectures in Chapter 12.

For the sake of completeness, we will mention that there is one more reason why this level is not interesting when we are looking at a single CDBE (as opposed to a DDBE or a Sub-DBE): the TV scenario is really the only possible situation for most CDBEs.

1.4.4   Schema and Data Control

The fourth level in our taxonomy is the schema and data control (SAD-CON) level. In this level, we are considering the set of all operations that we are allowed to perform using only the visible schema and the visible data content (we ignore any operation that would attempt to use hidden schema or content, since it would obviously fail). Once again, our primary focus is on the DDBEs. If the DDBA can perform any and every valid schema operation on the visible combined schema structures, then we have **total schema control (TSC)**. Similarly, if the DDBA can perform any and every possible data operation on the visible data content for the DDBE, then we have **total data control (TDC)**. When we have both TSC and TDC, we have the first extreme scenario, which we call **total control (TC)**. If there is at least one valid schema operation that the DDBA does not have permission to perform for some part of the visible combined schema, then we only have **partial schema control (PSC)**. If there is at least one data operation that the DDBA does not have permission to perform on some subset of the visible data content, then we have **partial data control (PDC)**. Having either PSC, PDC, or both PSC and PDC is referred to as **partial control (PC)**.

Again, it should be obvious that it is impossible for the other extreme scenario to \
exist in either a CDBE or a DDBE. In other words, if the DDBA cannot perform any
valid schema operation on any piece of visible schema, and also cannot perform any
valid data operation on any subset of the visible data, then the DBE is unusable for
any purpose. Like the previous level, the situation for a CDBE is not very interesting, because we would always expect TC. Although TC is possible for many DDBE
architectures (and even required for some of them), PC is also very common for many
DDBEs. For example, many DDBE architectures do not provide schema operations,
and many real-world implementations are fundamentally read-only with respect to the
data content. We will discuss some of these architectures in Chapter 12.

1.5 AN EXAMPLE DDBE

Suppose that our organization has three centralized DBEs deployed as depicted in
Figure 1.7. We have one instance of IBM's DB2 DBMS running on our IBM mainframe, which contains mission critical information about the entire organization and
supports our payroll, human resources, and customer fulfillment applications. We
also have two different departmental groups within our organization—one group is
using Oracle's DBMS to maintain project information and the other group is using
Microsoft's SQL Server DBMS to keep track of production information.

In this example, even though project information in the Oracle DBE and customer
information in the DB2 DBE are accessed independently most of the time, there are
times when we need to cross-reference the information in these two systems. Suppose a
manager wants to generate a report for each customer, listing details about the customer
as well as details about all the company projects involving that customer. In order to

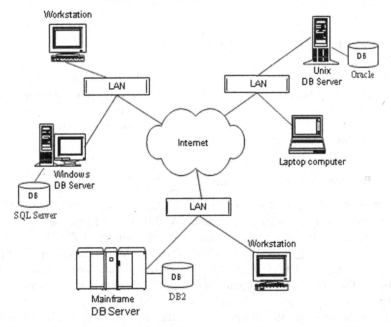

Figure 1.7 Example of the possible deployment of an organization's CDBEs.

satisfy this manager's requirements, we need to combine information that is stored in two different DBEs, controlled by two different types of DBMS. We could choose from two approaches when we attempt to satisfy this manager's requirements: a manual approach and an automated approach.

In the manual approach, we would log into each individual server, write some queries to get the information out of each DB, transfer results from each DB to our personal workstation, and then write a program that merges all the information into the final report format. This is a time-consuming process that requires someone familiar with each hardware platform, each DBE, the communications facilities needed to log into the systems and transfer the files, and the utilities or programming skills needed to fetch the information from each system and to merge the files into the final result. Even when we have someone who can perform all these tasks, we do not have any easy way to ensure that final report is valid.

For the automated approach, our company needs to combine the three CDBEs mentioned above into a new, single, DDBE that we need to implement. We can utilize the services of local DBMSs, each running on a separate computer, and the services of the communication subsystem (Ethernet, Token Ring, and Internet) to coordinate the necessary read or query operations. Ideally, users of our new DDBE will be completely unaware that the data content is dispersed across different computers and is controlled by different DBMS products—they have the illusion that all of our combined data content is stored and controlled locally by one system (the DDBE). Our DDBE users do not need to know anything about the DBMSs we have. They do not need to know the MLs required for each DBMS, anything about computer hardware running the DBEs, or any details about how these hardware and software systems are interconnected. Our users can send a query request to the DDBEs query processor that handles all the necessary coordination, execution, and merging automatically. Although using this new DDBE system is very easy, implementing it can be quite difficult.

1.6 A REFERENCE DDBE ARCHITECTURE

In discussing the theory behind a DDB, we will use the DDBE architecture discussed in this chapter as the reference. We will discuss other architectures in Chapter 12. For the rest of this chapter, and to set the basis for the discussion of theory and issues in a distributed database environment, we will further divide the architecture of a DDBE into an Information Architecture and a Software Architecture.

1.6.1 DDBE Information Architecture

The information architecture for a centralized database environment (CDBE) conforms to the American National Standards Institute (ANSI) standard proposed and approved by the Standard Planning and Requirements Committee (SPARC) [SPARC75] [SPARC76] [SPARC77] called the ANSI/SPARC three-level schema architecture as depicted in Figure 1.8. This architecture provides for three separate layers of abstraction—the external, conceptual, and internal schemas. Users of such a system are assigned external schemas (also known as external views), which they then use to access the information in the underlying database. These views are created from the conceptual schema that encompasses the entire set of data in the database. The

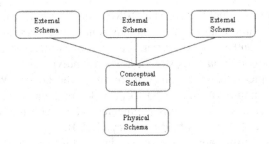

Figure 1.8   ANSI/SPARC three-level schema architecture.

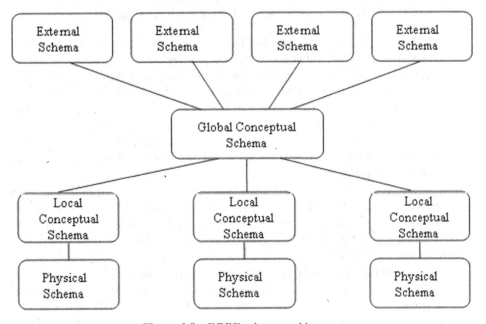

Figure 1.9   DDBE schema architecture.

conceptual schema in a relational system, for example, represents all the information in a database as a set of relations or tables. At the lowest layer of abstraction, the internal (or physical) schema represents the data in the raw format. This representation is not visible to the end user and provides for the application data independence feature of all DBMSs.

Although, the three-level schema architecture satisfies the needs of a CDBE, it is not sufficient for a DDBE [Sheth90]. In a DDBE, users' views must combine information across different S-DBEs. As such, their views need to be built on top of an integrated view of local conceptual schemas from the participating DBEs. This requirement adds a new level of abstraction, the **global conceptual schema (GCS)**, to the three-level schema architecture; this new architecture is depicted in Figure 1.9.

The GCS is an integrated view of all local conceptual schemas. It provides the basis for generating the external views for distributed system users. The local conceptual schemas provide a local view of data stored locally at each S-DBE. Therefore, GCS can only provide a global conceptual view of data and nothing more. In a distributed system where each individual S-DBE is a DBMS using the relational system, the GCS provides information about all tables in the environment, all primary keys, all foreign keys, all constraints, and so on. However, the GCS does not contain any information about where any individual table is stored, how any individual table is fragmented, or even how many copies of each fragment there are in the DDBE. We need additional information (not contained in the GCS) to provide for location, fragmentation, and replication transparencies. We call this augmented GCS (with the additional required information included) a **global data dictionary** (**GDD**).

The GDD contains information about all the data that is available to a distributed system user. The GDD contains, in addition to what is in the GCS, information pertaining to data location, data fragmentation, and data replication.

For example, in the relational world, GDD contains five submodels:

1. *Global Conceptual Schema (GCS).* The GCS has information about the tables, columns, data types, column constraints, primary keys, foreign keys, and so on. This part of the GDD provides for application data independence, which is required by all DBMS systems according to the ANSI/SPARC standard.

2. *Data Directory (DD).* The DD has information about the location of the data fragments. This information typically identifies the site location by specifying the Universal Resource Locator (URL), site name, IP address, and so on for the site containing the data. This part of GDD enables a DDBE to provide for location transparency.

3. *Fragmentation Directory (FD).* The FD has information about data fragments in the system. The FD typically contains conditions used for creation of horizontal fragments, join column for vertical fragments, columns that are part of the vertical fragments, primary key of the fragments, and so on. This part of GDD provides for fragmentation transparency.

4. *Replication Directory (RD).* The RD has information about replication. This typically includes the number of copies that exist for each table or a fragment of a table. Note that this information in conjunction with the DD information is enough to locate every copy of any fragment or a table. This part of GDD allows a DDBE to provide for replication transparency.

5. *Network Directory (ND).* The ND has information about the topology, communication link speed, and so on for all the sites participating in the DDBE. This part of GDD enables a DDBE to provide for network transparency.

1.6.2 DDBE Software Architecture

Like a centralized DBE, a distributed DBE consists of two main software modules called the **application processor** (**AP**) and the **data processor** (**DP**). Each DP provides the services necessary to connect a local DBE to the distributed environment. The actual DBE requirements and the specific requirements for the DP services depend on the approach we are using to implement the software components of the DDBE (Section 1.3 discussed these services, and Figure 1.6 provided four different examples of how a DP might bundle these services). There are two approaches to software implementation for a DDBE—they are called top–down and bottom–up. We will discuss the details of these approaches in Chapter 12. Here, we briefly outline the differences between them. Figure 1.10 depicts the architecture of a top–down DDBE implementation.

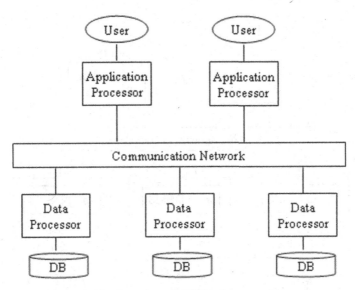

Figure 1.10   Top–down DDBE software architecture.

When we develop the software components of a DDBE, the APs and DPs can be deployed separately and can cooperate over a communication network. The AP is responsible for controlling the user interface and distributed transaction management, while the DP handles local query optimization, local transaction recovery, and local transaction execution support. This architecture parallels the information architecture discussed earlier. The AP uses the GCS and the GDD to handle users' requests at the global (distribution) level, while the DPs use the LCSs to execute the subrequests locally.

When we develop the software components of a DDBE bottom–up, we are really integrating existing database management systems as local DBEs into the DDBE. In this approach, many of the DP responsibilities can be delegated to the local DBEs. This reduces the DP component to nothing more than a thin wrapper surrounding the local DBE for each site. Figure 1.11 depicts the software components of this approach.

Figure 1.12 depicts the details of the application processor and data processor for both approaches mentioned above. This example shows a system with one AP and N DPs. Note that this is a generic logical architecture and does not imply deployment— we will cover software deployment in Chapter 12. The following two sections outline the software components of a DDBE. These components are necessary regardless of the approach used to develop the system.

1.6.2.1 Components of the Application Processor   The application processor is composed of two main subsystems. They are the **global transaction manager (GTM)** and the **distributed execution manager (DEM)**. The GTM itself is divided into five subsystems—the **user interface (UI)** module, the Decomposer, the Merger, the Optimizer, and the Planner. The GTM also contains the **global data dictionary (GDD)**. The GTM's overall responsibility is to manage user requests (queries and commands wrapped inside transactions). The UI accepts user requests and translates them into an internal representation suitable for processing. After translation, the request is passed to

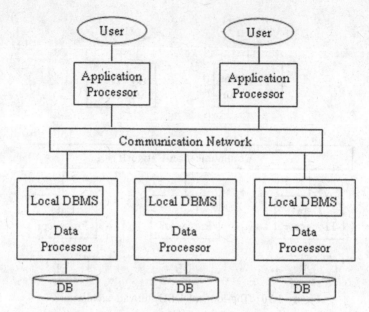

Figure 1.11 Bottom–up DDBE software architecture.

the Decomposer to break it up, if necessary, into subrequests that need to be processed by individual local DP (and DBMS) systems. The Decomposer parses the request first to find out the name of the tables (fragments), their columns, and predicates (join predicates and nonjoin predicates). The Decomposer then looks up the GDD to find out information about the location of the tables/fragments that are in the request. Based on this information, the Decomposer generates a set of local subrequests. These subrequests can run on individual local DP systems. The local subrequests are then handed out to the Optimizer. Similar to a local DBMS, the Optimizer and Planner work together and use the information they get from the GDD about replication, fragmentation, and communication link speeds to generate an optimized execution plan. The plan is then given to the DEM to be carried out.

The underlying DDBE Platform must supply the necessary services to guarantee the delivery of the requests and the responses. There are several implementation alternatives to choose from, but the primary role of whichever one we choose to use is to hide the specifics of these communication requirements from the DEM. We will discuss the DDBE Platform requirements in Chapter 14, and we will look at some of the implementation alternatives in Unit 3.

The job of the DEM is straightforward. The DEM simply executes the steps in the distributed execution plan by coordinating with the **local execution managers (LEMs)** contained within the DPs at the target sites. Once the local sites return the results to the DEM, they are passed to the Merger subsystem within GTM for assembly. For example, the Merger may have to join rows from two vertical partitions of a given table or may have to union rows from two horizontal partitions of a given table. We will discuss the rules for merging result fragments in Chapter 2.

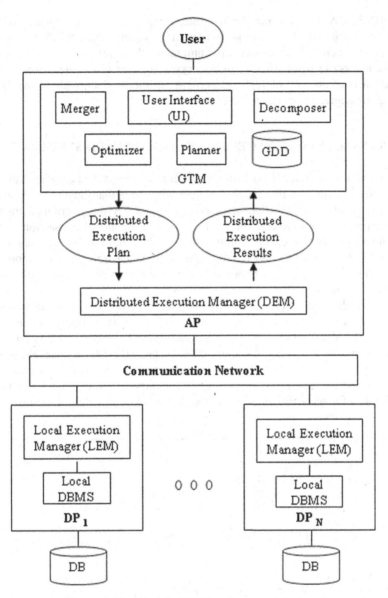

Figure 1.12 Generic DDBE software architecture.

1.6.2.2 Components of the Data Processor   The data processor consists of the LEM and the necessary data services we discussed in Section 1.3. Once again, the DDBE Platform is responsible for providing the necessary communications support at the local site. It guarantees end-to-end message delivery and hides details and issues with communications from the rest of the modules at each site. The primary responsibility of each LEM is to act on behalf of the DEM at the local site. It will receive the subrequests that pertain to the data at its site, interface with the local DB (through the local DBMS, DA, or DG), run the requests, collect the results, and then pass those results back to the DEM. When the subrequest is a query, these results contain actual data content; when the subrequests are commands, these results might contain details about the number of rows affected. In both cases, these results contain execution status information (success or failure), and perhaps additional details about the execution (warning messages, error messages, etc.)

1.7   TRANSACTION MANAGEMENT IN DISTRIBUTED SYSTEMS

As discussed, transactions in a distributed system can access data at more than one site. Each transaction consists of a number of subtransactions that must run at a site where the data is. Each subtransaction represents an agent for the distributed transaction. Each agent must be able to commit at a local site for the global transaction to commit. If the global transaction cannot commit, none of the subtransactions commit either. Figure 1.13 shows a fund transfer transaction (T1) that transfers the amount "amt" from account x at Site A to account y at Site B. We designate the agents of transaction T1 at Sites A and B as T1A and T1B.

How does the system carry out this distributed transaction? The answer depends on the overhead of communication involved in execution of the transaction. Before getting into the details of executing this transaction, let us review what we have already outlined in this chapter. The global transaction manager (GTM) produces the distributed execution plan. This plan, as we will discuss in Chapter 4, is an optimized plan that the DEM must execute. The DEM is responsible for carrying out the plan by coordinating the activities of some LEMs that act as the distributed transaction's agents.

```
begin T1
    begin T1A
            Read bal(x);
            if account not found then
            {abort(T1A); print "account not found"; exit;
            };
            bal(x) = bal(x) - amt;
            if bal(x) < 0 then
            {abort(T1A); print "insufficient funds"; exit;
            };
            write bal(x); commit T1A;
    end T1A;
    begin T1B
            Read bal(y);
            if account not found then
            {abort(T1B); print "account not found"; exit;
            };
            bal(y) = bal(y) + amt;
            write bal(y); commit T1B;
    end T1B;
    commit T1;
end T1;
```

Figure 1.13   A distributed fund transfer transaction.

```
Begin Tl
    Select Bal Into X From Acctl
    Where A# = 100;

    Select Bal Into Y From Acct2
    Where A# = 200;

    Select Bal Into Z From Acct3
    Where A# = 300;

    REPORT X+Y+Z TO USER
End Tl;
```

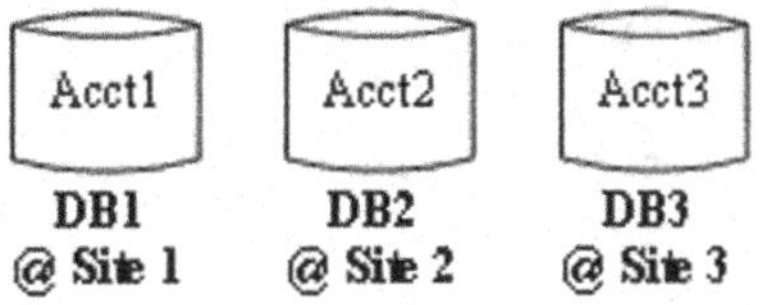

Figure 1.14   An example of a three-site distributed transaction.

Example 1.1   Consider a three-site system as shown in Figure 1.14, where transaction T1 enters the system at Site 1. Transaction T1 needs to reads the total balance for accounts 100, 200, and 300. Let's assume that the account table is horizontally fragmented across three sites. Site 1 holds accounts 1 to 150, Site 2 holds accounts 151 to 250, and Site 3 holds accounts 251 and higher. If X, Y, and Z represent the balances for accounts 100, 200, and 300, respectively, we can execute this distributed transaction as follows:

```
Send "necessary commands" to Site 1 to read "X" from DB1;
Send "necessary commands" to Site 2 to read "Y" from DB2;
Send "necessary commands" to Site 3 to read "Z" from DB3;
Receive "X" from Site 1;
Receive "Y" from Site 2;
Receive "Z" from Site 3;
Calculate Result = X + Y + Z;
Display Result to User;
```

Note that the Decomposer must know that the account table has three horizontal fragments called Acct1, Acct2, and Acct3. Based on the fragmentation assumptions we have made, account 100 is stored at Site 1, account 200 is stored at Site 2, and account 300 is stored at Site 3. For this example, the DEM needs to send two commands to the LEM at Site 2. One command is to read the balance of account 200. This command in SQL is "Select bal into Y from Account where A# = 200." The second command is an instruction to Site 2 to send the results back to Site 1. Site 1 packages these two commands in one message and sends the message to Site 2. In response, Site 2 sends the balance of account 200 in variable Y, as part of a response message, back to Site 1. Similar commands are sent to Site 1 and Site 3.

```
Distributed Execution Plan for DEM at Site 1:
Send "Select Bal into X From Acct1 Where A# = 100;
       Send X to Site 1"
to Site 1;
Send "Select Bal into Y From Acct2 Where A# = 200;
       Send Y to Site 1"
to Site 2;
Send "Select Bal into Z From Acct3 Where A# = 300;
       Send X to Site 1"
to Site 3;
Receive X from Site 1;
Receive Y from Site 2;
Receive Z from Site 3;
Calculate Result = X+Y+Z;
Display Result to User;


Plan for LEM at Site 1:
Select Bal Into X From Acct1 Where A# = 100;
Send X to Site 1;

Plan for LEM at Site 2:
Select Bal Into Y From Acct1 Where A# = 200;
Send Y to Site 1;

Plan for LEM at Site 3:
Select Bal Into Z From Acct1 Where A# = 300;
Send Z to Site 1;
```

Figure 1.15   Detailed execution plans for DEM and its LEMs.

Since Site 1 cannot add variables X, Y, and Z until all three variables arrive at its site, Site 1 must perform a blocking receive to achieve the necessary synchronization. A blocking receive is a receive command that blocks the process that executes it until the sought data has arrived at the site. Figure 1.15 shows the detailed distributed execution plan and individual plans for each of the three LEMs. In order for the DEM and the LEMs to be able to carry out their tasks, some services are required.

At a minimum, the system must have the ability to:

- Find the server address where the agent is going to run
- Remotely activate a process—DEM must activate its agents at remote sites
- Synchronize processes across sites—DEM must wait for LEMs to send their results to continue
- Transfer commands and receive results from its agents
- Transfer temporary data across sites—a select may return more than one row as its results

- Find out and ignore any commands that might be out of order or should not be processed
- Remotely deactivate a process—DEM needs to deactivate its agents

In the approach we used for coordinating the activities of the DEM and its LEMs, the DEM acted as the coordinator (Master) and the LEMs acted as the followers (Slaves) [Larson85]. Figure 1.16 depicts the Master–Slave approach to distributed execution management.

In the Master–Slave approach, the DEM synchronizes all temporary data movements. In this approach, LEMs send temporary data only to the DEM. Sometimes it is more beneficial to send temporary data from one LEM directly to another LEM. In this case, the DEM needs to send the proper commands and actions to the LEMs so that the LEMs can synchronize their own activities. Larson [Larson85] calls this type of control triangular distributed execution control. Figure 1.17 shows this type of control across one DEM and two LEMs.

Example 1.2   For this example, we assume the system has four sites. The user enters transaction T into the system at Site 0. There are three tables in the system defined as:

```
Person (SSN, Name, Profession, sal) stored at Site 1
Car (Name, Make, Year, SSN) stored at Site 2
Home (Address, No-of-rooms, SSN) stored at Site 3
```

For this distributed system, we want to print car and home address information for every person who makes more than $100,000. Applying a triangular distributed transaction control approach to this example results in the local execution plans shown in Figure 1.18. There are four LEMs in this system. These LEMs are numbered 0 through 3, indicating the site at which each runs. Although we do not have any data stored at Site 0, we must have one LEM there to perform the final join across the temporary tables that other LEMs send to it. This LEM acts as the merger, which we discussed in Section 1.1.

The synchronization mechanism used to coordinate the activities of the LEMs is implemented via the send and receive commands. When a LEM executes a receive command, it blocks itself until the corresponding data arrives at its site (this is an example of a blocking execution call or a blocking messaging call; see Section 14.3.1

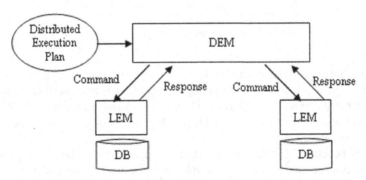

Figure 1.16   Master–Slave distributed transaction control.

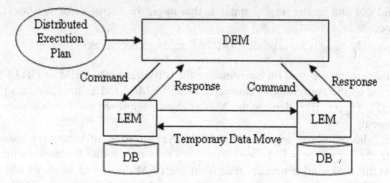

Figure 1.17 Triangular distributed transaction control.

```
@Site 1 do:
  Create table T1 as
    Select SSN, Name, Sal
    From Person
    Where sal > 100,000;
  Send T1 to S0;
  Create table T11 as
    Select SSN
    From Person
    Where sal > 100,000;
  Send T11 to Site 2;
  Send T11 to Site 3;
              (a)
```

```
@Site 2 do:
  Receive T11;
  Create table T2 as
    Select Name, Make, Year, T11.SSN
    From Car, T11
    Where T11.SSN = Car.SSN;
  Send T2 to Site 0;
              (b)
```

```
@ Site 3 do:
  Receive T11;
  Create table T3 as
    Select  Address, T11.SSN
    From Home, T11
    Where T11.SSN = Home.SSN;
  Send T3 to Site 0;

              (c)
```

```
@Site 0 do:
  Receive T1;
  Receive T2;
  Receive T3;
  Select *
  From T1, T2, T3
  Where T1.SSN= T2.SSN
  and T1.SSN=T3.SSN;
  Display Results to User;
              (d)
```

Figure 1.18 Local execution plans for Example 1.2.

for further details). For our example, the only LEM that can start processing immediately after activation is LEM 1 (see Figure 1.18a). That is because this LEM does not execute a receive command right away. On the other hand, all the other LEMs execute a receive command first. This action blocks these processes until the necessary data arrives at their sites.

It should be clear by now that the distributed execution plan—the plan that the DEM must run—contains the local commands that must be sent to the four LEMs.

```
Send            "Create table T1 as
                Select SSN, Name, Sal
                From Person Where sal > 100,000;
                Send T1 to Site 0;
                Create table T11 as
                Select SSN
                From Person
                Where sal > 100,000;
                Send T11 to Site 2;
                Send T11 to Site 3;"
To LEM @ Site 1;

Send            "Receive T11;
                Create table T2 as
                Select Make, Year, T11.SSN
                From Car, T11
                Where T11.SSN = Car.SSN;
                Send T2 to Site 0;"
To LEM @ Site 2;

Send            "Receive T11;
                Create table T3 as
                Select  Address, T11.SSN
                From Home, T11
                Where T11.SSN = Home.SSN;
                Send T3 to Site 0;"
To LEM @ Site 3;

Send            "Receive T1; Receive T2; Receive T3;
                Select *
                From T1, T2, T3
                Where T1.SSN= T2.SSN and T1.SSN=T3.SSN;
                Display Results to User;"
To LEM @ Site 0;
```

Figure 1.19   Distributed execution plan for Example 1.2.

Figure 1.19 depicts the distributed execution plan for this example. This execution strategy obviously uses a triangular control approach. As seen from this figure, the distributed execution plan contains only four messages that the DEM must send. Each one of these messages consists of the commands that one LEM must run. Obviously, since the DEM and LEM 0 are at the same site (Site 0), the message that the DEM sends to LEM 0 is a local message.

Example 1.3   Assume the table "EMP(EmpID, Name, Loc, Sal)" is horizontally fragmented into fragments MPLS_Farg, LA_Frag, and NY_Frag. Each horizontal fragment stores information about those employees who work at the corresponding location. LA_Frag stores information about employees who work in LA, NY_Frag contains information about employees who work in NY, and MPLS_Frag contains information about employees who work in MPLS. Transaction T enters the DEM deployed in St. Paul and needs to figure out the average salary for all employees in the company. An unoptimized query execution plan would try to reconstruct the EMP table from its fragments by sending all rows from all fragments to St. Paul and then using the SQL aggregate function AVG(sal) as

```
Select AVG(sal) From EMP;
```

If each row of the table takes one message to send from any site to any other site, this strategy would require as many messages as the total number of employees in the organization. However, we can execute this transaction using a small number of messages. The idea is not to materialize the EMP table but to figure out the average salary from the three fragments mathematically as

```
AVG(sal) =
(SAL_LA+SAL_MPLS+SAL_NY)/(count_LA+count_MPLS+count_NY)
```

In this formula, each "SAL" variable represents the total salary for the employees in its corresponding fragment, and each "count" variable indicates the total number of employees in its fragment. Once we realize this, we can use the Master–Slave control as shown Figure 1.20 to get the results. Note that in this figure, we use the LEM at St. Paul as the merger of the results from the local sites. Since this LEM does not have to perform any database operation, there is no need for a DBMS at St. Paul. In a

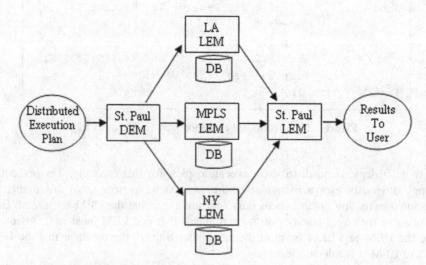

Figure 1.20   Master–Slave execution plan for query in Example 1.3.

```
LEM @ LA:
Select count(*), SUM(Salary) from LA_Frag into count_LA, SAL_LA;
Send "count_LA and SAL_LA" to LEM @ St. Paul;
Communication cost = 1 message

LEM @ MPLS:
Select count(*), SUM(Salary) from MPLS_Frag into count_MPLS, SAL_MPLS;
Send "count_MPLS and SAL_MPLS" to LEM @ St. Paul;
Communication cost = 1 message

LEM @ NY:
Select count(*), SUM(Salary) from NY_Frag into count_NY, SAL_NY;
Send "count_NY and SAL_NY" to LEM @ St. Paul;
Communication cost = 1 message

LEM @ St. Paul:
Receive count_LA and SAL_LA from LEM @ LA;
Receive count_MPLS and SAL_MPLS from LEM @ MPLS;
Receive count_NY and SAL_NY from LEM @ NY;
Calculate AVG = (SAL_LA+SAL_MPLS+SAL_NY)/(count_MPLS+count_LA+count_NY);
Display to the user;
Communication cost = 0

DEM @ NY:
Send "Select count(*), SUM(Salary) from MPLS_Frag into count_MPLS, SAL_MPLS;
     Send "count_MPLS and SAL_MPLS" to LEM @ St. Paul;" to LEM @ MPLS;
Send "Select count(*), SUM(Salary) from LA_Frag into count_LA, SAL_LA;
     Send "count_LA and SAL_LA" to LEM @ St. Paul;" to LEM @ LA;
Send "Select count(*), SUM(Salary) from NY_Frag into count_NY, SAL_NY;
     Send "count_NY and SAL_NY" to LEM @ St. Paul;" to LEM @ NY;
Communication cost = 3 messages
```

Figure 1.21 Distributed and local execution plans for query in Example 1.3.

nonoptimized approach as discussed above, the St. Paul LEM would require a DBMS to run the select statement that calculates the average salary.

Figure 1.21 shows the local execution plans for each LEM and the distributed execution plan for the DEM. As seen from this figure, the Master–Salve execution control takes six messages. A careful reader realizes that using a triangular execution control would require only four messages. We leave this as an exercise for the readers.

1.8 SUMMARY

Centralized database environments and specifically distributed database environments are complex systems composed of many subsystems, components, and services. This book discusses issues in implementing a DDBE. The emphasis of the book is on the practical aspects of implementing a DDBE. In this chapter, we have outlined the architecture of a DDBE and have discussed approaches to controlling the execution of a transaction.

1.9   GLOSSARY

Data Content   A data value (or set of data values) stored in a database.

Data Model (DM)   A representation of the structure of data.

Data Modeling Language (ML)   See **Modeling Language**.

Data Read Service (Drd-S)   A DBE service that provides the ability to retrieve data from the database.

Data Schema   See **Data Model**.

Data Write Service (Dwr-S)   A DBE service that provides the ability to write data to the database.

Database (DB)   A collection of data organized according to one or more data models.

Database Client (DB-Client)   An agent interfacing to a database either interactively or as an application.

Database Environment (DBE)   A collection of one or more DBs along with any software providing at least the minimum set of required data operations and management facilities.

Database Management System (DBMS)   A collection of software services or components that control access to, and modification of, data in a database.

Database Server (DB-Server)   A collection of software services (or a particular deployed instance of those services) that handles the interface to the database for database clients.

Deadlock Handling Service (Dead-S)   The service that handles deadlocks in a DBE.

Distributed Database (DDB)   A collection of software that allows several databases to operate as though they were part of a single database, even though they are actually separate and possibly deployed at different sites.

Execution Optimization Service (Eopt-S)   A DBE service that optimizes execution of the user's create, update, and delete commands.

Execution Service (Exec-S)   A DBE service that provides the ability to create, update, and delete data.

Fallback and Recovery Service (Rec-S)   A DBE service that guarantees availability of the database even when failures happen.

Locking Service (Lock-S)   A service that provides for data component locking capability.

Metadata   A piece or set of information about data.

Modeling Language (ML)   A vocabulary and set of rules used to define a model. Typically, there are also hints or suggestions for diagrammatic representations of the model, but this is not strictly speaking a requirement. For example, consider the Entity Relationship Modeling technique described by Dr. Chen, the Relational Model as formalized by Dr. Codd and the ANSI standard, or each proprietary Structured Query Language (SQL) defined by a particular RDBMS implementation.

Persistent Data   Data that is stored to secondary storage (hard drive).

Query   A formulation of a user's request to retrieve data, typically involving some criteria that control the filtering or formatting of the data that is returned.

Query Optimization Service (Qopt-S)   A DBE service that optimizes the plan used to execute queries.

Query Request Service (Qreq-S)   A DBE service that allows users to query the data in a database.

Replication Service (Repl-S)   A DBE service that manages multiple copies of the same data (including duplicate tables and/or duplicate databases).

Secondary Storage   A storage facility that does not lose its contents upon power shutdown (hard drive).

Security Service (Sec-S)   A service that guards the database against unwanted and unauthorized access.

Semantic Integrity Service (Semi-S)   A service that preserves the integrity and consistency of the data in a database.

Service   A logical collection (specification/design) of well-defined, cohesively related functionality or a software instance (physical collection) that implements this functionality.

Service Consumer   A component or subsystem that uses a set of functionality implemented by some other component or subsystem (consumes a service implemented by some service provider).

Service Provider   A component or subsystem that implements a set of functionality and makes it available to other components and subsystems (provides a service to be used by some service consumer).

Subsystem   A collection of components and/or subsystems that is part of a larger system but also a system in its own right.

Timestamping Service (Time-S)   A DBE service that creates a real and/or logical clock reading as a timestamp.

Transaction Management Service (Tran-S)   A DBE service guaranteeing that either all the CRUD operations within a well-defined set (called a transaction or a logical-unit-of-work) are committed to the database or none of them are committed to the database.

REFERENCES

[Larson85] Larson, J., and Rahimi, S., *Tutorial: Distributed Database Management*, IEEE Computer Society Press, New York, 1985, pp. 91–94.

[Sheth90] Sheth, A., and Larson, J., "Federated Database Systems for Managing Distributed, Heterogeneous and Autonomous Databases," *Computing Surveys*, Vol. 22, No. 3, September 1990, pp. 183–236.

[SPARC75] ANSI/X3/SPARC Study Group on Data Base Management Systems: (1975), *Interim Report. FDT*, ACM SIGMOD bulletin, Vol. 7, No. 2.

[SPARC76] "The ANSI/SPARC DBMS Model," in *Proceedings of the Second SHARE Working Conference on Data Base Management Systems*, Montreal, Canada, April 26–30, 1976.

[SPARC77] Jardine, D., *The ANSI/SPARC DBMS Model*, North-Holland Publication, Amsterdam, 1977.

2

DATA DISTRIBUTION ALTERNATIVES

In a distributed database management system (DDBMS) data is intentionally distributed to take advantage of all computing resources that are available to the organization. For these systems, the schema design is done top–down. A **top–down** design approach considers the data requirements of the entire organization and generates a **global conceptual model (GCM)** of all the information that is required. The GCM is then distributed across all appropriate local DBMS (LDBMS) engines to generate the **local conceptual model (LCM)** for each participant LDBMS. As a result, DDBMSs always have **one and only one** GCM and one or more LCM. Figure 2.1 depicts the top–down distribution design approach in a distributed database management system.

By contrast, the design of a federated database system is done from the bottom–up. A **bottom–up** design approach considers the existing data distributed within an organization and uses a process called schema integration to create at least one unified schema (Fig. 2.2). The **unified schema** is similar to the GCM, except that there can be more than one unified schema. **Schema integration** is a process that uses a collection of existing conceptual model elements, which have previously been exported from one or more LCMs, to generate a semantically integrated model (a single, unified schema). We will examine the details of federated database systems in Chapter 12.

Designers of a distributed database (DDB) will decide what distribution alternative is best for a given situation. They may decide to keep every table intact (all rows and all columns of every table are stored in the same DB at the same Site) or to break up some of the tables into smaller chunks of data called **fragments** or **partitions**. In a distributed database, the designers may decide to store these fragments locally (**localized**) or store these fragments across a number of LDBMSs on the network (**distributed**).

Distributed Database Management Systems by Saeed K. Rahimi and Frank S. Haug
Copyright © 2010 the IEEE Computer Society

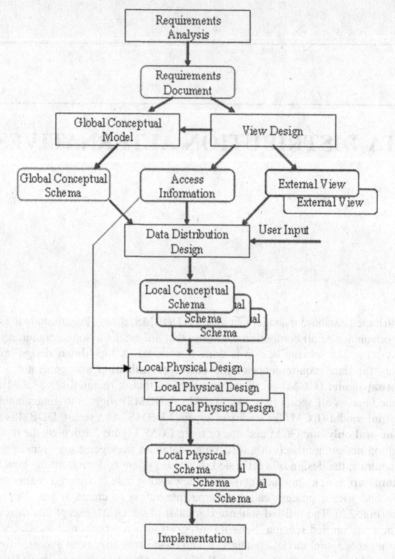

Figure 2.1   The top–down design process for a distributed database system.

Distributed tables can have one of the following forms:

- Nonreplicated, nonfragmented (nonpartitioned)
- Fully replicated (all tables)
- Fragmented (also known as partitioned)
- Partially replicated (some tables or some fragments)
- Mixed (any combination of the above)

The goal of any data distribution is to provide for increased availability, reliability, and improved query access time. On the other hand, as opposed to query access time,

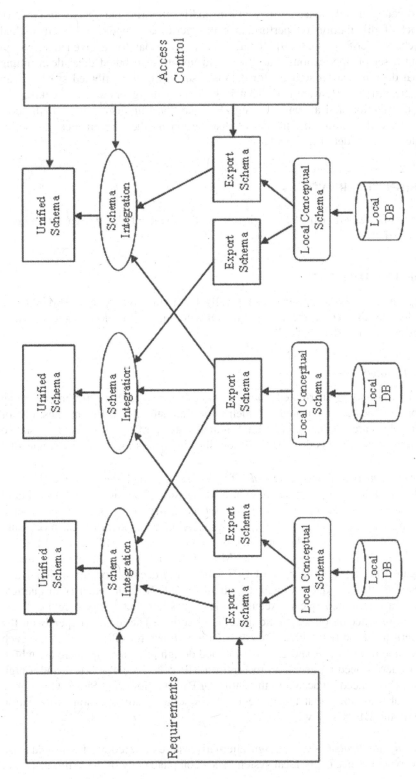

Figure 2.2 The bottom-up design process for a federated database system using schema integration.

distributed data generally takes more time for modification (update, delete, and insert). The impact of distribution on performance of queries and updates is well studied by researchers [Ceri87], [Özsu99]. It has been proved that for a given distribution design and a set of applications that query and update distributed data, determining the optimal data allocation strategy for database servers in a distributed system is an NP-complete problem [Eswaren74]. That is why most designers are not seeking the best data distribution and allocation design but one that minimizes some of the cost elements. We will examine the impact of distribution on the performance of queries and updates in more detail in Chapter 4.

2.1   DESIGN ALTERNATIVES

In this section, we will explore the details of each one of the design alternatives mentioned earlier.

2.1.1   Localized Data

This design alternative keeps all data logically belonging to a given DBMS at one site (usually the site where the controlling DBMS runs). This design alternative is sometimes called "not distributed."

2.1.2   Distributed Data

A database is said to be distributed if any of its tables are stored at different sites; one or more of its tables are replicated and their copies are stored at different sites; one or more of its tables are fragmented and the fragments are stored at different sites; and so on. In general, a database is distributed if not all of its data is localized at a single site.

2.1.2.1   Nonreplicated, Nonfragmented   This design alternative allows a designer to place different tables of a given database at different sites. The idea is that data should be placed close to (or at the site) where it is needed the most. One benefit of such data placement is the reduction of the communication component of the processing cost. For example, assume a database has two tables called "EMP" and "DEPT." A designer of DDBMS may decide to place EMP at Site 1 and DEPT at Site 2. Although queries against the EMP table or the DEPT table are processed locally at Site 1 and Site 2, respectively, any queries against both EMP and DEPT together (join queries) will require a distributed query execution. The question that arises here is, "How would a designer decide on a specific data distribution?" The answer depends on the usage pattern for these two tables. This distribution allows for efficient access to each individual table from Sites 1 and 2. This is a good design if we assume there are a high number of queries needing access to the entire EMP table issued at Site 1 and a high number of queries needing access to the entire DEPT table issued at Site 2. Obviously, this design also assumes that the percentage of queries needing to join information across EMP and DEPT is low.

2.1.2.2   Fully Replicated   This design alternative stores one copy of each database table at every site. Since every local system has a complete copy of the entire database, all queries can be handled locally. This design alternative therefore provides for the best possible query performance. On the other hand, since all copies need to be in sync—show the same values—the update performance is impacted negatively. Designers of a DDBMS must evaluate the percentage of queries versus updates to make sure that deploying a fully replicated database has an overall acceptable performance for both queries and updates.

2.1.2.3 Fragmented or Partitioned   Fragmentation design approach breaks a table up into two or more pieces called fragments or partitions and allows storage of these pieces in different sites.

There are three alternatives to fragmentation:

- Vertical fragmentation
- Horizontal fragmentation
- Hybrid fragmentation

This distribution alternative is based on the belief that not all the data within a table is required at a given site. In addition, fragmentation provides for increased parallelism, access, disaster recovery, and security/privacy. In this design alternative, there is only one copy of each fragment in the system (nonreplicated fragments). We will explain how each of the above fragmentation schemes works in Section 2.2.

2.1.2.4 Partially Replicated   In this distribution alternative, the designer will make copies of some of the tables (or fragments) in the database and store these copies at different sites. This is based on the belief that the frequency of accessing database tables is not uniform. For example, perhaps Fragment 1 of the EMP table might be accessed more frequently than Fragment 2 of the table. To satisfy this requirement, the designer may decide to store only one copy of Fragment 2, but more than one copy of Fragment 1 in the system. Again, the number of Fragment 2 copies needed depends on how frequently these access queries run and where these access queries are generated.

2.1.2.5 Mixed Distribution   In this design alternative, we fragment the database as desired, either horizontally or vertically, and then partially replicate some of the fragments.

2.2 FRAGMENTATION

As outlined earlier, fragmentation requires a table to be divided into a set of smaller tables called fragments. Fragmentation can be **horizontal, vertical**, or **hybrid** (a mix of horizontal and vertical). Horizontal fragmentation can further be classified into two classes: **primary horizontal fragmentation (PHF)** and **derived horizontal fragmentation (DHF)**. When thinking about fragmentation, designers need to decide on the degree of granularity for each fragment. In other words, how many of the table columns and/or rows should be in a fragment? The range of options is vast. At one end, we can have all the rows and all the columns of the table in one fragment. This obviously gives us a nonfragmented table; the grain is too coarse if we were planning to have at least one fragment. At the other end, we can put each data item (a single column value for a single row) in a separate fragment. This grain obviously is too fine: it would be hard to manage and would add too much overhead to processing queries. The answer should be somewhere in between these two extremes. As we will explain later, the optimal solution depends on the type and frequency of queries that applications run against the table. In the rest of this section, we explore each fragmentation type and formalize the fragmentation process.

2.2.1 Vertical Fragmentation

Vertical fragmentation (VF) will group the columns of a table into fragments. VF must be done in such a way that the original table can be reconstructed from the fragments. This fragmentation requirement is called "reconstructiveness." This requirement is used to reconstruct the original table when needed. As a result, each VF fragment must contain the primary key column(s) of the table. Because each fragment contains a subset of the total set of columns in the table, VF can be used to enforce security and/or privacy of data. To create a vertical fragment from a table, a select statement is used in which "Column_list" is a list of columns from R that includes the primary key.

```
Select Column_list from R;
```

Example 2.1   Consider the EMP table shown in Figure 2.3. Let's assume that for security reasons the salary information for employees needs to be maintained in the company headquarters' server, which is located in Minneapolis.

To achieve this, the designer will fragment the table vertically into two fragments as follows:

```
Create table EMP_SAL as
    Select EmpID, Sal
    From EMP;
```

EmpID	Name	Loc	Sal	DOB	Dept
283948	Joe	LA	25,000	2/6/43	Maintenance
109288	Larry	New York	35,200	12/3/52	Payroll
284003	Moe	LA	43,000	7/12/56	Maintenance
320021	Sam	New York	53,500	8/30/47	Production
123456	Steve	Minneapolis	67,000	5/14/78	Management
334456	Jack	New York	55,000	5/30/67	Production
222222	Saeed	Minneapolis	34,000	4/27/59	Management

EMP Table

Figure 2.3 The nonfragmented version of the EMP table.

```
Create table EMP_NON_SAL as
    Select EmpID, Name, Loc, DOB, Dept
    From EMP;
```

EMP_SAL contains the salary information for all employees while EMP_NON_SAL contains the nonsensitive information. These statements generate the vertical fragments shown in Figure 2.4a, 2.4b from the EMP table.

After fragmentation, the EMP table will not be stored physically anywhere. But, to provide for fragmentation transparency—not requiring the users to know that the EMP table is fragmented—we have to be able to reconstruct the EMP table from its VF fragments. This will give the users the illusion that the EMP table is stored intact. To do this, we will use the following join statement anywhere the EMP table is required:

EmpID	Sal
283948	25,000
109288	35,200
284003	43,000
320021	53,500
123456	67,000
334456	55,000
222222	34,000

(a) EMP_Sal Fragment

EmpID	Name	Loc	DOB	Dept
283948	Joe	LA	2/6/43	Maintenance
109288	Larry	New York	12/3/52	Payroll
284003	Moe	LA	7/12/56	Maintenance
320021	Sam	New York	8/30/47	Production
123456	Steve	Minneapolis	5/14/78	Management
334456	Jack	New York	5/30/67	Production
222222	Saeed	Minneapolis	4/27/59	Management

(b) EMP_NON_Sal Fragment

Figure 2.4 The vertical fragments of the EMP table.

```
Select EMP_SAL.EmpID, Sal, Name, Loc, DOB, Dept
From EMP_SAL, EMP_NON_SAL
Where EMP_SAL.EmpID = EMP_NON_SAL.EmpID;
```

Note: This join statement can be used in defining a view called "EMP" and/or can be used as an in-line view in any select statement that uses the virtual (physically nonexisting) table "EMP."

2.2.2 Horizontal Fragmentation

Horizontal fragmentation (HF) can be applied to a base table or to a fragment of a table. Note that a fragment of a table is itself a table. Therefore, in the following discussion when we use the term table, we might refer to a base table or a fragment of the table. HF will group the rows of a table based on the values of one or more columns. Similar to vertical fragmentation, horizontal fragmentation must be done in such a way that the base table can be reconstructed (reconstructiveness). Because each fragment contains a subset of the rows in the table, HF can be used to enforce security and/or privacy of data. Every horizontal fragment must have all columns of the original base table. To create a horizontal fragment from a table, a select statement is used. For example, the following statement selects the row from R satisfying condition C:

```
Select * from R where C;
```

As mentioned earlier, there are two approaches to horizontal fragmentation. One is called primary horizontal fragmentation (PHF) and the other is called derived horizontal fragmentation (DHF).

2.2.2.1 Primary Horizontal Fragmentation   Primary horizontal fragmentation (PHF) partitions a table horizontally based on the values of one or more columns of the table. Example 2.2 discusses the creation of three PHF fragments from the EMP table based on the values of the Loc column.

Example 2.2   Consider the EMP table shown in Figure 2.3. Suppose we have three branch offices, with each employee working at only one office. For ease of use, we decide that information for a given employee should be stored in the DBMS server at the branch office where that employee works. Therefore, the EMP table needs to be fragmented horizontally into three fragments based on the value of the Loc column as shown below:

```
Create table MPLS_EMPS as
     Select *
     From EMP
     Where Loc = 'Minneapolis';

Create table LA_EMPS as
     Select *
     From EMP
     Where Loc = 'LA';
```

```
Create table NY_EMPS as
    Select *
    From EMP
    Where Loc = 'New York';
```

This design generates three fragments, shown in Figure 2.5a,b,c. Each fragment can be stored in its corresponding city's server.

Again, after fragmentation, the EMP table will not be physically stored anywhere. To provide for horizontal fragmentation transparency, we have to be able to reconstruct the EMP table from its HF fragments. This will give the users the illusion that the EMP table is stored intact. To do this, we will use the following union statement anywhere the EMP table is required:

```
(Select * from MPLS_EMPS
Union
Select * from LA_EMPS)
    Union
    Select * from NY_EMPS;
```

EmpID	Name	Loc	Sal	DOB	Dept
123456	Steve	Minneapolis	67,000	5/14/78	Management
222222	Saeed	Minneapolis	34,000	4/27/59	Management

(a) MPLS_EMPS fragment

EmpID	Name	Loc	Sal	DOB	Dept
283948	Joe	LA	25,000	2/6/43	Maintenance
284003	Moe	LA	43,000	7/12/56	Maintenance

(b) LA_EMPS fragment

EmpID	Name	Loc	Sal	DOB	Dept
109288	Larry	New York	35,200	12/3/52	Payroll
320021	Sam	New York	53,500	8/30/47	Production
334456	Jack	New York	55,000	5/30/67	Production

(c) NY_EMPS fragment

Figure 2.5 The horizontal fragments of the EMP table with fragments based on Loc.

2.2.2.2 Derived Horizontal Fragmentation Instead of using PHF, a designer may decide to fragment a table according to the way that another table is fragmented. This type of fragmentation is called derived horizontal fragmentation (DHF). DHF is usually used for two tables that are naturally (and frequently) joined. Therefore, storing corresponding fragments from the two tables at the same site will speed up the join across the two tables. As a result, an implied requirement of this fragmentation design is the presence of a join column across the two tables.

Example 2.3 Figure 2.6a shows table "DEPT(Dno, Dname, Budget, Loc)," where Dno is the primary key of the table. Let's assume that DEPT is fragmented based on the department's city. Applying PHF to the DEPT table generates three horizontal fragments, one for each of the cities in the database, as depicted in Figure 2.6b,c,d.

Now, let's consider the table "PROJ," as depicted in Figure 2.7a. We can partition the PROJ table based on the values of Dno column in the DEPT table's fragments with the following SQL statements. These statements will produce the derived fragments from the PROJ table as shown in Figure 2.7b,c. Note that there are no rows in PROJ3, since department "D4" does not manage any project.

Dno	Dname	Budget	Loc
D1	Management	750,000	Minneapolis
D2	Payroll	500,000	New York
D3	Production	400,000	New York
D4	Maintenance	300,000	LA

(a) DEPT Table

Dno	Dname	Budget	Loc
D1	Management	750,000	Minneapolis

(b) MPLS_DEPTS Fragment

Dno	Dname	Budget	Loc
D2	Payroll	500,000	New York
D3	Production	400,000	New York

(c) NY_DEPTS Fragment

Dno	Dname	Budget	Loc
D4	Maintenance	300,000	LA

(d) LA_DEPTS Fragment

Figure 2.6 The fragments of the DEPT table with fragments based on Loc.

Pno	Pname	Budget	Dno
P1	Database Design	135,000	D2
P2	Maintenance	310,000	D3
P3	CAD/CAM	500,000	D2
P4	Architecture	300,000	D1
P5	Documentation	450,000	D1

(a) PROJ Table

Pno	Pname	Budget	Dno
P4	Architecture	300,000	D1
P5	Documentation	450,000	D1

(b) PROJ1

Pno	Pname	Budget	Dno
P1	Database Design	135,000	D2
P3	CAD/CAM	500,000	D2
P2	Maintenance	310,000	D3

(c) PROJ2

Figure 2.7   The PROJ table and its component DHF fragments.

```
Create table PROJ1 as
     Select Pno, Pname, Budget, PROJ.Dno
     From PROJ, MPLS_DEPTS
     Where PROJ.Dno = MPLS_DEPTS.Dno;

Create table PROJ2 as
     Select Pno, Pname, Budget, PROJ.Dno
     From PROJ, NY_DEPTS
     Where PROJ.Dno = NY_DEPTS.Dno;

Create table PROJ3 as
     Select Pno, Pname, Budget, PROJ.Dno
     From PROJ, LA_DEPTS
     Where PROJ.Dno = LA_DEPTS.Dno;
```

It should be rather obvious that all the rows in PROJ1 have corresponding rows in the MPLS_DEPTS fragment, and similarly, all the rows in PROJ2 have corresponding rows in the NY_DEPTS fragment. Storing a derived fragment at the same database server where the deriving fragment is, will result in better performance since any join across the two tables' fragments will result in a 100% hit ratio (all rows in one fragment have matching rows in the other).

Example 2.4 For this example, assume that sometimes we want to find those projects that are managed by the departments that have a budget of less than or equal to 500,000 (department budget, not project budget) and at other times we want to find those projects that are managed by the departments that have a budget of more than 500,000. In order to achieve this, we fragment DEPT based on the budget of the department. All departments with a budget of less than or equal to 500,000 are stored in DEPT4 and other departments are stored in the DEPT5 fragment. Figures 2.8a and 2.8b show DEPT4 and DEPT5, respectively.

To easily answer the type of questions that we have outlined in this example, we should create two derived horizontal fragments of the PROJ table based on DEPT4 and DEPT5 as shown below.

```
Create table PROJ5 as
    Select Pno, Pname, Budget, PROJ.Dno
    From PROJ, DEPT4
    Where PROJ.Dno = DEPT4.Dno;

Create table PROJ6 as
    Select Pno, Pname, Budget, PROJ.Dno
    From PROJ, DEPT5
    Where PROJ.Dno = DEPT5.Dno;
```

Figure 2.9 shows the fragmentation of the PROJ table based on these SQL statements.

Dno	Dname	Budget	Loc
D3	Production	400,000	New York
D4	Maintenance	300,000	LA

(a) DEPT4

Dno	Dname	Budget	Loc
D1	Management	750,000	Minneapolis
D2	Payroll	500,000	New York

(b) DEPT5

Figure 2.8 The DEPT table fragmented based on Budget column values.

Pno	Pname	Budget	Dno
P2	Maintenance	310,000	D3

(a) PROJ5

Pno	Pname	Budget	Dno
P1	Database Design	135,000	D2
P3	CAD/CAM	500,000	D2
P4	Architecture	300,000	D1
P5	Documentation	450,000	D1

(b) PROJ6

Figure 2.9   The derived fragmentation of PROJ table based on the fragmented DEPT table.

2.2.3   Hybrid Fragmentation

Hybrid fragmentation (HyF) uses a combination of horizontal and vertical fragmentation to generate the fragments we need. There are two approaches to doing this. In the first approach, we generate a set of horizontal fragments and then vertically fragment one of more of these horizontal fragments. In the second approach, we generate a set of vertical fragments and then horizontally fragment one or more of these vertical fragments. Either way, the final fragments produced are the same. This fragmentation approach provides for the most flexibility for the designers but at the same time it is the most expensive approach with respect to reconstruction of the original table.

Example 2.5   Let's assume that employee salary information needs to be maintained in a separate fragment from the nonsalary information as discussed above. A vertical fragmentation plan will generate the EMP_SAL and EMP_NON_SAL vertical fragments as explained in Example 2.1. The nonsalary information needs to be fragmented into horizontal fragments, where each fragment contains only the rows that match the city where the employees work. We can achieve this by applying horizontal fragmentation to the EMP_NON_SAL fragment of the EMP table. The following three SQL statements show how this is achieved.

```
Create table NON_SAL_MPLS_EMPS as
    Select *
    From EMP_NON_SAL
    Where Loc = 'Minneapolis';

Create table NON_SAL_LA_EMPS as
    Select *
    From EMP_NON_SAL
    Where Loc = 'LA';
```

```
Create table NON_SAL_NY_EMPS as
    Select *
    From EMP_NON_SAL
    Where Loc = 'New York';
```

The final distributed database is depicted in Figure 2.10.

Observation: The temporary EMP_NON_SAL fragment is not physically stored anywhere in the system after it has been horizontally fragmented. As a result, one can bypass generating this fragment by using the following set of SQL statements to generate the required fragments directly from the EMP table.

EmpID	Sal
283948	25,000
109288	35,200
284003	43,000
320021	53,500
123456	67,000
334456	55,000
222222	34,000

EMP_Sal

EmpID	Name	Loc	DOB	Dept
123456	Steve	Minneapolis	5/14/78	Management
222222	Saeed	Minneapolis	4/27/59	Management

NON_Sal_MPLS_EMPS

EmpID	Name	Loc	DOB	Dept
283948	Joe	LA	2/6/43	Maintenance
284003	Moe	LA	7/12/56	Maintenance

NON_Sal_LA_EMPS

EmpID	Name	Loc	DOB	Dept
109288	Larry	New York	12/3/52	Payroll
320021	Sam	New York	8/30/47	Production
334456	Jack	New York	5/30/67	Production

NON_Sal_NY_EMPS

Figure 2.10 The fragments of the EMP table.

```
Create table NON_SAL_MPLS_EMPS as
    Select EmpID, Name, Loc, DOB, Dept
    From EMP
    Where Loc = 'Minneapolis';

Create table NON_SAL_LA_EMPS as
    Select EmpID, Name, Loc, DOB, Dept
    From EMP
    Where Loc = 'LA';

Create table NON_SAL_NY_EMPS as
    Select EmpID, Name, Loc, DOB, Dept
    From EMP
    Where Loc = 'New York';
```

2.2.4 Vertical Fragmentation Generation Guidelines

There are two approaches to vertical fragmentation design—grouping and splitting—proposed in the literature [Hoffer75] [Hammer79] [Sacca85]. In the remainder of this section, we will first provide an overview of these two options and then present more detail for the splitting option.

2.2.4.1 Grouping Grouping is an approach that starts by creating as many vertical fragments as possible and then incrementally reducing the number of fragments by merging the fragments together. Initially, we create one fragment per nonkey column, placing the nonkey column and the primary key of the table into each vertical fragment. This first step creates as many vertical fragments as the number of nonkey columns in the table. Most of the time, this degree of fragmentation is too fine and impractical. The grouping approach uses joins across the primary key, to group some of these fragments together, and we continue this process until the desired design is achieved. Aside from needing to fulfill the requirements for one or more application, there are very few restrictions placed upon the groups (fragments) we create in this approach. For example, the same nonkey column can participate in more than one group—that is, groups can have overlapping (nonkey) columns. If this "overlap" does occur, obviously, it will add to the overhead of replication control in a distributed DBMS system. As a result, grouping is not usually considered a valid approach for vertical fragmentation design. For more details on grouping see [Hammer79] and [Sacca85]. Hammer and Niamir introduced grouping for centralized DBMSs and Sacca and Wiederhold discussed grouping for distributed DBMSs.

2.2.4.2 Splitting Splitting is essentially the opposite of grouping. In this approach, a table is fragmented by placing each nonkey column in one (and only one) fragment, focusing on identifying a set of required columns for each vertical fragment. As such, there is no overlap of nonprimary key columns in the vertical fragments that are created using splitting. Hoffer and Severance [Hoffer75] first introduced splitting for centralized systems, while Navathe and colleagues [Navathe84] introduced splitting for distributed systems. There is general consensus that finding an ideal vertical fragmentation design—one that satisfies the requirements for a large set of applications—is not feasible. In an ideal vertical fragment design, each application would only need to access the columns in one vertical fragment. If certain sets of columns are always processed together by the application, the process used to create this design is trivial. But real-life applications do not always behave as we wish. Hence, for a database that contains many tables with many columns, we need to develop a systematic approach for defining our vertical fragmentation.

As pointed out by Hammer and Niamir [Hammer79], there is a direct correlation between the number of columns in a table and the number of the possible vertical fragmentation options. A table with m columns can be vertically partitioned into $B(m)$ different alternatives, where $B(m)$ is the mth Bell number. For large m, $B(m)$ approaches m^m. For example, if a table has 15 columns, then the number of possible vertical fragments is 10^9 and the number of vertical fragments for a table with 30 columns is 10^{23}. Obviously, evaluating 10^9 (or 1,000,000,000) alternatives for a 15-column table is not practical. Instead of evaluating all possible vertical fragments, designers can use the metric **affinity** or **closeness** of columns to each other to decide whether or not a group of columns should be put in the same fragment. The affinity of columns expresses the extent to which they are used together in processing. By combining the access frequency of applications to columns of a table with the usage pattern of these applications, one can create the affinity matrix that forms the basis for vertically fragmenting the table.

Splitting in Distributed Systems   In this section, we will outline the proposal by Navathe and colleagues [Navathe84] in conjunction with an example. For further details about the approach, the reader should see the referenced publication.

Example 2.6   Consider applications "AP1", "AP2", "AP3", and "AP4" as shown. These applications work on the table "T" defined as "T(C̲, C1, C2, C3, C4)," where C is the primary key column of the table.

AP1: `Select C1 from T where C4 = 100;`
AP2: `Select C4 from T;`
AP3: `Update T set C3 = 15 where C2 = 50;`
AP4: `Update T set C1 = 5 where C3 = 10;`

UsAGE MATRIX   For a single site system, these applications are local and will have the usage matrix depicted in Figure 2.11. As can be seen, the usage matrix is a two-dimensional matrix that indicates whether or not an attribute (column) is used by an application. The cell in position (APi, Cj) is set to 1 if application "APi" accesses column "Cj," otherwise it is set to 0.

Observation 1: The **usage matrix** only indicates if a column is used by an application. However, the matrix does not show how many times an application accesses the table columns during a given time period. The **access frequency** is a term that represents how many times an application runs in a given period of time. The period of this measurement can be an hour, a day, a week, a month, and so on—as decided by the designer. Figure 2.12 depicts the expansion of the usage matrix to include the access frequency of each application.

	C1	C2	C3	C4
AP1	1	0	0	1
AP2	0	0	0	1
AP3	0	1	1	0
AP4	1	0	1	0

Figure 2.11   Single site usage matrix for Example 2.6.

	C1	C2	C3	C4	Access Frequency
AP1	1	0	0	1	3
AP2	0	0	0	1	7
AP3	0	1	1	0	4
AP4	1	0	1	0	3

Figure 2.12   Expansion of usage matrix.

Observation 2: Neither the usage matrix nor the access frequencies have any indication of distribution. In a distributed system, however, an application can have different frequencies at different sites. For example, in a four-site system, AP2 might run four times at S2 and three times at S3. It is also possible that AP2 might run seven times at site S2 and zero times everywhere else. In both cases, the frequency would still be shown as seven in the usage matrix. Also, each time the application runs at a site it might make more than one access to the table (and its columns). For example, suppose we had another application, AP5, defined as follows:

```
Begin AP5
    Select C1 from T where C4 = 100;
    Select C4 from T;
End AP1;
```

In this case, AP5 makes two references to T each time it runs. As a result, the actual access frequency for AP5 is calculated as "ACC(Pi) * REF (Pi)," where ACC(Pi) is the number of times the application runs and REF (Pi) is the number of accesses Pi makes to T every time it runs. To simplify the discussion, we assume "REF(Pi) = 1" for all processes, which results in "ACC(Pi) * REF(Pi) = ACC(Pi)."

If we include the access frequencies of the applications at each site for our original example (without AP5), this makes the usage matrix a three-dimensional matrix, where in the third axis we maintain the frequency of each application for each site. Since such

	C1	C2	C3	C4	Access Frequency			
					S1	S2	S3	S4
AP1	1	0	0	1	1	0	2	0
AP2	0	0	0	1	0	4	3	0
AP3	0	1	1	0	0	0	4	0
AP4	1	0	1	0	3	0	0	0

Figure 2.13 Access frequencies for a distributed system.

representation is difficult to display on two-dimensional paper, we flatten the matrix as shown in Figure 2.13.

By adding access frequencies for each application across all sites, we can get the affinity or closeness that each column has with the other columns referenced by the same application. This matrix is called the **process column affinity matrix**, and it is shown for this example in Figure 2.14.

The first row in this matrix shows the affinity of C1 to C4 (or C4 to C1) for AP1 being 3. Similarly, the third row indicates the affinity of C2 to C3 (or C3 to C2) for AP3 being 4; C1 to C3 (or C3 to C1) for AP4 being 3; and so on. Note that since AP2 only uses C4, for AP2 there is no affinity between C4 and other columns. In order to capture these affinities, we can remove the application names from the matrix and create a two-dimensional matrix as shown in Figure 2.15. This matrix shows the affinity of each column of the table with other column(s) regardless of the applications that use them. We call this the **affinity matrix**.

Notice in Figure 2.15 that the diagonal cells—cells in position "(i,i)" for "i = 1 to 4"—have value 0. Since the diagonal cells do not store any values, we can calculate the affinity of column Ci with respect to all the other columns and store this value in "Cell(i,i)" in the matrix. C1 has an affinity with C3 weighted at 3 and an affinity with C4 weighted at 3. Therefore, the affinity of C1 across all applications at all sites is found by summing its affinity weights with all the other columns, "3 + 3 = 6." We will insert this total affinity value in "Cell(1,1)." Similarly, C3 has two affinities—one with C1 weighted at 3 and one with C2 weighted at 4. C3 has the total affinity value of

	C1	C2	C3	C4	Affinity
AP1	1	0	0	1	3
AP2	0	0	0	1	7
AP3	0	1	1	0	4
AP4	1	0	1	0	3

Figure 2.14 Process column affinity matrix.

	C1	C2	C3	C4
C1	0	0	3	3
C2	0	0	4	0
C3	3	4	0	0
C4	3	0	0	0

Figure 2.15   The affinity matrix.

	C1	C2	C3	C4
C1	6	0	3	3
C2	0	4	4	0
C3	3	4	7	0
C4	3	0	0	3

Figure 2.16   Affinity matrix with diagonal values calculated.

"$3 + 4 = 7$" for all applications across all sites, which we insert in "Cell(3,3)." Adding up all affinities of each column (summing across the rows), we can calculate the total affinity for each column, storing them in the diagonal cells. Figure 2.16 shows the results. In the next section, we will discuss an algorithm that generates our vertical fragmentation design based on the affinity information contained in this matrix.

THE BOND ENERGY ALGORITHM   The information in the affinity matrix shown in Figure 2.16 can be used to cluster the columns of T together. McCormick and colleagues suggest using the **Bond Energy Algorithm (BEA)** [McCormick72] for this. This algorithm takes the affinity matrix as an input parameter and generates a new matrix called the **clustered affinity matrix** as its output. The clustered affinity matrix is a matrix that reorders the columns and rows of the affinity matrix so that the columns with the greatest affinity for each other are "grouped together" in the same cluster—which is then used as the basis for splitting our table into vertical fragments. Details of this algorithm are outside the scope of this chapter. In what follows, we will only discuss the steps in the algorithm for our example.

Step 1: Placement of the First Two Columns. In this step, we place the first two columns of the affinity matrix into a new matrix (the clustered affinity matrix). In our example, the first two columns are C1 and C2. According to McCormick and colleagues, the bond energy of any two columns such as "X1" and "X2"—shown as "Bond(X1, X2)"—is the row-wise sum of the product of the affinity values for X1 and X2, taken from the affinity matrix. Figure 2.17 shows this bond energy calculation for C1 and C2 of our example. In this figure, we created a new matrix

	C1	C2	product
C1	6	0	0
C2	0	4	0
C3	3	4	12
C4	3	0	0
Bond			12

Figure 2.17 The Bond calculation for columns C1 and C2 of Example 2.6.

by first copying the first two columns from the affinity matrix. Next, we augmented this new matrix by adding a new "product" column, where we show the result of the product (multiplication) of the two values in the same row, to the left of the column. For example, the product for row "C3" in this figure is 12, because "3 ∗ 4 = 12." Finally, we augmented it again by including the "Bond" row, which simply stores the sum of all the product column's values.

Step 2: Placement of Remaining Columns. In this step, we place each of the remaining columns (C3 and C4 in our example), one at a time, into the new clustered affinity matrix—which we have not actually shown yet, but since it only contains C1 and C2 we can understand what it looks like without presenting it in a separate figure. First, we will place C3, and then later C4, into the new matrix. The purpose of this step is to determine where each "new" column should be placed. In our example, first we need to decide "where" to add the C3 column from the affinity matrix to the matrix that already contains C1 and C2. For C3, there are three options—to place the C3 affinity information to the left side of C1 (making it the leftmost column in our new matrix), to place the C3 information in between C1 and C2, or to place the C3 affinity information on the right side of C2 (making it the rightmost column in the new table). We then need to calculate the contribution values of all these possible placements of the C3 affinity information, using the formula given in Equation 2.1. Once all contribution values are calculated, we choose the ordering that provides the highest contribution to the affinity measure.

Bond Contribution Calculation

$$\text{Cont}(X1, X2, X3) = 2 * \text{Bond}(X1, X2) + 2 * \text{Bond}(X2, X3) - 2 * \text{Bond}(X1, X3) \tag{2.1}$$

In general, when adding an affinity matrix column to the clustered affinity matrix, we must consider the two boundary conditions—leftmost and rightmost positions for the new column. The "X2" in the contribution formula is replaced with the column being considered, while the "X1" is the column to its left and "X3" is the column to its right. However, when we consider placing the new column in the leftmost position, there are no columns to the left of it—therefore, we use a pseudo-column named "C0" to represent this nonexistent column-to-the-left. Similarly, when we consider placing the new column in the rightmost position, we use another pseudo-column named "Cn" to represent the nonexistent column to its right. In our calculations, both C0 and Cn have an affinity of zero.

Therefore, when we consider adding C3 to the clustered affinity matrix for our example, there are three ordering options: "(C3, C1, C2)", "(C1, C3, C2)", or "(C1, C2, C3)." To determine which ordering yields the highest value for our affinity measure, we must calculate the contribution of C3 being added to the left of C1, between C1 and C2 and to the right of C2. Therefore, we need to calculate "Cont(C0, C3, C1)", "Cont(C1, C3, C2)," and "Cont(C2, C3, Cn)" and compare the results.

To calculate the contribution of "(C0, C3, C1)," we need to figure out the bonds for "(C0,C3)," "(C3, C1)," and "(C0, C1)." Once we have determined these bonds, we can use Equation 2.1 to calculate "Cont(C0, C3, C1) = 2* Bond(C0, C3) +2*

	C0	C3	product
C1	0	3	0
C2	0	4	0
C3	0	7	0
C4	0	0	0
Bond			0

(a)

	C3	C1	product
C1	3	6	18
C2	4	0	0
C3	7	3	21
C4	0	3	0
Bond			39

(b)

	C0	C1	product
C1	0	6	0
C2	0	0	0
C3	0	3	0
C4	0	3	0
Bond			0

(c)

Figure 2.18   Bonds for (C0, C3, C1) ordering.

Bond(C3, C1) $-2*$ Bond(C0, C1)." Figures 2.18a, 2.18b, and 2.18c depict these bond calculations. As these figures demonstrate, the Bond function will always return zero when either C0 or Cn is passed to it as a parameter, because C0 and Cn always have an affinity of zero.

By replacing the Bond functions with their values in the contribution formula, we calculate the contribution of this ordering as "Cont(C0, C3, C1) $= 2*0 + 2*$ $39 - 2*0 = 78$." Similarly, we can calculate the contributions of orderings "(C1, C3, C2)" and "(C1, C2, C3)" as

```
For ordering (C1, C3, C2):
Bond(C1, C3) = 39
Bond(C3, C2) = 44
Bond(C1, C2) = 12
Cont(C1, C3, C2) = 2*39 + 2*44 - 2*12 = 142

For ordering (C2, C3, Cn):
Bond(C2, C3) = 44
Bond(C3, Cn) = 0
Bond(C2, Cn) = 0
Cont(C1, C2, C3) = 2*44 + 2*0 - 2*0 = 88
```

Based on these calculations, the ordering "(C1, C3, C2)" provides the highest contribution. Using this ordering, Figure 2.19 shows the current definition of the new clustered affinity matrix. Since this matrix does not have C4 in it yet, it is called the partial clustered affinity matrix.

After adding C3 to the matrix, we are ready to add the affinity information for C4 as the final column. Adding C4 to the matrix requires calculating contributions of the orderings "(C0, C4, C1)," "(C1, C4, C3)," "(C3, C4, C2)," and "(C2, C4, Cn)." The following are the Bonds and contributions of these ordering options:

```
For ordering (C0, C4, C1):
Bond(C0, C4) = 0
Bond (C4, C1) = 27
Bond(C0, C1) = 0
Cont(C0, C4, C1) = 2*0 + 2*27 - 2 *0 = 54
```

	C1	C3	C2
C1	6	3	0
C2	0	4	4
C3	3	7	4
C4	3	0	0

Figure 2.19 The partial clustered affinity matrix.

```
For ordering (C1, C4, C3):
Bond(C1, C4) = 27
Bond(C4, C3) = 9
Bond(C1, C3) = 39
Cont(C1, C4, C3) = 2*27 + 2*9 - 2*39 = -6

For ordering (C3, C4, C2):
Bond(C3, C4) = 9
Bond(C4, C2) = 0
Bond(C3, C2) = 44
Cont((C3, C4, C2) = 2*9 + 2*0 - 2*44 = -70

For ordering (C2, C4, Cn):
Bond(C2, C4) = 0
Bond(C4, Cn) = 0
Bond(C2, Cn) = 0
Cont((C1, C4, C2) = 2*0 + 2*0 - 2*0 = 0
```

From these contribution calculations, the ordering "(C0, C4, C1)" yields the highest contribution and therefore is chosen. Figure 2.20 depicts the final ordering of affinity information for the columns of table "T" within the clustered affinity matrix.

Once the columns have been put in the right order, we order the rows similarly, ending up with the final clustered affinity matrix as shown in Figure 2.21.

	C4	C1	C3	C2
C1	3	6	3	0
C2	0	0	4	4
C3	0	3	7	4
C4	3	3	0	0

Figure 2.20 The clustered affinity matrix after rearranging the columns.

	C4	C1	C3	C2
C4	3	3	0	0
C1	3	6	3	0
C3	0	3	7	4
C2	0	0	4	4

Figure 2.21 The clustered affinity matrix after rearranging the rows and the columns.

Step 3: Partitioning the Table into Vertical Fragments. Step 3 is the last step in the process. In this step, we need to split the clustered affinity matrix into a top portion and a bottom portion as shown in Figure 2.22.

Among all applications that access this table, some access only the columns in the top corner (TC), some access only the columns in the Bottom Corner (BC), and the rest access columns in both corners (BOC). We consider $(n - 1)$ possible locations of the X point along the diagonal, where n is the size of the matrix (also the number of nonkey columns of the table). A nonoverlapping partition is obtained by selecting X such that the goal function "Z" as defined below is maximized.

```
Goal Function: Z = TCW * BCW - BOCW²
```

In Z, TCW is the total number of accesses by applications to columns in TC (**only** the columns in the top corner), BCW is the total number of accesses by applications to columns in BC (**only** the columns in the bottom corner), and BOCW is the total number of accesses by applications to columns in both quadrants (must access **at least one** column from TC and **at least one** column from BC).The partitioning that corresponds to the maximal value of Z is accepted if Z is positive and is rejected otherwise. This formula is based on the belief that "good" partitioning strategies increase the values of TCW and BCW while decreasing the value of BOCW. In order words, the approach tries to maximize the product TCW * BCW. This also results in the selection of values for TCW and BCW that are as close to equal as possible. Thus, the function will produce fragments that are "balanced." To find the splitting that yields the best partitioning of columns, we have to split the columns into a "one-column BC" and "$n - 1$ column TC" first. We calculate the value of Z for this starting point and then repeatedly add columns from TC to BC until TC is left with only one column. From these calculations, we choose the splitting that has the highest Z value. Recall the affinity matrix for our example (shown here again in

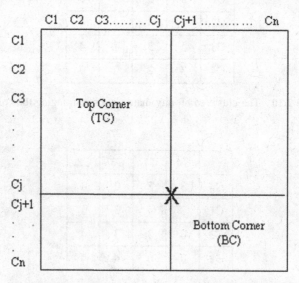

Figure 2.22 Partitioning of the clustered affinity matrix.

Figure 2.23a). As shown in Figure 2.23b, we begin partitioning the table by putting C4, C1, and C3 in TC and C2 in BC. In this figure, the "X icon" indicates the upper left corner of BC and the bottom right corner of TC.

The TC calculation will include the affinity value for all the applications that access one of the TC columns (C4, C1, or C3) but do not access any BC columns (C2). In this case, applications AP1, AP2, and AP4 access TC-only columns, AP3 accesses both TC and BC columns, and no application is BC-only. We use the function "AFF(a)" to represent the affinity for application "a." In other words, in our example, this is a short-hand notation for looking at the value for the affinity column in Figure 2.23a for the row corresponding to application "a." For this splitting option in our example, we calculate Z as follows:

```
TCW = AFF(AP1) + AFF(AP2) + AFF(AP4) = 3 + 7 + 3 = 13
BCW = none = 0
BOCW = AFF(AP3) = 4
Z = 13*0 - 4² = -16
```

In the next step, the splitting point is going to move to the middle of the matrix, leaving the TC and BC each with two columns as shown in Figure 2.24. Now, AP1 and AP2 remain the same, but AP3 uses BC-only columns, and AP4 uses columns that are from both-corners.

For this splitting option, the value of Z is calculated as follows:

```
TCW = AFF(AP1) + AFF(AP2) = 3 + 7 = 10
BCW = AFF(AP3) = 4
```

	C1	C2	C3	C4	Affinity
AP1	1	0	0	1	3
AP2	0	0	0	1	7
AP3	0	1	1	0	4
AP4	1	0	1	0	3

(a)

	C4	C1	C3	C2
C4	3	3	0	0
C1	3	6	3	0
C3	0	3	7	4
C2	0	0	4	4

(b)

Figure 2.23 The clustered affinity matrix partitioning starting point.

	C4	C1	C3	C2
C4	3	3	0	0
C1	3	6	3	0
C3	0	3	7	4
C2	0	0	4	4

Figure 2.24   Matrix for second split point.

```
BOCW = AFF(AP4) = 3
Z = 4*10 - 3² = 40 - 9 = 31
```

In the next step, the splitting point is going to move to the upper left corner as shown in Figure 2.25. Now, AP2 is still using only top-corner columns, but AP3 and AP4 are using bottom-only columns and AP1 is using columns from both-corners.

For this splitting option we have the following:

```
TCW = AFF(AP2) = 7
BCW = AFF(AP3) + AFF(AP4) = 4 + 3 = 7
BOCW = AFF(AP1) = 3
Z = 7*7 - 3² = 49 - 9 = 40
```

By now, it should be obvious that this approach creates nonoverlapping partitions by moving along the matrix diagonal. The proposed algorithm has the disadvantage of not being able to carve out an embedded or inner block of columns as a partition. To be able to do this, the approach has to place { C1, C3 } in one partition and { C4, C2 } in another partition as shown in Figure 2.26.

We can overcome this disadvantage by adding a SHIFT operation. When the SHIFT operation is utilized, it moves the topmost row of the matrix to the bottom and then it moves the leftmost column of the matrix to the extreme right. Figure 2.27a depicts the original matrix, along with an arrow indicating where the topmost row is supposed to be moved as part of the SHIFT. Figure 2.27b shows the

	C4	C1	C3	C2
C4	3	3	0	0
C1	3	6	3	0
C3	0	3	7	4
C2	0	0	4	4

Figure 2.25   Matrix for the third split point.

	C4	C1	C3	C2
C4	3	3	0	0
C1	3	6	3	0
C3	0	3	7	4
C2	0	0	4	4

Figure 2.26   Matrix for inner block of columns.

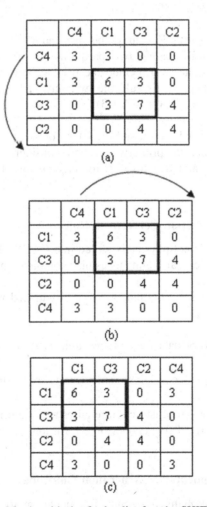

	C4	C1	C3	C2
C4	3	3	0	0
C1	3	6	3	0
C3	0	3	7	4
C2	0	0	4	4

(a)

	C4	C1	C3	C2
C1	3	6	3	0
C3	0	3	7	4
C2	0	0	4	4
C4	3	3	0	0

(b)

	C1	C3	C2	C4
C1	6	3	0	3
C3	3	7	4	0
C2	0	4	4	0
C4	3	0	0	3

(c)

Figure 2.27   Matrix with the final split after the SHIFT operation.

matrix after the rotation of the topmost row, with another arrow indicating where the leftmost columns are supposed to be moved as part of the same SHIFT operation. Figure 2.27c shows the matrix after the rightmost column is rotated. The SHIFT process is repeated a total of n times, so that every diagonal block gets the opportunity of being brought to the upper left corner in the matrix. For our example, we only need to utilize SHIFT once since all other combinations have already been covered.

After the SHIFT, AP4 is using TC-only columns, AP2 is using BC-only columns, and AP1 and AP3 are using columns from both-corners. For this splitting option we have the following:

```
TCW = AFF(AP4) = 3
BCW = AFF(AP2) = 7
BOCW = AFF(AP1) + AFF(AP3) = 3 + 4 = 7
Z = 3*7 - 7² = 21 - 49 = -28
```

Among all the positive Z values, the maximum value is 40. This value corresponds to the option creating two partitions "(C4)" and "(C1, C2, C3)." As mentioned before, we need to include the primary key column of the T table in every vertical fragment. As a result, the two vertical fragments will be defined as "VF1(C, C4)" and "VF2(C, C1, C2, C3)."

Final Note: We have only discussed the BEA for splitting the table into nonoverlapping vertical fragments (the primary key is not considered an overlap). Readers are referred to [Navathe84] and [Hammer79] for information about overlapping vertical fragments.

2.2.5 Vertical Fragmentation Correctness Rules

Since the original table is not physically stored in a DDBE, the original table must be reconstructible from its vertical fragments using a combination of some SQL statements (joins in this case).

As a result, the following requirements must be satisfied when fragmenting a table vertically:

- Completeness—every data item of the table is in, at least, one of the vertical fragments.
- Reconstructiveness—the original table can be reconstructed from the vertical fragments.
- Shared primary key—reconstruction requires that the primary key of the table be replicated in all vertical fragments (to perform joins).

2.2.6 Horizontal Fragmentation Generation Guidelines

As explained earlier, applying horizontal fragmentation to a table creates a set of fragments that contain disjoint rows of the table (horizontal disjointness). Horizontal fragmentation is useful because it can group together the rows of a table that satisfy the predicates of frequently run queries. As such, all rows of a given fragment should be in the result set of a query that runs frequently. To take advantage of this, the designer of a distributed database system should store each such horizontal fragment at the site where these types of queries run. This raises the question, "How do we decide which condition or conditions to use when we horizontally fragment a table?" The answer is formalized in [Özsu99] and also in [Bobak96]. We will summarize their discussion in this section and apply their formulation to an example in order to explain the general approach.

To fragment a table horizontally, we use one or more predicates (conditions). There are different types of predicates to choose from when fragmenting the table. For example, we can use **simple predicates**, such as "Sal > 100000" or "DNO = 1." In general, a simple predicate, P, follows the format "Column_Name **comparative_operator** Value." The comparative operator is one of the operators in the set $\{=, <, >, >=, <=, <>\}$. We can also use a **minterm predicate**, M, which is defined as a **conjunctive normal form** of simple predicates. For example, the predicates { Salary > 30,000 ˆ Location = "LA" } and { Salary > 30,000 ˆ Location<> "LA" } are minterm predicates. Here, the "ˆ" operator is read as "AND."

The set of all simple predicates used by all applications that query a given table is shown as "Pr = {p1, p2, ..., pn}." The set of all minterm predicates used by all applications that query the table is shown as " M = {m1, m2, ..., mk}." Applying the minterm predicates M to the table generates k minterm horizontal fragments denoted by the set "F = {F1, F2, ..., Fk}." For this fragmentation design, all rows in Fi, for "i = 1..k," satisfy mi.

2.2.6.1   *Minimality and Completeness of Horizontal Fragmentation*   It should be obvious that the more fragments that exist in a system, the more time the system has to spend in reconstructing the table. As a result, it is important to have a minimal set of horizontal fragments. To generate a minimal set of fragments, the following rules are applied.

> *Rule 1.* The rows of a table (or a fragment) should be partitioned into at least two horizontal fragments, if the rows are accessed differently by at least one application.
>
> When the successive application of Rule 1 is no longer required, the designer has generated a minimal and complete set of horizontal fragments. Completeness is, therefore, defined as follows.
>
> *Rule 2.* A set of simple predicates, Pr, for a table is complete if and only if, for any two rows within any minterm fragment defined on Pr, the rows have the same probability of being accessed by any application.

Example 2.7   Suppose application "AP1" queries the table "EMP" (see Figure 2.3), looking for those employees who work in Los Angeles (LA). The set "Pr = {p1: Loc = "LA"}" shows all the required simple predicates used by AP1. Therefore, the set "M = {m1: Loc = "LA", m2: Loc<>"LA"}" is a minimal and complete set of minterm predicates for AP1. M fragments EMP into the following two fragments:

```
Fragment F1: Create table LA_EMPS as
             Select * from EMP
             Where Loc = "LA";
```

```
Fragment F2: Create table NON_LA_EMPS as
             Select * from EMP
             Where Loc <> "LA";
```

If AP1 were to also (in addition to checking the value of Loc) exclude any employee whose salary was less than or equal to 30000, then the set of predicates would no longer be minimal or complete. This additional check would mean that the rows in F1 would be accessed by AP1 differently depending on the salary of each employee in F1. Applying the minimality rule mentioned above, we would need to further fragment the EMP table, if this were the case. The new simple predicates for AP1 would require changing Pr and M to the following:

```
Pr = {p1: Loc = "LA",
      p2: salary > 30000}
```

```
M = {m1: Loc = "LA"    Sal > 30000,
     m2: Loc = "LA"    Sal <= 30000,
     m3: Loc <>"LA"    Sal > 30000,
     m4: Loc <>"LA"    Sal <= 30000}
```

Observation 1: Since there are two simple predicates in Pr, and since for each predicate we have to consider the predicate and its negative, M will now have four minterm predicates in it. In general, if there are N simple predicates in Pr, M will have 2^N minterm predicates. As explained later in this section, not all minterm predicates are relevant—the irrelevant predicates must be removed from the set. Therefore, the actual number of horizontal fragments is usually fewer than 2^N.

Observation 2: In forming minterm predicates, we only use conjunctive normal form ("^") and do not use disjunctive normal form ("OR"). That is because disjunctive normal forms create coarser fragments than fragments generated by conjunctive normal form and hence are not needed.

Example 2.8   As another example, consider table "PROJ (<u>PNO</u>, Pname, Funds, Dno, Loc)," where the PNO column is the primary key as shown in Figure 2.28.

Also assume two applications ("AP1" and "AP2") query the PROJ table based on the following set of simple predicates:

Pno	Pname	Funds	Dno	Loc
P1	Requirements	135,000	D2	NY
P2	Design	310,000	D3	NY
P3	Code	300,000	D1	MPLS
P4	Documentation	450,000	D1	MPLS
P5	Testing	250,000	D4	LA

Figure 2.28   The PROJ table.

```
The AP1's simple predicates:
p1: Loc = "MPLS"
p2: Loc = "NY"
p3: Loc = "LA"

The AP2's simple predicates:
p4: Funds <= 300000
```

The two applications have a combined set of four simple predicates in Pr, defined as:

```
Pr = {Loc = "MPLS",
      Loc ="NY",
      Loc ="LA",
      Funds <= 300000}
```

Given the four simple predicates in Pr, M will have "$2^4 = 16$" different minterm predicates. The following depicts all these predicates.

```
m1  = {Loc =  "MPLS" ^ Loc =  "NY" ^ Loc =  "LA" ^ Funds <= 300000}
m2  = {Loc =  "MPLS" ^ Loc =  "NY" ^ Loc =  "LA" ^ Funds >  300000}
m3  = {Loc =  "MPLS" ^ Loc =  "NY" ^ Loc <> "LA" ^ Funds <= 300000}
m4  = {Loc =  "MPLS" ^ Loc =  "NY" ^ Loc <> "LA" ^ Funds >  300000}
m5  = {Loc =  "MPLS" ^ Loc <> "NY" ^ Loc =  "LA" ^ Funds <= 300000}
m6  = {Loc =  "MPLS" ^ Loc <> "NY" ^ Loc =  "LA" ^ Funds >  300000}
m7  = {Loc =  "MPLS" ^ Loc <> "NY" ^ Loc <> "LA" ^ Funds <= 300000}
m8  = {Loc =  "MPLS" ^ Loc <> "NY" ^ Loc <> "LA" ^ Funds >  300000}
m9  = {Loc <> "MPLS" ^ Loc =  "NY" ^ Loc =  "LA" ^ Funds <= 300000}
m10= {Loc <> "MPLS" ^ Loc =  "NY" ^ Loc =  "LA" ^ Funds >  300000}
m11= {Loc <> "MPLS" ^ Loc =  "NY" ^ Loc <> "LA" ^ Funds <= 300000}
m12= {Loc <> "MPLS" ^ Loc =  "NY" ^ Loc <> "LA" ^ Funds >  300000}
m13= {Loc <> "MPLS" ^ Loc <> "NY" ^ Loc =  "LA" ^ Funds <= 300000}
m14= {Loc <> "MPLS" ^ Loc <> "NY" ^ Loc =  "LA" ^ Funds >  300000}
m15= {Loc <> "MPLS" ^ Loc <> "NY" ^ Loc <> "LA" ^ Funds <= 300000}
m16= {Loc <> "MPLS" ^ Loc <> "NY" ^ Loc <> "LA" ^ Funds >  300000}
```

Observation 3: Simple predicates p1, p2, and p3 are mutually exclusive. This means that only p1 or p2 or p3 can be true and not any combination of them. For example, if Loc is set to "MPLS," then it cannot be equal to "NY" or "LA." As a result, m1, m2, m3, m4, m5, m6, m9, and m10 are invalid—we will remove them. This will leave the following eight minterm candidates:

```
m7  = {Loc =  "MPLS" ^ Loc <> "NY" ^ Loc <> "LA" ^ Funds <= 300000}
m8  = {Loc =  "MPLS" ^ Loc <> "NY" ^ Loc <> "LA" ^ Funds >  300000}
m11= {Loc <> "MPLS" ^ Loc =  "NY" ^ Loc <> "LA" ^ Funds <= 300000}
m12= {Loc <> "MPLS" ^ Loc =  "NY" ^ Loc <> "LA" ^ Funds >  300000}
m13= {Loc <> "MPLS" ^ Loc <> "NY" ^ Loc =  "LA" ^ Funds <= 300000}
m14= {Loc <> "MPLS" ^ Loc <> "NY" ^ Loc =  "LA" ^ Funds >  300000}
m15= {Loc <> "MPLS" ^ Loc <> "NY" ^ Loc <> "LA" ^ Funds <= 300000}
m16= {Loc <> "MPLS" ^ Loc <> "NY" ^ Loc <> "LA" ^ Funds >  300000}
```

Observation 4: m15 and m16 are invalid predicates, because Loc must have one of the three values mentioned (no blank values, no null values, and no other location values are allowed). After removing m15 and m16, we will have the following six minterm predicates:

```
m7 = {Loc =  "MPLS" ^  Loc <> "NY" ^  Loc <> "LA" ^ Funds <= 300000}
m8 = {Loc =  "MPLS" ^  Loc <> "NY" ^  Loc <> "LA" ^ Funds >  300000}
m11= {Loc <> "MPLS" ^  Loc =  "NY" ^  Loc <> "LA" ^ Funds <= 300000}
m12= {Loc <> "MPLS" ^  Loc =  "NY" ^  Loc <> "LA" ^ Funds >  300000}
m13= {Loc <> "MPLS" ^  Loc <> "NY" ^  Loc =  "LA" ^ Funds <= 300000}
m14= {Loc <> "MPLS" ^  Loc <> "NY" ^  Loc =  "LA" ^ Funds >  300000}
```

Observation 5: Since Loc can only have one value at a time, we can simplify the predicates to the following:

```
m7 = {Loc = "MPLS" ^   Funds <= 300000}
m8 = {Loc = "MPLS" ^   Funds >  300000}
m11= {Loc = "NY"   ^   Funds <= 300000}
m12= {Loc = "NY"   ^   Funds >  300000}
m13= {Loc = "LA"   ^   Funds <= 300000}
m14= {Loc = "LA"   ^   Funds >  300000}
```

Applying these minterm predicates to PROJ, we can generate fragments depicted in Figure 2.29. Although there are six minterm predicates, only five of them produce useful results from PROJ. For the current state of the table, only the five fragments shown actually contain rows, the sixth fragment does not. This fragmentation is minimal since rows within each fragment are accessed the same by both applications. This fragmentation is also complete since any two rows within each fragment have the same access probability for AP1 and AP2.

2.2.7 Horizontal Fragmentation Correctness Rules

Whenever we use fragmentation (vertical, horizontal, or hybrid), the original table is not physically stored. Therefore, the original table must be reconstructible from its fragments using a combination of SQL statements. Vertically fragmented tables are reconstructed using join operations, horizontally fragmented tables are reconstructed using union operations, and tables fragmented using hybrid fragmentation are reconstructed using a combination of union and join operations.

Any fragmentation must satisfy the following rules as defined by Özsu [Özsu99]:

- *Rule 1: Completeness.* Decomposition of R into R1, R2, ..., Rn is complete if and only if each data item in R can also be found in some Ri.
- *Rule 2: Reconstruction.* If R is decomposed into R1, R2, ..., Rn, then there should exist some relational operator, Δ, such that "R = $\Delta_{1 \leq i \leq n}$ Ri."
- *Rule 3: Disjointness.* If R is decomposed into R1, R2, ..., Rn, and di is a tuple in Rj, then di should not be in any other fragment, such as Rk, where k $\neq$ j.

Pno	Pname	Funds	Dno	Loc
P3	Code	300,000	D1	MPLS

(a) PROJ1: generated from applying m7

Pno	Pname	Funds	Dno	Loc
P4	Documentation	450,000	D1	MPLS

(b) PROJ2: generated from applying m8

Pno	Pname	Funds	Dno	Loc
P1	Requirements	135,000	D2	NY

(b) PROJ3: generated from applying m9

Pno	Pname	Funds	Dno	Loc
P2	Design	310,000	D3	NY

(c) PROJ4: generated from applying m11

Pno	Pname	Funds	Dno	Loc
P5	Testing	250,000	D4	LA

(d) PROJ5: generated from applying m13

Figure 2.29   The PROJ table fragmentation based on minterm predicates.

Rule 1 states that during fragmentation none of the data in the original table is lost. Every data item that exists in the original table is in at least one of the fragments. We use the term "at least" because vertical fragmentation always requires inclusion of the primary key column in all vertical fragments.

Rule 2 is required for reconstructiveness. This rule is required because, after fragmentation, the original table is not stored in the system anymore. Local DBMS servers will store fragments as part of their local conceptual schema. Globally, users of a distributed database system are not aware of the fragmentation that has been applied. To them, the original table exists as a whole. They will query the original table and not the fragments. Therefore, the system must be able to reconstruct the original table from its fragments on-the-fly.

Rule 3 applies to horizontal fragments. Each horizontal fragment is generated by the application of a minterm predicate to the original table. Therefore, each horizontal fragment houses only the rows that satisfy the corresponding minterm predicate. Since this is true for all horizontal fragments, rows are not shared across horizontal fragments.

2.2.8   Replication

During the database design process, the designer may decide to copy some of the fragments or tables to provide better accessibility and reliability. It should be obvious that the more copies of a table/fragment one creates, the easier it is to query that table/fragment. On the other hand, the more copies that exist, the more complicated (and time consuming) it is to update all the copies. That is why a designer has to know the frequency by which a table/fragment is queried versus the frequency by which it is modified—via inserts, updates, or deletes. As a rule of thumb, if it is queried more frequently than it is modified, then replication is advisable. Once we store more than one copy of a table/fragment in the distributed database system, we increase the probability of having a copy locally available to query.

Having more than one copy of a fragment in the system increases the resiliency of the system as well. That is because the probability of all copies failing at the same time is very low. In other words, we can still access one of the copies even if some of the copies have failed: that is, of course, if all copies of a fragment show the same values. Therefore, this benefit comes with the additional cost of keeping all copies identical. This cost, which could potentially be high, consists of total storage cost, cost of local processing, and communication cost. Note that the copies need to be identical only when the copies are online (in service). We will discuss the details of how copies are kept in sync as part of the replication control (in Chapter 7). We will also discuss calculating total cost of queries/updates as part of managing transactions (in Chapter 3) and query optimization (in Chapter 4).

2.3   DISTRIBUTION TRANSPARENCY

Although a DDBMS designer may fragment and replicate the fragments or the tables of a system, the users of such a system should not be aware of these details. This is what is known as **distribution transparency**. Distribution transparency is one of the sought after features of a distributed DBE. It is this transparency that makes the system easy to use by hiding the details of distribution from the users. There are three aspects of distribution transparency—location, fragmentation, and replication transparencies.

2.3.1   Location Transparency

The fact that a table (or a fragment of table) is stored at a remote site in a distributed system should be hidden from the user. When a table or fragment is stored remotely, the user should not need to know which site it is located at, or even be aware that it is not located locally. This provides for location transparency, which enables the user to query any table (or any fragment) as if it were stored locally.

2.3.2   Fragmentation Transparency

The fact that a table is fragmented should be hidden from the user. This provides for fragmentation transparency, which enables the user to query any table as if it were intact and physically stored. This is somewhat analogous to the way that users of a SQL view are often unaware that they are not using an actual table (many views are actually defined as several union and join operations working across several different tables).

2.3.3 Replication Transparency

The fact that there might be more than one copy of a table stored in the system should be hidden from the user. This provides for replication transparency, which enables the user to query any table as if there were only one copy of it.

2.3.4 Location, Fragmentation, and Replication Transparencies

The fact that a DDBE designer may fragment a table, make copies of the fragments, and store these copies at remote sites should be hidden from the user. This provides for complete distribution transparency, which enables the user to query the table as if it were physically stored at the local site without being fragmented or replicated.

2.4 IMPACT OF DISTRIBUTION ON USER QUERIES

Developers of a distributed DBMS try to provide for location, fragmentation, and replication transparencies to their users. This is an attempt to make the system easier to use. It is obvious that in order to provide for these transparencies, a DDBMS must store distribution information in its global data dictionary and use this information in processing the users' requests. It is expensive to give users complete distribution transparency. In such a system, although the users query the tables as if they were stored locally, in reality their queries must be processed by one or more database servers across the network. Coordinating the work of these servers is time consuming and hard to do. In Chapter 1, we discussed the issues related to distributed query execution. We will also address the performance impact of providing complete distribution transparency in Chapter 4. In the rest of this section, we will outline the impact of distribution on a user's queries.

Example 2.9   Let's assume that our database contains an employee table as defined below:

```
EMP (Eno, Ename, Sal, Tax, Mgr, Dno)
```

The column "Eno" is the primary key of this table. The column "Dno" is a foreign key that tracks the department number of the department in which an employee works. Suppose we have horizontally fragmented EMP into EMP1 and EMP2, where EMP1 contains only employees who work in a department with a department number less than or equal to 10, while EMP2 contains only employees who work in the departments with a department number greater than 10. Assume EMP2 has been replicated and there are two copies of it. Also assume that the company owns three database servers—one server is in Minneapolis (Site 1), one server is in St. Paul (Site 2), and the third server is located in St. Cloud (Site 3). The company decides to store EMP1 at Site 1, one copy of EMP2 at Site 2, and the other copy of EMP2 at Site 3. To see the impact of this database design on a user's queries, let's discuss a very simple query that finds salary information for "Jones," who is an employee with employee number 100. If the system were a centralized DBMS, a user would run the following SQL statement to find Jones' information:

```
Select * from EMP where Eno = 100;
```

In this example, our system is a distributed system and the table has been fragmented and replicated. How would a user write the query in this distributed system? The answer depends on whether or not the system provides for location, fragmentation, and replication transparencies. As mentioned in Chapter 1, the global data dictionary (GDD) stores distribution information for the environment. The impact of data distribution on user queries depends on how much of the distribution information is stored in the GDD and how many types of transparency are provided to the user.

Let's consider three different scenarios, with different degrees of transparency being provided to the user. For the first case, think of a GDD implementation that does not store any distribution information—the GDD is basically nonexistent. In this case, the design, implementation, and administration of the GDD would be trivial, but the GDD would provide absolutely no transparency to the user. This is clearly the simplest GDD implementation possible, but from the user's point of view, it is the hardest to use. The harder the system is to use, the less likely it will be used in the real world! Suppose we had the other extreme situation instead. This other case would be a very powerful GDD providing location, replication, and fragmentation transparencies to the user. While this would be nice for the user and it is the easiest for the user to use, this other extreme would obviously require a more complicated design and implementation, and would also be less trivial to administer. The more complicated a system is to implement and administer, the less likely it is to become ubiquitous. Somewhere between these two extremes, we are likely to find the right balance of transparency provided versus complexity required. In Sections 2.4.1, 2.4.2, and 2.4.3, we will attempt to illustrate the types of trade-offs that need to be considered as we move from case to case between these extremes.

2.4.1 No GDD—No Transparency

If the GDD does not contain any information about data distribution, then the users will need to be aware of where data is located, how it is fragmented and replicated, and where these fragments and replicas are stored. This means that the users need to know what information is stored in each of the local systems and then they need to incorporate this information into their queries. Figure 2.30 depicts the contents of the local data dictionaries at each of the three sites and the GDD.

Since the GDD does not store any distribution information, the users need to know this information. Figure 2.31 shows the program that a user writes to retrieve salary for Jones. **Note:** We have used the notation "EMP1@Site1" to indicate the need to run the SQL command against the EMP1 fragment at Site 1. Obviously, this is not a valid SQL statement and will **not** be parsed correctly by any commercial DBMS. We are assuming, however, that our DDBMS has a parser that understands this notation, translates it into the correct syntax, and actually sends the correct SQL statements to the right database servers. The notation /*... */ represents a comment in SQL.

In this program, the user assumes Jones is in EMP1 and queries EMP1 looking for Jones. The user had to "hard-code" the location for the table indicating which site contained the EMP1 table. Since there is only one copy of EMP1 in the system, the user specified Site 1. If the employee is not found there, then the employee might be in EMP2. We have two copies of EMP2 (at Site 2 and Site 3). There is no need to look in both of them since these are copies of the same fragment. The user has to decide which site to query for this fragment. In our example, the user has chosen Site 3. For this simple query, the user needed to write a rather long program,

```
GDD:Contains no distribution information

Site 1 Schema:
EMP1 (        Eno                         Integer,
              Ename                       Char (20),
              Sal                         Number(10,2),
              Tax                         Number(5,2),
              Mgr                         Integer,
              Dno                         Integer
                          );
Site 2 Schema:
EMP2 (        Eno                         Integer,
              Ename                       Char (20),
              Sal                         Number(10,2),
              Tax                         Number(5,2),
              Mgr                         Integer,
              Dno                         Integer
                          );
Site 3 Schema:
EMP2 (        Eno                         Integer,
              Ename                       Char (20),
              Sal                         Number(10,2),
              Tax                         Number(5,2),
              Mgr                         Integer,
              Dno                         Integer
                          );
```

Figure 2.30   The GDD and local schemas for Example 2.9.

```
If (select count (Sal) from EMP1@Site1 where Eno = 100) = 1
Then /* Jones is in fragment EMP1*/
            Select Sal
            From EMP1@Site1
            Where Eno =100
Else /* Jones is not in EMP1 - check EMP2 at Site 3 */
            If (select count (Sal)
                from EMP2@Site3 where Eno = 100) = 1
            Then /* Jones is in fragment EMP2 */
                        Select Sal
                        From EMP2@Site3
                        Where Eno = 100
            Else /* Jones is not in the database */
                        Output "No such employee"
            End if;
End if;
```

Figure 2.31   DDBMS with no transparency.

incorporating fragmentation, replication, and location information directly in the query. That is because distribution information is not stored in the GDD. In other words, if there is no GDD, then there is no distribution transparency provided to the user. If any of these details were to change (the fragmentation design, the number of fragments, the number of copies, or the locations for any of the tables/fragments/copies) then this program might stop working! This program would need to be modified, manually, to reflect the new information before it would work correctly again.

2.4.2   GDD Containing Location Information—Location Transparency

Now let's assume that the GDD contains location details for the tables/fragments in the environment, but no details about how the fragments relate to each other or to the EMP table as a whole. For example, the GDD could store location information in a special table called "Location_Table" as depicted in Figure 2.32. Assume we have the same local schemas for this case as we did for the pervious case (see Figure 2.30).

Since the GDD has location information for all the fragments, the system does provide for location transparency. As a result, the user does not need to specify location information in the SQL statements. Therefore, the user queries will be a bit simpler than they were in the previous case. Figure 2.33 shows the query we would write for

Table_Name	Site_Name
EMP1	Site1
EMP2	Site2
EMP2	Site3

Figure 2.32   The Location_Table of the GDD.

```
If (select count (Sal) from EMP1 where Eno = 100) = 1
Then /* Jones is in fragment EMP1*/
          Select Sal
          From EMP1
          Where Eno =100
Else /* Jones is not in EMP1 - check EMP2 */
          If (select count (Sal)
              from EMP2 where Eno = 100) = 1
          Then /* Jones is in fragment EMP2 */
                    Select Sal
                    From EMP2
                    Where Eno = 100
          Else /* Jones is not in the database */
                    Output "No such employee"
          End if;
     End if;
```

Figure 2.33   DDBMS with location transparency.

this environment in order to answer the same question we considered in the previous section.

As you can see from this program, all of the location information for the fragments has been removed from the select statements. In this case, the DDBMS looks up the location of EMP1 and EMP2 in the Location_Table in the GDD and sends the SQL statement to the desired site automatically. Although these select statements are less complicated to create than the ones given before, the user still needs to know that there are two fragments of the EMP table and that EMP2 has been replicated. The only benefit is that the user does not need to know where these fragments are stored. If the GDD stores additional details about each fragment (such as the fragmentation type for each table, how each fragment is generated, how it fits into the overall fragmentation plan, and the replication information for each fragment), then the user does not need to specify any of these details in the program.

2.4.3   Fragmentation, Location, and Replication Transparencies

To provide for location, fragmentation, and replication transparencies, the GDD has to store fragmentation, location, and replication information. This GDD implementation is the most complicated and difficult. Conversely, this environment is the easiest for the user to use. The GDD needs to contain additional tables to store the necessary information. For example, in addition to the Location_Table shown in Figure 2.32, we can create a table named "Fragmentation_Table." This new table contains information about real tables, real fragments, and "virtual tables." A virtual table refers to a table that is reconstructed from a set of fragments—recall that this table does not physically exist in the DDB! A simple GDD for this scenario is depicted in Figure 2.34. The local schemas for this example are the same ones we used in the previous sections (see Figure 2.30). In this case, the DDBMS provides the user with the illusion that the EMP table exists as a single physical table. As such, the DDBMS needs to store the definition of a virtual EMP table for users to access. Since the system is providing complete distribution transparency, the users query the system as if the system were a centralized system—just like a traditional, nondistributed system. Therefore, getting the salary for Jones can easily be achieved by the following SQL statement.

```
Select Sal
From EMP
Where Eno = 100;
```

Since the EMP table is a virtual table, when processing this query, the system generates all the proper subqueries (defined against the physical fragments) and then runs them at the sites where the fragments are stored.

2.5   A MORE COMPLEX EXAMPLE

Let's consider a more complicated example, in which we will apply a series of horizontal and vertical (hybrid) fragmentation to the table "EMP(eno, name, sal, tax, mgr, dno)." This fragmentation approach fragments the EMP table into four fragments called "EMP1," "EMP2," "EMP3," and "EMP4" as shown in Figure 2.35.

```
EMP (    Eno          Integer,
         Ename        Char (20),
         Sal          Number(10,2),
         Tax          Number(5,2),
         Mgr          Integer,
         Dno          Integer
                           );
```

EMP Virtual Table

Table_Name	Site_Name
EMP1	Site1
EMP2	Site2
EMP2	Site3

Location_Table

Table_Name	Fragment_Type	Virtual/Physical	Condition
EMP		Virtual	
EMP1	Horizontal	Physical	Dno <= 10
EMP2	Horizontal	Physical	Dno > 10

Fragmentation_Table

Figure 2.34   GDD for Example 2.9.

Obviously EMP1 and EMP2 both contain information about those employees who work in the departments numbered less than or equal to 10. Similarly, EMP3 and EMP4 both contain information about those employees who work in the departments numbered greater than 10. Figure 2.36 depicts the distribution of the EMP table and its fragments.

To show the effect of this fragmentation on our queries and commands, let's assume that "Smith" is an employee whose employee number is 100 (eno = 100). Smith currently works in department number 3 (dno = 3). Therefore, Smith's employee information is stored in EMP1 and EMP2. Suppose we need to move Smith to department number 15 (dno = 15). How do we achieve this? The answer, as explained in the previous case, depends on what is stored in the GDD. To illustrate the differences between the transparency alternatives, we will consider how the same operation is performed against the same schema, in three different scenarios. Each scenario will have a GDD that provides a different level of transparency.

Again, we will consider the following three levels of transparency:

• The system provides for fragmentation, location, and replication transparency.

```
Step 1: Generate temporary horizontal fragments
            Create table F1 as
                    Select * from EMP where dno <= 10;
            Create table F2 as
                    Select * from EMP where dno >10;

Step 2: Generate target vertical fragments from F1 and F2
            Create table EMP1 as
                    Select eno, name, sal, tax
                    From F1;
            Store a copy of this fragment at Site1 and Site5.
            Create table EMP2 as
                    Select eno, mgr, dno
                    From F1;
            Store a copy of this fragment at Site2 and Site6.
            Create table EMP3 as
                    Select eno, name, dno
                    From F2;
            Store a copy of this fragment at Site3 and Site7.
            Create table EMP4 as
                    Select eno, sal, tax, mgr
                    From F2;
            Store a copy of this fragment at Site4 and Site8.

Step 3: Drop the original EMP and temporary fragments F1 and F2
            Drop table EMP;
            Drop table F1;
            Drop table F2;
```

Figure 2.35   The EMP table fragmentation steps.

Emp1 (eno, name, sal, tax)	Emp2(eno, mgr, dno)	Emp3(eno, name, dno)	Emp4(eno, sal, tax, mgr)
Hybrid	Hybrid	Hybrid	Hybrid
Replicated at sites 1 & 5	Replicated at sites 2 & 6	Replicated at sites 3 & 7	Replicated at sites 4 & 8

Figure 2.36   The EMP table distribution.

- The system provides for location and replication transparencies, but no fragmentation transparency.
- The system does not provide for any transparency.

2.5.1   Location, Fragmentation, and Replication Transparencies

Because the system provides for location, fragmentation, and replication transparencies, we don't need to worry about any of the distribution details. As a result, our query can be written as if it were running in a centralized system. Because Smith needs to be moved from department 3 to department 15, we have to make a simple update to the database and indicate the new department number. We can do this move by using a single, simple SQL statement as shown:

```
Update Emp
Set dno = 15
Where eno = 100;
```

We do not need to add any complex logic to ensure the integrity of the database. The DDBMS knows that EMP is a virtual table. It looks up the fragmentation, location, and replication details in the GDD. The DDBMS uses this information to translate our update statement into the necessary SQL statements that need to run on the individual local systems. The DDBMS then executes the appropriate statements at the appropriate sites to make the requested updates to the necessary tables/fragments/copies.

2.5.2 Location and Replication Transparencies

In this case, the system provides for location and replication transparencies, but it does not provide for fragmentation transparency. Like the previous scenario, we do not need to include any location or replication details in our SQL. However, we do need to know the fragmentation details and we need to embed these details in our SQL. Unlike the previous case, our program is hard-coded to work for the old value of dno. In other words, because the old value of dno was less than or equal to 10, we cannot achieve this move in a single statement. First, we need to fetch the column values for EMP1 and EMP2 and store them into some program variables. Next, we need to delete the old values from the EMP1 and EMP2 fragments. Finally, we insert the values of our variables into the EMP3 and EMP4 fragments.

```
select name, sal, tax into $name, $sal, $tax
from Emp1
where eno = 100;

select mgr into $mgr
from Emp2
where eno = 100;

delete Emp1 where eno = 100;
delete Emp2 where eno = 100;

insert into Emp3 Values (100, $name, 15);
insert into Emp4 Values(100, $sal, $tax, $mgr);
```

In this case, we need to make sure that Smith's information is collected from the old fragments first to ensure that we do not lose them before we insert them in the new fragments. This means that we need to use some program variables to hold the selected information. Program variables $name, $sal, $tax, and $mgr are used to collect name, sal, tax, and mgr information from EMP1 and EMP2. After this information is collected, we delete Smith's information from EMP1 and EMP2 and insert Smith's information into EMP3 and EMP4. It should be obvious that the user would need to explicitly add transactions and/or locks to this program to ensure the integrity of the system during this move. We will not discuss locking and commitment/rollback of the transactions here (see Chapter 6 for details).

Note 1: This program only works when the old department number for Smith is less than or equal to 10 and the new department number is greater than 10. It should be obvious that moving Smith from department, say, 15, to department 3 would require a different program with the deletion of Smith's information from EMP3 and EMP4 and insertion of Smith's information back into EMP1 and EMP2. If, on the other hand, Smith is currently in department 12, then the move to department 15 only requires updating Dno in EMP3 and EMP4. Remember, any programs in this system must embed (hard-code) the fragmentation details defined in Figure 2.36 into the SQL statements. If any of the fragmentation details change, our program would be broken until we manually fixed it by hard-coding the new details.

Note 2: We have eliminated error checking in an attempt to not clutter the code. We should **always** implement error checking and validation checks in the real code. For example, in this case we should check whether or not Smith is an employee in the database, check the current department number, and other details before we perform the actual update. We will leave implementing the code of a general case as an exercise.

2.5.3 No Transparencies

This is the most complex case from the query-writer's perspective. In this case, the distributed database system does not provide for any of the fragmentation, location, or distribution transparencies. Since these transparencies are not provided by the system, we need to be aware of the location, fragmentation, and replication information. In Section 2.5.2, we analyzed the case of location and replication transparencies. Now that we do not have these transparencies, we have to manually hard-code in our program all the details that those transparences would normally provide. This makes the program very hard to write. The code snippet below shows the SQL-like program for this case. (Note that in the code, we have used the notation "@site X" to indicate that the SQL statement needs to run at Site X.)

```
select name, sal, tax into $name, $sal, $tax
from Emp1
where eno = 100 @site1;

select mgr into $mgr
from Emp2
where eno = 100 @site2;

delete Emp1 where eno = 100 @site 1;
delete Emp1 where eno = 100 @site 5;
delete Emp2 where eno = 100 @site 2;
delete Emp2 where eno = 100 @site 6;

insert into Emp3 values (100, $name, 15) @site 3;
```

```
insert into Emp3 values(100, $name, 15) @site 7;
insert into Emp4 values(100, $sal, $tax, $mgr) @site 4;
insert into Emp4 values (100, $sal, $tax, $mgr) @site 8;
```

This program resembles the program we presented in Section 2.5.2. However, since there are two copies of each fragment, we need to explicitly insert Smith's information into each copy of the new fragment and also explicitly delete Smith's information from each copy of the old fragment. Once again, we should really explicitly add transactions or locks to this program to ensure the integrity of the system. Notes 1 and 2 from Section 2.5.2 apply here as well.

2.6 SUMMARY

Distribution design in a distributed database management system is a top–down process. Designers start with the data access requirements of all users of the distributed system and design the contents of the distributed database as well as the global data dictionary to satisfy these requirements. Once the GDD contents are determined, the designers decide how to fragment, replicate, and allocate data to individual database servers across the network. In this chapter, we outlined the necessary steps for such a design.

We outlined the steps for creating horizontal fragments and vertical fragments of a table based on a set of requirements. We examined the rules for correct fragmentation design (such as completeness, reconstructiveness, and disjointness). We briefly discussed the impact of distribution on complexity of user programs to access and update distributed information.

2.7 GLOSSARY

Access Frequency   A measurement reflecting how often an application accesses the columns of a table during a defined period of time, for example, "fifteen accesses per day."

Affinity   A measure of closeness between the columns of a table as it relates to a given application or a set of applications.

Affinity Matrix   A matrix that contains the affinity of all columns of a table for all applications that refer to them.

Bond Energy Algorithm (BEA)   The algorithm that calculates a metric that indicates the benefits of having two or more columns to be put in the same vertical partition.

Bottom–Up   A methodology that creates a complex system by integrating system components.

Clustered Affinity Matrix   A matrix that is used for vertical partitioning of columns of a table based on the Bond Energy Algorithm.

Derived Horizontal Fragmentation   A horizontal fragmentation approach that fragments rows of a table based on the values of columns of another table.

Distribution Transparency   A type of transparency that hides the distribution details of database tables or fragments from the end users.

Fragmentation Transparency A type of transparency that hides fragmentation details of database tables or fragments from the end users.

Fragment A partition of a table.

Global Conceptual Model A repository of information such as location, fragmentation, replication, and distribution for a distributed database system.

Global Data Dictionary (GDD) The portion of global conceptual schema that contains dictionary information such as table name, column names, view names, and so on.

Horizontal Fragmentation The act of partitioning (grouping) rows of a table into a smaller set of tables.

Hybrid Fragmentation The application of horizontal fragmentation to vertical fragments of a table, or the application of vertical fragmentation to horizontal fragments of a table.

Local Conceptual Model The conceptual schema that users of a local DBMS employ.

Location Transparency A transparency that hides location of database tables or fragments from the end users.

Minterm Predicate A predicate that contains two or more simple predicates.

Partitions Either vertical or horizontal fragments of a table.

Primary Horizontal Fragmentation A horizontal fragmentation of a table based on the value of one of its columns.

Replication Transparency A transparency that hides the fact that there might be more than one copy of a database table or fragments from the end users.

Schema Integration The act of integrating local conceptual schemas of the component database systems into a cohesive global conceptual schema.

Simple Predicate A condition that compares a column of a table against a given value.

Top–Down A database design methodology that starts with the requirements of a distributed system (the global conceptual schema) and creates its local conceptual schemas.

Unified Schema An integrated, nonredundant, and consistent schema for a set of local database systems.

Usage Matrix A matrix that indicates the frequency of usage of columns of a table by a set of applications.

Vertical Fragmentation The act of partitioning the columns of a table into a set of smaller tables.

REFERENCES

[Bobak96] Bobak, A., *Distributed and Multi-Database Systems*, Artech House, Boston, MA, 1996.

[Ceri84] Ceri, S., and Pelagatti, G., *Distributed Databases—Principles and Systems*, McGraw-Hill, New York, 1984.

[Ceri87] Ceri, S., Pernici, B., and Wiederhold, G., "Distributed Database Design Methodologies," *Proceedings of IEEE*, Vol. 75, No. 5, pp. 533–546, May 1987.

[Eswaren74] Eswaren, K., "Placement of Records in a File and File Allocation in a Computer Network," in *Proceedings of Information Processing Conference*, Stockholm, pp. 304–307, 1974.

[Hammer79] Hammer, M., and Niamir, B., "A Heuristic Approach to Attribute Partitioning," in *Proceedings of ACM SIGMOD International Conference on Management of Data*, pp. 93–101, Boston, May 1979.

[Hoffer75] Hoffer, H., and Severance, D., "The Use of Cluster Analysis in Physical Database Design," in *Proceedings of the First International Conference on Very Large Databases*, Framingham, MA, pp. 69–86, September 1975.

[McCormick72] McCormick, W., Schweitzer, P., and White T., "Problem Decomposition and Data Reorganization by a Clustering Technique," *Operations Research*, Vol. 20, No. 5, pp. 993–1009, 1972.

[Navathe84] Navathe, S., Ceri, S., Wiederhold, G., and Dou, J., "Vertical Partitioning Algorithms for Database Design," *ACM Transactions on Database Systems*, Vol. 9, No. 4, pp. 680–710, December 1984.

[Özsu99] Özsu, M., and Valduriez, P., *Principles of Distributed Database Systems*, Prentice Hall, Englewood Cliffs, NJ, 1999.

[Sacca85] Sacca, D., and Wiederhold, G., "Database Partitioning in a Cluster of Processors," *ACM Transactions on Database Systems*, Vol. 10, No. 1, pp. 29–56, October 1985.

EXERCISES

Provide short (but complete) answers to the following questions.

2.1 Assume EMP has been fragmented as indicated in Figure 2.36. Also, assume the system **does not** provide for any transparencies. Write a SQL-like program that deletes the employee indicated by $eno from the database. Make sure you perform all the necessary error checking.

2.2 Answer true or false for the statements in Figure 2.37.

2.3 For the EMP table fragmented in Example 2.5, write a **single** SQL statement that reconstructs the original EMP table from its fragments.

2.4 An Employee table has the following relational scheme: "Employee (name, sal, loc, mgr)," where name is the primary key. The table has been horizontally fragmented into SP and MPLS fragments. SP has employees who work in St. Paul and MPLS contains all employees who work in Minneapolis. Each fragment is stored in the city where the employees are located. Assume transactions only enter the system in NY and there are no employees in NY. Write down the local schemas and global schema and indicate in which cities these schemas are located for the following three cases:

(A) The system does not provide for any transparencies.

(B) The system provides for location and replication transparencies.

(C) The system provides for location, replication, and fragmentation transparencies.

2.5 Consider table "EMP(EmpID, Name, Sal, Loc, Dept)." There are four applications running against this table as shown below. Design an optimal vertical

#	Statement	True/ False
1	In SQL, vertical fragments are created using the project statement.	
2	The external schemas define the database as the end users see it.	
3	Tuple is another word for a row in a relational database.	
4	Federated databases have three levels of schemas.	
5	Federated databases are formed from the Bottom–Up.	
6	Referential integrity enforced by a DDBMS does not span sites.	
7	Horizontal fragments need to be disjoint.	
8	Distributed DBMSs are formed Top–Down.	
9	Global data dictionary may be copied at some sites in a distributed DBMS.	
10	There are as many physical fragments as there are minterm predicates of a minimal and complete distribution design.	

Figure 2.37   True or false questions.

fragmentation strategy that satisfies the needs of these applications. Show steps for arriving at the answer.

A1: "Select EmpID, Sal From EMP;"

A2: "Select EmpID, Name, Loc, Dept From EMP Where Dept = 'Eng';"

A3: "Select EmpID, Name, Loc, Dept From EMP Where Loc = 'STP';"

A4: "Select EmpID, Name, Loc, Dept from EMP Where Loc = 'MPLS';"

3

DATABASE CONTROL

Database control is one of most challenging tasks that every **database administrator (DBA)** faces. Controlling a database means being able to provide correct data to valid users and applications. A data item must satisfy the correctness condition(s) that have been defined for it. The correctness conditions that are attached to a piece of data are called **constraints, semantic integrity rules, integrity constraints**, or **assertions**. We will use these terms interchangeably.

Let's consider the table "EMP (ENO, Ename, Sal, DNO)," where we store information about the employees of an organization. In this table, DNO represents the department in which the employee works.

Associated with DNO, there are a number of correctness criteria such as:

- DNO is an integer.
- DNO must be between 100 and 999.
- DNO must have a value for each employee.
- DNO value for a given employee must match the value of DNO in the DEPT table.

If any of these assertions for a given employee is violated, then the employee is not a valid employee. Semantic integrity rules must be defined before they can be enforced. Enforcing these assertions is the responsibility of the semantic integrity control module of the local DBE (see Chapter 1). These topics are discussed here under the topic of **semantic integrity control** or simply integrity control.

In addition to definition and enforcement of semantic integrity rules, the access to the database must be controlled. Only authenticated users with the proper authorization can be allowed to access the contents of the database. A DBA creates a list of valid

Distributed Database Management Systems by Saeed K. Rahimi and Frank S. Haug
Copyright © 2010 the IEEE Computer Society

users and defines the scope of their rights using the control language of the DBE. These issues are discussed under the topic of **access control**. Imposters and hackers must not be able to access and use the information in the database. An environment must have a sophisticated security mechanism in place to be able to thwart today's intruders. **Security** in a centralized DBE, and more importantly in a DDBE, is very difficult and costly to implement. We will discuss security issues and different threat types in Chapter 9.

There are two aspects to access control. The first has to do with **authentication** and the second with **access rights**. Authentication is used to make sure only preapproved applications and users can work with the database. Most of today's systems have a multilevel authentication system that checks the users' access to the database contents. Once a valid user has connected to the right database, the privileges that the user has must also be controlled. This is typically enforced by the DBE. Access rights of a given user can be defined, controlled, and enforced by the system to ensure that the user can only work with an allowed portion of the database and perform only allowed functions.

3.1 AUTHENTICATION

Authentication in a DBE guarantees that only legitimate users have access to data resources in a DBE. At the highest level of authentication, access to the client computer (the client is the front-end to the database server) or the database server is controlled. This is typically achieved by a combination of user-name/password and is enforced by the operating system. Other and more sophisticated approaches such as biometrics can also be used (see Chapter 9 for more detail).

Once the user is connected to the computer, accessing the DBE software is controlled by the second level of authentication. At this level, the user may use credentials that have been assigned by the DBE or the DBE can trust the operating system authentication and allow connection to the DBE software. The first approach is known as **database authentication** while the second is known as **operating system authentication**. SQL Server and Oracle have similar concepts, although they are not exactly the same concepts. A **login** (or **account**) is used to control access to the DBMS server while a **user** is used to control access to a database managed by a server. Sometimes in a DBE these concepts are implemented as separate things, sometimes a single implementation is used to represent both concepts.

In Oracle 10 g, a user account can use operating system (or external) authentication for validation. This allows operating system users to connect to the databases controlled by Oracle server. Oracle trusts the operating system's authentication and allows the current user to connect to a given database. Oracle can also use a database user-name and a password (maintained in the database) to authenticate an account. Assuming "saeed" is a database user-name with password "secret," the user will connect to a given database by providing the combination of saeed/secret and the database name.

In SQL Server 2005, the connection to the DBMS software is controlled by what is known as a login. A login is an authenticated connection to the server. An operating system user may login to a database server using two approaches similar to the way Oracle authenticates users. A login could be authenticated by the operating system (Windows) or by SQL Server. Again, operating system authentication is based on

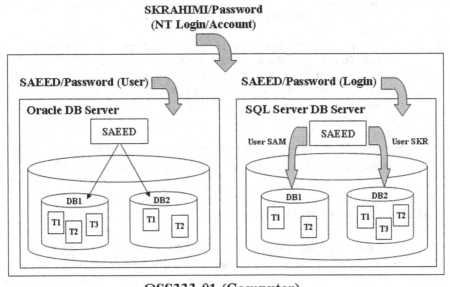

SKRAHIMI/Password
(NT Login/Account)

OSS333-01 (Computer)

Figure 3.1 Multilevel security example.

the trust relationship between the operating system and DBMS software. SQL Server authentication requires a login-name and a password. Regardless of how a login has been established, to work with a given database, a login must use a database user. A database user represents a login inside a database. As a result, a given login can work with multiple databases using multiple database users. Figure 3.1 depicts multilevel authentication approaches for Oracle and SQL Server. In a DBE, the DBA is responsible for managing user accounts, logins, and user-names.

3.2 ACCESS RIGHTS

In relational database systems, what a database user can do inside the database is controlled by the access rights that are given to that user. A user's access rights specify the privileges that the user has. For example, user "saeed" may have the right to create a table, to drop a table, or to add rows to a table. SQL, as the standard for relational model databases, can be used to specify at a very fine level of granularity (column level) the operations allowed and disallowed for a given user.

In any large database environment, there are many users, many databases, many tables with many columns, and many other database objects. As a result, in large systems, assignment of individual privileges to individual users is a time-consuming and error-prone task. To reduce the overhead associated with management of rights for a large system, the concept of a **role** is used. A role is a construct that can be given certain authorities within a database (or the server). Figure 3.2 shows the creation of a role called manager. This role is then given some privileges and, finally, user1 is given the manager role. After executing these statements, user1 will have all privileges that have been assigned to the role 'manager'—user1 plays the role of a manager.

```
Create role manager;
Commit;
Grant select, insert, delete on employee to manager;
Grant insert, update on project to manager;
Grant select on department to manager;
Grant execute on payroll to manager;
Commit;
Grant manager to user1;
Commit;
```

Figure 3.2 Creation of a role and its assignment to the user "user1."

3.3 SEMANTIC INTEGRITY CONTROL

A DBMS must have the ability to specify and enforce correctness assertions in terms a set of semantic integrity rules. The semantic integrity service (Semi-S), which we discussed in Chapter 1, Section 1.3.1, is used to define and enforce the semantic integrity rules for the system. This is true for both relational and nonrelational database systems, such as network, hierarchical, and object-oriented systems. For instance, the need to enforce uniqueness of the primary key (or its equivalent counterpart) is the same in all database types, although the approaches used by different systems are different. Similarly, the need to enforce the existence of a primary key value for a given foreign key is the same for all database types and data models.

Figure 3.3a depicts a network database DDL statement that declares a record type called "PART" with two fields, "PART-NO" and "AMOUNT." PART-NO is considered the primary key for the record since the field is not allowed to have duplicate values. PART-NO has an alphanumeric data type of length 5 and AMOUNT has a numeric data type that has four significant digits and two decimal places. The same record definition is shown in Figure 3.3b for a relational system.

Figure 3.4a shows an example of referential integrity across two record types in a network database type. For this system, the SET definition statement guarantees (forces the Semi-S to check for) a valid association between the two record types, PART and SUPPLIER. The same requirement in a relational system is shown in Figure 3.4b.

```
NETWORK DDL
RECORD NAME IS PART
            DUPLICATES ARE NOT ALLOWED FOR PART-NO
            PART-NO        PICTURE X99999
            AMOUNT         PICTURE 9999V99
                          (a)


RELATIONAL DDL
CREATE TABLE PART( PART-NO CHAR(5) NOT NULL PRIMARY KEY,
               AMOUNT DECIMAL(6,2));
                          (b)
```

Figure 3.3 Comparing network and relational model DDL statements.

```
Network Model
RECORD NAME IS PART
                DUPLICATES ARE NOT ALLOWED FOR PART-NO
                PART-NO      TYPE IS FIXED 6
                PART-NAME    TYPE IS CHAR 20
                QTY          TYPE IS FIXED 5

RECORD NAME IS SUPPLIER
                DUPLICATES ARE NOT ALLOWED FOR SUPPLIER-NO
                SUPPLIER-NO  TYPE IS FIXED 4
                SUPPLIER-CITY TYPE IS CHAR 30
                STATUS       TYPE IS FIXED 4

SET NAME IS PART-SUPPLIER
                OWNER        IS SUPPLIER
                MEMBER       IS PART
                INSERTION    IS AUTOMATIC (MANUAL)
                RETENTION    IS OPTIONAL (MANDATORY, FIXED)
                            (a)


Relational Model
CREATE TABLE PART (PART-NO DECIMAL (6) NOT NULL PRIMARY KEY,
                PART-NAME    CHAR(20) NOT NULL,
                QTY          DECIMAL(5)    NOT NULL,
                SNO          DECIMAL(4));

CREATE TABLE SUPPLIER (SNO DECIMAL (4) NOT NULL PRIMARY KEY,
                SCITY        CHAR(30) NOT NULL,
                STATUS       DECIMAL(4)    NOT NULL);

ALTER TABLE PART
ADD CONSTRAINT "PART-SUPPLIER-FKEY" FOREIGN KEY(SNO)
REFERENCES SUPPLIER(SNO);
                            (b)
```

Figure 3.4 Specifying referential integrity in network and relational models.

For the relational system, the referential integrity requirement is added to the table definitions using the "ALTER TABLE" statement after the two tables have been created.

When one or more semantic integrity rules are violated, Semi-S can report, reject, or try to correct the query or transaction that is performing an illegal operation. For example, Semi-S can evaluate the SQL query in Figure 3.5a and reject the query since it knows the Sal column has a numeric data type and the value being compared to it is a character string. In a smarter DBE, the Semi-S subsystem may try to correct the query by removing the single quotes from around 40000 and running the query. This issue has been resolved for the SQL statement in Figure 3.5b, but there is still a potential issue with the T1 table's existence (or lack thereof). If T1 exists, the statement is fine; otherwise, an "object not found" error message must be issued by the Semi-S.

```
Select Last_Name, Sal
From Emp
Where Sal >= '40000';
            (a)



Select Last_Name, Sal
From T1
Where Sal >= 40000;
            (b)
```

Figure 3.5   Example of two semantically incorrect SQL statements.

3.3.1   Semantic Integrity Constraints

A relational DBE supports four basic types of semantic integrity constraints or rules:

- Data type constraints
- Relation constraints
- Referential constraints
- Explicit constraints

The first three types are called **relational constraints** and are inherited from the entity relationship model (ERM); see Chapter 10. These integrity rules are an integral part of the relational model; see Chapter 11. These rules are often automatically generated by our data modeling tools—however, the last rule needs to be specified by the user explicitly in the relational model.

3.3.1.1 Relational Constraints   **Data type constraints** are semantic integrity rules that specify the **data type** for columns of relational tables. These are inherited from the ERM since the domains are tied to the underlying domains on which the attributes of an entity are defined in the ERM. Some relational database systems may allow specification of user-defined data types. A data type constrains the range of values and the type of operations that we can apply to the column to which the data type is attached. A **user-defined data type** is a data type that is based on a system data type and creates a specific data type on top of it. Examples of system-defined data types supported by most DBMS are Date, Integer, Decimal (X,Y), Float, Char(X), Varchar(X), Enumerated data types such as ('M', 'F') or ('Sat', 'Sun', 'Mon', 'Tue', 'Wed', 'Thu', 'Fri'), and Range data types such as (1–31). Figures 3.6a and 3.6b show two different database implementations of the same user-defined data type concept, for SQL Server 2005 and Oracle 11 g, respectively. In this example, we create the "salary" data type, basing it on the "numeric" system data type for SQL Server and the "number" data type for Oracle.

Relation constraints are the methods used to define a relation (or a table). The following codifies a table called Employee, which keeps track of the employees of an organization.

```
SQL Server User Defined Data Type:
CREATE TYPE salary FROM NUMERIC (8,2) NOT NULL
Go

CREATE TABLE EMP(Name      varchar (20)  NOT NULL ,
           Comp           salary        NOT NULL,
           Age            smallint      NULL )
Go
```
(a)

```
Oracle 11g User Defined Data Type:
CREATE TYPE salary AS OBJECT (salary number(8,2));

CREATE TABLE EMP (Name      varchar(20) NOT NULL,
           Comp           salary       NOT NULL,
           Age            number(3,0))NULL;
```
(b)

Figure 3.6 Example of a user-defined data type definition in SQL Server and Oracle.

```
Create table Employee (
     Emp#          integer not null,
     Name          varchar(20) not null,
     Emp_Nickname  char(10),
     DOB           date check (DOB LIKE 'MM-DD-YYYY'),
     Sex           char(1) in ('M', 'F'),
     Primary key (Emp#),
     Unique Emp_Nickname);
```

This code snippet conveys the following constraints:

- The table name "Employee" is unique within a database. This is called a relation constraint and is inherited from the fact that in the ERM there is a unique entity type called "Employee."
- Employees as objects of the real world are kept track of in the database as a set of rows in the Employee table.
- The Employee table has five columns: Emp#, Name, Emp_Nickname, DOB, and Sex. Each column has a data type constraint, may have a null or not null constraint, may have an enumeration constraint, and may have a range constraint.
- The Emp# column must be an integer and must have a value.
- The Name column is of type varchar(20) and must have a value. Since "varchar(20)" is used as the data type, the Name cannot be longer than 20 characters. If the Name is shorter than 20 characters, then the actual length of the name will be used.
- The DOB column is of type Date. This column may be left as null. If the column has a value for date it has to follow the format 'MM-DD-YYYY'. Otherwise, the row is not validated.

- The Sex column is a one-character field and can be left as null. The Sex column has an enumeration constraint on it. This constraint limits the value of the column Sex to either character 'M' or 'F'. Any other value is a violation of this constraint.
- The primary key constraint forces the Emp# column to be unique. If the value of this column is not unique, the employee is not validated.
- In addition to the Emp#, which is used as a primary key and is unique, each Employee row's nickname is also unique. Since a table cannot have two primary keys, the uniqueness of Emp_Nickname is enforced by a different type of constraint in the table, known as a unique constraint.

Referential integrity (RI) constraints restrict the values stored in the database so that they reflect the way the objects of the real world are related to each other. This constraint is inherited from the ERM by the relational systems. In the database, RI is implemented by controlling the way the rows in one table relate to the row(s) in another table. RI in relational systems forces the foreign key values in one table to correspond to a primary key value in another table. Another way of explaining this constraint is to say that in a relational database there exists no foreign key that does not correspond to a primary key. This constraint is enforced by the DBMS automatically.

Figure 3.7 outlines SQL statements that create two tables (Department and Employee) and enforce two referential integrity constraints defined across them. In this figure, we create the Department table first. This table has a clause that specifies the D# column as the primary key of the table. In the Employee table, SSN is defined as the primary key column of the table. MgrSSN, on the other hand, is defined as a foreign key that corresponds to the SSN column of the same table. This column keeps track of the manager of each employee. This constraint is inherited from the ER model, and it corresponds to the fact that in the real world an employee may be the manager of one or more employees. In the relational model, this is implemented by the RI constraint between the SSN and MgrSSN columns of the Employee table. In the relational model, the DBMS has to ensure that every employee in the database has a manager by forcing the value of MgrSSN for a given row to equal one other Employee rows' SSN value. Actually, the DBMS cannot prevent an employee from using its own SSN value for this purpose, but that is not a real issue for use here. We call the employee whose SSN value is used as the MgrSSN value the parent employee. All employees who use the parent's SSN as their MgrSSN are called the children. The DBMS must be told what to do when the SSN for a parent row is changed or deleted. This is specified in the code via 'on update' and 'on delete' clauses. In our example, the DBMS is told that when the parent row is deleted, it should set the value of MgrSSN for all its children to "111111111." The DBMS is also told that changing a SSN value that corresponds to one or more MgrSSN values in the Employee table is not allowed (Restricted). In this case, it does not make sense to allow an Employee's SSN value to be changed.

The DNO column in the Employee table is also defined as a foreign key, which refers to the primary key column of the Department table (D#). This RI keeps track of which department an employee works in. For this RI, we use the 'on update' clause to tell the DBMS to change the column value for DNO in the Employee table if the corresponding value of D# in the Department table changes. The 'on delete' clause of this RI indicates that the requirement is to set the DNO value for an employee to the

```
Create Table Department (D# Integer        not null,
               Name           char(10)       not null,
               Budget         Decimal(12,2)  not null,
               Primary Key (D#)};
                               (a)


Create Table Employee (SSN  char(9)         not null,
               Name           varchar(20)    not null,
               DOB            Date,
               DNO            Integer         default 1,
               MrgSSN         char(9)         not null,
               Primary Key (SSN),
        Foreign Key (MgrSSN) References Employee(SSN)
               On Delete Set 111111111  On Update Restrict,
        Foreign Key (DNO) References Department(D#)
               On Delete Set Default   On Update Cascade)};
                               (b)
```

Figure 3.7 Example of referential integrity across the Employee and Department tables.

default value when the corresponding department row is deleted from the Department table (i.e., when the department is closed).

Relation constraints as discussed above are typically applied to a single table. The SQL standard allows the use of the SELECT statement in the CHECK constraint to refer to other tables in the same database. To provide for general constraints that can refer to any number of tables, the SQL standard also allows creation of general assertions. Assertions are constraints that are not associated with any individual table. Figure 3.8b illustrates the use of an assertion in conjunction with the database tables shown in Figure 3.8a. As seen from this figure, the general assertion "No_loan_Issue" is applied when a customer requests a new loan from the bank. This assertion prevents the customer being given the loan if the average balance of all the customers' accounts is less than or equal to $5000. Similarly, this assertion ensures that the loan will be denied if the customer already has another loan from the bank (it will not allow the same customer to have more than one loan).

Some commercial databases, like Oracle, do not support the concept of assertions. For these products, explicit semantic integrity constraints have to be used. Explicit constraints are not inherited from the ERM like the other three constraints. We have to either code these constraints into the application programs that use the database or code them into the database using the concept of stored procedures and triggers.

Stored procedures and **triggers** are written programs that use SQL and extensions to the standard SQL—and, as a result, they are vendor specific. These programs are stored in the database as opposed to being compiled and stored as object code outside the database. Stored procedures, similar to any programming language procedures, are programs that accept input parameters, do some work, and can then return values through their output parameters. These procedures can be called from other procedures and/or be activated interactively by the DBMS users. The only difference between a stored procedure and other procedures is that stored procedures cannot request any user interaction once they have started. In other words, we cannot input additional

```
Table Customer(CID, Cname, Addr)
Table Account(A#, CID, bal)
Table Loan(L#, CID, amt)
                  (a)
```

```
Create Assertion No_loan_Issue
            Check (Select A.CID, Avg(bal)
                      From Account A
                      Group By A.CID
                      Having Avg(bal) > 5000
                      AND
                      Not Exists (
                            Select L.CID
                            From Loan L
                            Where L.CID = A.CID
                            )
                  );
                  (b)
```

Figure 3.8   An example of an assertion for a sample bank database.

information into the procedure besides what we have given it as input parameters. The general syntax of a stored procedure is given below:

```
Create Procedure Proc_Name (Param_list)
AS
Declaration section;
Begin
     Actions;
End Proc_Name;
```

A trigger is a special kind of stored procedure that is stored in the database. Triggers are an extension to the standard SQL. The only difference between a trigger and a stored procedure is that users cannot call a trigger—only the DBMS can do this. Triggers are run automatically (also known as fired) by the DBMS when certain changes (such as insert, delete, and update operations) are performed on tables of the database. When a table has associated triggers, modification statements performed on the table are monitored by the DBMS and the code of the trigger is fired if the trigger is defined for that action. For example, if we define a trigger for update on the EMP table, the trigger code will run automatically every time the value of a column of EMP is changed. The general syntax of a trigger code is shown below:

```
Create TRIGGER Trigger_Name ON Table FOR operation AS
Declaration section;
Begin
     If Trigger_Condition Exec Proc_Name (Param_list);
     ...
End Trigger_Name;
```

The language that Oracle uses for stored procedures and triggers is called PL/SQL, while SQL Server's language name is T/SQL. Both languages have many similarities but at the same time many differences. For example, Oracle allows for triggers to run either before the modification statement is performed or afterwards. If the trigger runs before the actual modification statement, it is called a **before trigger**; otherwise, it is called an **after trigger**. While Oracle allows both before and after triggers, SQL Server only allows after triggers. Also, Oracle trigger code can be defined to run as many times as the number of rows that are in the target of the modification statement (which is called a **row trigger)** or only once regardless of how many rows are affected (which is called a **statement trigger**). In the case of the SQL Server, only statement triggers are supported. A more detailed explanation of stored procedures and triggers is outside the scope of this book. We encourage interested readers to review any of the many good books written on the subject. In Examples 3.1 and 3.2, we use PL/SQL and T/SQL to write the same stored procedure and trigger for comparison purposes.

Example 3.1   Assume the DEPT and EMP tables are defined as shown in Figure 3.9a in Oracle. We would like to write a stored procedure that will, when given a department

```
EMP (Eno NUMBER(4) not null, Dno NUMBER(4) not null)
DEPT (Deptno NUMBER(4) not null, Mgr varchar(15))
                          (a)

1  Create or replace procedure delete_dept (v_dno   INTEGER)
2  Is
3  Begin
4             Delete from DEPT
5             Where deptno = v_dno;
6  End delete_dept;
7 /
                          (b)

1  create or replace trigger delete_emp
2  after delete on EMP
3  for each row
4  declare
5     v_dno EMP.dno%type;
6     cnt EMP.dno%type;
7  begin
8     select count(*) into cnt
9     From EMP
10    Where EMP.dno = :old.dno;
11    If cnt = 0 then
12    V_dno := :old.dno;
13    End if;
14    delete_dept (v_dno);
15  End delete_emp;
16 /
                          (c)
```

Figure 3.9   An example of a stored procedure and a trigger in PL/ SQL.

number (v_dno) as an input parameter, delete that department from the DEPT table. For simplicity, we assume that the department identified by v_dno is stored in the database. Figure 3.9b shows this procedure implemented in PL/SQL. This code simply deletes the department that has its Deptno column equal to the input parameter (see procedure lines 4 and 5). Now, we want to write a trigger that runs when rows are deleted from the EMP table. If the deleted employee is the last employee in the department, the trigger uses the above stored procedure to delete the department from the DEPT table as well. Otherwise, the trigger does not do anything. This trigger is designed to delete the departments when they lose all their employees and have no employees left in them. Figure 3.9c shows the PL/SQL code for this trigger. Since the delete operation may delete more than one row from the EMP table, we need to use a row trigger (see line 3). Since we are using an after trigger, the target employee row is already deleted from the EMP table by the time our code runs. To access the department number for this employee, Oracle maintains the image of the deleted/modified rows in the ":old" record structure (see line 10) during the execution of the trigger code. Here, the field ":old.dno" holds the department number for the row being deleted. The trigger code checks to see if there are any more employees in the department from where the current employee is being deleted (see lines 8 through 13). If this is the case, the department is deleted using the stored procedure in line 14.

Example 3.2 This example is exactly the same as Example 3.1, except that the stored procedure and trigger code are written in T/SQL for SQL Server 2005 DBMS. Note that since T/SQL does not support row triggers, we have to use the concept of a cursor (see lines 5 and 6 in Fig. 3.10) to analyze all the rows being deleted from the EMP table and perform the check for an empty department (see lines 11 through 15). In T/SQL, the table "deleted" holds an image of all the rows that are the target of the delete operation during the execution of the trigger code. We use this table to iterate through all rows that are being deleted. Note that since T/SQL only supports after triggers, during the execution of the trigger code the target rows have already been deleted from the EMP table. As a result, the only way to access the department number for the employees being affected is through the deleted table.

3.4 DISTRIBUTED SEMANTIC INTEGRITY CONTROL

In distributed systems, semantic integrity assertions are basically the same as in centralized systems (i.e., relation, data type, referential, and explicit constraints). When considering a distributed system, semantic integrity control issues become more complicated due to distribution. The first question that we have to answer is, "Where are the semantic integrity rules defined?" When thinking about the location of the rules, we have to be aware of the fact that some semantic integrity rules are local and some are distributed. After we define each rule, we need to consider which tables are affected or referenced by it. When all the tables are deployed in a single database (at a single site), the rule is a local rule; otherwise, it is a distributed rule. We also need to consider where each rule should be defined and enforced. It makes sense to have local rules defined and enforced at the site where all the tables involved are deployed. Deciding where to define and implement the enforcement for distributed (multisite) rules is a much bigger challenge. Let's consider two examples to illustrate these concepts.

```
EMP (Eno DECIMAL(4) not null, Dno DECIMAL(4) not null)
DEPT (Deptno DECIMAL(4) not null, Mgr varchar(15))
```
                                (a)

```
Create procedure delete_dept @dno   INT
As
Begin
                Delete from DEPT
                Where dno = @dno;
End
go
```
                                (b)

```
1   Create trigger emp_delete
2   on EMP for delete
3   AS
4   declare @dno int, @value Integer
5   declare C1 Cursor local for
6           select dno from deleted
7   Open C1
8           Fetch next C1 into @dno
9           While @@Fetch_Status = 0
10          Begin
11                      if (select count(*)
12                      From EMP, deleted
13                      Where EMP.dno = @dno) = 0
14                        execute delete_dept @dno
15                      fetch next C1 into @dno
16              end
17  close C1
18  deallocate c1
go
```
                                (c)

Figure 3.10   An example a stored procedure and a trigger in T/ SQL.

Example 3.3   The RI examples we discussed in Figure 3.7 apply to one database. In a distributed database, we have more than one DBE and might have an RI constraint that spans two or more servers because the tables involved may be deployed at different sites. We might also have an RI constraint that exists in two or more servers because of replication. For this example, assume a distributed database that consists of two servers at Site 1 and Site 2. The Department table, as defined in Figure 3.7a, is stored at Site 1 and the Employee table is stored at Site 2. We still have the same two RI requirements that we had in the previous example for MgrSSN and DNO. These reflect our business requirements and do not have anything to do with the way we have distributed our data. Our problem is with the enforcement of the RI requirement between the Employee and the Department tables. This is a problem, because the two tables are defined on two different DBMSs and neither system can enforce the RI constraint within a foreign system. In other words, when Site 2's DBMS analyzes the 'Create Table Employee...' statement, it will complain due to the fact that the Department table does not exist at Site 2—the Department table is defined at Site 1.

Example 3.4   As discussed in Chapter 2, replication is a design technique that attempts to provide more resiliency and availability of data by storing tables and their fragments multiple times. General issues with replication will be discussed in Chapter 7. As far as semantic integrity is concerned, replication creates a unique challenge in enforcing RI. Let's assume that CID is the primary key of the Customer table and that it has been used as a foreign key in the Order table to keep track of customers' orders. Furthermore, assume that both the Customer and Order table have been replicated at Site 1 and Site 2. Let's also suppose that Site 1 is an Oracle database while Site 2 is an IBM DB2 database.

If customer C1 places a new order at Site 1, then Oracle enforces the RI requirement and makes sure that this new order's CID in the Order table matches the Customer's CID. But Oracle does not know (and probably does not care) about the copy of the Order table deployed at Site 2, which is under the control of DB2. As a result, unless the DDBE software replicates this new order in the Order table at Site 2, the replicas of the table will diverge—they are no longer the same. We can also end up with a more interesting and challenging scenario. Let's suppose that at the same time that customer 100 places a new order for item 13 at Site 1, the DBA at Site 2 deletes item 13 from its database. The referential integrity of the Oracle and DB2 databases locally is enforced and the systems individually are consistent. But, as far as the overall distributed database is concerned, the database is mutually inconsistent. That is because at Site 1 we have an order for an item that does not exist at Site 2. These and similar issues related to semantic integrity constraints have to be addressed by the replication control software (see Chapter 7). These examples indicate many challenges involved in the declaration and enforcement of semantic integrity constraints in a distributed system.

The following outlines the additional challenges in distributed semantic integrity control:

- Creation of multisite semantic integrity rules
- Enforcement of multisite semantic integrity rules
- Maintaining mutual consistency of local semantic integrity rules across copies
- Maintaining consistency of local semantic integrity rules and global semantic integrity rules

It should be obvious that these challenges are due to database fragmentation, replication, and distribution. Obviously, the more a database is fragmented and/or replicated, the more overhead will be involved in creation and enforcement of the integrity rules. The main component of this overhead is the cost of communication between sites. An attempt to minimize the cost of communication can reduce the overall overhead associated with the creation and enforcement of integrity rules in a distributed database system. One approach for minimizing communication cost is to try to distribute a database in such a way that does not create multisite semantic integrity rules. For example, we should place the EMP and DEPT tables as shown in Figure 3.7a at the same site due to the existence of the RI rule between them. As another example, we could avoid vertical fragmentation of any table, since otherwise we would need to enforce relation constraints across the vertical fragments for each fragmented table.

Much of the work in semantic integrity area has been focused on the specification of the rules [Stonebreaker74] [Eswaran76] [Machgeles76] [McLeod79] as opposed to how the rules are validated [Eswaran76] [Stonebreaker76] [Hammer78]. Badal argues that, for a given distribution design, when we enforce the semantic integrity rules [Badal79] it has a big impact on the communication cost. According to Badal, semantic integrity rules for a transaction can be enforced when the transaction is compiled (compile time validation), during its execution (run time validation), or after the transaction has finished executing (postexecution time validation). In the following subsections, we briefly discuss these three approaches. For each approach, we calculate the cost of the approach, based on the number of required messages.

3.4.1   Compile Time Validation

In this approach to validation, transactions are allowed to run only after all the semantic integrity (SI) constraints have been validated. For this approach to work, SI data items need to be locked so that during validation and afterward, during transaction execution, they are not changed. It is easy to see that compile time validation is simple to implement and does not incur any cost for abort operations since we only run transactions when they are validated—transactions that violate the SI rule do not run at all. On the other hand, to implement this approach, all the constraint data items need to be locked for the duration of validation and transaction execution. After a transaction has been validated, it starts its execution. Note that a transaction that has been validated may still be rolled back due to concurrency control issues (such as locking and deadlock) or due to conflicts with other concurrent transactions.

3.4.2   Run Time Validation

In this validation scheme, there is no need to hold transactions back until they are validated (like we did in compile time validation). Here, transactions are validated during execution. When there is a need for validation, all the data items involved are locked and the transaction is validated. If semantic integrity rules are violated, the transaction is rolled back. There is a larger overhead associated with this approach, as compared to compile time validation, since invalid transactions need to be rolled back. On the other hand, the duration for which the constraint data items need to be locked is shorter. Once a transaction has been validated, it can commit.

3.4.3   Postexecution Time Validation

In this approach, validation is performed after the execution of the transaction but just before the transaction is committed. If validation fails, transaction will be aborted. It should be obvious that the cost of abort in this case is the highest since validation is performed last. Consequently, the lock duration for the data items with which a transaction is working is also long.

3.5   COST OF SEMANTIC INTEGRITY ENFORCEMENT

In centralized system, the cost of enforcing SI consists of the cost associated with accessing SI data items, locking these data items, calculating assertions associated with them, and then releasing the locks. This cost is dominated by the database access time, since compared to the CPU cost, database access time (disk I/O) is very slow. In a distributed system, on the other hand, the validation cost is dominated by the communication cost between the sites involved in a transaction. The cost of communication is directly associated with the number of required messages for coordination. Example 3.5 demonstrates this for a simple distributed system scenario.

Example 3.5   Consider a two-site system where the EMP table is stored at Site 1 and the DEPT table is stored at Site 2. The EMP table has column ENO as its primary key and a foreign key called "DNO" that indicates in which department the employee works. The DNO column in the DEPT table is the primary key. Suppose a human resource manager wants to add a new employee, say, employee 100, who works for department 10. Let's assume that this is achieved by a human resource manager issuing a transaction at Site 1. Obviously, department 10 must exist in this database since otherwise the referential integrity of the system would be violated. Before we run this transaction, we must validate the SI requirements of this transaction—we must confirm that department 10 exists in the system. We achieve this by sending a message from Site 1 to Site 2 asking if department 10 exists. Site 2's semantic integrity service checks the existence of the department and sends us an answer. If "DNO = 10" does not exist in DEPT, then this transaction is invalid and must be rolled back. Only if the validation is successful do we continue with the execution of this transaction.

Assuming that this transaction is valid and department 10 exists in the system, we have to make sure that, during the execution of this transaction, the DNO column of the DEPT table, representing department 10, does not change. This requires locking department 10's row at Site 2 before executing this insert transaction. To do this, Site 1 must send a message to Site 2 requesting it to lock the corresponding row in the DEPT table. Once the row has been locked, Site 2 sends an acknowledge message back to Site 1. Upon receiving this message, Site 1 will continue with the insert. If the execution of this transaction finishes without any problems, then Site 1 must release the lock on DNO at Site 2. This is accomplished by another message sent from Site 1 to Site 2 and another acknowledgment message sent back from Site 2.

A careful reader has noticed that this example uses a compile time validation approach—the transaction execution starts only after validation has completed. The total cost of this approach is six messages—two messages to validate the referential rule, two messages to lock the row in the DEPT table, and two messages to unlock the row after the transaction has committed. On the other hand, if we use run time validation, the total cost of validation will be four messages. We can achieve this by "piggybacking" the lock request on the validation request message. This also requires only one acknowledgment message back from Site 2, which reduces the total number of messages to four. The following three subsections outline the cost associated with each of the validation approaches in a distributed system.

3.5.1   Semantic Integrity Enforcement Cost in Distributed System

In calculating the cost of semantic integrity enforcement in distributed systems, we assume the cost of the CPU is negligible as compared to the communication cost. We also assume that communication cost is directly related to the number of messages required for each approach. This assumption ignores the amount of data transferred by each message and simply focuses on the number of messages. Example 3.6 presents a more complicated example.

Example 3.6   For this example, we are adding a new loan for a customer of the simple bank database given below (we will use this same database in Chapter 4 as well).

```
Customer (CID, CNAME,STREET, CCITY);
Branch (Bname, ASSETS, BCITY);
Account (A#,CID, Bname,BAL);
Loan (L#,CID, Bname, AMT););
Transaction (TID, CID, A#, Date, AMOUNT);
```

The following are semantic integrity requirements for this database:

- The CID column in Customer table is the primary key.
- CID is a foreign key in the Account, Loan, and Transaction tables.
- Bname is the primary key of Branch table.
- Bname is a foreign key in the Account and Loan tables.
- A customer can have any number of accounts in the bank.
- Each customer's account must have a positive balance.
- A customer can have any number of loans in the bank but the total amount of all loans for a customer at any point in time cannot be more than $500,000.

This database is distributed in a four-site system consisting of four database servers in Minneapolis (MPLS), St. Paul (StP), St. Cloud (StC), and Mankato (MK). The bank headquarters is in Minneapolis. The Customer table is stored in the Minneapolis server. There is a branch in St. Paul called the Grant branch, and a branch in St. Cloud called the Main branch. There are no branches in Mankato. Each branch server hosts fragments of the Loan and Account tables, for storing those loans and accounts that have been opened at that branch. Information about all the bank's branches is stored in the Branch table in Mankato. The Transaction table is also stored in Mankato and it stores all bank transactions, such as deposits, withdrawals, and loan payments. A new loan is added to the bank by performing an insert operation into the Loan table that provides values for L#, CID, Bname, and AMT. This insert operation must execute at the branch server where the loan is initiated. For our example, we assume the loan is initiated in St. Paul at the Grant branch, the loan number is 1234, the amount is $150,000, and the loan belongs to customer 1111.

The following rules must be validated when we add a new loan for a given customer:

- Since L# is the primary key of the Loan table, its value must be unique—no existing loan can have the same L# in the bank. Note that there are two loan tables in the bank, one in StP, and one in StC.
- CID must be associated with one customer in the Customer table.
- Bname must be associated with one branch name in the Branch table.
- A valid AMT value depends on how many other loans this customer has and whether or not the total of all of this customer's loan amounts is more than $500,000 or not.

The following outlines a compile time validation approach for this transaction:

- Since L# is the primary key in the Loan table, we must validate the nonexistence of "L# = 1234" in the two loan tables. To do this, the St. Paul site has to look up "L# = 1234" locally and at St. Cloud. The local lookup is achieved by a local select as "select count(*) from Loan where L# = 1234." If this count returns zero (0), then loan number 1234 is not used locally. After confirming this, the St. Paul site sends the same select statement to St. Cloud and asks that site to run the command and return the count. This validation step passes if the count received from St. Cloud is also zero.

- Since the loan belongs to customer 1111, we must also validate that "CID = 1111" exists in the Customer table. The Customer table is stored in Minneapolis. Therefore, the St. Paul site has to send a request to the MPLS site asking if "CID = 1111" is in the Customer table. When St. Paul gets a positive response back from Minneapolis, this validation step passes.

- Since the new loan is to open in Grant, we must validate the existence of "Bname = 'Grant'" in the Branch table. This is achieved by a local select against the Branch table, at Mankato, checking for existence of a row with "Bname = 'Grant'." If such a row exists, this validation step passes. Otherwise, the transaction fails.

- Due to the business rule that no customer should have more than $500,000 in total loan amounts, we need to validate that the sum of all existing loans combined with the new loan for this customer is less than $500,000. We can achieve this in three separate steps. In the first step, we need to calculate the sum of all loan amounts for customer 1111. We do this by running the SQL statement "select CID, SUM(AMT) from Loan Where CID = 1111 Group by CID" against the local Loan table and St. Cloud Loan table. In the second step, we add the two totals and the new loan amount together, resulting in the new total amount of loans for the customer. Finally, in the third step, we compare the new total amount from the second step with $500,000. If the new total amount is less than $500,000, the transaction is validated—otherwise, the transaction fails.

Figure 3.11 depicts a table that shows how validation steps are carried out by the St. Paul site.

As seen from this example, sometimes validation is performed by the site where the SI data item is stored—for example, checking the nonexistence of loan 1234 at St. Could—and at other times validation has to be performed by the site originating the transaction—for example, figuring out the new total loan amount for a customer. In the first case, we must use the site where the SI information is stored to validate; otherwise, the validation requires sending the entire Loan table from St. Could to St. Paul, where the existence of the account would be checked. This, obviously, would take many messages with a large communication cost—and it is not necessary. In the second case, the validation involves tables from two sites. In situations like this, where validation involves more than one site, it is better to have the validation performed by the transaction's originating site.

3.5.1.1 *Variables Used* By now, it should be rather clear that the more sites we have involved in validating a transaction, the more messages we must send for validation. In comparing the compile time, run time, and postexecution time validation, we are

Action	MPLS	StP (Transaction is here)	StC	MK
	Customer	Loan, Account	Loan, Account	Branch, Transaction
Validate non-existence of L# = 1234 in the two loan tables		• Validate non-existence of loan 1234 locally • If invalid, abort • Send a message to StC to verify existence of loan 1234 in StC • Get Ack message – if invalid, abort	• Receive message from StP • Validate • Send results back	
Validate the existence of CID = 1111 in the Customer table	• Receive message from StP • Validate • Send results back	• Send a message to MPLS to verify existence customer 1111 • Get Ack message – if invalid, abort		
Validate the existence of Bname ='StP' in the Branch table		• Send a message to MK to verify existence of branch 'StP' • Get Ack message – if invalid, abort		• Receive message from StP • Validate • Send results back
Validate that sum of all existing loans for this customer an the new loan is < $500,000		• Send a message to 'StC' to calculate total loan amounts for the customer there • Calculate total loan amounts locally • Add existing loan amounts for customer • Add up existing and new loan amounts • Validate if less than $500,000 • If invalid, abort	• Receive message from StP • Calculate values • Send results back	

Figure 3.11 Validation steps and messages required for adding a new loan.

not interested in costing individual transactions, but we are interested in figuring out the average cost of each approach for a large number of transactions. Therefore, we try to calculate the number of messages required for each option when considering a large number of transactions in the system. Also, for simplicity and efficiency we assume that when the transaction's originating site communicates with another site, it makes all of its requests together. For instance, suppose Site 1, where transaction T1 is originated at, needs to read-lock three items at Site 2. To do this, Site 1 sends one message requesting Site 2 to lock all three items as opposed to sending three individual read-lock requests. Therefore, it is not as important to know **how many items** a transaction needs to read-lock, write-lock, read, and write as it is to know **how many sites** these items are stored at, since this determines the number of messages involved.

Based on the above assumptions, the following are the terms we use in our calculations:

- There are **N** transactions in the system that we are trying to validate.
- Out of these **N** transactions, **M** will validate—the remaining **(N − M)** transactions will fail.
- Each transaction needs to know the average number of sites that it **only reads from**. This is necessary to figure out the cost for read-lock requests. We use **Ronly** as this average. Ronly indicates how many sites the transaction has to send a read-lock request to.
- Each transaction needs to know the average number of sites that it **only writes to**. This is necessary to figure out the cost for write-lock requests. We use **Wonly** as this average. Wonly indicates how many sites the transaction has to send a write-lock request to.
- Each transaction needs to know the average number of sites that it **both reads from and writes to**. We use **RW** as this average. This is necessary to figure out the cost for read-lock and write-lock requests. RW indicates how many sites the transaction has to send a read-lock and write-lock request to.
- All SI-related data items for each transaction need to be read-locked as well. This is necessary to prevent the SI rules from being changed while a transaction is validating. Therefore, each transaction needs to know the average number of sites at which its SI-related data items are stored. We use **SIS** as this average.

3.5.1.2 *Compile Time Validation*   The compile time SI validation algorithm works as follows:

1. Read-lock the SI-related data items at SIS sites.
2. These sites either evaluate SI and send the result to the control site or they send data to the control site, which does the SI validation.
3. If a transaction violates SI, then reject that transaction and terminate it. Otherwise, continue to step 4.
4. Lock data items at (Wonly + RW + Ronly) sites and execute the transaction. Note that requests to lock and commands to execute are piggybacked when the originating site sends a message to a remote site. This eliminates the need for multiple communications to the same site.

5. Unlock data items at the sites where successful transactions have committed.

We can figure out the locking/unlocking and validation cost for this algorithm by adding up the number of messages generated during each step of the algorithm. The following shows each individual algorithm step's cost:

1. Cost = N * SIS: this is the cost of read-locking the SI-related data items.
2. Cost = N * SIS: this is the cost of validating N transactions.
3. Cost = (N − M) * SIS: this is the cost of unlocking the SI-related data items locked in Step 1 for those transactions that have violated SI, been rejected, and then terminated.
4. Cost = M * (Wonly + RW + Ronly): this is the cost of locking the data items used by all the transactions that have successfully validated.
5. Cost = M * (Wonly + RW + Ronly + SIS): this is the cost of unlocking all data items (including the SI-related data items) for all the transactions that have validated.

3.5.1.3 *Run Time Validation*   The run time SI validation algorithm works as follows:

1. Read-lock all SI-related data items at SIS sites, read-lock data items for read-only at Ronly sites, and write-lock data items to read and write at RW sites.
2. Read, compute, and generate final values to write at RW and Wonly sites.
3. Read SI-related data items or ask for the results of validation from SIS sites.
4. If there is a violation, then reject the transaction and unlock by sending messages and terminating the transaction; otherwise, continue to Step 5.
5. Lock at Wonly sites and execute updates/commit for all successful transactions.
6. Unlock at sites for successful transactions and terminate.

For this algorithm, we can figure out the locking/unlocking and validation cost by adding up the number of messages generated during each step of the algorithm. The following shows each individual algorithm step's cost:

1. Cost = N * (RW + Ronly + SIS): this is the cost to read-lock SI-related and read-only data items plus the cost to write-lock read and write data items.
2. Cost = None: in this step the control site will perform the necessary computations.
3. Cost = N * SIS: this is the cost of reading the SI data items (or receiving the validation results from the sites that store SI data items).
4. Cost = (N − M) * (RW + Ronly + SIS): this is the cost of unlocking read and write, read-only, and SI data items for transactions that have failed the validation.
5. Cost = M * Wonly: this is the cost to write-lock data items that transactions write only.
6. Cost = M * (RW + Ronly + Wonly + SIS): this is the cost of unlocking all locked data items for transactions that have successfully finished.

3.5.1.4 Postexecution Time Validation   The postexecution time SI validation algorithm works as follows:

1. Read-lock data items to read at Ronly sites.
2. Write-lock data items to write or to read and write at Wonly and RW sites.
3. Compute new values to be written.
4. Send new values to the site where they need to be written at Wonly and RW sites.
5. Send read-lock messages to lock SI-related data items at SIS sites; ask them to send SI-related data items back or the results of their validation to the control site.
6. If a transaction fails validation, then send reject messages to all the sites at which the transaction has written, to undo the work.
7. Unlock the sites at which data items were locked and terminate.

For this algorithm, we can figure out locking/unlocking and validation cost by adding up the number of messages generated during each step of the algorithm. The following shows each individual algorithm step's cost.

1. Cost = N * Ronly: this is the cost to send the read-lock requests to all sites where the read-only data items reside.
2. Cost = N * (RW + Wonly): this is the cost to send the write-lock requests to all sites where the data items to be read and written as well as the data items to be only written reside.
3. Cost = None: the control site performs computation for new values during this step.
4. Cost = None: this is the cost of sending the new data item values to each site where they need to be written.
5. Cost = 2N * SIS: this is the cost of locking and either reading the SI-related data items or requesting and receiving the validation results for those data items from the SIS sites.
6. Cost = (N − M) * (Wonly + RW + Ronly + SIS): this is the cost of unlocking the data items that invalid transactions have used.
7. Cost M * (Ronly + Wonly + RW + SIS): this is the cost of unlocking all remaining locked data items.

Example 3.7   In this example, we present a simple eight-site system, location details for the data items used for a given transaction (T1), and a specific strategy for carrying out the transaction. We assume the cost of sending a message from any site to any other site is C units of time.

The following depicts the distribution setup for this example:

- There are eight (8) sites in the system.
- Sites 1 and 2 are the sites that T **only reads** from.
- Sites 3, 4, and 5 are the sites that T **only writes** to.
- Sites 6 and 7 are the sites that T **reads and writes**.

Site	1	2	3	4	5	6	7	8
Ronly	x	x						
Wonly			x	x	x			
RW						x	x	
SIS								x
				T enters here				

Figure 3.12   Summary of data item placement for Example 3.7.

- Site 8 is the site that transaction checks **SIS**.
- T enters the system at Site 4.

Figure 3.12 shows the placement of SIS, Ronly, Wonly, and RW data items for this transaction.

The following are the cost calculations for this example:

- The cost of locking all sites to write-only is 2C since the transaction enters at Site 4, which is where one of the needed items is, and it needs to send two messages to Sites 3 and 5.
- The cost of locking all sites to read-only is also 2C since the transaction needs to send two messages, one to Site 1 and one to Site 2, to read-lock the items there.
- The cost of locking all sites to read and write is 2C since the RW sites are Sites 6 and 7.
- The cost of locking all sites for transaction SI checks is 1C since all such items are stored at Site 8.
- The cost of reading all information that the transaction needs (after the data items have been locked) is 10C since the transaction needs to read items from Sites 1, 2, 6, 7, and 8. Since each read requires a message that is sent from Site 4 (where transaction is) to each site (where the data item is) and also requires that site to send the response message, the total cost is $(2 * 5)C = 10C$.
- The cost of writing all information that the transaction needs (after the data items have been locked) is 4C since Site 4 needs to send the values for the items that need to be written to Sites 3, 4, 5, 6, and 7. Note that the items on Site 4 are local and do not require a message. Therefore, we need four messages at the cost 4C.

Based on the costs calculated above, we can determine the cost of the following execution strategy. We will assume that lock and write commands do not require acknowledgment messages.

Strategy

- *Phase 1.* The originating site will lock items at all sites where it needs to lock them. This phase will cost 7C—2C to read-lock at Sites 1 and 2; 4C to write-lock at Sites 3, 5, 6, and 7; and 1C to read-lock at Site 8.

- *Phase 2.* The originating site will first send messages to read everything it needs. Then it will send messages to write everything it needs to write. This phase will cost 14C—10C to read data items at Sites 1, 2, 6, 7, and 8; and 4C to write data items at Sites 3, 5, 6, and 7.
- *Phase 3.* The originating site will validate the SI for transaction T. This phase will cost 2C since all SI data items are stored at Site 8.
- *Phase 4.* The originating site will unlock the sites it needs to unlock. This phase will cost exactly the same as Phase 1 (7C) since all data items locked in Phase 1 need to be unlocked.

3.6   SUMMARY

The issues with database control are some of the most challenging issues that a DBA must address. Controlling the database requires implementing tight security measures and correct security policies that define the access rights for users and guarantee the security of the database. This is vital to ensuring the database's consistency and its accessibility only by authorized users. Semantic integrity rules are defined when the database is designed and enforced by the DBMS when the database is used. Semantic integrity rules can be applied before a transaction runs, during a transaction's execution, or after a transaction's execution (but before it has been committed) with each approach having some drawbacks and some benefits.

3.7   GLOSSARY

Access Control   The action of controlling who can access what contents of the database.

Access Rights   The set of action privileges that are given to a user (or a group of users).

After Trigger   A trigger that runs after the triggering event has been run.

Assertions   A set of conditions/rules that are defined for the contents of the database.

Authentication   Any technique used to validate the identity of a source or destination of messages or data.

Before Trigger   A trigger that runs before the triggering event has been run.

Compile Time Validation   An approach to semantic integrity control that checks transactions before they run.

Constraints   A set of conditions/rules that are defined for the contents of the database.

Data Type   A constraint associated with the type of a data item in a database.

Database Administrator (DBA)   A person who has ultimate privileges on what can be done to the database.

Integrity Constraints   A set of conditions/rules that are defined for the contents of the database.

Postexecution Time Validation   An approach to semantic integrity control that checks transactions after they run.

Referential Integrity   The fact that for every foreign key value in a table there must be a corresponding primary key value in the database.

Relation Constraints   A set of rules that apply to the table as a whole.

Relational Constraints   A set of constraints that are inherited by the relational model from the ER (conceptual) model of the database.

Role   A grouping of privileges that can be assigned to a database user or another role.

Row Trigger   A trigger that runs as many times as the number of rows affected by the triggering event.

Run Time Validation   An approach to semantic integrity control that checks transactions during execution.

Semantic Integrity Rules   A set of conditions/rules that are defined for the contents of the database.

Statement Trigger   A trigger that runs only once regardless of how many rows are affected by the triggering event.

Stored Procedure   A procedure that is stored in the database.

Trigger   A stored procedure that can only be called by the DBMS when modifying events such as insert, delete, and update are issued by the database users.

User Defined Data Type   A data type that a database user can define, which is based on the base data types of a DBMS.

REFERENCES

[Badal79] Badal, D,, *The Proceedings of the Fourth Berkeley Conference on Distributed Data Management and Computer Networks*, pp. 125–137, August 1979.

[Eswaran76] Eswaran, P., *Specifications, Implementations and Interactions of a Trigger Subsystem in an Integrated Database System*, IBM Research Report RJ-1820, November 1976.

[Hammer78] Hammer, M., and Sarin, S., "Efficient Monitoring of Database Assertions," in *Proceedings of ACM SIGMOD International Conference on Management of Data*, pp. 38–48, Dallas, TX, June 1978.

[Machgeles76] Machgeles, C., "A Procedural Language for Expressing Integrity Constraints in the Coexistence Model," *Modeling in Database Management Systems*, pp. 293–301, edited by Nijssen, G., North-Holland, Amsterdam, 1976.

[McLeod79] McLeod, D., *High Level Expression of Semantic Integrity Specifications in a Relational Database System*, MIL Tech-Report TR-165, September 1979.

[Stonebreaker74] Stonebreaker, M., *High Level Integrity Assurance in Relational Data Management Systems*, Electronic Research Laboratory Memo ERL-M473, University of California, Berkeley, August 1974.

[Stonebreaker76] Stonebreaker, M., and Neuhold, E., *A Distributed Database Version of INGRES*, Electronic Research Laboratory Memo ERL-M612, University of California, Berkeley, August 1976.

EXERCISES

Provide short (but complete) answers to the following questions.

3.1   Assume the cost of sending a message from any site to any other site is C units of time for SI validation. Figure out the cost of each one of the phases of the following strategy. Also, assume that there are N transactions and, out of these, M will fail the validation.

Phase 1: Control site read-locks and reads all data that needs to be read.

Phase 2: Control site performs the validation.

Phase 3: Invalid transactions are rejected—locks are released for these transactions.

Phase 4: Control site calculates all the new values that need to be written.

Phase 5: Control site write-locks information at all the sites it needs (no ACK for locking is required).

Phase 6: Control site writes where it needs to write for successful transactions.

Phase 7: Control site unlocks at the sites that need to be unlocked.

3.2   Assume the following two tables in SQL Server 2005 where EMP(Dno) is a Fkey that points to DEPT(Dno).

```
EMP  (Eno Integer  not null, Dno Integer not null,
      primary key(Eno))
DEPT (Dno Integer not null, Mgr varchar(15),
      primary key(Dno))
```

(A) Write a stored procedure that when given a Dno checks the existence of it in the DEPT table. The procedure returns 1 if the Dno found and −1 if Dno is not found.

(B) Write a trigger that uses the procedure in part A to validate inserting a row into the EMP table. The trigger checks the existence of Dno in the DEPT table. If Dno is found, then the row is inserted. Otherwise, the trigger aborts the insert.

3.3   Assume the following two tables in Oracle 10 g:

```
EMP (Eno NUMBER(4) not null, sal NUMBER (10,2), Dno NUMBER
(3) not null)
DEPT (Dno NUMBER(3) not null, Mgr varchar(15), Tot_Emp_sal
NUMBER (12,2) not null)
```

EMP(Dno) is a Fkey that points to DEPT(Dno), which is a Pkey.

(A) Write a stored procedure that when given an amount increases the value of the column Tot_Emp_sal with this amount.

(B) Write a trigger that runs when employees are added to the database. The trigger uses the procedure in part A to update the column Tot_Emp_sal in the DEPT table to reflect the fact that the new employees are added to their corresponding departments.

3.4   Consider the bank database discussed in Example 3.6. This database has the integrity requirements that (1) a loan must belong to one, and only one, customer; (2) an account must belong to one, and only one, customer; and (3) a customer must own, at least, one loan or one account in the bank—otherwise, the customer cannot exist in the database. All branches in the bank are located in either Minneapolis (MPLS) or St. Paul (STP). All accounts belonging to a branch in MPLS are stored in the database in the MPLS server. Similarly, all accounts belonging to a branch in STP are stored in the database in the STP server. Smith is a customer with $CID = 100$. Smith decides to close the account with A# = 222 by issuing a delete command from an ATM in LA. Explain the steps required to maintain the integrity of this database when this account is closed.

4

QUERY OPTIMIZATION

In this chapter, we provide an overview of query processing with the emphasis on optimizing queries in centralized and distributed database environments. It is a well-documented fact that for a given query there are many evaluation alternatives. The reason for the existence of a large number of alternatives (**solution space**) is the vast number of factors that affect query evaluation. These factors include the number of relations in the query, the number of operations to be performed, the number of predicates applied, the size of each relation in the query, the order of operations to be performed, the existence of indexes, and the number of alternatives for performing each individual operation—just to name a few. In a distributed system, there are other factors, such as the fragmentation details for the relations, the location of these fragments/tables in the system, and the speed of communication links connecting the sites in the system. The overhead associated with sending messages and the overhead associated with the local processing speed increase exponentially as the number of available alternatives increases. It is therefore generally acceptable to merely try to find a "good" alternative execution plan for a given query, rather than trying to find the "best" alternative.

A query running against a distributed database environment (DDBE) will have to go through two types of optimization. The first type of optimization is done at the global level, where communication cost is a prominent factor. The second type of optimization is done at the local level. This is what each local DBE performs on the fragments that are stored at the local site, where the local CPU and, more importantly, the disk input/output (I/O) time are the main drivers. Almost all global optimization alternatives ignore the local processing time. When these alternatives were being developed, it was believed that the communication cost was a more dominant factor than the local processing cost. Now, it is believed that both the local query cost and the global communication cost are important to query optimization.

Distributed Database Management Systems by Saeed K. Rahimi and Frank S. Haug
Copyright © 2010 the IEEE Computer Society

Suppose we have two copies of a relation at two different servers, where the first server is a lot faster than the second server, but at the same time, the connection to the first server is a lot slower than the connection to the second server (perhaps we are closer to the second server). An optimization strategy that only considered communication cost would choose the second server to run the local query. This will not necessarily be the best strategy, due to the speed of the chosen (second) server. The overall time to run a query in a distributed system consists of the time it takes to communicate local queries to local DBEs; the time it takes to run local query fragments; the time it takes to assemble the data and generate the final results; and the time it takes to display the results to the user. Therefore, to study distributed query optimization, we need to understand how a query is optimized both locally and globally.

In this chapter, we introduce the architecture of the query processor for a centralized system first. We then analyze how a query is processed optimally, discussing the optimization techniques in a centralized system. The optimization of queries in a distributed system is explained last. We introduce a simple database that we use in our examples. We will also provide a brief introduction to **relational algebra (RA)** in this chapter, since most commercial database systems use this language as an internal representation of SQL queries.

4.1 SAMPLE DATABASE

We will use a small database representing a bank environment for our examples. This database has five relations: Customer, Branch, Account, Loan, and Transaction. In this database, customers, identified by CID, open up accounts and/or loans in different branches of the bank that are located in different cities. This is indicated by the CID and BNAME foreign keys in the Account and Loan relations. Customers also run transactions against their accounts. This is shown in the Transaction relation by the combined foreign key "(CID, A#)." Later in this chapter, when discussing query optimization alternatives, we will specify the statistics for this database. The following shows the relations of our example bank database.

```
CUSTOMER (CID, CNAME, STREET, CCITY);
BRANCH (BNAME, ASSETS, BCITY);
ACCOUNT (A#, CID, BNAME, BAL);
LOAN (L#, CID, BNAME, AMT);
TRANSACTION (TID, CID, A#, Date, AMOUNT);
```

4.2 RELATIONAL ALGEBRA

Since the introduction of the relational model by Codd in 1970 [Codd70], two classes of languages have been proposed and implemented to work with a relational database. The first class is called **nonprocedural** and includes **relational calculus** and **Quel**. The second class is known as **procedural** and includes relational algebra and the **Structured Query Language (SQL)** [SQL92]. In procedural languages, the query directs the DBMS on **how** to arrive at the answer. In contrast, in a nonprocedural language, the query indicates **what** is needed and leaves it to the system to find the process for arriving at the answer. Although it sounds easier to tell the system what is needed instead of how to get the answer, nonprocedural languages are not as popular as procedural languages. As a matter of fact, SQL (a procedural language) is the only widely accepted language for end user interface to relational systems today.

To start our query processing discussion, we will make the assumption that user requests are entered into the system as SQL statements. This is because, as we mentioned before, one of the goals of a distributed database management system is to provide a standards-based, uniform, high-level language interface to all the data that is stored across the distributed system. SQL is typically used as such a high-level language interface. Even though SQL is an accepted and popular interface for end users, it does not lend itself nicely to internal processing. Perhaps the most problematic aspect of SQL is its power in representing complex queries easily at a very high level without specifying how the operations should be performed. That is why most commercial database systems use an internal representation based on relational algebra that specifies the ordering of different operations within the query. Therefore, to understand how SQL queries are processed, we need to understand how their equivalent relational algebra commands work.

Since the detailed discussion of RA is outside the scope of this book, in this chapter we will only provide an overview of those RA operations that are of interest to query optimization. We recommend interested readers look at the discussion of the relational data model in Section 11.1 for a brief review of the terminology, and see [Codd70] for a more detailed review of the concepts and operations.

For the remainder of this section we will use the following notations:

- R and S are two relations.
- The number of tuples in a relation is called the cardinality of that relation.
- R has attributes a1, a2, ..., an and has cardinality of K.
- S has attributes b1, b2, ..., bm and has cardinality of L.
- r is a tuple in R and is shown as r[a1, a2, ..., an].
- s is a tuple in S and is shown as s[b1, b2, ..., bm].

4.2.1 Subset of Relational Algebra Commands

Relational algebra (**RA**) supports unary and binary types of operations. Unary operations take one relation (table) as an input and produce another as the output. Binary operations take two relations as input and produce one relation as the output. Note that regardless of the type of operation, the output is always a relation. This is an important observation since the output of one operation is usually fed as an input into another operation in the query. RA operators are divided into **basic operators** and **derived operators**. Basic operators need to be supported by the language compiler since they cannot be created from any other operations. Derived operators, on the other hand, are optional since they can be expressed in terms of the basic operators. Greek symbols are sometime used to represent the RA operators in many textbooks (see Table 4.1).

In this book, we will use the following notation instead:

- SL represents the relational algebra SELECT operator.
- PJ represents the relational algebra PROJECT operator.

TABLE 4.1   Symbols Often Used to Represent Relational Algebra Operators

Symbol	Name	RA Operator
σ	Sigma	Select
π	Pi	Project
$\bowtie$	Bowtie	Cross product or join

- JN represents the relational algebra JOIN operator.
- NJN represents the relational algebra natural JOIN operator.
- UN represents the relational algebra UNION operator.
- SD represents the relational algebra natural SET DIFFERENCE operator.
- CP represents the relational algebra CROSS PRODUCT operator.
- SI represents the relational algebra SET INTERSECT operator.
- DV represents the relational algebra DIVIDE operator.

4.2.1.1 Relational Algebra Basic Operators   Basic operators of RA are SL, PJ, UN, SD, and CP. In the following subsections, we briefly describe these operators.

Select Operator in Relational Algebra   The select operator returns all tuples of the relation whose attribute(s) satisfy the given predicates (conditions). If no condition is specified, the select operator returns all tuples of the relation. For example, "$SL_{bal=1200}$ (Account)" returns all accounts that have a balance of $1200. The result is a relation with four attributes (since the Account relation has four attributes) and as many rows as the number of accounts with a balance of exactly $1200. The predicate "bal $= 1200$" is a simple predicate. We can use "AND," "OR," and "NOT" to combine simple predicates, making complex predicates. For example, we can find the accounts with a balance of $1200 at branch "Main" using the select expression, "$SL_{bal=1200 \text{ AND } Bname='Main'}$ (Account)."

Project Operator in Relational Algebra   The project operator returns the values of all attributes specified in the project operation for all tuples of the relation passed as a parameter. In a project operation, all rows qualify but only those attributes specified are returned. For instance, "PJ $_{Cname,Ccity}$ (Customer)" returns the customer name and the city where the customer lives for each and every customer of the bank.

COMBINING SELECT AND PROJECT   We can combine the select and project operators in forming complex RA expressions that not only apply a given set of predicates to the tuples of a relation but also trim the attributes to a desired set. For example, assume we want to get the customer ID and customer name for all customers who live in Edina. We can do this by combining the SL and the PJ expressions as "PJ $_{CID, Cname}$ (SL $_{Ccity='Edina'}$ (Customer))." Note that operator precedence is enforced by parentheses. In this example, the innermost expression is the SL operation and is carried out first. This expression returns all customers who live in Edina. Subsequently, the PJ operator trims the results to only CID and Cname for those customers returned from the SL operation.

Union Operator in Relational Algebra   Union is a binary operation in RA that combines the tuples from two relations into one relation. Any tuple in the union is in the first relation, the second relation, or both relations. In a sense, the union operator in RA behaves the same way that the addition operator works in math—it adds up the elements of two sets. There are two compatibility requirements for the union operation. First, the two relations have to be of the same degree—the two relations have to have the same number of attributes. Second, corresponding attributes of the two relations have to be from compatible domains.

The following statements are true for the union operation in RA:

- We cannot union relations "R(a1, a2, a3)" and "S(b1, b2)" because they have different degrees.
- We cannot union relations "R(a1 char(10), a2 Integer)" and "S(b1 char(15), b2 Date)" because the a2 and b2 attributes have different data types.
- If relation "R(a1 char(10), a2 Integer)" has cardinality K and relation "S(b1 char(10), b2 Integer)" has cardinality L, then "R UN S" has cardinality "K + L" and is of the form "(c1 char(10), c2 Integer)."

Suppose we need to get the name and the address for all of the customers who live in a city named "Edina" or "Eden Prairie." To find the results, we first need to create a temporary relation that holds Cname and Ccity for all customers in Edina; then we need to repeat this for all the customers in Eden Prairie; and finally, we need to union the two relations. We can write this RA expression as follows:

PJ$_{CID, Cname}$ (SL$_{Ccity = 'Edina'}$ (Customer))
UN
PJ$_{CID, Cname}$ (SL$_{Ccity = 'Eden Prairie'}$ (Customer))

The union operator is commutative, meaning that "R UN S = S UN R." Also, the union operator is associative, meaning that "R UN (S U P) = (R UN S) UN P." Applying associativity and commutativity properties to union, we end up with 12 different alternatives for union of the three relations R, S, and P. We will leave it as an exercise for the reader to enumerate all the possible alternatives for the union of three relations.

Set Difference Operator in Relational Algebra   Set difference (SD) is a binary operation in RA that subtracts the tuples in one relation from the tuples of another relation. In other words, SD removes the tuples that are in the intersection of the two relations from the first relation and returns the result. In "S SD R," the tuples in the set difference belong to the S relation but do not belong to R. Set difference is an operator that subtracts the elements of two sets. In a sense, the set difference operator in RA behaves the same way that the subtraction operator works in math. There are again two compatibility requirements for this operation. First, the two relations have to be the same degree, and second, the corresponding attributes of the two relations have to come from compatible domains.

Assume we need to print the customer ID for all customers who have an account at the Main branch but do not have a loan there. To do this, we first form the set of all customers with accounts at the Main branch and then subtract all the customers with a loan at the Main branch from that set. This excludes the customers who are in the intersection of the two sets (those who have both an account and a loan at the Main branch) leaving behind the desired customers. The RA expression for this question is written as

PJ$_{CID}$ (SL$_{Bcity}$ = 'Main' (Account))
SD
PJ$_{CID}$ (SL$_{Bcity}$ = 'Main' (Loan))

Note: The SD operator is not commutative, that is, "R SD S ≠ S SD R." That is because the left-hand side of the inequality returns tuples in R that are not in S, while the right-hand side returns tuples in S that are not in R. Note, however, that unlike the union operator, the SD operator is not associative, meaning that "R SD (S SD P) ≠ (R SD S) SD P."

Cartesian Product Operator in Relational Algebra Cartesian product (CP), which is also known as cross product, is a binary operation that concatenates each and every tuple from the first relation with each and every tuple from the second relation. CP is a set operator that multiplies the elements of two sets. In a sense, the CP operator in RA behaves the same way that the multiplication operator works in math. This operation is hardly used in practice, since it produces a large number of tuples—most of which do not contain any useful information. "R CP S" is a relation with L*K tuples and each tuple is of the form "[a1, a2, ..., an, b1, b2, ..., bm]." For example, assume we have 1000 accounts and 200 loans in the bank. The cross product of the account and loan relations, written as "Account CP Loan," will have 8 attributes and as many as 200,000 tuples. Table 4.2 shows some of the tuples in the "Account CP Loan" results.

As seen from the sample tuples in this relation, account information for account number 100, for customer 111, has been concatenated with all the loans in the bank. Although this is a valid relation as far as the relational model is concerned, all the rows except for the ones that have equal values for the two CID attributes are useless (the tuple with "L# = 167" is valid, but the other tuples are not valid). Therefore, only tuple number 2, where the account and loan information for customer 111 have been concatenated, contains meaningful results. We will discuss how to eliminate the tuples that do not contain meaningful information when we discuss the join operator.

4.2.1.2 Relational Algebra Derived Operators In addition to the basic operators in RA, the language also has a set of derived operators. These operators are called "derived" since they can be expressed in terms of the basic operators. As a result, they are not required by the language, but are supported for ease of programming. These

TABLE 4.2 Partial Cartesian Products Results

A#	CID	Bname	Bal	L#	CID	Bname	Amt
100	111	Main	1000	212	312	Main	20000
100	111	Main	1000	167	111	Main	5000
100	111	Main	1000	435	217	Main	120000
100	111	Main	1000	900	222	Edina	63000

operators are SI, JN (NJN), and DV. The following sections represent an overview of these operators.

Set Intersect Operator in Relational Algebra   Set intersect (SI) is a binary operator that returns the tuples in the intersection of two relations. If the two relations do not intersect, the operator returns an empty relation. Suppose that we need to get the customer name for all customers who have an account and a loan at the Main branch in the bank. Considering the set of customers who have an account at the Main branch and the set of customers who have a loan at that branch, the answer to the question falls in the intersection of the two sets and can be expressed as follows:

$$PJ_{Cname} \ (SL_{Bcity \ = \ 'Main'} \ (Account))$$
$$SI$$
$$PJ_{Cname} \ (SL_{Bcity \ = \ 'Main'} \ (Loan))$$

SI operation is associative and commutative. Therefore, "R SI S = S SI R" and "R SI (S SI P) = (R SI S) SI P." As mentioned before, SI is a derived operator. That is because we can formulate the intersection of the two relations, "R SI S" as "R SD (R SD S)" by the successive application of the SD operator. We leave the proof as an exercise for the reader. *Hint*: Use a Venn diagram [Venn1880].

Join Operator in Relational Algebra   The join (JN) operator in RA is a special case of the CP operator. In a CP operation, rows from the two relations are concatenated without any restrictions. However, in a JN, before the tuples are concatenated, they are checked against some condition(s). JN is a binary operation that returns a relation by combining tuples from two input relations based on some specified conditions. These operations are known as **conditional joins**, where conditions are applied to the attributes of the two relations before the tuples are concatenated. For instance, the result of "R JN$_{a2 > b2}$ S" is a relation with "$<= L * K$" tuples and each tuple is in the form "[a1, a2, ..., an, b1, b2, ..., bm]," satisfying the condition "a2 > b2." One popular join condition is to force equality on the values of the attributes of the two relations. These types of joins are known as **equi-joins**. The expression "R JN$_{a2=b2}$ S" is a join that returns a relation with "$<= L * K$" tuples and each tuple is in the form "[a1, a2, ..., an, b1, b2, ..., bm]," satisfying the condition "a2 = b2."

In addition to these, RA supports the concept of **natural join**, where equality is enforced automatically on the attributes of the two relations that have the same name. For example, consider relations "Account(A#, CID, Bname, bal)" and "Branch(Bname, Bcity, Budget)." Although we can join these relations enforcing equality on any of their two attributes, the natural way to join them is to force equality on the Bname in Branch and the Bname in Account. A careful reader notices that this type of join forces equality on the value of the primary key with the value of the foreign key, resulting in groups of accounts for each branch. This join is written as "Branch JN$_{Branch.Bname=Account.Bname}$ Account." When performing joins of this nature, Relational Algebra knows that the values of attributes "Branch.Bname" and "Account.Bname" are the same, and therefore, showing both columns is not necessary. That is why RA drops one of the columns and only displays one. For our example, this type of join is called a natural join and is shown as "Branch NJN Account" knowing that equality is forced automatically on the

Bname attributes. Note that any natural join operation reduces to a Cartesian products operation if the two relations have no attributes in common.

Figure 4.1 depicts the union, SD, and SI operators in RA using Venn diagrams. The shaded areas for UN and SD and the cross-hatched area for SI represent the answer for each operator.

Divide Operator in Relational Algebra   Divide (DV) is a binary operator that takes two relations as input and produces one relation as the output. The DV operation in RA is similar to the divide operation in math. We will use an example to show how the divide operation works in relational algebra. Assume we want to find all customers who have an account at all of the branches located in the city MPLS (each and every branch). As a city, MPLS has multiple branches located in it. Suppose branches in MPLS are Main, Nicollet, and Marquette. We are looking for all customers who have at least one account in **every one of these three branches**. For instance, Jones who has one account in Main and one account in Nicollet is not part of the answer, while Smith who has an account in Main, an account in Nicollet, and an account in Marquette is part of the answer. Jones would be part of the answer if the question were, "Find customers who have an account at ANY branch in MPLS." The key difference between these two questions is "all" versus "any." To get the answer, we need to form two sets of tuples. The first is the set of all customers and the branches in which they have an account. The second set is the set of all branches in MPLS. A customer is part of the answer if for that customer the set of customers' branches **contains** the set of branches in MPLS. The operation that performs these steps is the division operation. Figure 4.2 depicts the two sets and the answer after the divide operation.

The expression "S = PJ bname (SL$_{bcity =\ ‘MPLS’}$ (Branch))" represents the set of all branch names in MPLS. The expression "R = PJ$_{cname,\ bname}$ (Account NJN Customer)"

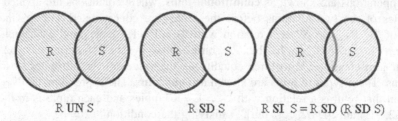

$$R\ UN\ S \qquad\qquad R\ SD\ S \qquad R\ SI\ S = R\ SD\ (R\ SD\ S)$$

Figure 4.1   Set operations in relational algebra.

R			S		Answer
cname	**bname**		**bname**	=	**cname**
Smith	b1	DV	b1		Smith
Rahimi	b3		b2		Rahimi
Jones	b2				
Rahimi	b2				
Smith	b2				
Rahimi	b1				
Love	b4				

Figure 4.2   Set divide operation example.

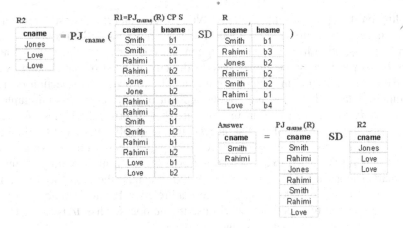

Figure 4.3   Divide operation using the basic RA operations.

represents the set of all customer names and their branch names for all customers in the bank. Hence, the answer can be arrived at by the following:

PJ_{cname, bname} (Account NJN Customer)
DV
PJ_{bname} (SL_{bcity = 'MPLS'} (Branch))

The following explains what the DV operator actually does:

- First, the DV operation performs a group-by on the Cname attribute of the first relation, which results in a set of branch names for each customer.
- Then, it checks to see if the set of Bname values associated with every unique value of Cname is the same set or a superset of the set of Bname values from the second relation. If it is (the same set or superset), then the customer identified by that Cname is part of the division result.

Since DV is a derived operation it can be expressed using the base RA operations expressed as follows:

R1 = PJ_{cname}(R) CP S
R2 = PJ_{cname} (R1 SD R)
R(cname, bname) DV S(bname) = PJ_{cname} (R) SD R2

We have shown the results of these steps in Figure 4.3 for the bank example.

4.3 COMPUTING RELATIONAL ALGEBRA OPERATORS

In the previous section, we discussed the use of some relational algebra operators. In this section, we briefly explain how each operator can be processed. As we will see in this section, an operator in relational algebra can be computed in many different ways depending on the operator type, the available memory, and the disk structures used in the system. Each execution alternative is known as an **access path**. The time it takes to perform any operation in RA has two components. The first component is the amount of time it takes to process the tuples. This is directly affected by the number of tuples that have to be examined in memory. For example, to process a selection on R with 1000 tuples, it takes $1000t$, where t is the amount of time to process one tuple. This time is usually much smaller than the time it takes to bring the tuples of a relation from the disk into memory. The disk access time is usually measured by the number of disk I/O operations. If R is stored on 100 disk pages, then it might take as many as 100 disk I/Os (in the worst case) to read the entire relation into memory. Many disks in the market today have a read speed of 9 milliseconds; therefore, we can estimate that it takes $(100 * 10)/1000$ or 1 second to read relation R into memory. For the rest of the discussions in this section, we will use the number of disk I/Os as the metric to measure the cost of each relational algebra operator.

4.3.1 Computing Selection

As discussed earlier, the select operator in RA examines all tuples in the source relation and only returns those tuples that satisfy the selection condition. The general form of a select statement is "SL_p (R)." Predicate p is either empty (in which case all tuples in R are returned), a simple predicate, or a complex predicate formed by combining simple predicates with "AND," "OR," or "NOT." How tuples within R are examined depends on the complexity of the predicate p and availability of indexes on attributes of R.

4.3.1.1 No Index on R If R does not have any index and it is not sorted, then the only way to process the select statement is to scan all disk pages (or disk blocks) of R. Each page is brought into memory and the tuples inside the page are examined against the predicate "p." Once a qualified tuple is found, it is put in the output of the select operator. Using a relation scan is the most expensive approach to processing a select, since every tuple in the relation must be examined. The disk I/O cost of performing a select on R using a relation scan is equal to the number of actual disk read operations. If we assume the worst case scenario, the pages will be stored on the disk out of sequence and in such a way that we cannot see two successive pages within the same read operation. This depends on the number of pages we can read at a time, the sequence that the pages are stored in on the disk, and the distance between these pages. If the page and buffer details conform to the worst case, we will need to read each page as an independent read operation. If the pages are also stored noncontiguously, and are scattered across the disk, the access time will be even greater because the performance will be worse than the average read speed. If an attribute of R is used many times in many select conditions, it might be a good idea to sort the tuples in R based on this attribute and then use a binary search for access. Similarly, we can create an index on the attribute and use the index. It is obvious that we have to spend the time to sort the relation or to create the index once. But in the long run, having the relation sorted or creating an index on R may be substantially beneficial for query operations.

4.3.1.2 B+Tree Index on R If R has an index—usually a B+Tree in most modern DBMSs—keyed on the attribute that is used in the select predicate, we also have the option of using this index instead of scanning the relation to qualify all the matching tuples in the relation. A B+Tree index sorts the key values (the attribute that the index is built on) at the leaves of the index. Whether or not an index should be used to process a select depends on the complexity of the select predicate.

Simple Predicates   A simple predicate is of the form **attribute op value**, where op is a relational operator (one of "=," "≠," ">," "<," "<>," "> =," and "<="). Finding every tuple in the relation whose attribute value satisfies this simple predicate requires traversing the index tree from the root node to a leaf. Assuming the worst case scenario, each node in the index tree requires a separate disk read (equivalent to needing one disk page per index node when no I/O blocking is used); therefore, the number of disk I/Os required to locate a given target leaf is the same as the height of the index. The existence of a key value in a leaf node of the index tree indicates that the matching tuple is in the database. Once a leaf node of the index has been identified, the next step is to read the disk page(s) containing the actual matching tuple (or tuples) in the relation. Usually a DBMS stores a **rowid** as one of the entries in the leaves of the index, which is then used to directly access the relation's tuples.

To calculate the actual disk I/O cost of using an index, we have to know (1) if the index is a **unique index** or a **nonunique index**, and (2) whether the index is **clustered** or **nonclustered**. In a unique index, the key value we are looking for can appear at most once in the leaves of the index, while in a nonunique index, the value may appear multiple times. In a clustered index, the tuples that are addressed by the key entries in adjacent leaves are stored "close to each other on the disk" (clustered). In a nonclustered index, the tuples may be scattered across the disk. As a result, finding a set of clustered tuples requires fewer disk I/Os than finding the same tuples if they were not clustered. This is important to know, since the time to access the actual tuples in the relation is directly affected by the number of key entries found in the index and how the tuples are stored on the disk.

If all of the matching tuples identified by the index are stored on only one disk page, we need to spend at most one additional disk access to get to the database page where the tuple(s) are stored. This is true for both a clustered and a nonclustered index. If, on the other hand, the index identifies matching tuple(s) that are stored across multiple pages, the access cost could be much greater. When multiple tuples are returned by the index search, it is important to know if the index is clustered or not. In a clustered index, all the tuples that have the same value for the key attribute are stored next to each other physically on the disk, in contiguous disk pages. Therefore, for a clustered index the cost of reading all tuples required is much less than it would be for the nonclustered case. In the best case scenario, it might require only a single disk I/O to read all the disk pages containing the matching tuples. But, if the index is not clustered, the matching tuples could be scattered on the disk, and hence, in the worst case scenario, the cost of retrieving the tuples could be as many additional disk I/Os as the number of data pages used by the matching tuples—that is, in the worst case, at least as many as the actual number of matching tuples.

Complex Predicates   A complex predicate for a select operation has either a **normal conjunctive** or **normal disjunctive** form. A predicate of normal conjunctive form uses "AND" to combine simple predicates, while a normal disjunctive form uses "OR."

An example of a complex normal conjunctive form is "(attribute **op1** value) **AND** (attribute **op2** value)." In this case, how the select operation is carried out depends on the availability of indexes on the two attributes used in the predicate. It is possible to have no such indexes, to have an index only on the first attribute, to have an index only on the second attribute, to have two indexes (one on each attribute), or to have one index including both attributes. We have already discussed the "no index scenario," which would require a relation scan. If we have an index only on the first attribute, we can use that index to find the tuple(s) that qualify the first simple component predicate and then check to see if the value of the second attribute matches the second condition. A similar process can be used when we have an index only on the second attribute. The case of having two indexes, one on each attribute, does not really provide any different access path than the cases we just mentioned involving one index. On the other hand, if there is a single index including both attributes, that index can be used to qualify the rows based on the values of both attributes.

When the complex predicate is a disjunctive normal form, such as "(attribute **op1** value) **OR** (attribute **op2** value)," the use of the index is not going to reduce the cost. That is because, although the use of the index on the first attribute would qualify the tuples that match the first simple predicate, there might be tuples that qualify the second simple predicate that are not returned by the first index lookup operation. Therefore, where disjunctive normal form is used, a relation scan usually performs better.

4.3.1.3   *Hash Index on R*   If R has a hash index keyed on the attribute that is used in the select predicate, we have the option of using this index to perform the selection. A hash index uses a hash function to calculate the address of a bucket where the key value corresponding to the hash value is to be stored. As a result, a hash index has only one level, as compared to the B+Tree, which has multiple levels. To find a key value in the index, the value is run through the hash function and a bucket address is generated. The key values in the bucket are then searched to see if a match exists. If it does, the rowid is used to read the actual tuple from the disk page in the database. Similar to the B+Tree index, the hash index can be clustered or not. In a clustered hash index, all the pages that correspond to a given set of keys in a bucket are clustered together as contiguous pages. In the best case scenario, all of these matching pages can be fetched by one disk I/O operation; even in the worst case scenario, the number of read operations required and the delay between the reads will be minimal.

One of the issues with using hash indexing is collision handling. A collision happens when two different keys hash into the same value. All keys that collide have to be put in the same bucket. This can cause a bucket overflow, requiring additional pages to accommodate the collided keys. Collisions and bucket overflows can cause additional disk I/Os when the index is used to find matching tuples. In a perfect world, when there are no collisions, finding the right bucket in the hash index requires only one disk I/O. If there are collisions, then the bucket itself may span multiple pages, requiring more disk I/Os just to read all the key values in the bucket. The number that is typically used to estimate/adjust for overflow is 1.2 disk I/Os. When the search returns more than one tuple in the result set, we may require as many additional disk I/Os as the number of tuples returned for a nonclustered hash index. For a clustered hash index we might need as few as one disk I/O to access all the matching tuples.

4.3.2   Computing Join

Joins are the most expensive operations in relational algebra. When joining R and S, every tuple in R needs to be compared with every tuple in S to see if the join condition across their attributes is satisfied. When the condition is met, the rows are **concatenated** and copied into the result relation. There are many approaches for performing a join. We will analyze the nested-loop approach (with and without indexes), the sort–merge approach, and the hash-join approach.

4.3.2.1   Nested-Loop Joins   The classical approach to performing a join operation is a row-based, nested-loop join, which is illustrated in the code snippet given below. Here, R and S are joined over the attribute "a" of R and the attribute "b" of S. Note that the operator "||" represents a concatenation operation.

```
For Each r in R Do /* r is a tuple in R */
    For Each s in S Do /* s is a tuple in S */
        If r.a = s.b
        then add r||s to the output
    Next s
Next r
```

In order to analyze the cost of performing the joins we are going to discuss, we need to make some assumptions about the two relations involved in the join.

The following assumptions have been made for our discussion example:

- There are "M = 1000" disk pages in R.
- There are "N = 500" disk pages in S.
- R has 100,000 tuples; that is, it has cardinality of "K = 100,000."
- S has 40,000 tuples; that is, it has cardinality of "L = 40,000."
- We have allocated three buffers to be used while processing tuples in memory; each buffer is only as big as a single disk page.
- We use the first buffer to process pages of R, the second buffer to process pages of S, and the third buffer (the output buffer) for preparing the tuples of the result.
- As the output buffer fills up, its contents are written to the disk to make room for more result tuples to be prepared.
- All of the tuples are smaller than the disk page size, and just to simplify the calculations, we will assume that one or more tuples can fit within the disk page without overlap or wasted space.

To perform the join using a nested-loop approach, we have to spend M disk I/Os to bring all the pages of R (one-by-one) into memory. For each tuple of R, we have to bring all the pages of S (one-by-one) into memory and then examine each tuple in S. Therefore, the number of disk I/Os required is going to be "M + K * N." Substituting 1000 for M, 100,000 for K, and 500 for N, the actual cost is "1000 + 100,000 * 500" or 50,001,000 disk I/Os! If each disk I/Os takes roughly 9 milliseconds, then this approach is going to take over 125 hours to complete. This is not an acceptable performance for two relatively small relations even for today's high-speed disks.

To reduce the cost of nested-loop join, we can use a block-oriented nested-loop join instead. In this approach, we still scan all pages for relation R. For every page of R, we scan all pages in S. In this case, the cost of the join is "1000+1000 * 500" or 501,000 disk I/Os. Even with this improvement, the amount of time required is over 75 minutes.

Other improvements to block-oriented nested-loop joins are possible. For example, we can increase the number of buffers to hold all the pages of R in memory and have two additional buffers, one for the pages of S and one for the output. In this case, the cost will be as small as "1000 + 500" or 1500 disk I/Os (or 0.225 minutes). In reality, we may not have buffer space to put all pages in R into memory at once. In this case, we have to bring a subset of pages of R into memory together. Let's assume we have 202 buffers. We use 200 of these for R, 1 for S, and 1 for output. The cost in this case is "1000 + (1000/200) * 500" or 3500 disk I/Os (less than a minute). DBMSs today allocate a large number of buffers to join relatively large relations in subseconds. We will discuss these approaches in the next few sections.

Nested-Loop Joins with Indexes   What if the two relations involved in the join have an index on the attribute that is being used for the join? Let's assume R has an index on attribute "a" but S does not have an index on attribute "b" as the first scenario. In this case, we use S as the outer relation and scan all of its tuples first. For each tuple of S, we use the index on R and check to see if the value of attribute "b" of S is in the index of R. When a match is found the two tuples are concatenated and the result is added to the output. This eliminates the need to scan R altogether. The cost of this approach depends on the type of index on "a." For our example, if the index on "a" is a hash index and it is clustered, the cost is "500 + 40000 * (1.2 + 1)" or 88,500 disk I/Os (a little over 13 minutes). The cost for a nonclustered hash index depends on how many actual tuples in R qualify for the join. We leave this calculation as an exercise for the reader.

As the second scenario, let's assume that there is an index on attribute "b" of S but no index on attribute "a" of R. In this case, R will be used as the outer relation and S as the inner relation. The final scenario is where both R and S could have an index on their join attribute. This setup is not any different from the previous two we considered, since only one of the indexes can be used. Having an index on each of the attributes that are used for the join can help to join them, but not when we are using a nested-loop join—instead this can help a sort-merge join as we will discus in the next section.

4.3.2.2   Sort–Merge Join   In this join approach, the two relations involved are **sorted** based on the join attribute and then the sorted relations are **merged**. The overall cost of the join is the sum of the sort cost and the merge cost.

External Sort   The sort–merge join approach requires sorting both relations involved in the join. The main issue with sorting a large relation is our inability to sort the relation using one of the popular memory-based sort approaches (such as quick sort, binary sort, or heap sort) due to insufficient memory. As a result, typical internal sort approaches cannot be used. Instead, we use an external sort, where the pages of the relation are brought into memory and sorted internally before the sorted pages are merged. The number of pages of a relation that can be sorted together in memory at the same time depends on the number of buffers available for the sort. The external sort contains two phases. In Phase 1, an internal sort is used to sort all of the tuples within each page. In Phase 2, these sorted pages are merged. We will explain a setup known as a two-way merge that uses three buffers—two input buffers and one output buffer. Let's try to sort R consisting of "M = 1000" pages—once again, we will assume that the tuples fit nicely within the page size and that each buffer is the same size as a single disk page.

Phase 1: The Sort Phase. In this phase, each page of R is brought into memory and is then sorted using one of the fast, internal sort techniques mentioned above. Once the tuples in the page are sorted, the page is written back to the disk. The cost of this phase for R is "2 * M" or 2000 disk I/Os since each and every page has to be read once and written once.

Phase 2: The Merge Phase. In this phase, the now-sorted pages of R are merged, by processing two pages at a time—that is, two sorted pages are read in, and then they are merged. As the tuples are sorted across the two pages, the output is written to the output buffer. When the output buffer is full, it is flushed (emptied) by writing its contents to the disk and then resetting the buffer. After each pair of pages is merged, the tuples in the two pages are sorted. This is known as a run of two pages. After the first iteration of the merge, we end up with the ceiling of "M/2" runs, each consisting of two pages. In subsequent merge steps, the results of two such runs are merged to create runs that are twice as long. This process continues until all pages have been merged. The cost of the merge phase depends on how many merge passes we make. Since we use a two-way merge, the number of passes is the ceiling of "$Log_2 M$," which is the height of a balanced binary tree with M nodes. In each pass we read every page of R and write every page. Therefore, the cost of the merge phase is

```
2W_phase_two_cost = 2 * M * ⌈Log₂M⌉
```

Therefore, the total cost of the sort is

```
2W_Total_cost = (2 * M) + (2 * M * ⌈Log₂M⌉)
              = 2 * M * (1 + ⌈Log₂M⌉)
```

For our example, since R has 1000 pages, the cost of sorting R is "2 * 1000 * (1 + 10)" or 22,000 disk I/Os. It should be obvious that the more buffers we allocate to the sort process the faster the sort can be. At one end of the spectrum, we can sort the entire relation in memory if we allocated M buffers for input and one buffer for output. We cannot do this for large relations due to insufficient available memory. We can, however, allocate the highest number of buffers possible to the sort. If B is the highest number of buffers we can use, we can allocate "B−1" buffers to the merge and one buffer to the output and perform a "B−1 way" merge. In this case, the first phase still takes "2 * M" disk I/Os to sort the tuples in all pages, but it creates "M/B" sorted runs, each of which is B pages long.

In the merge phase, we merge the pages in "$⌈Log_{B-1}⌈M/B⌉⌉$" passes. Therefore, the total cost of the sort is

```
BW_Total_cost = 2 * M * (1 +⌈Log_B-1⌈M / B⌉⌉)
```

Assuming we have 201 buffers for the sort, relation R can be sorted in

```
BW_Total_cost = 2 * 1000 * (1 + ⌈Log₂₀₀5⌉)
              = 2 * 1000 * (1 + 1)
              = 4000 disk I/Os
```

The typical number of buffers allocated to the sort in today's DBMSs is 257. This allows for a 256-way sort–merge and requires only three passes for a relation with 1,000,000 pages and only four passes for a relation of 1,000,000,000 pages!

Merge   Merge is the last step in joining two relations using the sort–merge approach. To merge, each page of the sorted relations must be brought into memory and then written out. The total cost of merging R and S, for example, is "2 * (M + N)." The total cost of the sort–merge join for R and S using B buffers is

```
Total_cost =   2 * M * (1 + ⌈Log_{B-1}⌈M / B⌉⌉)
             + 2 * N * (1 + ⌈Log_{B-1}⌈N / B⌉⌉)
             + 2 * (M + N)
```

4.3.2.3   *Hash-Join*   The last alternative access path we will consider in this section is the hash-join. The hash-join has been gaining a lot of popularity in today's DBMSs. The hash-join approach consists of two phases: the **partitioning** phase and the **probing** phase. In the partitioning phase, R and S are each broken up (partitioned) into two separate collections of nonoverlapping subsets (partitions). A tuple is assigned to a particular partition by using the same hash function for both relations. When partitioning R, attribute "a" is passed to the hash function, while the partitioning of S passes attribute "b." Since we use the same hash function for both relations in the partitioning phase, the matching tuples from both relations, if any, end up in the buckets with the same address. For example, if all key values between 100 and 200 are hashed to partition 5 of R, then all tuples with the same key value range in S will also be hashed into partition 5 of S. In the probing phase of the join, tuples in a partition of R are only compared to the tuples in the corresponding partition of S. There is no need to compare the tuples in partition 5 of R, for example, with tuples in partition 7 of S. This is a very important observation that gives a hash-join its speed. Of course, we still have to spend the time it takes to partition the two tables based on the values of the join attribute. But, once we have done that, the probing phase can be carried out very quickly.

The cost of hash-join is the total cost of partitioning both relations and the cost of probing. In the partitioning phase, each relation is scanned and is written back to the disk. Therefore, the partitioning phase cost is "2 ∗ (M + N)." In the probing phase, each relation is scanned once again. Hence, the total cost of a hash-join is "3 ∗ (M + N)." Using the statistics we used earlier in this section, the hash-join of R and S will take "3 ∗ (1000 + 500)" or 4500 disk I/Os or 40.5 seconds. Compared to the nested-loop join access path, this is a much smaller cost!

4.4   QUERY PROCESSING IN CENTRALIZED SYSTEMS

The goal of the query processing subsystem of a DBMS should be to minimize the amount of time it takes to return the answer to a user's query. Obviously, the response time metric is the most important to the user. However, there are other cost elements that the system is concerned with, which do not necessarily result in the best response time. For example, the system may decide to optimize the amount of resources it uses to get the answer to a given user's query or the answers to queries requested by a group of users. In other cases, we may try to maximize the throughput for the entire system. This may translate into a "reasonable" response time for all queries rather than focusing on the response time for a specific query. These goals are sometime contradictory and do not always mean the fastest response time for a given user or group of users.

In a centralized system, the goals of the query processor may include the following:

- Minimize the query response time.
- Maximize the parallelism in the system.
- Maximize the system throughput.
- Minimize the total resources used (amount of memory, disk space, cache, etc.).
- Other goals?

The system might be unable to realize all of these goals. For example, minimizing the total resource usage may not yield minimum query response time. It is understood that minimizing the amount of memory allocated to sorting relations can have a direct impact on how fast a relation can be sorted. Faster sorting of the relations speeds up the total amount of time needed to join two relations using the **sort–merge** (see Section 4.3.2.2) strategy. The more **memory pages** (**memory frames**) allocated to the sort process the faster the sort can be done, but since total physical memory is limited, increasing the size of sort memory decreases the amount of memory that can be allocated to other data structures, temporary table storage in memory, and other processes. In effect, this **may increase** the query response time.

The center point of any query processor in a centralized or distributed system is the **data dictionary** (DD) (the **catalog**). In a centralized system, the catalog contains dictionary information about tables, indexes, views, and columns associated with each table or index. The catalog also contains statistics about the structures in the database. A system may store the number of pages used by each relation and indexes, the number of rows per page for a given relation, the number of unique values in the key columns of a given relation, the types of keys, the number of leaf index pages, and so on. In a distributed system, the catalog stores additional information that pertains to the distribution of the information in the system. Information on how relations are fragmented, the location of each fragment, the speed of communication links connecting sites, the overhead associated with sending messages, and the local CPU speed are all examples of the details the catalog may contain in a distributed system.

4.4.1 Query Parsing and Translation

As shown in Figure 4.4, the first step in processing a query is parsing and translation. During this step, the query is checked for syntax and correctness of its data types. If this check passes, the query is translated from its SQL representation to an equivalent relational algebra expression.

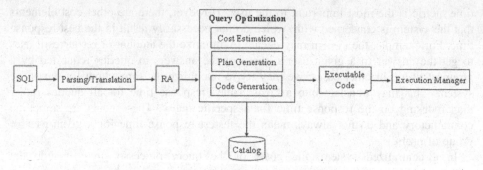

Figure 4.4 Query processing architecture of a DBE.

Example 4.1 Suppose we want to retrieve the name of all customers who have one or more accounts in branches in the city of Edina. We can write the SQL statement for this question as

```
Select  c.Cname
From    Customer c, Branch b, Account a
Where   c.CID   = a.CID
AND     a.Bname = b.Bname
AND     b.Bcity = 'Edina';
```

There are two join conditions and one select condition (known as a filter) in this statement. The relational algebra (RA) expression that the parser might generate is shown below:

$$PJ_{cname} \ (SL_{Bcity \ = \ 'Edina'} \ (Customer \ CP \ (Account \ CP \ Branch)))$$

The DBMS does not execute this expression as is. The expression must go through a series of transformations and optimization before it is ready to run. The query optimizer is the component responsible for doing that.

4.4.2 Query Optimization

There are three steps that make up query optimization. These are cost estimation, plan generation, and query plan code generation. In some DBMSs (e.g., DB2), an extra step called "Query Rewrite" is performed before query optimization is undertaken. In query rewrite, the query optimizer rewrites the query by eliminating redundant predicates, expanding operations on views, eliminating redundant subexpressions, and simplifying complex expressions such as nesting. These modifications are carried out regardless of database statistics [Pirahesh92]. Statistics are used in the optimization step to create an optimal plan. Again, an optimal plan may not necessarily be the best plan for the query.

The RA expression for Example 4.1 does not run efficiently, since forming Cartesian products of the three tables involved in the query produces large intermediate relations. Instead, join operators are used and the expression is rewritten as

$$PJ_{cname} \ (Customer \ NJN \ Account)NJN$$
$$(Account \ NJN \ (SL_{Bcity \ = \ 'Edina'}(Branch)))$$

This expression can be refined further by eliminating the redundant joining of Account relation as

PJ$_{cname}$ (Customer NJN (Account NJN (SL$_{Bcity='Edina'}$ (Branch))))

As we will see later, there are other equivalent expressions that can also be used. All available alternatives are evaluated by the query optimizer to arrive at an optimal query expression.

4.4.2.1 Cost Estimation   Given a query with multiple relational algebra operators, there are usually multiple alternatives that can be used to express the query. These alternatives are generated by applying the associative, commutative, idempotent, distributive, and factorization properties of the basic relational operators [Ceri84].

These properties are outlined below (the symbol "≡" stands for equivalence):

- Unary operator (Uop) is commutative:

Uop1(Uop2(R)) ≡ Uop2(Uop1(R))

   For example,

SL$_{Bname = 'Main'}$ (SL$_{Assets > 12000000}$ (Branch) ≡
SL$_{Assets > 12000000}$ (SL$_{Bname = 'Main'}$ ((Branch))

- Unary operator is idempotent:

Uop((R)) ≡ Uop1(Uop2((R))

   For example,

SL$_{Bname = 'Main'\ AND\ Assets > 12000000}$ (Branch) ≡
SL$_{Bname = 'Main'}$ (SL$_{Assets > 12000000}$ (Branch)

- Binary operator (Bop) is commutative except for set difference:

R Bop1 S ≡ S Bop1 R

   For example,

Customer NJN Account ≡ Account NJN Customer

- Binary operator is associative:

R Bop1 (S Bop2 T) ≡ (R Bop1 S) Bop2 T

   For example,

Customer NJN (Account NJN Branch) ≡
(Customer NJN Account) NJN Branch

- Unary operator is distributive with respect to some binary operations:

$$Uop(R \; Bop \; S) \equiv (Uop(R)) \; Bop \; (Uop(S))$$

For example,

$SL_{sal > 50000}$ (PJ$_{Cname, \; sal}$ (Customer)
UN PJ$_{Ename, \; sal}$ (Employee)) $\equiv$
(SL$_{sal > 50000}$ (PJ$_{Cname, \; sal}$ (Customer))
UN ((SL$_{sal > 50000}$ (PJ$_{Ename, \; sal}$ (Employee)))

- Unary operator can be factored with respect to some binary operation:

$$(Uop(R)) \; Bop \; (Uop(S)) \equiv Uop(R \; Bop \; S)$$

For example,

$SL_{sal > 50000}$ (PJ$_{Cname, \; sal}$ (Customer))
UN (SL$_{sal > 50000}$ (PJ$_{Ename, \; sal}$ (Employee))) $\equiv$
SL$_{sal > 50000}$
(PJ$_{Cname, \; sal}$ (Customer)) UN (PJ$_{Ename, \; sal}$ (Employee))

This is the inverse of the distributive property.

Applying the above properties to the operators of an RA query can create multiple equivalent expressions. For example, the following eight expressions are equivalent. It is the responsibility of the query optimizer to choose the most optimal alternative.

Alt1: (SL$_{Bname}$ = 'Main' (Account)) NJN Branch
Alt2: Branch NJN (SL$_{Bname}$ = 'Main' (Account))
Alt3: (SL$_{Bname}$ = 'Main' (Branch)) NJN Account
Alt4: Account NJN (SL$_{Bname}$ = 'Main' (Branch))
Alt5: SL$_{Bname}$ = 'Main' (Account NJN Branch)
Alt6: SL$_{Bname}$ = 'Main' (Branch NJN Account)
Alt7: (SL$_{Bname}$ = 'Main' (Account)) NJN (SL$_{Bname}$ = 'Main' (Branch))
Alt8: (SL$_{Bname}$ = 'Main' (Branch)) NJN (SL$_{Bname}$ = 'Main' (Account))

For query optimization discussion, it is more convenient to use a **query tree** instead of the RA expression. A query tree is a tree whose leaves represent the relations and whose nodes represent the query's relational operators. Unary operators take one relation as input and produce one relation as output, while binary operators take two relations as input and produce one relation as output. That is why every operator's output can be fed into any other operator. Results from one level's operators are used by the next level's operators in the tree until the final results are gathered at the root. All operators have the same relation-based interface for input and output. This helps with a uniform interface implementation for the query execution manager. This uniformity has given rise to the use of this operator model in most commercial systems such as System R (DB2), Oracle, Informix, and Ingres. In such systems, each operator's implementation is based on the concept of an **iterator** [Graefe93].

Each iterator has a set of functions (methods in object-orientated terminology) that can be called when needed. An iterator acts as a producer for the iterator at the next level and as a consumer for the iterator(s) above it—remember in our representation of a query tree the leaves are on the topmost level. An iterator has three functions—to prepare, to produce, and to wrap-up production. These functions are called "Open," "Get_Next," and "Close." For example, to perform a select using a scan access path, the operator opens the file that contains the relation to be scanned and allocates enough input and output memory buffers for the operation. Once opened, the Get_Next function is called repeatedly to process tuples from the input buffer(s), it qualifies them and puts them in the output buffer(s). Once there are no more tuples to process, the Close function is activated to close the file and deallocate the memory buffers. Note that although the Open and Close functions for all iterators perform similar tasks, depending on the operator, the work that Get_Next function has to do may vary tremendously. For instance, a sort–merge to join two relations requires reading the pages for each relation into memory, sorting them, writing them out, bringing them back, and merging them to produce the output, as explained in Section 4.3. One of the advantages of the iterator model is that it naturally supports pipelining, where the output tuples of one operator can be fed as input into another operator without needing to store them on the disk (materializing them).

For a given query expression, the query optimizer analyzes all equivalent query trees that represent the **solution space** for the query. For the SQL query used in Example 4.1, the solution space (not considering the trees that produce Cartesian products) consists of five query trees that can be used to produce the same results as shown in Figure 4.5 [Larson85].

The optimizer analyzes all these trees in the solution space and selects a tree that is optimal for the query. The first step in the optimization is pruning. In the pruning step, the "bad" alternative trees are eliminated. The optimizer usually uses a small set of rules for pruning. One such rule requires that "before joining two relations, the relations should be reduced in size by applying the select and the project operations." Considering this rule, alternatives 2 and 5 perform better than the others do, since they perform the select operation before the join operation. In the next step, the optimizer selects trees 2 and 5 and runs them through the cost analysis. In the cost analysis step, statistics are used to determine/estimate the cost of each candidate tree. In this step, the tree with the smallest cost is chosen.

The following are statistics about our database:

- There are 500 customers in the bank.
- On average, each customer has two accounts.
- There are 100 branches in the bank.
- There are 10 branches in Edina city.
- Ten percent of customers have accounts in the branches in Edina.

Since there are 1000 accounts in the bank, and 50 customers have accounts in the branches in Edina resulting in 100 accounts in that city. Let's also assume that it takes "t" units of time to process each tuple of each relation in memory. Using the statistics

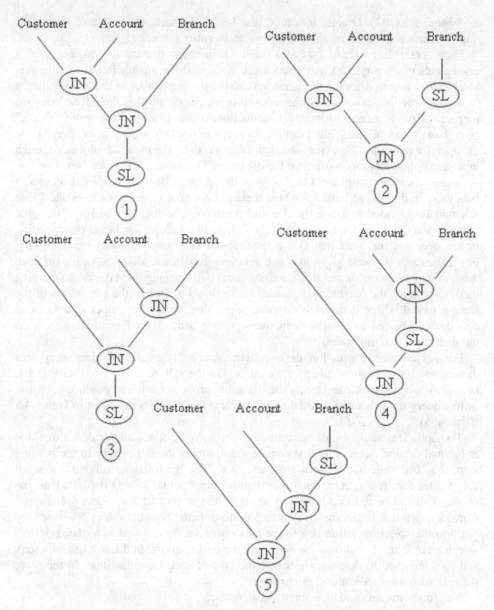

Figure 4.5   Alternative query tree for the Example 4.1.

we just discussed, we can calculate the cost of the two chosen alternatives based on the number of rows that each one processes. Figure 4.6 shows the cost analysis for these two alternatives.

Analysis of Alternative 2: The first operation in this alternative is the join between the Customer and the Account relations. The cost of this join is "500 * 1000t," since there are 500 tuples in the Customer relation and 1000 tuples in the Account relation. The join results in the temporary relation "R1." R1 has 1000 tuples, since every account must belong to a customer. The second operation selects those branches that are in city

```
Cost of alternative 2:
Operation                                    Cost            Number/Rows
Customer NJN Account -> R1                    500 * 1000t     1000 tuples
SL Rcity = 'Edina' (Branch) -> R2             100t            10 tuples
R1 NJN R2 -> Result                           1000 * 10t      100 tuples
Total cost:                                   510,100t


Cost of alternative 5:
Operation                                    Cost            Number/Rows
SL Rcity = 'Edina'.(Branch) -> R1             100t            10 tuples
R1 NJN Account -> R2                           1000 * 10t      100 tuples
R2 NJN Customer -> Result                      500 * 100       100 tuples
Total cost:                                   60,100t
```

Figure 4.6   Cost analysis for Example 4.1.

Edina as temporary relation "R2." Since there are 100 branches in the bank, the select cost is 100t and R2 has 10 tuples in it. The last operation joins R1 and R2, picking up the customers for accounts in Edina's branches. The cost of this join is "1000 * 10t." Since there are 100 accounts in branches in Edina, it returns 100 tuples. The total cost of this alternative therefore is 510,100t.

Analysis of Alternative 5: The first operation in this alternative is the select with the cost of 100t resulting in relation "R1" with 10 tuples. The second operation joins the Account relation with R1, storing the accounts that are in Edina in the temporary relation "R2." This operation's cost is "1000 * 10t" and it returns 100 tuples. The last operation joins Customer and R2, picking up the customers for the accounts in Edina. The cost of this operation is "500 * 100t" and it returns 100 tuples, which represent the accounts in Edina.

Since query tree 5's cost is smaller than query tree 2's cost, alternative 5 is chosen for the query. We could have arrived at the same conclusion by noticing that we join the Account and Customer relations, which are the largest relations in the database, first in query tree 2—resulting in a higher cost. As a general rule, most DBMSs postpone joining the larger relations until the select operations and other joins have reduced the number of tuples in the join operands to a more manageable number.

4.4.2.2 Plan Generation   In this optimization step, the **query plan** is generated. A query plan (or simply, a plan, as it is known by almost all DBMSs) is an extended query tree that includes **access paths** for all operations in the tree. Access paths provide detailed information on how each operation in the tree is to be performed. For example, a join operation can have an access path that indicates the use of the block-nested loop join, hash-join, or sort–merge join, while a select access path can specify the use of an index (a B+Tree index or a hash index) or a table scan. See Section 4.3 for more details on access paths.

In addition to the access paths specified for each individual RA operator, the plan also specifies how the intermediate relations should be passed from one operator to the next—**materializing** temporary tables and/or **pipelining** can be used. Furthermore, operation combinations may also be specified. For example, select and project operations can be combined. In this case, after a tuple is qualified, unwanted attributes are projected out while the tuple is still in memory. This eliminates reprocessing qualified rows in a project operation after a select. Other examples of operator combination include select and join; select and union; project and join; project and union; and select, project, and join.

Query optimization has been researched for many years and is still the focus of research due to its importance in centralized and distributed DBEs. Steinbrunn provides an excellent overview of an alternative approach to query optimization [Steinbrunn97]. Among the proposed algorithms, **exhaustive search** and **heuristics-based** algorithms are most popular. The difference between these two approaches is in the time and space complexity requirements and superiority of the plans they generate. We will review these two approaches to optimization next.

Exhaustive Search Optimization   Algorithms in this class will first form all possible query plans for a given query and then select the "best" plan for the query. **Dynamic programming (DP)** [Selinger79] (see Section 4.4.2.3) is an example of an algorithm in this class. Since the solution space containing all the possible query execution alternatives using DP is very large—it has an exponential time-and-space complexity. Many different DP algorithms attempting to reduce the solution space and lower the time and/or complexity have been proposed [Graefe87] [Ono90] [Pellenkoft97]. We will review two such algorithms in Section 4.4.2.4.

Heuristics-Based Optimization   Originally, most commercial DBMSs used **heuristics-based approaches**, which are also known as **rule-based optimization (RBO) approaches**, as their optimization technique. The algorithms in this class have a polynomial time-and-space complexity as compared to the exponential complexity of the exhaustive search-based algorithms, but the heuristics-based algorithms do not always generate the best query plan [Steinbrunn97]. In this approach, a small set of rules (heuristics) are used to order the operators in an RA expression without much regard to the database's statistics. One such heuristic is based on the observation that if we reduce the size of the input relations to a join, we reduce the overall cost of the operation. This rule is enforced by applying the select and/or project operations before the join. This rule is also known as "pushing" the select and project toward the leaves of the query tree. Another heuristic joins the two smallest tables together first. This is based on the belief that since not all tuples from the relations being joined qualify the join condition, fewer tuples will be used in the next operation of the query tree, resulting in a smaller overall cost for the query. Another popular heuristic is simply to disallow/avoid using the cross-product operation, which is based on the fact that the intermediate result of this operation is usually a huge relation.

These rules (and others like them) are used in many of today's commercial systems. In DB2, for example, there is a rule that forbids/avoids the use of an intermediate relation as the right operand of a join operation. In Oracle 10g, the rule-based optimizer (RBO) associates weights with each operation and uses the operation with the smallest weight first. For example, Oracle associates a weight of 5 with a select operation that uses a unique index, while it assigns a weight of 20 to a relation scan. As a result, when given the choice, the RBO will use the index lookup to find a single tuple rather than scanning the table. Oracle's RBO generates the query plan by applying this rule repeatedly to all operations in the query tree. One advantage of using a small set of rules like these is that the optimizer can generate a plan quickly. Although Oracle's RBO is fast, because it applies rules statically—without considering available statistics—it does not always generate an optimal plan. For instance, perhaps the RBO only considers nested-loop joins for a particular query, even when a sort–merge join or a hash-join would perform better (see Section 4.3) for the current state of the database.

4.4.2.3 Dynamic Programming   Dynamic programming (DP) is an exhaustive search-based algorithm used today by most commercial DBMSs. The approach uses a cost model, such as query response time, to generate a plan with the optimal cost. This approach is also known as **cost-based optimization (CBO)**. In this section, we will summarize dynamic programming. For a more detailed explanation of DP, we refer the reader to [Selinger79]. A good overview of the alternatives for dynamic programming can be found in [Kossmann00b] and [Steinbrunn97]. Surveys of query optimization techniques in centralized systems can be found in [Jarke84] and [Ioannidis96].

For the sake of simplicity when discussing dynamic programming, let's consider the case of joining N relations together in an N-way join, that is, "R1 **JN** R2 ... **JN** RN−1 **JN** RN." The number of alternatives for joining the N relations is "$(2*(N-1))!/(N-1)!$" For example, there are 12 alternatives for joining three tables, 120 alternatives for joining four tables, and 1680 alternatives for joining five tables. Dynamic programming uses a cost model to dynamically reduce the solution space and generates an optimal plan by building the plan one step at a time, from the bottom–up. The algorithm iterates over the number of relations that have been joined so far and prunes the alternatives that are inferior (cost more), keeping only the least costly alternatives. In addition to keeping optimal alternatives, the algorithm may also keep plans that generate a sorted intermediate relation. These plans are of an "interesting order" and are kept because having a sorted intermediate relation helps the next join, encouraging it to apply a sort–merge join as discussed before (since the intermediate result is already sorted, the overhead is less than it would be otherwise). To illustrate how DP works, let's examine a few steps in the DP processing of this N-way join.

Step 1: Generate All 1-Relation Plans.   This step generates the access plans for each of the relations involved in the query. Select and project are the only operations we consider in this step. All other operations are binary operations, which involve more than one relation by definition. When considering 1-relation plans, the access paths for each select and project operation are evaluated and we choose the path with the smallest cost, discarding the others. For instance, we know that a predicate of the form "attribute = constant" for a uniquely valued attribute will return either one tuple or zero tuple. In this case, if a unique index has been created on the attribute, we have an access path based on a unique index lookup. Alternatively, we could scan the relation to find the matching tuple. It should be obvious that between these two access paths, the unique index lookup is faster than the scan, especially for large relations that occupy many disk pages. Therefore, the plan that utilizes the index is chosen for the select operation using this relation. Let's assume that the optimal access plans, P_1, P_2, ..., PN, are kept for relations R1, R2, ..., RN correspondingly.

Step 2: Generate All 2-Relation Plans.   In this step, the algorithm combines all the 1-relation plans we kept from Step 1 into 2-relation plans and chooses those with the smallest cost for each pair of relations. Again, the cost of each combination is determined by the different access paths available for the join. The 2-relation plans with the smallest cost are chosen in this step. For example, we know that there are two alternatives for joining R_1 and R_2, based on the order of operands—"R1 JN R2" and "R2 JN R1." For each alternative, it is also possible to join the two relations based on any of the join strategies we discussed in Section 3.4. Let's assume that our system only supports nested-loop row-based joins and sort–merge joins. For this system, there will be two ways to join R1 and R2 and two ways to join R2 and R1. Depending on the availability of indexes keyed on the join attributes of the two relations, the nested-loop join can be implemented in two different ways—one using the index and one not using the index. As a result, for each pair of relations, this system has to consider six different join alternatives (each operand ordering alternative can use one of the two nested-loop join alternatives or the sort–merge alternative). Since the sort–merge join produces a sorted intermediate relation, this plan is kept as an interesting order plan, as we discussed earlier. When we consider the two nested-loop join alternatives, we only keep the plan with the smallest cost if its cost is less than the cost of the sort–merge join. Assuming that we only keep one plan for each pair of relations, we can indicate these plans as $P_{12}, P_{13}, \ldots, P_{1N}$, $P_{21}, \ldots, P_{NN-1}$, where the two digits in the indexes refer to the relations and the order of their join. In other words, the plan we keep for the join between R1 and R2 is called "P_{12}," while the plan we keep for the join between R2 and R1 is called "P_{21}."

Step 3: Generate All 3-Relation Plans. In this step, the algorithm combines all the 2-relation plans from Step 2, with the 1-relation plans from Step 1 to form 3-relation plans. For example, assume the query calls for "R1 JN R2 JN R4." Furthermore, assume that the 2-relation plan P_{12}, which joins R1 and R2 and produces R12, is kept from Step 2. In this case, "R12 JN R4" and "R4 JN R12" must be considered. For each one of these alternatives, we consider all the access paths for the join and keep the optimal plan along with any plans with interesting orders.

Step 4: Generate All 4-Relation Plans. In this step, the algorithm joins the 3-relation plans from Step 3 with the 1-relation plans from Step 1 to form 4-relation plans. The algorithm also joins all the 2-relation plans from Step 2 with each other to form 4-relation plans. Again, for each of these alternatives, we consider all the access paths for each join, keeping the optimal plan and the plans with interesting orders.

Subsequent Steps: The pattern is repeated for each subsequent step, to incrementally create bigger plans until all N relations have been joined.

Example 4.2   In this example, we will apply dynamic programming to the query expressed in Example 4.1. We show this query here again for ease of reference.

```
Select  c.Cname
From    Customer c, Branch b, Account a
Where   c.CID   = a.CID
AND     a.Bname = b.Bname
AND     b.Bcity = 'Edina';
```

Before applying dynamic programming to optimize this query, we need to collect some additional statistics about our database. This collection of statistics should include things like a cost model and further details about the indexes, potential select and join approaches, and the number of sort buffers available.

For this example, suppose we have collected the following information:

- We use disk I/O as our cost model.
- We have a B+Tree index on attribute Bcity of Branch relation.
- We have 257 buffers allocated for sorting.
- There is a nonunique clustered index on attribute Bname of Account.
- There is a hash index on attribute CID of Customer.
- Each B+Tree has two levels since the relations are relatively small (one or two pages each).
- Each hash index has 1.2 bucket access I/O cost.
- Select operations can only use scan and index lookup.
- The system only allows nested-loop and sort–merge joins.

Dynamic Programming Steps for Example 4.2

Step 1: 1-Relation Plans. The only select operator in this example is on the Branch relation looking for branches in city Edina. There are only two possible access paths that can be considered for the select operation on the Branch relation. One approach is to scan the entire relation and the other is to use the B+Tree index. Since there are only 100 branches in the bank, the entire relation can be stored in one or two disk pages. Therefore, the cost of scan is two disk I/Os. The other access plan uses the index on Bname to locate each leaf where Edina is stored as the value. Since the primary key of the Branch relation is Bname, Edina is stored 10 times (one for each branch in Edina). Even though there are multiple values of Edina stored in the leaves, since the B+Tree index sorts the keys in the leaves, all values of Edina will probably be stored in one leaf. It takes two disk I/Os to traverse from the root of the index to reach this leaf. Once we have found the desired leaf, we have to find database pages where the needed tuples are stored. Since Branch relation occupies only two disk pages, we have to spend two additional disk I/Os to read in the tuples. This makes the total cost of using the index four disk I/Os. As a result, scanning the relation is more efficient than using the index. Scanning the Branch relation will be used as its access path. This is also what is called the 1-relation plan for Branch. There are no select operations defined for Customer or Account. Therefore, scan is the only 1-relation plan that can be used. Let's assume plan P_b for Branch, P_c for Customer, and P_a for Account are the ones we have chosen from the first step. These will be used as the 1-relation plans in Step 2.

Step 2: 2-Relation Plans. Let's assume that Rb is a relation that represents the results of "SL $_{Bcity='Edina'}$ Branch." In forming the 2-relation plans, we have to enumerate all possible ways that our three relations can be joined. Listed in no particular order, these are:

Group 1:
P_{ba}: Rb JN Account
P_{ab}: Account JN Rb

```
Group 2:
Pac: Account JN Customer
Pca: Customer JN Account
Group 3:
Pbc: Rb JN Customer
Pcb: Customer JN Rb
```

Among these groups, the "Group 3" alternatives (P_{bc} and P_{cb}) are not considered since they join two relations that do not have a common attribute; that is, they perform cross products. The other four plans in "Group 1" and "Group 2" are analyzed next. In comparing P_{ba} and P_{ab}, we realize that it is better to use P_{ba} because this plan does not materialize the temporary results of "$SL_{Bcity='Edina'}$ Branch" and performs the join on-the-fly using R_b as the driver of the join. In this approach, the value of Bname from the tuples that are returned from the selection is used to probe into the Account relation. Each probe uses the index on Bname and takes three disk I/Os (two for tree traversal and one for the cluster of branches with the same name). Since there are 10 branches in Edina, the total cost of this plan is "10 * 3 = 30" disk I/Os. In contrast, plan P_{ab} is more expensive since it requires scanning the Account relation, which takes 1000 I/Os. Therefore, P_{ba} is chosen for this join. This plan corresponds to "($SL_{Bcity='Edina'}$ Branch) NJN Account," which we indicate by the intermediate relation Rba. In comparing P_{ac} and P_{ca}, we realize that there is an index on the attribute Bname of the Account relation. Since the join between Account and Customer is on CID, this index cannot be used in the nested-loop join. As a result, both joins have to be done using sort–merge access paths. The cost of each alternative using sort–merge is the same since the order of the join operands does not impact the cost of this join strategy. Therefore, we keep P_{ac} indicated as the intermediate relation Rac for the next step.

Step 3: 3-Relation Plans. With P_{ba} chosen as the 2-relation plan from Group 1 and P_{ac} as the plan from Group 2, we need to form all possible 3-relation plans. Since there are only three relations in the query, we need to join Customer with P_{ba} and Branch with P_{ac}. The options for this step are

```
Pbac: Rba JN Customer
Pcba: Customer JN Rba
Pacb: Rac JN Branch
Pbac: Branch JN Rac
```

We have to choose the least expensive alternative as the final plan for the query. Since there are four plans and each join can be done utilizing nested-loop or sort–merge, we will have eight different options. Among these, plan P_{bac} costs the least since it can be done on-the-fly. All other plans require scanning of at least one relation and therefore cost more. The optimizer produces the plan shown in Figure 4.7 as the optimum plan. Surprisingly enough, this plan is what we indicated as the best plan in our analysis in Section 4.4.2.1.

Example 4.3   In this example we will use dynamic programming (DP) to join five relations. In Example 4.2, we applied DP to a three-way join. Although the details of DP were highlighted in Example 4.2, the example had a small number of alternatives

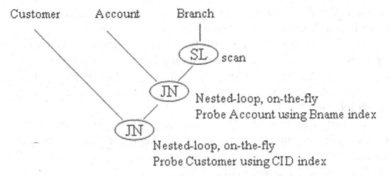

Figure 4.7   Dynamic programming optimum plan for Example 4.2.

to deal with and therefore did not show how large the solution space for DP can really be. To appreciate the time-and-space complexity of DP, we will join five relations: A, B, C, D, and E. In what follows, we will show all plans generated for each step of the algorithm. For simplification, we will not consider any plans with "interesting orders." Figure 4.8 shows the results from Steps 1 and 2 of the algorithm. In this figure, we have used the symbol ⋈ instead of JN to represent the join operation. We assume that A, B, C, D, and E indicate access plans (1-relation paths) chosen from Step 1. In Step 2, all alternatives for joining the 1-relation plans together to form 2-relation plans are shown. The 2-relation plans that are kept from Step 2 are named AB for "A JN B." This indicates not only the two relations that are joined but also the order of the operands passed to the join operation. In this respect, AB is different from BA, since

```
Kept one-relation plans (Access paths):
     A      B      C      D      E

   Two-relation plans:
     A ⋈ B        A ⋈ C        A ⋈ D        A ⋈ E
     B ⋈ A        B ⋈ C        B ⋈ D        B ⋈ E
     C ⋈ A        C ⋈ B        C ⋈ D        C ⋈ E
     D ⋈ A        D ⋈ B        D ⋈ C        D ⋈ E
     E ⋈ A        E ⋈ B        E ⋈ C        E ⋈ D

Kept two-relation plans:
     AB = A ⋈ B
     AC = A ⋈ C
     AD = A ⋈ D
     AE = A ⋈ E
     BC = B ⋈ C
     BD = B ⋈ D
     BE = B ⋈ E
     CD = C ⋈ D
     CE = C ⋈ E
     DE = D ⋈ E
```

Figure 4.8   Steps 1 and 2 of dynamic programming for Example 4.3.

in AB relation A is the outer relation (e.g., in a nested-loop join) and B is the inner relation, while in BA the inner and outer relations are reversed.

Figure 4.9 shows all the 3-relation plans that are generated by combining the kept 2-relation plans from Step 2 and the 1-relation plans from Step 1. From among these plans we have to choose the 3-relation plans with the smallest cost for each combination of three relations. Again, ABD is a plan that indicates "AB JN D" and is different from DAB, which indicates "D JN AB."

Each 4-relation plan is generated by joining together the plans we kept in the previous steps. We can join two 2-relation plans (kept from Step 2) together or join a 1-relation plan (kept from Step 1) with a 3-relation plan (kept from Step 3). Figure 4.10 shows all the possible 4-relation plans.

Figure 4.10 also depicts all the 5-relation plans we generated. As shown in this figure, the 5-relation plans are formed by combining the 1-relation plans from Step 1 with the 4-relation plans we just generated or by combining the 2-relation plans from

```
Three-relation plans:
        AB ⋈ C          AB ⋈ D          AB ⋈ E
        AC ⋈ B          AC ⋈ D          AC ⋈ E
        AD ⋈ B          AD ⋈ C          AD ⋈ E
        AE ⋈ B          AE ⋈ C          AE ⋈ D
        BC ⋈ A          BC ⋈ D          BC ⋈ E
        BD ⋈ A          BD ⋈ C          BD ⋈ E
        BE ⋈ A          BE ⋈ C          BE ⋈ D
        CD ⋈ A          CD ⋈ B          CD ⋈ E
        CE ⋈ A          CE ⋈ B          CE ⋈ D
        DE ⋈ A          DE ⋈ B          DE ⋈ C

        C ⋈ AB          D ⋈ AB          E ⋈ AB
        B ⋈ AC          D ⋈ AC          E ⋈ AC
        B ⋈ AD          C ⋈ AD          E ⋈ AD
        B ⋈ AE          C ⋈ AE          D ⋈ AE
        A ⋈ BC          D ⋈ BC          E ⋈ BC
        A ⋈ BD          C ⋈ BD          E ⋈ BD
        A ⋈ BE          C ⋈ BE          D ⋈ BE
        A ⋈ CD          B ⋈ CD          E ⋈ CD
        A ⋈ CE          B ⋈ CE          D ⋈ CE
        A ⋈ DE          B ⋈ DE          C ⋈ DE

Kept three-relation plans:
ABC = AB ⋈ C
DAB = D ⋈ AB
ABE = AB ⋈ E
ACD = AC ⋈ D
ACE = AC ⋈ E
ADE = AD ⋈ E
BCD = BC ⋈ D
BCE = BC ⋈ E
BDE = BD ⋈ E
CDE = CD ⋈ E
```

Figure 4.9 Step 3 of dynamic programming for Example 4.3.

Four-relation plans:

AB ⋈ CD	AB ⋈ CE	AB ⋈ DE
AC ⋈ BD	AC ⋈ BE	AC ⋈ DE
AD ⋈ BC	AD ⋈ BE	AD ⋈ CE
AE ⋈ BC	AE ⋈ BD	AE ⋈ CD

CD ⋈ AB	CE ⋈ AB	DE ⋈ AB
BD ⋈ AC	BE ⋈ AC	DE ⋈ AC
BC ⋈ AD	BE ⋈ AD	CE ⋈ AD
BC ⋈ AE	BD ⋈ AE	CD ⋈ AE

ABC ⋈ D	ABC ⋈ E	D ⋈ ABC	E ⋈ ABC
DAB ⋈ C	DAB ⋈ E	C ⋈ DAB	E ⋈ DAB
ABE ⋈ C	ABE ⋈ D	C ⋈ ABE	D ⋈ ABE
ACD ⋈ B	ACD ⋈ E	B ⋈ ACD	E ⋈ ACD
ADE ⋈ B	ADE ⋈ C	B ⋈ ADE	C ⋈ ADE
BCD ⋈ A	BCD ⋈ E	A ⋈ BCD	E ⋈ BCD
BCE ⋈ A	BCE ⋈ D	A ⋈ BCE	D ⋈ BCE
BDE ⋈ A	BDE ⋈ C	A ⋈ BDE	C ⋈ BDE
CDE ⋈ A	CDE ⋈ B	A ⋈ CDE	B ⋈ CDE

Kept four-relation plans:
    AB ⋈ CD
    ABC ⋈ E
    ACD ⋈ E
    B ⋈ CDE
    E ⋈ DAB

Five-relation plans:
    (AB ⋈ CD) ⋈ E
    (ABC ⋈ E) ⋈ D
    (ACD ⋈ E) ⋈ B
    (B ⋈ CDE) ⋈ A
    (E ⋈ DAB) ⋈ C

Figure 4.10   Steps 4 and 5 of dynamic programming for Example 4.3.

Step 2 with the 3-relation plans from Step 3. There are five such plans that can be generated based on what was kept in different steps of the DP algorithm. From these plans, we choose the one with the smallest cost as the final plan, which is shown in Figure 4.11.

4.4.2.4 Reducing the Solution Space   As discussed earlier in this chapter and as demonstrated by Example 4.3, dynamic programming generates a large solution space even for a small number of relations. Therefore, it is fairly common for the query optimizers to sacrifice some of the query response time in return for faster query plan generation by reducing the solution space. This means the optimizer tries to find an optimal plan and not necessarily the best plan. The optimizer may actually miss some better plans trying to save time to generate the plan.

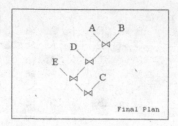

Figure 4.11 Dynamic programming final plan for Example 4.3.

For instance, the optimizer may only consider a left-deep (or a right-deep) query tree instead of a bushy tree when analyzing different access paths as depicted in Figure 4.12. Although a bushy tree may perform better in some situations, the left-deep plan lends itself better to do the operations on-the-fly. The left-deep plan is the only type of tree that DB2 allows. Using a left-deep query plan, the execution manager can perform the second and third joins in our example on-the-fly. As the tuples from the previous join are produced, they are joined with the relation at the next level. This eliminates the need to materialize the results of the joins that are necessary for the bushy plan. For large relations, the intermediate join results could potentially be large and could not be kept in memory for the next step. Storing these large intermediate relations on disk can take a considerable number of disk I/Os.

Even considering only one shape for the query tree does not reduce the solution space dramatically. Consider the case of having to join three relations: A, B, and C. With a left-deep type of tree, joining these relations can be done in six different ways, as depicted in Figure 4.13.

Note: In this example, we assume that any relation can be joined with any other relation. In reality, this may not be the case; that is, A can be joined with B if there is a common attribute between A and B but not with C if there are no common attributes between A and C.

Other alternatives to reduce solution space and the cost-and-time complexity of DP are **iterative dynamic programming** (**IDP**) [Kossmann00a] and the **greedy** approach [Shekita93], both of which we will review next.

Iterative Dynamic Programming   The main issue with dynamic programming is the space-and-time complexity of the algorithm. DP selects the best possible approach by forming all possible alternatives for joining the relations in a query from the bottom

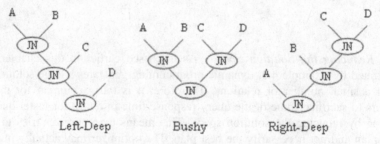

Figure 4.12 Left-deep, bushy, and right-deep plan examples.

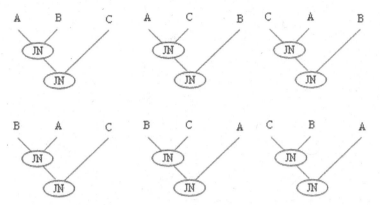

Figure 4.13   Left-deep trees to join three relations.

up. The time and space requirements of DP grow exponentially as the number of relations grows. For a large number of relations, it is fairly common for the algorithm to exhaust the available memory since DP keeps all the plans generated throughout the entire process. Thrashing—the constant exchange of information between the memory and the disk—starts when the computer runs out of memory. One alternative that specifically addresses the issue with the size of memory is called iterative dynamic programming (IDP). The IDP algorithm divides the optimization process into a set of iterations. In each iteration, the algorithm only enumerates up to k relation plans and then stops. Parameter "k" is carefully defined ahead of time to prevent exhausting the available memory based on the number of relations in the query.

For example, if "$k = 3$", then in iteration one the algorithm forms only 1-relation, 2-relation, and 3-relation plans. From the first iteration the best 3-relation plan is selected. All 1-relation and 2-relation plans that include one or more of the three relations participating in the chosen 3-relation plan are discarded. Other plans are carried over to the second iteration. Assuming the same five relations that we used in Example 4.3, Iteration 1 of IDP generates the same plans as generated by DP for up to 3-relation plans (see Figures 4.8 and 4.9). From these plans, the plans shown in Figure 4.14a are kept for Iteration 2. In Iteration 2, the 2-relation plans are formed. Note that although these are called 2-relation plans, in reality they may contain more than two relations. If two base relations are joined the plan is a 2-relation plan. If one 2-relation plan is combined with one 3-relation plan, the result is a 5-relation plan. Figure 4.14b indicates all the 2-relation plans generated from Iteration 2 for our example. As seen from this figure, "CE JN DAB" is actually the 5-relation plan that we are seeking. Figure 4.14c shows the final query plan based on this strategy.

The basic strategy behind IDP is this: if we keep the cheapest k-way plan in each step, the final plan costs the least based on the chosen plans. What we must keep in mind is that since we do not consider all possible plans in each step, IDP may actually miss the optimal overall plan.

Greedy Algorithms   Greedy algorithms have a much smaller time-and-space complexity requirement compared to dynamic programming. However, they do not necessarily produce superior plans [Steinbrunn97]. One can categorize greedy algorithms as a special case of IDP with k = 2. Greedy algorithms behave exactly the same as IDP except

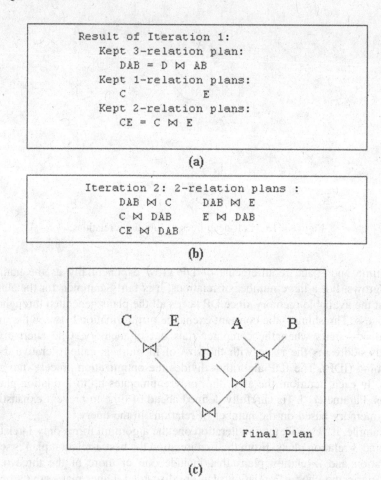

Figure 4.14 Iterative dynamic programming results for Example 4.3.

that only 1-relation and 2-relation plans are formed from plans kept from the previous iteration. Let's apply the greedy algorithm to joining five relations A, B, C, D, and E. For the first iteration, the greedy algorithm generates the same plans as generated by DP for up to 2-relation (see Figure 4.8). At this point, as shown in Figure 4.15, the greedy algorithm breaks and selects the best 2-relation plans and all 1-relation plans that do not include a relation in the chosen 2-relation plan.

Figure 4.15 also shows the 3-relation, 4-relation, and 5-relation plans that the greedy algorithm generates in the second, third, and fourth iterations, respectively. The final plan, which is shown in Figure 4.16, is chosen from all the 5-relation plans that we formed.

4.4.3   Code Generation

The last step in query optimization is code generation. Code is the final representation of the query and is executed or interpreted depending on the type of operating system or hardware. The query code is turned over to the **execution manager** (EM) to execute.

```
Iteration 2: Kept plans:
      AD      B      C      E
      New Plans:
      AD ⋈ B        AD ⋈ C        AD ⋈ E
      B ⋈ AD        B ⋈ C         B ⋈ E
      C ⋈ AD        C ⋈ B         C ⋈ E
      E ⋈ AD        E ⋈ B         E ⋈ C
      Chosen plan:
      ADB = AD ⋈ B
Iteration 3: Kept plans:
      ADB     C      E
      New plans:
      ADB ⋈ C       ADB ⋈ E
      C ⋈ ADB       C ⋈ E
      E ⋈ ADB       E ⋈ C
      Chosen plans:
      ABD            EC = E ⋈ C
Iteration 4: Kept plans:
      ABD            EC
      New plans:
      ABD ⋈ EC    EC ⋈ ABD
      Kept plan (Final plan)
      EC ⋈ ABD
```

Figure 4.15   Greedy algorithm applied to Example 4.3.

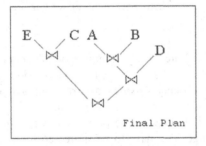

Figure 4.16   Plan generated by greedy algorithm for Example 4.3.

4.5   QUERY PROCESSING IN DISTRIBUTED SYSTEMS

As mentioned in Chapter 2, there are two distinct categories of distributed systems:
(1) distributed homogeneous DBE (what we called a DDBE) and (2) distributed heterogeneous DBE (what we called a MDB). In both of these systems, processing a
query consists of optimization and planning at the global level as well as at the local
database environment (LDBE) level. Figure 4.17 depicts how queries are processed
in a DDBE.

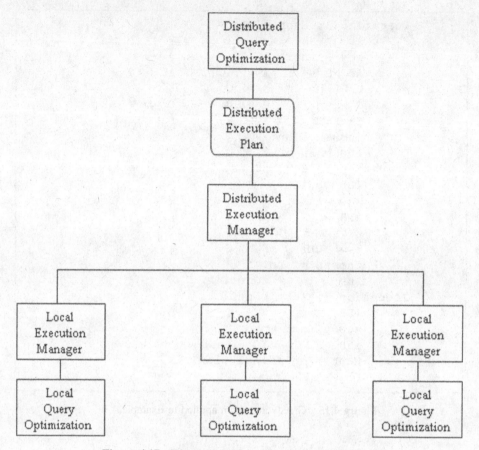

Figure 4.17 Distributed query processing architecture.

The site where the query enters the system is called the client or controlling site. The client site needs to validate the user or application attempting to access the relations in the query; to check the query's syntax and reject it if it is incorrect; to translate the query to relational algebra; and to globally optimize the query. In the rest of this chapter, we will discuss how queries are processed in a traditional DDBMS first and then point out the challenges that have to be addressed for a MDB or a heterogeneous database environment.

4.5.1 Mapping Global Query into Local Queries

Recall from Chapter 2 that a global query is written against the global schema. The relations used in the global query may be distributed (fragmented and/or replicated) across multiple local DBEs. Each local DBE only works with the local view of the information at its site and is unaware of how the data stored at its site is related to the global view. It is the responsibility of the controlling site to use the global data dictionary (GDD) to determine the distribution information and reconstruct the global view from local physical fragments.

Example 4.4   Suppose the EMP relation is horizontally fragmented based on the value of the LOC attribute as discussed in Chapter 2. Each employee works at one of three possible locations (LA, NY, or MPLS). The LA server stores the information about employees who work in LA. Similarly, NY and MPLS servers store the information about employees who work at these locations. Now we will consider a query that needs to retrieve the name of all employees who make more than $50,000. Since EMP does not physically exist, the global query has to be mapped to a set of local queries that run against the fragments of EMP as shown below.

```
Global Query: PJEname (SLsal > 50000 (EMP))
LA's Query:   PJEname (SLsal > 50000 (LA_EMP))
Ny's Query:   PJEname (SLsal > 50000 (NY_EMP))
MPLS's Query: PJEname (SLsal > 50000 (MPLS_EMP))
```

The GDD contains rules for reconstructing the original relation from its fragments. Because the EMP relation is horizontally fragmented, we need to union the fragments together to reconstruct the original relation. After adding this reconstruction step, the global query looks like the following:

```
PJEname (SLsal > 50000 (LA_EMP))
UN
PJEname (SLsal > 50000 (NY_EMP))
UN
PJEname (SLsal > 50000 (MPLS_EMP))
```

It should be obvious that, just like a local query, there are multiple equivalent expressions (or query trees) for any extended global query. These alternatives are generated when we take into account the associative and commutative properties of the relational algebra binary operators in a query. For instance, applying the associative property of the UN operation, we can also express the above query by

```
PJEname (SLsal > 50000 (LA_EMP))
UN
(
     PJEname (SLsal > 50000 (NY_EMP))
     UN
     PJEname (SLsal > 50000 (MPLS_EMP))
)
```

There are 12 different alternatives that we can use to union these relations, as discussed before $(2 * (3-1)!/(3-1)!)$. Specifying when and where the SL operation is performed creates more alternatives to consider. One such alternative is shown below:

```
SLsal > 50000 (
          PJEname (LA_EMP)
          UN
          (
          PJEname (NY_EMP)
```

$$\text{UN}$$
$$\text{PJ}_{Ename} \ (\text{MPLS\_EMP})$$
$$)$$
$$)$$

For each alternative, the global optimizer must also decide where to union these results together. One approach would be to union all three intermediate relations at the client or controlling site. Another approach is to use one of the database servers at MPLS, LA, or NY to perform the union. The anticipated size of each intermediate relation, the local database server speed, and the communication link speed are factors that are used to decide on a plan with the smallest communication cost.

The cost of executing each alternative query tree must be examined by the distributed query optimizer to arrive at the most optimal answer. In a centralized system, the query tree shape and the available access paths are main drivers of this decision. In a distributed system, the query tree shape and the associated communication cost are the main factors. At the global level, the optimizer is not aware of the access paths that are available at the local sites. Choosing the access paths for a local query is solely the local optimizer's responsibility. What impacts the global optimization the most is the communication cost. The global optimizer must generate a distributed execution plan for the query that uses the least amount of data transfer. The plan has to specify where each fragment of data must be accessed, in what order the query steps must be carried out, and furthermore, how intermediate results are transferred from site to site.

Example 4.5   Consider a simple query that performs a select operation on the Branch relation in our example bank database. This query enters Site 1 of a three-site system. To analyze the impact of distributing the Branch relation on the overall execution, we consider three cases. In the first case, the Branch relation is stored at Site 2 and it is not fragmented or replicated. In the second case, the Branch relation is replicated and there are two copies of it, one at Site 2 and one at Site 3. In the third case, the Branch relation is fragmented horizontally with one fragment stored at Site 2 and another at Site 3.

Case 1: The Branch relation is stored entirely at Site 2. In this case, since the Branch relation is not fragmented or replicated, the global query is mapped directly to a local query that must run at Site 2. The results of the select operation need to be sent back to Site 1 to be displayed to the user. To run the query at Site 2, Site 1 sends a message to Site 2 passing the SL expression to it. We will assume that the SL command takes one message to send. The number of messages required to return the results to Site 1 depends on how many tuples of the Branch relation qualify. For simplicity, we assume that each row of the relation takes one message to be sent. Therefore, the results require N messages if there are N tuples that are returned from the select. This alternative requires "N + 1" messages.

Case 2: The Branch relation is replicated with copies stored at Site 2 and Site 3. In this case, since Branch is replicated but not fragmented, the global query still maps to a single site local query. Since there are two copies of the relation in the system, the global optimizer will have to decide where it is best to run the query. In either case, the number of messages to run the command at the remote site and send the results back is "N + 1"—the same as Case 1. In this case, the optimizer has to consider factors such as the local processing speed of each server as well as the communication link speed between Site 1 and each of the two candidate sites. If the link speed for both sites is the same, the processing speed and workload are used to break the tie. But if the link between Site 1 and Site 2 is much faster than the link between Site 1 and Site 3, running the select operation at Site 2 is better only if the processing speed and load of servers at Site 2 and Site 3 are the same.

Case 3: The Branch is horizontally fragmented with fragments at Site 2 and Site 3. In this case, the global query is mapped into two local queries, each running against one of the two fragments. Since fragments of the Branch relation are not replicated, the global optimizer has only one option for the site where it needs to run each local query. As assumed before, the query returns N tuples. In this case, however, the N tuples reside on two different sites. Let's assume that N2 and N3 represent the qualified number of tuples at Site 2 and Site 3, respectively, where "N = N2 + N3." We need to union the tuples from Site 2 and Site 3 as the answer to the query.

There are three sites where we can perform the union:

1. Union is performed at Site 1. In this case, as shown in Figure 4.18a, the communication cost is "2 + N2 + N3."
2. Union is performed at Site 2. In this case, as shown in Figure 4.18b, the communication cost is "2 + N + N3."
3. Union is performed at Site 3. In this case, as shown in Figure 4.18c, the communication cost is "2 + N + N2."

Clearly, the lowest communication cost is associated with Plan 1. If Site 1 does not have a database server to perform the union, Plan 2 or Plan 3 must be considered. If "N2 > N3," then Plan 2 is superior. If "N2 < N3," then Plan 3 is better. If "N2 = N3,"

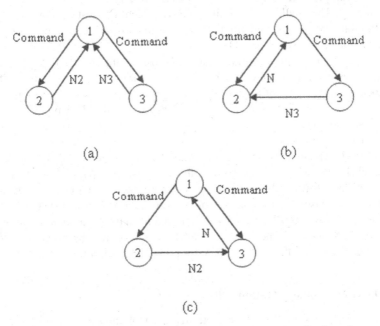

(a)   (b)

(c)

Figure 4.18 Alternatives for performing union in a three-site distributed system.

then both plans have the same communication cost. In this case, the optimizer must consider each database server's speed and/or load factors to decide where to run the query. From this discussion, we can summarize that the total processing cost of a query in a distributed database consists of the amount of time it takes to generate the distributed query execution plan; the time it takes to send the commands that each local server must run; the time it takes for the local DBEs to execute the local queries; and the additional communication cost required between the controlling site and the local sites for transferring the intermediate and/or final results.

We can draw the following conclusions from Example 4.5:

- The global query is mapped to one or more local queries.
- An extended global query reconstructs the results from local results based on distribution information.
- Without replication, the global optimizer should run a local query at the site where the needed fragment is stored.
- With replication, the global optimizer has more than one site where a local query can run. Given the choice, the global optimizer selects the site that requires the least amount of communication, has the lowest workload, or is the fastest.
- Each local query is optimized by the local database server as discussed earlier in this chapter.
- The local query results are merged together using join for vertical fragments and union for horizontal fragments.

We might conclude that running a query in a distributed system is more expensive since it requires more than one site to communicate and cooperate their activities. Although on the surface this seems reasonable, we should not lose sight of the fact that having multiple database servers gives us the ability to explore parallel execution of local queries. The challenge is to find a global execution strategy that minimizes the overall communication cost and at the same time maximizes the amount of parallelism among available database servers. Query optimizers in distributed systems try to exploit the hidden parallelisms in executing a query across multiple DBEs. A good database distribution design fragments and/or replicates a relation in a manner that allows the most expensive operations of a query to run in parallel. For example, to join two large relations may require allocation of each relation to an individual processor to utilize parallel scan, sort, and merge. Query processing can benefit from data distribution if we can capitalize on the vast amount of processing power available in a distributed system. These same advantages exist in parallel databases. The difference between distributed and parallel databases is that the communication cost of a parallel database is much smaller than that of a distributed system. Therefore, the same amount of data transfer in a parallel database takes a fraction of the time it takes in a distributed database. On the other hand, a parallel database environment may use a shared disk or shared memory or both, which could be a source of contention for the processors involved. In a distributed system, there is no contention between individual DBEs.

4.5.2   Distributed Query Optimization

As discussed in Section 4.5.1, global optimization is greatly impacted by the database distribution design. Just like a local query optimizer, a global query optimizer must evaluate a large number of equivalent query trees, each of which can produce the desired results. In a distributed system, the number of alternatives increases drastically as we apply replication, horizontal fragmentation, and vertical fragmentation to the relations involved in the query.

Example 4.6   Let us consider joining three relations—A, B, and C—as "A JN B JN C" in a three-site distributed system. As discussed in Section 4.4.2.2, there are 12 different query trees alternatives that can be used for this purpose. Let's now assume that although A is not fragmented, it is replicated, and there are two copies of it; that B is horizontally fragmented into B1, B2, and B3; and finally, that C is vertically fragmented into C1 and C2. For this distributed database, since B and C do not physically exist, we need to reconstruct them from their fragments. To include reconstruction steps for relations B and C, the global query changes to

A JN B JN C $\equiv$ A JN (B1 UN B2 UN B3) JN (C1 JN C2)

As seen from the mapped global query, the number of relations involved in the query is raised from three to six, increasing the number of available alternatives to $(2 * (6-1)!/(6-1)! = 30,240$. For each alternative, there are many approaches that we can use to formulate the answer for each intermediate result. This adds another order of magnitude to the size of the solution space. To analyze the impact of distribution, let's assume that we decide to use "B1 UN (B2 UN B3)" to reconstruct B from its fragments. For this specific alternative, we have the option of running both union operations at Site 1, both at Site 2, both at Site 3, one at Site 1 and one at Site 2, one at Site 1 and one at Site 3, and so on. We have two operations and each can be performed at three sites, which results in "$3^2 = 9$" alternatives for where the unions are performed. This example clearly shows that evaluating all possible plans for a distributed query is not practical. Instead, we must find a way to arrive at an optimal plan without spending a great amount of time on it.

4.5.2.1 *Utilization of Distributed Resources*

In a distributed system, there are many database servers available that can perform the operations within a query. There are three main approaches on how these resources are utilized. The difference among these approaches is based on whether we perform the operation where the data is; send the data to another site to perform the operation; or a combination of the two. We will examine these three approaches next.

Operation Shipping   In this approach, we run the operation where the data is stored. In order to achieve this, the local DBE must have a database server that can perform the operation. A good example of the kind of operation that lends itself nicely to operation shipping is any unary operation such as relational algebra's select (SL) and project (PJ). Since a unary operation works on only one relation, the most logical and most economical in terms of communication cost is to run the operation where the data fragment is stored. Even for binary operations, such as join and union, we prefer operation shipping if the two operands of the operation are stored at the same site. Most of today's DBMSs such as Oracle, SQL Server, and DB2 prefer operation shipping. In these systems, an interactive query that enters the system at a client computer does not run at the client but at the database server, where the data is stored. The results are then transferred back to the client. These systems store canned queries such as stored procedure on the database server as well. The database server activates these stored procedures upon request from an application or an interactive user at the server, simulating operation or query shipping.

Data Shipping   Data shipping refers to an alternative that sends the data to where the database server is. This obviously requires shipment of data fragments across the network, which can potentially lead to a high communication cost. Consider the case of having to select some tuples from a relation. We can perform the SL operation where the data is as explained in operation shipping. We can also send the entire relation to another site and perform the SL operation there. One can argue that in a high-speed fiber optic communication network, it might be faster to send the entire relation from a low-speed processor to a high-speed processor and perform the SL operation there.

Data shipping is also used in object-oriented databases as a preferred approach. Page-based data caching, close to where the use is, will presumably speed up the response time for queries that run frequently when data does not change often [Dewitt90a] [Franklin93]. A similar caching approach is proposed for an index lookup by Lomet [Lomet96]. An index page fault happens when data required by a query is not in the cache. In this case, the page containing the data is brought into memory. If the cache is full, the least recently used page will be written back to the disk to make room available for the required page.

Hybrid Shipping   Hybrid shipping combines data and operation shipping. This approach takes advantage of the speed of database servers to perform expensive operations such as joins by transferring the smaller relation to the server where the larger relation resides. Figure 4.19 depicts the three alternatives mentioned above.

4.5.2.2 Dynamic Programming in Distributed Systems   The dynamic programming principles we discussed for centralized systems can also be used for query optimization in distributed systems. The following example applies dynamic programming to a distributed database.

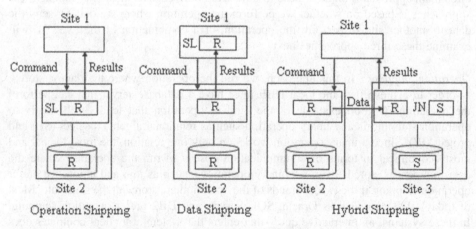

Figure 4.19   Operation, data, and hybrid shipping examples.

Example 4.7   Let's apply dynamic programming to a simple query in a simple distributed system. We use the query in Example 4.2. This query prints the name of all customers who have an account in any branch in city Edina. For ease of reference we have copied the SQL query for this example here again.

```
Select  c.Cname
From    Customer c, Branch b, Account a
Where   c.CID   = a.CID
AND     a.Bname = b.Bname
AND     b.Bcity = 'Edina';
```

The following describes the distributed database set up for this example:

- There are three sites to this system.
- The user enters the query at Site 1, making it the controlling site.
- The Branch relation is not fragmented and is stored at Site 3.
- There are two copies of the Customer relation (C1 and C2). C1 is stored at Site 1, and C2 is stored at Site 2.
- The Account relation is horizontally fragmented based on the value of the balance attribute. All accounts with balances of less than $5000 are in fragment "A1" and are stored at Site 1, the rest are in fragment "A2" and are stored at Site 2.
- We assume that the network is a high-speed local Ethernet and therefore each message takes "t" units of time to get from any site to any other site.
- We also assume that sending any tuple from any site to any other site takes one message and therefore also takes "t" units of time.
- For simplicity, we will assume that all three database servers have the same load and have the same processing speed.
- Also for simplicity, we will refer to each relation with their alias used in the query, i.e., Branch is referred to as B, Account as A, and Customer as C.
- We will use operation shipping, that is, perform the operation where the data is stored.

1-Relation Plans: There are three relations involved in the query. B is not fragmented and/or replicated and is stored at Site 3. The 1-relation plan for this relation is to send the "SL$_{Bcity='Edina'}$ (Branch)" command to Site 3. The results of this SL operation are 100 tuples that we capture in an intermediate relation called "B3." The Account relation is fragmented into two fragments. Since we are looking for accounts in the city of Edina and do not know which of the Edina city accounts have a balance of more than $5000, we have to query both fragments of Account—A1 and A2. The Customer relation is replicated. We can use the copy at Site 1 or at Site 2. Since the communication link speeds, processor load, and processor speed are the same for Site 1 and Site 2, there is no difference between the two 1-relation plans for Customer. We will choose Site 1 as the target site for the Customer relation. The following are chosen 1-relation plans for each relation or a fragment of a relation.

```
P_b: Access Branch relation at Site 3 and run SL there
     Results in B3 relation at Site 3
```

P_{a1}: Access A1 relation at Site 1
P_{a2}: Access A2 relation at Site 2
P_{c1}: Access C1 relation at Site 1

2-Relation Plans: Since there are three relations and two joins in our query, we have six different query trees that we can choose from.

P_{ba}: B3 JN A
P_{ab}: A JN B3
P_{bc}: B3 JN C
P_{cb}: C JN B3
P_{ac}: A JN C
P_{ca}: C JN A

Note that among these, P_{bc} and P_{cb} cannot be considered since they try joining two relations that do not have a common attribute; that is, they are cross products. We will consider the other four plans in the next step:

P_{ba}: B3 JN A
P_{ab}: A JN B3
P_{ac}: A JN C
P_{ca}: C JN A

Relation "A" consists of two horizontal fragments "A1" and "A2" that need to be unioned together. For relation "C," we have chosen to use copy "C1." Taking these into account, the plans are changed into five groups as follows:

Group1:
P_{ba1}: B3 JN A1
P_{a1b}: A1 JN B3

Group2:
P_{ba2}: B3 JN A2
P_{a2b}: A2 JN B3

Group3:
P_{a1c}: A1 JN C1
P_{ca1}: C1 JN A1

Group4:
P_{a2c}: A2 JN C1
P_{ca2}: C1 JN A2

Group5:
P_{a1a2}: A1 UN A2

In analyzing the 2-relation plans, we use the rule that says, "When joining two relations that are stored at different sites, the smaller relation should be sent to where the larger relation is."

Analysis of 2-Relation Plans

- Group 1: For this group, we apply the rule to send the smaller relation to where the larger relation is for join. As a result, the plan we will take to the next step is "P_{ba1}: B3 JN A1."
- Group 2: For this group, the same argument we used for Group 1 applies. We take "P_{ba2}: B3 JN A2" to the next step.
- Group 3: For this group, we know that both relations are at the same site (Site 1). This makes the JN a local join. The communication costs of the two alternatives are also the same. We choose "P_{a1c}: A1 JN C1" for the next step.
- Group 4: In this case, C1 is a smaller relation and should be sent to where the larger relation is in order to join them. Therefore, we choose "P_{ca1}: C1 JN A2" for the next step.
- Group 5: This group has only one plan for it and is therefore kept. In order to know the cost of this union we need to know how many tuples are in each relation. Assuming that there are more tuples in A1 than A2, we need to send A2 to Site 1 to union with A1.

The plans that need to be considered in the next phase of dynamic programming are

```
Pba1:   B3 JN A1 runs at Site 1
Pba2:   B3 JN A2 runs at Site 2
Pa1c:   A1 JN C1 runs at Site 1
Pca1:   C1 JN A2 runs at Site 2
Pa1a2:  A1 UN A2 runs at Site 1
```

3-Relation Plans: For this example, we assume that we do not allow bushy plans. Therefore, to form a 3-relation plan, we have to combine a base relation with one of the 2-relation plans we have kept. The following are the 3-relation plan alternatives we have:

```
Pba1c:   (B3 JN A1 runs at Site 1) JN C1
Pba2c:   (B3 JN A2 runs at Site 2) JN C1
Pa1cb:   (A1 JN C1 runs at Site 1) JN B3
Pca1b:   (C1 JN A2 runs at Site 2) JN B3
Pa1a2b:  (A1 UN A2 runs at Site 1) JN B3
```

All these plans are needed for the next step since they produce different results. The decision that we have to make is where to run the new joins. The following indicates the site where the operation should be performed based on the rule we mentioned above.

```
Pba1c:   (B3 JN A1 runs at Site 1) JN C1 runs at Site 1
Pba2c:   (B3 JN A2 runs at Site 2) JN C1 runs at Site 1
Pa1cb:   (A1 JN C1 runs at Site 1) JN B3 runs at Site 1
         (B3 was shipped there)
Pca1b:   (C1 JN A2 runs at Site 2) JN B3 runs at Site 2
Pa1a2b:  (A1 UN A2 runs at Site 1) JN B3 runs at Site 1
```

4-Relation Plans: Although we logically have three relations, we have to consider 4-relation plans since the Account relation has been fragmented into two fragments. The following are the alternatives:

```
Pba1c  UN Pba2c  runs at Site 1
Pa1cb  UN Pca1b  runs at Site 1
Pa1a2b JN C1     runs at Site 1
```

Among these alternatives, the cheapest is the first plan since both relations involved in the operation are locally available at Site 1. This site is also where the user and the final results need to be displayed. We showed how dynamic programming principles can be used in conjunction with distributed queries. For the simple example we discussed above, and even with all the simplifying assumptions we made, application of dynamic programming to a three-site system created a lot of alternatives. The reason is that, in distributed systems, fragmentation, replication, availability of different communication paths for command, and alternatives to data exchange among sites tremendously increase the number of available alternatives. This creates a solution space that is very large, even for the simplest of queries. As a result, it is impractical to try to enumerate all of the alternative query trees in dynamic programming for distributed queries. Therefore, we need to use heuristics to reduce the solution space as much as possible before applying dynamic programming.

4.5.2.3 Query Trading in Distributed Systems

An alternative to dynamic programming that is based on the principles of trading negotiation is called query trading (QT), which was proposed by Pentaris and Ioannidis [Pentaris06]. In the QT algorithm, the control site for a distributed query is called the buyer and each site where a local query runs is called a seller. The buyer has different alternatives for choosing sites where data fragments are and also different choices for reconstructing the global results. In this algorithm, the buyer tries to achieve the optimal total cost for the query by negotiating services from different local sellers.

For example, assume a relation is replicated at two sites. When the buyer asks each seller about the cost of performing a select operation on a given relation, each seller (local server) bids on the select based on the facilities and services that are locally available. The difference between the prices that two sellers offer for the same select operation on the same relation is due to differences between each local server's processing speed, workload, method of local optimization, and available indexes. The buyer decides on which seller's offer to choose to lower the overall cost of the query. A cost function is used by the buyer to choose the right seller(s). As an example, assume we need to join relations R1 and R2. Suppose Site 1 has already been chosen to perform a select on R1. In the next step the buyer needs to decide where the join operation is going to be performed. It might be cheaper to join R1 and R2 at Site 1 by sending R2 to this site than sending the results of the select from Site 1 to Site 2 where the join will be performed. The buyer's decision in this case depends on the prices that Site 1 and Site 2 offer for the join operation. In subsequent steps, the buyer negotiates with chosen sellers to see if they can perform a larger portion of the query. This process is repeated until the entire query execution is planned.

The query trading algorithm works by gradually assigning subqueries to local sites. A site may be a buyer, a seller, or both a buyer and a seller depending on the data stored at the site and/or the query that is being performed. During the negotiation, the buyer simply puts the plan together from the bottom up. The query is not actually executed until the overall global plan has been determined. The goal of the algorithm is to create the most optimal plan from local optimized query plans that have been proposed by the sellers together with the communication cost of reconstructing the final results.

4.5.2.4 Distributed Query Solution Space Reduction   As explained earlier in this chapter, both dynamic programming and query trading algorithms have to deal with a large number of alternatives even for simple queries. Attaining the absolute best distributed query plan, therefore, is too expensive to achieve. The following is a summary of the rules that can be applied to a query tree in a distributed system to reduce its solution space [Ceri84].

Apply Select and Project as Soon as Possible   This rule is similar to the rule we discussed earlier for a centralized system. The difference is that in distributed systems, if the select condition includes the attribute that is used for fragmenting a relation horizontally, the distributed select may reduce to a single site select.

Example 4.8   Let's reconsider the EMP relation as defined in Chapter 2, Section 2.2.2. For ease of reference we have shown the EMP relation and its horizontal fragments here again.

```
EMP (EmpID, Name, LOC, SAL, DoB, Dept);

Create MPLS_EMPS
AS SELECT * FROM EMP WHERE LOC = 'Minneapolis';

Create LA_EMPS
AS SELECT * FROM EMP WHERE LOC = 'LA';

Create NY_EMPS
AS SELECT * FROM EMP WHERE LOC = 'NY';
```

We issue the following global query against EMP.

```
Select Name
From EMP
Where LOC = 'LA' and Sal > 30,000.
```

Figure 4.20 shows the query tree that corresponds to this SQL statement.

Since EMP does not exist as a physical relation, to retrieve the tuples of EMP that satisfy the select condition, we have to qualify the tuples in MPLS_EMPS, LA_EMPS, and NY_EMPS. To reconstruct EMP, we must union these three horizontal fragments. Figure 4.21 depicts the expanded global query to include the fragments of the EMP relation.

Without optimization, the select operation must run against the union of EMP's fragments. This approach requires materializing EMP from its fragments at one site

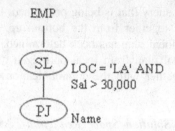

Figure 4.20 Global query tree for Example 4.8.

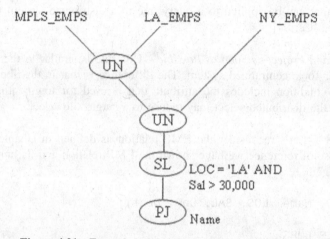

Figure 4.21 Expanded global query tree for Example 4.8.

and then executing the select against it. To reduce the communication overhead, we can apply the select to each fragment and only send the qualified tuples across the network. Figure 4.22 shows how we reduce communication cost by pushing the select operation toward the leaves of the tree to get the results.

Simplify Operations on Horizontal Fragments In the query tree just generated, the optimizer can recognize that the LOC attribute is used as both the predicate for the select and the condition for horizontal fragmentation. Since the select predicate requires "LOC = 'LA'," the select operations on MPLS_EMPS and NY_EMPS will not return any tuples. Similarly, the select operation on LA_EMPS does not need to check the LOC value since all tuples at this site will match that condition. Therefore, the optimizer should only run the select operation at the LA site. The query tree then is reduced to what Figure 4.23 shows as a single site query. This rule works well when the select predicate and the horizontal fragmentation condition are compatible.

Perform Operations Where Most of the Data Is Performing union and join operations in distributed systems is more expensive when the join and union operands are at different sites. Example 4.9 explains this.

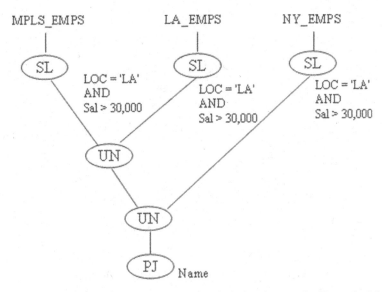

Figure 4.22   The "more optimized" expanded global query for Example 4.8.

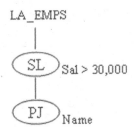

Figure 4.23   The optimized global query tree for Example 4.8.

Example 4.9   In this example, we try to find the name of each employee who works in LA or NY and makes more than $30,000. As part of this same query, we also want to find the the name of the project that has at least one of these employees working on it. Let's assume that the EMP relation is horizontally fragmented as discussed earlier in Example 4.8 and that the PROJ relation is also horizontally fragmented based on the location of the project. In other words, employees working in LA are only assigned to the projects originated in LA, while employees working in NY are only assigned to the projects originated in NY. Figure 4.24 depicts the query tree for this example.

The global optimizer should realize that LA_EMPS and LA_PROJS are colocated in LA while NY_EMPS and NY_PROJS are colocated in NY. Hence, as shown in Figure 4.25, the optimizer should first join the corresponding fragments locally and then union the join results together.

Simplify Join Operations   Assume that we have used a hybrid fragmentation for the EMP relation as discussed in Section 2.2.3 of Chapter 2. In this distribution design, EMP is first vertically fragmented into two fragments. The first fragment is called

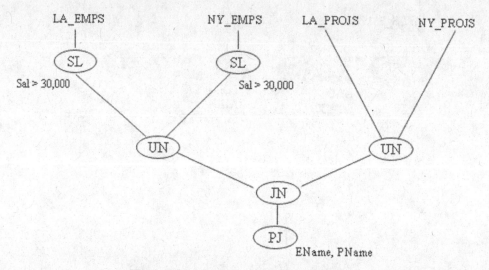

Figure 4.24   The query tree for Example 4.9.

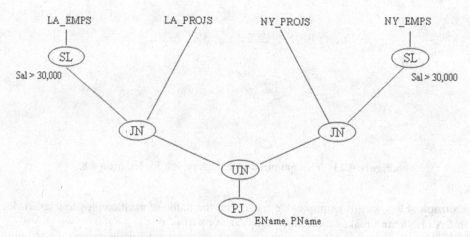

Figure 4.25   Colocalizing global operations for Example 4.9.

"EMP_SAL" and contains the EmpID and Sal attributes. The nonsalary vertical fragment of EMP is further fragmented horizontally into three fragments that we call "LA_EMPS", "NY_EMPS", and "MPLS_EMPS" for this discussion.

Example 4.10   In this example, a user issues a query that prints the salary for those employees who make more than $30,000. The query in relational algebra is written as

$$PJ_{Name,\ Sal}\ (SL_{Sal\ >\ 30,000}\ (EMP))$$

Since the EMP relation uses a hybrid fragmentation, as shown in Figure 4.26, the query needs to be expanded to include the fragments.

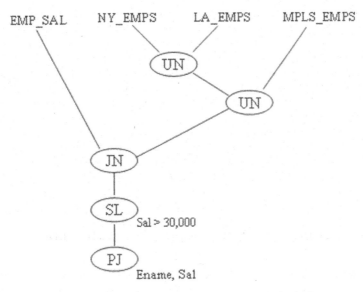

Figure 4.26   The expanded query for Example 4.10.

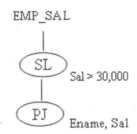

Figure 4.27   Reduced query for Example 4.10.

Because all the predicates and attributes that need to be displayed to the user are within EMP_SAL, the global optimizer can reduce the query as shown in Figure 4.27 to a single site query.

Materialize Common Subexpressions Once   This rule is equivalent to merging the common leaves and subtrees in a distributed query tree. Example 4.11 explains the use of this rule.

Example 4.11   Suppose we need to find the manager name and project names for all employees who work in LA and make more that $30,000. Again, without optimization, Figure 4.28 represents the global query tree that is created for the query.

In this case, the global query optimizer realizes that the left and right subtrees of this query are identical and therefore should be materialized once. Based on this observation, the optimizer creates the optimized query tree depicted in Figure 4.29.

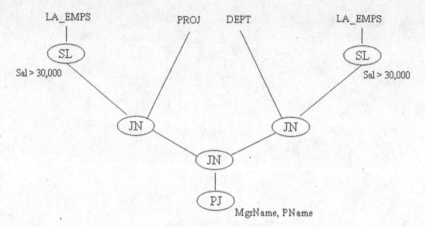

Figure 4.28 Unoptimized query tree for Example 4.11.

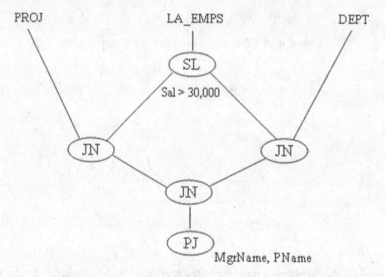

Figure 4.29 Optimized query tree for Example 4.11.

Use Semi-join to Reduce Communication Cost The semi-join operation is a supportive operation in relational algebra. It is a different, multistep approach for joining two relations. Semi-join attempts to qualify the tuples before the relations are actually joined. In distributed systems, we can use semi-join to qualify the tuples in both relations that match the join conditions before we send the tuples across the network. As a result, we do not send any tuples that are not part of the final join results, which reduces our communication costs. Suppose we were joining two relations with 1000 tuples each. If joining these two relations would ultimately result in only 50 rows, it would be very beneficial to avoid sending the 950 (or more) rows in each relation that are not part of the final answer across the network.

Semi-join was first used in SDD−1 [Bernstein81] and then extended and applied by Apers, Hevner, and Yao [Apers83] to reduce the overall communication cost and/or total query cost of simple distributed queries. The proposal of using semi-join for distributed joins was attractive because original experimental distributed systems had a slow communication network. As a result, the cost of running distributed queries in older distributed systems was greatly impacted by the amount of information that was sent across the network. To explain how the semi-join approach works, we use an example.

Example 4.12   Let's consider a distributed system with three sites, where relation "R" is at Site 1, relation "S" is at Site 2, and the user is at Site 3. The user issues a query to join R and S over attribute "a" of R and attribute "b" of S as "R $JN_{a=b}$ S." As discussed earlier in this chapter, this join can be performed at Site 1 or Site 2 with different cost ramifications. Either way, one of the relations needs to be shipped across the network to the other site, where it will then be joined with the other relation. The rule of thumb is to send the smaller relation to where the larger relation is to reduce the communication cost. Even for small relations, the cost of sending the entire relation across the network can be large since every tuple might require more than one message (for wide relations).

Suppose that R has 500 tuples, S has 200 tuples, and that the number of tuples in these relations where "a = b" is 50. As a rough estimate, suppose that each tuple is sent as a single message. Hence, an optimal strategy to performing the join will require 250 messages (200 messages to send S from Site 2 to Site 1 to perform the join and 50 messages to send the results from Site 1 to Site 3 to display to the user).

Semi-join attempts to minimize the communication cost by first finding the tuples that qualify the join condition and then performing the actual join. To apply semi-join to join these two relations, we proceed as follows:

```
Step 1: Do PJa(R) at Site 1 producing temporary relation R1(a)
Step 2: Send R1 from Site 1 to Site 2
Step 3: Do R1 JNa = b S at Site 2 producing temporary relation S1
Step 4: Send S1 from Site 2 to Site 1
Step 5: Join S1 with R producing the final results in R JNa = b S
Step 6: Send results to Site 3 where the user is
```

Figure 4.30 depicts the steps used in the semijoin for our example.

In Step 1, we cut out attribute "a" of R and create a one-column relation "R1(a)." The reason for doing this is that attribute "a" is all we need to qualify the tuples in S. Step 2 is where the main difference between a join and semi-join occurs. In this step, we send only attribute "a" of R to where S is instead of sending the entire relation R. Sending a relation with only one attribute is a lot cheaper than sending a wide relation across the network—perhaps we can even send many tuples in a single message. Once we join R1 and S at Site 2 into S1, we have identified all of the tuples that qualify the join condition. But, what is missing from the results are the other attributes of R. For example, if R is defined as "R(a, c, d, f)," then S1 is lacking "c," "d," and "f" attributes of R. To add these attributes to the rows in S1, we have to send S1 back to where R is (Step 4) and then join S1 with R (Step 5). Note that in Step 4 we do not send any tuple that is not part of the final answer and therefore we are not wasting any messages.

The semi-join approach to joining R and S requires fewer messages. Before presenting the actual number of messages, let's make an assumption about sending a column of a relation. We assumed that each tuple of each relation takes one message

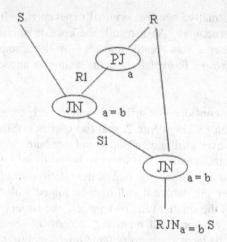

Figure 4.30   Use of semi-join to join relations R and S in Example 4.12.

to send. Suppose that each column of a relation, regardless of the number of tuples in the relation, takes one message to send as well. Based on this assumption, Step 2 would require 1 message; Step 4 would require 50 messages; and Step 6 would require 50 messages. The overall cost of this strategy is 101 messages.

The semi-join approach produces the final results at the site where we start the semi-join process. In Example 4.12, we started with R relation at Site 1 and the results were produced at the same site. We could have started with the S relation and have accumulated the results at Site 2. For this example, the cost would have been the same for both approaches since the final results had to be sent to Site 3. But for a setup where the user is at Site 2 and runs the same query, it will be much cheaper to start with S at Site 2 since the final results will be gathered where the user resides.

Note that in Example 4.12, we could have reduced the communication cost by not sending the attributes that were not necessary for the final results in S1. Example 4.13 includes more optimization for the semi-join approach.

Example 4.13   A more complete form of the query that was used in Example 4.12 is used in this example. Let "R(a, c, d, f)" and "S(b, m, n)" be the two relations we would like to join. We will consider the following query issued by a user at Site 3.

```
Select a, c, m
From R, S
Where R.a = S.b;
```

An optimized semi-join strategy considers what needs to finally be displayed to the user and only includes the attributes that are either required for the join or part of the final answer. We have outlined the semi-join steps for this example below:

```
Step 1: Do PJₐ (R) at Site 1 producing temporary relation R1(a)
Step 2: Send R1 from Site 1 to Site 2
Step 3: Perform R1 JNₐ₌ᵦ S at Site 2 resulting in S2(b, m, n)
```

```
Step 4: Apply PJb, m (S2) at Site 2 producing S1(b, m)
Step 5: Send S1 from Site 2 to Site 1
Step 6: Do S1 JN R resulting in relation R2(a, c, d, f, b, m)
Step 7: Apply PJa, c, m (R2) producing the final results in R3
Step 8: Send R3 to Site 3 where the user is
```

It should be obvious that since this strategy reduces the number of attributes being sent (as part of the temporary relation "S1" in Step 5 and the final results in Step 8), the overall communication cost is reduced. Applying the semi-join algorithm to a join involving more than two relations requires repeated application of the steps outlined above. For example, suppose we are joining three relations: "R" (at Site 1), "S" (at Site 2), and "T" (at Site 3) over a common attribute "a." This requires identifying which pairs of relations are joined first. The temporary relation produced is then joined with the third relation. As discussed earlier in this chapter, there are many alternatives for doing this. One such join ordering is "T $JN_{a=a}$ (R $JN_{a=a}$ S)." To apply the semi-join approach to this query requires the following steps:

```
Step 1: Apply PJa (R) at Site 1 producing temporary relation R1
Step 2: Send R1 from Site 1 to Site 2 where S is
Step 3: Join R1 and S at Site 2 producing temporary S1
Step 4: Send S1 from Site 2 to Site 1 where R is
Step 5: Join S1 with R producing the temporary R2 at Site 1
Step 6: Apply PJa (T) at Site 3 producing temporary relation T1
Step 7: Send T1 to Site 1 where R2 is
Step 8: Join R2 and T1 at Site 1 producing temporary relation R3
Step 9: Send R3 to Site 3 where T is
Step 10: Join R3 and T producing the final results
```

Apers, Hevner, and Yao discuss several algorithms that use semi-join to optimize simple distributed queries [Hevner79] [Sacco82] [Apers83]. These algorithms focus on optimizing the overall communication cost or the total query cost for distributed queries. Interested readers are referred to these references for further readings.

Use Bit Vectors to Reduce Communication Cost   Approaches using **bit vector filters** instead of join attributes for semi-joins across multiple sites have also been proposed (see [Babb79] and [Valduriez84]). A similar approach (known as **Bloom vectors**) was also proposed by Bloom [Bloom70]. In a 2-relation join, Bloom's approach uses a bit vector filter that approximates the join attribute of the first relation. This is sent across the network from the first site to the second site, where it is used to qualify the tuples in the second relation involved in the join. Once the tuples from the second relation are qualified, these tuples are sent back to the first site, where they are joined with the first relation. Bit vectors are created using a hash function to approximate the values of the join attributes in a multirelation query. Bit vectors have been used extensively in parallel databases. Specifically, Dewitt and his colleagues have demonstrated bit vectors in the Gamma parallel database machine with distributed memory [Dewitt86] [Dewitt88] [Dewitt90a]. We will use an example to explain their approach.

Example 4.14   In this example, we will try to join two relations "R(a, c, d, f)" and "S(b, m, n)" as explained in Example 4.13. Let's assume that attribute "a" is the primary key of R, attribute "b" is a foreign key in S pointing to "a", R has 500 tuples, and S has 200 tuples. Being a primary key, there are 500 unique values for the attribute "a" in R. To start, we use a bit vector with 500 bits, each set to zero. We then run each unique value of the attribute "a" through a hash function, for example, "$f(a) =$ **a MOD 500**," that maps the value of "a" to a number in the range of $\{0, 1, \ldots, 499\}$. The corresponding bit for the hashed value is set to 1. For instance, running the key value 1002 through the hash function turns on bit 2 in the bit vector. Once all values of "a" have been hashed, we use this vector to qualify the tuples in S. To do so, we run each value of the attribute "b" of S through the same hash function and generate a hash value. We then check to see if the bit corresponding to this new hash value is set in the bit vector. If it is, then the tuple in S qualifies the join condition.

Whenever two or more different values map to the same hash value (or address), we call it a collision. In our example, our hash function maps both "a = 2" and "a = 502" to value 2. As a matter of fact, all key values 2, 502, 1002, and so on collide to value 2. It is not necessary to keep track of which values of the join attribute collide in this approach. That is because it is not necessary to know what the actual values of "a" or "b" are; we simply need to know each value for "a" that hashes to the same location as some value of "b" did. For our example, values 2, 502, 1002, and so on for the attribute "b" also map to 2 and therefore all of these tuples from relation S are qualified. It is clear that bit vectors can be used to qualify the tuples of two relations in a join before the join is actually performed in a distributed system. Like the semi-join, a bit vector filter eliminates the need to send any tuple that is not part of the join across the network. This results in lower communication costs for distributed queries.

Although Example 4.14 pointed out the usefulness of using a bit vector filter for joining only two relations, the idea can easily be extended to cover multirelation joins. Mullin proposed the idea of sending bit vector filters back and forth between the sites where the relations involved in a multi-join query reside to discard the tuples that are not part of the final answer [Mullin90]. This reduction process is continued as long as the number of useful tuples for the join can be reduced.

A Multiphase Approach   We have reviewed many alternatives for query optimization in centralized and distributed database systems. In what follows, we use an example to bring together some of the ideas that we have discussed so far in this chapter as a set of simplified rules in a multiphase approach that could generate a near optimal distributed query plan at a very low communication cost.

The approach works as follows:

- In the first phase, we ignore distribution and decide on a query plan that is best suited to execute the query.
- In the second phase, we decide on the sites that we will use to access the required data. The rule we use for site selection is simple. When there is no replicated data, the site where the required fragment resides is chosen. When there is replication, we have the choice of selecting any site among all the sites where the copies of a replicated fragment reside. In this case, we choose the replication site that has the largest amount of data required by the query.

- In phase three of the algorithm, we run the operations at the sites where the data is stored. In other words, we utilize function shipping rather than data shipping. This phase is carried out as a set of local queries that the chosen sites will optimize locally and run locally.
- In the last phase of the algorithm, we decide on the sites where we perform the reconstruction operations, that is, the joining of vertical fragments and the unioning of the horizontal fragments. Our decision in this phase is again based on a simple rule. We choose to run the operations at the site(s) where the most data is located. Since some of the operations may require data that is stored across two sites (such as join and union), we have no choice but to move the data between sites—this requires data shipping. Deciding which data to ship is also governed by a simple rule. We send the smaller operand of any binary relational algebra operator to where the larger operand is stored.

The following example explains the steps in this approach for a simple distributed database system.

Example 4.15   In this example, we will use the same relations that we used for query optimization in a centralized system in Example 4.1. Furthermore, we will assume that we have a two-site distributed database system where the Customer relation is replicated at Site 1 and Site 2; the Account relation is stored at Site 1; and the Branch relation is stored at Site 2. We have shown the query here again for ease of reference.

```
Select  c.Cname
From    Customer c, Branch b, Account a
Where   c.CID   = a.CID
AND     a.Bname = b.Bname
AND     b.Bcity = 'Edina';
```

This query prints the name of all customers who have an account at any one of the branches located in city Edina. To optimize the query in our distributed system, we proceed as follows.

Phase 1: Tree Selection. Disregarding distribution, as discussed for Example 4.1, there are five alternatives that are candidates for running this query. In Figure 4.31, we have shown these alternatives again for ease of reference. From these alternatives, we need to eliminate the ones that do not apply the select before the join. Applying this rule leaves us with alternatives 2 and 5 as the only two viable options. Next, we use cost estimation to determine which one of the two alternatives performs better. We select alternative 5 as the candidate tree since it has a smaller processing cost.

Up to this point in the discussion, we have not considered distribution. In order to run this query optimally in our two-site distributed system, we need to decide where each operation is performed. We also need to decide which sites are used to access the relations and how the intermediate results will be merged to form the final results.

Phase 2: Data Localization. In this phase, we need to decide which sites we will use to access the relations we need. The rule that we apply here says, "Select the sites where the most data is." In our example, Site 1 has a copy of the Customer relation and the Account relation, while Site 2 has a copy of the Customer relation and the Branch relation. We know that there are 500 customers in the database and each customer

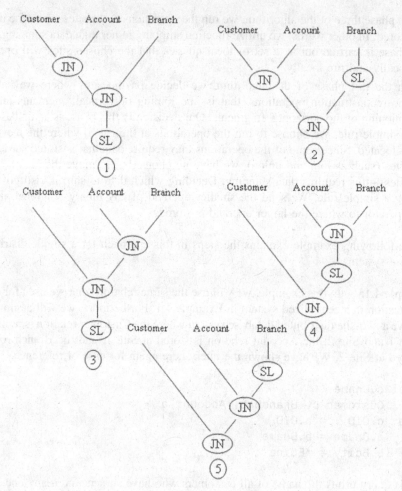

Figure 4.31 Five alternative query trees for Example 4.15.

has two accounts. This means that the largest relation in the database is the Account relation, with 1000 tuples. We also know that the Branch relation has 100 tuples. Based on these statistics, Site 1 stores much more information than Site 2 does. Applying the rule above, we choose to access the Customer and the Account relations at Site 1 and to access the Branch relation at Site 2. Once we have decided where each relation is going to be accessed, we use the site ID as the subscript of the relation as shown in Figure 4.32.

Phase 3: Function Shipping. In this step, we will decide where each operation of the query tree will run. Since there is only one completely local operation in the query tree (the select on the Branch relation), we must perform the SL at Site 2 (where the Branch relation is stored). The results of the select are stored at Site 2 as well.

Phase 4: Data Shipping for Binary Operations. Since there are three operations in the query and each operation can run at either of the two sites, we will have eight different alternatives to perform the operations of this query as indicated in Figure 4.33. In each tree, each operation has a subscript indicating the Site ID where the operation

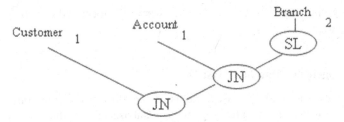

Figure 4.32 The query tree chosen for Example 4.15.

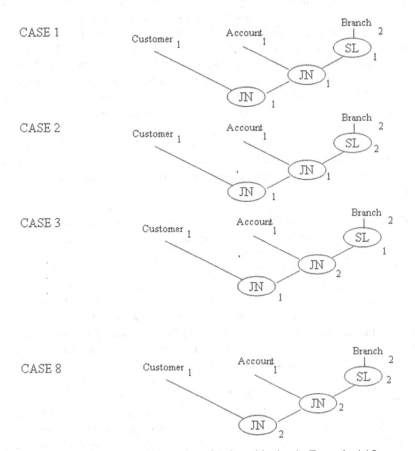

Figure 4.33 All possible options for data shipping in Example 4.15.

must run. For example, the first option indicates that the SL runs at Site 1; the first JN runs at Site 1; and the second JN runs at Site 1. The rule that we follow for data shipping is this: "Always send the smaller relation to the site where the larger relation is located." The application of this rule eliminates seven of the alternatives, making Case 2 the optimal tree for this query.

Stonebreaker has utilized an extended variation of this approach in the Mariposa system [Stonebreaker96]. Stonebreaker uses ideas from microeconomics and iterative dynamic programming to decide on the sites where the local and distributed operations of the query must run.

4.5.3 Heterogeneous Database Systems

Heterogeneous distributed database systems behave differently from homogeneous distributed database systems. In a heterogeneous database system, the underlying database systems are different, maintain their autonomy, and may hide the details of how they process queries from the outside world. These systems are also called federated database systems or multidatabase systems in the literature [Sheth90]. The individual DBEs that make up a heterogeneous database system can support different database models, for example, relational, hierarchical, network, object-oriented, or text databases such as BigBook (www.bigbook.com). DBEs in a heterogeneous database system may also utilize different query processing and optimization approaches. They can be closed or open to the outside world. If open, they provide an application programming interface (API). These differences make processing a distributed query in heterogeneous database systems a lot more difficult than processing queries in a homogeneous distributed database system. Kossmann in [Kossmann00b] provides an excellent survey and an overview of issues involved in query processing and optimization in heterogeneous database systems. In this section, we summarize some of the challenges that must be overcome in query processing and optimization in heterogeneous database systems.

4.5.3.1 Heterogeneous Database Systems Architecture
The underlying DBEs of a heterogeneous system are different in nature and may provide different interfaces to the outside world. One of the first challenges in integrating heterogeneous DBEs is to hide the difference in the interfaces these systems expose. Wrappers have been used ubiquitously in the industry as the approach for doing this [Roth97] [Nelson03]. A wrapper is a software module that uses the open (or the proprietary) interface of an underlying DBE and provides a uniform interface to the outside world based on the capabilities that the DBE provides. Since the de facto standard for query processing in any heterogeneous database system is SQL, a wrapper exposes a relational model and SQL as the interface for the system is wraps.

Depending on the capabilities of the underlying component DBEs, wrappers provide different sets of functionalities. For instance, a relational DBMS wrapper can support all of the capabilities that a relational DBMS provides. An Excel wrapper can provide the ability to enumerate the rows in an Excel worksheet as tuples in a relation. This ability can be utilized to perform a select on the contents of a worksheet very much like performing a select operation on a relation. As a result, we can use an Excel wrapper to join the rows in an Excel worksheet with the rows of a table exposed by a relational DBMS wrapper. Because of limitations of the BigBook database, a wrapper for the BigBook database can only provide capability of selecting limited information such as business category and the city where the business is located. The BigBook wrapper is not able to provide the capability to enumerate rows and, therefore, cannot support joins. Several systems using the wrapper approach to integrating heterogeneous database systems have been researched and developed over the past few years. IBM WebSphere Federation Server 9.5, Disco [Tomasic97], Garlic project at IBM [Carey95], and TSIMMIS [Papakonstantinou95] are examples of

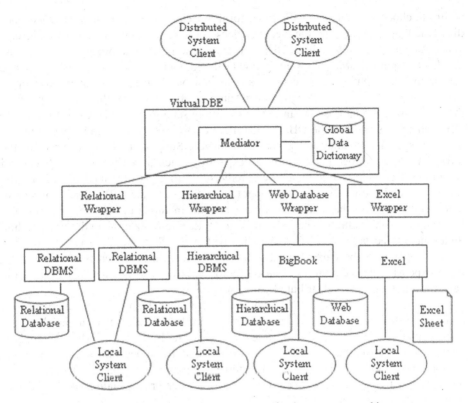

Figure 4.34 Wrapper-based heterogeneous database system architecture.

such systems. Figure 4.34 illustrates a wrapper based architecture for a heterogeneous database system.

As illustrated in Figure 4.34, each data source in the system is wrapped by a specific wrapper. Depending on the underlying DBE, a wrapper may be able to provide either tuple level or block level (a set of tuples that are grouped together) access to the information that the database controls. The wrapper may also be able to cache information outside the database for faster access. According to Wiederhold, wrappers are not directly used by the client of the heterogeneous database system, but interact with a layer of software called the mediator [Wiederhold93]. The mediator does not have the capability to interface directly to the underlying DBE. The mediator can access the global data dictionary (see Chapter 12 for details) to find out the schema of the local DBEs and the functionality they provide. The mediator processes the queries that are posted by the global users; determines the location details for each piece of required data for the queries being processed by looking up the details in the GDD; exploits the functionalities that each local DBE provides through its wrapper; and optimizes the queries at the global level.

4.5.3.2 Optimization in Heterogeneous Databases   Query optimization in a heterogeneous DDBE is a much more difficult task than query optimization in a homogeneous DDBE. The reason is that in a homogeneous distributed database system all the DBEs provide the same and uniform capabilities. This provides the global optimizer with the ability to choose any of the DBEs to perform, for example, a join. In a heterogeneous distributed database system, the mediator does not have the same freedom. In a heterogeneous database system, a local DBE may be able to perform a join and the other may not. Lack of join capability by some of the DBEs (or their wrappers) creates a challenge for the mediator that does not exist in a homogeneous distributed database system.

For example, in a homogeneous distributed database system, the global optimizer that needs to join relations "R" and "S" can simply send R from where it resides to the DBE where S is and ask the DBE server there to process the join. In a heterogeneous database system, this may not be easily achieved. Suppose that the wrapper for the DBE that stores S does not have a join capability (such as a BigBook database) and can only select tuples based on a given predicate. In this case, the mediator has to first retrieve all tuples for R from the wrapper that interfaces to the DBE where R is stored. Once all the tuples of the R relation are received, the mediator iterates through all tuples in R and uses the value of the join attribute of R, one-by-one, to find corresponding tuples in S. The lack of a join capability within the S wrapper, in effect, forces a nested-loop join to be carried out by the mediator. This approach is probably a lot more expensive than having the join be performed by the component DBE, as is the case for a homogeneous distributed database system.

Another set of differences that may exist between the DBEs in a heterogeneous database system are called semantic heterogeneity [Sheth90]. For example, Wrapper 1 may interface to a DBE that uses letter grades {A, B, C, D, F} while Wrapper 2 interfaces to a DBE that uses scores between 1 and 10. When integrating the results from these two local DBEs or when transferring the grade from one DBE to the other, the mediator has to convert scores of 1 to 10 to letter grades and/or letter grades to scores in the range of 1 to 10.

Once the capability differences between the local DBEs have been dealt with, the approach to global optimization for both homogeneous and heterogeneous database systems is very similar. Once the capabilities of the underlying DBEs are encapsulated by the wrapper and are presented to the mediator as a set of enumeration rules, dynamic programming or iterative dynamic programming (see Sections 4.4.2.3 and 4.4.2.4 of this chapter) can be used by the mediator to optimize global queries in heterogeneous database systems [Haas97]. In Chapter 12, we provide more details about integration challenges in heterogeneous database systems.

4.6 SUMMARY

In this chapter, we outlined the available techniques for query optimization in both centralized and distributed DBEs. We discussed the fact that query optimization is a complex component of query processing. We provided an overview of relational algebra as an internal language representation used by all commercial DBMSs to process user commands. Access path strategies for different relational algebra operations were also discussed. We pointed out that even for queries of moderate complexity the solution space was large. Approaches to reducing the solution space and dealing with the complexity of the query optimization were outlined. Rules and heuristics for query optimization were investigated. We reviewed dynamic programming, iterative dynamic programming, and greedy methods as three alternatives widely used in query optimization.

Ideas and techniques used in centralized query optimization were then expanded to include distribution. We analyzed approaches that were used for query optimization in homogeneous as well as heterogeneous DDBEs. Most notably, we studied semi-join and dynamic programming for distributed database environments.

4.7 GLOSSARY

Access Path   The method by which a table is accessed as part of an overall query processing.

Bit Vector Filter   A bit-oriented encryption of the join columns to reduce the communication cost between the sites involved in a distributed query.

Bloom Vector   A bit-oriented encryption of the join columns proposed by Bloom to reduce the communication cost between the sites involved in a distributed query.

Catalog   A set of system-defined tables that maintain information about structures defined within one or more databases. "Catalog" is another term for "data dictionary."

Centralized Database Environment (CDBE)   A database environment in which one computer (server) carries out the users' commands.

Clustered Index   An index in which the table rows that are addressed by sorted key values are clustered (adjacent) to each other.

Conditional Join   A join that requires a condition that two or more columns of the two tables being joined will have to satisfy.

Cost-Based Optimization (CBO)   An optimization approach in which the cost method is used to find the query plan with the smallest cost out of the possible query plans for the query.

Data Dictionary   A collection of system tables that hold information about the structures of a database. Data dictionary is also known as the meta-data for the databases in a DBMS.

Data Shipping   An execution strategy in which data is shipped to another computer to be used in the operation.

Disk I/O   The process of reading or writing from/to the hard disk.

Distributed Database Environment (DDBE)   A collection of one or more DBs along with any software providing at least the minimum set of required data operations and management facilities capable of supporting distributed data.

Dynamic Programming   A phased approach to query optimization which eliminates suboptimal plans until the optimal plan is arrived at.

Equi-join   A conditional join that forces equality across two columns of the two tables being joined.

Global Query   A query whose target tables are distributed across multiple computers or database environments.

Greedy Algorithm   An optimization approach that limits the amount of disk storage and memory used by dynamic programming by only forming 2-relation plans at each step of the process.

Hash-Join   A specific join strategy that uses a hash function to partition the rows of the two tables being joined and then only joins rows in corresponding partitions.

Heterogeneous DDBE   An environment in which the DBEs are from different vendors and/or support different data models.

Heuristics-Based Optimization   An optimization approach that uses heuristics to eliminate alternatives that do not provide or lead to an optimal query plan.

Homogeneous DDBE   An environment in which all DBEs are from the same vendor and/or support the same data model.

Hybrid Shipping   A mix of data and operation shipping.

Iterative Dynamic Programming   An iterative approach to dynamic programming that limits the memory and storage requirements.

Local Query   A query whose target tables are on the same computer or database environment.

Materialization   The act of forming and storing the temporary results of a relational operator.

Memory Frame   A container for storing a page in memory.

Memory Page   A unit of storage allocation in memory.

Modulus (MOD) Function   An operation that returns the remainder of dividing two numbers.

Nonclustered Index   An index in which the table rows are not forced to be adjacent to each other for consecutive key values of the index.

Nonprocedural Language   A language in which the user specifies what is needed and the system determines the process of arriving at the answer.

Nonunique Index   A nonunique index allows key duplication in the index.

Normal Conjunctive Form   A complex predicate in which the component predicates are tied together by the logical operator "AND."

Normal Disjunctive Form   A complex predicate in which the component predicates are tied together by the logical operator "OR."

On-the-Fly   The process of feeding the results of one relational operator into another without having to store the results on the disk.

Operation Shipping   An execution strategy in which the operation is carried out where the data is.

Partitioning   The act of dividing the rows in a table based on a given condition applied to a column of the table.

Probing   The act of finding a qualified row based on the value of a column typically using an index.

Procedural Languages   A language in which the user specifies the process of arriving at the answer.

Quel   A higher level language based on relational calculus.

Query Optimization   The process of finding an optimal query execution plan for a given query.

Query Plan   A plan that specifies a detailed step-by-step execution strategy for a given query.

Query Processing   The process of executing a user's query.

Query Trading   A specific query optimization approach that uses negotiation to arrive at an optimal query execution strategy.

Query Tree   A binary tree that indicates the steps required to arrive at the answer for the query.

RA Expression   A query in a relational algebra representation of a SQL query.

RA Subexpression   A subquery in a relational algebra that corresponds to a SQL query.

Relational Algebra   A procedural language in which the programmer specifies the steps required to get the answer.

Relational Calculus   A nonprocedural language in which the programmer specifies what is needed and the system determines how to get the answer.

Rowid   An internal representation of a row inside a relational database.

Rule-Based Optimization (RBO)   An optimization approach that uses a small set of rules to arrive at a near optimal query execution plan.

Semi-join   An approach for joining two tables that minimizes the amount of data transfer between DBEs in a distributed environment.

Solution Space   The set of all possible solutions to a problem, for example, all the implementation alternatives to carry out a given query.

Sort–Merge   A join strategy that is carried out in two phases—the sort phase and the merge phase.

Structured Query Language (SQL)   The de facto standard procedural language for all relational database management systems.

Unique Index   An index that allows only unique key values.

Wrapper   A software component that wraps a data source and provides a uniform interface to the outside world by hiding the specifics of its representation and command interface.

REFERENCES

[Apers83]   Apers, P., Hevner, A., and Yao, S., "Optimization Algorithms for Distributed Queries," *IEEE Transactions on Software Engineering*, Vol. 9, No. 1, pp. 57–68, 1983.

[Babb79]   Babb, E., "Implementing a Relational Database by Means of Specialized Hardware," *ACM Transactions on Database Systems*, Vol. 4, No. 1, pp. 1–29, March 1979.

[Bernstein81]   Bernstein, P., Goodman, N., Wong, E., Reeve, C., and Rothnie, J., "Query Processing in a System for Distributed Databases (SDD-1)," *ACM Transactions on Database Systems*, Vol. 6, No. 4, pp. 602–625, December 1981.

[Bloom70]   Bloom, B., "Space/Time Tradeoffs in Hash Coding with Allowable Errors," *Communications of ACM*, Vol. 13, No. 7, July 1970.

[Carey95]   Carey, M., Haas, L., Schwarz, P., Arya, M., Cody, W., Fagin, R., Flickner, M., Luniewski, A., Niblack, W., Petkovic, D., Thomas, J., Williams, J., and Wimmers, E., "Towards Heterogeneous Multimedia Information Systems: The Garlic Approach," in *Proceedings of the 1995 IEEE Workshop on Research Issues in Data Engineering (RIDE-95)*, Taipei, Taiwan, March 1995.

[Ceri84]   Ceri, S., and Pelagatti, G., *Distributed Databases Principles and Systems*, McGraw-Hill, New York, 1984.

[Codd70]   Codd, E., "A Relational Model for Large Data Banks," *Communications of the ACM*, Vol. 13, No. 6, pp. 377–387, 1970.

[Dewitt86] DeWitt, D., Gerber, R., Graefe, G., Heytens, M., Kumar, K., and Muralikrishna, M., "Gamma—A High Performance Dataflow Database Machine," in *Proceedings of the International Conference on Very Large Data Bases*, VLDB Endowment, 1986. Reprinted, *Readings in Database Systems*, Morgan Kaufmann, San Francisco, CA, 1988.

[Dewitt88] DeWitt, D., Ghandeharizadeh, S., and Schneider, D., "A Performance Analysis of the GAMMA Database Machine," in *Proceedings of ACM SIGMOD Conference*, ACM, New York, 1988.

[Dewitt90a] DeWitt, D., Ghandeharizadeh, S., Schneider, D., Bricker, A., Hsaio, H., and Rasmussen, R., "The Gamma Database Machine Project," *IEEE Transactions on Knowledge Data Engineering*, Vol. 2, No. 1, pp. 44–62, March 1990.

[DeWitt90b] DeWitt, D., Futtersack, P., Maier, D., and V'elez, F., "A Study of Three Alternative Workstation Server Architectures for Object-Oriented Database Systems," in *Proceedings of the 16th Conference on Very Large Data Bases*, pp. 107–121, Brisbane, Australia, 1990.

[Franklin93] Franklin, M., Carey, M., Livny, M., "Local Disk Caching for Client-Server Database Systems," in *Proceedings of the 19th International Conference on Very Large Data Bases (VLDB)*, pp. 641–655, Dublin, Ireland, August 1993.

[Graefe87] Graefe, G., and Dewitt, D., "The EXODUS Optimizer Generator," in *Proceedings of the ACM SIGMOD Conference on Management of Data*, pp. 160–172, San Francisco, CA, May 1987.

[Graefe93] Graefe, G., "Query Evaluation Techniques for Large Databases," *ACM Computing Surveys*, Vol. 25, No. 2, pp. 73–170, June 1993.

[Haas97] Haas, L., Kossmann, D., Wimmers, E., and Yang, J., "Optimizing Queries Across Diverse Data Sources," in *Proceedings of the Conference on Very Large Data Bases (VLDB)*, pp. 276–285, Athens, Greece, August 1997.

[Hevner79] Hevner, A., and Yao, S., "Query Processing in Distributed Database Systems," *IEEE Transactions on Software Engineering*, Vol. 5, No. 3, pp. 177–182, March 1979.

[Ioannidis96] Ioannidis, Y., "Query Optimization," *ACM Computing Surveys*, Vol. 28, No. 1, pp. 121–123, March 1996.

[Jarke84] Jarke,M., and Koch,J., "Query Optimization in Database Systems," *ACM Computing Surveys*, Vol. 16, No. 2, pp. 111–152, June 1984.

[Kossmann00a] Kossmann, D., and Stocker, K., "Iterative Dynamic Programming: A New Class of Query Optimization Algorithms," *ACM Transactions on Database Systems*, Vol. 25, No. 1, March 2000.

[Kossmann00b] Kossmann, D., "The State of Art in Distributed Query Processing," *ACM Computing Surveys*, Vol. 32, No. 4, pp. 422–469, December 2000.

[Larson85] Larson, J., and Rahimi, S., *Tutorial: Distributed Database Management*, IEEE Computer Society Press, New York, 1985, pp. 91–94.

[Lomet96] Lomet, D., "Replicated Indexes for Distributed Data," in *Proceedings of the International IEEE Conference on Parallel and Distributed Information Systems*, Miami Beach, FL, December 1990.

[Mullin90] Mullin, J., "Optimal Semi joins for Distributed Database Systems," *IEEE Transactions on Software Engineering*, Vol. 16, No. 5, May 1990.

[Nelson03] Nelson, M., "Integrating Information for On Demand Computing," in *Proceedings of the 29th VLDB Conference*, Berlin, Germany, 2003.

[Ono90] Ono, K., and Lohman, G., "Measuring the Complexity of Join Enumeration in Query Optimization," in *Proceedings of the 16th International Conference on Very Large Data Bases, VLDB*, pp. 314—325, Brisbane, Australia, August 1990.

[Papakonstantinou95] Papakonstantinou, Y., Gupta, A., Garcia-Molina, H., and Ullman, J., "A Query Translation Scheme for Rapid Implementation of Wrappers," in *Proceedings of the Conference on Deductive and Object-Oriented Databases* (*DOOD*), pp. 161–186, December 1995.

[Pellenkoft97] Pellenkoft, A., Galindo-Legaria, C., and Kersten, M., "The Complexity of Transformation-Based Join Enumeration," in *Proceedings of the 23rd International Conference on Very Large Data Bases, VLDB*, pp. 306–315, Athens, Greece, August 1997.

[Pentaris06] Pentaris, F., and Ioannidis, Y., "Query Optimization in Distributed Networks of Autonomous Database Systems," *ACM Transactions on Database Systems*, Vol. 31, No. 2, pp. 537–583, June 2006.

[Pirahesh92] Pirahesh, H., and Hasan, W., "Extensible/Rule Based Query Rewrite Optimization in Starburst," in *Proceedings of the ACM SIGMOD Conference on Management of Data*, pp. 39–48, San Diego, CA, June 1992.

[Ramakrishnan03] Ramahrishnan, R., and Gehrke, J., *Database Management Systems*, 3rd edition, McGraw-Hill, New York, 2003.

[Roth97] Roth, M., and Schwarz, P., "Don't Scrap It, Wrap It! A Wrapper Architecture for Legacy Data Sources," in *Proceedings of the 23rd Conference on Very Large Data Bases*, Athens, Greece, August 26–29, 1997.

[Sacco82] Sacco, M., and Yao, S., "Query Optimization in Distributed Database Systems," in *Advances in Computers*, Vol. 21, Academic Press, New York, 1982, pp. 225–273.

[Selinger79] Selinger, P., Astrahan, M., Chamberlin, D., Lorie, R., and Price, T., "Access Path Selection in a Relational Database Management System," in *Proceedings of ACM SIGMOD Conference on the Management of Data*, pp. 23–34, Boston, MA, June 1979.

[Shekita93] Shekita, E., Young, II., and Tan, K., "Multi-join Optimization for Symmetric Multiprocessors," in *Proceedings of the 19th International Conference on Very Large Data Bases, VLDB*, Dublin, Ireland, Morgan Kaufmann Publishers, San Francisco, CA, August 1993, pp. 479–492.

[Sheth90] Sheth, A., and Larson, J., "Federated Database Systems for Managing Distributed, Heterogeneous and Autonomous Databases," *Computing Surveys*, Vol. 22, No. 3, pp. 183–236, September 1990.

[Steinbrunn97] Steinbrunn, M., et al., "Heuristics and Randomized Optimization for the Join Ordering Problem," *The Very Large Databases Journal*, Vol. 6, No. 3, pp. 191–208, August 1997.

[Stonebreaker96] Stonebraker, M., Aoki, P., Litwin, W., Pfeffer, A., Sah, A., Sidell, J., Staelin, C., and Yu, A., "Mariposa: A Wide-Area Distributed Database System," *VLDB Journal*, Vol. 5, No. 1, pp. 48–63, 1996.

[SQL92] Database Language SQL (SQL-92), BNF Grammar for ISO/IEC 9075: 1992.

[Tomasic97] Tomasic, A., Amouroux, R., Bonnet, P., Kapitskaia, O., Naacke, H., and Raschid, L., "The Distributed Information Search Component (Disco) and the World Wide Web," *ACM SIGMOD Records*, Vol. 26, No. 2, pp. 546–548, June 1997.

[Valduriez84] Valduriez, P., and Gardarin, G., "Join and Semi-join Algorithms for a Multiprocessor Database Machine," *ACM Transactions on Database Systems*, Vol. 9, No. 1, pp. 133–161, March 1984.

[Venn1880] Venn, J., "On the Diagrammatic and Mechanical Representation of Repositions and Reasoning," *Dublin Philosophical Magazine and Journal of Science*, Vol. 9, No. 59, pp. 1–18, 1880.

[Wiederhold93] Wiederhold, G., "Intelligent Integration of Information," in *Proceedings of the ACM SIGMOD Conference on Management of Data*, pp. 434–437, Washington DC, May 1993.

EXERCISES

Provide short (but complete) answers to the following questions.

4.1   How many alternatives exist for joining three tables together? How many alternatives exist for joining four tables and five tables together? Can you extrapolate from these numbers to arrive at the number of alternatives that can be used to join N tables together?

4.2   A four-site system has tables R, S, T, and M stored as depicted in Figure 4.35. The user is at Site 1. Assume each row of any table that has more than one column can be sent in one message. You can also assume that a one-column table can be sent in one message. Also assume that the cost of sending each message is C units of time. There are no costs associated with sending commands. What is the cost of "(S JN R) JN (T JN M)" if "S JN R" and "T JN M" are done using semi-join and the final join is done normally? Make sure you show all steps and cost of communication for each step.

4.3   Assume the four-site system shown in Figure 4.36—the table distribution and the query tree that prints all information about the employees who work for the engineering department and have an account in a branch in the city of Edina. Also assume the user is at Site 2. Let's assume that 40% of accounts are in branches in Edina; 50% of employees work for the engineering department; and 10% of employees who work for the engineering department have an account in a branch in Edina. If each row being sent from each site to any other site takes C units of time, what is the communication cost of the optimized query tree (results must be displayed to the user) in terms of C? Make sure you show individual step's cost and the total cost. Assume there is no cost associated with sending the commands.

4.4   In the four-site system shown in Figure 4.37, the user is at Site 1. We need to print all information about all sales persons who have accounts in a branch in the city of Edina. We know that 5% of branches are in Edina; 10% of all accounts

Site 1			Site 2		Site 3			Site 4	
S			R		T			M	
A	B	C	A	D	A	E	F	A	G
1	b1	c1	1	d1	1	e1	f1	1	g1
2	b2	c2	2	d2	2	e2	f2	2	g2
3	b3	c3	3	d3	3	e3	f3	3	g3
4	b4	c4	5	d4	4	e4	f4	5	g4
9	b5	c5	6	d5	5	e5	f5		
					6	e6	f6		
					7	e7	f7		

Figure 4.35   Relations for Exercise 4.2.

Emp (Ename, Sal, D#)
Dept (D#, dname, Budget)
Account (A#, bal, bname, cname)
Branch (bname, bcity)

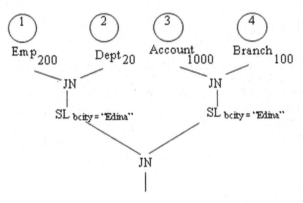

Figure 4.36   Database setup for Exercise 4.3.

Emp (Ename, Sal, D#, Position)
Dept (D#, dname, Budget)
Account (A#, bal, Bname, Ename)
Branch (Bname, bcity)

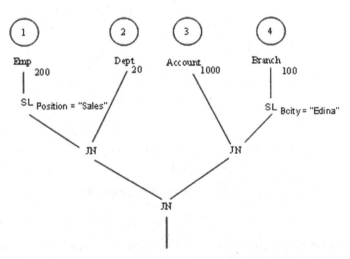

Figure 4.37   Query tree for Exercise 4.4.

Sailors(<u>sid</u>, sname, rating check (1-10), age)
Boats(<u>bid</u>, bname, type)
Reserves(<u>sid, bid, day</u>, mame, desc)

Sailors table stats:

> There are 40,000 sailors – 40,000 rows
> Each row is 50 bytes long
> A page can hold 80 sailor rows
> There are 500 pages to sailor table

Reserves table stats:

> There are 100,000 reserves – 100,000 rows
> Each row is 40 bytes long
> A page can hold 100 reserves rows
> There are 1000 pages to sailor table

Boats table stats:

> There are 100 boats

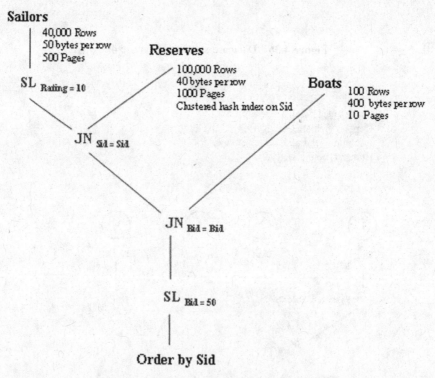

Figure 4.38 ·Relations for Exercise 4.6.

are in branches in Edina; and 20% of employees are in sales. If processing each row takes "t" units of time, what is the processing cost of this tree? Make sure you show all steps and the cost of each step.

4.5   For the distributed database given in Exercise 4.3, what is the cost of an optimal distributed execution strategy for this query in terms of the number of messages required? Assume the cost of sending each row of any table is C units of time. Assume there is no cost associated with sending the commands. Make sure you show all steps and the cost of each step.

4.6   For this question, we use a sail club database used in [Ramakrishnan03]. This database has three tables as shown in Figure 4.38. Suppose we have a query that returns a sorted order of the sailors with a rating of 10 who have reserved the boat with ID = 50. The query plan for this question is depicted in Figure 4.38. Assume the page size is 4000 usable bytes after the page overhead. If the first join is done by a nested-loop, row-based join and the second join is done by a sort–merge join, what is the cost of this plan in number of disk I/Os? Assume that we have five buffers for sorting and all distributions are uniform.

5

CONTROLLING CONCURRENCY

In this chapter, we will discuss the concepts of transaction management and database consistency control. We start by defining the terms we will use in the rest of the chapter. We then focus on transaction management as it relates to **online transaction processing (OLTP)** systems. The concurrency control service is the DBE service that is responsible for consistency of the database. In a nutshell, it controls the operations of multiple, concurrent transactions in such a way that the database stays consistent even when these transactions conflict with each other. Approaches to **concurrency control** are explained next. We introduce concurrency control for centralized DBE first and then consider distributed DBE. In Section 5.3, we formalize the algorithms for concurrency control in a centralized DBE. In Section 5.4, we expand the concurrency control for a centralized DBE to cover the issues in concurrency control for distributed DBEs.

5.1 TERMINOLOGY

Before we discuss how concurrency control applies to the centralized and distributed databases, it is important to understand the terminology that we are using to describe the different approaches and issues involved. In particular, we need to have a better understanding of exactly what a database and a transaction are.

5.1.1 Database

A **database** is a collection of data items that have a name and a value. The set $D\{i_1, i_2, \ldots, i_N\}$ represents a database with N data items. Some of these data items must have a value, they are NOT NULL, and some may have a value, they are NULL. Although this definition of the database seems simplistic, in reality it is comprehensive and can represent relational databases, object-oriented databases, hierarchical databases,

Distributed Database Management Systems by Saeed K. Rahimi and Frank S. Haug
Copyright © 2010 the IEEE Computer Society

NAME	ADDRESS	CITY
Paul Jones	1437 Washington	St. Paul
Cindy Smith	2645 France	Edina

Figure 5.1   A generic database example.

network databases, spreadsheet databases, and flat file databases. Even though we assume each data item has a name, in reality, all we are saying is that every item is accessible and/or addressable. Figure 5.1 depicts an example of a database. According to our definition, there are six data items in this database.

To a person familiar with an Excel spreadsheet, this database represents a sheet with two rows and three columns. Each cell is addressable by the combination of a row and column address. The value "2645 France" represents the address for Cindy Smith. Now assume this is an object-oriented database. For an object-oriented database, "2645 France" presents the address property for the Cindy Smith object while "Paul Jones" represents a name property for the Paul Jones object. In a relational database, this example represents a table with two rows and three columns. In a relational database, the value, "2645 France" is associated with the address column of Cindy Smith's row.

5.1.1.1   Database Consistency   Each data item in the database has an associated correctness assertion. For example, the social security number for an employee must be a unique value, age for an employee needs to be a positive number, an employee must work for one and only one department, the balance of an account needs to be positive and more than $100, and so on. These are all examples of assertions in a database. A database is said to be consistent if and only if the correctness criteria for all the data items of the database are satisfied.

5.1.2   Transaction

A **transaction** is a collection of operations performed against the data items of the database. There have been many references to the **ACID** properties (**atomicity, consistency, isolation**, and **durability**) of a transaction in the literature. Instead of simply repeating these properties, we will use an example to explain a transaction's properties.

In order to know what a transaction does, we need to know when it starts and when it ends. We do that by delineating the boundaries of the transaction either explicitly or implicitly. For our discussions, we will indicate the transaction boundaries using **Begin_Tran** and **End_Tran**. Note that when working interactively with the DBMS we may not need to use Begin_Tran and End_Tran. That is because, in most DBMSs, either every user's operation is considered a transaction or the entire user's session is considered as one large transaction. Similarly, when a programmer implements a transaction, the use of Begin_Tran and End_Tran might be required. The syntax and precise mechanism used to perform these operations varies, depending on the DBMS, the database/transaction API, and the programming language/platform being used to implement the program (we will look at some different mechanisms in Chapters 15–19). In the body of the transaction, one can find some control statements, some read operations, some write operations, some calculations, zero or more aborts, and finally zero or one commit operation.

Example 5.1   This example shows pseudocode (an implementation independent form
of an algorithm) for a transaction that transfers $500 from account X to account Y.

```
Begin_Tran T1:
      Read (account X's balance) into X
      If account X not found Then
            Print 'Invalid source account number'
            Abort
      End If
      Read (account Y's balance) into Y
      If account Y not found Then
            Print 'Invalid target account number'
            Abort
      End If
      Calculate X = X - 500
      If X < 0 Then
            Print 'Insufficient funds'
            Abort
      End If
      Calculate Y = Y + 500
      Write (account X's balance) with X
      Write (account Y's balance) with Y
      Ask user if it is OK to continue
      If Answer is "Yes" Then
            Commit
                  Else
            Abort
      End If
End_Tran T1;
```

To simplify our discussion when working with transactions, we will disregard the
calculations performed and only focus on the read and write operations within the
transaction. No information is lost when we do this. That is because the results of
the calculations are reflected in the values that the transaction writes to the database.
The following is the simplified pseudocode for the previous transaction:

```
Begin_Tran T1:
      Read(X(bal))
      Read(Y(bal))
      Write(X(bal))
      Write(Y(bal))
End_Tran T1;
```

It is important to realize that each transaction contains an ordered list of operations. It
is also important to realize that in a multi-user transaction processing environment, there
could be many transactions running in the system at the same time and their operations
might be interleaved. Therefore, it is important to identify to which transaction each
operation belongs. To do this, we will use a compact (but easy to understand) notation.

In this notation, read operations are represented by an "R" and write operations are represented by a "W." The R and W are followed by a number representing the transaction to which the operation belongs. We will also use generic data item names such as "X" and "Y" and put the data item name in parentheses for each operation. Applying this convention to our fund transfer transaction, we will have the following new representation of our transaction:

```
Begin_Tran T1:
    R1(X)
    R1(Y)
    W1(X)
    W1(Y)
End_Tran T1;
```

We can represent this in an even more compact notation, by using a single formula—"T1 = R1(X), R1(Y), W1(X), W1(Y)" is a straight-line representation of our T1 transaction. In this representation, it is understood that R1(X) happens before R1(Y), R1(Y) happens before W1(X), and so on, meaning that the time increases from left to right.

Now, let's assume that Alice is a customer who owns account X and account Y. Let's also assume that account X has a balance of $1500 and account Y has a balance of $500. As far as Alice is concerned, the database is in a correct state as long as the two accounts show the balances we just indicated. Suppose Alice wants to transfer $500 from account X to account Y. When the transaction completes, the database is in correct state if both accounts have a balance of $1000. If either account shows any other balance value, it would indicate that the database is in an inconsistent state (and Alice would probably be upset). In order to ensure that the database remains correct and consistent, there are four properties (the ACID properties we mentioned earlier) that every transaction must satisfy.

- The **atomicity** property of a transaction indicates that either all of the operations of a transaction are carried out or none of them are carried out. This property is also known as the "all-or-nothing" property.

- The **consistency** property of a transaction requires a transaction to be written correctly. It is the programmer's responsibility to implement the code in the program correctly—so that the program carries out the intention of the transaction correctly. For the fund transfer transaction example, if we are given two account numbers representing the source and the target accounts, the programmer has to make sure the transaction debits the balance of the first account and credits the balance of the second account. If any other modifications are made to the balances of these accounts, the program is invalid. The program implementing the fund transfer transaction must also verify the existence of the account numbers it was given by the user. In addition to these requirements, the program implementing the transaction must also check to see if there is enough money in the source account for the transfer. Note that if Alice inputs the account numbers in the wrong order, the money will be transferred in the wrong direction, that is, the reverse order of what she intended. In this case, it was Alice's mistake—there is nothing wrong with the program implementing the transaction, and it cannot do anything about the mistake. Therefore, the burden of enforcing transaction consistency is shared between the programmer who codes the transaction and the user who runs the transaction.

- The **isolation** property of a transaction requires that the transaction be run without interference from other transactions. Isolation guarantees that this transaction's changes to the database are not seen by any other transactions until after this transaction has committed.

- The **durability** property of a transaction requires the values that the transaction commits to the database to be persistent. This requirement simply states that database changes made by committed transactions are permanent, even when failures happen in the system. When a failure happens, there are two types of changes that can be found in the database. The first type refers to all the changes made by transactions that committed prior to the failure. The other type refers to all the changes made by transactions that did not complete prior to the failure. Since changes made by incomplete transactions do not satisfy the atomicity requirement, these incomplete transactions need to be undone after a failure. This will guarantee that the database is in a consistent state after a failure. We will address durability and handling failures in conjunction with commit protocols in detail in Chapter 8.

As an example of how failures can result in an inconsistent database, assume the system loses power at some point during the execution of the fund transfer transaction. This leads to the transaction's abnormal termination. One can imagine the case where the debit portion of the transaction has completed but the credit portion has not. In this case, the savings account balance will be $1000 but the checking account balance is still $500. This obviously indicates an inconsistent state for the database. The DBMS has to guarantee that when the power is restored, the savings account balance will be restored to $1500. Let's consider another example that demonstrates the ACID properties.

Example 5.2   To see what can go wrong when two transactions that interfere with each other run concurrently (i.e., what would happen if we did not have the isolation property), consider the following scenario. Transaction T1 is transferring $500 from account X to account Y at the same time that transaction T2 is making a $200 deposit into account Y. We can show the operations of these two transactions as follows:

```
Begin_Tran T1:
    Read (account X's balance) into X
    Read (Account Y's balance) into Y
    Calculate X = X - 500
    Calculate Y = Y + 500
    Write (account X's balance) with X
    Write (account Y's balance) with Y
End_Tran T1;

Begin_Tran T2:
    Read (account Y's balance) into Y
    Calculate Y = Y + 200
    Write (account Y's balance) with Y
End_Tran T2;
```

Assuming the same starting balances as before (account X has a balance of $1500 and account Y has a balance of $500), we can say that after these two transactions complete, the database is correct if account X's balance is $1000 and account Y's balance is $1200. Any other values for the balances of these accounts will leave the database in an inconsistent state. Without isolation, one possible scenario interleaves the operation of T1 and T2 as "R1(X), R1(Y), R2(Y), W1(X), W1(Y), W2(Y)." This scenario results in account X's balance being $1000 and account Y's balance being $700, which makes the database inconsistent. Another possible scenario interleaves the operations as "R1(X), R1(Y), R2(Y), W1(X), W2(Y), W1(Y)." This scenario also produces an inconsistent database since account X's balance will be $1000 and account Y's balance will be $1000. Lack of isolation is the cause of the inconsistency of the database in both of these two scenarios. In the first scenario, the value of Y that was written by T1 was lost, and in the second scenario, the value of Y that was written by T2 was lost. Similar issues can occur when the temporary values of one transaction are seen by other transactions.

In environments such as banking systems or airline reservation systems, there are a large number of transactions that run concurrently against the database. In concurrent transaction processing systems like these, the isolation property enables each transaction to perceive itself as the only transaction running in the system. The concurrency control subsystem of the DBMS achieves this perception by enforcing transaction isolation using either **locking** or **timestamping**. We will discuss how isolation maintains the consistency of the database later in this chapter.

5.1.2.1 *Transaction Redefined*

Previously, we defined a transaction to be a collection of operations against the data items of a database without talking about any of the properties the transaction must satisfy. Now that we have introduced transaction atomicity, consistency, isolation, and durability, we need to refine the definition of a transaction. Jim Gray [Gray81] defines a transaction as follows:

> A transaction is a collection of user actions mapped to operations against the data items of the database that, if runs uninterrupted by other transactions and by system failures, transfers the database from one consistent state into another consistent state. If the transaction aborts, it does not change the state of the database.

Figure 5.2 depicts the life cycle of a transaction as Jim Gray defines it. It is important to notice that when a transaction finishes (either successfully or unsuccessfully), the database is left in a consistent state. A successful termination, indicated by a commit, creates a new consistent state for the database, while an unsuccessful termination, caused by an abort, restores the consistent state prior to the start of the transaction. What is equally important is that during the execution of the transaction the database may or may not be in a consistent state. In our fund transfer example, the state of the database after the debit has been done, but before the credit is applied, is an example of an inconsistent state. The database can never be left in this inconsistent state. In case of a failure in this state, a rollback is required to undo the incomplete work of the transaction to restore the previous consistent state.

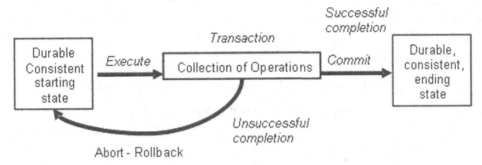

Figure 5.2 Transaction life cycle.

5.2 MULTITRANSACTION PROCESSING SYSTEMS

Our focus on concurrency control is on on-line transaction processing (OLTP) systems. An OLTP system is a system with many transactions running at any given point of time. One characteristic of these systems is the fact that transactions in an OLTP environment are short-lived transactions and make many changes to the database. These systems are somewhat different from **on-line analytical processing (OLAP)** systems that support **decision support system (DSS)** or data warehousing. Transactions in OLAP systems are long-lived and may make little changes to the data warehouse.

Banking systems, airline reservation systems, and systems that monitor the stock market are typical examples of multitransaction processing environments. At any given point in time, there may be hundreds or thousands of transactions running concurrently in the system. Some of these concurrent transactions may interfere with each other. In these cases, it is important to keep track of how the multiple transactions' operations are interleaved. This is what modern database management systems maintain as a **schedule**.

5.2.1 Schedule

A schedule is the total order of operations for a set of transactions. A schedule has sometimes been called a **history** in the industry. When different transactions run in a system, they sometimes create a **serial schedule** and other times a **parallel schedule**.

5.2.1.1 Serial Schedule A serial schedule is one that contains transactions whose operations do not overlap in time. This means that at any point in time only one transaction is running in the system. This schedule is also known as a **sequential schedule**. The schedule "S1 = R1(X), R1(Y), W1(X), R2(Y), W2(Y)" is an example of a serial schedule. This schedule indicates that transaction T1 commits before T2 starts. We show this order as "T1 → T2," where the "→" indicates commitment precedence. Figure 5.3 depicts an example of a serial schedule.

5.2.1.2 Parallel Schedule A **parallel schedule** is one that may contain transactions whose operations do overlap in time. This means that at any point in time there can be

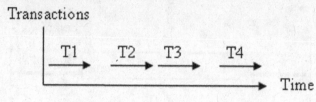

Figure 5.3   An example of serial schedule.

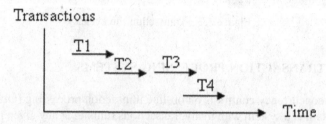

Figure 5.4   An example of parallel schedule.

more than one transaction active. This schedule is called parallel or concurrent. The schedule "S2 = R1(X), R1(Y), R2(Y), W1(X), W2(Y), W1(Y)" is an example of a parallel schedule. It is not clear what the commitment order is for transactions T1 and T2 in this case. Figure 5.4 shows an example of a parallel schedule.

Observation: Two or more transactions running in series maintain the consistency of the database. Figure 5.5 depicts two transactions running in series. It should be obvious that when transaction T1 starts the database is in Consistent State 1. Without interference, T1 transforms the database from Consistent State 1 to Consistent State 2. When T2 starts, it works on the database that is in Consistent State 2 and it transforms the database to Consistent State 3. Since we cannot expect to run all transactions in the system in series, we have to be able to determine if a parallel schedule preserves the consistency of the database. This observation helps to determine if a parallel schedule preserves the consistency of the database (see Section 5.2.4). The main issue with any parallel schedule is the fact that the transactions might interfere with one another. Two transactions interfere with each other when they perform conflicting operations on the same data item.

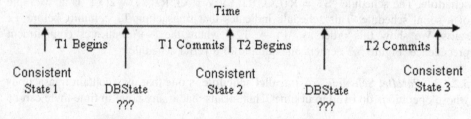

Figure 5.5   An example of two transactions running in series.

	Read T2	Write T2
Read T1	No Conflict	Conflict
Write T1	Conflict	Conflict

Figure 5.6 Conflict matrix.

5.2.2 Conflicts

A **conflict** occurs when two running transactions perform noncompatible operations on the same data item of the database. Transactions perform either read or write operations on data items in the database. A conflict occurs when one transaction writes an item that another transaction is reading or writing. Figure 5.6 shows the conflict matrix for two transactions.

As indicated in this matrix, the two transactions can read the same data item without causing any conflicts, but if either one of them writes to it, at any given point in time, then the other transaction cannot access it at all. When transactions run concurrently, the data items they change are not necessarily part of a consistent state of the database. As a result, isolation is required to hide these inconsistent data items. If isolation is not enforced, two conflicting transactions may cause some unexpected results. These unexpected results are called **anomalies**. In the following, we describe three specific anomalies caused by conflicts. Assume the following three schedules:

```
S1= ..., R1(X), ..., W2(X), ...
S2= ..., W1(X), ..., R2(X), ...
S3= ..., W1(X), ..., W2(X), ...
```

Each of these schedules produces some anomalies that need to be dealt with by the scheduler. These anomalies are **unrepeatable read** anomaly (in S1), **reading uncommitted data** (or **dirty read**) anomaly (in S2), and **overwriting uncommitted data** anomaly (in S3). We will discuss each of these anomalies separately and identify what the scheduler has to do to address them.

5.2.2.1 Unrepeatable Reads   In schedule S1, transaction T1 reads data item X before transaction T2 writes it. The value that is returned by R1(X) is the value of X in the database. The problem with this schedule is that it can lead to unrepeatable reads. Assume that T1 issues a second read on X. This changes the schedule to "S1 = ... R1(X), ..., W2(X), ..., R1(X)." It is easy to see that T1 reads a different value when it issues the second R1(X) from the value it gets when it issues the first R1(X). This is because T2 changes the value of X before T1 reads it again.

5.2.2.2 Reading Uncommitted Data   In schedule S2, transaction T2 reads the value that transaction T1 has written. The problem with this schedule is that it allows transaction T2 to see the uncommitted value of X, which was modified by transaction T1. This can lead to schedule "S2 = ... W1(X), ..., R2(X), ..., W2(X), ..., Commit T2, ..., Abort T1." In the modified schedule, T2 reads the value of X written by T1, computes a new value for X based on this value, writes it to the database, and then commits the new value to the database. This is OK as long as T1 also commits. But, the

schedule we are considering indicates that T1 actually aborts after T2 has committed. T1's abort requires the value of X to be changed back to what was in the database before T1 started. This rollback invalidates the value that T2 wrote to the database. As a result, it requires that T2 also be rolled back. If other transactions have used the value written by T2, they also need to be rolled back. This leads to cascading aborts that are time consuming and error prone.

5.2.2.3 Overwriting Uncommitted Data   As an example of this, assume transaction T2 writes the same data item that T1 has already written. The problem with allowing overwriting of uncommitted data is that it could lead to the schedule "S3 = ... W1(X), ..., W2(X), ..., Commit T2, ..., Abort T1." In this schedule, what T2 has written to the database is lost, since after T1 is aborted T2 needs to be aborted as well. Note that these writes are not preceded by a read in the schedule. What causes the problem is allowing transactions to write an item without first reading it. This type of write is known as **blind write**. An example of a blind write is shown in the following SQL statement:

```
Update Employee
Set salary = 2000
Where EmpID = 1234;
```

5.2.3 Equivalence

Transactions that run concurrently can cause conflicts that lead to the above-mentioned anomalies. These anomalies can destroy the consistency of the database. Therefore, the scheduler must control the conflicting operations of concurrent transactions. The scheduler has two options to preserve the consistency of the database. The first option is to run all transactions in-series, allowing only serial schedules. This, for today's system, is not an acceptable approach. The second option is to run transactions concurrently. In this case, the scheduler has to make sure that the parallel schedule preserves the consistency of the database. How does the scheduler achieve this? The scheduler achieves this goal by making sure that the allowed parallel schedule is equivalent to a serial schedule for the same set of transactions. Two schedules are said to be equivalent if they both produce the same state for the database and every transaction reads the same value(s) and writes the same value(s). Figure 5.7 shows a parallel schedule and an equivalent serial schedule for it.

It is easy to see why these schedules are equivalent. T1 reads the value of X, which was in the database before transaction T1 started in both schedules. Therefore, the value of X written by T1 is the same in both schedules. T2 reads the same value for X in both schedules since the same value is written by T1 in both schedules. Since T2 sees the same value for X, it also produces the same value for X in both schedules. With the same reasoning, both schedules produce the same value for Y when they finish.

$$S1 = R1(X)\ W1(X)\ R2(X)\ W2(X)\ R1(Y)\ W1(Y)\ R2(Y)\ W2(Y)$$
$$S2 = R1(X)\ W1(X)\ R1(Y)\ W1(Y)\ R2(X)\ W2(X)\ R2(Y)\ W2(Y)$$

Figure 5.7   An example parallel schedule and its equivalent serial schedule.

Therefore, the database state for either schedule shows the same values for X and Y. It is obvious that schedule S2 is serial and therefore produces a consistent database. Since schedule S1 is equivalent to S2, it also produces a consistent database. We therefore say that schedule S1 is serializable.

5.2.4 Serializable Schedules

A schedule is said to be serializable if it is equivalent to a serial schedule. The check for serial schedule equivalence is known as **serializability**. A DBE guarantees the consistency of the database by enforcing serializability. To understand serializability, we need to focus on how the DBE handles conflicts. As mentioned before, the scheduler schedules operations for each transaction. When a transaction enters the system, it is assigned to a **transaction monitor** (**TM**). Every TM works with the scheduler to schedule the operations of the transaction it monitors. A TM submits the transaction's operations to the scheduler one operation at a time. The scheduler will determine if the requested operation from a TM is in conflict with any other operations it has already granted—the operations that are part of the schedule at this point in time. If the request is not in conflict with any operation already scheduled, then the scheduler grants the operation and adds that operation to the schedule. If, on the other hand, the request is in conflict with one or more of the already granted operations, the scheduler only grants the operation if the resulting schedule will still remain serializable. Otherwise, the requesting transaction is rolled back.

It is neither practical nor efficient for the scheduler to **only** look for serial schedules that are equivalent to the current parallel schedules. That is because serial schedules can slow down even a high-powered database server's CPUs. The scheduler needs to allow those parallel schedules that are equivalent to a serial schedule to run to promote concurrency and increase throughput. The scheduler focuses on the impact that conflicts have on the commitment order of transactions in the schedule. To understand this better, let's focus on all possible conflicts between two transactions. The conflict matrix (see Section 5.2.2) shows three types of conflicts between the operations of two transactions. These are the read–write, the write–read, and the write–write conflicts. We use the notation RW, WR, and WW to indicate these conflicts. The following three schedules show possible conflicts between T1 and T2 for three separate scenarios. Note that for clarity we are using a separate schedule to show only one of the conflicts and are not showing other transactions' operations in the schedules.

```
S1= ... R1(X) ... W2(X) ...
S2= ... W1(X) ... R2(X) ...
S3= ... W1(X) ... W2(X) ...
```

Let's assume that S1S is a serial schedule that is equivalent to S1. In S1S, R1(X) has to appear before W2(X) appears in the schedule, because T1 reads what was written by other transactions, but not what was written by T2. Because of this, in S1S, T1 must commit before T2. That is because S1S is a serial schedule and in any serial schedule one transaction cannot start before the other transaction commits. As a result, the order in which T1 and T2 commit is the order in which two conflicting operations R1(X) and W2(X) appear in the serial schedule. We therefore conclude that "the order of two conflicting operations by two different transactions determines the order of their commitment in an equivalent serial schedule." The same holds true for serial schedules that are equivalent to S2 and S3. In all three schedules, since transaction T1 performs a conflicting operation on data item X before T2 performs its operation, then T1 needs to commit before T2 commits.

Two transactions may conflict more than once, depending on the data items in each and the operations being performed. Each pair of conflicting operations in the schedule puts a commitment order requirement on the transactions that request the operations. We call the commitment order that a pair of conflicting operations put on the system a **partial commitment order** (**PCO**). We know that there are multiple transactions in the system and there can be many conflicts among them. Considering all possible PCOs for a schedule, we conclude that the schedule is serializable if and only if none of the PCOs are contradictory. We can validate that there is no contradiction among PCOs by forming a graph that contains all PCOs and checking the graph for nonexistence of cycle(s). We call this graph the **total commitment order** (**TCO**) graph. To summarize the above discussion, we say a schedule is serializable if and only if its TCO is acyclic.

Example 5.3   Let's consider the schedule "S1 = R1(X), R2(X), W2(X), W1(X)." There are three conflicts in this schedule between transactions T1 and T2. The first conflict is between R1(X) and W2(X). Because of this conflict, T1 must commit before T2 commits. We show this by the order "T1 → T2." The conflict between R2(X) and W1(X) requires that "T2 → T1." The conflict between W2(X) and W1(X) requires that "T2 → T1." As a result, the total commitment order graph has a cycle in it. That is because, on the one hand, we have the requirement that transaction T1 needs to commit before T2 and, at the same time, we also have the requirement that transaction T2 needs to commit before transaction T1 commits. Since this is not possible, the schedule is not serializable.

Example 5.4   As another example, consider the schedule "S2 = R2(X), R1(X), W2(X), W3(X)." For this schedule, the four PCOs are "T2 →T3," "T1 → T2," "T1 → T3," and "T2 → T3." We can satisfy all these requirements if we commit T1 before T2 and commit T2 before T3, which means that we need to have the total order "T1 → T2 → T3." Since this total ordering does not have any cycles in it, schedule S2 is serializable. This also means that S2 is equivalent to the serial schedule "R1(X), R2(X), W2(X), W3(X)."

5.2.4.1   *Serializability in a Centralized System*

In a centralized DBMS, a schedule is serializable if and only if it is equivalent to a serial schedule. The scheduler checks for conflicts between each pair of transactions' operations. For each conflict found, it imposes a partial commitment order (PCO). Putting all such partial commitment orders together, the system generates a total commitment order graph. Existence of a cycle in this graph indicates that the schedule is not serializable. Otherwise, the schedule is serializable to one or possibly more serial executions of the transactions in the schedule. The scheduler checks for serializability every time a TM requests to schedule a new operation. If granting the operation does not result in a cycle in the total commitment order of all transactions whose operations have already been scheduled, the operation is granted and the new operation is scheduled. Otherwise, the requesting transaction is rolled back.

5.2.4.2 Serializability in a Distributed System   In a distributed system, transactions run on one or more sites. Therefore, the global schedule consists of a collection of local schedules—each site involved has a local schedule that may or may not be serializable. It should be obvious that in a distributed system, if there is a local schedule that is not serializable, then the global schedule that contains it is not serializable. The question we need to address now is whether or not the global schedule is serializable when all local schedules are. The answer depends on whether or not the database is replicated. It should be rather obvious that if the database is not replicated there is no mutual consistency requirement. The mutual consistency requirement states that copies of data items of a database must have the same value. In a nonreplicated database, there is no mutual consistency requirement. As a result, as long as local schedules are serializable, the global schedule is serializable as well.

When we replicate a database in a distributed system, we need to maintain mutual consistency of the database. The issue with replication and mutual consistency is that just because local schedules are serializable, it does not necessarily mean that the global schedule is serializable. Example 5.5 demonstrates this.

Example 5.5   Suppose we have a database for a company whose headquarters is in LA while their development department is in NY. Smith is a developer who makes $1000 monthly. Smith's manager (who is also located in NY) wants to adjust Smith's salary by issuing an equity adjustment increase of $200. In addition, the company is giving everybody in the organization a 10% increase (it has been a good year for the company!). The latter is issued by the human resources manager, who is in LA. The company's intention is to raise everybody's adjusted salary. It should be obvious that Smith's salary must be $1320 after these two adjustments. This distributed database has two copies, one in LA and one in NY. The equity adjustment transaction, T1, enters into the system in NY while the raise transaction, T2, enters in LA. Assuming X represents Smith's salary, transactions T1 and T2 are written as

```
Begin_Tran T1:                    Begin_Tran T2:
    R(X)                              R(X)
    Calculate X = X + 200             Calculate X = X *1.10
    W(X)                              W(X)
    End_Tran End T1;              End_Tran End T2;
```

Each transaction runs at the site where it has entered the system, moves to the other site, and then runs there. Therefore, T1 runs in NY first and then in LA, while T2 runs in LA first and then in NY. If these two transactions start at almost the same time, we would have the following two local schedules:

```
Schedule at NY: S1 = R1(X), W1(X), R2(X), W2(X)
Schedule at LA: S2 = R2(X), W2(X), R1(X), W1(X)
```

It is obvious that both schedules are serial schedules and are consistent. As a result, both local schedulers would allow the schedules. But, globally the database is inconsistent because after both schedules complete the salary for Smith in LA is $1320 but in NY it is $1300.

Serializability in Replicated Databases To consider mutual consistency in a replicated database, we need to extend the local serializability definition. In a replicated database, schedule S is globally serializable if and only if all local schedules are serializable and the order of commitment for two conflicting transactions is the same at every site where the two transactions run. Applying these requirements to our example, we see that for conflicting transactions T1 and T2, at the LA site the commitment order is "T1 → T2" but in NY, the commitment order is "T2 → T1." Since the two transactions do not commit in the same order across both sites, they leave the database copies in an inconsistent state.

5.2.4.3 Conflict Serializable Schedules The serializability concept we have discussed so far is known as **conflict serializability**, which was first discussed in [Eswaran76]. Although it is true that conflict serializable schedules produce a consistent database, they are not the only schedules that do so.

5.2.4.4 View Serializable Schedules Consider schedule "S = R1(X), W2(X), W1(X), W3(X)." This schedule is not conflict serializable since it implies the PCOs "T1 → T2," "T1 → T3," "T2 → T1," and "T2 → T3," which cannot all be satisfied—the total order graph is not acyclic. After a closer look, however, we notice that this schedule produces the same result as the following two schedules:

```
S1 = R1(X), W1(X), W2(X), W3(X)
S2 = R1(X), W2(X), W1(X), W3(X)
```

Schedule S1 is a serial schedule and preserves the consistency of the database. Schedule S2, on the other hand, is not a serial schedule. However, S2 is equivalent to S1 and therefore preserves the consistency of the database as well. Since S is equivalent to S1, S also preserves the consistency of the database. What is peculiar about schedules S1 and S2 is that they allow blind writes—transactions that write a data item without having read it first. Note that in S1 and S2, whatever transactions T1 and T2 write into the database for X is immediately overwritten by what T3 writes and hence it does not matter what T1 and T2 have read or written. This type of schedule is called **view serializability** by Silberschatz and Korth [Silberschatz05]. According to Silberschatz and Korth, view serializability is based on the concept of view equivalency.

Schedules S1 and S2 are view equivalent if they satisfy the following two conditions:

- Condition 1: A transaction that performs a read for a data item, reads the same value in both schedules.
- Condition 2: The final value of X is written by the same transaction in both schedules.

For schedules S1 and S2, the only read operation is R1(X). The value that R1(X) returns to T1 is the value that was initially in the database—what was written by T0 before T1, T2, and T3 started. This satisfies Condition 1. Condition 2 also holds true for these two schedules since the final value of X is written by T3. As a result, S, S1, and S2 are view equivalent.

As we argued before, these three schedules are conflict serializable. It is not too difficult to observe that every conflict serializable schedule is also view serializable.

However, not every view serializable schedule is conflict serializable. Schedule "S2 = R1(X), W2(X), W1(X), W3(X)" is not conflict serializable but it is view serializable as discussed above. Silberschatz and Korth also show that the problem of checking if a schedule is view serializable is a **NP-complete** problem. Therefore, finding an efficient or even feasible algorithm to check for view serializability is **extremely** unlikely.

5.2.4.5 Recoverable Schedules   Recoverable schedules are those schedules that allow recovery of the database to a consistent state after the failure of one or more transactions. As an example, assume schedule "S = R1(X), W1(X), R2(X), W2(X), C2, R1(Y)." This schedule is conflict serializable to "T1 → T2." But, this is only true if T1 eventually commits. On the other hand, if T1 aborts in addition to rolling back T1, what T2 has written to the database needs to also be undone by rolling back T2. Furthermore, every transaction that used what T2 wrote to the database must also be rolled back. The steps necessary to recover the consistent state of the database prior to when schedule S started are very difficult, if not impossible, to determine. As a result, this schedule is not recoverable. To recover the consistent state of the database, as it was before S began, we can restore the database from a backup prior to S and roll all the committed transactions forward. This process is known as **point-in-time** (**PIT**) **recovery**, which we will explain in Chapter 8.

The only way to avoid the need for PIT recovery is to reject all unrecoverable schedules. If we allow unrecoverable schedules, then we must use PIT recovery. In our example, by forcing T2 to delay its commit until after T1 commits, we make the schedule recoverable as "S = R1(X), W1(X), R2(X), W2(X), R1(Y), C1, C2." The issue with unrecoverable schedules is the potential for cascading rollback—when the rollback of one transaction requires rollback of some other transactions.

5.2.4.6 Cascadeless Schedules   Assume in schedule "S = R1(X), W1(X), W1(Y), R2(X), W2(X), R3(X), W3(X)" that none of the transactions have committed. At this point in time, the schedule is recoverable according to the above definition. However, if transaction T1 rolls back, it necessitates rolling back T2 and T3 as well. The reason for this is that T2 and T3 have used what T1 has written to the database. This type of rollback is called a **cascading rollback**, which requires a significant amount of work. To eliminate cascading rollbacks, we can restrict the scheduler to allow only cascadeless schedules. A schedule is cascadeless if whenever we have a pair of conflicting transactions (Ti and Tj) and one transaction (Tj) reads a data item that was written by the other transaction (Ti), the reading transaction commits after the writing transaction (i.e., Tj commits after Ti). It should be obvious that a cascadeless schedule is a recoverable schedule as well. By applying this rule, expanding schedule S to "R1(X), W1(X), W1(Y), R2(X), W2(X), R3(X), W3(X), C1, C2, C3" makes it a cascadeless schedule.

5.2.5 Advanced Transaction Types

The transaction model we have discussed so far is used to enforce the ACID properties. This transaction model is intended to support transactions that take a short amount of time (usually measured in seconds) to finish. These types of transactions are called **short-lived transactions** (**SLTs**). SLTs form most of the transactions in today's computer systems. For SLTs, the decision to commit or abort a transaction is made in a relatively short amount of time. But, there are **long-lived transactions** (**LLTs**) that take a long time (compared to SLTs) to finish. LLTs may take minutes, hours, or even days to finish. An example can be a transaction that consists of a series of tests that must be done on a given patient in a hospital. This transaction can obviously take a day, or more than a day, to finish. Another property of this transaction is that, although considered one transaction, the transaction itself consists of multiple transactions (each test is also a transaction). LLT can hold on to the database resources (data items, locks, etc.) for long periods of time. Therefore, they can negatively impact the overall performance of the system by denying SLTs access to the same set of resources. The longer duration is caused by factors such as waiting for user input or for the collaboration of multiple parties before committing the transaction.

5.2.5.1 Sagas

5.2.5.1 Sagas   Garcia-Molina introduced the concept of sagas [Garcia-Molina87] to allow for management of long transactions. A saga is an LLT that is written as a series of transactions that can be interleaved with other transactions. Transactions within a saga must be carried out in the order specified. But, a transaction within the saga can be committed in an interleaved fashion with respect to the other transactions outside the saga. This means that the subresults of a transaction are released to other transactions or sagas. Both the concept of a saga and its implementation are relatively simple, but they have the potential to improve performance significantly for certain classes of applications.

It should be obvious that as long as a saga completely commits, releasing the results of one or more transactions within a saga to other transactions has no potential performance issues. The problem is when a saga cannot commit completely. In that case, one or more **compensating transactions** must be run, usually in the reverse order of the transactions in the saga, undoing the effects of what has been committed to the database. Since sagas release partial results to other sagas and transactions, compensating one or more transactions within one saga may necessitate compensating other transactions within other sagas as well. Sometimes a compensating transaction for a transaction within a saga may not be possible or may not make sense. For example, consider a saga that consists of a test, a treatment, a second test, and second treatment for a patient. Suppose the second test indicates a situation that necessitates undoing the effect of the first treatment. Undoing the first treatment may or may not be possible. As another example, consider trying to compensate a transaction with a saga that bought 1000 shares of a company. Although compensating this transaction is possible technically, the results (financially, legally, ethically, etc.) may be disastrous.

The kind of recovery we just discussed for a failed transaction within a saga is called **backward recovery**. Backward recovery obviously leads to the potential for cascading compensation, which may take a long time to carry out and in some cases may not be possible. Such cases would require restoring the database from a consistent backup and rolling forward good transactions (see Chapter 8 on failure and recovery for more details). This second type of recovery is called **forward recovery**. The third alternative for recovery of a failed transaction within a saga uses a mixed approach. In this alternative, instead of using a backup as the starting point for the forward recovery, a **save point** is used. The database is first rolled back to the save point and then is rolled forward by running all the good transactions.

Sagas can also cause database consistency loss. This can happen since transactions within sagas are interleaved. When running sagas, we must make sure that the effect of running transactions within sagas creates a serializable schedule. Sagas are a form of nested transactions. As discussed later in this chapter, a nested transaction model nicely supports distributed database systems. Being a nested transaction, a saga can act as a global transaction and transactions within it as local transactions. Sagas support two types of nesting called closed nesting and open nesting. In a closed nested transaction, the intermediate results of a subtransaction are not seen by other transactions. In an open nested transaction, the intermediate results are exposed to other transactions. Therefore, a saga is an open nested transaction.

Various implementation issues related to sagas exist—for example, how can sagas be run on an existing system that does not directly support them? Another issue has to do with the creation of compensating transactions for those transactions that have used the results of one or more transactions contained within a saga. To address this issue, Garcia-Molina and his colleagues introduced the concept of nested sagas [Garcia-Molina91]. In a nested saga, a transaction within a saga can be a saga itself, and therefore contain steps that can also be compensated.

5.2.5.2   ConTracts   Reuter introduced the concept of ConTract [Reuter89] as an extension of sagas, in order to deal with some of the issues found in long running transactions. In a ConTract, embedded transactions are defined as a set of nested steps that can be compensated independently. In addition, the control flow among these steps is not sequential the way that the transactions within a saga flowed. The steps within a ConTract are capable of defining the control flow for themselves. In a ConTract, the failure of a step can be compensated and the ConTract can continue from the point of failure. This requires saving of state information for steps (subtractions), which the underlying DBE may support.

There are many other transaction models that have been discussed and proposed in the literature to deal with long running transactions, addressing their ACID property and performance issues. Some of these models have been used to deal with transaction management issues in the **federated** and **multidatabase** systems (see Chapter 12). Barker [Barker99] provides a good summary of these models including a summary for ACTA [Chrysanthis90], sagas, ConTracts, split transactions [Kaiser92], flex transactions [Emagarmid90] [Leu91], S-transactions [Veijalainen92], multilevel transactions [Weikum91], polytransactions [Sheth92], and epsilon transactions [Pu93].

5.2.6   Transactions in Distributed System

In a distributed system, a transaction can either be a **local transaction** or a **global transaction**. A local transaction is a transaction that performs all its work at the site where it originates. In other words, a local transaction does not leave its originating site. A global transaction, on the other hand, is a transaction that has to perform work at one or more sites different from its originating site. The originating site is the site where the transaction first enters the system. That is where the transaction is assigned to a transaction monitor, TM, as mentioned before. A global transaction is carried out as a set of local transactions each running as an agent of the global transaction at a given site. Each local transaction is a subtransaction of a global transaction. This introduces a new degree of difficulty in committing a global transaction. Using this model, we can write the equity adjustment transaction we discussed in Example 5.5 as global transaction T1 consisting of two local transactions T1LA and T1NY:

```
Begin_Tran T1
     Begin_Tran T1LA
          R(X)
          Calculate X = X + 200
          W(X)
          Commit T1LA
     End_Tran T1LA

     Begin_Tran T1NY
          R(X)
          Calculate X = X * 1.10
          W(X)
          Commit T1NY
     End_Tran T1NY

     Commit T1
End_Tran T1;
```

Note that we commit T1 only when both its subtransactions have been committed. Rollback of T1 necessitates the rollback of its subtransactions. But, commitment of one of the subtransactions does not necessarily mean the commitment of the other subtransaction and/or the global transaction. In reality, the global transaction has one or more nested transactions, where each nested transaction is a local transaction that is to run at a particular site. The global transaction is also called the **parent transaction** and each subtransaction is called a **child transaction**. Each child transaction can have its own children transactions. For any nested transaction, the order of commitment is important. A parent transaction can only commit after all its child transactions have committed. In Chapter 8, we will discuss the impact of nested transactions in distributed commit protocols to maintain durability in a distributed database management system. As discussed in Chapter 8, distributed commit reduces the site autonomy of the local DBEs by requiring them to defer the commitment of a local transaction until the global transaction wants to commit. This deferred commit potentially causes problems for the local DBEs; in addition to reducing their autonomy, it is not always possible to implement a distributed commit since a local site may not support the idea of deferring a transaction's commit. This is especially true for nonrelational legacy DBMS systems.

5.3 CENTRALIZED DBE CONCURRENCY CONTROL

Concurrency control algorithms for a centralized database have been studied in detail by many researchers. Therefore, we will summarize these approaches for completeness but will not provide any further details. We will, however, discuss the implication of distribution on these algorithms in detail. We will use the transaction model that was discussed in Chapter 1 for this concurrency control discussion. Recall that in our model, a transaction was initiated at a site and assigned to a transaction monitor (TM), which was responsible for running the transaction. The TM is part of the application processor (AP), as we discussed. The TM uses the scheduler to schedule its transaction's operations. The scheduler generates a serializable schedule for all running transactions.

The scheduler is a part of the concurrency control module of the DBE. There are two basic approaches to enforcing isolation in a centralized system. They are based on the concepts of **locking** and **timestamping**. Locking-based concurrency control algorithms use locking to isolate the data items that one transaction is using from other transactions. Although we focus our discussion on locking data items, in reality, lock granularity may be different. For example, one can lock a table row, a database page, a tablespace, or the entire database. We will discuss the impact of locking granularity on performance later in this chapter. Timestamping does not use locking to isolate data items. Instead, timestamps are used to order transactions and their operations in the schedule. Sometimes timestamps are used in conjunction with locking to improve performance.

We can also classify the concurrency control algorithms based on when serializability is enforced. A system can have a high rate of conflicts or a low rate of conflicts. Concurrency control algorithms that work in systems with a high rate of conflict are called **pessimistic concurrency control** algorithms. Concurrency control algorithms that work in systems with a low rate of conflicts are called **optimistic concurrency control** algorithms. For pessimistic concurrency control (where the conflict rate is high), we try to identify conflicts and synchronize transactions as soon as possible. Transactions executing in a system with a high conflict rate are more likely to need a restart than those executing in a system with a lower conflict rate. When a transaction needs to restart, we must undo all of the operations it has performed up to that point. Therefore, in systems where restarts are very likely (high conflict rates), we try to identify conflicts and synchronize transactions as soon as possible, reducing the chance of restarts. On the other hand, if the rate of conflict in a system is low, it might be better to delay the synchronization of transactions. That is because conflict identification and transaction synchronization are nontrivial tasks (requiring time and other resources): we try to delay these actions as much as possible for systems where restarts are rare (low conflict rates). In the next four subsections, we study the approaches to concurrency control in a centralized DBE.

5.3.1 Locking-Based Concurrency Control Algorithms

In this section, we summarize concurrency control algorithms for a centralized DBMS that uses locking. Locking-based concurrency control algorithms use a lock compatibility matrix to determine if a data item can be locked by more than one transaction at the same time. The **lock matrix** is a matrix that indicates compatibility of locks on a data item by two transactions. The lock matrix shown in Figure 5.8 mirrors the conflict matrix discussed in Section 5.2.2. A data item must be locked exclusively when it is being written, but an item can be locked in a shared mode when it is being read.

Locking-based concurrency control systems can utilize either **one-phase** or **two-phase** locking.

	Read Lock	Write Lock
Read Lock	Allowed	Not Allowed
Write Lock	Not Allowed	Not Allowed

Figure 5.8 Lock compatibility matrix.

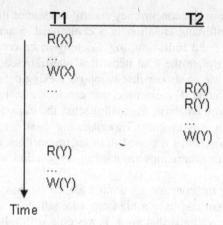

Figure 5.9   Example of two concurrent transactions.

5.3.1.1 One-Phase Locking   **One-phase locking(1PL)** is a method of locking that requires each transaction to lock an item before it uses it and release the lock as soon as it has finished using it. Obviously, this method of locking provides for the highest concurrency level but does not always enforce serializability. Figure 5.9 depicts an example to two concurrent transactions T1 and T2.

Applying one-phase locking principles to scheduling the requests from these two transactions result in the schedule "S = WL1(X), R1(X), W1(X), LR1(X), RL2(X), R2(X), LR2(X), WL2(Y), R2(Y), W2(Y), LR2(Y), WL1(Y), R1(Y), W1(Y), LR1(Y)." The schedule utilizes three new notations that relate to locking and unlocking of data items. RLj(x) indicates a read lock request on X by transaction j; WLj(x) indicates a write lock request on data item X by transaction j; and finally LRj(x) indicates a release of lock by transaction j. To see the actual schedule that has been formed by using one-phase locking, we need to remove the lock and unlock requests from the schedule. Doing so results in "S = R1(X), W1(X), R2(X), R2(Y), W2(Y), R1(Y), W1(Y)" as the schedule. This schedule is not serializable since the PCOs "T1 → T2" and "T2 → T1" cannot both be satisfied.

What is the problem with one-phase locking and why does it produce schedules that are not serializable? This approach is too aggressive in releasing the locks acquired by a transaction. The idea of releasing the locks as soon as possible to provide for more parallelism causes the schedule to be nonserializable. In other words, transactions using 1PL do not keep their locks long enough to ensure serializability—the locks are released prematurely. To ensure serializability, two-phase locking must be utilized.

5.3.1.2 Two-Phase Locking   **Two-phase locking (2PL)** [Eswaran76] is a locking approach in which transactions do not interleave their lock acquisition and lock release. The approach consists of two phases. In the first phase, transactions only acquire locks and do not release any lock until all the locks they need have been granted. In the second phase, transactions start releasing locks and do not request any more locks. That is why the first phase of this locking approach is known as **growing phase** while the second phase is known as **shrinking phase**. The growing and shrinking terms reflect the number of locks a transaction is holding at any given point in time during its execution.

Applying the 2PL principles to the example in Figure 5.9 results in schedule "S = WL1(X), R1(X), W1(X), WL1(Y), LR1(X), R1(Y), W1(Y), LR1(Y), RL2(X), R2(X), WL2(Y), LR2(X), R2(Y), W2(Y), LR2(Y)." Note that, in this schedule, transaction T1 does not release the lock on X until after it has locked data item Y. Again, removing the lock and unlock operations from the schedule, we simplify the schedule as "S = R1(X), W1(X), R1(Y), W1(Y), R2(X), R2(Y), W2(Y)." This schedule is serializable since the two PCOs in the schedule are "T1 → T2" and "T1 → T2," which correspond to the serial execution of T1 followed by T2. We should note that transaction T1 does not have to hold the lock on X until just before it commits. As a matter of fact, the sooner that transaction T1 releases X the sooner T2 can start. This provides for better throughput and parallelism. The approach in which transactions hold all their locks until just before they commit is known as **strict two-phase locking**. Strict 2PL provides for the least amount of parallelism between two conflicting transactions. Figure 5.10 illustrates the two alternatives for 2PL. In 2PL, if a schedule contains a transaction that needs to lock a data item that is already locked in a conflicting mode by another transaction, the transaction needing the lock will wait until it has been granted the lock. This wait is necessary to guarantee that the schedule of running conflicting transactions is always serializable.

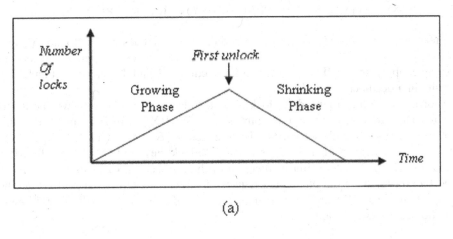

(a)

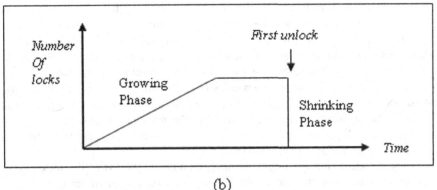

(b)

Figure 5.10 Two-phase locking alternatives.

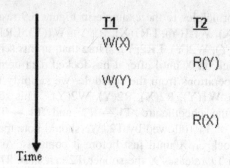

Time

Figure 5.11 Example of two-phase locking with deadlock.

Applying 2PL to the two transactions in Figure 5.9 results in many schedules including the following three schedules. Schedule S1 is based on the application of strict 2PL while schedules S2 and S3 result from the application of (nonstrict) 2PL. All three schedules are serializable.

```
S1 = R1(X), W1(X), R1(Y), W1(Y), R2(X), R2(Y), W2(Y)
S2 = R1(X), W1(X), R2(X), R1(Y), W1(Y), R2(Y), W2(Y)
S3 = R1(X), W1(X), R1(Y), R2(X), W1(Y), R2(Y), W2(Y)
```

The formal proof that 2PL produces serializable schedules can be found in [Bernstein87]. Although 2PL guarantees serializability, it does not prevent deadlocks—for example, applying the 2PL approach to transactions T1 and T2 shown in Figure 5.11 results in a deadlock.

For this example, T1 needs to lock X first. Since X is available, it will be locked by T1. The partial schedule at this point is "S = WL1(X), W1(X)." Shortly after this, T2 needs to lock Y and the schedule is expanded to "S = WL1(X), W1(X), RL2(Y), R2(Y)." Now, neither T1 nor T2 can release the lock they are holding since they both need to lock another item. But neither one of the transactions can lock the other item that they need, since the other item required by each of them is locked by the other transaction. This will cause an indefinite wait or a **deadlock**. We will discuss how to handle deadlocks in Chapter 6.

5.3.1.3 Locking in Relational Databases
Up to now, we have been talking about locking data item X and have not specified what X actually is. In a relational database, locks can be acquired for different parts of the database and at different levels of database hierarchy. For example, a relational DBMS may allow database, table, page, and row-level locking. This hierarchy indicates coarse level granules (databases) at the top of the hierarchy and fine level granules (rows) at the bottom of the hierarchy. A database lock covers everything in the database. A table lock covers all pages (and rows) in the table, while a page lock covers all the rows in the page. Finally, a row-level lock covers all columns in a particular row. Figure 5.12 depicts the granules used by the lock hierarchy for a relational DBMS.

It should be clear that the larger the lock granule is, the lower the lock overhead is, and at the same time, the lower the concurrent access to the database objects. To maximize concurrency and at the same time to minimize the locking overhead, a DBMS may utilize **multiple-granularity locking** in conjunction with **intention locking**. Many

Database							
Table 1				Table 2			
Page 1		Page 2		Page 1		Page 2	
Row	Row	Row	Row	Row	Row	Row	Row

Figure 5.12 Lock granularities in a relational database.

relational DBMSs also allow for **lock conversion, lock upgrade, lock downgrade**, and **lock escalation** for better utilization of system resources such as tables, pages, and rows.

Most relational DBMSs allow the following locking principles:

- *Lock Conversion.* If the transaction already holds a lock on a data item, it can convert the lock type from one lock mode to another. There are two alternatives to lock conversion: lock upgrade and lock downgrade.
- *Lock Upgrade.* This happens when a transaction converts a read lock to a write lock. When the write lock request is issued, the lock manager grants the upgrade if the requesting transaction is the only one holding a read lock on the data item. Otherwise, the requesting transaction must wait for readers to release the locks.
- *Lock Downgrade.* This happens when a transaction converts a write lock to a read lock. There is no issue with the downgrade since the downgrading transaction is the only transaction that is holding the lock on the data item.
- *Lock Escalation.* This happens when a transaction tries to avoid acquiring too many fine grain locks by requesting to lock a larger granule. This might be requested by the transaction or may be applied automatically by the DBMS. In the latter case, the DBMS can set a lock escalation threshold. For example, if more row locks than indicated in the threshold are requested, the DBMS might automatically escalate the row locks to a table lock.
- *Multiple-Granularity Locking (MGL).* This approach allows transactions to lock items at multiple levels of the hierarchy. When a transaction locks a granule at a higher level of the hierarchy, the transaction is also given the lock to all the granules in the subtree below it. The locks can be, as usual, read (shared), write (exclusive), or intention locks. MGL is enforced by requiring the transaction that wants to lock a granule to lock the ancestor(s) of it first. For instance, if a transaction wants to lock a row of a table it must hold a lock on the table that the row is in.
- *Intention Locking.* This is a method in which a transaction must tell the DBMS its intention to lock before it actually locks the granule. The intention (what the transaction is planning to do) is represented by an intention lock. For example, a transaction may want to lock a table in the shared mode but intends on modifying some (but not all) of the rows. This transaction must request a shared lock on the table with the intention to exclusively lock some of its rows. Before locking a granule, a transaction must set intention locks on all its ancestors.
- *Intention Lock Modes.* There are five intention lock modes:

  S: the transaction locks the entire subtree in shared (S) mode.
  X: the transaction locks the entire subtree in exclusive (X) mode.

		Mode of lock Requested				
		S	X	IS	IX	SIX
Mode of locks	S	Y	N	Y	N	N
currently	X	N	N	N	N	N
held by another	IS	Y	N	Y	Y	Y
Transaction	IX	N	N	Y	Y	N
	SIX	N	N	Y	N	N

Figure 5.13   Intention lock compatibility matrix for Oracle 10 g.

IS: the transaction intends to lock some descendant in S mode.

IX: the transaction intends to lock some descendant in X mode.

SIX (= S + IX): the transaction locks the entire subtree in S mode; intends to lock some descendant in X mode.

With the introduction of intention locking, the lock compatibility matrix must be changed to include intention lock types. Figure 5.13 depicts the lock compatibility matrix for Oracle 10 g. As shown in Figure 5.13, an exclusive lock is not compatible with any other type of lock. As a result, when a transaction puts an exclusive lock on a table, no other transaction can read or modify any of the table's rows or columns. But, a request for an IX lock on a table that is already locked in IS, a request for an IS lock on rows of a table that is already locked in IX, and a request for an IX lock on a table that is already locked in IX mode are all allowed. This flexibility allows for better concurrency and parallelism in the system. The belief is that although two transactions are intending on changing some rows of the table, the actual rows that are going to be changed by them are different. Therefore, Oracle, for example, locks the rows exclusively when it has to and not ahead of time, allowing for more concurrency.

Oracle 10 g uses two simple rules: one rule to lock, and one rule to unlock a granule in MGL. To lock a granule, Oracle requires a transaction to acquire intention locks on all the granule's ancestors. To get a shared lock (S), the transaction must hold an IS on the parent; to get an X or IX lock, the transaction must hold an IX or SIX on the parent. To unlock a granule, Oracle requires a transaction to release the locks from the bottom of the hierarchy up. For instance, if transaction T1 wants to read all rows of table R, T1 is required to get a shared lock (S) on table R. If T2 wants to read all rows of R and may want to update a few rows, then T2 must get an SIX lock on table R, and then, occasionally, get an X lock for the rows it wants to change. If T3 wants to use an index to read only part of R, then T3 gets an IS lock on R, and repeatedly gets an S lock on each row it needs to access.

5.3.1.4 Phantom Issue   The term "phantom" refers to an issue that is specific to the way relational DBMSs use row-level locking. Phantoms occur when one transaction's updates or inserts change the scope of rows that another transaction has locked. Figure 5.14 illustrates how the phantom issue occurs between two transactions working on the rows of the same table.

In this example, transaction T1 locks and reads the total of Saeed's account balances first. The first select statement in T1 finishes before the insert statement of T2 starts. Although T1 has a shared lock on the rows of the table, it does not prevent T2 from

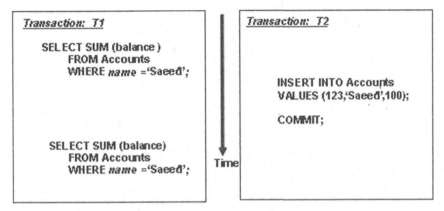

Figure 5.14   An example of phantom issue.

inserting a new row into the table. This new row for Saeed's new account is exclusively locked by T2 until it commits. At this time, T2 releases the lock, and when T1 audits the table again, it gets a different value ($100 more than before) for Saeed's accounts. This phenomenon is known as the **phantom issue** in relational databases. Phantoms occur when row locking is used and one transaction issues a SELECT, UPDATE, or DELETE using a predicate P, and another transaction creates a row (using INSERT or UPDATE) that satisfies P. In other words, the DBMS does not prevent creation of new rows satisfying the predicate of rows locked by another transaction.

The phantom issue may or may not be an issue for a given application. In general, the impact of conflict in relational systems is dictated by the level of exposure of items between two transactions. **ANSI** (the American National Standards Institute) suggests four isolation levels for its **SQL92** standard and indicates the ramification of each level of exposure as shown in the Table 5.1.

DBMSs can employ different approaches to overcome the phantom issue. The two most commonly used approaches are **index page locking** and **predicate locking**. As an example of index page locking, assume transaction T1 is printing the name of all employees whose salaries (hopefully, weekly salaries) are in the range "$5K< salary <= $10K." Suppose there are three employees who satisfy this condition. These employees make $6K, $9K, and $10K. Then, during the execution of T1, transaction T2 inserts a new employee with the salary of $7K. Obviously, the new row that transaction T2 is inserting satisfies the predicate for the select issued by T1. Therefore, it is a phantom row. The phantom issue in this case is remedied by index page locking. To show how this approach works, assume there is a B^+Tree index on the salary column

TABLE 5.1   ANSI Isolation Levels

Level	Isolation Name	Dirty Reads	Unrepeatable Reads	Phantom
Level 1	Read Uncommitted	Maybe	Maybe	Maybe
Level 2	Read Committed	No	Maybe	Maybe
Level 3	Repeatable Reads	No	No	Maybe
Level 4	Serializable	No	No	No

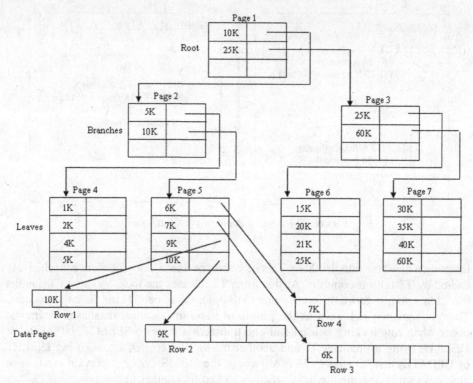

Figure 5.15   Example of index page locking.

of the employee table as shown in Figure 5.15. In this case, transaction T1 must get
an IS lock on the employee table, shared locks on the data pages that contain rows 1,
2, and 3, and shared locks on the index pages 1, 2, and 5. The index entry for the new
employee's salary is also in page 5 of the index. Therefore, in order for T2 to insert the
new employee row, T2 must acquire an exclusive IX lock on the employee table, X
locks on index page 5, and X locks on the data block that contains row 4. There is no
issue with T2 getting an IX lock on the employee table since this IX lock is compatible
with the IS lock that T1 holds on the table. There is also no issue with T2 getting the
exclusive (X) lock on the block that row 4 is going into since this block is compatible
with the IS lock T1 holds on the table. But, the X lock on page 5 of the index cannot be
granted to T2 since it is not compatible with the S lock that T1 is holding on this index
block. Therefore, T2 cannot insert the new row until after T1 finishes, which prevents
the phantom issue. If there were no such index on the column that the predicate is based
on, transaction T1 would need to lock all the employee table pages to prevent phantoms.

In predicate locking the DBMS deals with the phantom issue by not only locking
all the rows that satisfy the predicate of the SQL statements, but also by denying any
insertions of new rows and/or updates of existing rows that would change the scope of
a conflicting transaction. Index page locking is a special case of predicate locking for
which an index provides an efficient implementation of the predicate lock. Because of
the overhead associated with the implementation of predicate locking, many DBMSs
(such as Microsoft SQL Server and Sybase) use index page locking to deal with the
phantom issue.

5.3.2 Timestamp Concurrency Control Algorithms

As discussed in Section 5.3.1, locking-based concurrency control algorithms use locks to isolate the data items that one transaction is working with from other transactions—the other transactions are denied access to those locked data items. A transaction's **timestamp** (age) can also be used to coordinate concurrent access to the database's data items in such a way that the schedule is conflict serializable. This approach is known as **timestamp ordering (TO)** [Bernstein80b]. In TO concurrency control, each transaction is given a timestamp when it enters the system. The timestamp is set to the computer's clock reading at the time that the transaction enters the system. Since a single processor can only handle one transaction entry at a time, timestamps generated by the system are unique for a single computer. Handling only one transaction at a time is a necessary requirement since each transaction must be given a unique timestamp. The timestamp acts as the "birthdate" of the transaction. We use the notation ts(Ti) to indicate the timestamp of transaction Ti. If ts(Ti)< ts(Tj) then Ti is older than Tj.

Instead of using the actual physical clock reading as the timestamp, we can use a **logical clock** reading. The logical clock is a counter that is initially set to one (1) and incremented as each transaction enters the system. The transaction that first enters the system gets a logical clock reading of one (1), the second transaction gets a reading of two (2), and so on. If we refer to the first transaction as T1 and the second transaction as T2, then ts(T1) = 1 and ts(T2) = 2. Obviously, since ts(T1)< ts(T2), T1 is older than T2. The use of transaction subscripts, instead of an actual physical clock reading for timestamps, will simplify our discussion

The main philosophy behind the TO approach is to coordinate the access to a data item based on the age of the transactions involved. TO concurrency control based algorithms force transactions to commit in the order dictated by their ages. It is expected that an older transaction must commit before a younger transaction, since the older transaction enters the system before the younger one does. For example, if transactions T1, T2, ..., T10 are all running in the system, then TO concurrency control expects that T1 must commit before T2, T2 must commits before T3, and so on. This does not mean that all 10 transactions will commit, but it does mean that those that do commit must be committed in the proper order (using their ages). In other words, TO concurrency control algorithms generate schedules that are serializable and the transactions in the equivalent serial schedule are arranged in order, from oldest to youngest based on each transaction's age.

5.3.2.1 *Basic TO Concurrency Control Algorithm*   There are three rules that enforce serializability based on the age of a transaction. In what follows we outline these rules for two conflicting transactions. It should be noted that in a concurrent transaction processing system, there are many transactions running at the same time. For these systems, the serializability rules are applied to each pair of conflicting transactions.

These three rules are:

- *Access Rule.* When two transactions try to access data item X at the same time, with conflicting operations, priority is given to the older transaction. This priority forces the younger transaction to wait for an older transaction to commit first.
- *Late Transaction Rule.* An older transaction is not allowed to read or write a data item that has already been written by a younger transaction. This rule prevents the

older transaction from needing to commit after the younger transaction has already been committed, which would be a violation of the age order if we allowed it to happen.

- *Younger Transaction Wait Rule.* A younger transaction is allowed to read or write a data item that has already been written by an older transaction.

In this approach, a transaction's writes are divided into two phases—the **pre-write** phase and the **commit** phase. When transaction Ti wants to write data item X, it calls the algorithm shown in Figure 5.16a, passing parameter Ti to it as the transaction ID and X as the data item name and value. Once Ti is ready to commit the new value for X, it calls the algorithm in Figure 5.16b to commit the new value for X to the database. If transaction Ti needs to read a data item such as X, then it needs to call the algorithm shown in Figure 5.16c, passing it Ti as the transaction ID and X as the data item name. If the algorithm actually performs the read, we can use X as an output value or return the new value as a return value—the mechanism is not important to the algorithm, and therefore not shown here.

In the algorithms shown in Figure 5.16, ts(Ti) represents the timestamp for transaction Ti. The TO algorithms also need to maintain two other timestamps—these timestamps are maintained for each data item stored in the database. We use rts(X) to represent the read timestamp of data item X—rts(X) holds the timestamp of the **youngest** transaction that has ever read data item X. Similarly, we use wts(X) to represent the write timestamp of data item X—wts(X) holds the timestamp of the last (most recent) transaction that wrote to data item X. The notation "/* ... */" indicates a comment to help understand the algorithm.

During the pre-write phase, the changes for the transaction are kept in memory—not stored in the database. During the commit, the changes are transferred from memory to the database. When changes from more than one transaction are buffered, the order of committing these transactions is dictated by the ages of the transactions as well. If two conflicting transactions are ready to commit, the system allows the younger one to commit only after the older one has been committed or restarted. Each transaction's reads are always processed from the information stored on the disk. Based on this, if transaction T1 reads X, writes X, and then reads X again, the value it reads for the second time is the same value that it read the first time. If the intention of T1 is to use the new value it generated for X, then T1 should not issue a new read and should continue using what is stored in memory for X.

The implementation of the TO concurrency control algorithm shown in Figure 5.16 suffers from many unnecessary restarts. Assume there are 15 transactions currently running in the system. Let's consider the case where the system receives a write request from transaction T14 for item X. Also, assume that X has not been requested by any other transaction so far. In this case, the system is going to allow T14 to pre-write and then commit a new value to the database. This commitment of T14 invalidates any read or write request from transactions T1 through T13. This results in many restarts for transactions that are older than T14. That is why this algorithm is also known as the **aggressive TO algorithm**.

5.3.2.2 Conservative TO Algorithm   A variation of the basic TO concurrency control algorithm that can eliminate some of the unnecessary restarts is known as **conservative TO ordering**. In the conservative TO algorithm, the concurrency control does not

```
Begin pre-write (Ti and X as inputs)
   /* Ti attempts to pre-write X */
            If ts(Ti) < rts(X) or ts(Ti) < wts(X) Then
                  /* X has been accessed by a younger T */
                  /* Ti is too late */
                  Rollback Ti;
                  Restart Ti with a new timestamp later;
            Else Buffer changes for Ti with ts(Ti)
                  /* Ti is now pending */
            End if;
End pre-write;
```

(a)

```
Begin Commit (Ti and X as inputs)
    /* Ti attempts to commit item X */
            For all Tj that are older and are pending
                  Ti waits unit Tj to commit or abort
                  Else Ti commits X and sets wts(X) = ts(Ti)
            End For;
End Commit;
```

(b)

```
Begin Read (Ti and X as inputs)
    /* Ti attempts to read data item X */
            If ts(Ti) < wts(X) Then
                  X has been written by a younger transaction
                  Rollback Ti; restart later with a new ts
            Else
                  For all Tj that are older and are pending
                      Ti waits unit Tj to commit or abort
                      Else Ti Reads;
                          Set rts(X) = max{ts(Ti), rts(X)}
                  End For;
            End if;
End Read;
```

(c)

Figure 5.16 Basic timestamp ordering algorithm.

act on a request from a much younger transaction until the system has processed requests from a large enough number of the older transactions. Therefore, any potential conflict of a younger transaction with older transactions will be detected before the system commits a much younger transaction. For instance, in the above example, the concurrency control algorithm will delay responding to the write request from T14 until such time as the other 13 older transactions have had a chance to make a request to access X. This is done by maintaining a queue in which requests from transactions are put in order of their age—requests from older transactions are in the front of the queue. The concurrency control algorithm processes the requests in the queue from the front. However, in practice it is not possible to eliminate all restarts. In order to implement this goal, the concurrency control algorithm must wait until it has received requests from all currently running transactions. This in effect will force the execution of transactions to a serial schedule based on the age of transactions, which is not desirable.

5.3.2.3 Multiversion Concurrency Control Algorithm The **multiversion** (**MV**) algorithms for concurrency control [Papadimitriou82] are mostly used in engineering databases, where the system needs to maintain the history of how a data item has changed over time. In other words, instead of saving only one value for data item X, the system maintains multiple values for X known as versions. Every time a transaction is allowed to write to data item X, it creates a new version of X. If X has been written N times, then there are N versions of X in the database. One of the benefits of having multiple versions for every data item is that the MV algorithm does not have to block any read requests. That is because for any read request, say, from Ti, it can find a version of X that has been written by, say, Tj, such that the ts(Tj) < ts(Ti) and Tj is the youngest transaction among all transactions that have written X. Figure 5.17 illustrates this example. For this example, data item X has N versions. Transaction Ti must read the most recent version of X that precedes it chronologically. This is the version of X that was written by the youngest transaction older than Ti, that is, version Xk in the diagram.

In order to maintain consistency, the MV algorithm must reject Ti's request to write X if any younger transaction has read X before Ti makes the request to write it. In this case, Ti is too late—meaning that Ti should have made its write request before the read requests from the younger transactions. Since age is used to enforce serializability, Ti should have written X before a younger transaction had read it. In Figure 5.18, we have outlined the MV algorithm. In this figure, data item X has N versions indicated as x1, x2, ..., xN. This MV algorithm handles timestamping similar to the basic TO algorithm, with one exception. Since the MV algorithm must consider multiple versions of an item, we must also consider multiple timestamps for each data item—there is a read timestamp and a write timestamp associated with each version. In the MV algorithm, each version has a value, a read timestamp (rts), and a write timestamp (wts). In this algorithm, "value(xk)" represents the value of version

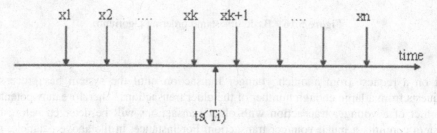

Figure 5.17 Version creation in multiversion concurrency control.

```
Algorithm Multi-Version (Ti and X as Input)
Let xk be a version of X such that wts(xk) is the largest ts <= ts(Ti)
     If "operation of Ti is a read request"
     Then
            Let Ti read xk
            Set rts(xk) to max {ts(Ti), rts(xk)}
     Else "operation of Ti is a write request"
            If ts(Ti) < rts(xk)
            Then
                   Rollback Ti
                   Restart Ti later with a new timestamp
            Else
                   Create a new version of x (say xm)
                   Rts(xm) = ts(Ti)
                   Wts(xm) = ts(Ti)
            End if;
     End if;
End Algorithm Multi-version;
```

Figure 5.18   Multiversion concurrency control algorithm.

xk; "wts(xk)" represents the timestamp of the transaction that has written version xk; and "rts(xk)" represents the read timestamp of the youngest transaction that has read version xk.

5.3.3 Optimistic Concurrency Control Algorithm

Kung and Robinson proposed an alternative to concurrency control [Kung81] that is based on the assumption that, in some systems, the conflict rate is very low and therefore validating every request from every transaction when the request is made is not necessary. If the check for serializability is postponed until just before a transaction commits, they believe it will provide better performance in a low conflict system. It is true that some transactions may have to be aborted, since committing them generates a schedule that is not serializable. But, since we are optimistic, the probability of this happening is very low. There are two approaches to implementing optimistic concurrency control; both locking and timestamping can be utilized by the proposed algorithm. Since the first proposal by Kung and Robinson used timestamping and it was this proposal that is extended for distributed database, we will only discuss the timestamp-based approach. Interested readers are referred to [Kung81] for the details of the locking-based optimistic concurrency control algorithm.

In optimistic concurrency control, a transaction's life cycle is divided into three phases, **execution phase (EP)**, **validation phase (VP)**, and **commit phase (CP)** as outlined below:

- *Execution Phase (EP)*. In this phase, transaction performs its actions and buffers the new values for data items in memory.
- *Validation Phase (VP)*. In this phase, transaction validates itself to assure that committing its changes to the database does not destroy the consistency of the database (i.e., generates serializable schedule).
- *Commit Phase (CP)*. In this phase, transaction writes its changes from memory to the database on disk.

To ensure serializability, this approach, like other concurrency control algorithms, must check for read–write, write–read, and write–write conflicts between transactions. To explain how this approach achieves serializability, let rs(Tj) be the set of data items that transaction Tj reads (the read-set) while ws(Tj) represents the set of data items that Tj writes (the write set). During the execution phase, transaction only reads data items from the database and does not write anything to the database. During the validation phase, serializability is checked and transaction does not read from or write to the database. During the commit phase, transaction only writes to the database.

There are three rules that this algorithm uses to enforce serializability during validation:

- *Rule 1.* For two transactions Ti and Tj, where Ti is reading what Tj is writing, Ti's EP phase cannot overlap with Tj's CP phase. Tj has to start its CP after Ti has finished its EP.
- *Rule 2.* For two transactions Ti and Tj, where Ti is writing what Tj is reading, Ti's CP phase cannot overlap with Tj's EP phase. Tj has to start its EC after Ti has finished its CP.
- *Rule 3.* For two transactions Ti and Tj, where Ti is writing what Tj is writing, Ti's CP phase cannot overlap with Tj's CP phase. Tj has to start its CP after Ti has finished its CP.

Unlike the previous algorithms, this algorithm uses a timestamp that is assigned to a transaction when the transaction is ready to validate. Delaying the assignment of the timestamp until validation time reduces the number of unnecessary rejections. Suppose transaction Tj has completed its EP. Tj can only be committed after it has been validated against all the other transactions currently running in the system. There are three cases that cover all possible conflicts between Tj and other transactions. We use Ti as a representative of other transactions.

These three cases are as follows:

- *Case I.* Tj starts its read phase after Ti has finished its commit phase as seen in Figure 5.19a. It is obvious that, in this case, Ti and Tj are running in series and there are no issues with committing Tj.
- *Case II.* Tj starts its commit phase after Ti completes its commit phase. In this case, as seen in Figure 5.19b, the only potential overlap is between the CP of Ti and the EP of Tj. Therefore, we must make sure that "ws(Ti) intersect rs(Tj) = empty."
- *Case III.* Tj completes its execute phase after Ti completes its execute phase. In this case, as shown in Figure 5.19c, there may be an overlap between the execute and commit phase of Tj with the commit phase of Ti. Therefore, we must make sure that "ws(Ti) intersect (rs(Tj) union ws(Tj)) = empty."

5.3.4 Concurrency Control in a Real DBMS (Oracle)

To discuss how a real DBMS implements concurrency control, we will use Oracle 10 g as an example. The reason for choosing Oracle as opposed to other database management systems is that Oracle is one of the databases that we are mostly using in our university. Oracle uses the multiversion concurrency control approach. Oracle

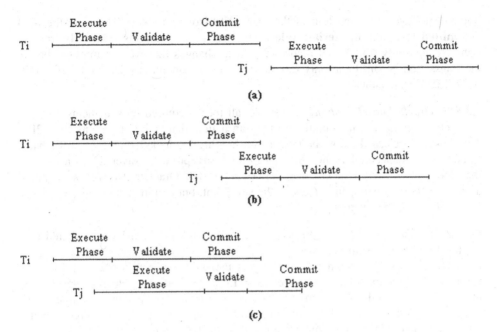

Figure 5.19   Optimistic concurrency control algorithm overlap cases.

achieves this by maintaining multiple values for each data item in the database. Oracle maintains a consistent version of each data item for readers. A reader does not see what another transaction writes, until after the transaction commits. This allows Oracle to provide for read consistency—it guarantees that a user reading the database always sees a consistent view. Oracle returns the value of the data item from the database, if there are no current writers writing the item. Oracle returns the "before value" of a data item to a reader if there is a concurrent writer writing the item. The "before value" is obtained from the database's rollback segment (the log that Oracle maintains to roll transactions back).

As an example, assume User 1 is querying the table at the same time that User 2 is making changes to some of the rows in the table. As User 2's transaction makes changes to the rows, Oracle maintains a "before image" in its rollback segment (the value that was stored in the database before User 2's transaction changed them) for every row being changed. This view provides a consistent view of the database that User 1's query can see regardless of the outcome of User 2's transaction. In Oracle, each transaction is given a **system change number** (SCN). This is a logical timestamp that records the order in which transactions enter the system. Oracle stores the SCN in its log to enable it to undo the work of a transaction if necessary. By using the SCN, Oracle can determine what the consistent view of the database for the readers should look like.

Oracle's approach to concurrency control uses implied locking—users never explicitly need to lock resources (but they can if they want to). The default locking mechanism is row-level locking. Because Oracle maintains multiple versions of rows, read operations are always allowed. In addition to this benefit, read operations do not block write (update) operations. Write operations block other write operations to the same row. Oracle automatically detects and rolls back deadlocks. Oracle's concurrency control implements levels two and four of the four ANSI isolation levels. These are the **read committed** level and the **serializable** level. Oracle also supports **read-only** transactions. A read-only transaction reads only those changes that were committed before the transaction began. Read-only transactions cannot contain any INSERT, UPDATE, or DELETE statements.

5.3.4.1 Oracle Lock Duration

In Oracle, all locks acquired by statements within a transaction are held for the duration of the transaction, that is, it implements strict 2PL. The locks are released when the transaction holding the locks commits or rolls back. In addition, Oracle implements the concept of a **savepoint**. A savepoint is a point in the transaction to which the changes can be rolled back. Oracle releases locks acquired after a savepoint when rolling back to the savepoint, but continues to hold those locks obtained before the savepoint.

5.3.4.2 Oracle Lock Modes

In general, Oracle employs exclusive and shared lock modes. Locks with **exclusive lock mode** (**ELM**) are obtained to modify data. The first transaction to lock a resource exclusively is the only transaction that can alter that resource, until the exclusive lock is released. Locks with **share lock mode** (**SLM**) are used to allow several transactions to acquire share locks on the same resource, at the same time, so they can read the resource. Holding share locks on a resource prevents concurrent access by transactions trying to modify the resource.

5.3.4.3 Oracle Lock Types

From a different viewpoint, Oracle supports three types of locks: **DML locks, DDL locks**, and **system locks**.

The following summarizes these three lock types:

- A DML lock (data lock) is used by any SQL statement that modifies data—such as INSERT, DELETE, UPDATE, and SELECT . . . FOR UPDATE. These statements can acquire row-level locks or table-level locks. A row-level lock acquired for the rows of a table is automatically upgraded to a table-level lock when the number of rows updated by a transaction exceeds a threshold value.

- A DDL lock (also known as a dictionary lock) prevents changes to the underlying tables and views, when the data in these tables and views is being accessed by multiple transactions. Oracle can place exclusive DDL locks or shared DDL locks on its dictionary objects.

- A system lock can be placed on memory contents, buffers, and sort area. Interested readers are referred to the Oracle manuals for more details. System locks include internal locks/latches, parallel cache management locks, and distributed transaction locks.

5.3.4.4 Enforcing Serializability in Oracle

Oracle also utilizes intention locking (see Section 5.3.1.3) combined with row- and table-level DML lock types to enforce serializability as outlined below.

Oracle Row-Level Locks   Row-level locking is the default locking granule for Oracle. There are two flavors of row-level locks:

1. *Shared Row-Level Lock.* This type of lock is acquired by a read-only transaction. A read lock like this never blocks writers (as discussed earlier).

2. *Exclusive Row-Level Lock.* This type of lock is acquired by transactions that execute the INSERT, DELETE, UPDATE, and SELECT ... FOR UPDATE statements. To obtain a row-level lock, a transaction also acquires a table lock for the corresponding table to prevent conflicting DDL operations.

Table-Level Locks   There are five types of table locks in Oracle. These are **row Share (RS)**, **row exclusive (RX)**, **share (S)**, **share row exclusive (SRX)**, and **exclusive (X)** table locks as explained below:

- *Row Share (RS) Table Lock.* This indicates that a transaction is holding shared row locks on rows of the table and intends to update them. A row share table lock is automatically acquired for a table when one of the following SQL statements is executed:

```
SELECT ... FROM table_name ... FOR UPDATE OF ... ;
LOCK TABLE table_name IN ROW SHARE MODE;
```

  A shared row lock allows for most concurrency in an Oracle system. Even when a table is locked in RS mode, other transactions are allowed to query, insert, update, delete, or lock rows concurrently in the table that has the RS lock on it. The only operation that is blocked by a RS lock is "LOCK TABLE table_name IN EXCLUSIVE MODE," which gives the transaction executing the statement exclusive write access to the table named "table_name."

- *Row Exclusive (RX) Table Lock.* This indicates that the transaction holding the lock has made one or more updates to rows in the table. A row exclusive table lock is acquired automatically for a table modified by the following types of statements:

```
INSERT INTO table_name ... ;
UPDATE table_name ... ;
DELETE FROM table_name ... ;
LOCK TABLE table_name IN ROW EXCLUSIVE MODE;
```

  A row exclusive table lock is slightly more restrictive than a row share table lock. Even when a table is locked in RX mode, other transactions are allowed to query, insert, update, delete, or lock rows concurrently in the same table. The belief is that the specific rows being worked on by these different transactions do not usually overlap. If two transactions try to update the same row, for example, one of them has to wait. This type of uncontrolled wait can lead to deadlocks. Oracle employs deadlock detection to deal with deadlocks. When a deadlock is detected, a victim transaction is chosen, rolled back, and restarted by Oracle. A row exclusive table lock held by a transaction prevents other transactions from manually locking the table for exclusive reading or writing. Therefore, other transactions cannot concurrently execute:

```
LOCK TABLE table_name IN SHARE MODE;
LOCK TABLE table_name IN SHARE EXCLUSIVE MODE;
LOCK TABLE table_name IN EXCLUSIVE MODE;
```

- Share (*S*) Table Lock. This is acquired automatically for the table specified in the following statement:

```
LOCK TABLE table_name IN SHARE MODE;
```

A share table lock held by a transaction allows other transactions to execute:

```
SELECT ... FROM table_name ... FOR UPDATE;
LOCK TABLE table_name ... IN SHARE MODE;
```

Multiple transactions can hold share table locks for the same table concurrently, but none of the transactions can update the table. A transaction that has a share table lock can update the table only if no other transactions have a share table lock on the same table.

The following are not allowed on a table that is locked in a shared mode:

```
LOCK TABLE table_name IN SHARE ROW EXCLUSIVE MODE;
LOCK TABLE table_name IN EXCLUSIVE MODE;
LOCK TABLE table_name IN ROW EXCLUSIVE MODE;
```

- *Share Row Exclusive* (SRX) Table Lock. This is more restrictive than a share table lock. A share row exclusive table lock is acquired for a table when a transaction executes:

```
LOCK TABLE table_name IN SHARE ROW EXCLUSIVE MODE;
```

Only one transaction at a time can acquire a share row exclusive table lock on a given table. Other transactions can query or lock specific rows using "SELECT" with the "FOR UPDATE" clause but cannot update the table. A SRX lock on a table prevents other transactions from obtaining row exclusive table locks and modifying the same table. This type of lock prohibits execution of the following statements by other transactions:

```
LOCK TABLE table_name IN SHARE MODE;
LOCK TABLE table_name IN SHARE ROW EXCLUSIVE MODE;
LOCK TABLE table_name IN ROW EXCLUSIVE MODE;
LOCK TABLE table_name IN EXCLUSIVE MODE;
```

- *Exclusive (X) Table Lock*. This is the most restrictive mode of table lock, allowing the transaction that holds the lock to have exclusive write access to the table. An exclusive table lock is acquired for a table as follows:

```
LOCK TABLE table_name IN EXCLUSIVE MODE;
```

Only one transaction can obtain an exclusive table lock for a table. An exclusive table lock permits other transactions only to query the table. An exclusive table lock held by a transaction prohibits other transactions from performing any type of DML statement against the table and also prevents them from placing any type of lock on the table. Figure 5.20 outlines the lock types that Oracle uses for different types of SQL statements.

DML Statement	Mode of Row Locks	Mode of Table Lock
	No Lock	No Lock
SELECT ... FROM table_name ...		
INSERT INTO table_name ...	X	RX
UPDATE table_name ...	X	RX
DELETE FROM table_name ...	X	RX
SELECT ... FROM table_name ... FOR UPDATE OF ...	X	RS
LOCK TABLE table_name IN ...		
ROW SHARE MODE		RS
ROW EXCLUSIVE MODE		RX
SHARE MODE		S
SHARE EXCLUSIVE MODE		SRX
EXCLUSIVE MODE		X

Figure 5.20 Intention locking in Oracle DBMS.

	RS	RX	S	SRX	X
RS	Y	Y	Y	N	N
RX	Y	Y	N	N	N
S	Y	N	Y	N	N
SRX	N	N	N	N	N
X	N	N	N	N	N

Figure 5.21 Oracle lock compatibility matrix.

Oracle Lock Escalation   Oracle automatically converts a table lock of lower restrictiveness to one of higher restrictiveness as appropriate. As an example, assume a transaction issues a "SELECT . . . FOR UPDATE" statement. In this case, the transaction acquires an exclusive row lock and a row share table lock on the table. If this transaction later updates one or more of the locked rows, the row share table lock is automatically converted to a row exclusive table lock by Oracle. As another example, if a transaction holds many row locks on a table, the database will automatically escalate the row locks to a single table lock for the transaction.

Oracle Lock Compatibility Matrix   Figure 5.21 summarizes the lock types and compatibilities that are supported by Oracle 10 g.

Example 5.6   The following cases illustrate some of the row- and table-level lock compatibilities as indicated in Figure 5.21. These cases are run against Oracle's sample database schema called "Scott" (traditionally accessed with the password "tiger"). The Scott schema has two tables—DEPT and EMP—created as follows:

```
create table DEPT (
     DEPTNO NUMBER(2) NOT NULL ,
     DNAME VARCHAR2(14),
     LOC VARCHAR2(13),
PRIMARY KEY (DEPTNO));

create table EMP (
     EMPNO NUMBER(4) NOT NULL,
     ENAME VARCHAR2(10),
     JOB VARCHAR2(9),
     MGR NUMBER(4),
     HIREDATE DATE,
     SAL NUMBER(7,2),
     COMM NUMBER(7,2),
     DEPTNO NUMBER(2),
PRIMARY KEY (EMPNO),
FOREIGN KEY (DEPTNO) REFERENCES DEPT(DEPTNO));
```

To run these cases, we used Oracle's SQL * PLUS tool (a command-based interactive user interface) to set up two concurrent sessions with the server. Each session simulates one transaction. The session on the left represents transaction T1, which is

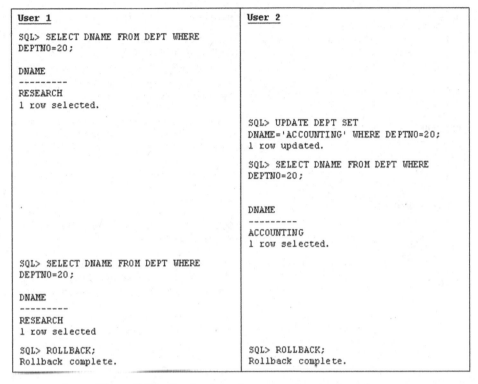

User 1	User 2
SQL> SELECT DNAME FROM DEPT WHERE DEPTNO=20;	
DNAME	

RESEARCH	
1 row selected.	
	SQL> UPDATE DEPT SET DNAME='ACCOUNTING' WHERE DEPTNO=20;
	1 row updated.
	SQL> SELECT DNAME FROM DEPT WHERE DEPTNO=20;
	DNAME

	ACCOUNTING
	1 row selected.
SQL> SELECT DNAME FROM DEPT WHERE DEPTNO=20;	
DNAME	

RESEARCH	
1 row selected	
SQL> ROLLBACK;	SQL> ROLLBACK;
Rollback complete.	Rollback complete.

Figure 5.22 Oracle transactions see only committed data.

running on behalf of User 1, and the session on the right is for transaction T2 running on behalf of User 2. At the end of each case, the transactions are rolled back to restore the database.

Case 1. Figure 5.22 shows how Oracle locking prevents one transaction from reading uncommitted changes of another transaction. In this example, User 1 does not see the changes that User 2 is making to the data item it is reading, until after User 2 commits or aborts.

Case 2. As shown in Figure 5.23, one transaction blocks the other transaction since they both try to update the same row in the EMP table. The waiting transaction (User 2) continues once User 1 aborts/commits.

Case 3. The example shown in Figure 5.24 illustrates how explicit table-level locking works. The example demonstrates that a row share table-level lock is compatible with other row share, row exclusive, and share table locks, but it is not compatible with an exclusive table lock.

Case 4. The example in Figure 5.25 shows that a row exclusive table lock is compatible with another row exclusive or row share table lock, but it is not compatible with share, share row exclusive, or exclusive table locks.

User 1	User 2
SQL> SET TRANSACTION ISOLATION LEVEL READ COMMITTED; Transaction set.	SQL> SET TRANSACTION ISOLATION LEVEL READ COMMITTED; Transaction set.
SQL> SELECT EMPNO, SAL FROM EMP WHERE ENAME='SMITH';	SQL> SELECT EMPNO, SAL FROM EMP WHERE ENAME='SMITH';

```
User 1

SQL> SET TRANSACTION ISOLATION
LEVEL READ COMMITTED;
Transaction set.

SQL> SELECT EMPNO, SAL FROM EMP
WHERE ENAME='SMITH';

EMPNAME        DEPTNO
----------    ----------
7369          800
1 row selected.

SQL> UPDATE EMP SET SAL=SAL+50
WHERE ENAME='SMITH';
1 row updated.

SQL> SELECT EMPNO, SAL FROM EMP
WHERE ENAME='SMITH';

EMPNAME    SAL
----------  ----------
7369       850
1 row selected.

SQL> Rollback;
Rollback complete.
```

```
User 2

SQL> SET TRANSACTION ISOLATION
LEVEL READ COMMITTED;
Transaction set.

SQL> SELECT EMPNO, SAL FROM EMP
WHERE ENAME='SMITH';

EMPNAME        DEPTNO
----------    ----------
7369          800

1 row selected.



SQL> UPDATE EMP SET SAL=SAL+100
WHERE ENAME='SMITH';

This transaction will wait since
T1 is updating the same row and
has not committed the update yet.



1 row updated.

SQL> SELECT EMPNO, SAL FROM EMP
WHERE ENAME='SMITH';

EMPNAME        DEPTNO
----------    ----------
7369          900
1 row selected.
SQL> Rollback;
Rollback complete.
```

Figure 5.23   Writers using "Update" block other writers in Oracle.

Case 5. As depicted in Figure 5.26, this experiment uses share table lock mode and creates a deadlock between T1 and T2. Both transactions lock the table in shared mode. Then, they both try to update the same row. This causes a deadlock since both transactions wait for the lock on the row to be released by the other.

Case 6. This example uses a share row table lock. This scenario (Figure 5.27) is the same as above except that transaction T2 locks the table in shared row mode. This experiment also shows that share table lock and row share table locks are compatible.

5.4   CONCURRENCY CONTROL IN DISTRIBUTED DATABASE SYSTEMS

In this section, we extend the centralized concurrency control algorithms we discussed in Section 5.3 for a distributed database system. Distributed locking, timestamping, and

User 1	User 2
SQL> LOCK TABLE DEPT IN ROW SHARE MODE; Table(s) Locked.	SQL> LOCK TABLE DEPT IN ROW SHARE MODE NOWAIT; Table(s) Locked. SQL> LOCK TABLE DEPT IN ROW EXCLUSIVE MODE NOWAIT; Table(s) Locked. SQL> LOCK TABLE DEPT IN SHARE MODE NOWAIT; Table(s) Locked. SQL> LOCK TABLE DEPT IN SHARE ROW EXCLUSIVE MODE NOWAIT; Table(s) Locked. SQL> LOCK TABLE DEPT IN EXCLUSIVE MODE NOWAIT; ERROR at line 1: ORA-00054: resource busy and acquire with NOWAIT specified
SQL> rollback; Rollback complete.	
	Now that T1 has finished, T2 can lock the table in exclusive mode SQL> LOCK TABLE DEPT IN EXCLUSIVE MODE NOWAIT; Table(s) Locked. SQL> UPDATE DEPT SET LOC='NEW YORK' WHERE DEPTNO=20; 1 row updated.
SQL> SELECT LOC FROM DEPT WHERE DEPTNO=20 FOR UPDATE OF LOC; T1 will wait since T2 has locked the table exclusively.	
LOC ------------- DALLAS SQL> rollback; Rollback complete.	SQL> ROLLBACK; Rollback complete.

Figure 5.24 Writers using explicit locking block other writers in Oracle.

optimistic concurrency control algorithms are discussed. As discussed before, when extending an algorithm that is designed to work on a centralized system, we have to consider the issue of control. In a centralized system, there is only one site and that site is the center of control. This is the site where transactions enter the system and where the concurrency control module of the DBMS resides. In a distributed system, on the other hand, the control may reside at a site different from the site where a transaction enters the system. The control may be centralized, residing at only one site, or distributed—where multiple sites cooperate to control execution of transactions.

User 1	User 2
SQL> LOCK TABLE DEPT IN ROW EXCLUSIVE MODE NOWAIT; Table(s) Locked.	
	SQL> LOCK TABLE DEPT IN ROW SHARE MODE NOWAIT; Table(s) Locked.
	SQL> LOCK TABLE DEPT IN ROW EXCLUSIVE MODE NOWAIT; Table(s) Locked.
	SQL> LOCK TABLE DEPT IN SHARE MODE NOWAIT;
	ORA-00054: resource busy and acquire with NOWAIT specified
	SQL> LOCK TABLE DEPT IN SHARE ROW EXCLUSIVE MODE NOWAIT;
	ORA-00054: resource busy and acquire with NOWAIT specified
	SQL> LOCK TABLE DEPT IN EXCLUSIVE MODE NOWAIT;
	ORA-00054: resource busy and acquire with NOWAIT specified
	UPDATE DEPT SET LOC='NEW YORK' WHERE DEPTNO=20; 1 row updated.
SQL> SELECT LOC FROM DEPT WHERE DEPTNO=20 FOR UPDATE OF LOC; This transaction will wait.	
LOC -------------- DALLAS	SQL> rollback; Rollback complete.
SQL> rollback; Rollback complete.	

Figure 5.25 Writers using RX locks block other writers in Oracle.

Before discussing the extensions made to the algorithms we introduced in Section 5.3, we need to generalize the serializability requirements for a distributed DBE. Serializability in a centralized DBE stated that all partial commitment orders (PCOs) imposed by the conflicts between operations in concurrent transactions have to be compatible. As such, if we have the precedence "Ti → Tj" for the commitment order of Ti and Tj, as a result of one conflict, we need to have the same order requirement for all the conflicts between these two transactions. In a distributed system, each transaction may run on multiple sites. As a result, we have to address local serializability as well as global serializability issues. We showed in Section 5.3 that local schedules for concurrent transactions running at any site must

User 1	User 2
SQL> LOCK TABLE DEPT IN SHARE MODE; Table(s) Locked.	
	SQL> LOCK TABLE DEPT IN SHARE MODE NOWAIT; Table(s) Locked. SQL> UPDATE DEPT SET LOC='NEW YORK' WHERE DEPTNO=20; T2 will wait since it needs exclusive lock on this row and with Shared lock mode by T1 it cannot get it.
SQL> SELECT LOC FROM DEPT WHERE DEPTNO=20 FOR UPDATE OF LOC; T1 will wait as well. This causes a deadlock between t1 and T2. LOC ------------- DALLAS SQL> Rollback; Rollback complete.	ORA-00060: deadlock detected while waiting for resource SQL> Rollback; Rollback complete.

Figure 5.26   Deadlocks in Oracle.

User 1	User 2
SQL> LOCK TABLE DEPT IN SHARE MODE; Table(s) Locked.	
	SQL> LOCK TABLE DEPT IN ROW SHARE MODE NOWAIT; Table(s) Locked. SQL> UPDATE DEPT SET LOC='NEW YORK' WHERE DEPTNO=20; T2 will wait.
SQL> SELECT LOC FROM DEPT WHERE DEPTNO=20 FOR UPDATE OF LOC; LOC ------------- DALLAS	
SQL> Rollback; Rollback complete.	1 row updated.
	SQL> rollback; Rollback complete.

Figure 5.27   Row share table lock with the intent to exclusive access.

be serializable. But, what does it mean to have global serializability? We will use Example 5.7 to explain the issues with global serializability.

Example 5.7   Let's look at the issues from a different angle. Suppose, in a two-site system, data item X is stored at Site 1 and data item Y is stored at Site 2. Assume that transaction T1 enters Site 1 at the same time that T2 enters Site 2, and these transactions are defined as follows:

```
T1: R1(X), W1(Y)
T2: R2(Y), W2(X)
```

Obviously, these are two global transactions—each of them must perform work at both Site 1 and Site 2. T1 must first read X at Site 1 and then write Y at Site 2. Meanwhile, T2 must read Y at Site 2 and then write X at Site 1. There are two local schedules that will be formed as a result of running these global transactions. Schedule "R1(X), W2(X)" is formed at Site 1, while schedule "R2(Y), W1(Y)" is formed at Site 2 if these two transactions enter the system at roughly the same time. It should be obvious that both local schedules are serializable. At Site 1, we have a serializable schedule indicating "T1 → T2," while at Site 2, we have a serializable schedule indicating "T2 → T1." Now, we must determine whether or not the schedule is globally serializable.

Before addressing the global serializability issue across these two transactions, let's assume the same two transactions run in a centralized system consisting of data items X and Y stored at one server. In the centralized system, the following six schedules are possible:

```
LS1 = R1(X), W1(Y), R2(Y), W2(X), schedule serializable to
T1 → T2
LS2 = R2(Y), W2(X), R1(X), W1(Y), schedule serializable to
T2 → T1
LS3 = R1(X), R2(Y), W1(Y), W2(X), schedule is not serializable
LS4 = R1(X), R2(Y), W2(X), W1(Y), schedule is not serializable
LS5 = R2(Y), R1(X), W1(Y), W2(X), schedule is not serializable
LS6 = R2(Y), R1(X), W2(X), W1(Y), schedule is not serializable
```

Among these schedules, only S1 and S2 are serializable and the other four are not. That is because the following holds for these schedules:

- In LS1, "R1(X), W2(X)" requires "T1 → T2" and "W1(Y), R2(Y)" requires "T1 → T2," resulting in the total serialization order of "T1 → T2."
- In LS2, "R2(Y), W1(Y)" requires "T2 → T1" and "W2(X), R1(X)" requires "T2 → T1," resulting in the total serialization order of "T1 → T2."
- In LS3, "R1(X), W2(X)" requires "T1 → T2" and "R2(Y), W1(Y)" requires "T2 → T1," which cannot be satisfied together.
- In LS4, "R1(X), W2(X)" requires "T1 → T2" and "R2(Y), W1(Y)" requires "T2 → T1," which cannot be satisfied together.
- In LS5, "R2(Y), W1(Y)" requires "T2 → T1" and "R1(X), W2(X)" requires "T1 → T2," which cannot be satisfied together.
- In LS6, "R2(Y), W1(Y)" requires "T2 → T1" and "R1(X), W2(X)" requires "T1 → T2," which cannot be satisfied together.

In the distributed system discussed above, the order in which the operations of these two transactions are performed globally is not clear. That is because there is no global clock in the system and the local clocks might not be synchronized. So, we do not know the real execution order for these operations. As an example, assume there are two copies of data item X, with each site storing one copy. Let's suppose that T1 issues the "W1(X)" operation at Site 1 when the clock at Site 1 shows "10:00." Suppose T2 issues the "W2(X)" operation at Site 2 when the local clock at Site 2 indicates "10:02." The question is: Do we really know that "W1(X)" happened before "W2(X)"? If the two clocks are synchronized, then obviously "W1(X)" starts before "W2(X)" in real time. If the two clocks are not synchronized with a global clock, there is no way to know the order of these operations. A commitment order of "T1 → T2" or "T2 → T1" may be the case. As a direct result of this, we cannot rely on global ordering of operations across sites for global serializability. We have to devise a mechanism by which we can definitely determine if a global schedule is serializable. Fortunately, the solution to the problem is not as difficult as it sounds. The point that we must keep in mind is that, from a global perspective, it is not that important to know the absolute order of scheduling for conflicting operations from different transactions across sites. Instead, it is more important to know the relative order of scheduling conflicting operations across transactions within each site.

In order to arrive at the solution, we need to introduce a new notation that allows us to incorporate site information with the data items our transactions are using. We use the notation "Oi(X@j)" to indicate that Ti performs operation "O" on data item "X" at Site "j." For example, "R1(X@1), W2(X@1)" indicates a part of the schedule where transaction T1 performs a read of X at Site 1 and then T2 performs a write on X at the same site. Obviously, these two operations are conflicting and both are happening at Site 1. The local concurrency control at Site 1 will detect this conflict and will require "T1 → T2" at this site. In this notation, data item "X@1" is not considered the same data item as "X@2." In fact, X@1 and X@2 are two different copies of X and are stored at two different sites. Applying this concept to distributed systems, the global schedule "W2(X@1), W3(X@1), W3(X@2), W2(X@2)" contains two local conflicts. The first conflict is "W2(X@1), W3(X@1)," indicating that T2 must commit before T3 at Site 1 and the second conflict is "W3(X@2), W2(X@2)," which requires T3 to commit before T2 at Site 2. Note that the two operations "W2(X@1), W3(X@2)" and "W3(X@1), W2(X@2)" are not considered conflicts since the items are different (they are stored at different sites.)

Now let's revisit the distributed situation we considered in Example 5.7. In this example, X is stored at Site 1 and Y is stored at Site 2. We apply the site information to the schedules that we formed earlier. Again, it is not clear which of the six possible schedules is formed globally but, as we will explain later, that is not important. We have called these schedules GS1, GS2, ..., GS6 as shown below:

```
GS1 = R1(X@1), W1(Y@2), R2(Y@2), W2(X@1)
GS2 = R2(Y@2), W2(X@1), R1(X@1), W1(Y@2)
GS3 = R1(X@1), R2(Y@2), W1(Y@2), W2(X@1)
GS4 = R1(X@1), R2(Y@2), W2(X@1), W1(Y@2)
GS5 = R2(Y@2), R1(X@1), W1(Y@2), W2(X@1)
GS6 = R2(Y@2), R1(X@1), W2(X@1), W1(Y@2)
```

Globally, if these schedules are serializable they must be equivalent to some serial schedule. The check for serializability for these global schedules is the same as the check for serializability in a centralized system. We have to identify all conflicts in the schedule and make sure that the total commitment order graph is acyclic. Applying this check to the above schedules, we conclude that, among these six schedules, only GS1 and GS2 are serializable. That is because, in GS1, we have the PCO requirement that "T1 → T2" (for conflict on X@1) and "T1 → T2" (for conflict on Y@2). In GS2, we have the requirement that "T2 →T1." What is different between GS1, GS2, and the other four schedules that are not serializable is that, in GS1 and GS2, the commitment order of T1 and T2 at Site 1 and Site 2 are compatible, but that is not the case for the other four schedules.

From the above observation, we conclude that in order for a set of transactions in a distributed DBE to be serializable, the following two requirements must be satisfied:

1. All local schedules must be serializable.
2. If two transactions conflict at more than one site, their PCO requirements at all sites where they meet must be compatible for all their conflicts.

In this example, we assumed schedules "S1 = R1(X), W2(X)" and "S2 = R2(Y), W1(Y)." Using our rules for global serializability, we conclude that, since at Site 1 we have the requirement "T1 → T2" and at Site 2 the requirement "T2 → T1," the global schedule is not serializable.

The above-mentioned requirements work for distributed systems with or without replication. Example 5.7 provided the case in which the data items were not replicated. In Example 5.8, we will use a replicated database. Before discussing this example, we need to briefly discuss what replication is. In replicated databases, we have multiple copies of each replicated data item and store different copies of the same data item at different sites. Having more than one copy of the data allows us to have more availability and more resiliency. We will discuss more details of replication in Chapter 7. As we will see, in order for replication to work, a replicated data item must have the same value for all its copies. This requirement allows us to read from any copy. To satisfy this requirement, any update of replicated data item X must be propagated to all replicas. In other words, if transaction Ti wants to update X, it must do so by updating all copies of X. This is achieved by modifying transaction Ti to explicitly include the updates for all copies of X as if they were different data items. In general, data item X may have N copies. We use X1, X2, ..., XN to refer to these copies. Suppose transaction Ti wants to write a value to data item X. To make sure all copies of X show the same value after the change, we rewrite transaction Ti to include operations updating all the copies: in other words, we substitute "Wi(X1), Wi(X2), ..., Wi(XN)" for "Wi(X)."

Example 5.8   In this example, we use the same two transactions we did in Example 1, but for a three-site system. For this example, data item X is replicated and stored at Sites 1 and 2. Data item Y, on the other hand, is not replicated, but it is stored at Site 3. As assumed in Example 5.7, transaction T1 enters Site 1 at the same time that T2 enters Site 2. Since X is replicated at Site 1 and Site 2, transaction T2 has to be changed to include the operations that write to both copies. Using the site inclusion notation we introduced in Example 5.7, we can rewrite transactions T1 and T2 as follows:

```
T1: R1(X@1), W1(Y@3)
T2: R2(Y@3), W2(X@1), W2(X@2)
```

Since Y is stored at Site 3 and X is stored at Site 1 and Site 2, we have schedules "S1 = R1(X@1), W2(X@1)," "S2 = W2(X@2)," and "S3 = R2(Y@3), W1(Y@3)." Using our rules for global serializability, we conclude that, since at Site 1 we have the requirement "T1 → T2" and at Site 3 the requirement "T2 → T1," the global schedule is not serializable.

Distributed 2PL, timestamping, and optimistic concurrency control algorithms can be used to make sure that the above two rules are enforced. The difference between these algorithms is in the way they enforce these two requirements.

5.4.1 Two-Phase Locking in Distributed Systems

Implementing 2PL for a centralized system is straightforward. Because a centralized system contains only one site, the lock manager sees all transactions and can control lock acquisition requests from all transaction monitors (TMs). In a distributed system, that is not the case. A transaction may enter the system at Site 1, but request a lock from Site 5. At the same time, a conflicting transaction may enter the system at Site 2 and request a lock from Site 4. If there isn't any coordination between the lock managers at Sites 4 and 5, the conflict will not be detected, which may result in an inconsistent database.

To deal with distribution issues, a common requirement for all alternatives for implementing 2PL in a distributed system is that the lock conflicts must be seen by at least one site. In the centralized implementation, the central lock manager sees all lock requests from all sites and enforces 2PL principles. In the distributed implementation, the conflict must be detected by at least one site but may be detected by more than one site. In a distributed system, when the control of 2PL is given to one site, the algorithm is called centralized 2PL. Alsberg and Day first proposed the centralized 2PL in 1976 [Alsberg76]. When the control is shared by multiple sites, the algorithm is called primary copy 2PL and, finally, when the lock responsibility is given to all sites, the algorithm is called distributed 2PL.

5.4.1.1 Centralized 2PL   **Centralized 2PL** is an implementation of the two-phase locking approach in a distributed system where one site is designated as the **central lock manager (CLM)**. All the sites in the environment know where the CLM is. Each site is directed to obtain locks, according to 2PL rules, from the CLM. To request a lock, a TM sends a lock request to the CLM instead of its local lock manager. If the data item to be locked is available, the CLM locks the item on behalf of the transaction and sends a "lock granted" message to the requesting TM, thereby granting the lock. If the data item cannot be locked, because it is locked by one or more conflicting transactions, the lock is not granted and the transaction is added to the list of transactions that are waiting for this item.

Upon receiving a "lock granted" message, the requesting TM can continue to run. Note that the data item that is locked on behalf of the transaction may be local to the site where the transaction is or it may be located elsewhere. It is the responsibility of the TM to access the data item wherever it is. If the data item is replicated, then the requesting TM will decide which copy to read. In this case, the requesting TM also makes sure that a write operation is applied to all copies. Once a transaction is done, a TM notifies the CLM that a data item lock is no longer needed by sending a "lock release" message to the CLM. Upon receipt of a "lock release" message, the CLM releases the data item and grants the lock to the transaction in front of the wait queue for the item. If this "lock release" is the first one from a particular TM, the CLM also makes a note that the corresponding TM has entered the second phase of 2PL. This is done to ensure that the TM does not misbehave—that it does not ask for more locks after this point.

Example 5.9   Figure 5.28 depicts an example of a centralized 2PL implementation for a four-site system. In this example, transaction "T1 = R(X), R(Y), W(Y)" enters the system at Site 1. Data item X is stored at Site 2 and data item Y is stored at Site 4. The central lock manager (CLM) runs at Site 3. As seen from this figure, all lock requests are sent to Site 3 by Site 1's TM. The transaction accesses X and Y at Sites 2 and 4 only after the lock manager has granted it the necessary locks. Once T1 is done, the TM releases its locks by informing the CLM at Site 3. The main issue with centralized 2PL is reliability of the CLM. The site where the CLM runs may become overloaded by all the lock request/release messages. Furthermore, if the CLM fails, it will cause an overall system failure. To overcome these issues, we can use either the **primary copy 2PL** or the **distributed 2PL** approaches.

5.4.1.2 *Primary Copy 2PL*

This alternative for implementing 2PL was first proposed by Stonebreaker [Stonebreaker77]. In this alternative, a number of sites are designated as control centers. Each one of these sites has the responsibility of managing a number of locks. For example, one site may have the responsibility of locking rows in the EMP table, while another site manages the locks for rows in the DEPT table. Obviously, how EMP and DEPT are distributed and/or replicated is known by all sites—each site knows which site controls EMP and which site controls DEPT. As such, when a TM needs to lock EMP, it directs its lock requests to the primary site responsible for locking EMP and does the same for DEPT when it needs to lock it. Beyond this difference in the distribution of control, the primary copy 2PL is basically the same as centralized 2PL implementation. Similar to the centralized 2PL implementation, if there are multiple copies of the EMP and DEPT tables, the requesting TM decides which copy to read and makes sure that all copies are written to in the case of any write operations.

5.4.1.3 *Distributed 2PL*

Variations of this approach have been implemented in IBM's system R* by Mohan [Mohan86] and Tandem's Nonstop SQL engine [Tandem87] [Tandem88]. Distributed 2PL requires each lock manager (LM) to manage the data items stored at its local site. Where the lock manager resides depends on the data distribution and/or replication.

There are three alternatives:

- At one end of the spectrum, the distributed database maintains no replicated data items. In this case the site where the only copy of the data item resides acts as the lock manager for the item.

Site 1		Site 2		Site 3		Site 4
		Data Item X		CLM		Data Item Y
T1: R(X), R(Y), W(Y)						
Read Lock(X) to Site 3	→					
				Read Lock(X) from Site 1		
			←	Read Lock (X) Granted to Site 1		
Read Lock (X) Granted						
R(X) to Site 2	→					
		R(X) from Site 1				
	←	Value of X to Site 1				
Value of X from Site 2						
Write Lock (Y) to Site 3	→					
				Write Lock (Y) from Site 1		
			←	Write Lock (Y) Granted to Site 1		
Write Lock(Y) Granted						
W(Y) to Site 4	→					
						W(Y) from Site 1
					←	Done to Site 1
Done from Site 4						
Unlock (X and Y) to Site 3	→					
				Unlock (X and Y) from Site 1		
			←	Locks Released to Site 1		
Lock released from Site 3						
Start 2PH commit						

Figure 5.28   Example of centralized 2PL implementation.

- At the other end of the spectrum, all data items are replicated. In this case, one of the sites is chosen as the lock manager for each data item. If the responsibility of managing the locks for all items is given to one site, the approach reduces to the centralized 2PL implementation.

- Finally, some of the data items in the system may be replicated while the others are not. For the data items that are not replicated, the site where the data item resides acts as the lock manager for that item. For the replicated data items, one site is chosen as the lock manager for each item. It is the responsibility of the TM to acquire the lock from each data item's lock manager. The TM is also responsible for ensuring any updates to a data item are reflected in all the sites where that data item resides.

Once the LM for each item is chosen, the approach for enforcing the distributed concurrency control is the same for all three of the distribution alternatives mentioned above.

Example 5.10 This example uses a distributed 2PL for nonreplicated distributed database. Assume Site K's lock manager locks data item X for Ti before Tj requests to lock X. In this case, Tj must wait for Ti to release X at Site K. Because of this wait, if both Ti and Tj commit, Ti commits before Tj commits at Site K. If Ti and Tj conflict on another item, say, Y at Site L, then two scenarios are possible. In the first scenario, Ti locks Y before Tj at Site L, causing Ti to commit before Tj at Site L as well. These two local PCOs are consistent across Sites K and L. There is no issue with global serializability between Ti and Tj as long as Ti locks data items it needs before Tj locks them at any site. The global serialization order for Ti and Tj is "Ti→ Tj." In the second scenario, Tj locks a data item before Ti gets to it, thereby forcing Ti to wait for Tj. Because of this wait, the system will be in a distributed deadlock (see distributed deadlock detection in Chapter 6). The direct result of this second scenario is a nonserializable schedule across the two sites. Example 5.10 also points out that, similar to the case in centralized systems, a 2PL implementation in a distributed system results in serializable schedules, but can cause deadlocks.

Figure 5.29 shows an example implementing distributed 2PL in a four-site system. In this case, transactions T1 and T2 will create a distributed deadlock. A distributed deadlock is a deadlock that involves more than one site. For this example, each local site controlling a given item is responsible for handling the lock requests for that item. Site 2 is the lock manager for X while Site 3 manages the lock requests for data item Y. Note that at Sites 2 and 3, the local schedules are serializable. However, at Site 2 the serialization order is "T1 → T2," while at Site 3 the order is "T2 → T1." These two serializable orders are not compatible globally and create the deadlock.

5.4.2 Distributed Timestamp Concurrency Control

The basic concept of timestamp concurrency control algorithms in centralized systems can easily be extended to a distributed database. Since both the basic and conservative TO algorithms (discussed earlier in this chapter) rely on timestamps for resolving conflicts, it is important that timestamps be a good representative of the relative age of each transaction. In a centralized system, the physical clock reading is used as the timestamp. The physical clock obviously produces a true indication of each transaction's age—the smaller the timestamp the older the transaction is. As mentioned earlier, we do not actually have to use the physical clock reading of the local system as the timestamp. We can use a logical clock (LC) that is incremented for each event in the system as the transaction timestamp, since it provides for the same relative ordering for a transaction's age.

In a distributed system, on the other hand, we cannot use any local physical clock readings or any site's logical clock readings as our global timestamps, since they are not globally unique. An indication of the site ID (which is globally unique) needs to be included in the timestamp of a transaction. The issue with using a site's physical clocks is called "drifting"—when two or more clocks show numbers that are different from each other. To see the impact of clock drifting on the TO algorithms, consider two sites, S1 and S2, that generate the same number of transactions during a period of time. If the clocks at these two sites are relatively close, then the ages of transactions at these sites are also relatively close. But, if the clock at S1 is much faster than the

Site 1		Site 2		Site 3		Site 4
		Data Item X; LM (X)		Data Item Y; LM(Y)		
T1: R(X), R(Y), W(Y)						
Read Lock(X) to Site 2	→					
		Read Lock(X) from Site 1				
		← Read Lock (X) Granted to Site 1				
Read Lock(X) Granted						
R(X) to Site 2	→					
		R(X) from Site 1				
		← Value of X to Site 1				
Value of X from Site 2						T2: W(Y), R(X), W(X)
					←	Write Lock(Y) to Site 3
				Write Lock (Y) from Site 4		
				Write Lock (Y) Granted to Site 4	→	
						Write Lock(Y) Granted
					←	W(Y) to Site 3
				W(Y) from Site 4		
				Done writing(Y) to Site 4	→	
						Done Writing(Y) from Site 3
Write Lock(Y) to Site 3	→					
				Write Lock(Y) from Site 1		
				T1 waits for T2		
						Write Lock(X) to Site 2
					←	
		Write Lock(X) from Site 4				
		T2 waits for T1				
		System is globally deadlocked				

Figure 5.29   Example of primary 2PL implementation with a deadlock.

clock at S2, after a period of time, transactions generated at S1 are going to be much younger than the transactions generated at S2. This will cause S1's transactions to be given a lower priority when they conflict with S2's transactions. To solve this problem, we can either use a system clock with which all sites synchronize their local clocks or we can periodically synchronize all the sites' clocks with each other. Using either approach will require a large number of messages. Because of this problem, we can use the logical clock readings at each site as part of the global timestamps.

When using logical clock (LC) readings drifting can still occur. In this case, sites that generate more transactions have larger LC readings. This again will negatively impact the site's transactions when conflicts occur. Let's assume site S1 generates a lot more transactions than site S2 does within a given period of time. If at time t1 the LCs at sites S1 and S2 are both set to 5, it is possible that, at time t2, S1's clock might be 50 while S2's clock might only be 20. From this point on, transactions at S1 will get lower priority than the ones at S2. To resolve this issue, we need to synchronize the logical clocks at S1 and S2. Note that it is only important to achieve clock synchronization if transactions at S1 and S2 conflict. If they do, the TMs at these sites will have to communicate with each other. We can use the messages that are sent from one site to the other for synchronization. When one site communicates with another site, it can piggyback its LC reading on the message. The receiving site then examines the LC reading received and compares it to its own. If its clock is slower than the clock at the other site, then it will advance its clock accordingly. Sites do not decrement their LCs since this would cause duplicate clock readings. This idea can be implemented with a simple comparison:

```
LC at local site = Max(Local LC, LC received with the message)
```

In the above example, when S2 sends a message to S1, no adjustment is made. On the other hand, when S1 sends a message to S2, site S2's clock will be advanced to 50. Implementing the basic TO algorithm in a distributed database is not cost effective due to the substantial number of messages required to enforce the read, pre-write, and commit phases of the algorithm.

Implementation of the conservative TO algorithm proposed by Herman and Verjus [Herman79] in a distributed system is straightforward. The basic idea is to maintain a queue for each TM in the system at each site. For example, for a system with five sites and five TMs, each site's scheduler will maintain five queues, one for each TM. Each TM sends the lock request to each site's scheduler. The receiving scheduler puts the requests in that site's queue, in increasing timestamp order (oldest first). It should be obvious that the queues for a given TM have the operations in the same order at all sites. Requests are then processed from the front of the queues in the order of their age—the oldest first. Although this approach reduces the number of restarts, it does not completely eliminate them. Suppose when processing operations from the front of queues at Site 5, the scheduler finds the queue for Site 3 empty. This indicates a lack of requests from Site 3. It is possible that Site 3 has transactions that are older than the ones in the other queues—processing the requests from younger transactions in the queues for Sites 1, 2, and 4 invalidates all such older transactions initiated at Site 3, resulting in restarts for those transactions.

One way to get around this problem is to force the schedulers to process the queues only when there is at least one request in every queue. There are two issues with this approach. First, this very conservative TO approach forces the system to execute transactions sequentially. Second, the queues for sites that do not have any transaction waiting to be processed will be empty. A site with an empty queue cannot process transactions in the other queues until a request from the corresponding site arrives. To circumvent this problem, we can require each site that does not have any transaction waiting to be processed to send a dummy request periodically in order ensure that it does not delay the processing of transactions from other sites.

Note that using timestamps to order the commitment of transactions according to their age has an advantage over locking—in TO algorithms, local sites will only allow schedules that are age-sensitive (older transactions commit before younger transactions). For example, assume transaction T4 commits before T6 at Site 5. If T4 and T6 also run at Site 7, the local scheduler at Site 7 only allows T4 to commit if it commits before T6, and not the other way around. Consequently, the second requirement we explained in Section 5.4 is automatically enforced by the local schedulers.

5.4.2.1 Conflict Graphs and Transaction Classes   SDD-1, a system for distributed databases that was developed at the Computer Corporation of America, uses the conservative distributed timestamp algorithm with some modifications [Bernstein80a]. The following provides an overview of SDD-1's concurrency control implementation. SDD-1 recognizes different classes of transactions and levels of conflict. Each class contains one set of data items as its read set (RS) and another set of data items as its write set (WS). As we discussed before, two transactions are in conflict if one writes a data item that the other reads or writes. This concept is extended to the definition of conflicts between two transaction classes, TCi and TCj. Two transaction classes are in conflict if one of the following is true:

```
WS(TCi) ∩ (WS(TCj) U RS(TCj)) ≠ Ø
WS(TCj) ∩ (WS(TCi) U RS(TCi)) ≠ Ø
```

A given transaction belongs to a particular class if all of the data items in the transaction's read set are contained within the class' read set and all of the data items in the transaction's write set are contained within the class' write set. In other words, Ti belongs to transaction class TCj if and only if

```
RS(Ti) is a subset of  RS(TCj), and
WS(Ti) is a subset of WS(TCj)
```

Each transaction issues its read requests for the data items contained within its read set during its read phase. Each transaction issues its write requests during the second phase, which is called the write phase. Based on the data items currently being read and written, we create a **conflict graph** for the classes to which the active transactions belong. A conflict graph is a nondirected graph that has a set of vertical, horizontal, and diagonal edges. A vertical edge connects two nodes within a class and indicates a conflict between two transactions within the class. A horizontal edge connects two nodes across two classes and indicates a write–write conflict across different classes. A diagonal edge connects two nodes within two different classes and indicates a write–read or a read–write conflict across two classes. The following is an example that shows how a conflict graph is created. Assume the following read sets and write sets for transactions T1, T2, and T3:

```
T1: (RS1) = {a} and (WS1) = {b}
T2: (RS2) = {c} and (WS2) = {d}
T3: (RS3) = {e} and (WS3) = {a, b}
```

Also, assume that transactions T1, T2, and T3 belong to transaction classes TC1, TC2, and TC3, respectively, and that Figure 5.30 shows the conflict graph for these transactions.

Analysis of the conflict graph determines if two transactions within the same class or across two different classes can be run parallel to each other. In the above example, transactions T1 and T3 cannot run in parallel since their classes are connected (both diagonally and horizontally) in the conflict graph. This means that they have both a write–write conflict and a read–write conflict. On the other hand, transaction T2 can run in parallel to T1 and T3 since there are no edges between TC2 and TC1 and no

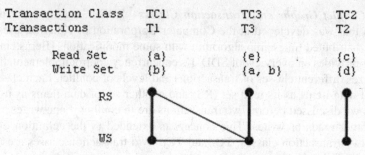

Transaction Class	TC1	TC3	TC2
Transactions	T1	T3	T2
Read Set	{a}	{e}	{c}
Write Set	{b}	{a, b}	{d}

Figure 5.30   A conflict graph example for SDD-1.

edges between TC3 and TC2. By knowing to which class a transaction belongs, the scheduler at a given site knows whether the transaction can be safely processed or not. Within a class, conflicting transactions are processed in order, according to their timestamps. Across classes, transactions only conflict with each other if the classes they belong to conflict. This allows SDD-1 to statically define classes that can run in parallel and to statically define classes whose transaction-execution needs to be controlled.

In SDD-1, if a transaction needs to read or write data items at a remote site, it does not start a child process there—instead it issues a remote read or remote write request. The implementation assumes that remote requests arrive at their destination in the order of their timestamp as well. To guarantee this, a younger transaction at a given site (Site K) that wants to issue a remote read or write request to some other site (Site L) must wait until all older transactions at Site K have issued their reads and writes to Site L. This requirement further restricts concurrency among distributed transactions.

Each site maintains two queues (a read queue and a write queue) for each site in the system. Assuming that there are N sites in the system, each site will have 2 * N queues, out of which, two queues are set aside for the local operations from the local transactions. In order to handle read–write conflicts, special processing must be performed when the next read request is taken from the front of a read queue at a given site. In particular, we must examine all the write requests that are at the front of all write queues at this site. If any of these write operations are for an older transaction than the read request we are processing, we must delay the read. If all these write operations are for younger transactions, we may proceed with the read operation. Otherwise, the read is delayed. To take care of write–write conflicts, a write request at front of a write queue at a given site is processed only when all write requests at the front of all write queues at this site are from younger transactions. Otherwise, the write is delayed. To deal with a read–write conflict, similar checks are necessary when a read request in the front of a queue at a site is processed. A careful reader observes that this distributed implementation serializes the transactions based on their age and therefore reduces the amount of parallelism across transactions from different sites.

5.4.3 Distributed Optimistic Concurrency Control

In Section 5.3.3, we discussed the optimistic concurrency control for a centralized system. This section discusses the extensions that need to be made to the centralized optimistic concurrency control in order to use it in a distributed system.

To extend the optimistic concurrency control algorithm to a distributed implementation, two rules must be applied:

- The first rule applies to validating transactions locally. Transaction Ti must be locally validated at all the sites where it runs. The local optimistic concurrency control algorithm outlined in Section 5.3.3 is used to apply this rule. If Ti is invalid at one or more sites, then it is aborted. Local validation guarantees that Ti is part of a serializable schedule at the sites where it has been run. After Ti has been validated at all the sites where it has run, then it needs to be globally validated.
- The second rule applies to validating transactions globally. When two conflicting transactions run together at more than one site, the global validation requires that these two transactions commit in the same relative order at all the sites they run together. Suppose transactions Ti and Tj run at two sites (Site 1 and Site 2). Ti can globally validate if and only if the relative commit order of Ti and Tj is the same at both Site 1 and Site 2. Otherwise, Ti cannot validate. To apply this rule, Ti's commitment at a site is delayed until all conflicting transactions that precede Ti in the serialization order are committed or aborted. Note that this requirement makes the algorithm pessimistic since Ti cannot commit as soon as it is validated at a site.

One way to implement optimistic concurrency control is to require that all local schedulers maintain a total commitment order for all local transactions. These schedulers are required to send their total commitment order graphs to the responsible global TM when they validate a transaction locally. The global TM receiving all such graphs will only commit the transaction globally if the order of committing the transaction in all local graphs is compatible. Otherwise, the global TM aborts the transaction.

5.4.4   Federated/Multidatabase Concurrency Control

The concurrency control methods we have discussed in this chapter apply only to centralized databases or homogeneous distributed databases. There are other kinds of distributed database systems, however. In particular, a different class of distributed database systems known as federated or multidatabase (see Chapter 12) also exists—its databases are heterogeneous. For this class of distributed database systems, implementing the concurrency control algorithms that we discussed in this chapter is not practical for various reasons. The first and foremost issue is that federated and multidatabase systems integrate both relational and nonrelational (e.g., flat file based) systems, and these systems do not always expose their transaction management functions (Transaction_Begin, Transaction_End, Commit, Abort, Lock, Unlock, etc.). As a result, implementation of the concurrency control algorithms mentioned above is not possible. Even for newer relational systems, where the distributed database software has access to the transaction management functions, implementing 2PL negatively affects the sites' autonomy and performance. We will look at some of these issues in more detail in Chapter 12, and discuss the changes that are necessary to address concurrency control algorithms for federated and multidatabase systems.

5.5 SUMMARY

In this chapter, we discussed approaches to concurrency control in centralized and distributed DBEs. The main focus of our discussion was maintaining the atomicity property of transactions. We pointed out that atomicity was maintained by providing the illusion that transactions were running alone in the system. We argued that in order for the concurrency control to provide such an illusion, every transaction's changes needed to be isolated from the other transactions, until such a time as the transaction decided to commit or abort.

Since the focus of our discussion was OLTP systems, we introduced transaction concepts first. The ACID properties for transactions were defined and studied. We categorized two main approaches to concurrency control: pessimistic and optimistic concurrency control. Serializability was identified as the basis for preserving the consistency of a database in a centralized or distributed DBE. Issues regarding the conflicting operations from different transactions and their impact on the schedule that a DBE generates were discussed. We also discussed how locking and/or timestamping can be used to handle concurrent access to the database and to generate a serializable schedule. We identified deadlocks as a potential problem for locking-based approaches, but the discussion of deadlocks was delayed until Chapter 6. We discussed how locking and timestamping differ in the way they schedule transactions. We pointed out that the locking approach resulted in a nondeterministic commitment order for concurrent transactions, while timestamping provided for a deterministic order based on the age of each transaction.

The centralized concurrency control concepts then were extended to cover the issues in distributed DBEs. We explained the difference between a local schedule and a global schedule and outlined the rules for global serializability. Global serializability had two requirements—that local schedules be serializable and that all conflicting transactions commit in the same order at all the sites where they create a conflict.

We did not address the issue of atomicity when failures happen, because Chapter 8 discusses how atomicity is provided when there are failures in the system.

5.6 GLOSSARY

ACID Properties   The properties that a transaction maintains in a traditional DBMS.

Aggressive TO Algorithm   A version of the TO algorithm that tries to resolve conflicts as soon as possible.

ANSI   American National Standards Institute.

ANSI Isolation Levels   The set of concurrency control isolation levels that are part of the ANSI standard (four levels).

Atomicity   A property of a transaction that requires all change or none of the changes of a transaction must be applied.

Backward Recovery   The act of recovering a database to a consistent state in the past.

Blind Write   The type of database write operation that does not require reading the value being changed.

Cascadeless Schedules A category of schedules that do not require cascade rollback when problems arise.

Cascading Rollback A transaction rollback operation that requires other transactions' rollback.

Centralized 2PL A version of 2PL algorithm that controls transactions from a centralized site.

Child Transaction A transaction that is activated as part of another transaction (usually a parent transaction).

Compensating Transaction A transaction that is run to compensate for the effect of a committed transaction.

Concurrency Control A database subsystem that is responsible for providing consistency of the database when there are multiple transactions running concurrently in the system.

Conflict A situation where two or more operations from different transactions are not allowed to be processed concurrently (typically a read and write or two writes).

Conflict Graph A graph that includes all conflicts across running transactions.

Conflict Matrix A matrix that shows compatible and incompatible transactions' operations.

Conflict Serializability A type of serializability that serializes conflicting operations from different transactions.

Conflict Serializable Schedules A schedule that is conflict serializable.

Conservative TO Algorithm A version of the TO algorithm that does not act on resolving conflicts immediately.

Consistency A requirement that every transaction must satisfy.

ConTracts A long transaction that consists of other long transactions.

Database A collection of data items where each item has a name and a value.

Database Consistency A requirement that guarantees database data items are consistent/correct.

DDL Lock A type of lock that is placed on database dictionary items.

Decision Support System A system that supports management of an organization in making business decisions.

Dirty Read A read operation where the changed value of a data item is read before the transaction that is changing it has been committed.

Distributed 2PL A version of 2PL that shares the control across all sites.

DML Lock A type of lock that is placed on behalf of a transaction's DML statements.

Durability A property of a transaction that requires writing its changed values to a persistent medium.

Exclusive Lock Mode A type of data item lock that cannot be shared.

Federated Databases An integration strategy for existing databases and database systems.

Forward Recovery An approach of recovering a database from an image in the past and reapplying each transaction's changes.

Global Transaction A transaction that works with data at more than one site in a distributed system.

Growing Phase   The initial phase of 2PL when a transaction acquires locks.

History   A total ordering of concurrent transactions' operations.

Index Page Locking   An approach to dealing with the phantom issue, which utilizes locks on an index of a table.

Intention Locking   A specific approach to locking, which requires a transaction to identify its intent on making changes to a lockable database granule.

Isolation   A property of a transaction that forces the concurrency control to hide the changes of one transaction from the other transactions until it terminates.

Local Transaction   A transaction that does not run at any site but the local site.

Lock Conversion   The act of changing a lock from a finer granule to a coarser granule or vice versa.

Lock Downgrade   The situation when a lock on a coarser granule is changed to a finer granule.

Lock Escalation   The situation when a shared lock mode is changed to an exclusive lock mode.

Lock Matrix   A matrix that outlines compatible and incompatible lock modes for a DBE system.

Lock Upgrade   The situation when a lock on a finer granule is changed to a coarser granule.

Locking   The act of isolating data items that are being accessed by transactions.

Logical Clock   A counter that resembles the physical clock at a site.

Long-Lived Transaction   A transaction that runs for a long time, usually minutes, hours, or even days.

Multidatabase   An approach to integrating multiple existing databases and/or database systems.

Multiple-Granularity Locking   A locking approach, which is usually used in conjunction with intention locking, that requires a transaction to lock not only the desired database granule but also the ancestors of it.

Multiversion Concurrency Control   An approach to concurrency control that maintains multiple copies of each data item of the database.

One-Phase Locking   A locking approach to concurrency control that allows transactions to lock and release items as they wish.

On-Line Analytical Processing   A database environment in which reporting in support of management decisions is a prominent factor.

On-Line Transaction Processing   A database environment in which many transactions run concurrently.

Optimistic Concurrency Control   An approach to concurrency control that is designed to work well with low conflict environments.

Overwriting Uncommitted Data   A type of isolation that allows one transaction to write what is being changed by another transaction.

Parallel Schedule   An ordering of transactions in which one transaction starts before others finish.

Partial Commitment Order   The commit order requirement that a conflicting operation from two different transactions puts on the system.

Pessimistic Concurrency Control An approach to concurrency control that is designed for high conflict environments.

Phantom Issue An issue that exists in relational database systems when the scope of rows that one transaction is working with is changed by other transactions' inserts or updates.

Point-in-Time Recovery A type of database recovery that restores a consistent database as of a point in time.

Predicate Locking An approach to dealing with the phantom issue in relational databases.

Pre-write The act of buffering the changes of one transaction in memory until the transaction is ready to commit/abort.

Primary Copy 2PL An approach to 2PL that uses a primary site for every data item of the database that is replicated.

Read Committed An isolation requirement that forces transactions to read only committed values.

Read Uncommitted Data An isolation requirement that allows transactions to read committed or uncommitted values.

Read-Only Transaction A transaction that does not make any changes to the database (a query).

Recoverable Schedules A schedule that can be recovered after a system or database failure of the system.

Saga A long transaction that contains other transactions nested in it.

Savepoint A consistent point in the life of Oracle transactions to which the database can be rolled back.

Schedule The total order of operations of concurrent transactions.

Sequential Schedule A schedule that only allows transactions to run serially (also known as serial schedule).

Serial Schedule A schedule that only allows transactions to run serially.

Serializability The requirement that forces the concurrency control of a database system to guarantee that any parallel schedule is equivalent to a serial schedule.

Serializable Schedule A parallel schedule that is equivalent to a serial schedule.

Shared Lock Mode A mode of database granule locking that can be used simultaneously by multiple transactions.

Short-Lived Transaction A transaction that runs for a very short period of time, usually subseconds.

Shrinking Phase The phase in 2PL when the transaction only releases the locks it has acquired.

SQL92 The Structured Query Language as per ANSI Standard 1992.

Strict Two-Phase Locking A specific type of 2PL where transactions have to hold the locked items until just before the commit.

System Lock A kind of lock that Oracle puts on objects in memory.

Timestamp Ordering An approach to concurrency control that uses the age of transactions as a way of enforcing serializability.

Total Commitment Order   The commitment order of all concurrent transactions in the system.

Transaction   A collection of reads, calculations, and writes of data items in a database.

Transaction Monitor   A component or subsystem of a DBE that is responsible for managing the execution of a transaction.

Two-Phase Locking   An approach to locking that disallows a transaction to request a lock after it has released a lock.

Unrepeatable Read   An isolation level that does not guarantee the same value for what is read, if the same data item is accessed by the same transaction more than once.

View Serializability   A serializability requirement that guarantees consistency of the database even though it does not produce a conflict serializable schedule.

View Serializable Schedule   A schedule that is equivalent to a serial schedule.

REFERENCES

[Alsberg76] Alsberg, P., and Day, J., "A Principle for Resilient Sharing of Distributed Resources", In *Proceedings of 2nd International Conference on Software Engineering, San Francisco, CA*, pp. 562–570, 1976.

[Barker99] Barker, K., and Elmagarmid, A. "Transaction Management in Multidatabase Systems: Current Technologies and Formalisms," in *Heterogeneous and Autonomous Database Systems* (A. Elmagarmid et al., editors), Morgan Kaufmann, San Francisco, 1999, pp. 277–297.

[Bernstein80a] Bernstein, P., and Shipman, D., "The Correctness of Concurrency Control Mechanisms in a System for Distributed Databases (SDD-1)," *ACM Transactions on Database Systems*, Vol. 5, No. 1, pp. 52–68, March 1980.

[Bernstein80b] Bernstein, P., and Goodman, N., "Timestamp-Based Algorithms for Concurrency Control in Distributed Database Systems," in *Proceedings of the Sixth International Conference on Very Large Data Bases*, 1980.

[Bernstein87] Bernstein, P., Hadzilacos, V., and Goodman, N., *Concurrency Control and Recovery in Database Systems*, Addison-Wesley, Reading, M.A., 1987.

[Chrysanthis90] Chrysanthis, P. K., and Ramamritham K., "ACTA: A Framework for Specifying and Reasoning About Transaction Structure and Behavior," in *Proceedings of the ACM SIGMOD International Conference on Management of Data*, pp. 194–203, 1990.

[Elmagarmid90] Elmagarmid, A., Leu, Y., Litwin, W., and Rusinkiewics, M., "A Multidatabase Transaction Model for InterBase," in *Proceedings of the 16th International Conference on VLDB*, pp. 507–518, 1990.

[Eswaran76] Eswaran, K., Gray, J., Lorie, R., and Traiger, I., "The Notion of Consistency and Predicate Locks in a Database System," *Communications of the ACM*, pp. 624–633, 1976.

[Garcia-Molina87] Garcia-Molina, H., and Salem, K., "Sagas," in *Proceedings of the ACM SIGMOD International Conference on Management of Data*, pp. 249–259, 1987.

[Garcia-Molina91] Garcia-Molina, H., Salem, K., Gawlick, D., Klein, J., and Kleissner, K. "Modeling Long-Running Activities as Nested Sagas," *Database Engineering*, Vol. 14, No. 3, pp. 10–25, 1991.

[Gray81] Gray, J., "Transaction Concept: Virtues and Limitations," in *Proceedings of the 7th International Conference on Very Large Databases*, September 1981.

[Herman79] Herman, D., and Verjus, J., "An Algorithm for Maintaining Consistency of Multiple Copies," in *Proceedings of 1st International Conference on Distributed Computing Systems*, pp. 625–631, 1979.

[Kaiser92] Kaiser, G., and Pu, C., "Dynamic Restructuring of Transactions," in *Database Transaction Models for Advanced Applications* (A. Elmagarmid, editor), Morgan Kaufmann, San Francisco, 1992, pp. 265–295.

[Kung81] Kung, H., and Robinson, J., "On Optimistic Methods for Concurrency Control," *ACM Transactions on Database Systems*, Vol. 6, No. 2, pp. 213–226, June 1981.

[Leu91] Leu, Y., "Computing Multidatabase Applications Using Flex Transactions," *IEEE Data Engineering Bulletin* Vol. 14, No. 1, March 1991.

[Mohan86] Mohan, C., Lindsay, B., and Obermarck, R., "Transaction Management in the System R* Distributed Database Management System," *ACM Transaction Database System*, Vol. 11, No. 4, pp. 378–396, 1986.

[Papadimitriou82] Papadimitriou, C., and Kanellakis, P., "On Concurrency Control by Multiple Versions," in *Proceedings of the 1st ACM SIGACT-SIGMOD Symposium on Principles of Database Systems*, March 1982.

[Pu93] Pu, C., and Chen, S. W., "ACID Properties Need Fast Relief: Relaxing Consistency Using Epsilon Serializability," in *Proceedings of the Fifth International Workshop on High Performance Transaction Systems*, 1993.

[Reuter89] Reuter A., "Contracts: A Means for Extending Control Beyond Transaction Boundaries," in *Third International Workshop on High Performance Transaction Systems*, 1989.

[Sheth92] Sheth, A., Rusinkiewics, M., and Karabatis, G., "Using Polytransactions to Manage Interdependent Data," in *Database Transaction Models for Advanced Applications* (A. Elmagarmid, editor), Morgan Kaufmann, San Francisco, 1992, pp. 555–581.

[Silberschatz05] Silberschatz, A., Korth, H., and Sudarshan, S., *Database System Concepts*, McGraw-Hill, New York, 2005.

[Stonebreaker77] Stonebreaker, M., and Neuhold, E., "A Distributed Version of INGRES," in *Proceedings of the 2nd Berkeley Workshop on Distributed Data Management and Computer Networks*, Berkeley, CA, pp. 9–36, May 1977.

[Tandem87] The Tandem Database Group, "Non-stop SQL—A Distributed High Performance, High Availability Implementation of SQL," in *Proceedings of International Workshop on High Performance Transaction Systems*, September 1987.

[Tandem88] The Tandem Performance Group, "A Benchmark of Non-stop SQL on Debit Credit Transaction," in *Proceedings of ACM SIGMOD International Conference on Management of Data*, pp. 337–341, June 1988.

[Veijalainen92] Veijalainen, J., Eliassen, F., and Holtkamp, B., "The S-Transaction Model," in *Database Transaction Models for Advanced Applications* (A. Elmagarmid, editor), Morgan Kaufmann, San Francisco, 1992, pp. 467–513.

[Weikum91] Weikum, G., "Principles and Realization Strategies of Multilevel Transaction Management," *ACM Transactions on Database Systems*, Vol. 16, No. 1, March 1991.

EXERCISES

Provide short (but complete) answers to the following questions.

5.1 Check the serializability of each one of the following schedules:

```
S1 = R1(X), R2(X), R3(X), W1(X), W3(X)
S2 = R2(X), R1(Y), W3(X), W2(X)
S3 = W1(X), R2(X), W3(X), W2(X)
```

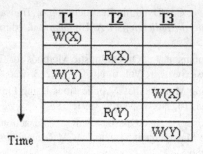

T1	T2	T3
W(X)		
	R(X)	
W(Y)		
		W(X)
	R(Y)	
		W(Y)

Time

Figure 5.31 Concurrent transactions for Exercise 5.2.

S4 = R1(X), R3(X), R2(X), W2(Y), W3(X)
S5 = R3(X), W1(X), R1(X), W2(X)

Indicate all RW, WR, and WW conflicts and show all partial commitment orders forced by these conflicts. Indicate if the schedule is serializable. If it is, what is the total commitment order? If it is not, indicate the first operation that causes the problem.

5.2 Assume the following three transactions in Figure 5.31 and the order in which they work with data items X and Y. Show three schedules that are created by applying (A) no-locking, (B) 1PL, and (C) 2PL to these transactions. For each schedule in (A), (B), and (C), you should show all partial commitment orders (PCOs) caused by all RW, WR, and WW conflicts. Are these schedules serializable? If yes, what is the serialization order? If not, why?

5.3 Assume the three transactions in Figure 5.32 and the order in which they work with items X and Y. Answer the following for these three transactions, if we use (A) no-locking, (B) 1PL, and (C) 2PL for concurrency control. Show the schedules for (A), (B), and (C). Find out all partial commitment orders for RW, WR, and WW conflicts. If the schedule is serializable, what is the serialization order? If not, why? Are there any deadlocks?

5.4 Assume transactions T1, T2, T3, T4, and T5 generate schedules SA and SB as shown below. (A) Are the local SA and SB schedules serializable? If so, what are the equivalent local serial schedules? If not, why? (**Show all partial commitment**

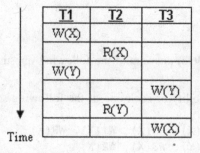

T1	T2	T3
W(X)		
	R(X)	
W(Y)		
		W(Y)
	R(Y)	
		W(X)

Time

Figure 5.32 Concurrent transactions for Exercise 5.3.

orders.) (B) Are they globally serializable? If so, what is the equivalent global serial schedule? If not, why?

```
SA = R1(x1), W1(x1), R2(x2), R4(x1), W2(x2), W3(x2), R4(x2)
SB = R5(x3), R1(x3), R3(x4), W2(x4), R5(x4), R3(x3)
```

5.5 What is the condition for the optimistic concurrency control for transactions overlapping as (A) Ti completes its write phase before Tj starts its read phase, (B) Ti and Tj complete their validation phase at the same time, (C) Ti completes its validation phase before Tj completes its validation phase, (D) Ti completes its read phase after Tj completes its validation, and (E) both Ti and Tj complete their read phase exactly at the same time?

6

DEADLOCK HANDLING

As we discussed in Chapter 5, both centralized and distributed database environments (DBEs) can utilize locks to enforce concurrency control. To access a data item, a transaction must put the right type of lock on it—a read lock to read the item or a write lock to modify the item. Suppose we have a transaction called T1. If T1 wants to lock some particular data item, but that item is already locked by some other transaction such as T2, then T1 must wait for T2 to release the lock before it can proceed. When any transaction waits for another transaction, there is always a potential for a **deadlock**. In this chapter, we will first introduce what a deadlock is and then discuss alternatives for dealing with deadlocks. Deadlock handling alternatives are outlined for centralized systems first. Then we will continue our discussion to include deadlock handling alternatives in a distributed system.

6.1 DEADLOCK DEFINITION

Deadlock, or **deadly embrace**, is a state of the system in which two or more transactions wait forever. This is indicated by a cycle in the **wait-for-graph** (**WFG**). A WFG is a directed graph in which the circles indicate transactions and the arcs indicate waits. Sometimes, we put the name of the data item in contention (the item we are waiting for) on the arc, but often, for simplicity, the item name may not be shown. Figure 6.1 depicts the classical example of a two-transaction deadlock. As seen from this WFG, transaction T1 has locked item Y and needs to lock item X, while T2 has locked item X and needs to lock item Y. In this case, since both transactions are waiting, no transaction can continue and a deadlock is formed.

There are three classical approaches to deadlock handling. These approaches can be used in either a centralized or a distributed database system. These are **deadlock prevention, deadlock avoidance**, and **deadlock detection and removal**.

Distributed Database Management Systems by Saeed K. Rahimi and Frank S. Haug
Copyright © 2010 the IEEE Computer Society

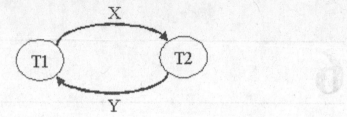

Figure 6.1   Classical example of a deadlock between two transactions.

6.2   DEADLOCKS IN CENTRALIZED SYSTEMS

All three approaches mentioned earlier can be used in a centralized system. Most current DBMS vendors, such as Oracle, Microsoft, IBM, and Sybase, utilize deadlock detection and removal in their products. We will outline each alternative and discuss their advantages and disadvantages in this section.

6.2.1   Deadlock Prevention

Deadlock prevention is an approach that prevents the system from committing to an allocation of locks that will eventually lead to a deadlock. In other words, it is impossible (both theoretically and practically) for a deadlock to occur in a system using a deadlock prevention approach. There are several possible implementations of this approach, but all of them follow the rule that "when two or more transactions require conflicting locks for the same data item, only one of them will be given the lock." One example of such implementation is the **preacquisition of all locks** algorithm that we describe in Section 6.2.1.1.

6.2.1.1   The Preacquisition of All Locks Algorithm   The preacquisition of all locks is an implementation example of deadlock prevention. In this scheme, transactions are required to lock all the data items they need before they are allowed to start their work and are also required to hold onto these locks for the entire duration of the transaction. For example, suppose a transaction needs three data items. This transaction will ask the lock manager to lock all three items before it starts executing any commands inside the transaction. If any data item this transaction needs is locked by another transaction, then this transaction will have to wait. As soon as all the locks needed by the transaction are obtained, this transaction proceeds. Although this transaction may have to wait before it starts executing, the system will never be deadlocked since waiting transactions are not running, and therefore not holding any locks yet. Another way of thinking about this approach is to say that deadlock prevention deals with deadlocks "ahead of time."

Observation 1: It should be obvious that in order for this approach to work, each and every transaction in the system must know all the data items they need to lock before they start executing. If any of this information is missing, the deadlock prevention approach is not going to work. Therefore, this approach is suitable for transactions that know all the data items they need a priori. This is, of course, somewhat limiting with respect to the types of transactions that can be processed. Data driven transactions cannot use this approach since, for them, what the transaction needs to lock is only known at runtime.

Observation 2: It should also be obvious that this system has no overhead for locking. At the same time, this approach may cause some transactions to wait indefinitely. This phenomenon is known as **transaction starvation**. Transaction starvation usually happens to large/long transactions that need to lock many data items. Because a long transaction needs to lock many data items, it is possible (and likely) that while it is waiting, some other smaller/shorter transactions (requiring fewer data item locks) will succeed in locking the items that it needs. If these other transactions keep locking items required by our long transaction, the long transaction might be forced to wait for a long time.

6.2.2   Deadlock Avoidance

Deadlock avoidance is a deadlock handling approach in which deadlocks are dealt with before they occur. The deadlock avoidance approach uses knowledge about the system in determining whether or not a wait can lead to a deadlock. If deadlock prevention deals with deadlocks ahead of time, deadlock avoidance deals with deadlocks "just in time."

In this scheme, transactions can start executing and can request data items to be locked as needed. If a data item to be locked is available, then the lock manager will allocate that item to the requesting transaction. On the other hand, if the data item is locked by another transaction, then the requesting transaction has to wait. If transactions are made to wait without any control, deadlocks will undoubtedly occur. Therefore, to avoid deadlocks, we must also define a deadlock avoidance approach. When one transaction requests a lock on a data item that has already been locked by another transaction in an incompatible mode, the algorithm decides if the requesting transaction can wait or if one of the transactions needs to abort. Sometimes it is easy to determine when one transaction can safely wait for another transaction. However, it is not easy to see if allowing a transaction to wait will cause a deadlock in future.

The database deadlock avoidance approach proposed by Garcia-Molina uses a variation of the deadlock avoidance approach employed in operating systems [Garcia-Molina79]. In this approach, data items are ordered in the system and transactions are required to access data items following this predefined order. Implementing this approach in a centralized system is straightforward. Implementing the approach in a distributed database system requires numbering the sites and then numbering the data items within each site as well. For distributed systems, the combination of site number and data item number is unique, and the ordering is defined based on this combination. In a distributed system, transactions are required to request locks on data items determined by the combined site and item number. This is achieved by transactions visiting sites in order identified by their site number, and within the site, transactions access the required data items in order. Garcia-Molina shows that such requirements guarantee that deadlocks never occur.

Two algorithms proposed by Rosenkrantz can be used to address the uncertainty about deadlock creation caused by allowing transactions to wait for each other [Rosenkrantz78]. These algorithms are known as the **wait–die** and the **wound–wait** algorithms, which we explain next.

6.2.2.1   The Wait–Die Algorithm   Consider two transactions, called "Ta" and "Tb." Let's assume that Ta issues a lock request on data item "X" and that Tb holds an

exclusive lock on "X." In this case, we do not want to allow Ta to wait for Tb if this wait will eventually cause a deadlock. To make sure that deadlocks are avoided at all costs, we will utilize each transaction's age as a way of deciding whether we should allow or disallow the wait. Obviously, in order to be able to do this, we need to know the age of each transaction in the system. As a result, we need to keep track of when each transaction entered the system; in other words, we need to maintain a timestamp for every transaction in the system. A timestamp is a unique ID that carries site information as well as the local clock reading at the site where the transaction enters the system. Think of a timestamp as a sort of "birth date" for each transaction. Because the timestamp contains a site component and a time component, we can guarantee uniqueness quite easily, by merely restricting timestamp generation to "one transaction at a time" on each site. Since a transaction can only be "born" at one site and each site can only create one transaction at a given "local time," we can be sure that the timestamp is unique across all sites in the system.

If we timestamp each transaction when it enters the system, we can use the algorithm depicted in Figure 6.2 as our wait–die algorithm. Recall that a timestamp is like a birth date. This means that the smaller a timestamp is, the older the transaction is. For example, a person born in 1908 is older than a person born in 2007, and, of course, 1908 is less than 2007. Therefore, if the timestamp of Ta, which is written as "ts(Ta)," is less than the timestamp of Tb, we know that Ta is older than Tb.

This algorithm simply states that when an older transaction (the transaction with the smaller timestamp) needs to lock an item that has already been locked by a younger transaction (the transaction with a larger timestamp), the older transaction waits. If, on the other hand, a younger transaction requests a lock that is held by an older transaction, then the younger transaction will be killed. Because timestamps are unique, it is impossible for two transactions to have the same age. Therefore, because we only allow the older transactions to wait, there is no way that the wait-for-graph can contain a cycle (i.e., a deadlock). The reason the algorithm kills younger transactions, as opposed to killing older transactions, is a simple priority mechanism. The belief is that because older transactions have been in the system for a longer period of time and have done more work, killing them is not advisable. If the younger transaction is killed, it will be "reborn" later, but when this "rebirth" happens, the transaction will retain its current timestamp instead of obtaining a new timestamp.

```
Algorithm Wait-Die (Ta and Tb as Input)
Begin
              /* Ta is requesting a lock already held by Tb        */
              If ( ts(Ta) < ts(Tb))
              Then
                          /* Because Ta is older, it waits for Tb*/
                          Ta waits for Tb to finish or abort;

              Else
                          /* Because Ta is younger, Ta dies        */
                          /* Ta will be reborn later with the same timestamp */
                          Ta dies;

              End if;
End Algorithm Wait-Die;
```

Figure 6.2 The wait–die algorithm.

6.2.2.2 The Wound–Wait Algorithm Because the wait–die algorithm is very straightforward, it does not recognize some special cases. For example, there is no special handling in it to address the scenario where a younger transaction that is a candidate to be killed is very close to being done. Obviously, killing such transactions can add to the overall system overhead and can delay the average response time. Because of this shortcoming, a modified approach to the wait–die algorithm, known as the wound–wait algorithm, can be used instead. This new algorithm has the same assumptions as those we stated for the wait–die algorithm in Section 6.2.2.1. Let's consider two transactions, Ta and Tb, and suppose that Ta needs a data item that is locked by Tb. Using the wound–wait algorithm, if Ta is older than Tb, then Ta "wounds" Tb. Notice that we did not "kill" the transaction, we "wounded" it. If instead, Ta were younger than Tb, then Ta would wait for Tb instead of wounding it. Figure 6.3 depicts the wound–wait algorithm.

Observation 1: As before, priority is given to older transactions by allowing them to wound younger transactions and thereby access the data items that were locked by the younger transactions. The wound process deserves some explanation. Once the transaction is wounded, the transaction has a small amount of time to finish processing. If the wounded transaction does not finish within the specified period of time, then the transaction is killed. It is worth noticing that, during the wound period, the system may actually "sort of" be in a deadlock. This deadlock, however, is not an indefinite deadlock, and therefore it is not really a deadlock—it is merely an apparent one. As soon as the wounded transaction is finished or killed, the apparent deadlock is broken.

Observation 2: The wound period will give the younger transaction that is holding the data item required by the older transaction a chance to finish. If the younger transaction does finish within this "grace period," it will not be killed. This obviously eliminates some of the drawbacks of the wait–die algorithm.

Observation 3: Both algorithms are run from the "second" transaction's point of view. In other words, we are always looking from the transaction (Ta) toward the other transaction (Tb)—from the transaction requesting the lock (Ta) toward the transaction that "got there first" and already obtained the lock (Tb) on the data item in conflict. Both names reflect the same processing order (and this "second" transaction's point of view): "wait–die" means "if Ta is older-then-wait-else-die." "Wound–wait" means "if Ta is older-then-wound-else-wait." Both algorithms avoid deadlocks by ensuring the "death" of the younger transaction.

```
Algorithm Wound-Wait (Ta and Tb as Input)
Begin
                /* Ta is requesting a lock already held by Tb    */
                If ( ts(Ta) < ts(Tb))
                Then
                                /* Because Ta is older, it wounds Tb*/
                                /* to either finish or abort        */
                                Ta wounds Tb;
                Else
                                /* Because Ta is younger, Ta waits  */
                                Ta waits;

                End if;
End Algorithm Wound-Wait;
```

Figure 6.3 The wound–wait algorithm.

6.2.3   Deadlock Detection and Removal

In this approach, the lock manager component of the concurrency control subsystem does not check for deadlocks when a transaction requests a lock. The approach is designed for fast response to lock requests. If the data item in question is not locked, the lock manager grants the requested lock to the requesting transaction. If the data item in question is already locked by some other transaction and the lock type is not compatible with the new lock request, the lock manager makes the requesting transaction wait. It is obvious that, without precautions, some of these transactions may end up in a deadlock after awhile. To handle this, the lock manager checks the WFG for cycles (deadlocks) at regular time intervals based on the system load.

Typically, a timer is used to initiate the deadlock detection process. Checking for deadlocks is initiated when the timer goes off. At that time, the lock manager looks for cycles in the WFG. It is possible that there are no cycles and therefore no deadlocks at that time, in which case there is nothing more that needs to be done. If there are any cycles in the graph, the lock manager will have to select a transaction, a victim, that needs to be rolled back to break the deadlock. Sometimes, there might be more than one cycle, meaning that there can be more than one independent (nonoverlapping) deadlock. In this case, one victim from each cycle will have to be rolled back. Sometimes, two deadlocks may overlap (have one or more transactions in common). In this case, an efficient lock manager will choose a victim that is present in both cycles to reduce the overhead of rollback and restart. Once deadlocks are dealt with, the lock manager resets the timer and continues. Victim selection can be based on many parameters.

Possible approaches to choosing the victim include the following:

- Choosing the youngest transaction as the victim
- Choosing the shortest transaction (transaction with fewest required data items) as the victim
- Choosing the transaction with the lowest restart overhead as the victim

6.3   DEADLOCKS IN DISTRIBUTED SYSTEMS

Use of timestamps in dealing with deadlocks is basically the same for both centralized and distributed DBMSs. We discussed how global timestamps are generated in distributed systems briefly in Section 6.2.2 (for further details, see the timestamp-based concurrency control section in Chapter 5). We also discussed how age could be used as a tiebreaker for conflicting transactions for a centralized system in Section 6.2.2. In a distributed system, we will rely on the global timestamps and use a relative order based on age among all transactions in the system. As discussed, this can be achieved using a combination of site ID and local logical clock readings to guarantee global uniqueness as well as age fairness. Therefore, with respect to relative age of transactions, the global timestamps are good indicators and can be used in the wait–die and the wound–wait algorithms.

Because data is distributed in a DDBMS, the transaction processing is also distributed. This means that the same transaction might require processing at multiple sites within the DDBE. Because of this, there are two main issues that we have to deal with when implementing deadlock handling algorithms in a distributed database system.

The first issue deals with where and when a transaction is active at any given point in time. Transactions must be processed at each site that contains one or more of the data items used by the transaction. The amount of processing required at each site is not necessarily divided equally across all the sites. The start and stop times at each site are dependent on the global transaction processing model, as well as site-specific details, such as the amount of work required and the other work being done at that site. This means that processing within a single distributed transaction does not occur at exactly the same time at all the sites. In other words, we can consider the distributed transaction to be active at a given site when work is being done there and inactive when work at the site is either completed, not yet started, or placed on hold for some time. Depending on our implementation, a given transaction might be active at one or more sites at any given time, but we cannot guarantee that it is active at any particular site or at any particular time. As a result, the first issue we have to deal with for a distributed implementation is directly related to the active/inactive status at a given site for a given transaction. When a conflict happens between two transactions at a given site, it is possible that one of the transactions might not be active at that site. This is not an issue in a centralized system since there is only one DBE that contains all active transactions. We call this issue the **transaction location issue**.

The second issue is related to where the algorithms are actually implemented—in other words, which sites are responsible for carrying out the steps in the deadlock-handling scheme. This is not an issue in a centralized system since there is only one DBE that handles all algorithms. In a distributed system, since there are multiple local DBE servers, we have several alternatives to choose from when deciding where to implement our algorithms. We could designate one server as the center of control, we could have a floating control center that travels from server to server as needed, or we could have a number of servers share the control responsibility. We call this issue the **transaction control issue**.

6.3.1   The Transaction Location Issue

In order to better understand why there is an issue with the location of the transaction that is in conflict with another transaction, we have to understand the processing model we use in distributed systems. In our processing model, transactions initiate at a single site and get a transaction ID at that site. This ID is unique throughout the entire distributed database management system. Once a transaction has been given an ID, it can start processing. If all the data required by the transaction is locally available, this transaction does not leave its originating site and is therefore called a **local transaction**. If the transaction needs to access data items on other databases at other sites, then the transaction is called a **global transaction** or a **distributed transaction**.

There are two approaches for processing global transactions. In the first approach, the transaction is broadcast to all sites that contain any data items needed by the transaction and these sites can then perform the transaction's work concurrently. In the second approach, the transaction is not broadcast to all sites but moves from site to site. The difference is that, in the first case, the transaction might be active at multiple sites at any given point in time, while in the second case, the transaction is only active at one site at any given point in time. For simplicity of our discussion, we will only consider the second approach.

In our chosen model—which is also called the daisy-chain model [Obermarck82]—a transaction carries some needed information with it when it moves from one site to another. As the transaction moves from site to site, it includes details such as the list of databases (and sites) that the transaction has already visited and the number of sites yet to be visited, items the transaction has already locked, and lock types for items locked. When the transaction terminates, either by committing (successful termination) or aborting (unsuccessful termination), it sends a message to all the sites it previously visited informing them of the decision to commit or abort. Figure 6.4 shows an example of two transactions in a three-site system. In this figure, T1 initiates at Site 1, does some processing at Site 1, moves to Site 2 where it performs more work, and finally moves to Site 3 where it needs to complete its processing. At the same time, T2 initiates at Site 2, performs some work there, and then moves to Site 3 where it is supposed to finish its processing as well. It is plausible that the two transactions running at Site 3 cause a conflict. We will discuss in detail how to handle situations like this, once we explain the details of the **distributed wait–die algorithm**.

6.3.2 The Transaction Control Issue

By definition, a distributed system consists of more than one server. This raises an issue that does not exist in a centralized system where there is only one server that controls everything. In a distributed system, we have to decide whether the control is given to one site or more than one site. If the control is given to only one site, we call the control approach "centralized." If multiple sites share the control, we call the control approach "distributed." Variations of these approaches are also possible. For example, in the centralized control approach, we can have one fixed site that is always the center of control or the control can be given to a site for awhile and then transferred to another site. Although different sites may be the center of control, at any given point in time there is only one controlling site in the system. In distributed control, we can have all sites be involved in controlling deadlocks or only a subset of the sites. We will discuss the ramification of each of these alternatives in conjunction with each algorithm.

6.3.3 Distributed Deadlock Prevention

Deadlock prevention in a distributed system is implemented in exactly the same way that it is implemented in a centralized system. All resources needed by the transaction,

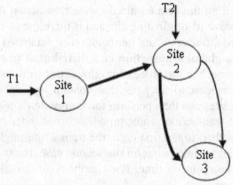

T1 and T2 will cause a conflict at Site 3

Figure 6.4 An example of two conflicting transactions.

in this case a global transaction, must be locked before the transaction starts its processing. For this alternative to distributed deadlock handling, the site where the transaction enters the system becomes the controlling site. Since the transaction does not actually start processing until all required locks are secured, deadlocks are prevented. All performance issues mentioned for centralized deadlock prevention are still present in a distributed system. In addition, since the resources that a transaction needs are potentially stored at different sites on different database servers, preacquisition will take a longer amount of time to complete due to communication delays. One side effect of a long wait time is an increased susceptibility to starvation for large/long transactions.

Aside from this issue, the implementation of distributed deadlock prevention is fairly straightforward. The controlling site informs the servers where the items the transaction needs are located, to lock the desired items. The controlling site waits until it receives confirmation that all items have been locked before it starts processing the transaction. If there are any site failures or communication failures, it is possible that one or more of the required sites might not be available. In this case, the transaction cannot start until all failed sites and/or communication lines have been repaired.

Obviously, the controlling site can also fail while waiting and this can be a complex problem for this approach to handle. Consider the case where the controlling site fails after lock acquisition has begun. In this case, all sites that have already locked items must unlock those items but they will not be able to do that since they cannot communicate with the controlling site. These sites will need to wait. This is an example of a larger issue known as blocking. With respect to this issue, if a site failure or communication failure happens, then either the controlling site blocks other sites or other sites block the controlling site. We will discuss how to deal with the blocking nature of this and other deadlock algorithms in Chapter 8.

6.3.4 Distributed Deadlock Avoidance

Distributed deadlock avoidance can have one of the two alternatives that we discussed for centralized deadlock avoidance. The distributed wait–die and the distributed wound–wait algorithms essentially work the same as the centralized versions of the algorithms. The major difference, as mentioned earlier, is that we need to address the transaction location issue and the transaction control issue. Because each transaction may perform its work on multiple sites, a given transaction may cause a conflict with some transaction at one site and also cause another conflict with a different transaction at a different site. It is also possible for one or more of the conflicting transactions to be inactive at the site where the conflict happens.

6.3.4.1 The Distributed Wait–Die Algorithm   As mentioned earlier, the basic wait–die algorithm in a distributed system is essentially the same as it is in the centralized system. When a conflict happens between two transactions, age (based on the global timestamp) is used as a way of deciding which transaction is to be killed. The algorithm states that if a younger transaction requests a lock that is already held by an older transaction, then the younger transaction will die and be reborn later with the same timestamp it has now if the user still wants to run the transaction. On the other hand, if an older transaction needs to lock an item that a younger transaction has already locked, the older transaction will wait for the younger transaction. There are two issues with respect to implementing this algorithm in a distributed system. Example

6.1 explains the transaction location issue. We will explain the transaction control issue of the distributed wait–die algorithm in conjunction with the distributed wound–wait algorithm in Example 6.3.

Example 6.1   Let's assume that transaction "Ta" arrives at Site K, where it needs to lock data item "X." By the time Ta gets to Site K, suppose transaction "Tb" has already locked X exclusively at that site. When the conflict happens, Ta's age is compared to Tb's age. The action to be taken depends on which transaction is older and which one is younger. Keep in mind that even though Ta and Tb have a conflict at Site K, Tb might be active at some other site and therefore not be active at Site K.
There are two possible cases:

- *Case 1: Ta Is Older than Tb.* In this case, Ta has to wait for Tb. Since Ta is only active at Site K, this wait will completely block Ta's processing. Ta will continue only when Tb has successfully committed, aborted, or decided to die. How does Ta know how long to wait? Ta will wait at Site K until the site receives a message that indicates the termination of Tb—either successful termination or unsuccessful termination. Remember, Site K is in the list of sites that Tb has visited and, therefore, the broadcast from the concurrency control at the site at which Tb terminates will include Site K.
- *Case 2: Ta Is Younger than Tb.* In this case, Ta will have to die. Again, since Ta is only active at Site K, the concurrency control at Site K kills Ta and sends a message to all of the sites that Ta has already visited, telling them to also kill Ta. Once Ta has successfully died at all sites, the user is notified.

6.3.4.2   The Distributed Wound–Wait Algorithm
Similar to the centralized wound–wait algorithm, when a conflict happens between two transactions in the distributed wound–wait algorithm, age is used to decide which transaction waits or is wounded. The algorithm states that if a younger transaction requests a lock on an item that is already locked by an older transaction, then the younger transaction will wait for the older transaction. On the other hand, if an older transaction needs to lock an item that a younger transaction already holds, then the older transaction has the right to wound the younger transaction to access the resource. Again, there are two issues with respect to implementing this algorithm in a distributed system. Example 6.2 explains the transaction location issue, while Example 6.3 discusses the transaction control issue.

Example 6.2   Continuing with the scenario of Example 6.1, Ta arrives at Site K, where it needs to lock X. Suppose that by the time Ta gets to Site K, Tb has already locked X exclusively. When the conflict happens, Ta's age is compared to Tb's age. The action to be taken depends on which transaction is older and which one is younger. Once again, keep in mind that even though Ta and Tb have a conflict at Site K, Tb might be active at some other site and, therefore, not be active at Site K.
Case 1 and Case 2 outline the steps required for implementation of this algorithm.

- *Case 1: Ta Is Younger than Tb.* According to the rule, Ta has to wait for Tb. Since Ta is only active at Site K, this wait will completely block Ta's processing. Ta will continue only when Tb has successfully committed or aborted.

- *Case 2: Ta Is Older than Tb.* According to the rule, Ta wounds Tb. In this case, what happens next depends on where Tb is active. There are three possible scenarios: (1) Tb is also active at Site K, (2) Tb has left Site K and is active at some other site, say, Site L, or (3) Tb has left Site K but is waiting (blocked) at some other site, say, Site N, because the resource it needs is locked by another transaction that is older than Tb.

Scenario 1: Tb is active at Site K. The concurrency control at Site K will enforce the wound rule. In this case, Tb is given the wound period of time to finish. If Tb does not finish within the specified period of time, Site K will roll back Tb locally and broadcast the wound-rollback message to all the sites that Tb has already visited. Each of these sites will roll back Tb locally, once they receive this message from Site K.

Scenario 2: Tb has left Site K, so it is not active there, but Tb is active at Site L. In this case, the concurrency control at Site K broadcasts the fact that Tb has been wounded to all sites. When Site L receives the wound message, that site carries out the wound rule. Again, if Tb does not finish within the time period specified by the wound process, then Site L kills Tb locally and broadcasts the wound-rollback message to all sites where Tb had previously done work. If Tb does finish within the wound period, then Site L broadcasts the committed message to all sites where Tb had previously done work.

Scenario 3: Tb has left Site K but Tb is waiting (blocked) at Site N. This scenario is the same as Scenario 2 with one minor difference. Since Tb is blocked at Site N, Site N will carry out the wound rule rather than Site L, and there is very little chance of Tb committing during the wound period.

In general, when a wound message is broadcast for a given transaction, the site at which Tb is active or is blocked has the responsibility of carrying out the wound process. According to our processing model, Tb cannot be both active at one site and blocked at another site. Thus, there is only one site that carries out the wound process and there is no need for further synchronization. Note also that there is a case when Tb might not be active at any site: this transaction is not blocked (not waiting for a locked resource), and this transaction is not active. This transaction is in transit from one site to another. As soon as the transaction arrives at its destination, it becomes active there. This can be handled simply by caching the message that was broadcast from Site K and applying it when the transaction arrives at the site with the newly activated transaction.

6.3.4.3 Distributed Wound–Wait Control Alternatives

6.3.4.3 Distributed Wound–Wait Control Alternatives   From the control point of view, there are two approaches to implementing deadlock avoidance algorithms in a distributed system. These are, as mentioned earlier, centralized control and distributed control. In the centralized implementation, one site has total control, while in the distributed implementation, two or more sites share the control. Generally, centralized control is simple to implement since all decisions are made by one site. At the same time, centralized control suffers from reliability issues, since the center of control is a weak point in the system. To overcome this issue, distributed control is used to allow the system to operate even when one or more sites fail. The main issue with distributed control is how sites agree on applying the same decision. Distributed control requires additional synchronization steps that sites have to take. In Example 6.3, we discuss the centralized approach to the distributed wound–wait algorithm, while in Example 6.4, we outline implementation of a distributed control.

Example 6.3   In this example, we describe the centralized control implementation for the distributed deadlock avoidance algorithm. Let's assume there are four sites in the system and they are numbered "S0," "S1," "S2," and "S3." Furthermore, data item "X" is stored at S1, Y is at S3, Z is at S2, and there are no data items at S0. Let transactions "T1" and "T2" enter the system at roughly the same time and let T1 be older than T2. T1 is issued at S1 while T2 is issued at S3. S0 is the center of control running the wound–wait algorithm. Transaction T1 needs to perform operations "R(X), W(X), R(Z), W(Z)," while T2 wants to perform operations "R(Y), W(Y), R(Z), W(Z)." Obviously, T1 must perform R(X) and W(X) locally and then move to S2 to perform R(Z) and W(Z). Similarly, T2 must perform R(Y) and W(Y) locally and move to S2 to perform R(Z) and W(Z). Figure 6.5 displays data distribution as well as what each transaction does locally and remotely for this example.

To run their operations locally, T1 and T2 send their lock requests to S0. Since X and Y are available, S0 will grant the lock requests to allow T1 and T2 to perform their local reads and writes. Since T1 and T2 enter the system at roughly the same time, the local operations happen in parallel. After T1 and T2 have finished their local operations, they have to move to S2 to work on Z. Now, the questions we have to answer are related to the order in which these transactions arrive at S2 and how the conflict is handled by S0. There are two possible scenarios for T1 and T2 running at S2.

In the first scenario, we assume that T1 arrives at S2 first and write locks Z by sending a request to S0. Since at this point in time Z is not locked, T1's request will be granted and T1 will lock the item. Later on, when T2 arrives at S2, the item is already locked by T1. In this case, T2's request to lock the item will not be granted. The controlling site (S0) will apply the wound–wait rule. Since T2 is younger than T1, T2 will have to wait for T1 to finish or to roll back. In the second scenario, T2

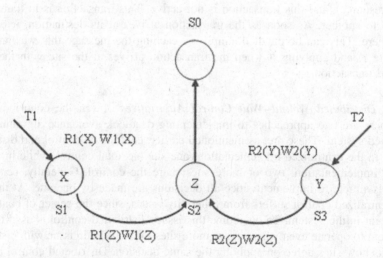

Figure 6.5   Data distribution and transaction steps for Example 6.3.

gets to site S2 first and locks item Z. In this case, when T1 requests to lock Z, the controlling site cannot grant the lock to T1 immediately and will have to wound T2.

It is easy to see that the outcome of applying the wound–wait algorithm depends on when transactions request the lock. What happens strongly depends on the timing of transactions and what operations they perform as part of their processing at any given site. This version of the algorithm is straightforward and has the lowest overhead for implementing the wound–wait rules. That is because all of the information necessary to decide whether or not a transaction could wait or be wounded is stored at one site (site S0 in this case). Although centralization helps with simplicity of implementing the algorithm, centralization has a major drawback, namely, having the control site as a potential bottleneck. That is why most distributed database management systems implement a distributed wound–wait deadlock avoidance approach as explained in Example 6.4.

Example 6.4   In this example, we outline the details of the distributed wound–wait deadlock avoidance algorithm.

We need to recall two familiar terms and introduce two new terms:

- *Local Transaction.* A **local transaction** is a transaction that does not leave the initiation site (as discussed in Section 6.3.1).
- *Global Transaction.* A **global transaction** is a transaction that moves from the initiation site to other sites (as discussed in Section 6.3.1).
- *Awaits.* We say that "transaction S **awaits** transaction T" at a particular site if both S and T are local and S is waiting for T at that site, or if both S and T are global and have already visited this site.
- *Can-Wait-for.* We say that "transaction Q **can-wait-for** transaction P" at a particular site if there is no chain of transactions from P to Q in which each process awaits the next at that site.

With these new definitions, we can expand the wound–wait algorithm to incorporate distributed control. The algorithm is shown in Figure 6.6.

In this algorithm, Ta and Tb are both global transactions. As a result, we have to consider not only the local waits but also the global waits (which are denoted as "awaits" in this discussion). Local deadlock detectors can detect deadlocks among local transactions but cannot detect global deadlocks. To make sure that we do not have

```
Dist_Wound_Wait(Ta and Tb as Input)
Begin
      If (Ta can-Wait-for Tb) Then
           Ta waits-for Tb;
      Else If (ts(Ta) < ts(Tb)) Then
                Ta wounds Tb;
           Else Ta dies;
      End If;
End;
```

Figure 6.6   Distributed wound–wait algorithm.

a global deadlock—a deadlock spanning the sites in the global wait-for-graph—we include the condition "If (Ta can-wait-for Tb)." To demonstrate how this new algorithm works, we apply the distributed wound–wait deadlock avoidance to a three-site system as shown in Figure 6.7.

How a distributed wound–wait algorithm works for this setup depends on the age of these three transactions and the order in which they work on the data items they need at different sites. Let Q be the oldest transaction, P the next oldest, and N the youngest. Figure 6.8 depicts one possible scenario where these three transactions enter the system at almost the same time, do some work locally, and then move to another site to perform the rest of their actions. Note that transaction actions are ordered from the top of the page to the bottom, that is, "WLQ(b)" happens before "WQ(b)," "WQ(b)" happens before "WLN(c)," and so on. Based on the ordering shown, schedule "WLQ(b),WQ(b),WLN(c),WN(c),WLP(a),WP(a),WLQ(d),WQ(d),RLN(d),WLP(c)" will be formed at time 13. At this point in time, Q needs to lock item "a" at Site 1 but the item has already been locked by P. The question that the distributed wound–wait algorithm has to answer is: "If Q can-wait-for P," can transaction Q wait for transaction P without the probability of a deadlock?

The answer to the question in this instance is, "No, we cannot allow Q to wait for P." Since P is already waiting for N, and N is already waiting for Q, making Q wait for P would cause a distributed deadlock. Since the answer is no, we have to figure out what to do with Q. That is when we apply the distributed wound–wait rule that says "if (ts(Q) < ts(P)) then Q wounds P." Because Q is older than P, Q will wound P. Since P is waiting for N at Site 2, it does not finish within the wound period, and it will be killed. In this case, Q is then free to finish its execution, which will then allow N to complete. At this point, P would be free to run if it were executed again.

6.3.5 Distributed Deadlock Detection

In this deadlock-handling approach, deadlocks are allowed to happen and the system periodically checks for them. Deadlock detection in a distributed system works exactly the same as deadlock detection in a centralized system, but it requires the creation of global wait-for-graphs (WFGs). In this approach, when a transaction requests a lock for a data item, it is not checked by the system at the time the lock request is made.

```
Set-up:
    There are four data items a, b, c, and d
    There are three transactions P, Q, N

    Data item a is stored at site 1
    Data item b is at stored site 3
    Data item c is at stored site 2
    Data item d is at stored site 2

    P is issued at site 1 and needs to do W(a) W(c)
    Q is issued at site 3 and needs to do W(b) W(d) W(a)
    N is issued at site 2 and needs to do W(c) R(d)
```

Figure 6.7 Distributed wound–wait algorithm example.

Time	Site 3 Q: W(b) W(d)W(a) Data Items: b	Site 2 N: W(c) W(d) Data Items: c, d	Site 1 P: W(a) W(c) Data Items: a
1	WLQ(b)		
2	WQ(b)	WLN(c)	
3	Q Moves to Site 2	WN(c)	WLP(a)
4			WP(a)
5		WLQ(d)	
6		WQ(d)	
7		N needs to lock d	
8		N awaits Q	
9			
10		P needs to lock c	P moves to Site 2
11		P awaits N	
12		Q moves to Site 1	
13			
14			
15			Q needs to lock a
16			Q can-wait-for P?

Figure 6.8 Example of distributed wound–wait algorithm application.

Sometimes, this will result in one or more deadlocks. To make sure that the deadlocks are eventually detected, the system maintains what is known as a global WFG that indicates which transactions are waiting for which other transactions. The existence of a directed cycle in this global WFG indicates a deadlock. It is not too complicated to detect deadlocks that are local to a site. This has been done by all centralized database management systems for many years. In a distributed database management system, however, the problem arises from having transactions wait for resources across the network. In this section, we describe how to extend the approach to local deadlock detection in a centralized system to detect deadlocks in a distributed system.

Deadlock detection algorithms use the concept of a timer. The timer is set to the prespecified amount of time in which a transaction is expected to finish. If the transaction does not finish within a predetermined amount of time and the timer goes off, we suspect that the transaction is in a deadlock and needs our intervention. The other mechanism required for deadlock handling is the concept of a deadlock detector. In a centralized system, there is one deadlock detector that is located with the local database management system. In a distributed system, we can have one or more deadlock detectors. Each deadlock detector is responsible for detecting deadlocks for the site or sites that are under its control. There are three alternatives for deadlock detection in a distributed system. They are **centralized, hierarchical**, and **distributed** deadlock detectors.

6.3.5.1   Centralized Deadlock Detectors   We can designate one site in a distributed system as the centralized deadlock detector. Periodically, each site sends its **local WFG (LWFG)** to this controlling site. The control site then assembles a **global wait-for-graph (GWFG)** to determine if there are any local or distributed deadlocks. If the controlling site detects any deadlock, it must choose a victim transaction, which will be aborted to break the deadlock. Once the victim transaction is chosen, the controlling site will send information to the site where the transaction was initiated to roll back the transaction.

Although centralized deadlock detectors are easy to implement, they are not very reliable. Often, the controlling site will create a bottleneck, which means that the communication lines to the site are overwhelmed and the site may be overloaded if there are too many transactions in the system and the LWFGs contain long chains. To overcome the bottleneck issues with centralized deadlock detectors, we can implement a hierarchical or a distributed deadlock detection mechanism.

6.3.5.2   Hierarchical Deadlock Detectors   In this approach to deadlock detection, there can be more than one deadlock detector in the system, organized into a hierarchy. Each deadlock detector in the hierarchy is responsible for collecting the wait-for-graph information from all sites that are under its control. In turn, each detector can then send the collected wait-for-graph information to a deadlock detector that is at a higher level in the hierarchy. The site at the top of the hierarchy tree (the root) is responsible for detecting deadlocks across all sites. This approach works well for a system that consists of multiple regions. Each region's deadlock detection responsibilities are assigned to a particular site in that region. Since most deadlocks occur among transactions that only run within a region, regional deadlock detectors work well. If deadlocks occur across regions, then the site that is designated as the root of the hierarchy can detect them by merging the WFGs from each regional deadlock detector involved. It should be obvious that this approach is more reliable than the centralized deadlock detection approach because there is more than one detector in the system at any given point in time.

6.3.5.3   Distributed Deadlock Detectors   In this approach to deadlock detection, all the sites participate in detecting and resolving potential deadlocks. Ron Obermarck first introduced an approach to distributed deadlock detection that shares the responsibility of detecting distributed deadlocks among all sites in the system [Obermarck82]. This approach has the highest level of reliability since the system can continue working even when one or more sites have failed. Before we talk about how distributed deadlock detection works, we should describe what makes up a distributed deadlock. In order to understand how transactions can create a distributed deadlock, we have to understand the transaction-processing model we introduced earlier in this chapter. We discussed the fact that in our model a transaction carries out its work by moving from site to site. We now extend that concept to include the concept of subtransaction. In Section 6.3.4.3, we defined a global transaction as one that leaves its initiation site after performing some work locally. To perform work at another site, a global transaction spawns a subtransaction at that site. All spawned subtransactions are called children of the global transaction. Because of the processing model we described earlier in this chapter, a global transaction can be active at only one site at any given point in time, which means that only one subtransaction can be active for a given transaction at any time.

For example, assume that T1 is a transaction initiated at Site 1 and it needs to perform some database access operations at both Site 1 and Site 2. T1 performs its intended work at Site 1 by spawning a subtransaction at Site 1. Once T1 has finished working with the local database at Site 1, it spawns another subtransaction at Site 2 to access the database at that site. At this point in time, the child of T1 at Site 2 is the only child of T1 that is active. In some respects, we can consider T1's child at Site 1 to be waiting for T1's child at Site 2. Figure 6.9 depicts the WFG for two transactions (Ti and Tj) in a distributed deadlock for a two-site system.

Observation 1: As Figure 6.9 shows, the only time we allow "waiting" to span sites is when the subtransactions are children of the same global transaction. In other words, a distributed (cross-site) wait must be between two children of the same transaction at two different sites. In Figure 6.9, this is denoted by the two dashed lines.

Observation 2: In Figure 6.9, we can also see that the only time we allow local "waiting" is when the subtransactions are children of different global transactions. In other words, a local (within-site) wait must be between children of two different transactions at the same site. In Figure 6.9, this is denoted by the two solid lines.

Observation 3: In order for a global deadlock to happen, we must have at least two cross-site waits in the global WFG.

Observation 4: Although there are no local deadlocks, Figure 6.9 clearly indicates that transactions Ti and Tj are in a distributed/global deadlock, because there is a cycle where all the arrows flow in the same direction.

Figure 6.10 depicts an example of a three-site system in which T7, T8, and T9 are globally deadlocked.

We should recognize that just because there are cross-site waits, it does not mean that there is always a global deadlock. For example, in a two-site system shown in Figure 6.11, there is no distributed deadlock even though we have cross-site waits.

If the existence of cross-site waits does not always indicate the presence of a deadlock, how do we determine if the system is, in fact, in a distributed deadlock state? To examine the issue, we consider the example WFG depicted in Figure 6.12. It is clear that locally (at Site 1) there are no local deadlocks. How do we know if the transactions on this site participate in a global deadlock?

Site 1 knows that Ti's child at Site 1 is waiting for another child of Ti outside Site 1. Site 1 also knows that Tj's child at Site 1 has been spawned from outside Site 1. The rest of transactions on Site 1 are all local transactions and, therefore, Site 1 knows

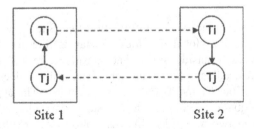

Figure 6.9   Example of two-site distributed deadlock.

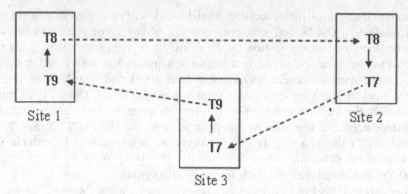

Figure 6.10   Example of three-site distributed deadlock.

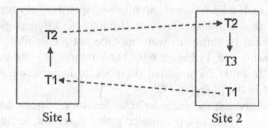

Figure 6.11   Example of three-site system with no distributed deadlock.

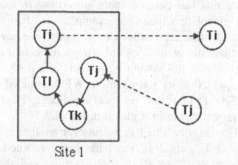

Figure 6.12   Potential for global deadlock.

their status completely. Based on the information that Site 1 has, it determines that there is a "potential" for a global deadlock. As far as Site 1 is concerned, if there is a chain of global waits outside Site 1 that transitively makes Ti wait for Tj, then there is a distributed deadlock. The issue here is that Site 1 does not know what is going on with transactions Ti and Tj outside of its control. The approach that realizes the potential for a global deadlock and detects such deadlocks requires the definition of two new terms and two new rules. In what follows, we explain these two terms and rules and then provide the algorithm for distributed deadlock detection. Note that this is a summary of the approach that Obermarck proposed [Obermarck82]. For more details, readers are encouraged to review the cited paper.

Definition 1: Input and Output Ports. Let's focus on one site. If a transaction at this site spawns a child at some other site (outside this site), we create an output port at this site. If some transaction at some other site (outside this site) spawns a subtransaction on this site, we create an input port at this site. In Figure 6.13, transaction Ti has created an output port at Site 1, while transaction Tj has created an input port at Site 1. To distinguish these ports from subtransactions we use a square instead of a circle as depicted in Figure 6.13

As far as Site 1 is concerned, if the two ports are connected by a chain of other transactions, such that the output port is forced to wait for the input port, then there is a global deadlock as depicted in Figure 6.14.

To simplify the process of identifying potential global deadlocks, we can collapse the output ports and input ports into one port called an "external" port, abbreviated as "Ex."

Definition 2: External Port. An external port is a port that represents the world outside a site. Figure 6.15 shows the external port (Ex) for Site 1.

With this definition of an external port, each site can identify the potential for a global deadlock locally if Rule 6.1 as discussed below applies.

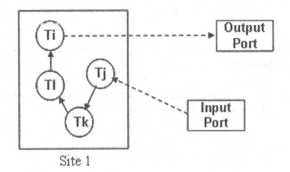

Figure 6.13 Example of input and output ports for a site.

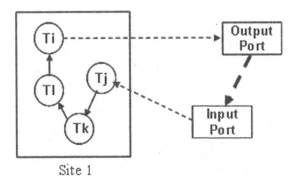

Figure 6.14 Potential for a global deadlock using input ports and output ports.

Rule 6.1: Potential for a Global Deadlock   There is a potential for a global deadlock at a site if and only if there exists a directed chain of waits that start with Ex and end with Ex at that site. In other words, there is a potential for global deadlock if a site has a directed cycle of waits including Ex. For example, in Figure 6.15, the cycle "Ex→Tj→Tk→Tl→Ti→Ex" indicates a potential for a global deadlock including Tj, Tk, Tl, and Ti.

Now, we can formally define the algorithm for distributed deadlock detection.

Algorithm 6.1

- All input and output ports at a site are collected into one port called external (Ex).
- A potential global deadlock is detected by the local deadlock detector when there is a cycle in the LWFG that includes Ex.
- When such a LWFG is detected, the site sends the LWFG information (including the Ex) to the other site(s).
- A site combines its local graph with LWFGs received from other sites and checks for cycles in the combined graph.
- Any cycle in the combined graph indicates a global deadlock.
- Upon detecting a global deadlock, the site selects a victim transaction to be rolled back.
- The site rolls back the selected transaction locally and broadcasts a kill message to other sites.
- Every site receiving the kill message also kills the transaction and releases the resources it is holding.

Example 6.5   Figure 6.16 shows the use of Ex in a two-site system running transactions T1 and T2. As mentioned in Chapter 5, Section 5.3.2, let's assume that the transaction subscript is a reflection of the timestamp/age for each transaction. In other words, T1 is older than T2 because one is less than two.

The following should be obvious from Figure 6.16:

- Both Sites 1 and 2 detect a potential global deadlock.

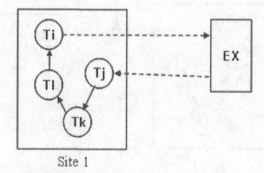

Site 1

Figure 6.15   External port for Site 1.

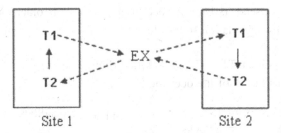

Figure 6.16 Deadlock detection process.

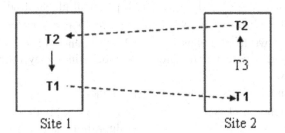

Figure 6.17 A three-site system with no deadlocks.

- Site 1 sends the LWFG "Ex→T2 →T1 →Ex" to Site 2.
- Site 2 sends the LWFG "Ex→T1 →T2 →Ex" to Site 1.
- Site 1 detects a global deadlock.
- Site 2 detects the same global deadlock.
- Either T1, T2, or both will be selected as a victim and will be rolled back.

As indicated above, the direct application of the algorithm without additional information detects the deadlock but has the potential of killing both transactions instead of killing only one. That is because the same deadlock will be detected by both sites. Not knowing what the other site decides, each site may decide on aborting a different transaction and therefore causing unnecessary slowdown of the system. Also, sending both LWFGs puts an additional and unnecessary communication cost on the system. To eliminate these issues, every site will use Rule 6.2, as discussed below, before sending their local WFG information.

Rule 6.2: Graph Sending Rule   When a site detects a potential for global deadlock, the site sends its graph information if and only if "the Ex is waiting for a transaction that is younger than the transaction that is waiting for Ex."

Applying Rule 6.2 to the above example results in the following sequence of events:

- Both sites detect a potential global deadlock.
- Site 1 detects "Ex→T2 →T1 →Ex" as a potential for distributed deadlock.
- Site 2 detects "Ex→T1 →T2 →Ex" as a potential for distributed deadlock.
- Site 1 sends "Ex→T2 →T1 →Ex" to Site 2.

- Site 2 does not send its LWFG since in its graph T1 is older then T2.
- Site 2 receives information from Site 1, combines the two graphs, and detects the deadlock.
- Site 2 selects either T1 or T2 to be killed (but not both).
- Site 2 informs Site 1 of the decision.

Example 6.6   This example shows how we apply the deadlock detection algorithm to a system that is not in deadlock.
Transactions are the ones used in Figure 6.11.

- Site 1 detects "Ex→T1 →T2 →Ex" as a potential global deadlock.
- Site 1 does not need to send information since T1 is older then T2.
- Site 2 detects two local graphs: "Ex→T2 →T3" and "T1 →Ex." Neither one of these graphs is a potential for global deadlock since they do not have a cycle including Ex.
- Site 2 does not send its graph information either.
- In the next iteration of the deadlock detection process, both Site 1 and Site 2 will examine their own graphs and apply the algorithm again. Suppose that, by then, T3 at Site 2 has finished, which allows T2 to continue at Site 2. Once T2 finishes at Site 2, T2 at Site 1 will commit and allows T1 to continue.

Example 6.7   This example uses a three-site system depicted in Figure 6.17.
The application of the deadlock detection algorithm results in the following steps:

- Site 1 detects "Ex→T2 →T1 →Ex" as a potential global deadlock.
- Site 1 will send information to Site 2.
- Site 2 detects "Ex→T1" and "T3 →T2 →Ex."
- Neither graph indicates a potential for global deadlock.
- Site 2 does not send any information to Site 1.
- Site 2 combines the graph "Ex→T2 →T1 →Ex" that it has received from Site 1 with its local graphs.
- After combining the graph, Site 2's graphs are "Ex→T1" and "T3 →T2 → T1 →Ex."
- Rightly, neither graph shows any cycle and therefore no deadlocks.

Example 6.8   Up to this point, we have used examples of two-site systems. For these examples, it is easy to know where each site sends its LWFG information—which is always the other site. In a system that has more than two sites, the question of where to send the LWFG information must be answered. Assume we have the three-site systems shown in Figure 6.18.
Application of the deadlock detection algorithm results in the following:

- At Site 1, "Ex→T9 →T8 →Ex" is a potential for global deadlock.
- At Site 2, "Ex→T8 →T7 →Ex" is a potential for global deadlock.
- At Site 3, "Ex→T7 →T9 →Ex" is a potential for global deadlock.

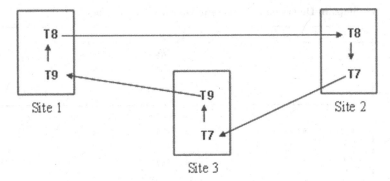

Figure 6.18   A three-site deadlock.

- Site 1 must send its LWFG information.
- Site 2 must send its LWFG information.

Question: Where do Sites 1 and 2 send their LWFG information?

For each site, there are three alternatives that answer this question. In the first alternative, we broadcast the LWFG to all sites. This alternative is too costly and wasteful. The broadcast might include sites that are not part of the deadlock and do not need to receive the information. The second alternative suggests sending the graph information along the input port. Applying this alternative, Site 2 will need to send its LWFG to Site 1. This is not possible since Site 2 may not know which site has spawned T8 at its site. The third alternative suggests sending the LWFG information along the output port. Obviously, Site 2 knows that it has spawned T7's child transaction at Site 3 as an output port. Applying this rule, Site 2 will have to send its graph to Site 3. Therefore, the rest of the steps involved in this example are for Site 1 to send its LWFG to Site 2, and Site 2 to send its LWFG to Site 3.

In the next iteration of the distributed deadlock detection algorithm, sites that receive graphs from other sites combine these graphs with their local information and apply the algorithm again. We have outlined all steps for detecting the deadlock in this example in Table 6.1.

We have used the following notation in Table 6.1:

- For simplicity, we have used only numbers to refer to transactions. For example, we have used "7" to represent "T7" and so on.
- The "Iteration" column indicates when the deadlock detection process starts. This corresponds to the deadlock timer going off.
- The "Site" column indicates a site number, using roman numerals. All the subsequent rows are for that site, until a new value is seen in this column.
- The "Receive" column indicates the graph information that the corresponding site receives.
- The "From" column indicates the site number from which the information was received.
- The "Graph" column contains either the LWFG or the combined WFG for each site.

TABLE 6.1   Steps in Detecting a Three-Site Distributed Deadlock

Iteration	Site	Receive	From	Graph	Send	To	
1	I			ex,9,8,ex	ex,9,8,ex	II	Potential
	II			ex,8,7,ex	ex,8,7,ex	III	Potential
	III			ex,7,9,ex			Potential
2	I			ex,9,8,ex	ex,9,8,ex	II	Potential
	II	ex,9,8,ex	I	ex,8,7,ex	ex,8,7,ex	III	Potential
				ex,9,8,7,ex	ex,9,8,7,ex	III	Potential
	III	ex,8,7,ex	II	ex,7,9,ex			Potential
				ex,8,7,9,ex			Potential
3	I			ex,9,8,ex	ex,9,8,ex	II	Potential
	II	ex,9,8,ex	I	ex,8,7,ex			Potential
				ex,9,8,7,ex	ex,9,8,7,ex	III	Potential
	III	ex,8,7,ex	II	ex,7,9,ex			
		ex,9,8,7,ex	II	ex,8,7,9,ex			
				ex,7,9,8,7,ex	Kill7	I&II	
				Results			
				9,ex			
				ex,8			
				9,8			

- The "Send" column indicates the graph information that a site will be sending in this iteration.
- The "To" column indicates the number of the site that will be receiving the graph we "Send."
- The "Potential" column indicates if a graph is a potential for global deadlock.

Several variations of this algorithm have been proposed [Hass82] [Chandy82] [Chandy83]. All of these deadlock detection algorithm variations propose that when a transaction is blocked because of a conflict with another transaction, the blocked transaction can start the deadlock detection process. Details of these approaches are left as an exercise for the reader.

6.4   SUMMARY

Locking is one of the approaches that both centralized and distributed systems use to provide isolation for the data items in a database that are being accessed by concurrent transactions. When one transaction locks a data item exclusively, it forces other transactions to wait. If not controlled, this waiting can create a deadlock. Deadlock is a directed cycle in the wait-for-graph (WFG) of the system, either local or distributed. Once a deadlock happens, all transactions involved in the deadlock are blocked and cannot be processed anymore. An intervention from the system (or the user) is required to break the deadlock cycle so that transactions can continue.

In this chapter, we presented three approaches for handling deadlocks in centralized and distributed database systems. Deadlock prevention, deadlock avoidance, and deadlock detection and removal algorithms were discussed. Although all three approaches are used in the industry, these approaches have their own strengths and weaknesses. Deadlock prevention has the least amount of overhead and is the most restrictive approach. Deadlock avoidance offers more flexibility than deadlock prevention but has more overhead. Deadlock detection offers the most flexibility but also has the highest overhead. Deadlock detection is the standard in centralized and distributed database systems.

6.5 GLOSSARY

Awaits   A wait between two transactions that spans sites.

Can-Wait-For   A condition that when satisfied allows one transaction to wait for another local or global transaction.

Deadlock   A state of the DBE in which two or more transactions block each other's process because of locked items.

Deadlock Avoidance   A deadlock handling scheme that uses time as a priority scheme to avoid deadlocks.

Deadlock Detection   A deadlock-handling scheme in which deadlocks are allowed to happen and then are dealt with.

Deadlock Prevention   The most restrictive deadlock handling scheme in which transactions have to secure all the data item locks they need before they are allowed to start.

Deadly Embrace   Another term used for deadlock.

Distributed Transaction   A transaction that leaves its originating site to work on data items that are remote.

Distributed Wait–Die   A distributed deadlock-handling scheme that uses the wait–die algorithm.

Distributed Wait-for-Graph   A wait-for-graph that includes waits across sites.

Distributed Wound–Wait   A distributed deadlock-handling scheme that uses the wound–wait algorithm.

External Port   A perception of all transactions outside any site.

Global Timestamp   A timestamp that includes local time reading and a site ID for global unique identification of all transactions.

Global Transaction   A transaction that works with data at more than one site in a distributed system.

Global-Wait-For-Graph (GWFG)   A wait-for-graph that includes waits for transactions across sites.

Input Port   A port that is used by processes outside a site to invoke a child transaction at the site.

Local Timestamp   A timestamp that is generated locally for a local transaction.

Local Transaction   A transaction that does not run at any site but the local site.

Local Wait-For-Graph (LWFG)   A wait-for-graph that includes only local transactions' waits.

Output Port   A port that is used by a local process to invoke a child transaction at a remote site.

Potential for a Global Deadlock The probability that local transactions might be involved in a global deadlock.

Preacquisition of All Locks A deadlock-handling scheme that requires all transactions to secure all the data item locks they need before they run.

Timestamp An identification of a transaction based on the time.

Transaction Starvation A phenomenon that prevents a transaction from ever securing all the data item locks it needs.

Wait–Die An approach to deadlock avoidance that uses age to allow a transaction to wait or to die.

Wait-For-Graph (WFG) A direct graph that shows how transactions are waiting for items locked by other transactions.

Wound–Wait An approach to deadlock avoidance that uses age to allow a transaction to try to preempt the lock another transaction is holding or to wait for it.

REFERENCES

[Chandy82] Chandy, K., and Misra, J., "A Distributed Algorithm for Detecting Resource Deadlocks in Distributed Systems," in *Proceedings of ACM SIGACT-SIGOPS Symposium on Principles of Distributed Computing*, ACM, New York, 1982.

[Chandy83] Chandy K., Hass L., and Misra, J., "Distributed Deadlock Detection," *ACM Transactions on Computer Systems*, Vol. 1, No. 2, pp. 144–156, 1983.

[Garcia-Molina79] Garcia-Molina, H., "Performance of Update Algorithms for Replicated Data in a Distributed Databases," Ph.D. thesis, Department of Computer Sciences, Stanford University, Stanford, CA, 1979.

[Hass82] Hass, L., and Mohan, C., "A Distributed Deadlock Detection Algorithm for Resource-Based System," IBM Research Report RJ3765, San Jose, CA, 1982.

[Obermarck82] Obermarck, R., "Distributed Deadlock Detection Algorithm," *ACM Transactions on Database Systems*, Vol. 7, No. 2, pp. 187–208, 1982.

[Rosenkrantz78] Rosenkrantz, D., Stearns, R., and Lewis, P., "System Level Concurrency Control for Distributed Database Systems," *ACM Transactions on Database Systems*, Vol. 3, No. 2, pp. 178–198, 1978.

EXERCISES

Provide short (but complete) answers to the following questions.

6.1 In Figure 6.19, there are two concurrent global transactions "T1" and "T2," local transactions "T3" (at Site A) and "T4" (at Site B), and local schedules "SA" and "SB" at Sites A and B, respectively. These two schedules are serializable to "T2 → T3 → T4 → T1" or "T2 → T4 → T3 → T1." Data items "x1" and "x2" are stored at Site A, while "x3" and "x4" are stored at Site B. We use a distributed wound–wait algorithm for deadlock control. Write all awaits that exist in the above two schedules. Assume all transactions have entered the system at Site C. Suppose T2 makes a new request at Site B to do R2(x3) after the current request R4(x4). Can "T2-wait-for-T1"?

```
T1 = R1(x1), W1(x1), R1(x3), W1(x3)
T2 = R2(x2), W2(x2), R2(x4), W2(x4)

T3 = R3(x1), R3(x2) at site A
T4 = R4(x3), R4(x4) at site B

SA  = R3(x1), R1(x1), W1(x1), R2(x2), W2(x2), R3(x2)
SB  = R4(x3), R1(x3), W1(x3), R2(x4), W2(x4), R4(x4)
```

Figure 6.19   A three-site deadlock.

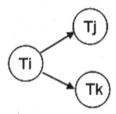

Figure 6.20   WFG for Exercise 6.2.

6.2 Briefly explain how the WFG given in Figure 6.20 can be formed.

6.3 Consider Figure 6.21 with three sites and the local WFGs for them. How many cycles of the distributed deadlock detection are required to detect all existing deadlocks? Show all steps required in a table similar to Table 6.1.

6.4 Assume a three-site distributed system that uses a distributed wound–wait for concurrency control. Assume T1 enters Site 1, T2 enters Site 2, and T3 enters Site 3. T1 is the oldest transaction while T3 is the youngest. These transactions enter the system at exactly the same time. Assume x is stored at Site 1, y is at Site 2, and z is at Site 3. The three schedules shown in Figure 6.22 have been formed. Also assume that T1 gets to Site 2 before T2 gets to Site 3. T3 gets to Site 1 last. Answer the following questions:

(A) What are all the partial commitment orders for S1, S2, and S3?

(B) Is S1 serializable? If yes, show serialization order.

(C) Is S2 serializable? If yes, show serialization order.

(D) Is S3 serializable? If yes, show serialization order.

(E) What are all the waits and/or awaits in the system?

(F) How do you apply the distributed wound–wait algorithm and what are the results?

6.5 Suppose schedules "SA" and "SB" are produced by the local schedulers at Site A and Site B, respectively, as shown. Assume that all transactions enter the system at Site C (making all transactions global). Transaction ID shows the timestamp (the smaller the ID, the older the transaction).

```
SA = r1(x1), w1(x1), r2(x2), r4(x1), w2(x2), w3(x2), r4(x2)
SB = r5(x3), r1(x3), r5(x4), w2(x4), r3(x4), r3(x3)
```

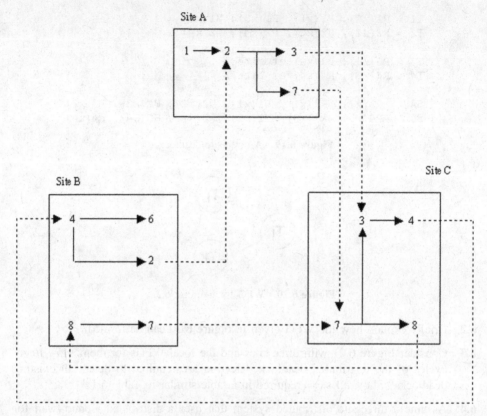

Figure 6.21   WFG for Exercise 6.3.

```
S1 at Site 1 = r1(x)w1(x)r3(x)
S2 at Site 2 = r2(y)w2(y)r1(y)
S3 at Site 3 = r3(z)w3(z)r2(z)
```

Figure 6.22   Schedules formed at Sites 1, 2, and 3.

(A) Are the local SA and SB schedules serializable? If so, what are the equivalent local serial schedules? If not, why? Show all partial orders.

(B) Are these schedules globally serializable? If so, what is the equivalent global serial schedule? If not, why?

(C) Write all awaits that exist at Sites A and B (separate them by site).

(D) Are there any deadlocks in the local schedules and the global schedule?

(E) Suppose transaction T3 makes a new request to write x4 at Site B, resulting in the following schedule at Site B: "SB = r5(x3), r1(x3), r5(x4), w2(x4), r3(x4), r3(x3), **w3(x4)**." How is this new request handled in a distribution wound–wait algorithm? Briefly explain.

7

REPLICATION CONTROL

Replication is a technique that only applies to distributed systems. A database is said to be replicated if the entire database or a portion of it (a table, some tables, one or more fragments, etc.) is copied and the copies are stored at different sites. The issue with having more than one copy of a database is maintaining the **mutual consistency** of the copies—ensuring that all copies have identical schema and data content. Assuming replicas are mutually consistent, replication improves availability since a transaction can read any of the copies. In addition, replication provides for more reliability, minimizes the chance of total data loss, and greatly improves disaster recovery. Although replication gives the system better read performance, it does affect the system negatively when database copies are modified. That is because an update operation, for example, must be applied to all of the copies to maintain the mutual consistency of the replicated items.

Example 7.1 This example shows how the mutual consistency of two copies of a database can be lost when the copies are subjected to schedules that are not identical. In this example, the value of data item "X" is 50 at both the LA and NY sites before transactions "T1" and "T2," as shown below, start.

```
Begin_Tran T1;              Begin_Tran T2;
    R(X);                       (R(X);
    X = X - 20;                 X = X * 1.1;
    W(X);                       W(X);
End_Tran T1;                End_Tran T2;
```

Distributed Database Management Systems by Saeed K. Rahimi and Frank S. Haug
Copyright © 2010 the IEEE Computer Society

T1 runs in LA before it moves to NY to run there. T2, on the other hand, runs in NY first and them moves to LA to run there. Based on this ordering of the transactions' operations, the following two schedules are formed at LA and NY:

```
SLA = R1(X), W1(X), R2(X), W2(X)
SNY = R2(X), W2(X), R1(X), W1(X)
```

When we apply these schedules to the copies of X in LA and NY, we end up with "X = 33" in LA and "X = 35" in NY as shown below:

```
At Los Angeles
Initial Value        X = 50
T1 Subtracts 20      X = 30
T2 Increases 10%     X = 33

At New York

Initial Value        X = 50
T2 Increases 10%     X = 55
T1 Subtracts 20      X = 35
```

Recall from Chapter 5 that SLA is a serial schedule as "T1 → T2" and SNY is also a serial schedule as "T2 → T1." Although both local schedules are serial schedules and maintain the consistency of the local copies, the system has a cycle in its global schedule, which leads to the inconsistency between the copies. To maintain the mutual consistency of the data items in the replicated database, we must enforce the rule that "two conflicting transactions commit in the same order at every site where they both run." See Section 5.2.4.2 in Chapter 5. Guaranteeing this requirement is the topic of replication control, which we will discuss in this chapter.

7.1   REPLICATION CONTROL SCENARIOS

It should be clear by now that replication control algorithms must maintain the mutual consistency of the copies of the database. One way to categorize the approaches is based on whether or not the copies are identical at all times. From this perspective, there are two approaches to replication control: **synchronous replication control** and **asynchronous replication control**.

In synchronous replication, replicas are kept in sync at all times. In this approach, a transaction can access any copy of the data item with the assurance that the data item it is accessing has the same value as all its other copies. Obviously, it is physically impossible to change the values of all copies of a data item at exactly the same time. Therefore, to provide a consistent view across all copies, while a data item copy is being changed, the replication control algorithm has to hide the values of the other copies that are out of sync with it (e.g., by locking them). In other words, no transaction will ever be able to see different values for different copies of the same data item. In asynchronous replication, as opposed to synchronous replication, the replicas are **not** kept in sync at all times. Two or more replicas of the same data item can have different values sometimes, and any transaction can see these different values. This happens to be acceptable in some applications, such as the warehouse and point-of-sales database copies.

7.1.1 Synchronous Replication Control Approach

In this approach, all copies of the same data item must show the same value when a transaction accesses them. To ensure this, any transaction that makes one or more changes to any copy is expanded to make the same change(s) to all copies. The two-phase commit protocol (see Chapter 8) is used to ensure the atomicity of the modified transaction across the sites that host the replicas. For example, assume we have copied the "EMP(Eno, Ename, Sal)" table in all the sites in a three-site system. Also, assume transaction "T1" has the following operations in it:

```
Begin T1:
    Update EMP
    Set Sal = Sal *1.05
    Where Eno = 100;
End T1;
```

This transaction gives a 5% salary increase to employee 100. To make sure that all copies of the EMP table are updated, we would change T1 to the following:

```
Begin T1:
    Begin T11:
        Update EMP
        Set Sal = Sal *1.05
        Where Eno = 100;
    End T11;

    Begin T12:
        Update EMP
        Set Sal = Sal *1.05
        Where Eno = 100;
    End T12;

    Begin T13:
        Update EMP
        Set Sal = Sal *1.05
        Where Eno = 100;
    End T13;
End T1;
```

where T11 is a child of T1 that runs at Site 1, T12 is a child of T1 that runs at Site 2, and T13 is a child of T1 that runs at Site 3. Because of this modification, when T1 commits all three copies will have been updated accordingly. It is important to note that, during the execution of T1, employee 100's salary is locked and therefore no other transaction can see a mutually inconsistent value for this employee's salary.

The lock is removed when T1 commits, at which time T1 reveals the new salary for employee 100 in all copies of the EMP table.

It should be obvious that enforcing synchronous replication control has major performance drawbacks. Another major issue is dealing with site failures. If one of the sites storing a replica of a data item modified by T1 goes down during the execution of T1, T1 is blocked until the failed site is repaired. We will discuss the impact of site failure on transaction execution in Chapter 8. For these reasons, synchronous replication is only used when one computer is a backup of the other. In this scenario, two computers act as a hot standby for each other. Suppose we have two servers, "A" as the primary and "B" as the backup, that need to be identical at all times. In this setup, when A fails, transaction processing continues on B without interruption. Meanwhile, transactions that run on B are kept in a pending queue for application to A when it is repaired. When the A server restarts, it is not put back in service until it is synchronized with the B server. During synchronization, new transactions that arrive at either site are held in the job queue and are not run. Synchronizing A means that the pending transactions from B are applied to A in the same order that they ran on B. After all of the transactions in the pending queue have been processed against A, both servers are put back in service. At this time, transactions are processed from the front of the job queue and run against both copies.

7.1.2 Asynchronous Replication Control

In this approach, copies do not have to be kept in sync at all times. One or more copies may lag behind the others (be out of date) with respect to the transactions that have run against the copies. These copies need to eventually catch up to the others. In the industry, this process is known as **synchronization**. How and when the out-of-date copies are synchronized with the others depends on the application. There are multiple approaches to implementing the required synchronization. Most commercial DBMSs support what is known as the **primary copy** approach. This approach is also known as the **store and forward** approach. The site that is updated first is called the **primary** site, while others are known as the **secondary** sites. Some DBMS vendors call the primary site the **publisher** and the secondary sites the **subscribers**. All transactions are run against the primary site first. This site determines a serialization order for the transactions it receives and applies them in that order to preserve the consistency of the primary copy. The transactions are then queued for application to the secondary sites. Secondary sites are updated with the queued transactions using a batch-mode process. This process is known as the **rollout**. The database designer or the DBA decides on the frequency of rolling out transactions to the secondary sites.

The secondary copies can be kept in sync with the primary copy by either rolling out the transactions that are queued or rolling out a snapshot of the primary copy. To roll out queued transactions, the transactions are run from the front of queue against all secondary sites. In the snapshot rollout, the image of the primary copy is copied to all secondary sites. The advantage of rolling out a snapshot of the primary is speed. Most databases support unloading a database to a file and reloading the database from a file. Snapshot replication can be implemented using these database capabilities to speed up the synchronization of the secondary sites with the primary. Snapshot replication can be done on demand, can be scheduled, or can simply run periodically.

In asynchronous replication, the failure of the primary is troublesome, since the primary is the only copy that is updated in real time. To deal with the failure of the primary, the system may use a hot standby as a backup for the primary. When the primary fails, the standby will continue to act as the primary until the primary is repaired and is synchronized as explained in Section 7.1.1. Instead of having a fixed site as the primary, an approach that allows for a floating primary can also be utilized. In this approach, the responsibility to be the hot standby for the primary is passed from one site to another in a round-robin fashion. As another alternative, sites may also be allowed to compete to be the primary's hot standby, if the designers choose.

Other alternatives to asynchronous replication control can also be implemented. In one approach, instead of having one primary and many secondary sites, a system can have multiple primaries and a single secondary. In this case, transactions are applied to each primary when they arrive at a secondary. Since there is no immediate synchronization between the primaries, the primary copies may diverge. To synchronize all the copies, transactions that are queued at each primary are sent to the single secondary for application. This copy will then generate a serialization order that is applied to the secondary and is then rolled out to all the primaries. In another approach, as opposed to having sites designated as primary and secondary, we can have all sites act as peers. In this approach to replication, we utilize **symmetric replication** in which all copies are treated the same. Transactions are applied to the local copy of the database as they arrive at a site. This approach potentially causes the divergence of the replicas. Example 7.1 in Section 7.1.1 discusses this approach to replication control. Since the copies of the database in this approach may diverge, occasionally the system has to synchronize all the copies. Most DBMS vendors ship the necessary software to compare the contents of the copies and also provide tools for synchronization and identification of differences in the copies. When synchronization is required, tools from the DBMS allow the database designer or a DBA to synchronize the replicas before they are put back in service again.

7.2 REPLICATION CONTROL ALGORITHMS

Many replication control algorithms have been studied and proposed in the literature [Ellis77] [Gifford79] [Rahimi79] [Thomas79] [Rahimi80]. All these approaches focus on providing synchronous replication control. The algorithms can be categorized in two general categories of centralized and distributed control. In the centralized approach, the control is given to one site while in the distributed approach the control is shared among the sites. Before discussing replication control algorithms, we need to define the architectural aspects of a replicated database environment (DBE).

7.2.1 Architectural Considerations

As mentioned in Chapter 2, a database can be fully or partially replicated. A fully replicated database stores one complete copy of the database at each database server. A partially replicated database, on the other hand, does not store a copy of every table of the database at every site. Instead, some of the tables (or some of the table fragments) are copied and stored at two or more sites. To simplify the discussion of the

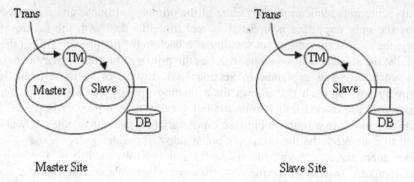

Figure 7.1   Master–salve replication control algorithm placement.

replication control algorithms, we assume the database is fully replicated. Extension of the algorithms to cover partially replicated databases is left as an exercise.

We also make the following assumptions with regard to the communication subsystem:

- Message delays are viable, meaning that there is a time delay between when a message is sent and when it is received.
- Messages are received in the same order in which they are sent. To guarantee this, the communication subsystem must use some form of queuing mechanism to order the delivery of the messages.
- Finally, we assume that all messages that are sent will be received (no messages are lost).

The last two points are referred to as "reliable messaging," which is discussed in Section 15.1.2.5. General messaging issues are also discussed in Section 14.3.1.2.

7.2.2   Master–Slave Replication Control Algorithm

The master–slave replication control algorithm was first proposed by C. Ellis [Ellis77]. In this implementation, as shown in Figure 7.1, there is one master algorithm and N slave algorithms for an N-site system. The master algorithm runs at only one site and is responsible for conflict detection. A copy of the slave algorithm runs at every site where there is a copy of the database. The implementation of this approach consists of two phases: the transaction acceptance/rejection phase and the transaction application phase.

Ellis uses a modified Petri net [Petri62] diagram notation known as an evaluation net [Nutt72]. In this notation, squares represent events, circles represent states, large arrows represent tasks, and small arrows represent transitions. A dot next to the large arrow indicates a single message being sent as one of the actions in the task, while three dots (an ellipsis) indicate a broadcast. We have used a Petri net to discuss the master algorithm in Figure 7.2. We will not show the slave algorithm diagrammatically here—this is left as an exercise for the reader. We will explain how the two algorithms work to ensure consistency of the copies of the database in the next section.

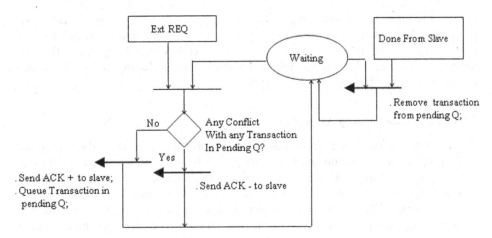

Figure 7.2 Petri net for the master algorithm in a master–slave replication algorithm.

7.2.2.1 Centralized Transaction Acceptance/Rejection Phase   When a transaction enters a site, the local transaction monitor (TM) sends a request to the slave at that site asking it to run the transaction. Upon receiving this request, the slave sends a request to the master asking if it is okay to run this transaction. The box labeled "Ext REQ" in Figure 7.2 indicates this request. To be able to detect conflicts between running transactions, the master maintains a pending queue of such transactions. The master's pending queue holds all the currently running transactions that have been approved by the master (the master voted OK to each of them) but have not been committed yet. When the master receives a request from a slave, it checks for conflicts between this transaction request and all the transactions that are already in its queue. If the new request is not in conflict with any transaction in its pending queue, the master enters the transaction in its pending queue and sends an "ACK+" (positive acknowledgment) message to the requesting slave indicating that it is OK to run the transaction. If, on the other hand, the new request is in conflict with one or more of the transactions in the pending queue, the master responds with an "ACK−" (negative acknowledgment) message to the slave indicating that it is not OK to run this transaction. When the requesting slave receives a favorable response from the master, it starts the transaction application phase. On the other hand, if the response from the master is not favorable, then the slave rejects the transaction.

7.2.2.2 Centralized Transaction Application Phase   When a slave receives the OK for its transaction from the master, it broadcasts a request to update by sending a "UPD" message to all other slaves. Slaves that receive this request must run the transaction and acknowledge it by sending an "ACK" message back to the requesting slave. The requesting slave waits until it receives acknowledgments from all its peers. This is an indication that the transaction has been applied successfully to all database copies at all sites. Only then does this slave send a "DONE" message to the master and the TM, letting them know that the transaction has been applied successfully. Upon receiving the "DONE" message from the slave, the master removes the transaction from its pending queue.

Like any other centralized control algorithm, the centralized voting algorithm has the drawback of overloading the center of control, which is the weakest point of the architecture. The failure of the center causes the overall system to collapse. To overcome issues of load balancing and improve resiliency, Ellis also proposed a distributed voting algorithm, which we discuss next.

7.2.3 Distributed Voting Algorithm

This implementation of the distributed voting algorithm is similar to the centralized version, in that a transaction has to be "accepted" before it is actually applied to all copies. The difference lies in how the transaction acceptance is carried out. In this approach, since there is no master algorithm, all the sites act as peers. In this scenario, they all have to "OK a transaction" before it runs. Any objection from any site will cause the rejection of the transaction. In other words, this implementation requires consensus on applying a transaction, that is, the decision to approve the transaction must be unanimous. Once consensus is reached, the transaction is applied by all the slaves (peers) at all the sites.

7.2.3.1 Distributed Transaction Acceptance Phase As in the centralized case, when a transaction enters a given site, the local TM sends a local request to the slave at that site asking it to run the transaction. Upon receiving this request, the slave broadcasts a request to all other slaves asking them if it is OK to run this transaction. The requesting slave then waits until it receives responses from all other slaves. If they all OK the transaction, the requesting slave proceeds to the transaction application phase. If, on the other hand, one or more slaves are NOT OK to run the transaction, the requesting slave rejects the transaction. Each and every site uses a set of priority-based voting rules to resolve conflicts. There are three basic conflict cases that a slave needs to handle.

Assuming sites are voting on transaction Ti, the following rules are applied:

- *Case 1:* The voting slave is not currently working on a transaction that has been initiated at its site. In this case, the slave votes OK to applying Ti.
- *Case 2:* The voting slave is currently working on transaction Tj that has been initiated at its site and Tj is NOT in conflict with Ti. In this case, the slave votes OK to Ti since both Ti and Tj can run concurrently.
- *Case 3:* The voting slave is currently working on transaction Tj that has been initiated at its site and Tj is in conflict with Ti. Since Ti and Tj cannot run concurrently, one of them has to be rejected (aborted). To sort out the conflict, age is used as a priority. If Tj has a higher priority than Ti, because it is older, the slave votes NOT OK to Ti, causing Ti to die. If, on the other hand, Tj has lower priority than Ti, because it is younger, then the slave votes OK to Ti, causing its own transaction Tj to die.

7.2.3.2 Distributed Transaction Application Phase The slave that has started the transaction acceptance phase for its transaction can start the transaction application phase when it receives an OK from all other slaves. In this phase, the slave applies the transaction to all copies by sending a new broadcast. The broadcast requests all other slaves to run the transaction. Slaves that receive this request simply run the transaction and acknowledge it by sending an "ACK" message back to the requesting slave. The requesting slave waits until it receives acknowledgments from all its peers. This is an indication that the transaction has been applied successfully to all database copies at all sites. At this time, the slave will let the TM know that the transaction has been applied successfully.

Note: During the transaction application phase, a slave defers voting on a new transaction until it has completed applying its own transaction. This is to make sure that newer transactions are serialized after older transactions at all sites.

7.2.4 Majority Consensus Algorithm

The two variations of the algorithms proposed by Ellis are examples of centralized and distributed replication control. In the centralized case, the algorithm is susceptible to the failure of the center of control. In the distributed case, the algorithm requires consensus to detect conflicts. The consensus requirement may result in more than one slave detecting the same conflict, which is not necessary. To overcome this drawback, the consensus requirement could be lessened to a majority requirement. In other words, when a transaction enters the system it must collect OKs from more than half of the slaves before it is applied. When two conflicting transactions run concurrently in a system that is using this approach, it is obvious that there is at least one site that sees both conflicting transactions. In this case, that site detects and resolves the conflict. Thomas first introduced the majority voting algorithm to overcome the drawback of the consensus approach [Thomas79] We briefly discuss Thomas' algorithm in the next section.

In Thomas' proposal, the transaction life cycle is divided into two phases similar to what we discussed before. These are the transaction acceptance/rejection phase and the transaction application phase. In order to make this concept work, Thomas makes use of timestamps for the transaction and data items in his proposal. When transaction "Ti" enters the system, it is tagged with the local site ID and the local clock reading as its timestamp, which is shown as "ts(Ti)." In addition, each data item is given a timestamp, which is the timestamp of the last transaction that has written the item. When a transaction enters a site, it collects the values of all data items it needs to read and write. The data items a transaction needs to read are called the read set (RS), while the data items it needs to write are called the write set (WS). In addition to the RS and the WS, the transaction also collects the timestamps of these items. Once all this information has been collected into a structure called the update list (UL), the voting starts. The UL carries the number of OK votes that a transaction has collected so far.

There are two alternatives to achieve voting—the slave broadcasts the UL to all slaves to vote on, or the slave forwards the UL to another site for voting. The difference between the two approaches is that in the first approach all slaves vote in parallel on a transaction while in the second approach only one site votes on a transaction at any given point in time. The first approach is known as the **broadcast** approach while the second approach is known as **daisy chaining**. We will discuss only the daisy chaining approach, leaving the broadcast approach as an exercise.

Thomas' algorithm requires a majority of sites to OK a transaction before a transaction is applied to all copies. If one site rejects a transaction before a majority decision is reached, then the transaction will be aborted. The following outlines the voting, transaction acceptance, transaction application, and transaction rejection steps of the algorithm.

7.2.4.1   The Voting Rule   Suppose a site receives a UL for transaction Ti to vote on. Once the site receives the UL, it compares the timestamps of all items in the UL with the timestamps of the items in its local copy.

After the comparison, the slave applies the following rules:

- If the timestamp of any data item in the UL is **not** the same as the timestamp from the local copy, then the site votes REJECT. That is because the local copy has been written by a different transaction since the voting began for the new transaction. In this case, the new transaction cannot continue, which is what the REJECT vote achieves.

- If timestamps are equal but there is a conflicting transaction with a higher priority (such as Tj) pending at this site (i.e., ts(Tj)< ts(Ti)), then the site votes REJECT. This is to prevent the lower priority transaction, Ti, from running while the higher priority transaction, Tj, is running.

- If the timestamps are equal but there is a conflicting transaction with lower priority (such as Tj) pending at this site (i.e., ts(Tj)> ts(Ti)), then the site votes DEFER and puts the transaction in its deferred list. The site then forwards the transaction and its UL to another site.

- Otherwise, the site votes OK for Ti, increments the number of OK votes in the UL, and appends the transaction to its pending list.

7.2.4.2   The Resolution Rule   If a site votes OK on a transaction and a majority is reached, then the site accepts the transaction and broadcasts acceptance to all sites. If a site votes REJECT, then the site broadcasts a "REJECT" message to all sites. Otherwise, the site forwards the transaction.

7.2.4.3   The Transaction Application Rule   Once a decision has been made to accept or reject a transaction, that decision is broadcast to all sites.

A site that receives the resolution message has to act on the message as follows:

- If the transaction is accepted, then the site removes the transaction from its pending list (if it is in there), applies the transaction, and rejects all conflicting transactions that were deferred because of the accepted transaction.

- If the transaction is rejected, then the site removes the transaction from its pending list (if it is in there) and reconsiders all conflicting transactions that were deferred because of the rejected transaction.

7.2.5   Circulating Token Algorithm

This approach to replication control is different from the other approaches that we have discussed so far. In previous alternatives, some transactions may, in fact, be rejected to protect the database against mutual inconsistency. In this approach, all transactions are accepted and none are rejected. This approach uses a circulating token to serialize all transactions in the system. Once the serialization order has been determined for a transaction, the transaction runs in that order against every copy of the database. We call this approach the **circulating token** approach.

Similar to the other approaches, the circulating token algorithm has transaction acceptance and transaction application phases. During the transaction acceptance phase, all transactions in the system are sequenced to run—their serialization order is determined. This is achieved by assigning every transaction at every site a unique ticket from a sequential series, which indicates the order of that transaction in the serialization schedule. Once a transaction has been ticketed, it is broadcasted to all sites. The sites then run their transactions in the order of their tickets.

7.2.5.1 *Circulating Token Implementation*

To implement the algorithm, a token is utilized to allow the sites to ticket their transactions. A site can only ticket its transactions when it is holding the token. The token circulates in a virtual ring and carries the available ticket number from site to site. This allows all sites the opportunity to ticket their transactions. To be fair, the system utilizes either a maximum amount of time that a site can hold the token or a maximum number of transactions that a site can ticket while holding the token. When a site pulls a ticket out of the token, it assigns it to a transaction and increments the ticket on the token. Once the site has reached the maximum number of tickets allowed or the maximum time to hold the token is reached, the site forwards the token with the available ticket to the next site in the ring. To be able to do this, every site must know the address of its successor in the ring. To deal with failures, as we will discuss later, each site must also know its predecessor.

The ticketing of transactions constitutes the transaction acceptance phase of this algorithm. Once a transaction is ticketed, the algorithm starts the transaction's application phase. During this phase, a transaction and its ticket are broadcast to all sites. In the transaction application phase, all transactions must be applied in the order of their tickets at all sites. In order to achieve this, every site maintains the ticket number of the last applied transaction (LAP). When a new transaction and its ticket arrive at a site, the ticket number of this transaction is compared to the LAP. If the incoming transaction's ticket number is equal to "LAP + 1," then this transaction is ready to be applied at the site. Otherwise, the transaction is queued until such time as all transactions with smaller ticket numbers have been applied at the site. Example 7.2 shows how token passing can be used in a four-site system. Example 7.3 extends the concept of token passing to handle loss of the token during transmission and/or as a result of a site failure.

Example 7.2 Suppose we have the following four-site system using the token passing replication control on a virtual ring as shown in Figure 7.3. Site 1 sends the token to Site 2, Site 2 sends the token to Site 4, Site 4 sends the token to Site 3, and Site 3 sends the token back to Site 1, completing the ring. Also, for fairness, assume that when a site receives the token it can ticket a maximum of three transactions.

When the system starts, the token is at Site 1 and has ticket 1 on it. Before Site 1 sends the token forward, it tickets its two transactions. Transactions T11 and T12 are given tickets 1 and 2. The ticket number for a transaction is indicated in **bold** next to the transaction number in Figure 7.3. When the token leaves Site 1, it carries ticket 3. Site 2 pulls ticket 3 and assigns it to transaction T21; Site 4 tickets T41, T42, and T43 with tickets 4, 5, and 6. Finally, Site 3 tickets T31, T32, and T33 with tickets 7, 8, and 9. Therefore, when the token arrives at Site 1 again, it is carrying ticket 10. In the first circulation of the token, transactions T11, T12, T21, T41, T42, T43, T31, T32, and T33 are ticketed with ticket numbers 1 through 9. If the state of the system does not change when token rotation number 2 starts, transactions T44 and T34 are

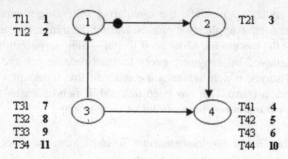

Figure 7.3 A token passing replication control example.

given tickets 10 and 11, respectively. As a result, after the token arrives at Site 1 again it carries ticket 12. This results in a serial schedule as "T11 → T12 → T21 → T41 → T42 → T43 → T31 → T32 → T33 → T44 → T34."

The replication control algorithm is able to deal with the loss of the token as well. The token may be lost in transition (from one site to another) or disappear when it is at a site and the site fails. In either case, a replacement token is generated by the site that recognizes the loss of the token and the process continues. The issue with token recovery is to make sure that the tickets on the new token do not duplicate the tickets that were on the old token, to avoid confusion in the serialization order of transactions. We explain how to deal with the loss of the token in Example 7.3.

Example 7.3 Suppose we have the following four-site system using the token passing replication control on a virtual ring as shown. Site 1 sends the token to Site 2, Site 2 sends it to Site 3, Site 3 sends it to Site 4, and Site 4 sends the token back to Site 1, completing the ring. Also, for fairness, assume that when a site receives the token it can ticket a maximum of two transactions as shown in Figure 7.4.

When the system starts, the token is at Site 1 and has ticket 1 on it. Before Site 1 sends the token forward, it tickets its only transaction, T11, with ticket 1 and forwards the token. When the token leaves Site 1, it carries ticket number 2. Site 2 pulls ticket 2 and assigns it to transaction T21; Site 3 tickets T31 and T32 with tickets 3 and 4. Finally, Site 4 tickets T41 and T42 with tickets 5 and 6. Therefore, when the token arrives at Site 1 again it is carrying ticket 7. In the first circulation of the token, transactions T11, T21, T31, T32, T41, and T42 are ticketed with ticket numbers 1 through 6.

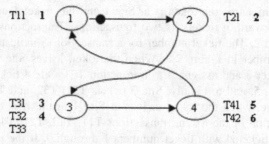

Figure 7.4 Token passing replication control example with failures.

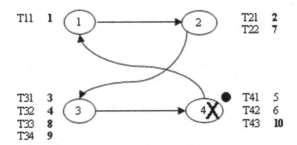

Figure 7.5 Site failure in token passing replication control.

Now assume, that when the second circulation of the token starts, the system has changed as depicted in Figure 7.5. During this token rotation, Site 2 tickets transaction T22 with ticket number 7 and passes the token to Site 3. Site 3 pulls tickets 8 and 9 from the token and passes the token to Site 4. After the token arrives at Site 4 and the site tickets transaction T43 with ticket 10, the site goes down. Site 4, therefore, cannot forward the token to Site 1. Site 1, waiting to receive the token from Site 4, times out while waiting for its predecessor site and starts investigating the status of the token. The first step in this process for Site 1 is to check with its predecessor, that is, Site 4. Site 1 sends a message to Site 4 asking about the token. Since Site 4 is down, it cannot respond. Once Site 1 does not hear back from Site 4 in a predetermined amount of time, it assumes Site 4 has failed and bypasses the site and communicates with Site 4's predecessor (Site 3). Site 1 sends a request to Site 3, asking if it had sent the token to Site 4 and, if yes, what the ticket number on the token was. Site 3 responds with ticket 10 to Site 1. At this time, Site 1 declares Site 4 dead and regenerates a new token (with a new token ID) and puts ticket 10 on it. Up to this point, transactions T11, T21, T31, T32, T41, T42, T22, T33, T34, and T43 have been ticketed with tickets 1 through 10, respectively, from the previous token. Since the previous token was invalidated by Site 1, ticket 10 from this token (assigned to T43 by Site 4) would also be invalid. Site 4's transaction T43 must be given a valid ticket from the new token. The process then continues.

Now suppose Site 4 is repaired when iteration 3 of the token starts. When Site 4 comes back on line, the ring is repatched but Site 4 is told that the previous token at its possession is invalid and transaction T43 must get a new ticket. Suppose when the third circulation of the token starts, the transactions that are in the system are as shown in Figure 7.6. By the time the token arrives at Site 1 again—at the completion of the third circulation of the token—transactions T11, T21, T31, T32, T41, T42, T22, T33, T34, T23, T35, T43, and T44 are given tickets 1 through 13. As seen in Figure 7.6, transaction T43 at Site 4 has been given 12 as its new ticket number.

As mentioned earlier, this algorithm can also deal similarly with the loss of the token in transition from a site to a site. We leave the details of this case as an exercise.

7.2.6 Generalized Voting Algorithm for Replication Control

Recall that in order for copies of a database to show the same consistent state, they all have to run the same serializable schedule. To guarantee that a local schedule is

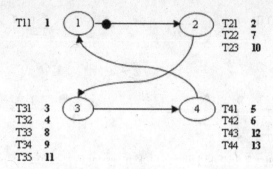

Figure 7.6   Token circulation after a site failure repair.

serializable, two conflicting operations must be seen by at least one site's concurrency control. Although many algorithms such as centralized control, decentralized control, and voting for replication control have been proposed with different names, they are all specific implementation of the **generalized voting** algorithm proposal by Gifford [Gifford79]. In this approach to replication control, each database server in the system is given a number of votes. The decision on how many votes a server should have depends on the importance of the server in the system. For example, a mainframe should have more votes than a departmental server, which might have more votes than a group database sever. Generally, there are N copies of a data item denoted as {X1, X2, ..., XN}. Each database server that hosts a copy of X is assigned a number of votes shown as "V(Xi) for i = 1, 2, ..., N." There are also two quorums defined for reading a data item or writing a data item. Vr(X) is the number of votes required to read X (we call this the **read quorum**). Vw(X) is the number of votes required to write X (we call this the **write quorum**).

Voting starts when a transaction enters the system. If a transaction needs to read X, it needs to collect Vr(X) votes from the copies of the database first. Once this quorum is reached, the transaction can read the data item. If a transaction needs to write X, it needs to collect Vw(X) votes from the copies of the database first. Again, once the write quorum is reached, the transaction can write the data item. When a site casts its vote for a transaction to read or write an item, it cannot vote again until that transaction is completed. The key to the success of this algorithm is the fact that it makes sure that two conflicting transactions that run concurrently cannot reach conflicting quorums—only one quorum can be reached by one of the two transactions requiring the other one to abort and restart. The success lies in defining the read and write quorums in such a way that all read–write, write–write, and write–read conflicts are detected.

To make sure that only one of the two concurrent transactions with a read–write conflict on X can run, the algorithm requires that "Vr(X) + Vw(X)> sum(V(Xi)) for i = 1 to N"—meaning that "read quorum + write quorum" requires more votes than the system has. This guarantees that two transactions trying to read and write the same data item cannot both succeed. Similarly, to make sure that only one of the two concurrent transactions with a write–write conflict on X can run, the algorithm requires that "Vw(X)> sum(V(Xi))/2"—meaning that the quorum to write is more than half the votes. This guarantees that two transactions conflicting to write an item cannot both succeed. To show why this algorithm is known as the generalized voting approach for replication, we explain how deciding on the number of votes, how deciding on the number of votes allocated to different sites, and how deciding on the read and write quorums can implement other approaches by a series of examples.

Example 7.4   This example shows how "Write all sites–Read all sites" works. Assume we have five copies of the database and each copy has one vote. Therefore, the total number of votes in the system is five. Let's decide on "Vr(X) = 5" and "Vw(X) = 5." This means that any transaction that wants to read or write X must collect five votes. Since each site has one vote, all sites must OK every read and every write from every transaction. Suppose transactions Ti and Tj are conflicting and running concurrently in this system. Also, assume that Ti enters the system at Site 1 while T2 enters the system at Site 2. Site 1 votes OK to run T1 while Site 2 votes OK to T2. At this point, these two sites do not have any more votes left. As a result, at most T1 can have four votes, which would mean that T2 would have only one vote. It is also possible that T2 might end up with four votes, but then T1 could only have one vote. In both cases, neither one of the two transactions can collect the required number of votes to succeed.

The above implementation of the voting approach requires consensus for writing or reading a data item—all sites have to OK a transaction's read or write. If there is any site that has already cast its vote to allow a conflicting transaction to read or write the data item, consensus for a new transaction is not possible. This guarantees the consistency of the copies of the database.

Example 7.5   This example shows how "Write all sites—Read any sites" works. Assume we have five copies of the database and each copy has one vote. Therefore, the total number of votes in the system is five. Now let's decide on "Vr(X) = 1" (instead of 5 in Example 7.4) and "Vw(X) = 5." In this case, a transaction can read any of the five copies as long as the slave at that site votes OK to read the data item X. Allowing every transaction to be able to read any copy, we must make sure that we do not allow a conflicting transaction to write the same data item. Since Vw(X) is set to 5, another transaction, like Tj, that wants to write X must get the OK from all five sites. This requires that Tj to collect OK votes from the site that has already said OK to Ti to read X. The site that has voted OK to Ti will say NOT OK to Tj, causing Tj to collect only four OK votes, which is not enough to write X—Tj restarts.

Example 7.6   This example shows how "Write any 3 sites–Read any 3 sites" works. Assume the same five site system as before with every site having one vote. Now assume that "Vr(X) = 3" and "Vw(X) = 3." In this case, a transaction that wants to read or write an item must collect three OK votes from any three sites before it can perform its operation. Since there are five sites in the system, one site will see any read–write conflict or any write–write conflict between two transactions. That site will have to decide how to cast its vote. If the site votes OK for a transaction that reads, then all conflicting writers will be aborted. If the site votes OK to write X, then all conflicting writers or conflicting readers will be aborted.

The above implementation of the algorithm results in a majority algorithm for replication control. Since majority is required for a transaction to read or write only one of the conflicting transactions can succeed.

Example 7.7 This example shows how "All reads and writes to one site" works. Assume the same five- site system as before but four sites have zero votes and one site has one vote. A transaction that wants to read has to reach a read quorum of one, that is, "Vr(X) = 1." A transaction that wants to write has to reach a write quorum of one, that is, "Vw(X) = 1." Since the only vote in the system is given to one site, all transactions have to compete for that site's vote. The site, therefore, will see all requests from all transactions. By casting its vote for only one of the conflicting transactions, the database consistency is preserved. That is because, when the site casts its vote for one transaction, other concurrently running conflicting transactions will not be able to get the necessary vote to run and are restarted. Although straightforward, this implementation of the replication control mechanism is centralized and has all the drawbacks associated with such an implementation.

7.2.7 Posted Update Approach

The **posted update approach** (PUA) was proposed by Rahimi [Rahimi80]. The main advantage of this algorithm over distributed and majority voting algorithms is that it can deal with partially replicated databases. The PUA preserves the consistency of a database by producing serializable schedules. The approach also maintains consistency across copies by applying the same serializable schedule to all copies of the database and/or database partitions.

The PUA uses one queue for each partition to order how conflicting transactions run against the partition and its copies. Once in a partition's queue, transactions run on the partition from the front of the queue one at a time. The PUA only processes one transaction at a time from the front of the queue, hence eliminating concurrent application of conflicting transactions to the partition and its copies. Therefore, the PUA creates a serial schedule for the conflicting transactions against each partition and its copies. To make sure that all copies of a partition are mutually consistent, the PUA guarantees conflicting transactions are queued in the same order in all queues for a given partition. The decision whether or not to queue a transaction for a partition is made between the slaves and the master similar to the master–slave control approach discussed before (see the centralized voting approach in Section 7.2.2).

In the PUA, there are three algorithms called "Master," "Slave," and "LDM," which stands for local data manager. The master algorithm runs at the site where the transaction enters the system. If there are N copies of a partition of the database, then there are N slaves, each running at one of these sites. Each slave is responsible for controlling the entrance of the transactions in its associated partition queue. Transactions waiting for services in each queue are called "Posted Updates." The LDM algorithm is responsible for processing transactions from the front of its queue against the partition. While slaves enter transactions at the back of the queue, the LDM services these transactions from the front of the queue. By doing so, the concurrent transaction threat is eliminated at each site. To ensure mutual consistency among the copies, it is required that all transactions are applied in the same order to all the partition copies. In the PUA, this is made possible by making sure that while a transaction is being queued, no other conflicting transaction is placed in partition queues.

Both the master and slave algorithms have three states: "Idle," "Active," and "Queuing." In the Idle state, the algorithm is not working on any transaction. In the Active state, the algorithm is working on establishing a serializable order for a transaction. In the Queuing state, the algorithm has determined the order for a transaction and has entered the transaction in the queue. The protocols for achieving the goals of the PUA are similar to the two-phase commit (see Chapter 8). During the first phase of processing transaction "Ti," which is also called the "Voting" phase, the master of Ti asks all involved slaves to ready their queues for its transaction. Once all slaves have replied favorably, the master enters the second phase—the "Queuing" phase. To allow priority and fairness, the master can abort a transaction during the voting phase. However, once the queuing phase has started, the transaction will be queued and applied.

In response to the request to ready the queue, slaves act according to the state they are in:

- If a slave is in the idle state (i.e., not currently working on a transaction), then it votes "Ready."
- If a slave is in the active state (i.e., it has readied its queue for a conflicting transaction of higher priority), then it votes "Not Ready."
- If a slave has readied its queue for a conflicting transaction of lower priority, such as Tj, it will defer voting and tries to find out if it can change its vote for Ti. To do this, the slave sends a message to the master of Tj asking if its previous "Ready" vote can be changed to "Not Ready." If the master of Tj has not started its queuing phase, it will allow the vote change and aborts transaction Tj. Otherwise, the master of Tj will deny the vote change. The slave that deferred voting on Ti can then proceed accordingly.

It should be obvious that at any point in time the slave algorithm maintains two lists. The first list tracks all nonconflicting transactions that are pending to be queued. The second list tracks transactions that are deferred. Transactions are only vulnerable when they are in one of these lists. Once a transaction is queued, it is removed from the list it is in and it is guaranteed to be completed. To deal with failures, the two-phase commit is utilized between the master and corresponding LDMs. Before applying a transaction from the front of a queue, the LDM informs the master that it is ready to run the transaction. The master can then decide to continue with the transaction or abort it. If the decision is to abort, then this decision is communicated to all LDMs working on the corresponding transaction.

7.3   SUMMARY

In this chapter, we extended the concurrency control algorithms we discussed in Chapter 5 to include replication control. The issue with replication, as discussed in this chapter, is maintaining the mutual consistency of copies. Approaches were grouped into two categories. The first group, known as synchronous replication control, maintains identical database copies at all times. The second group, known as asynchronous replication control, allows the copies to show different values sometimes. We pointed out that, to detect a conflict, two conflicting transactions must be seen by at least one site. We exploited this concept for different algorithms that are proposed for replication control. We also discussed how voting was used to achieve the goal of replication control and concluded that different algorithms proposed for replication control, such as consensus, majority, master–slave, posted updates, and token passing, were special cases of the generalized voting approach.

7.4 GLOSSARY

Asynchronous Replication   An approach to replication control that allows copies of the database data items to show different values.

Broadcast   The act of sending the same message to all sites in a network.

Circulating Token   An approach to replication control that uses a token with a ticket to serialize transactions in a distributed database.

Consensus   An approach to replication control that requires all sites to OK a transaction before it is run.

Daisy Chaining   A distributed transaction execution application that requires a transaction to move from a site to a site that only allows it to be active at one site at any given point in time.

Fully Replicated Database   A replication design that requires copying all tables of the database at all sites in the system.

Generalized Voting   A comprehensive voting approach to replication control.

Majority Voting   A voting approach to replication control that only requires a majority of sites to agree on applying a transaction.

Master–Slave   A replication control strategy that assigns one site as the master and the others as the slaves.

Mutual Consistency   The consistency requirement across copies of the same table and/or partition.

Partially Replicated Database   A replication design that does not require copying all tables of the database at all sites in the system.

Posted Updates   An approach to replication control that uses queues to order transactions for application to the copies of database tables.

Primary Copy   The copy of a database that is designated at the primary—transactions are applied to this copy first.

Publisher   The copy of a database that is designated at the publisher—transactions are applied to this copy first.

Read Quorum   The number of votes required to read a data item in a replicated database.

Secondary Copy   The copy of a database that is designated at the secondary—transactions are applied to this copy after they are applied to the primary.

Store and Forward   Another terminology for primary–secondary replication control.

Subscriber   The copy of a database that is designated at the subscriber—transactions are applied to this copy after they are applied to the publisher.

Symmetric Replication   A replication control approach in which transactions are applied to the database copy at the site where they arrive.

Synchronous Replication   An approach to replication control that does not allow copies of the database data items to show different values.

Transaction Acceptance Phase   The phase in a replication control algorithm that decides whether or not to accept a transaction and orders its execution with other transactions.

Transaction Application Phase   The phase in a replication control algorithm that applies a transaction that has already been serialized.

Weighted Voting   A voting approach to replication control in which sites are given different numbers of votes to use during the transaction acceptance phase.

Write Quorum   The number of votes required to write a data item in a replicated database.

REFERENCES

[Ellis77]   Ellis, C., "A Robust Algorithm for Updating Duplicate Databases," in *Proceedings of the 2nd Berkeley Workshop on Distributed Data Management and Computer Networks*, pp. 146–158, 1977.

[Gifford79]   Gifford, D., "Weighted Voting for Replicated Data," in *Proceedings of the 7th Symposium on Operating Systems Principles*, Pacific Grove, CA, ACM, New York, 1979, pp. 150–162.

[Nutt72]   Nutt, G., "Evaluation Nets for Computer Analysis," in *Proceedings of FICC*, 1972, and also Ph.D. thesis, University of Washington, 1972.

[Petri62]   Petri, C., "Kommunikation Mit Automation," Ph.D. thesis, University of Bonn, 1962.

[Rahimi79]   Rahimi, S., and Franta, W., "The Effects of Topological, Replication, and Loading Factors on Concurrent Update Algorithm Performance: A Case Study," University of Minnesota, Computer Sciences Department Tech Report, 79-25, November 1979.

[Rahimi80]   Rahimi, S., "A Posted Update Approach to Concurrency Control in Distributed Database Systems," Ph.D. thesis, University of Minnesota, 1980.

[Thomas79]   Thomas, R., "A Majority Consensus Approach to Concurrency Control for Multiple Copy Databases," *ACM Transactions on Database Systems*, Vol. 4, No. 2, pp 180–209, June 1979.

EXERCISES

Provide short (but complete) answers to the following questions.

7.1   Assume weighted voting is used for replication control of a five-site system, shown in Figure 7.7. Also assume that X as a data item is copied at all sites. How do you decide on the total number of votes, the number of votes assigned to each site, the read quorum ($Vr(x)$), and the write quorum ($Vw(x)$) that satisfies the following conditions:

(A) The number of votes assigned to each site is the absolute minimum? (**Note:** Zero is NOT accepted as the number of votes assigned to a site.)

(B) Site 1 can read if it decides to read X?

(C) X could be written if and only if Site 1 and at least two other sites vote to write?

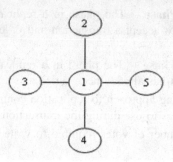

Figure 7.7   Network topology for Exercise 7.1.

7.2   There are two parts to the token passing replication control algorithm as mentioned in this chapter. The first part consists of ticketing transactions and the second part includes applying transactions. Draw the Petri net for each part of the algorithm. Do NOT worry about dealing with failures.

7.3   Assume the four-site system given in Figure 7.8 for the token passing replication control. Suppose, for fairness, when a site receives the token it can ticket a maximum of three transactions. A token is generated at Site 1 to start with. Answer the following questions for this setup for cycle 1 of the algorithm.

   (A) What is the ticket number when the token leaves Site 1?
   (B) What is the ticket number when the token comes back to Site 1?
   (C) How many transactions and in what order are they serialized for the first cycle of the token (cycle starts at Site 1 and ends when the token arrives at Site 1 again)?

7.4   As depicted in Figure 7.9, during the second cycle, the communication line between Sites 3 and 4, when the token is on it, goes down. For this cycle, answer the following questions:

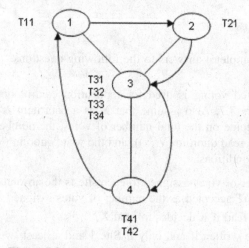

Figure 7.8   Network topology for Exercise 7.3.

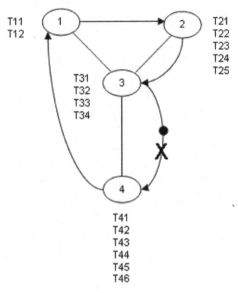

Figure 7.9   Network topology for Exercise 7.4.

(A) What is the ticket number when the token leaves Site 1?

(B) What is the ticket number when the token comes back to Site 1?

(C) How many transactions, and in what order, are serialized at the completion of cycle 1 and cycle 2?

7.5   At the beginning of cycle 3, the network looks like the one shown in Figure 7.10. Show the serialization order of all transactions at the completion of cycle 3.

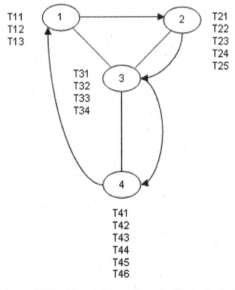

Figure 7.10   Network topology for Exercise 7.5.

8

FAILURE AND COMMIT PROTOCOLS

Any database management system needs to be able to deal with failures. There are many types of failures that a DBMS must handle. Before discussing failure types and commit protocols, we need to lay the foundation by defining the terms we will use in the rest of this chapter.

8.1 TERMINOLOGY

We define the terms we need here to make sure that the reader's understanding of these terms is the same as what we have in mind.

8.1.1 Soft Failure

A **soft failure**, which is also called a **system crash**, is a type of failure that only causes the loss of data in nonpersistent storage. A soft failure does not cause loss of data in persistent storage or disks. Soft failures can range from the operating system misbehaving, to the DBMS bugs, transaction issues, or any other supporting software issues. We categorize these under the soft failure, since we assume that the medium (the disk) stays intact for these types of failure. A soft failure can also be caused by the loss of power to the computer. In this case, whatever information is stored in the volatile storage of the computer, such as main memory, buffers, or registers, is lost. Again, the assumption we make is that power loss does not cause disk or database loss. This assumption does not mean that we do not deal with disk failure issues but that we treat the disk loss under the hard failure that we discuss next. Note that soft failures can leave the data stored in persistent storage in a state that needs to be addressed; for example, if the software was in the middle of writing information to the disk, and only

Distributed Database Management Systems by Saeed K. Rahimi and Frank S. Haug
Copyright © 2010 the IEEE Computer Society

some data items were written before the failure, then, obviously, the data content might be inconsistent, incomplete, or possibly corrupted. However, the persistent storage did not lose any data. This is true in the sense that the persistent storage still contains everything we wrote to it—it just does not contain all the things we intended to write to it.

8.1.2 Hard Failure

A **hard failure** is a failure that causes the loss of data on nonvolatile storage or the disk. A disk failure caused by a hard failure destroys the information stored on the disk (i.e., the database). A hard failure can be caused by power loss, media faults, IO errors, or corruption of information on the disk. In addition to these two types of failures, in a distributed system network failures can cause serious issues for a distributed DBMS. Network failures can be caused by communication link failure, network congestion, information corruption during transfer, site failures, and network partitioning. There have been many studies on the percentage, frequency, and causes of soft and hard failures in a computer system over the years [Mourad85] [Gray81] [Gray87]. We will not repeat these finding here.

As a rule of thumb, the following can be used as the frequency of different types of failures:

- Transaction failures happen frequently—maybe as many as a few times a minute. This is usually for high-volume transaction processing environments like banking and airline reservation systems. The recovery is usually fast and is measured in a fraction of a second.
- System failures (power failure) can happen multiple times a week. The time it takes to recover is usually minutes.
- Disk failures can happen once to maybe twice a year. Recovery is usually short (a few hours), if there is a new, formatted, and ready-to-use disk on reserve. Otherwise, duration includes the time it takes to get a purchase order, buy the disk, and prepare it, which is much longer (could be a number of days to a week or two).
- Communication link failures are usually intermittent and can happen frequently. This includes the communication link going down or the link being congested. Recovery depends on the nature of the failure. For congestion, typically the system state changes over time. For link failure, the link will be bypassed by the routing protocols until after the link is repaired. Sometimes the link failure is caused by the failure of a hub or a router. In this case, the links that are serviced by the hub or the router are disconnected from the rest of the network for the duration of the time the device is being repaired or replaced.

8.1.3 Commit Protocols

A DBMS, whether it is centralized or distributed, needs to be able to provide for atomicity and durability of transactions even when failures are present. A DBMS uses **commit protocols** to deal with issues that failures raise during the execution of transactions. The main issue that the commit protocols have to deal with is the ability to guarantee the "all or nothing" property of transactions. If a failure happens during the execution of a transaction, chances are that not all of the changes of the transaction have been committed to the database. This leaves the database in an inconsistent state as discussed in Chapter 5. Commit protocols prevent this from happening either by continuing the transaction to its completion (roll forward or redo) or by removing whatever changes it has made to the database (rollback or undo). The commit protocols guarantee that after a transaction successfully commits, all of its modifications are written to the database and made available to other transactions. Commit protocols also guarantee that all the incomplete changes made by the incomplete transactions are removed from the database by rollback when a failure happens.

8.1.3.1 Commit Point   A **commit point** is a point in time when a decision is made to either commit all the changes of a transaction or abort the transaction. The commit point of a transaction is a consistent point for the database. At this point, all other transactions can see a consistent state for the database. The commit point is also a restart point for the transaction. This means that the transaction can be safely undone. Finally, the commit point is a release point for the resources that the transaction has locked.

8.1.3.2 Transaction Rollback (Undo)   Transaction rollback or undo is the process of undoing the changes that a transaction has made to the database. Rollback is applied mostly as the result of a soft failure (see Section 8.1.1). Rollback is also used as a necessary part of transaction semantics. For example, in the fund transfer transaction in a banking system, there are three places from which a transaction should abort. It is necessary to abort this transaction if the first account number is wrong (it does not exist), if there is not enough money in the first account for the transfer, and finally, if the second account number is wrong (it does not exist). The following shows the fund transfer transaction that is written as a nested transaction consisting of two subtransactions—a debit and a credit transaction. This nesting of the two transactions allows the program to run on a distributed DBMS, where accounts are stored on two different servers.

```
Begin Transaction Fund_Transfer(from, to, amount);
    Begin Transaction Debit
          Read bal(from);
          If account not found then
          Begin
               Print "account not found";
               Abort Debit;
               Exit;
          End if;
          bal(from) = bal(from) - amount;
          if bal(from) < 0 then
          Begin
               Print "insufficient funds";
               Abort Debit;
               Exit;
          End if;
```

```
            write bal(from);
            Commit Debit;
      End Debit;
      Begin Transaction Credit
            Read bal(to);
            If account not found then
            Begin
                  Print "account not found";
                  Abort Credit;
                  Exit;
            End if;
            bal(to) = bal(to) + amount;
            write bal(to);
            Commit Credit;
      End Credit;
      Commit Fund_Transfer;
End Fund_Transfer;
```

This transaction transfers the "amount" from the "from" account to the "to" account. The debit subtransaction checks the validity of the account from which funds are to be taken. If that account does not exist, then the transaction is aborted. If the account exists but there is not enough money to transfer—the resulting balance after the debit is less than zero—the transaction has to abort again. The credit subtransaction does not need to worry about the amount of money in the "to" account since money will be added but needs to make sure that the "to" account exists. If the "to" account does not exist, then the transaction aborts again.

If all three abort conditions are false, then the transaction is at the commit point. At this point, as mentioned before, the user needs to make a decision to commit the transaction or roll it back. For an ATM transaction, this point in time is when the ATM machine gives the customer the option to complete the transaction or cancel it. At this point, each account's balance has been updated and everything is ready to be committed. The two database servers—local systems where the accounts are stored—have the accounts' balances still locked. Once the user decides to commit the transaction, the locks are released and the new accounts' balances are available to other transactions.

8.1.3.3 *Transaction Roll Forward (Redo)*

Transaction roll forward or redo is the process of reapplying the changes of a transaction to the database. Since the changes are reapplied to the database, typically a transaction redo is applied to a copy of the database created before the transaction started. As we will discuss in Section 8.2, redo is mostly necessary for recovery from a hard failure.

8.1.4 Transaction States

A transaction goes through the following set of steps during execution:

```
1. Start_Transaction
2. Repeat
```

    2.1 Read a data item's value
    2.2 Compute new values for the data item
    2.3 If abort condition exists then abort and exit
    2.4 Write the new value for the data item
    2.5 If abort condition exists then abort and exit
3. Until no more data items to process
4. Commit
5. End_Transaction

Statement 1 indicates a transaction's activation by a user or the system. Similarly, statement 5 indicates the successful termination of the transaction. The transaction can also terminate unsuccessfully, as shown in statements 2.3 and 2.5, if abort conditions exist. Some DBMSs require explicit "Start Transaction" and "End Transaction" while others use implicit start and end statements. For example, in Oracle a begin transaction is assumed when changes are made to the database. In this context, an implicit "End Transaction" is assumed when a commit is issued. On the other hand, in SQL Server the "Start Transaction" and "End Transaction" are explicit. As seen in the code snippet above, once a transaction starts, it repeatedly reads the data items from the database, calculates new values for them, and writes new values for the data items to the database. Obviously, in this algorithm we assume the operation being performed inside the transaction is an update operation. In case of an insert into the database, no data items need to be read. Conversely, when a delete command is executed, no new values are written to the database.

One formal specification of a transaction uses a finite state automaton (FSA) that consists of a collection of states and transitions. This is typically shown as a state transition diagram (STD). In a STD, states are shown as circles and transitions as arrows, where the tail is connected to the state the program leaves and the tip is connected to the state the program enters. The state of the STD that a transaction is in at the time of a failure, tells the local recovery manager (LRM) what needs to be done for a transaction. Figure 8.1 depicts the STD for a transaction.

In this diagram, the double-lined circles are terminal states and the single-lined states are transitional. The "Idle" state corresponds to when the transaction is not running.

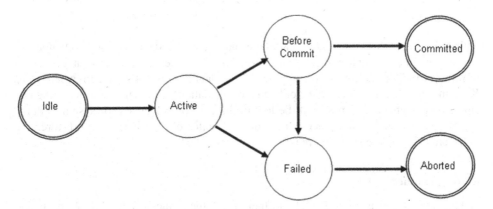

Figure 8.1   State transition diagram for a transaction.

Once started, a transaction changes state to the "Active" state. In the "Active" state, the transaction performs its work. In this state, the transaction reads, performs calculations, and writes data items. If any of the abort conditions hold, the transaction issues an abort and changes state to the "Failed" state. Entry into the "Failed" state causes the local recovery manager to undo the transaction. The transaction enters its commit point by transitioning to the "Before Commit" state. As mentioned before, at the commit point a transaction holds a consistent state for the database. It can back out of the transaction by canceling the transaction or it can complete the work by committing. Cancellation is performed by a transition from the "Before Commit" state to the "Failed" state, which causes the LRM to undo the transaction. The successful termination is initiated by transitioning from the "Before Commit" state to the "Committed" state.

It is important to remember the following:

- In the "Active" state, the transaction has not completed all the work necessary—not all changes have been made.
- In the "Before Commit" state, the transaction has completed all the work necessary—all transaction changes have been made.
- In the "Failed" state, the transaction has decided to abort or it has been forced by the DBMS to abort due to concurrency control and/or deadlock issues.
- In the "Committed" state, the transaction has terminated successfully.
- In the "Aborted" state, the transaction has terminated unsuccessfully.

A careful reader notices that actions of a transaction when it commits or aborts depend on whether or not the transaction changes have been written to the database. In other words, the update mode of the DBMS is important in what needs to be done to commit or rollback a transaction.

8.1.5 Database Update Modes

A DBMS can use two update modes:

- Immediate update mode—a DBMS is using immediate updates, if it writes the new values to the database as soon as they are produced by a transaction.
- Deferred update mode—a DBMS is using deferred update, if it writes the new values to the database when a transaction is ready to commit.

In the case of the immediate update, the old value of a data item being changed is overwritten in the database by the transaction. As a direct result of this, it is not possible to rollback the transaction if the old value of the data item is not stored anywhere else. Keep in mind that maintaining the old value of the data item in memory is not sufficient since the contents of memory will be lost in the case of power loss or system failure. Therefore, we need a safe place where the old values of data items can be stored. A transaction log is used for this purpose.

8.1.6 Transaction Log

A **transaction log** is a sequential file that stores the values of the data items being worked by transactions. Like the blocks written on a magnetic tape, a transaction log is a sequential device. To reach a certain record within the log, the log must be processed sequentially, either from the beginning or from the end. Typically, log records for a given transaction are linked together for ease of processing.

The transaction log is used for two purposes. The first use of the log is to support commit protocols to commit or abort running transactions. The second use of the log is to allow recovery of the database in case of a failure. In the first case, we use the log information to redo—repeat the changes of a transaction—or undo—remove the changes of a transaction from a database. Redo and undo are sometimes called transaction roll forward and rollback, respectively. When a transaction is rolled forward its changes are redone—rewritten to the database. When a transaction is rolled back, its changes are undone—removed from the database. In the second case, the log information is used to recover a database after a power failure or a disk crash. As we will discuss later, if power fails, incomplete transactions have to be undone. The log information is used to achieve this. Also, as we will discuss later, if the disk crashes, completed transactions need to be redone. Again, the log information is used to achieve this.

Information that is written to the log is used for recovering the contents of the database to a consistent state after a transaction rollback or after a failure. Without this information, recovery may not be possible. Technologically, today the safest place a log can be stored is on the disk. However, if the disk fails and the log is on it, the log is lost. That is, of course, not too troubling if the database is still intact. Losing the log and the database at the same time, obviously, is disastrous.

To make sure this is not the case, one of the following alternatives can be utilized:

1. Use tapes for the log. Although this separates the database storage (disk) and log storage (tape), this is not typically the choice of DBAs because writing to and reading from the tape is very slow. Some of the DBMSs, such as Oracle, archive the inactive portion of the log—the log portion that pertains to transactions that have been competed—on tape.

2. In smaller systems where the log and the database share the same disk, one can use different disk partitions for the database and the log files. Doing so reduces the probability of loss of the database and the log at the same time when a portion of the disk is damaged. In this case, if the disk completely fails or the disk controller goes bad, both the log and the database will be lost.

To guard against the issue with the second alternative, we can store the log and the database on separate disks. This is typically the case for larger systems where the database may require more than one disk for its storage. In this case, we can use a separate disk for the log files. In very large systems, a **RAID (redundant array of independent disks)** system may be used to provide for recovery of the disk contents by rebuilding the contents of a failed disk from other disks. Regardless of the alternative used for maintaining the log, the goal is to keep the log safe from power loss and/or disk failure. The storage type that is used for the log is known as the "stable storage" as categorized below.

8.1.7 DBMS Storage Types

There are three types of storage in the storage hierarchy of a DBMS:

1. *Volatile Storage (Memory).* Memory is a fast magnetic device that can store information for the computer to use. It is called volatile storage since loss of

electrical power causes it to lose its contents. That is why memory is used for temporary storage of information to serve the need of the CPU. During normal operations of the system, memory-based log files can be used for database rollback, since during the rollback, the transactions are still running and the memory contents are still intact. On the other hand, the memory cannot serve as a storage medium for logs required for database recovery after a failure since the memory contents of a failed system are lost.

2. *Nonvolatile Storage (Disk, Tape).* Disk and tape are magnetic devices that can store information in a way that withstands shutdowns and power losses. The information written to a disk or a tape stays intact even when the power is disconnected. Although disks and tapes are nonvolatile with respect to power loss, they are still volatile to medium failure—a disk crash causes the loss of information on the disk. As a result, a log that is stored on the disk is lost when the disk crashes.

3. *Stable Storage.* Stable storage is a storage type that can withstand power loss and medium failure. The log is written to stable storage so that the information in the log is not lost when the system is subjected to power failure or disk failure. DBMSs usually maintain duplicate or triplicate copies of the log files for resiliency. Lampson and Sturgis assume that replicating the log on the disk (persistent storage) is stable [Lampson76]. For the rest of our discussion in this chapter, we also assume a replicated log on the disk and we refer to the disk as stable storage.

8.1.8   Log Contents

As mentioned earlier in this chapter, the log is a sequential device consisting of a set of records. A log record stores information about a change from a single transaction. In addition to the time of the change, specific information about the transaction ID, the DML operation, the data item involved, and the type of operation are recorded. Specific record contents depend on the mode of update. To represent a log record, we use the notation "<record_type>." A typical transaction log has records of the type <transaction start>, <transaction commit>, <transaction abort>, <insert>, <delete>, <update>, and <checkpoint>. Obviously, since read operations do not change data item values, they are not tracked in the log. There are many types of log records that support different strategies for updating the database—immediate versus deferred—and recovery alternatives for power and disk failures. We will start by investigating the transaction update modes and their impact on what the log should contain.

8.1.8.1   *Deferred Update Mode Log Records*   In this mode of update, the DBMS does not write the changes of a transaction to the database until a transaction decides to commit (the commit point). There are two basic approaches used for deferred updates. Özsu and Valduriez [Özsu99] outline the details of these approaches in what they call "out-of-place" update. We briefly mention the two approaches here.

The first approach uses the concept of differential files, which has been used in the operating system for file maintenance for many years. Severance and Lohman proposed to extend the concept to database updates [Severance76]. In this approach, changes are not made to the database directly, but instead, they are accumulated in a separate file as the difference. A file could accumulate changes from a single transaction or from multiple transactions. There are two approaches to merging the changes from the differential files with the database. A transaction's changes can be merged into the database when the transaction commits. Alternatively, changes can be left in the file and be used as the new values for the changed data items. In this case, the DBMS has to keep track of the new values for data items that have been worked on in the files. Once these files become too large and the overhead becomes too high, the files are merged into the database and the differential files are discarded.

The second approach uses the concept of "shadow paging" [Astrahan76]. In this approach, the database page containing the data item being changed is not modified. Instead, the change is made to a copy of the page called the "shadow page." The actual database page holds the old data item value (used for undo) and the shadow page contains the new data item value (used for redo). If the transaction decides to commit, the shadow page becomes part of the database and the old page is discarded. Logging in conjunction with shadow paging has been used to enable database recovery after a failure in IBM's System R [Gray81].

As a direct result of deferred updates, for each data item being changed, the old value (also known as the "before-image") is in the database until just before the transaction commits. Therefore, the log only needs to tack the new value (also known as the "after-image") for the data item being changed in the log. Therefore, in the deferred update mode, the old values of the data items being changed by a transaction do not need to be written to the log. To see what is stored in the log for a database that uses the deferred update mode, let T5 be a fund transfer transaction that transfers $200 from account A1 with the balance of $1000 to account A2 with the balance of $500. For this example, the records written to the log for T5 are

```
<T5, t1, Start>
<T5, t2, update, Account.A1.bal, after-image = $800>
<T5, t3, update, Account.A2.bal, after-image = $700>
<T5, t4, Before Commit>
<T5, t5, Commit>
```

Notice that every record has a time marker indicating the time of the event. The first record indicates that transaction T5 has started. The second and third records track the writes that T5 makes, the time of these events, and the after-images for the data items being changed. The fourth record indicates that there will be no more changes made by this transaction; that is, the transaction has entered its commit point at time t4. This log shows a successful completion of T5, which is indicated by the existence of the commit record at time t5. During normal operations, transferring the new values for the two data items from the memory buffers is followed by writing a commit record to the log. If, on the other hand, T5 had decided to abort the transaction, the log would have contained the following records:

```
<T5, t1, Start>
<T5, t2, update, Account.A1.bal, after-image = $800>
<T5, t3, update, Account.A2.bal, after-image = $700>
```

```
<T5, t4, Before Commit>
<T5, t5, Abort>
```

For deferred updates, when T5 aborts there is no need to undo anything. That is because T5 does not write anything to the database until it decides to commit. If a failure happens, depending on the time and type of failure, T5 needs to be undone or redone (see Section 8.4). If T5 needs to be redone, the after-images from the log are used. Again, there is nothing to do to undo T5.

8.1.8.2 Immediate Update Mode Log Records In this mode of update, the DBMS writes the changes of a transaction to the database as soon as the values are prepared by the transaction. As a direct result of this, the old values of the data items are overwritten in the database. Therefore, the log not only needs to track the after-images but also the before-images of the data items changed by the transaction. If T5, as discussed above, runs a system with immediate update, the log records will look like the following:

```
<T5, t1, Start>
<T5, t2, update, Account.A1.bal, before-image = $1000,
                 Account.A1.bal, after-image = $800>
<T5, t3, update, Account.A2.bal, before-image = $500,
                 Account.A2.bal, after-image = $700>
<T5, t4, Before Commit>
<T5, t5, Commit>
```

When T5 decides to commit, the new values for the two data items are already in the database. Therefore, the only action required is indicating the successful completion of the transaction by writing a "Commit" record to the log. In immediate update mode, the DBMS has access to the before-and after-images of data items being changed in the log. The DBMS can undo T5 by transferring the before-images from the log to the database and can redo T5 by transferring the after-images of the data items to the database when needed. It should be obvious that in a multitransaction system the records that different transactions write to the log are interleaved.

The log record contents discussed above are generic and do not indicate implementation by any specific DBMS. Most DBMS vendors use two or three additional fields in each record to help traverse the records for a given transaction. A linked list is used to connect together all records that belong to the same transaction. Table 8.1 depicts an example of log records for four transactions "T1," "T2," "T3," and "T4," including the link fields (Record ID and Link Info in the table). This information is helpful in locating records for a given transaction quickly during recovery from a failure. Another point worth mentioning is that commercial DBMSs do not include "before commit" and "failed" records in the log and therefore eliminate these states. These states are recorded as part of the commit and the abort states. In other words, the state transition diagram for transactions is reduced to what is shown in Figure 8.2.

This approach speeds up the log management for committed and/or aborted transactions. The assumption is that most of the time transactions succeed and they are not subjected to failures. As a result, it seems unnecessary to do a lot of recordkeeping for dealing with failures. The drawback to this approach, therefore, is the payback when failures do happen.

TABLE 8.1   Example of Log Records

Record ID	Tid	Time	Operation	Data Item	Before-Image	After-Image	Link Info
1	T1	t1	Start				3
2	T2	t2	Start				2
3	T1	t3	Update	Account.A1.bal	1000	800	8
4	T2	t4	Insert	Account.A3.No		1111	5
5	T2	t5	Insert	Account.A3.bal		750	6
6	T2	t6	Update	Account.A4.bal	600	550	9
7	T3	t7	Start				17
8	T1	t8	Before Commit				11
9	T2	t9	Before Commit				10
10	T2	t10	Commit				2
11	T1	t11	Commit				1
12	T4	t12	Start				13
13	T4	t13	Delete	Account.A5.No	2222		14
14	T4	t14	Delete	Account.A5.bal	650		15
15	T4	t15	Failed				16
16	T4	t16	Abort				12
17	T3	t17	Update	Account.A1.bal	800	1200	18
18	T3	t18	Before Commit				19
19	T3	t19	Commit				7

As an example, assume a system that does not write the "Before Commit" to the log to indicate that the transaction has finished preparing the new values for the data items. When a failure during the commitment of the transaction happens, since there is no "Before Commit" record in the log, the LRM has to assume that the transaction was active when the failure happened and will have to rollback the transaction. It should be easy to see that the existence of the "Before Commit" record in the log tells the LRM to commit the transaction using the new values of the changed data items from the log. We encourage readers to map the structure discussed above with specific DBMS

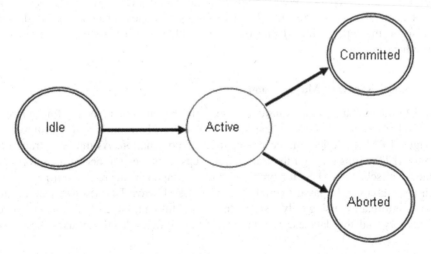

Figure 8.2   Reduced state transition diagram for a transaction.

implementation. For example, the following displays an update statement that changes the balance of account 1111 and the log records that are extracted by Oracle Log Miner from the log running the select statement shown against the "v$logmnr_contents" dictionary view.

```
Update account
Set bal = 800
Where No = 1111;
Commit;

SELECT  sql_redo, sql_undo, ph1_name, ph1_redo, ph1_undo
FROM    v$logmnr_contents;

update ACCOUNT set BAL = 800 where ROWID = 'AAABGpAABAAABdQAAA';
update ACCOUNT set BAL = 700 where ROWID = 'AAABGpAABAAABdQAAA';
BAL 800 700
```

As can be seen from the results of the select statement, Oracle records the actual SQL statement in the log record to be able to undo or redo a column change. In addition, Oracle tracks the operation type, before-image, and after-image for the column being changed. Note that there are many other columns used in this dictionary view in Oracle that we did not print. These columns record transaction ID, transaction name, timestamp, table, tablespace, and so on.

8.2   UNDO/REDO AND DATABASE RECOVERY

Now that we have discussed what the log for immediate and deferred update modes contains, we can discuss what actions are required to recover a database when a failure happens. There are only two actions the DBMS recovery manager performs to recover a database. These actions are the redoing or undoing of transactions. The question that needs to be answered is, "What action is required for each type of recovery?" The answer depends not only on the mode that the system uses for updating the database but also on the type of failure and on the state that each transaction is in when the failure happens.

8.2.1   Local Recovery Management

A DBMS tracks changes that transactions make to the database in the log for transaction abort and recovery purposes. To be able to do this, the DBMS utilizes the local recovery manager (LRM) to collect the necessary logging information. As the local transaction monitor (LTM) runs through the transaction steps, it passes the necessary information to the local scheduler (LS) for processing (see Chapter 5 on transaction processing). Each LS subsequently passes the request to the LRM. Most DBMSs today do not read or write information using only a single table row. Instead, the unit of transfer between the memory and the database is a larger unit of storage. A DBMS uses the concept of a **block** or a **page** as the smallest unit of storage for the database. The page size in some databases, like SQL Server, is fixed at 8 Kbytes where each Kbyte is 1024 bytes. In some other systems such as Oracle, the page size can be decided by the DBA and can be 4, 8, 16, or 32 Kbytes. To read a row in a table, a DBMS needs to transfer the page that contains the desired row into memory. Most DBMSs also do not simply bring a single page into memory. Instead, they transfer the **extent** that contains the page. An extent is typically eight contiguous pages, which is the smallest allocation unit in Oracle and SQL Server today. For simplicity, for the rest of the discussion in this chapter, we assume that a single page is the unit of transfer.

Storage of information in the main memory has to match the storage of information on the disk. A DBMS assumes the memory is divided into a set of equal size blocks called **frames**. A frame can hold exactly one page. Any page can go into any frame available. To speed up the reading and writing of information, a DBMS sets aside a number of main memory frames known as the **cache** or the **buffer**. The cache or buffer size is decided by the DBA and is measured in the number of frames or pages. The program that manages the transfer of information between the buffer and the stable storage (the disk) is known as the local buffer manager (LBM). A read is complete when the page that contains the desired information is transferred from the disk into a frame in memory. If the page containing the desired information is already in the buffer, the read does not necessitate a disk access. Similarly, it is assumed that a write is complete when the changes are made to the target buffer in memory. It is the responsibility of the local recovery manager to write the page (or the extent where the page is) to the stable storage successfully. This obviously requires proper log management by the LRM that we will discuss next. Figure 8.3 shows the local recovery manager and its interfaces to the LTM, LS, and LBM.

8.2.1.1 Database Buffers and Log Buffers

A DBMS maintains two types of buffers—the **database buffers** and the **log buffers**. The database buffers host database pages that have been read or written by transactions. The pages that have been written are sometimes called **dirty pages** as well. When a required page is not in the cache, it is **read** or **fetched**. When a page needs to be written to the stable storage it is **flushed** or **forced**. We would like to cache as much information as possible to speed up reading and writing.

Write-ahead-logging(WAL) [Lindsay79] was proposed to protect against loss of information being written to the database. Any change to the database is recorded in two places—in a database page in the database buffers, and in a log page in the log buffers. As long as these pages are maintained in memory, there should be no problem. If the contents of memory are lost—due to a failure—transactions whose changes were not recorded in the database must run again. According to WAL, once we decide to flush the dirty pages to the database, the log pages must be written to the stable storage before the dirty pages are written to the database on disk. That is because once we have successfully written the log in the stable storage, the database changes are guaranteed.

To see how this is possible, consider the fund transfer transaction we discussed earlier in this chapter. There are two data items that this transaction changes. Let us assume these two data items are on two separate pages in two separate extents, and that

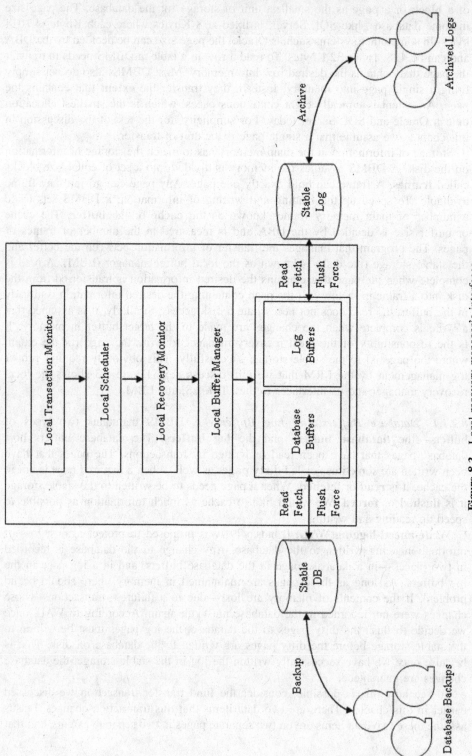

Figure 8.3 Local recovery manager's interfaces.

the changes are recorded in one log page. To commit this transaction, the LRM issues a force command to the LBM for the log page. The LBM may fail to complete this command or may succeed. In case of a failure, the contents of the memory buffers are lost. When the system restarts, the fund transfer transaction must be run again. In the absence of failures, the page is successfully written to the log in the stable storage. After the log page force command is completed, the LRM sends a force database page command to the LBM to write the two dirty pages for the transaction to the database. Again, there are two possible scenarios. In the first scenario, there are no failures, which allows the LBM to successfully write. In the second, during the writing of the dirty pages, there is a failure. In this case, after the failure is repaired, the changes can be made to the database pages by transferring the after-images from the log in the stable storage to the database pages.

8.2.1.2 *Log Archival and Database Backups*   Log records are associated with two types of transactions—transactions that are still running (**active transactions**) and transactions that have either committed and/or aborted (**completed transactions**). It should be obvious that the log records pertaining to the running transactions need to be readily available and therefore should be cached in the memory buffers. This speeds up the rollback of currently running transactions. Once a transaction commits (or aborts), its log records are not going to be needed unless there is a failure. As a result, the log records that correspond to terminated transactions can be transferred to the disk to make memory available for active transactions.

Note that if the amount of memory we allocate to the log buffers is not large enough, there may not be enough memory for all active transactions in the cache. This can be the case for a high-volume, concurrent transaction processing environment. In these environments, the log tends to grow very rapidly. The log size could easily reach and exceed the amount of memory allocated to the cache. Therefore, it is not possible to maintain the entire log in memory due to lack of space. In this case, even some of the active transactions' log records have to be forced to the disk.

On the disk, the log typically consists of two or more log files. For example, an Oracle 10 g log consists of three log files by default. The space on these files is considered sequential from File 1 to File 2, and File 2 to File 3. As the space on File 1 is used up, File 2 becomes the active file. Once the space on File 2 is completely used, File 3 becomes the active file. Once the space on all of the log files has been used, the DBA has to either archive inactive (committed/aborted) transaction records to the tape or add more files to the log to provide space for more logging. Otherwise, the DBMS cannot continue. **Note:** Although in Figure 8.3 we refer to archiving as writing the log or the database pages to magnetic tapes, some DBAs prefer archiving of information on disks instead of tapes.

Despite the fact that the database and the log are maintained on the stable storage, recovery from a failed database is not possible without a database backup. We can back up a database on a disk during the normal operation of the system. The backup on the disk is periodically archived onto a set of tapes for recovery from a major disk failure when the database is lost. We will discuss the alternatives for the database backup in the next section.

8.2.1.3 *Backup Types*   DBMSs use two alternatives to back up the database—a **complete backup** or an **incremental backup**. A complete backup is a backup of the

entire database contents. This is also known as a **full-image** backup. This backup can be done when the database is quiescent—there are no transactions running in the system. This type of backup is also known as **cold backup**. Alternatively, the backup can also be done when transactions are running in the system. This type of backup is known as a **hot backup**. When the backup is a cold backup, the log can be cleared since all transactions prior to the backup time have terminated. If, on the other hand, the backup is a hot backup, the log from previous cold backup is required for the recovery process. Figure 8.4 depicts examples of a cold and a hot backup.

In Figure 8.4a, the backup is a cold backup since no transactions were running at the time of the backup. In this case, since every transaction prior to the backup has terminated, there is no need to keep the log from prior to the backup. In Figure 8.4b, a hot backup was performed when transactions T2 and T3 were running. As a result, the log from prior to the last backup is needed. This also indicates the fact that as long as the backups are hot the log needs to be kept. Therefore, the log is probably going to grow very large. To prevent this from happening, a DBA must perform a cold backup periodically to be able to discard the log from the previous hot backups. Note also that a cold backup always corresponds to a consistent point of time for the database since all active transactions have been completed. Some DBMS vendors provide the capability to force the database to be quiescent. If the DBMS provides for the quiescent

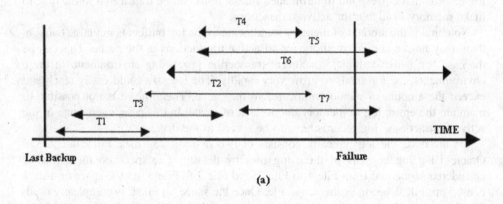

(a)

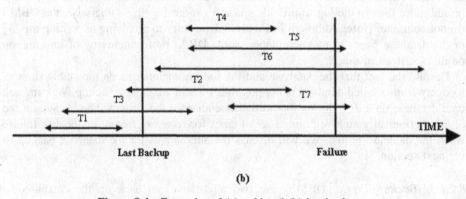

(b)

Figure 8.4 Examples of (a) cold and (b) hot backups.

option, then the DBA can force it, perform a cold backup, and discard the old log. Without an automatic quiescent option, the DBA needs to establish the point manually.

The following options can be used to force a quiescent point for a database:

- Put the database in read-only mode until after the backup.
- Bring the database off-line.
- Halt application processes.

An **incremental backup** is a backup that contains only the changes to the database from the previous complete backup or incremental backup. Since performing a complete database backup is time consuming, a DBA performs multiple incremental backups in between two consecutive complete backups. When needed, a complete image of the database is formed by merging the previous complete backup with individual incremental backups in order, up to the point of failure. Incremental backups are done when transactions are running—they are hot backups.

8.2.1.4 Rolling a Database Forward   A compete backup is a consistent snapshot of the database used for recovery. A complete backup is required for recovery from a failed disk when the database is lost. However, this is not the only use of the backup. The backup is also used for other types of recovery, as we will discuss later (see Section 8.5.2). A backup is used to restore the database to a consistent point in the past (as compared to the current time). To recover a failed database, we need to reapply those transactions that have committed between the backup time and the present to the restored image of the database. The LRM achieves this by using the log to redo committed transactions after the failure. This action is known as rolling the database forward.

8.2.1.5 Rolling a Database Back   The LRM rolls back a database by undoing the effects of one or more transactions. It starts with the current image of the database and rolls back transactions. This action is required when the current image of the database is inconsistent and we need to restore the database to a consistent point in the past.

8.3 TRANSACTION STATES REVISITED

Recall transaction states outlined in Section 8.1.4. We can extend the steps for a running transaction to include logging to support the transaction abort and database recovery. Note that what is logged depends on the mode of update—deferred versus immediate—as shown below (Sections 8.3.1 and 8.3.2).

8.3.1 Deferred Update Transaction Steps

The following depicts the transaction steps extended to include logging for a system that implements deferred updates.

```
1. Start_transaction
2. Log "Start"
3. Repeat
     3.1 Read a data item's "before-image"
```

```
   3.2 Compute the "after-image" for the data item
   3.3 If must abort then log "Abort" and exit
   3.4 Log the "after-image" of the data item
   3.5 Write the "after-image" of the data item
4. Until no more rows to process
5. Log "Commit"
6. Commit_transaction
7. End_transaction
```

8.3.2   Immediate Update Transaction Steps

The following depicts the transaction steps extended to include logging for a system that implements immediate updates.

```
1. Start_transaction
2. Log "Start"
3. Repeat
   3.1 Read a data item's "before-image"
   3.2 Log the "before-image" for the data item
   3.3 Compute the "after-image" for the data item
   3.4 If must abort then log "Abort" and exit
   3.5 Log the "after-image" of the data item
   3.6 Write the "after-image" of the data item
4. Until no more rows to process
5. Log "Commit"
6. Commit_transaction
7. End_transaction
```

A careful reader notices that the difference between the two sets of steps is the logging of the before-image of the data item for the immediate update approach. This step is not necessary for the deferred updates, since the old values of the items are in the stable storage and do not need to be logged.

8.4   DATABASE RECOVERY

In order to properly recover a database from failures and enable the transaction abort/restart, the LRM has to log the necessary information as part of the logging process. When a failure happens, the log information is used in the recovery process. In the following two sections, we discuss what the LRM logs in response to requests from the TM and then outline the steps that the LRM takes in the recovery process.

8.4.1   Logging Process

The LRM responses to the requests made by the transaction monitor are as follows:

- *Transaction Start.* The TM issues a transaction start request to the LRM with the transaction ID. The LRM then writes a transaction start record to the log for this transaction. As mentioned before, in addition to the transaction ID, timestamp and other system information are also stored as part of the record. What the LRM does in response to the transaction start is the same for immediate and deferred updates.

- *Transaction Read.* The TM issues a read request to the LRM for the data item. The LRM then tries to read the data item from the cached pages that belong to the transaction. If the data item is in the cache, its value is given to the transaction. If the data item is not cached, then the LRM issues a fetch command to the LBM, which then loads the page into the cache. In addition, the LRM has to record the value of the data item in the log for the immediate update case.

- *Transaction Write.* The TM issues a write request to the LRM by specifying a value for the data item. The LRM then tries to locate the data item in the transaction's cache. In this case, the data item is changed in the cache and the new value is written to the log. Note that, in this case, the old value has already been written to the log by the transaction before. If the data item is not cached, the LRM issues a fetch command to the LBM to cache the page containing the data item. The LRM also records the before value of the data item in the log for the immediate update case. The data item is then changed in the cache, and the new value is also recorded in the log. Note that when the data item is changed in the cache we assume that it is written to the database. When immediate update is used, the LBM transfers the page containing the data item to the database immediately. In the case of deferred update, the page is forced to the stable database when the transaction commits. In either case, WAL rules apply when writing dirty pages to the database.

- *Transaction Abort.* An abort request indicates an unsuccessful termination of the transaction. In response to an abort request, the LRM's actions depend on the mode of update. In the case of immediate updates, since the database has been changed for the data items that the transaction has written, the LRM has to undo the changes. To do this, the LRM restores the before-images of the data items that the transaction has written from the log into the database. Then the LRM records the termination of the transaction with a transaction abort record in the log. When deferred update is used, since database pages have not been written yet, the abort does not necessitate any database page changes. In this case, the buffer database pages that belong to the aborting transaction are simply discarded. Similar to the immediate case, the LRM records the termination of the transaction with a transaction abort record in the log.

- *Transaction Commit.* The TM issues either a commit transaction or end transaction to the LRM to indicate a successful termination. The LRM's actions in response to the commit request depend on the mode of update. If the update mode is deferred, then the LRM sends a flush/force command to the LBM to write the log pages and dirty pages for this transaction to the stable storage. Obviously, the WAL rules, which require log pages be written before database dirty pages are written, are enforced. Once the LBM has flushed the pages, the LRM writes a commit record for the transaction to the log. In the case of immediate update, changed pages for the transaction have already been flushed to the database and therefore the only action for the LRM to do is to write a transaction commit record to the log.

Note: In the above discussion, we indicated the completion of transaction commit and abort by writing a corresponding record to the log. In practice, the system may add the transaction that has committed/aborted to the list of committed/aborted transactions, and carry the actual commit and abort action later. This is an attempt to reduce the number of disk I/Os by attempting to write as many pages as possible together to the disk.

8.4.2 Recovery Process

The recovery process is initiated after a failure. The failure, as mentioned before, can be a soft failure, power loss, hard failure, or disk crash. Once the computer fails, it needs to be restarted. If the cause of the failure is a software failure, normally a reboot of the system is all that is needed. If the failure is due to power loss, power has to be restored to the system and then the system is restarted. Our assumption is that a power failure does not cause any disk damage or database information loss. This does not mean that we do not deal with disk damage caused by a power loss; it simply means that we categorize such failure as a hard failure or disk crash.

Typically, a failed disk requires replacement. If the disk failure is not catastrophic, some information on the disk will be recoverable. That would be the case when a portion of the disk, such as a logical partition, is damaged but the rest of the disk and the electronics controlling the disk head movement are still intact. In either case, we assume total database loss and outline the process for its recovery. After total loss of the database, recovery is not possible by only utilizing the information on the log. Such failure requires not only the information on the log but also a backup of the database on either another disk or a magnetic tape.

8.4.2.1 *Log Information Analysis*
The LRM processes the information in the log to determine the state of each transaction at the time of the failure. To help with this process, as explained before, log records are linked together for each transaction. In addition, DBMSs maintain a transaction table that holds the transaction IDs and a pointer to the transaction start record for each transaction in the log. Like the log, this table is also maintained in the stable storage. The LRM determines what to do for each transaction by following the transaction's link in the transaction table and then finding the log records for each transaction.

As such, the LRM categorizes transactions in the log in the following manner:

- If a transaction has a transaction start record and a transaction commit record, then this transaction belongs to the list of committed transactions.
- If a transaction has a transaction start record and a transaction failed but not a transaction abort record, then this transaction belongs to the list of failed transactions.
- If a transaction has a transaction start record and a transaction abort record, then this transaction belongs to the list of aborted transactions.
- If a transaction has a transaction start record and a transaction before-commit record but not a transaction commit or abort record, then this transaction belongs to the list of before-commit transactions.
- If a transaction has a transaction start record and a no before-commit, commit, abort or failed record, then this transaction belongs to the list of active transactions.

8.4.2.2   Recovery from a Power Failure   Remember we assumed that power failure does not cause loss of database information. It only causes the loss of information in the volatile storage (memory). After power is restored to the system, the OS and DBMS software restart. The OS issues a new type of command (i.e., recover command) to the LRM. The LRM's recovery from a power failure depends on the mode of update. The LRM processes the log information and categorizes transactions according to the above categories. The LRM then performs the following to recover a consistent state of the database as close as possible to the time of failure.

In the case of **immediate update**, the LRM will take the following steps:

- It will undo transactions that are in the active list. For each such transaction, the LRM also writes a transaction abort record to the log indicating the transaction's abort.
- It will redo transactions that are in the before-commit list. For each such transaction, the LRM also writes a transaction commit record to the log indicating the transaction's abort.
- It will undo transactions that are in the failed list. For each such transaction, the LRM also writes a transaction abort record to the log indicating the transaction's abort.
- The LRM does not have to do anything for transactions that are in committed and/or aborted lists since they had completed before the failure.

In the case of **deferred update**, the LRM will take the following steps:

- It will write a transaction abort record to the log for each active transaction. This is to indicate these transactions have been aborted. Note that LRM does not actually have to undo such transactions, since they have not written anything to the stable database yet.
- It will redo transactions that are in the before-commit list. For each such transaction, the LRM also writes a transaction commit record to the log indicating the transaction's abort.
- It will write a transaction abort record for each transaction in the failed list. This will indicate these transactions have been aborted. Again, the LRM does not actually have to undo such transactions since they have not written anything to the stable database yet.
- The LRM does not have to do anything for transactions that are in committed and/or aborted lists since they had completed before the failure.

8.4.2.3   Recovery from Disk Failure   We assume a "hard crash" will cause a total database loss. This is a catastrophic failure that requires a new disk, a complete database backup, and a log that is in sync with the backup. The computer operator will prepare the new disk for restoration. Similar to the case of a power failure, once the OS is restored, it sends a recover command to the LRM to recover the database. In this case, the mode of the update does not matter since the newly restored disk does not contain any of the running transactions' changes at the time of failure. Therefore, recovery from a disk crash is the same for the immediate and the deferred update modes. The LRM processes the log information and categorizes the transactions according to the above categories.

The LRM performs the following to recover the database as close as possible to the time of failure:

- It will redo all transactions that are in the committed transactions list.
- It will also redo all transactions that are in the before-commit list. For each one of these transactions, the LRM also writes a commit record to the log indicating that these transactions have been committed.
- For each transaction in the list of failed transactions, the LRM writes an abort record to the log indicating their termination.
- For each transaction in the list of active transactions, the LRM writes an abort record to the log indicating their termination.

Note: It is a good idea for a DBA to perform a complete backup of the database immediately after recovery and before the database is put online for general use. As a result, it seems unnecessary to log the cleanup actions that the LRM takes. After all, after the complete backup, the old log has to be discarded and a new one started. Although that is the case for a successful recovery, chances are that, during the recovery, a new failure might happen. The recovery from this new failure needs a log that represents the state of the database as of the time of the second failure and not the first one. The cleaned up log correctly portrays the new state and will be used for the new recovery process. Once the database is successfully recovered, the DBA should perform a full backup and discard the updated log.

8.4.2.4 *Checkpointing*   **Checkpointing** is used by different DBMSs to shorten the recovery process. There are different alternatives for checkpointing. We will cover two types of checkpointing—**fuzzy checkpointing** and **consistent checkpointing**.

Fuzzy checkpointing writes the list of active transactions at the time of the checkpoint to the log. Fuzzy checkpointing is very inexpensive and can be done while transactions are running in the system. The usefulness of this type of checkpointing is seen in recovery from a power failure. Recall that the LRM will have to undo all transactions that are active at the time of a power failure. Without a checkpoint in the log, the LRM has to process the entire log to determine which transactions were active when the power failure happened. This, obviously, is very time consuming and prolongs the recovery. With checkpointing, the LRM only has to process those transactions that are active at the time of the checkpoint and later. It should be obvious that all transactions prior to the last checkpoint have terminated and, therefore, cannot be active. Since fuzzy checkpointing is cheap to do, frequent use of it improves the power failure recovery. However, this type of checkpointing does not help with recovery from disk failure.

Consistent checkpointing is done for a consistent snapshot of the database. As a result, consistent checkpointing is very expensive and has to be done when the database is quiescent. Lindsey calls this type of a checkpoint a transaction-consistent-checkpoint [Lindsey79].

Consistent checkpointing is carried out as follows:

- A checkpoint start record is written to the log.
- Information about the running transactions is recorded in the log.

- Processing of new transactions that enter the system after the time of the start checkpoint record is halted until the checkpoint is complete.
- Once all running transactions have completed, all dirty pages of the database are flushed to the disk.
- An end checkpoint record is written to the log.

This type of checkpointing establishes a consistent image of the database at the time of the checkpoint. Therefore, it can help in power failure recovery. When recovering from a power failure, the only transactions that are on the right side of the last consistent checkpoint are processed. Only these transactions have to be undone or redone. All transactions to the left side of the last consistent checkpoint are ignored since they have completed. Just like fuzzy checkpointing, this type of checkpointing does not help with disk failure recovery unless we back up the database at the time of the consistent checkpoint. In the absence of a backup at the time of consistent checkpoint, the database has to be restored to the consistent image as of the time of the last backup. Therefore, all completed transactions from before the checkpoint and afterwards have to be redone. It is a good idea to back up the database when a consistent checkpoint is performed since the database has already been forced to a quiescent state.

Microsoft's SQL Server DBMS performs a semiconsistent checkpoint when the log file is 75% full. By default, SQL Server flushes all the dirty database pages to the stable storage when this threshold is reached. SQL Server also truncates the log at this time by removing all records for completed transactions from it. This is an attempt to make room available for currently running and future transactions. The issue with this idea is that if a quiescent point is not established soon after and/or if the database is not backed up, recovery from a disk failure is not possible. That is because information about all completed transactions prior to the checkpoint have been removed from the log. That is also why SQL Server DBAs must make a point of disabling "truncate log on checkpoint" and/or make a habit of performing a complete backup of the database immediately following a checkpoint.

8.5   OTHER TYPES OF DATABASE RECOVERY

Database recovery can be based on transactions or time. Recovery based on time is either recovering the database to current (now or the time of failure) or recovery to a point-in-time in the past.

8.5.1   Recovery to Current

This type of recovery is usually for disk and power failures. We have already explained the steps necessary to perform this type of recovery in Section 8.4.2.3.

8.5.2   Recovery to a Point-in-Time in the Past

This type of recovery (also known as PIT recovery) is usually performed to reestablish the database to a consistent point in the past. Typically, PIT is a quiescent point when there are no active transactions running. This type of recovery is not done because of a failure.

PIT recovery is done either by transaction rollback or transaction roll forward.

- *PIT Using Rollback.* For this approach, the LRM will put the database offline; will undo all active and completed transactions from the current time to a PIT; and then will put the database back online.
- *PIT Using Roll Forward.* For this approach, the LRM will put the database offline; will restore the database from the most recent complete cold backup; will roll all completed transactions prior to the PIT forward; and will put the database back online.

The question that comes to mind is: "Which type of PIT recovery is better?" The answer depends on the amount of work that the LRM has to perform for each case. If the number of transactions that need to be undone is smaller than the number of transactions that have to be redone, then rollback is used. Otherwise, roll forward is used.

8.5.3 Transaction Recovery

This type of recovery is usually performed to remove the effect of some bad transactions from the database. This does not necessarily indicate a failure, but perhaps we must address the fact that some transactions that ran previously need to be compensated for. Similar to the PIT recovery, the transaction recovery can be done by UNDO scripts or REDO scripts. UNDO scripts are generated first and then applied to remove the work that the "bad" transactions have performed. REDO scripts are generated first for the "good" transactions—that is, all transactions except the bad ones. The REDO scripts are then applied to an image of the database in the past. The REDO and UNDO scripts are generated from the log contents.

8.5.3.1 *Transaction Recovery Using UNDO Scripts* For this type of transaction recovery, the LRM forces a quiescent point, puts the database in the "DBA use only" mode, analyzes the log, and generates the UNDO scripts for bad transactions. Once the scripts are generated, they are run against the database. The scripts can be run with the database online.

The following are steps to generate the UNDO scripts:

- If the transaction has performed an insert, the LRM compensates that by generating a delete from the after-images in the log.
- If the transaction has performed a delete, the LRM compensates that by generating an insert from the before-images in the log.
- If the transaction has performed an update, the LRM compensates that by generating an update from the after-images and before-images in the log.

Note: Bad transactions in this case include the target transactions as well as all transactions that have used what the bad transactions have written to the database.

8.5.3.2 Transaction Recovery Using REDO Scripts For this type of transaction recovery, the LRM forces a quiescent point, analyzes the log, and generates the REDO scripts for the transactions since the last backup, but not including the bad transactions. The scripts can run with the database online.

The following are steps to generate the REDO scripts:

- If the transaction has performed an insert, the LRM generates an insert from the after-images in the log.
- If the transaction has performed a delete, the LRM generates a delete from the before-images in the log.
- If the transaction has performed an update, the LRM generates an update from the after-images and before-images in the log.

The LRM then restores the last cold backup, applies the REDO scripts to the database, and then opens the database for public use.

Example 8.1   In this example, we perform recovery with incremental logs for deferred updates. Assume the five transactions depicted in Figure 8.5, the time of failure, the checkpoint, and the database backup.

What are the recovery steps if the system utilizes deferred updates?

- *Recovery from Power Failure.* If transactions T3 or T5 have written before-commit records to the log, then redo them and write commit records for them to the log. If T3 or T5 have NOT written before-commit records to the log, then write abort records for T3 or T5 to the log.
- *Recovery from Disk Failure.* Restore the database from the last backup. Redo T1, T2, and T4. If T3 or T5 have logged before-commit, then redo T3 or T5 and log that have been committed; otherwise, log that they have been aborted.

Example 8.2   In this example, we perform recovery with incremental logs for immediate (instead of deferred) updates. Assume the same five transactions in Example 8.1, the time of failure, the checkpoint, and the database backup.

What are the recovery steps if the system utilizes immediate updates?

- *Recovery from Power Failure.* If T3 or T5 have written before-commit records to the log, then write two commit records to the log indicating that they have committed; otherwise, undo T3 or T5 and log that they have been aborted.

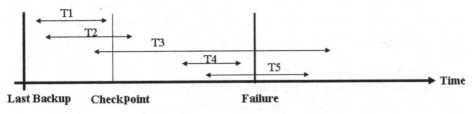

Figure 8.5   Failure recovery example.

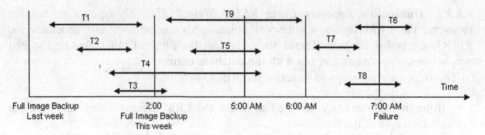

Figure 8.6 Transactions involved in Example 8.3.

- *Recovery from Disk Failure.* Restore the database from the backup. Redo T1, T2, and T4. If T3 or T5 have logged before-commit, then redo T3 or T5 and log that have been committed; otherwise, log that they have been aborted.

Example 8.3   Assume the transactions, the backup time, and failure time indicated in Figure 8.6. Assume the system uses an immediate update strategy and that neither T6 nor T8 has entered its commit process when the failure happens at 7:00 A.M.
The following statements are true for this system:

- We do not need to maintain the logs for the backup taken last week since that backup was taken at a quiescent time—a cold backup.
- We do need to maintain the logs for the backup taken this week since there are transactions running at the time of the backup—a hot backup.
- After a power failure, we must undo T6 and T8 and write an abort record for each transaction to the log.
- After a disk failure, we must restore from this week's full backup image. Roll forward (redo) T3, T4, T5, T7, and T9. Write abort records to the log for T6 and T8.
- At 7:00 A.M. and without any failure, we can use two approaches to recover to 6:00 A.M. as a PIT recovery. Approach 1: Do not restore; undo T6, T7, and T8. Approach 2: Restore from this week's backup; redo T3, T4, T5, and T9. The first approach is better since there are fewer transactions to recover.
- To recover from running transactions T1, T2, and T5, we restore to last week's cold backup; generate the redo scripts for T3, T4, T7, and T9; run the redo scripts; and rerun T6 and T8 if necessary.

8.6   RECOVERY BASED ON REDO/UNDO PROCESSES

We have discussed four recovery classes, which were based on the failure types and mode of updates:

- Recovery from power failure with immediate updates
- Recovery from power failure with deferred updates
- Recovery from disk failure with immediate updates
- Recovery from disk failure with deferred updates

Researchers have classified these approaches from another angle based on whether or not redo and undo is used [Bernstein87]. If the recovery process uses redo, it is known as "redo recovery," and if it uses undo, then it is known as "undo recovery." The recovery process could also choose not to use redo—known as "no-redo," or could choose not to use undo—known as "no-undo" recovery.

This provides for four alternatives for the recovery process as classified below:

- *Class 1 Recovery: Redo/Undo.* The redo in this approach applies to those transactions that are at the commit point. Analyzing the log, the LRM will redo transactions in the "Before Commit" state as well as committed transactions reflecting their effects on the stable database. Afterwards, a commit record is written to the log for each transaction in the "Before Commit" state. The undo in this approach applies to those transactions that are incomplete at the time of the failure. The LRM will undo transactions that are in the "Active" state. Afterwards, an abort record is written to the log for each one of these transactions. Comparing this approach to what we discussed in Section 8.4.2.3, we realize that the redo/undo recovery is the same as the **recovery from a disk failure** in the **immediate update** strategy.

- *Class 2 Recovery: Redo/No-Undo.* The redo in this approach is the same as Class 1. This approach does not require undo since the transactions are only written to the database after the transactions enter the "Before Commit" state. That is, changes of a transaction are deferred until a decision is made to commit the transaction. Comparing this approach to what we discussed in Section 8.4.2.3, we realize that the redo/no-undo recovery is the same as **recovery from a disk failure** in the **deferred update** strategy.

- *Class 3 Recovery: No-Redo/Undo.* The no-redo in this approach indicates that transactions are never redone. That is because changes of a transaction have been written to the database immediately. At the commit point, there is no work to be done except writing a commit record to the log. Since transactions' changes are reflected in the database immediately, if a transaction decides to abort, its changes have to be undone and the action has to be recorded by the LRM in the log. Obviously, this class corresponds to what we called **recovery from a power failure** for the **immediate update** strategy in Section 8.4.2.2.

- *Class 4 Recovery: No-Redo/No-Undo.* This approach writes changes for a transaction to the database at the commit point and therefore requires no-redo when a transaction actually commits. The approach does not require undo since changes are not written to the database if the transaction aborts. Again, comparing this to what we discussed in Section 8.4.2.2, we realize that the approach corresponds to what we called **recovery from a power failure** for the **deferred update** strategy.

8.7   THE COMPLETE RECOVERY ALGORITHM

The following code snippet outlines the complete recovery process for power and disk failures. Both immediate and deferred updates are included in the code. Note in this code that the notation "<Ti, Action>" indicates a log record for transaction "Ti" and the action it logs. The notation "/*...*/" indicates a comment.

```
Begin recovery
    Analyze the log
    Create list 1 containing those transactions that have
    a <T, Begin> record but not a <T, Before commit> record
        these are incomplete transactions.
    Create list 2 containing those transactions that have
    a <T, Begin> record and a <T, Before commit> record
        these are before committed transactions.
    Create list 3 containing those transactions that have
    a <T, Begin> record and a <T, Commit> record
        these are committed transactions.

Case (a):
    Power Failure without database loss
    If deferred updates
    Then
            Redo transactions in list 2;
            Write Commit to the log for transactions in list 2;
            For transactions in list 1 write abort to the log;
    Else /*Immediate updates*/
            Undo transactions in list 1;
            Write abort for transactions in list 1;
            Write commit for transactions in list 2;
    End if;

Case (b):
    Disk crash with database loss
            Restore database from tape;
            For transactions in 1 write abort to the log;
            Redo transactions in list 2;
            Write commit to the log for them;
            Redo transactions in list 3;

Case (c):
    Database, backup and log loss
            Look for another job;
    End Case;
End recovery;
```

8.8 DISTRIBUTED COMMIT PROTOCOLS

In the previous section, we described the centralized fault tolerance and commit protocol. We discussed how the commit protocol guarantees the atomicity of a transaction
in a centralized system even when failures happen. In this section, we will discuss
extensions to the centralized fault tolerance concepts to support transaction atomicity
in a distributed database.

In a centralized system, the issues with atomicity were related to the transaction's abort, concurrency control issues such as deadlocks, system failures, and disk failures. The collection of local systems that form a distributed system use a communication network for their interconnection. In addition to having to deal with issues that a local server handles in committing a local transaction, in a distributed system we must be able to deal with a local server's system crash, disk failures, and also with communication link failures. Network partitioning, especially, is very difficult to deal with in supporting the distributed commit protocols.

To understand why distributed commit protocols are necessary, we should use an example. Let us assume that a distributed system consists of two servers. Let us also assume that the fund transfer transaction transfers money from an account on the first server to an account on the second server. Locally, each server runs a transaction—the first server runs the debit transaction while the second server runs the credit transaction. Once each local server is done executing, it indicates that the local transaction has entered the "Before-Commit" state in its STD—the local transaction is then ready to commit. However, the local servers cannot commit the transaction unilaterally until it is guaranteed that both servers can commit. If one server is ready to commit and the other is not, the transaction as a whole cannot commit. Distributed atomicity requires that either all servers commit the transaction or none of them commits.

The steps that are required to globally commit a distributed transaction are therefore different from the steps required to commit a local transaction. In a local system, once the transaction monitor decides to commit a transaction, it simply communicates the decision to the local LRM to do so. In a distributed system, on the other hand, the decision to commit or abort a transaction must not only be communicated to all the local servers involved, but also be uniformly enforced. Problems arise when a local server that has been involved in a distributed transaction cannot be reached or is not available to commit or abort the global transaction. Failures that directly impact the distributed commit protocols are loss of data during communication, data corruption, network failure, site crash, network congestion, and network partitioning. As we will show, some of these protocols are blocking—the failure of one server blocks the process of other servers—while some of these protocols are nonblocking—the failure of one server does not block other servers.

8.8.1 Architectural Requirements

Before discussing the distributed commit protocols, we would like to outline the required architectural elements. The distributed commit protocols assume the existence of a process called the **coordinator**. Typically, the coordinator is the **transaction monitor** (**TM**) that runs at the site where the transaction enters the system. All other servers or sites involved in a transaction act as **slaves** or **followers**. The transaction coordinator is responsible for carrying out the transaction across all slave sites involved in the transaction. Once the transaction has been executed successfully by all slaves, the coordinator needs to make a decision to either commit or abort the transaction. After the decision has been made, the coordinator is responsible for making sure that all slaves carry out the decision uniformly—meaning that either all sites commit the transaction or all sites abort the transaction.

To detect failures, sites use a timeout mechanism. Local timers are used for this purpose. The timer at a site is set to a predetermined time interval. The timer at a site starts when the site sends a message. The site expects to get a response from a remote site before the timer goes off (expires). For example, when the coordinator sends a command to a slave to execute a transaction, it starts the timer. If the coordinator does not hear from the slave before the timer goes off, the coordinator suspects that this slave has failed. To make sure, the coordinator sends a message requesting a response from the allegedly failed slave. This message is known as a **ping**—similar to the sonar signals submarines use to detect the existence of an external object. If there is no response from the slave, the coordinator knows the slave has failed. To be able to recover from a failure, a site must be able to determine its transactions' states at the time of the failure after the site is repaired. This, as mentioned before, assumes that each site properly writes the necessary records to the site's log for all local transactions.

Recall that in our transaction model a distributed transaction consists of a set of subtransactions (**local transactions**), each one of which runs at a local site. Each local site runs through the states of the local STD for its transaction. That includes the local transaction running at the coordinator site as well as slave sites. Without orchestration from the coordinator, the subtransactions of a global transaction could end up in different terminal states of abort and commit. The coordinator has to make sure that all its local transactions forming the global transaction terminate in either the commit state or in the abort state but not in both states at the same time.

8.8.2 Distributed Commit Protocols

There are many **distributed commit protocols** (**DCPs**) proposed and studied over the years [Gray78] [Gray87] [Lampson76] [Lindsey79] [Skeen81] [Skeen82] [Skeen83]. These include **one-phase commit** (**1PC**), **two-phase commit** (**2PC**), **three-phase commit** (**3PC**), or **quorum-based commit** (**QBC**), which we will discuss next. In discussing DCPs, researchers have used the concept of phase to differentiate alternatives. What is not clear is whether or not the execution phase of the transaction is counted as part of the protocol. For instance, Skeen and Stonebraker present a formal model for DCPs [Skeen83]. The example they use for the two-phase commit protocol in a two-site system is explained as follows:

Phase 1: Site 1 (the coordinator) sends the transaction to Site 2 (the only slave). Site 2 starts the local transaction, executes the transaction, but does not commit. If the execution is successful, Site 2 sends a "Yes" message to Site 1 to commit; otherwise, it sends a "No" message to abort.

Phase 2: Site 1 receives the response (vote) from Site 2. If the vote is "Yes" and Site 1 agrees, then it sends a "Commit" message to Site 2; otherwise, it sends an "Abort" message.

As a contrast to this, Özsu and Valduriez use a STD for the two-phase commit that starts with an initial state [Özsu99]. The initial state concept used by Özsu and Valduriez does not correspond to the transaction start state used by Skeen. When we examine these two definitions of the two-phase commit protocol side-by-site, it is clear that there is no general agreement on how to count the number of phases of the protocol. According to Skeen and Stonebraker, the transaction's overall life cycle is divided into two phases—the execution phase and the commit phase. While according to Özsu and Valduriez, the overall life cycle of the transaction is divided into three phases—the execution phase, the preparing phase, and the commit phase. However, all these researchers call the approach "two-phase commit."

There is general agreement that every local transaction that acts as a subtransaction of a global transaction enters the "Before Commit" state after it finishes its active state and before it enters the commit or abort state. Our discussion of different distributed commit protocols assumes the distributed commit process starts when all subtransactions have entered the "Before Commit" state (see Section 8.1.4).

8.8.3   One-Phase Commit

One-phase commit (1PC) is the simplest form of the distributed commit. In the 1PC, once the coordinator makes a decision to commit or abort a distributed transaction, it communicates that decision to the slaves in one broadcast. The slaves that receive the message carry out the decision and acknowledge the action. Figure 8.7 depicts execution of a distributed transaction in a three-site system using the 1PC protocol.

As shown in the picture, the 1PC protocol starts once all the slaves have executed the transaction locally but have not committed it. Upon completion of the transaction at a local site, each slave sends a "Done" message to the coordinator. After that, all slaves involved in the transaction are waiting to hear the coordinator's decision to either commit the transaction or abort it. This period of time is known as the **window of vulnerability (WoV)**. During this window, slaves will be waiting to hear the decision from the coordinator and cannot unilaterally commit or abort the transaction. The failure of the coordinator during this window will block the continuation of the transaction by the slaves. When the coordinator receives the "Done" messages from all slaves, it will make a decision to commit or abort the transaction. This point in time corresponds to the commit point of the distributed transaction. The decision to commit or abort is communicated to the slaves by the coordinator broadcasting the "Commit" or the "Abort" message. Once the message is received by a slave, it executes the decision and acknowledges the action.

The 1PC is straightforward to implement, but at the same time it is a blocking protocol and lacks resiliency. One major issue with the 1PC is that a slave cannot back out of the transaction after it has sent the "Done" message to the coordinator. In a sense, slaves who execute a transaction are bound to whatever the coordinator decides. This is not necessarily bad, if the coordinator communicates the final decision to the slaves in a short period of time. However, since the coordinator must wait to receive the "Done" messages from all slaves before it decides what to do with the transaction, the slaves that have finished working on the transaction early may be waiting for a long time. The state of the sites that are waiting may change if the elapsed time is too long. Keep in mind that, during the wait period, the slave has to keep the resources it has used for the transaction locked. Obviously, locked resources are not available to other local transactions (even the read-only transactions). This negatively impacts the performance of the local system. Nevertheless, the slaves cannot release the resources until the coordinator communicates the final decision to them. Slaves that are waiting for the coordinator are blocked.

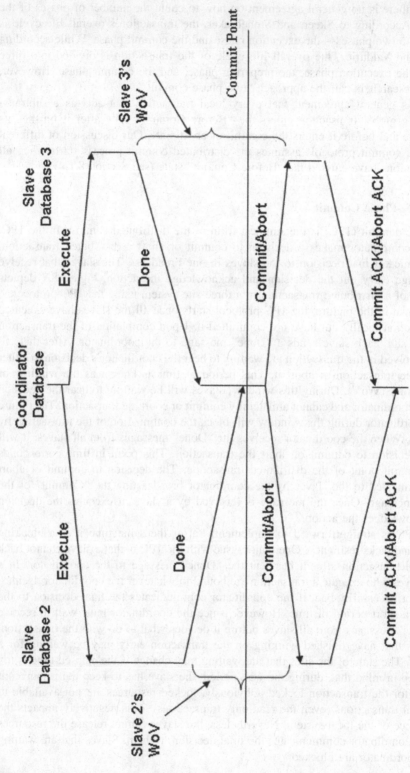

Figure 8.7 One-phase commit protocol in a three-site distributed system.

328

The more problematic issue with the 1PC is the failure of the coordinator during the WoV. In this case, the slaves will be blocked for a much longer period of time. Without the failure of the coordinator, the WoV of a slave, in the worst case, is as long as the time it takes for all other slaves to execute the transaction and the coordinator to broadcast the "Commit" message. The failure of the coordinator extends this window to include the time it takes to repair the coordinator as well.

Note that slaves cannot unilaterally decide to commit or abort a transaction if the coordinator fails. It is true that once the coordinator fails, the slaves can communicate with each other and try to determine the coordinator's decision. The coordinator's decision must have been to commit the transaction if one or more slaves have received the "Commit" message. If one such slave is found, then all slaves commit the transaction. However, if none of the slaves has received the "Commit" message, then all of the slaves are blocked. That is because the coordinator may have carried out the decision locally on the local copy of the database but failed before the message was sent out of the coordinator's site. If we allowed the slaves to make a decision here, any decision that the slaves collectively might make, may or may not be the same as the one the coordinator had carried out locally. The WoV and the blocking properties of the 1PC are reduced to some degree by the two-phase commit protocol.

Example 8.4   Consider transaction "T: $Z = X + Y$" issued at Site 1 in a two-site system, where data item "X" is at Site 1 and data items "Y" and "Z" are at Site 2. Since this transaction enters the system at Site 1, it makes Site 1 the coordinator and Site 2 the only slave. Figure 8.8 depicts the communication between the two sites to execute the transaction, using locks as the approach for concurrency control and the one-phase commit protocol.

8.8.4 Two-Phase Commit Protocol

Although, the 1PC is straightforward and easy to implement, due to its lack of resiliency it is not the industry standard. Two-phase commit (2PC) extends the 1PC to reduce the vulnerability of the servers involved in the transaction [Gray78]. Figure 8.9 illustrates the execution of a distributed transaction in a three-site system using the 2PC protocol.

As in the 1PC, the commit point for the 2PC is reached when the coordinator has received the "Done" messages from all slaves. At this time, like before, the coordinator will make a decision to commit or to abort the transaction. The decision to abort is communicated to the slaves by a "Global Abort" message, upon receipt of which the slaves abort the transaction locally and acknowledge the action. The coordinator has globally aborted the transaction once it receives the "Abort ACK" messages from all slaves.

If the coordinator decides to commit the transaction, it enters the first phase of the protocol by sending a "Prepare" message to all slaves. The slaves vote on whether they still want to commit the transaction or not by sending a "Ready" or a "Not Ready" message, respectively. A slave that does not want to continue with the transaction votes "Not Ready" to force the transaction to abort. This decision can be based on the change of state in the slave due to conflicting local concurrent transactions or just the fact that the coordinator waited too long before starting the commit process. Upon receipt of the first "Not Ready" message, the coordinator starts the global abort

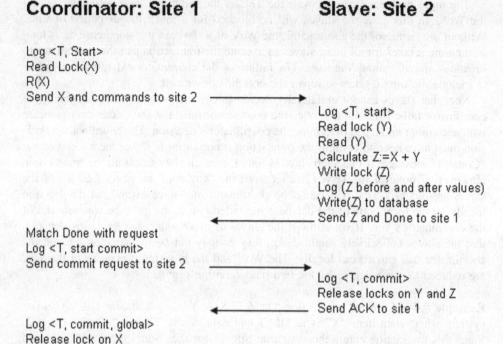

Coordinator: Site 1

```
Log <T, Start>
Read Lock(X)
R(X)
Send X and commands to site 2  ──────────────►
```

Slave: Site 2

```
                                    Log <T, start>
                                    Read lock (Y)
                                    Read (Y)
                                    Calculate Z:=X + Y
                                    Write lock (Z)
                                    Log (Z before and after values)
                                    Write(Z) to database
                    ◄──────────────  Send Z and Done to site 1
```

```
Match Done with request
Log <T, start commit>
Send commit request to site 2  ──────────────►
                                    Log <T, commit>
                                    Release locks on Y and Z
                    ◄──────────────  Send ACK to site 1
Log <T, commit, global>
Release lock on X
Display Z to user
```

Figure 8.8   One-phase commit protocol example in a two-site distributed system.

process by sending a "Global Abort" message to all slaves. This signifies the start of the second phase of the 2PC. Once the "Global Abort" message is received, slaves abort the transaction and acknowledge the action. Again, the coordinator has globally aborted the transaction once it receives the "Abort ACK" messages from all the slaves. Note: Since the coordinator starts the global abort process as soon as it receives the first "Not Ready" message, it might receive other votes on the same transaction from other slaves after this point. The coordinator simply ignores these votes once it has started the global abort process.

On the other hand, if all slaves are willing to commit the transaction, they will send a "Ready" message to the coordinator. Once the "Ready" messages from all of the slaves are received, the coordinator starts the second phase of the protocol by sending the "Global Commit" message to all slaves. Slaves then apply the transaction and acknowledge the action. Once the coordinator has received the "Commit ACK" messages from all slaves, the transaction has globally been committed. Note that sending a "Ready" message indicates the willingness of a slave to continue with a transaction's commit. The slave who sends a "Ready" message cannot change its decision and it is bound to whatever decision the coordinator makes with respect to the faith of this transaction.

The simplified version of the 2PC does not require commit and abort acknowledgments from the slaves. In this variation, the commit and abort states are terminal states for the programs. We have chosen to require the acknowledge messages as part of the protocol and therefore have introduced an intermediate state before commit and abort

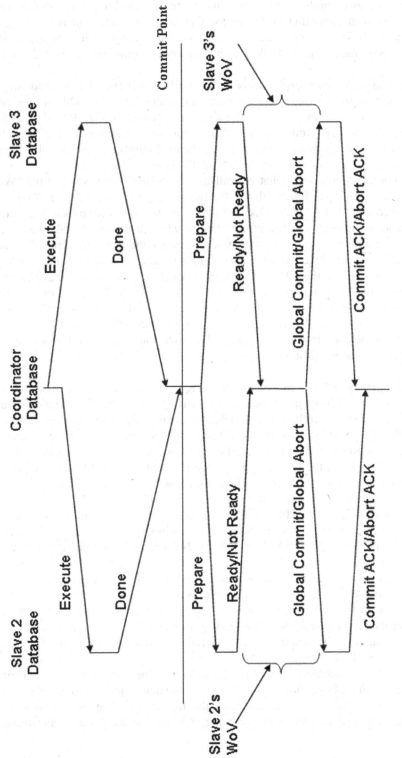

Figure 8.9 Two-phase commit protocol example.

331

states for this reason. In these states, both the coordinator and the slaves will do some cleanup work such as writing to the log the fact they are aborting or committing the transaction. Inclusion of these states in the protocol helps explain the cleanup actions of the local systems and helps to deal with recovery from failures, as we will explain later.

We have also chosen to use a variation of the Petri net [Petri62] methodology to depict the details of algorithms for the coordinator and the slaves. Others have used the state transition diagram to discuss the algorithms [Gray87] [Özsu99]. Figures 8.10 and 8.11 show the algorithms for the coordinator and the slaves for the no failure case. Note: In these figures, we have assumed the total number of sites involved in the transaction is "N", one coordinator, and "N − 1" slaves.

Note: For the coordinator, what we call the "Preparing" state is called the "Wait" state by others [Gray87] [Özsu99] and for the slaves, what we call the "Prepared" state is called the "Ready" state. Once all slaves are ready to commit the transaction, the coordinator enters the "Committing" state in which it makes sure all slaves have successfully committed the transaction before it enters the final "Committed" stated. Similarly, to abort a transaction when the coordinator receives a "Not Ready" message, we have chosen to use the "Aborting" state in which the coordinator makes sure all slaves abort the transaction before it enters the final "Aborted" state. For the slave, the "Aborting" state is entered when the slave replies with a "Not Ready" message, aborts the transaction locally, and is then waiting to acknowledge the "Global Abort" message from the coordinator. Figure 8.12 shows the state transition diagrams for the coordinator and slave algorithms.

8.8.4.1 *Resiliency of 2PC and Failure Handling*

The 2PC protocol is more resilient than the 1PC since it has a much smaller WoV. The WoV in the 2PC is much smaller than the one in 1PC, since it does not include the transaction execution time. Prior to entering the "Prepared" state, if the coordinator fails, slaves can abort the transaction by voting "Not Ready." This protocol, however, is not capable of dealing with the coordinator's failure in the second phase of the protocol. It should be easy to see that the only time when the slaves are blocked from making a unilateral decision to abort a transaction is when they have entered their "Prepared" states.

To deal with failures, the 2PC must be extended to include a **termination protocol** and a **recovery protocol**. These protocols together guide sites through a set of steps to deal with failures. The termination protocol is intended to terminate a transaction when one or more sites fail. This protocol is invoked by all operational sites after a failure of a site is detected. The termination protocol tries to commit or abort the transaction after a failure as soon as possible to release data resources locked by the sites involved in the transaction. The recovery protocol is run by the sites that have failed after they are repaired. A failed site is not involved in the decision that is made about termination of the transaction and, therefore, it must terminate the transaction exactly as others have.

We assume the inclusion of a timeout mechanism that allows the coordinator to detect the failures of the slaves and the slaves to detect the coordinator's failure. All transitions in the 2PC require writing the log and sending one or more messages. We assume that a site writes the log, submits the messages to the message

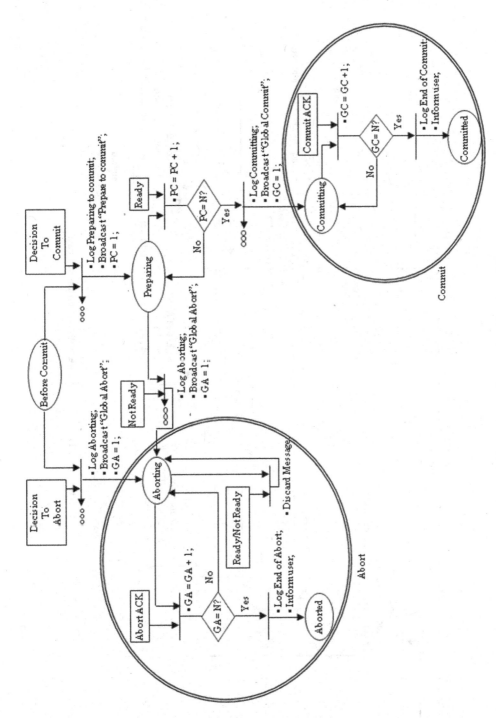

Figure 8.10 2PC coordinator algorithm—no failure case.

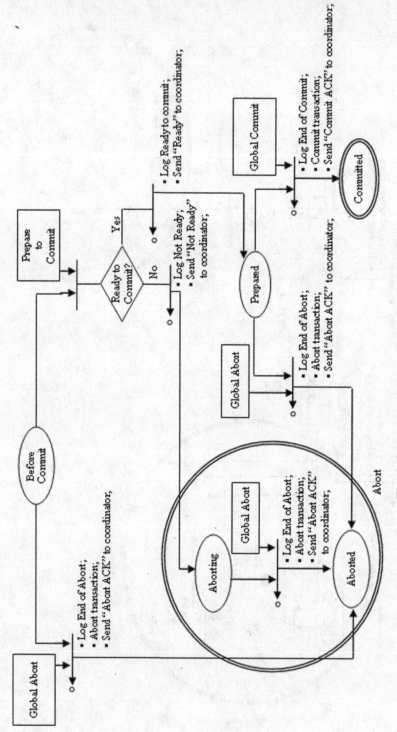

Figure 8.11 2PC slave algorithm—no failure case.

334

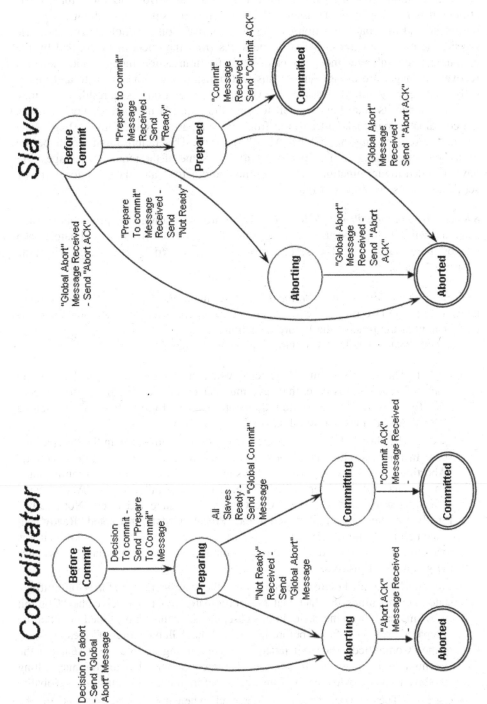

Figure 8.12 State transition diagrams for the 2PC coordinator and slave algorithms.

queue, and then makes the transition. Although it is reasonable to assume these three actions are atomic (the site cannot fail in the middle of performing these three operations), it is not reasonable to assume that the actual transmission of the messages in the queue and the state transition can be done as one atomic action. That is because physical removal and transmission of messages from the queue is performed by the communication sublayer independent of what the transaction monitor and the local recovery manager are doing. This means that transitioning to a new state and physically sending the required message are two separate operations. As a result, a site may actually change its state but may fail to send the required message(s). For example, the coordinator may make a transition from the "Preparing" state to the "Abort" state but fail before sending the "Global Abort" message. This failure might occur before it has sent any messages, or after it has sent only some of the required messages. We have included the termination protocol in the coordinator's and slaves' algorithm as a set of new steps, as shown in Figure 8.13.

8.8.4.2   Termination Protocols in 2PC   There are two termination protocols that are activated when failures occur. The first protocol is activated by the coordinator when one or more slaves fail. The second protocol is activated by the slaves when the coordinator fails.

2PC Coordinator Termination Protocol   The termination steps that the coordinator takes after the failure of a slave has been detected depend on the state that the coordinator is in at the time of the failure detection.

The coordinator handles the failure of a slave as follows:

- Case 1: The slave's failure is detected when the coordinator is in the "Before Commit" state. In this case, the slave must have failed during transaction execution. To terminate the transaction, the coordinator will log "Aborting" and send a "Global Abort" message to all slaves.

- Case 2: The slave's failure is detected when the coordinator is in the "Preparing" state. In this case, the slave could have been in any of the "Before Commit," "Aborting," or "Prepared" states. If the slave failed in the "Before Commit" state, it never received the "Prepare" message. If the slave failed in the "Abort" state, it must have received the "Prepare to Commit" message and voted "Not Ready." Finally, the slave must have failed in the "Prepared" state, if it voted "Ready" but failed before it sent out the message. In any case, the decision by the coordinator is to assume that the slave did not want to commit the transaction, which necessitates the global abort process.

- Case 3: The slave's failure is detected when the coordinator is in the "Committing" state. This signifies the fact that the coordinator did not receive the "Commit ACK" message from the slave. In this case, the slave must have failed in either the "Prepared" state—it failed before it received the "Global Commit" message—or in the "Committed" state—it failed after committing and before it sent out the "Commit ACK" message. In either case, the coordinator has to continue polling the slave for acknowledgment of the action before it ends the transaction globally.

- Case 4: The slave's failure is detected when the coordinator is in the "Aborting" state. This signifies the fact that the coordinator did not receive the "Abort ACK" from the slave. In this case, the slave could have been

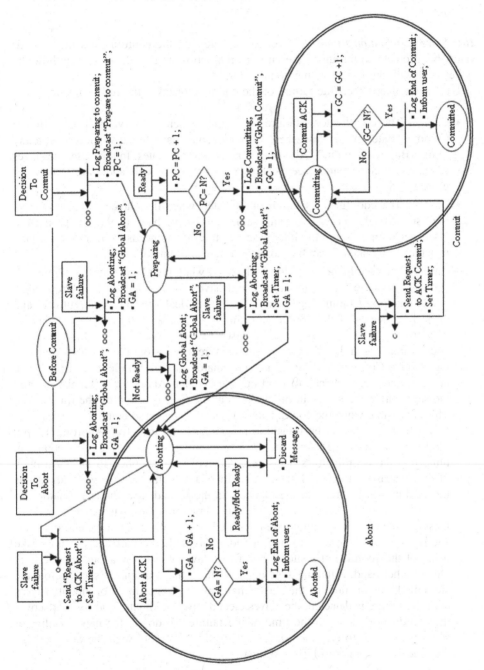

Figure 8.13 Coordinator algorithm with slave's failure.

in any of the "Before Commit," "Prepared," "Aborting," or "Aborted" states. Regardless of the state in which the slave failed, the coordinator must poll the slave for acknowledgment of the abort before it ends the transaction globally.

2PC Slave Termination Protocol Each slave detecting the coordinator's failure activates this protocol to terminate the current transaction. Figure 8.14 explains how the slaves deal with the failure of the coordinator.

Each slave that detects the failure of the coordinator takes the following steps:

- Case 1: The coordinator's failure is detected when the slave is in the "Before Commit" state. In this case, the coordinator must have failed when it was in any of the "Before Commit," "Aborting," or "Preparing" states. In this case, the slaves elect a new coordinator (see Section 8.8.4.6), which will abort the transaction globally.
- Case 2: The coordinator's failure is detected when the slave is in the "Aborting" state. In this case, the coordinator could have been in the "Preparing" or "Before Commit" state. In either case, the transaction needs to be aborted, which is achieved by slaves deciding to elect a new coordinator.
- Case 3: The coordinator's failure is detected when the slave is in the "Prepared" state. In this case, the coordinator could have failed in any of the "Preparing," "Aborting," or "Committing" states. The slaves deal with the "Committing" and "Aborting" states of the coordinator similarly, and, therefore, we will consider only two cases. Let's discuss these cases in more detail. In the first case, the coordinator dies in the "Preparing" state before it sends out the "Global Abort" or the "Global Commit" message. The coordinator that dies in the "Preparing" state and does not get a chance to send out the "Global Abort" or "Global Commit" message leaves the slaves in the dark about the final decision on the transaction. This is possible when the coordinator makes the decision to commit (or abort) the transaction and makes the transition to the "Committing" (or "Aborting") state, but before the message leaves the site's message queue, the site fails. Keeping in mind that the coordinator's decision could have been applied to the local copy of the database at the coordinator's site, the slaves cannot do anything about this transaction—therefore, they are blocked. In the second case, the coordinator dies in the "Committing" (or "Aborting") state. For this case, it is possible that the message to globally commit the transaction did not make it out of the coordinator's site or that it did make it to one or more slaves. If the message did not make it out of the coordinator's site, none of the slaves will know about the decision. On the other hand, if the message made it out of the coordinator's site before the site failed, one or more of the slaves may know the decision. For the latter case, after the failure is detected, the slaves elect a new coordinator and try to discover the coordinator's state at the time of the failure. To do so, the new coordinator sends a message to all other slaves asking them to reply with the last message they received from the failed coordinator.

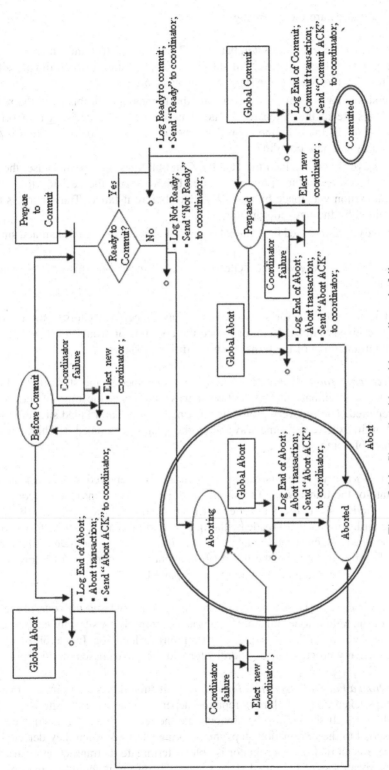

Figure 8.14 Slave algorithm with coordinator's failure.

Possible scenarios are the following:

1. No slave has received the "Global Abort" or "Global Commit" message. This corresponds to Case 1 above. All slaves are blocked until the coordinator site is repaired and the coordinator starts the recovery process.
2. Some slaves have received the "Global Abort" message. In this case, the rest of the slaves are in the "Prepared" state. This indicates the decision to abort the transaction was made by the coordinator before it failed. The transaction is then aborted by the new coordinator.
3. Some slaves have received the "Global Commit" message. In this case, the rest of the slaves are in the "Prepared" state. This indicates the decision to commit the transaction was made by the coordinator before it failed. Transaction is then committed by the new coordinator.
4. All slaves have received the "Global Abort" message. This case is handled similar to Case 2.
5. All slaves have received the "Global Commit" message. This case is handled similar to Case 3.

Note: It is not possible for some slaves to have received "Global Abort" while others have received "Global Commit" since the coordinator would not have decided on contrary terminations of the transaction for different slaves.

8.8.4.3 Recovery Protocols in 2PC
These protocols specify the steps that a failed site must take to terminate the transaction it was running at the time of the failure after it is repaired. The recovery protocols must make sure that a failed site terminates its transaction in exactly the same way the working sites terminated it. There are two possible ways of doing this.

Recovery by Discovery The first approach requires the repaired site to ask around about the fate of the transaction. The site then terminates the transaction accordingly. If the failed site is a slave, it can ask the coordinator about the transaction. If the failed site is the coordinator, it can broadcast the question to all slaves. Either all the other slaves or the newly elected coordinator will send the answer to the requesting site. In order for this protocol to work, the information about the termination of a transaction must be held by each site until all failures are repaired.

Independent Recovery The second approach relies on the site and the state of the site at the time of the failure to terminate the transaction properly. A site can determine the state it was in when the failure happened by examining its local log. In the following, we discuss the recovery process for the coordinator and the slaves based on this approach.

Recovering from a Failure Using State Information It should be rather obvious that the recovery steps taken after a failure is repaired depend on the state the site is in when the failure happens. It should also be obvious that the recovery steps a failed site takes must correspond to the termination steps the working site took when they detected the site's failure. Recall that the coordinator is able to terminate its transaction even when a slave fails, regardless of the failed slave's state. Therefore, it should be possible for a failed slave to recover without asking the coordinator. On the other hand, the failure of the coordinator does block the slaves when the coordinator is in specific states. As a result, when a failed coordinator is repaired, in some cases, it has to continue the transaction to unblock the slaves.

8.8.4.4 2PC Coordinator Recovery Process   After a coordinator is repaired, it will read the local log, determine the state it was in at the time of the failure, and take the necessary steps for recovery.

Here are the possible cases:

- The coordinator was in the "Before Commit" state when it failed. In this case, the coordinator did not send the decision to commit or abort the transaction to slaves. The termination protocol for this case forces the slaves to abort the transaction. Therefore, the coordinator must also abort the transaction. As part of this process, the coordinator will send an "Abort ACK" to the newly elected coordinator.

- The coordinator was in the "Preparing" state when it failed. In this case, according to the termination protocol the slaves are blocked. The coordinator restarts the voting process to terminate the transaction. This is necessary since some of the slaves' responses may have been lost in the coordinator's message queue when the site failed.

- The coordinator was in the "Aborting" state when it failed. In this case, the decision was to abort the transaction because either one or more slaves voted to abort, or the coordinator decided to abort. The recovery process in this case requires the coordinator to communicate with the new coordinator, which was elected as part of the termination protocol. Two subcases are possible. If all the slaves were ready to commit, but the coordinator had decided to abort, and none of the slaves had received the "Global Abort" message, then the slaves are blocked. For this subcase, the coordinator will have to inform all slaves that the transaction is being aborted by sending a "Global Abort" message to terminate the transaction. In the second subcase, one or more slaves had received the "Global Abort" message. Here, the new coordinator has aborted the transaction according to the termination protocol. Therefore, the repaired coordinator will simply abort the transaction and acknowledge the action to the new coordinator.

- The coordinator was in the "Committing" state when it failed. In this case, the decision was to commit the transaction, and all slaves were ready to do so. The recovery process in this case requires the coordinator to communicate with the new coordinator, which was elected as part of the termination protocol. Two cases are possible. If the "Global Commit" message was received by one or more slaves, then the new coordinator has committed the transaction. If the "Global Commit" message was not received by any transaction, then the slaves are blocked. If the slaves are blocked, the old coordinator will commit the transaction globally. If slaves have already committed the transaction, then the old coordinator commits the transaction as well.

- The coordinator was in the "Aborting" state when it failed. In this case, the decision was to abort the transaction. Again, either the slaves are blocked or they have aborted the transaction. The recovery process in this case requires the coordinator to communicate with the new coordinator, which was elected as part of the termination protocol. If the "Global Abort" message was received by one or more slaves, then the new coordinator has aborted the transaction. In this case, the old coordinator will abort the transaction as well. If slaves are blocked, the old coordinator will abort the transaction globally.

- Recovery in the states "Committed" and "Aborted" does not require any action from the coordinator.

8.8.4.5 2PC Slave Recovery Process

After a slave is repaired, it will read the local log, determine the state it was in at the time of the failure, and take the necessary steps for recovery.

Here are the possible cases:

- The slave was in the execute phase of the transaction when it failed. In this case, the coordinator aborted the transaction according to the termination protocol and, therefore, the slave can safely abort the transaction. As part of the abort, it will send an "Abort ACK" message to the coordinator.

- The slave was in any of the "Before Commit," "Aborting," or "Prepared" states when it failed. In this case, the coordinator aborted the transaction according to the termination protocol, and, therefore, the slave can safely abort the transaction. As part of the abort, it will send an "Abort ACK" message to the coordinator.

- The slave was in the "Committed" or "Aborted" state when it failed. In this case, the coordinator must have committed or aborted the transaction according to the termination protocol. As a result, the slave will send "Commit ACK" if it is in the "Committed" state or "Abort ACK" if it is in the "Aborted" state to the coordinator. Note: In the above, we assume the acknowledge message got lost due to a failure and therefore requires resending. If the message was in fact received by the coordinator, the coordinator will simply ignore the new response.

8.8.4.6 New Coordinator Election in 2PC

Sometimes, when the coordinator fails, the slaves in the 2PC are forced to elect a new coordinator from among the slaves to continue a stalled transaction. This can be done by the slaves voting, based on the priority of the sites or based on a predetermined order. Once elected, the new coordinator will have the responsibility to try to commit or to try to abort the transaction globally. This responsibility includes informing the original coordinator after it has been repaired. It should be easy to see that the election process is time consuming and may necessitate a large number of messages to be exchanged.

8.8.4.7 Multiple Site Failures in 2PC

Skeen and Stonebraker show that when two or more sites fail at the same time, the 2PC is not capable of performing independent recovery [Skeen83]. It should be obvious that failure of a single slave or multiple slaves does not block the coordinator. However, as we have discussed, the coordinator's failure may be blocking, depending on the coordinator's state. As a result, the 2PC cannot guarantee a consistent state for the database when two or more sites fail and the coordinator is one of the failed sites. Skeen and Stonebraker further argue that no protocols can deal with multiple site failures when the coordinator is one of the failed sites. This includes the 2PC, as we have discussed, and also includes the 3PC that we will discuss in Section 8.8.5.

8.8.4.8 Two-Phase Commit Performance   The two-phase commit protocol is an expensive protocol since it requires three broadcasts and acknowledgments. The cost of the protocol depends on the number of messages that are sent over different phases and the number of log records that the coordinator and the slaves write to the stable storage. The protocol requires additional messages to be sent, and log records to be written when failures happen. Mohan and Lindsay propose variations of this protocol that try to reduce the number of messages and the number of log records [Mohan85]. We will briefly discuss two specific alternatives known as "presumed commit" and "presumed abort" next.

Presumed Commit and Presumed Abort   The 2PC presumed abort (PA) and presumed commit (PC) rely on the existence as well as the absence of certain log records to decide the fate of the transaction after a failure. The PA is a protocol that works best for systems with many aborts. This pessimistic view assumes that most of the time transactions are going to abort and therefore it forgets about the transaction as soon as it logs abort. Similarly, the PC is a protocol that works best for systems with many commits. This is an optimistic view that assumes most transactions are going to commit and therefore it forgets about the transaction as soon as it logs commit. The reasoning in either case is very simple. For the PA, sites are told "When in doubt, abort," and for the PC, sites are told "When in doubt, commit." A site that does not find an abort or a commit record in its log after recovery is in doubt. In other words, since the log does not contain either a commit record or an abort record, the recovery manager must make a presumption for committing or aborting the transaction.

In the absence of failures, the coordinator guides the slaves to terminate the transaction properly. When a failure happens, the log contents that are not forced (written) to the stable storage are lost. After recovery, the site cannot find the abort/commit record in the stable storage and will be in doubt. The sites will make the right decision about the transaction depending on what presumed protocol they are using. The protocols also use the concept of "forgetting about a transaction," which means removing the log records for a given transaction from the memory even when there are no failures. The protocols allow sites to ignore writing all the log records that we discussed in the 2PC protocol. Both the coordinator and the slaves apply these rules uniformly. The decision to follow the rule for the PA or the PC is made ahead of time for the entire system. A system that implements the PA cannot also implement the PC and vice versa.

In applying the PA, if the coordinator decides to abort a transaction after the votes are in, it writes an abort log record but does not force the log to the stable storage, forgets about the transaction, and does not send the "Global Abort" message to the slaves. Slaves that are waiting to hear from the coordinator will time out the coordinator and abort the transaction. The slaves do not force their logs to the stable storage and they forget about the transaction as well. This includes not only the slaves that voted to abort the transaction, but also the slaves that voted to commit the transaction. If there are failures, after repair, a failed slave or a failed coordinator will be in doubt about the transaction since the log on the stable storage does not contain a commit or an abort record for the transaction.

The lack of the abort record for a transaction in the log on the stable storage works well for a site that is recovering to abort the transaction. On the other hand, it is not acceptable for a failed site to abort a transaction that the working sites have committed. As an example, let us assume that "Site 1" (a slave site) fails and the coordinator guides other slaves to abort transaction "Ti." When Site 1 comes up, it must determine what to do with Ti. The site looks in its log on the stable storage and searches for a commit or an abort record for Ti. It does not find either. The absence of a commit or an abort record for Ti is a directive to Site 1 to abort the transaction. All sites now have terminated the transaction the same way. In this case, the database stays consistent. However, if the working sites decide to commit the transaction, their decisions will be different from the decision that Site 1 makes for Ti. In this case, the database will be inconsistent. To prevent the above scenario from happening, the protocol requires writing the commit record to the log and forcing the log to the stable storage before a transaction enters the commit phase. Doing so guarantees that Site 1 finds a commit record in its log for Ti if the working sites commit the transaction. In this case, the failed site also commits the transaction and the database stays consistent.

In applying the PC, the coordinator explicitly logs which transactions have aborted but does not force the commit records to the log for those transactions that are being committed. After a failure and during recovery, a site that does not find a commit or an abort record for a transaction in its log presumes commit and commits a transaction. That is where the similarity between the PC and the PA protocols ends. In the PA, once the decision to abort is made, the coordinator can forget about the transaction since the transaction will be aborted by all slaves due to lack of further information. In the PA, this philosophy works even if the coordinator or slaves fail. However, in the PC, the coordinator cannot forget about the transaction as soon as it decides to commit the transaction. Further communications from the coordinator are required to successfully commit the transaction at all slaves. To do this and to protect against failures, the coordinator writes the name of all slaves as a "collecting" log record to the stable storage before the coordinator sends out the "Prepare" message. The coordinator then starts preparing the slaves. Suppose the coordinator fails in the preparing state. Once restarted, the coordinator finds the collecting record in the log but does not find a commit or abort record. This tells the independent recovery mechanism that the transaction must be aborted. From the collecting record, the coordinator knows exactly which slaves need to be told to abort the transaction. If we did not use the collecting record, upon recovery from the preparing state, the coordinator would have committed the transaction, which would not be correct.

Slaves vote on the transaction, log abort if the decision is to abort, log ready to commit if the decision is to commit, and send their votes back to the coordinator. Once all slaves have voted to commit, the coordinator writes the commit record to its log, sends the "Global Commit" message to the slaves, and forgets about the transaction. The coordinator does not need to force the log to the stable storage and does not need to wait for the acknowledge message from the slaves. In this case, slaves are waiting in the prepared state. When they receive the "Global Commit" message, they commit the transaction and forget about it as well. Again, since this protocol presumes commit when in doubt, aborting a transaction requires all sites to log the abort record and force the log to the stable storage for the transaction. This prevents a failed site from committing a transaction that the working sites abort. Therefore, if the decision is to abort the transaction, coordinator writes and forces its log, sends the "Global Abort" message to all slaves, waits until the abort is acknowledged by all slaves, and writes the end of the transaction record to the log.

Other variations of the presumed abort and presumed commit have been proposed. The emphasis is sometimes on minimizing the number of messages sent and sometimes on the total amount of information communicated [Lampson93] [Attaluri02].

8.8.5 Three-Phase Commit Protocol

As explained in Section 8.8.4, the 2PC is a blocking protocol. To overcome the blocking property of the 2PC, Skeen proposed the three-phase commit (3PC) protocol [Skeen81]. In the 2PC, the coordinator and the slaves can only be one state apart in their transitions—the coordinator decides to change its state, informs that slaves to do the same, and changes its state. The coordinator and the slaves are therefore synchronous within one state. The problem is that the state transition diagram (the STD) of the 2PC does not contain the same state adjacent to the commit and abort states for the coordinator and the slaves. The STD for the slaves contains the "Prepared" state for the slave and the "Preparing" state for the coordinator. As a result, when failures happen, it is possible that when the coordinator changes its state to "Committed" (or "Aborted"), the slave changes its state to "Aborted" (or "Committed"), which are contradictory states for the two parties. The 3PC protocol overcomes this problem by introducing a new state that both the coordinator and the slaves enter as a buffer until such time as both parties are sure they can commit the transaction. With this "buffer" state, there is no way the two parties act differently on a given transaction—since at no time are the coordinator and the slave more than one state apart during execution.

In the 3PC, as shown in Figure 8.15, the second phase of the protocol calls for the coordinator to initiate another broadcast informing the slaves of the final decision. The coordinator broadcasts an "Enter Prepared State" message. In response, the slaves vote "OK." Then the final phase of the 3PC, the commit phase, resumes as in the 2PC. In the 3PC, the "Commit ACK" response from slaves is not required. The intension of Phase 2 in the 3PC is to inform all slaves that Phase 1 (the voting phase) was completed in favor of committing the transaction. Having sent the voting result to all slaves enables the protocol to recover from the failure of the coordinator as long as there is at least one slave that has received the "Enter Prepared State" message.

As mentioned earlier, the introduction of this new phase adds a "buffer" state before the terminal commit state. The introduction of this "buffer" state changes the state transition diagrams of the 3PC (as compared to the 2PC) for the slaves and the coordinator as shown in Figure 8.16.

8.8.5.1 Resiliency of 3PC   Like the 2PC, the 3PC has two protocols that are used for termination and recovery purposes. The termination protocol is used to properly terminate a transaction when a failure happens. The recovery protocol is used to make sure that after recovery a failed site's state is consistent with the state of active sites.

Termination Protocols in 3PC   The coordinator activates its termination protocol when it realizes that a slave has failed. Similarly, the slaves activate the termination protocol when they detect the coordinator's failure.

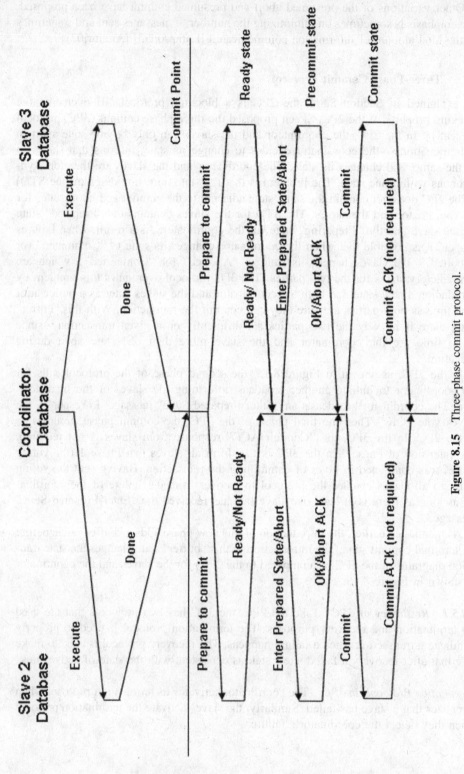

Figure 8.15 Three-phase commit protocol.

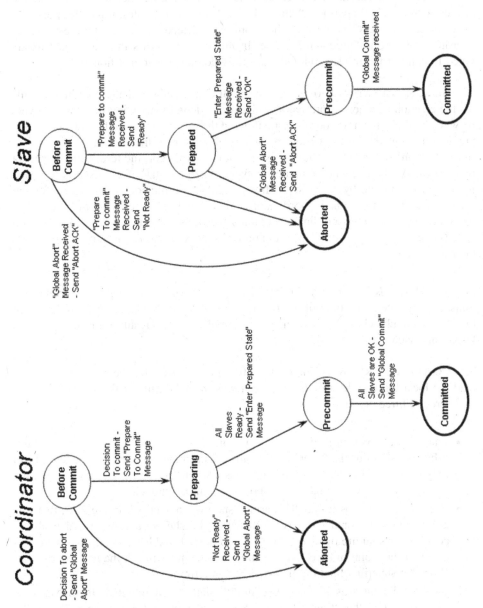

Figure 8.16 Three-phase commit state transition diagrams.

3PC COORDINATOR TERMINATION PROTOCOL   The termination protocol in the 3PC is similar to the one we discussed in the 2PC. The difference between the 2PC and the 3PC is the "Precommit" state. Therefore, the steps that the coordinator takes to handle the slave's failure are the same for both protocols in all states except the "Precommit" state. Hence, if the coordinator detects the slave's failure when the coordinator is in the "Before Commit," "Preparing," "Aborted," or "Committed" states, it handles it exactly the same as in the 2PC. Otherwise, the coordinator detects the slave's failure when the coordinator is in the "Precommit" state. In this case, it knows the slave had already voted to commit the transaction and can safely commit the transaction.

3PC SLAVE TERMINATION PROTOCOL   In the 3PC, the failure of the coordinator calls for the election of a new coordinator. This can be done by allowing the slaves to vote on who should be the new coordinator, allowing them to compete for the role, or simply pre determining who the next coordinator should be (sort of like a chain of command). In order to protect against the failure of this new coordinator, the termination protocol requires the newly elected coordinator to synchronize the states for all slaves to match its own. This is done by a broadcast, from the new coordinator to the slaves, forcing them to transition to the new coordinator's state. Once all slaves have transitioned to the same state, the new coordinator commits the transaction if the new coordinator's state is one of the "Precommit" or "Committed" state. Otherwise, the coordinator aborts the transaction.

Recovery Protocols in 3PC   As in 2PC, the log information is used to determine the transaction's state at the time of the failure in the 3PC. It should be obvious that since the 3PC is a nonblocking protocol, no slaves are blocked as a result of the coordinator's failure and vice versa.

3PC COORDINATOR RECOVERY PROCESS   After a coordinator has been repaired, it will read the local log and determine the state it was in at the time of the failure.
There are three possible cases:

- The coordinator was in the "Before Commit" state when it failed. In this case, it has not sent out the "Prepare to Commit" message. As a result, the slaves can only be in the "Before Commit" state. As a result, slaves unilaterally aborted the transaction. The coordinator will abort the transaction locally.
- The coordinator was in the "Preparing" state when it failed. In the 2PC, this was a blocking state for the slaves. In the 3PC, the slaves have recovered from the coordinator's failure by electing a new coordinator and have terminated the transaction at this point in time. The repaired coordinator will ask the new coordinator about the state in which the transaction was terminated.
- The coordinator was in the "Precommit" state when it failed. In this case, it is possible that the "Enter Prepared State" message did not make it out of the coordinator's site before the site failed. As a result, the slaves may have committed or aborted the transaction. Therefore, the repaired coordinator needs to ask the newly elected coordinator how to terminate the transaction locally.

3PC Slave Recovery Process   After a slave is repaired, it will read the local log and determine the state it was in at the time of the failure. All the slaves' states in the 3PC are the same as they were in the 2PC except the "Precommit" state. Recovery in the 3PC is the same as it was in the 2PC, from all states except the "Precommit." When the slave recovers from the "Precommit" state, it has already received the "Enter Prepared State" message. The slave must have failed before committing the transaction and entering the terminal state committed. Therefore, the slave commits the transaction and writes an end of transaction record to its log.

8.8.5.2 *Multiple Site Failures in 3PC*   This protocol blocks slaves when multiple sites fail at the same time. Consider the case when the coordinator receives ready messages from all slaves, decides to commit, makes a transition to its "Precommit" state, starts sending out "Enter Prepared State" messages, and fails after sending the message to the first slave. This failure is recoverable as long as the only slave that received the message does not fail. On the other hand, if this slave also fails, all other slaves will be blocked.

8.8.6   Network Partitioning and Quorum-Based Commit Protocol

As discussed in Section 8.8.5, the 3PC is a nonblocking protocol with respect to the failure of the coordinator or the failure of only one slave. However, as Skeen explains in [Skeen81] and [Skeen83] the protocol is blocking if multiple sites fail. In addition to this problem, the 3PC is not able to deal with communication link failures when such failures partition the network. A network is said to be partitioned if communication link failures divide the network into multiple sets. Each set is called a partition. A partition consists of a set of interconnected operational computers that cannot communicate with any computers in another partition. Figure 8.17 shows an example network and how it can be partitioned.

In this example, if the communication link between computers C4 and C5 fails, the network will be partitioned into two partitions. The left partition will have C1, C2, C3, and C4 computers, and the right partition will have C5 through C10 computers in it. If, on the other hand, C5 fails (a site crash), the network will be partitioned into three partitions. In this case, C1 through C4 will be in partition P1, C6 and C7 will be in partition P2, and C8, C9, and C10 will be in partition P3.

When a network partitioning happens, the coordinator of a transaction will be in one partition isolated from the slaves in the other partitions. Both the coordinator and

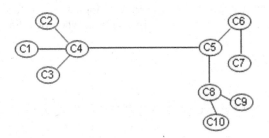

Figure 8.17   A network example.

the slaves in the other partitions will activate their termination protocols to deal with the failure. Note that the coordinator cannot reach the slaves that are not in its partition and assumes they have failed, and, similarly, the slaves that are in a partition without a coordinator assume the coordinator has failed and activate their termination protocol. It is possible that the computers in one partition decide to abort a transaction while the computers in another partition decide to commit the transaction. As a result, a partitioned network can create an inconsistent database. To see how this is possible, assume the network depicted in Figure 8.18 with C3 being the coordinator. Also assume that C3 is preparing the slaves to vote on its transaction. Furthermore, let's assume that when the link between C2 and C3 fails, C4 and C5 have voted to commit the transaction but C1 and C2 have not voted yet.

When the network becomes partitioned, C3 assumes that C1 and C2 have failed and starts its termination protocol. Since C4 and C5 are ready to commit, C3 will commit the transaction on the computers in its partition. On the other hand, C1 and C2 realize that they have lost communication with the coordinator and elect a new coordinator, say, C1. If both C1 and C2 are also ready to commit the transaction, there should be no problem and the database will remain consistent. But, if C1 or C2 vote abort, they will abort the transaction, which results in an inconsistent database across the two partitions.

To deal with this problem, Skeen proposes an extension to the 3PC, called the **quorum-based commit (QBC)** protocol [Skeen82]. We discussed the idea of using votes to deal with concurrency control and replication control issues in Chapters 5 and 7. Recall that voting-based replication algorithms use a number of votes, V, and allocate them to different sites in the system based on some kind of priority. In order for a transaction to read a data item, it must collect the required number of votes called the read quorum, Vr, from the sites that have a copy of the data item. Also, in order for a transaction to write a data item, it must collect the required number of votes called the write quorum, Vw. The first requirement is that the total number of votes must be less than "Vr + Vw," which makes it impossible for two conflicting transactions to both read and write the copies at the same time. The second requirement is that the total number of votes must be less than "2 * Vw," which makes it impossible for two conflicting transactions to both write the copies at the same time.

In the QBC, the same idea is utilized by the termination protocol to make sure that the same transaction is not committed and aborted by different partitions in the system. The 3PC protocol is extended to require the sites to reach a commit quorum, Vc, in order to commit a transaction; and to reach an abort quorum, Va, to abort a transaction. There are V total votes in the system that has been allocated to the N sites as V1, V2, ..., VN. When a site votes, it casts all its votes for commit or abort but cannot split its votes across both alternatives. If there are V total votes in the system, Va and Vc are allocated such that "Va + Vc> V." In addition, when deciding on Vc and Va, we

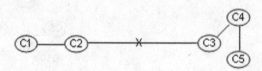

Figure 8.18 A partitioned network with inconsistent databases.

must also have "0 < = Vc < = V" and "0 < = Va < = V." This simple idea makes it impossible for a partitioned network to commit and abort the same transaction at different partitions.

To make this work, the third phase of the 3PC is changed to count votes for abort or commit and to check to see which quorum, if any, is reached. This means that the sites are now required to attach their votes to the response they send to the coordinator when they receive the "Enter Prepared State" message. Under normal operations, the coordinator will collect the votes, which should be a quorum for commit, and then it will commit the transaction. Now suppose a failure partitions the network into two partitions when the system is the "Precommit" state. The coordinator will check the number of votes from the sites in its partition and it will decide if it can commit or abort the transaction. The slaves in the other partition elect a new coordinator and count their votes as well. With correct allocation of V, Vc, and Va, there is no way the two partitions can reach different quorums.

Let us apply this idea to the example discussed in Figure 8.18. Assume that each site is given one vote, making the total number of votes "V = 5." Let's also assume that "Va = 3" and "Vc = 3." This satisfies the requirement that "Va + Vc> V." In the partitioned network, if all computers in the right partition vote for commit, they have three votes to commit and have reached the commit quorum and will commit the transaction. Computers in the left partition, however, do not have enough votes to commit or abort and will be blocked from terminating the transaction. Although this is an undesirable situation, it is better than having the database become inconsistent. Obviously, the QBC protocol is blocking when a partition does not have a quorum to commit or abort the transaction.

8.9 SUMMARY

In this chapter, we analyzed the fault tolerance and recovery concepts for centralized and distributed databases. To guard against loss of database consistency, databases use a persistent medium, called a log, to store state information for transactions. After a failure, a system is brought back up; the log(s) are analyzed and depending on the state each transaction was in at the time of the failure, certain steps are taken. The overall approach for centralized and distributed systems is the same. What is different is that in a distributed system all sites must be recovered to the same consistent state. To achieve this, different distributed commit protocols are used. We analyzed one-phase, two-phase, three-phase, and quorum-based commit protocols for distributed database systems.

8.10 GLOSSARY

Active Transaction   A transaction that is running at the time of the failure.

Before Commit State   The state that a transaction enters just before it commits.

Checkpoint   The process of writing the logged completed transactions to the stable storage.

Cold Backup   A backup that is performed when there are no transactions running.

Commit Point   A point in the life of a transaction when a decision has to be made to either commit or abort the transaction.

Commit Protocols   A set of protocols that guarantee the consistency of the database even if failures happen.

Compete Backup   A backup of the database that includes a complete snapshot of the database at the time of the backup.

Consistent Checkpointing   The process that halts accepting new transactions, completes all active transactions, writes the proper log records to the log, and writes completed transactions to the stable storage.

Database Recovery   The process of recreating a consistent snapshot of the database at a given point in time (usually as close as possible to the time of the failure).

Database Rollback   The process of undoing the effects of some transactions to reinstantiate a consistent state of the database in the past.

Database Roll Forward   The process of starting with a consistent snapshot of the database in the past and recreating a consistent state after that point by reapplying transactions.

Deferred Update   An approach to database update that does not write the changes of a transaction to the database until the transaction is ready to commit.

Fuzzy Checkpointing   The act of writing the list of active transactions to the log. It is usually used for recovery from power failure.

Global Transaction   A transaction that works with data at more than one site in a distributed system.

Hard Failure   A failure that causes loss of data in the database (the disk).

Hot Backup   A backup that is performed while transactions are running in the system.

Immediate Update   An approach to database update that writes the changes of a transaction to the database as soon as the transaction comes up with them.

Inactive Transactions   A transaction that is not currently running because it is committed and/or aborted.

Incremental Backup   A backup approach that only tracks changes since the last complete and/or incremental backup.

Local Transaction   A transaction that does not run at any site but the local site.

Log Archival   The process of writing the inactive portion of the log files to a secondary medium such as tape.

Log Buffers   A prespecified amount of memory designated to the log records.

Nonvolatile Storage   A storage medium that can withstand power failures.

One-Phase Commit (1PC)   A distributed commit approach in which the decision to commit and/or abort is communicated in one broadcast.

Point-In-Time (PIT) Recovery   The process of recovering a consistent snapshot of the database to a point in time.

Quiescent Point   A point in time when no transactions are running in the system.

Quorum-Based Commit (QBC)   A modified version of the 3PC that uses voting to deal with network failures during the third phase.

Recovery Protocol   The protocol that a failed system must follow after it has been repaired.

Recovery to Current   The process of recovering the database to the present time (usually the time of the failure or as close to it as possible).

Redo   The process of reapplying the changes of a transaction.

Redo Scripts   A set of redo operations for some transactions.

Soft Failure   A failure that does not cause loss of data on disk—usually caused by some form of "unclean" shutdown, such as a power failure, operating system misbehavior, or DBMS bug.

Stable Storage   A storage medium that does not lose its contents even when disk failures happen.

System Crash   A failure caused by loss of power to the system; a failure that does not cause loss of data on disk.

Termination Protocol   The process that a site must follow when the site notices that its counterpart has failed.

Three-Phase Commit (3PC)   A distributed commit approach in which the decision to commit and/or abort is communicated in three broadcasts.

Transaction Log   A record of all changes that transactions have made to the database.

Transaction Recovery   The process of reapplying the changes of a transaction.

Two-Phase Commit (2PC)   A distributed commit approach in which the decision to commit and/or abort is communicated in two broadcasts.

Undo   The process of getting rid of the changes of a transaction from the database.

Undo Scripts   A set of undo operations for a set of transactions.

Volatile Storage   A storage medium that loses its contents when power to it is lost.

REFERENCES

[Astrahan76] Astrahan, M., Blasgen, M., Chamberlin, D., Eswaran, K., Gray J., Griffiths, P., King, W., Lorie, R., McJones, P., Mehl, J., Putzolu, G., Traiger, I., Wade, B., and Watson V., "System R: A Relational Approach to Database Management," *ACM Transactions on Database Systems*, Vol. 1, No. 2, pp. 97–137, June 1976.

[Attaluri02] Attaluri, G., and Salem, K., "The Presumed-Either Two-Phase Commit Protocol," *IEEE Transactions on Knowledge and Data Engineering*, Vol. 14, No. 5, pp. 1190–1196, September 2002.

[Bernstein87] Bernstein, P., Hadzilacos, V., and Goodman N., *Concurrency Control and Recovery in Database Systems*, Addison-Wesley Longman Publishing Company, Boston, MA, 1987.

[Gray78] Gray, J., Bayer, R., Graham, R., and Seegmuller, G., "Notes on Data Base Operating Systems," in *Operating Systems: An Advanced Course*, Notes in Computer Science, Vol. 60, Springer-Verlag, New York, 1978, pp. 393–481.

[Gray81] Gray, J., McJones, P., Blasgen, M., Lindsay, B., Lorie, R., Price, T., Putzolu, F., and Traiger, I., "The Recovery Manager of the System R Database Manager," *ACM Computing Survey*, Vol. 13, No. 2, pp. 223–242, June 1981.

[Gray87] Gray, J., "Why Do Computers Stop and What Can Be Done About It?" Technical Report 85-7, Tandem Corporation, 1985. Also in "Tutorial Notes, Canadian Information Processing Society," Edmonton '87 Conference, Edmonton, Canada, November 1987.

[Lampson76] Lampson, B., and Sturgis, H., "Crash Recovery in Distributed Data Storage System," Tech Report, Xerox Palo Alto Research Center, Palo Alto, CA, 1976.

[Lampson93] Lampson, B., and Lomet, D., "A New Presumed Commit Optimization for Two Phase Commit," in *Proceedings of the 10th VLDB Conference*, Dublin, Ireland, pp. 630–640, 1993.

[Lindsay79] Lindsay, B., "Notes on Distributed Databases," IBM Technical Report RJ2517, San Jose, CA, July 1979—also Tandem Technical Report 81.3, June 1981.

[Mohan85] Mohan, C., and Lindsay, B., "Efficient Commit Protocols for the Tree of Processes Model of Distributed Transactions," *ACM SIGOPS Operating Systems Review*, Vol. 19, No. 2, pp. 76–88, April 1985.

[Mourad85] Mourad, S., and Andres, D., "The Reliability of the IBM/XA Operating System," in *Proceedings of the 15th Annual International Symposium on Fault-Tolerant Computing Systems*, pp. 93–98, 1985.

[Özsu99] Özsu99, M., and Valduriez, P., *Principles of Distributed Database Systems*, Prentice Hall, Englewood Cliffs, NJ, 1999.

[Petri62] Petri, C., "Kommunikation Mit Automation," Ph.D. thesis, University of Bonn, 1962.

[Severance76] Severance, D., and Lohman, G., "Differential Files: Their Application to the Maintenance of Large Databases," *ACM Transactions on Database Systems*, Vol. 1, No. 3, pp. 256–261, September 1976.

[Skeen81] Skeen, D., "Non-blocking Commit Protocols," in *Proceedings of ACM SIGMOD International Conference on Management of Data*, pp. 133–142, 1981.

[Skeen82] Skeen, D., "A Quorum-Based Commit Protocol," Tech Report TR82–483, Cornell University, Ithaca, NY, 1982.

[Skeen83] Skeen, D., and Stonebraker, M., "A Formal Model of Crash Recovery in a Distributed System," *IEEE Transactions on Software Engineering*, Vol. 9, No. 3, pp. 219–228, May 1983.

EXERCISES

Provide short (but complete) answers to the following questions.

8.1 A quorum-based commit protocol is implemented to deal with network partitioning of a four-site system. Sites 1 and 3 have the same importance. Sites 2 and 4 are more important than Sites 1 and 3. Site 2 is more important than Site 4. How do you decide on the **smallest** number of votes for V (total votes), V1, V2, V3, V4, Vc, and Va if we want the partitioned system to abort if and only if Sites 2 and 4 are in the same partition (**but** cannot abort if Sites 2 and 4 are in different partitions)?

8.2 Assume the transactions shown in Figure 8.19, the time of checkpoints, and the time of failure. Suppose the log contains the "Before Commit" records for T5 and T6 but does not contain the "Before Commit" record for T7.

    (A) Assume that we utilize a deferred update approach. Explain the recovery steps from a soft crash (power failure). Explain the recovery steps from a disk failure (hard crash).

    (B) Now assume that the update approach is immediate updates. Explain the recovery steps from a soft crash (power failure). Explain the recovery steps from a disk failure (hard crash).

    (C) Assume that during the recovery from a power failure in the deferred update case, a disk crash happens. Explain the recovery steps from this failure.

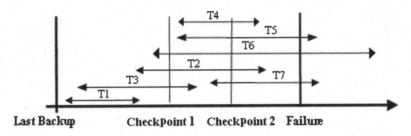

Figure 8.19 Transactions for Exercise 8.2.

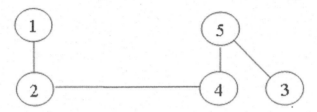

Figure 8.20 Topology for computers in Exercise 8.3.

8.3 Assume every site in Figure 8.20 has the same weight for voting in a quorum-based commit protocol. What are "Vi (for i = 1 to 5)," V, Vc, and Va for the following cases?

(A) We do NOT want the system to commit or abort any transaction when the link between 2 and 4 goes down.

(B) We want each partition to commit but no partition is able to abort when the link between 2 and 4 goes down.

(C) We want each partition to abort but no partition is able to commit when the link between 2 and 4 goes down.

(D) If Site 4 goes down, can the partitions in the partitioned system achieve a different quorum if each site is given one vote? Explain your answer.

9

DDBE SECURITY

BRADLEY S. RUBIN
University of St. Thomas

Security is a key facet of any database deployment. It is essential that we **authenticate** database users (ensuring that they are who they claim to be), allow only **authorized** users access to information, and maintain overall system data integrity. There are also many subtle security issues, specific to databases, such as SQL injection and inference attacks. Distributed database environments (DDBEs) require communication, so we must ensure not only that the data in databases is secure but that the communication links between users and their data and among the communicating DDBE components are also secure.

This chapter provides an overview of database and communications security. We begin by covering the basics of cryptography and outline the key building blocks and some common algorithms and best practices using those building blocks. Next, we will examine several higher-level security protocols composed of these building blocks. We then look at some security issues specific to communications and data. After examining some high-level architectural issues, we conclude this chapter with an example of how pieces in this chapter integrate.

For a comprehensive overview of security engineering, see [Anderson08]. For a more detailed look at cryptographic building blocks and specific algorithms, see [Stallings05] and [Ferguson03]. For an expanded database-specific security discussion, see [Natan05].

9.1 CRYPTOGRAPHY

Cryptography is the science of creating secrets. **Cryptanalysis** is the science of breaking secrets. The related science of hiding secrets is called **steganography**. To create a secret, we can use either **codes**, which map whole words to other words, or **ciphers**, which map individual characters (bytes) to other characters (bytes). The use of codes

Distributed Database Management Systems by Saeed K. Rahimi and Frank S. Haug
Copyright © 2010 the IEEE Computer Society

declined after World War II and today ciphers are most commonly used with digital data. The original (unencrypted) words or characters are referred to as the original message, the unencrypted message, or more specifically as the **plaintext**, while the characters we map to are referred to as the encrypted message or, more specifically, as the **ciphertext**.

Specific cryptographic functions include the following:

- **Confidentiality** keeps messages private between parties even in the face of eaves- droppers attempting to snoop while data is transported over communication net- works or while it resides in the database.
- **Authentication** allows message receivers to validate the message source and to ensure the integrity of the message.
- **Nonrepudiation** validates the message source so strongly that the message sender cannot deny being the message sender (this is a stronger form of authentication).

There are a number of cryptographic building blocks that provide these functions:

- **Conventional cryptography** provides confidentiality with previously distributed keys.
- **Message digests (MDs)** and **message authentication codes (MACs)** provide authentication.
- **Public key cryptography** provides confidentiality without prior key distribution.
- **Digital signatures** provide nonrepudiation.
- **Digital certificates** and **certificate authorities** authenticate public keys.

We will now examine each of these cryptographic building blocks in more detail.

9.1.1 Conventional Cryptography

Conventional cryptography is a simple concept. Suppose we have two parties who want to communicate securely with each other; let's call them Alice and Bob. Further suppose that Alice and Bob each have their own copy of the same secret **key**, which is a random string of bits. When Bob wants to send a message to Alice and wants to ensure that no eavesdroppers can read it, he **encrypts** his message with an encryption algorithm that uses his copy of the secret key before he sends it. After receiving the encrypted message from Bob, Alice uses a corresponding decryption algorithm that uses her copy of the same secret key to **decrypt** the message so she can read it. If Alice wants to send a message to Bob, she can use exactly the same process (sending an encrypted message to Bob by encrypting her message using her copy of the secret key and then sending the encrypted message to Bob so that he can decrypt the message using his copy of the key). This is shown in Figure 9.1, with M representing the message, E representing the encrypt operation, D representing the decrypt operation, and "secret" representing the secret key.

There are a variety of algorithms that can provide the encrypt and decrypt operations, but we always assume that the algorithm is known (or at least knowable). The security of these algorithms does not depend on the obscurity of the algorithms themselves; it depends solely on the strength and obscurity of the secret key. Because a key is just a

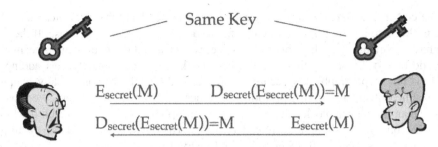

$$E_{secret}(M) \qquad D_{secret}(E_{secret}(M))=M$$
$$D_{secret}(E_{secret}(M))=M \qquad E_{secret}(M)$$

Figure 9.1   Alice and Bob use conventional cryptography.

string of bits (typically 128 or 256 bits long) that determines the mapping from plaintext to ciphertext for encryption and from ciphertext to plaintext for decryption, an attacker can always try to break the encryption by trying all of the possible keys. This is called a **brute force attack**. In order to defend against this attack, we try to use a key space large enough such that the attacker can never, even with large networks of fast computers, try all of the possible keys in any realistic amount of time. Today, a typical key size for conventional cryptography is 128 bits, which yields 2^{128} or 3.4×10^{38} keys. On average, we need to try half of all the possible keys before we will find the correct one using a brute force attack. If we deployed a million computers, each trying a million keys per second, it would take on average 5.4×10^{18} years to find the key needed to decrypt the message. This is about a billion times the estimated age of the universe!

All of the security in conventional cryptography depends on only two things: a sound algorithm (assumed to be known to all) and a long, randomly generated key kept secret between communicating parties. Of course, it is possible that the brute force attack could find the key in a shorter than average time (or take longer than the average time). Since we can never prevent these attacks against the key space, we must use an algorithm that has no weakness that would allow an attacker to find the key or the plaintext more efficiently than brute force.

Let us now consider how we can securely transport the shared secret key from Alice to Bob. We cannot encrypt the key—what key would we use to encrypt the key and how would we get that encryption key to the other party? In practice, we could send the key via some alternative communication channel that is hopefully free from eavesdropping, such as email or the telephone or a person with a handcuffed briefcase, but these are cumbersome alternatives. This form of cryptography (and its cumbersome key transfer methods) is known as conventional cryptography because it was the only type of cryptography known before the mid-1970s (and the invention of **public key cryptography**).

There are two families of conventional cryptographic algorithms: **block ciphers** and **stream ciphers**. Block ciphers encrypt a block of bits, typically 128 bits long, at a time and do not maintain state. This means that each resulting ciphertext block does not depend on the encryption of previous blocks (although we will soon see how to add dependency with a concept called **modes**). Stream ciphers encrypt a bit or a byte at a time while maintaining state from previous encryptions. This means that the same plaintext byte or bit will result in a different ciphertext byte or bit depending on the previous encryption result. These state-dependent mappings help thwart cryptanalysis. Over the years, many conventional cryptographic algorithms have emerged.

With block ciphers (and also, as we will see, with public key cryptography), we need to consider the problem of encrypting data when it does not match the block size of the cipher. The data we have can be smaller or larger than the cipher block size. We use **padding** to handle the smaller case and **modes** to handle the larger case. If the data we have is smaller than the cipher block size, we must pad the data, which means that we add bits to the data until it matches the block size. Unfortunately, just adding 0s or 1s is not cryptographically secure, so special padding algorithms, usually matched to specific cipher algorithms, perform this function securely. If the data we have is larger than the cipher block size, we must split it up into chunks that match the block size. The options for doing this are called modes. The obvious way to do this is to just take each block size worth of plaintext and encrypt it independently of any previous encryptions. This is known as **electronic code book (ECB)** mode. Unfortunately, this approach creates several problems. Since each block of plaintext is encrypted to the same value ciphertext each time, an attacker can build a dictionary of ciphertext values knowing that they are repeats of the same plaintext values. An attacker can also carry out a replay attack by injecting or rearranging ciphertext blocks, causing unexpected results for the receiver.

A better solution is to chain together successive blocks of encryption so that the encryption of one block is dependent on the previous encryptions. This yields ciphertext for a block that is different from the ciphertext generated for the exact same plaintext block elsewhere in the message. This causes any rearrangement of the encrypted ciphertext blocks to result in an incorrect (and incomprehensible) decrypted version of the plaintext because of the broken dependency chain. Many different modes can accomplish this, with different engineering considerations, but the most common one is **cipher block chaining (CBC)**. When using this mode, we have to start the chain with a value called an **initialization vector (IV)**. The IV does not have to be encrypted, but it should be integrity protected and never be reused.

We will now examine three of the most common conventional algorithms: two block ciphers (DES/Triple DES, AES) and one stream cipher (RC4).

9.1.1.1 DES/Triple DES   Historically, the most famous algorithm for conventional cryptography was the **Data Encryption Standard** (**DES**). IBM submitted an internally developed cipher for a National Institute of Standards and Technology (NIST) standardization effort and it became DES, and reigned from 1976 to 2002. DES uses a 64-bit block size and a 56-bit key length. Unfortunately, it is no longer recommended due to the general vulnerability to brute force attacks (but it has no severe breaks). Several factors contributed to this vulnerability, including the 56-bit key length, the increasing pace of CPU speed improvement, and the ease of harnessing large networks to provide parallel computing capacity. A cipher based on DES as a building block has extended its life. By increasing the key length (to either 112 bits or 168 bits depending on the specific implementation), and encrypting data with DES three times in succession, we get an effective strength of about 2^{56} that of DES alone. This approach is known as **Triple DES, 3DES**, or **DESede**. Note that there is no "Double DES" algorithm because an attack called the **meet-in-the-middle attack** is known. This attack weakens the strength of a Double DES approach—and actually degrades it to the same strength as the original DES. This attack also explains why the strength of Triple DES is only 2^{56} instead of 2^{112} times as strong as DES alone. While Triple DES is an improvement, it should be viewed as a stopgap solution because of the performance inefficiencies of using DES three times in succession.

9.1.1.2 AES In 2002, NIST selected an algorithm called **Rijndael** [Daemen02] as the successor to DES and renamed it. The new name they gave it is the **Advanced Encryption Standard (AES)**. AES has a block size of 128 bits and a choice of three key lengths (128, 192, or 256 bits). The criteria for its selection as the replacement for DES included many factors, such as resistance to all known attacks, good performance when implemented in both hardware and software, efficient resource usage (small memory footprint and small CPU requirements for smart card implementations), and fast key changing times. Currently, best practice is to use the AES algorithm in new applications, typically with a 128-bit key length.

9.1.1.3 RC4 Ron Rivest of RSA, Inc. created **RC4** but never officially released it. Ironically, it was leaked to the public, and once it was leaked, it became commonplace in many applications, ranging from wireless network encryption to browser security via Transport Layer Security (TLS)/Secure Sockets Layer (SSL). RC4 is a stream cipher that encrypts and decrypts one byte at a time. It uses a shared secret key as the seed for a pseudorandom number generator. At the sender side, each successive byte of the random stream is Exclusive-ORed (XORed) with each successive byte of plaintext to produce each successive byte of ciphertext. At the receiver side, each successive byte of the regenerated random number stream (which is the same as the sender's stream because of the common key/seed) is XORed with each successive byte of ciphertext to recreate the original plaintext byte.

There are several bitwise operations (meaning that the operation is conceptually done on a single bit but logically can be extended to a byte, or any number of contiguous bits) defined for computers, but here we are using the "Exclusive OR" (XOR), which takes two binary operands and returns a single binary result. There are only four possible combinations to consider: the first operand (A) is a bit that is either a zero or a one, and the second operand (B) is also a bit that is also either a zero or a one. The XOR operation returns a zero when the bits in the two operands are the same and returns a one when the bits in the two operands are different. For example, extending this to a sequence of bits, if the first operand was the binary number 1100, and the second operand was the binary number 1010, the result of 1100 XOR 1010 would be 0110. Notice that the operation is commutative: in other words, 1010 XOR 1100 also results in 0110. Also, XORing A to B and then XORing the result to B again yields A once again, which is an important property for its use in cryptography.

XOR Operation Summary

A	B	A XOR B
0	0	0
0	1	1
1	0	1
1	1	0

This approach takes advantage of two properties of XOR. First, if we XOR the same bits twice (in this case, the pseudorandom number stream), the result will be the same as the original data. Second, if we XOR with random bits, then the result (in this case, the ciphertext) will also look like random bits. RC4 can be viewed as a pragmatic implementation of a theoretical cipher known as a **one time pad (OTP)**. When using an OTP, the sender XORs the plaintext with the key (a string of random bits, which is exactly the same length as the plaintext), thereby producing the ciphertext, which is then sent to the receiver. The receiver receives the ciphertext and then XORs it with the same shared key (that string of random bits used by the sender), thereby producing the plaintext. OTPs are impractical because the key lengths need to be as long as the plaintext, the shared key must be perfectly random, and it can never be reused. RC4 makes this idea more practical by generating the key using a pseudorandom number stream. This stream can be exactly as long as needed and uses a shared secret seed value, which can then be viewed as the conventional shared secret key.

9.1.2 Message Digests and Message Authentication Codes

Ensuring data **integrity** is a fundamental requirement for any database. We must guard against both accidental database modification and malicious attempts to modify the data. Simple error detection and correction algorithms, such as cyclic redundancy codes (CRCs), which were designed to detect errors due to noise and other communication faults, cannot be used for security. If we did use one of these algorithms, an attacker could easily modify both the data and the CRC designed to protect the data in such a way that the receiver would be unaware of the data modification. There are two classes of cryptographic building blocks designed to ensure data integrity, message digests (MDs) and message authentication codes (MACs). MD algorithms take a message of unlimited size as input and produce a fixed sized (often several hundred bits long) output. The output is often referred to as a **hash** of the input. The algorithm used for MD is designed to quickly process the large number of input bits into the fixed sized output. It is essential that this function is one way, meaning that it is computationally infeasible to reverse engineer the input bit stream from a given output hash value. This means that an attacker cannot modify the data to match the MD value in an attempt to fool the receiver into thinking that the data still has integrity. MACs operate similarly to MDs, except that they use a shared secret key to control the mapping from input message to output hash. Because they use a secret key, MACs can also authenticate data origin.

9.1.2.1 MD5 and SHA MD5 was the most popular MD algorithm. It generates a 128-bit output hash. But, because of weaknesses identified with the algorithm, it is no longer recommended. Despite these weaknesses, it does still exist in many legacy implementations. Its replacement, an algorithm called **SHA-1**, has a 160-bit output. However, weaknesses were found in SHA-1 as well, so it also is no longer recommended (and it also still exists in many legacy applications). A stronger form of SHA, called **SHA-256**, is currently recommended while a NIST-sponsored effort is underway to develop a replacement standard MD algorithm. A popular framework for turning an MD algorithm into a MAC algorithm is called **HMAC (hash message authentication code)**. Common versions include HMAC-MD5, HMAC-SHA1, and HMAC-SHA256, which are based on the named MD algorithms.

9.1.3 Public Key Cryptography

The biggest drawback of conventional cryptography is the requirement for a shared secret key (and the awkward or insecure options for distributing that key). In the mid-1970s, a number of solutions to this problem appeared. All of these solutions extended the notion of a single key to a key pair, consisting of a **private key** (similar to the secret key of conventional cryptography) and a mathematically related partner called a **public key**. The public key can safely be revealed to the world. The public key can be sent to any party that wants to send a secret message to the key's owner without any communication channel protection or prior prearranged secret. Consider the example shown in Figure 9.2. Whenever Bob wants to send a secret message to Alice using public key cryptography, he first needs to have a copy of Alice's public key. Because this is a public key, Alice can make her public key available to Bob using any mechanism she wants to use (including any nonsecure mechanism). Once Bob has Alice's public key, he can encrypt the plaintext of the message he wants to send using Alice's public key, and then send the resulting ciphertext to Alice. The ciphertext can also be sent using any mechanism, since it is encrypted. Once Alice receives the ciphertext message from Bob, she can decrypt it using her private key. Because Alice is the only one with her private key, she is also the only one who can decrypt messages encrypted using her public key. If she wants to send a message to Bob, she would do the same thing Bob did (obtain a copy of Bob's public key, use it to encrypt the message, and send it to him). With this technology, any two parties can ensure the confidentiality of their communication without previously exchanging any secret information.

Unfortunately, public key cryptography algorithms are much less efficient than conventional cryptography algorithms, typically by several orders of magnitude. This means that it is usually not practical to encrypt or decrypt long messages with public key cryptography. However, we can use it to encrypt a secret key. Then, we can simply send the encrypted secret key using a nonsecure communication channel. Now, we can use conventional cryptography without the awkward secret key distribution issue. By using this hybrid approach, public key cryptography is used for its strength (privately distributing a secret key without prior secret sharing) and conventional cryptography is used for its strength (speed).

We will now look at two algorithms for public key cryptography: the **RSA** algorithm and the **Diffie–Hellman** algorithm. There is also a new family of algorithms called

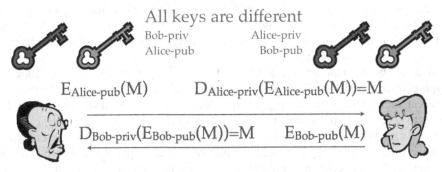

Figure 9.2   Alice and Bob use public key cryptography.

elliptic curve cryptography (ECC), which might emerge in the future, but we will not cover them here. Note, as previously discussed, we must pad data that is smaller than a block size and choose a mode for data that is larger than a block size.

9.1.3.1 RSA and Diffie–Hellman   Although there are a few different algorithms that can be used for public key encryption, we will only mention two of them. The RSA algorithm [Rivest78] is one of the oldest yet still the most popular public key cryptographic algorithm. It is based on the computational difficulty of factoring large numbers into component prime factors. Typically, a user generates a key pair of size 1024 bits (although the best practice is moving to 2048 bits). The RSA block size is typically the same as the key length.

The Diffie–Hellman algorithm [Diffie76] does not directly perform encryption. It is an algorithm run between two parties. Each party performs a calculation based on secret information. This secret information is not preshared with the other party. Instead, the two parties exchange some public results of those calculations with each other and then perform another calculation. The algorithm ensures that both parties will have calculated the same result, which can then be treated as a secret key and used with a subsequent conventional cryptographic algorithm such as AES. Diffie–Hellman is an example of a class of algorithms known as key agreement algorithms.

9.1.4 Digital Signatures

Digital signatures (DSs) are an authentication technique based on public key cryptography. A DS can provide authentication, just like a MAC can, but a DS can also provide a more advanced function, namely, nonrepudiation. There is a subtle distinction between authentication and nonrepudiation. Suppose Alice receives a message from Bob, and that message has an associated and appended MAC. Also, suppose that Alice and Bob had previously obtained the secret MAC key. Alice can then take her key and run the message through the MAC algorithm to verify that she generates the same MAC code as the one appended to Bob's message. Because Alice and Bob are the only ones with the shared secret key, Alice knows that only Bob could have originated this message and associated MAC. Therefore, Alice has authenticated Bob as the source of the message (and authenticated the integrity of the message). But, what would happen if Bob denied that he ever sent Alice this message? If Alice took Bob to court, could Alice prove that Bob originated the message? Although Alice knows that Bob is the only one who could have sent this message (because Bob is the only one who had the other copy of the secret key), Bob could claim that since Alice also has a copy of the secret key, she could have composed the message and sent it to herself! Alice would not be able to prove him wrong, so although MACs provide authentication, they do not provide nonrepudiation.

With a DS, we can use the public and private key pair and certain public key cryptographic algorithms (RSA is the most popular choice) to perform a completely different function than the encryption function we've already discussed. When Bob wants to send a signed message to Alice, he uses his private key to "encrypt" or sign the message. While this action uses an encryption algorithm, it isn't true encryption because anyone with the corresponding public key can decrypt the message, and anyone can potentially get access to the public key. While the message is not encrypted, it is authenticated, because the message receiver can use Bob's public key to "decrypt" or verify the message. This not only authenticates the message origin to Alice as Bob, but (since Bob is the only holder of Bob's private key) this provides the even stronger notion of nonrepudiation. If Alice takes Bob to court, Alice can prove that Bob is the only one who could have originated the message since he is the only holder of the private key that was used to sign the message. So, Bob cannot completely deny that he originated the message. However, there is still a problem in attaining perfect nonrepudiation from digital signature technology. Bob can claim that his private key was stolen and the thief, not Bob, signed the message. A family of protocols called **arbitrated digital signatures** can partially address this "stolen key" issue, but we will not discuss them here.

For performance reasons, we typically do not sign an entire message. The sender takes a message and calculates the message digest of the message, and signs ("encrypts") that digest with a private key and appends the signed digest along with the plaintext message. The receiver removes the appended signed digest and verifies ("decrypts") the digest with the corresponding public key. The receiver then takes the plaintext message and runs it through the same message digest algorithm. If the results of the verified message digest match the results of the message digest calculation, then the receiver knows that the message has integrity and authenticates the message to the sender such that the sender cannot deny message origination. Notice that public key cryptography can be used for two completely different purposes. If we encrypt a message with the receiver's public key, we get an encrypted message, but no authentication. If we sign a message with the sender's private key, we get authentication (and nonrepudiation), but no privacy. We can, however, use both of these functions in sequence.

If Bob wants to send a signed, encrypted message to Alice, the following sequence must occur:

- Bob signs the message he wants to send with his private key.
- Bob encrypts his (already signed) message using Alice's public key.
- Bob sends the signed, encrypted message to Alice.

If Alice wants to receive a signed, encrypted message from Bob, the following sequence must occur:

- Alice receives the signed, encrypted message from Bob.
- Alice decrypts the message using her private key.
- Alice verifies the unencrypted message using Bob's public key.

9.1.5   Digital Certificates and Certification Authorities

While public keys are designed to be publicly shared and distributed, they must also be authenticated to their owners. Otherwise, anyone could generate a key pair and then distribute it. The attacker could claim that the public key belonged to someone else, and then use the private key to intercept and decrypt messages meant for the legitimate receiver. The most famous scenario for this attack is called the **man-in-the-middle attack** in which a malicious entity in the middle of a communication path can make two legitimate parties think that they are securely communicating with each other while the malicious entity can decrypt all the traffic.

The most common solution for this problem is to employ a **digital certificate**. A digital certificate for a user or machine consists of a public key, some identifying information (name, location, etc.), and some dates indicating the certificate validity period. All of this information is unencrypted, but it is signed with the private key of a trusted third party known as a **certificate authority (CA)**, such as Verisign, Inc. For a fee, the CA will verify the identity of a party requesting a certificate and then sign the certificate with their private key. The certificates are in a format defined in a standard called X.509. The CA public key is distributed in browsers and operating systems. Using this technology, users do not send their public keys directly to another party. Instead, they send their digital certificates. Certificate receivers can then verify the CA signature using their own copy of the CA public key (in their browser or operating system). This authenticates the owner of the public key contained inside the certificate, which can then be used for subsequent conventional key distribution, encryption, or digital signature verification. If a security problem with the key or certificate is found, then the certificate serial number is placed on the CA's **certificate revocation list (CRL)**, which should always be checked prior to using any certificate. Most browsers have a setting that automates this checking, but for performance reasons, the default is usually set to not check the CRL.

Note that digital certificates do not need to be signed by a CA, but can be self-signed or signed by a company for its own use. This works well for internal applications (and there is no external CA cost). External web users, however, must be presented with a CA-signed certificate or they will see a message box in their web browser indicating that the certificate cannot be trusted.

9.2   SECURING COMMUNICATIONS

DDBEs require secure communications, both between users and the DDBE and among the Sub-DBEs themselves. Secure communication typically demands privacy, authentication, and integrity. This means that we must protect against both passive eavesdroppers who can monitor messages passed over the network and active attackers who can not only monitor messages but can also inject new or modified messages into the network. In general, whenever we need to implement some security capability, we should use an existing, well-hardened protocol. This protocol should, in turn, use one or more of the existing, well-hardened cryptographic building blocks. We should use building blocks that were written by an experienced vendor or a trusted open-source project. Security algorithms, protocols, and implementations are extremely hard to design, implement, and deploy, and history is littered with well-intentioned, failed attempts. We will look at two well-known, well-hardened technologies for achieving end-to-end secure communications: **SSL/TLS** and **Virtual Private Networks (VPNs)**.

9.2.1   SSL/TLS

The most common protocol for securing communications is the Secure Sockets Layer (SSL) protocol, which is now known as the Transport Layer Security (TLS) protocol. This protocol, originally developed by Netscape, makes use of all of the cryptographic building blocks we have discussed. Here is a conceptual sketch of how this protocol works. Suppose Bob wants to communicate with his bank's web server via a web browser. The TLS protocol provides two services in this scenario: it provides end-to-end communication link privacy via encryption and it provides an authentication service that allows Bob to authenticate the identity of his bank's server via digital signatures and digital certificates. Bob begins by opening a Transmission Control Protocol (TCP) connection from his browser to his bank's server, as shown in Figure 9.3. Usually we want to use a **Uniform Resource Locator (URL)** that begins with "https://," which will attempt to open port 443 on the bank's web server. Using this port indicates a desire to use TLS communications instead of the normal, insecure communications, which uses a URL beginning with "http://" and usually uses port 80. Note, however, that some web servers are configured to treat "http://" requests as "https://" requests.

After the TCP connection is established, Bob's browser and the bank's server negotiate a cipher suite, indicating the specific algorithms that they will use for subsequent communication. For example, RC4 might be used for the conventional cryptography, RSA for the public key cryptography, and SHA-1 for MD. After this negotiation, the bank's server sends its digital certificate to Bob's browser. This digital certificate is signed by a CA and contains the bank's server name, public key, validity dates, and other information. Bob's browser then verifies this certificate using the CA's public key, which was preinstalled in Bob's operating system or browser. Bob's browser can then verify that the machine he is communicating with matches the one named in the certificate, which authenticates the bank's server to Bob. Now that Bob's browser has an authenticated public key for the bank's server, his browser can generate a conventional cryptographic key and encrypt it using this public key. Once the conventional key is encrypted, Bob's browser sends it to the bank's server. Finally, the bank's server decrypts the conventional key that Bob's browser sent, and they can begin to communicate privately (using RC4 in this example).

There is an optional TLS protocol phase that also allows the server to authenticate the client, but it requires a client digital certificate so it is rarely found in consumer scenarios like the one we just described. This optional phase is useful for securing dedicated TLS links between two machines. When the TLS protocol is used without a web browser for these purposes, it is often called TLS secure socket communication. Note that TLS is a form of end-to-end security, meaning the entire communication path from client to server is protected. This means that every message sent using this protocol is protected, even when they pass through insecure links along the way, such as an unencrypted wireless network.

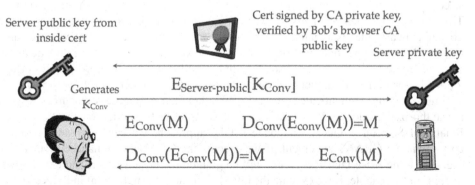

Figure 9.3   Bob uses TLS/SSL to connect to his bank's server.

9.2.2   VPN, IPSec, and SSH

Briefly, here are three other examples of technologies (like TLS) that can be used to provide end-to-end secure communications. One approach to securing communication links is to use a technology called **Virtual Private Networks (VPNs)**. This technology was originally designed to allow the insecure Internet to be used securely with an additional layer providing security services. This is useful for both remote worker-to-business and site-to-site security, such as between DDBE components. Another approach is to use a protocol called **IPSec**, which provides both encryption and digital signature services to the IP layer of the Internet. This allows all of the higher layers (TCP, UDP, and applications) to benefit from this security service. The IPSec protocol is optional for IP Version 4, but it is mandatory for the next generation, IP Version 6. Often, VPN services are built on top of IPSec. **Secure Shell (SSH)** is a similar authentication/encryption protocol that can also be used to build secure tunnels between two endpoints.

9.3   SECURING DATA

While secure communication between users and DDBEs, and between DDBE components themselves, is necessary for overall system security, it is not always sufficient. Sometimes, we must also protect the data residing in the databases from unauthorized viewing and modification. Even when these security measures are in place, we can be vulnerable to various other attacks. In this section, we will begin by examining some techniques for authorizing data access. Then, we will consider techniques for encrypting data. Next, we will look at two classes of database-specific security attacks. The first class of attacks (unvalidated input and SQL injection) depends on deployment and implementation details, while the second (data inference) has more subtle causes. We will close this section with an overview of data auditing.

9.3.1   Authentication and Authorization

Authentication for both DDBE users and components can be implemented using digital certificates, as described above in the TLS protocol using client certificates, or with user ID and password. Security tokens (in the form of a key fob or a credit card-sized device) are increasingly popular extensions to the user ID/password approach. They display a sequence of digits, which randomly change every 30 seconds or so. To authenticate, the user enters his/her user ID, the displayed digit sequence, and his/her PIN, creating a one-time password. This is known as two-factor authentication: something you have (the token) and something you know (the PIN). Biometrics offers a third factor to use for authentication: something you are (such as a fingerprint).

After users are authenticated to the DDBE, they can only access resources if they are authorized to do so. If we model our DDBE security service on the traditional Relational Structured Query Language (SQL) approach, we can offer authorization control via the GRANT statement. If we execute the GRANT command on the left in Figure 9.4, the Alice DDBE Account will be granted the right to insert and delete rows in the Employee table. If we execute the GRANT command on the right in Example 9.1, the Alice User Account will be granted the right to read rows from the Employee table

```
GRANT INSERT, DELETE
ON    Employee
To    Alice;
```

```
GRANT SELECT
ON     Employee
TO     Alice
WITH   GRANT OPTION;
```

Figure 9.4   Granting the Alice DDBE User privileges on the Employee table.

and her account will also be granted the right to extend this authorization (SELECT) to other DDBE Accounts.

A technology called **Lightweight Directory Access Protocol (LDAP)** can also support authentication and authorization. Within this context, a directory is a collection of generic information (such as white pages listing people, their phone numbers, addresses, email addresses, etc.) Directories can also contain authentication information such as user ID and password information. Similarly, directories can contain authorization information that specifies what software an authenticated user can or cannot access. By using either a single LDAP server or a collection of cooperating LDAP servers, administrators can use a single facility to control distributed authentication and authorization details. This strategy is called **single sign on (SSO)**. Microsoft Windows Active Directory provides a similar capability. We must secure all the communication links to LDAP servers too, which is often done using TLS.

Firewalls, often specialized for use with databases, can control access at the network level. Administrators can specify parameters such as a list of IP addresses, ports, protocols, dates, and times for which accesses are allowed or denied. This enables the firewall to filter unauthorized network traffic before it arrives at the DDBE components. **Intrusion detection systems (IDSs)** can monitor network traffic for patterns of malicious traffic (such as viruses, worms, or live attackers) that can potentially compromise a database. The IDS can then alert an administrator to take action. Note that IDSs can be human resource intensive because they typically generate many false positives.

9.3.2 Data Encryption

If the physical hardware systems used by our DDBE components are ever physically compromised, the disks could be removed and scanned for sensitive data. Even if they are never physically compromised, these systems could be attacked across a network from remote machines, from local machines on the network, or even from processes running directly on the host server itself. This means that sensitive data should be encrypted inside the database storage.

Encrypted file systems (EFSs) are becoming increasingly popular for protecting hard disk drives (especially on laptops) containing sensitive data. All the data on the disk is encrypted with a conventional key and accessed via a user password. However, this technology can often create performance problems when used with database systems because database system designers have taken great care to optimize data access assuming specific physical disk layouts that might be disrupted when data is encrypted.

A better approach for encrypting database data is to encrypt the data being stored rather than the underlying file system. There are two basic approaches: internal to the DBE, and external from the DBE. In the first approach, we use components or applications to encrypt the data prior to sending it to the DBE for storage and then use similar components or applications to decrypt the data after it is retrieved from the DBE. Since the DB is storing the encrypted version of the data, the data types used inside our DBs must be modeled to hold the encrypted ciphertext, not the plaintext. This often requires extensive use of binary data types in the database, such as variable-length binary (varbinary) types or binary large objects (BLOBs). In the second approach, because the DBE directly supports encryption, the DDBE users can simply read and write their data normally while the DBE handles the encryption "under the covers." This is generally the most efficient approach to data encryption for centralized DBMS.

With any type of encryption, we must be careful with key handling, because a compromised key means compromised data. Often, the key is protected by a password. This password must be stronger than the key it is protecting. In this context, stronger has a very specific, technical meaning, called **entropy**, that refers to more than just the literal password length. A long password consisting of words easily found in a dictionary and using only a subset of possible characters (such as all lowercase letters) has lower entropy than a password that is the same length but uses random, uniformly distributed characters.

Users must never store their passwords directly on a machine unless the passwords are also encrypted using a sufficiently strong encryption mechanism. Software providing password vaulting, a technique where a master password is used to decrypt a list of other passwords, is a reasonably safe way to store passwords. The master password must be at least as strong as the contained passwords. The Mac OS X keychain is an example of a password vault.

We must also be careful when the password is supplied by a machine or process instead of a person. Hard-coding passwords in command scripts can make them vulnerable to both snooping and to system utilities that list the command lines of running processes. Hard-coding passwords in source code can make the passwords vulnerable to string extraction utilities. The best options use operating system provided key-protection constructs such as keychains and ACL protected registries. In the future, secure hardware module key storage will probably become increasingly popular.

9.3.3 Unvalidated Input and SQL Injection

Unvalidated user input is one of the most common software security flaws. It is responsible for exploits ranging from buffer-overruns, to command injection, to cross-site scripting. It is also responsible for a class of exploits specific to databases known as **SQL injection**. This attack takes advantage of a lack of user input validation, usually in web-based input fields for forms and in URLs containing post data. The attack uses cleverly crafted input values to sneak in SQL commands that can expose confidential information, allow unauthorized data modification, or even destroy or corrupt the data in the database.

Suppose we have a web-based application that uses web-forms for user input, which it then uses to build SQL commands dynamically. It creates these SQL commands at runtime by concatenating SQL command fragments and the user-supplied input values. Although the actual DDBE authorization and authentication would **never** be based on this user input, this is an easy example to explore. For each of these scenarios, suppose our web-based application is an online storefront of some kind, and the web-form in the scenario is the customer login and password entry form. Assume we have a relational table named "CustomerLogin" in the DDB that contains a unique "CustomerId" value for each unique pair of "CustomerName" and "CustomerPassword" values. Our web-form must have two user-supplied data fields; let's call them "inputName" and "inputPass." Now let's consider what happens when this form is attacked using a SQL injection technique.

9.3.3.1 Bypassing the Password for Customer Login

9.3.3.1 Bypassing the Password for Customer Login Suppose our application dynamically builds a SQL Select statement using the hard-coded strings shown in Figure 9.5, and the user input values. Notice that String2 and String3 have a leading space. Both String3 and String4 have a single-quote (apostrophe) at the end, and both String4 and String5 have a single-quote (apostrophe) at the beginning. String5 ends with a semicolon, which is the "end of command" character for SQL. When the customer logging in provides values via the input fields in this form, our application creates a SQL query by concatenating String1, String2, and String3 together, followed by the value of inputName field, then String4, followed by the value of inputPass, and then, finally, String5. This SQL query will return the CustomerId value from the relational table where the CustomerName value and CustomerPassword value each match the values specified in the web-form fields.

For an example of what we intended to have happen, if a customer named Alice used this form to enter her name and password (let's suppose she enters the value "Alice" for inputName and "Rabbit" for inputPass), our application would create the SQL query in Figure 9.6. If the specified values (CustomerName equal to "Alice" and CustomerPassword equal to "Rabbit") do **not** exist for any row in the table, then the SQL query will return an empty set (zero rows returned, a "SQL-Not-Found" error raised, etc.). If this happens, since there is no "CustomerId" value returned for this query, the login attempt will fail. On the other hand, if the SQL query returns a nonempty result set, then it will contain Alice's CustomerId value, and the login attempt will succeed.

For an example of an unintended consequence, if we have "unvalidated" input for this web-form (if our code does not adequately check for malicious or invalid customer input), it is possible that some attacker could cleverly construct values for these input

```
String1 = SELECT CustomerId
String2 =  FROM CustomerLogin
String3 =  WHERE CustomerName = '
String4 = ' AND CustomerPassword ='
String5 = ';
```

Figure 9.5 Hard-coded strings used to build SQL query.

```
SELECT CustomerId
FROM    CustomerLogin
WHERE   CustomerName = 'Alice'
AND     CustomerPassword = 'Rabbit';
```

Figure 9.6 SQL query built for customer "Alice" with password "Rabbit."

fields to circumvent both our authentication and authorization mechanisms. Suppose our attacker provides the input values shown in Figure 9.7. The value for each field is the same: a single-quote, followed by a space, the word "OR," and another space, and then two single-quotes followed by an equal-sign and another single-quote. What will happen next?

Figure 9.8 shows the SQL query that our application would create and execute in this scenario. Notice that the single-quotes changed the logic of the WHERE clause. Now, we will return the CustomerId value wherever the CustomerName value is empty OR wherever an empty string equals an empty string. This would effectively return a random CustomerId value and allow the attacker to be logged in as this random customer. By specifying a known customer name for the inputName field, along with this same malicious password value, an attacker can impersonate any customer.

9.3.3.2 Bypassing the Password for Change Password

This same technique can be used to circumvent other unvalidated web-forms, even when we attempt to enforce security. For example, suppose our attacker has logged in using CustomerName "Alice" and obtained her CustomerId as shown in Figure 9.8. Suppose Alice's CustomerId value is "1234." Now, suppose the attacker wants to change Alice's password—effectively preventing Alice from being able to log in to her own account. Suppose we had another (unvalidated) web-form for changing passwords. Even if this form attempted to provide additional security by requiring the customer to enter the old password value along with the new, the attacker could again use the technique (and values) shown in Figure 9.8. Here, the system would provide the CustomerId value, and our attacker would provide the "old CustomerPassword value" (same as shown in Figure 9.7), and a "new CustomerPassword value" (suppose the new password is "newValue"). Figure 9.9 shows how the exploited SQL Update command might look in this scenario.

9.3.3.3 Vandalizing the DDBE

In the previous examples, our attacker was attempting to impersonate one of our customers. Suppose we encounter an attacker who wants

```
inputName =' OR ''='
inputPass =' OR ''='
```

Figure 9.7   Malicious input values entered by an attacker.

```
SELECT  CustomerId
FROM    CustomerLogin
WHERE   CustomerName = '' OR ''=''
AND     CustomerPassword = '' OR ''='';
```

Figure 9.8   SQL query built from malicious input (shown in Figure 9.7).

```
Update  CustomerLogin
SET     CustomerPassword = 'newValue'
WHERE   CustomerId =1234
AND     CustomerPassword = '' OR ''='';
```

Figure 9.9   SQL update built from malicious input.

to vandalize our website and DDBE. There are several scenarios where the same SQL injection technique can allow such an attacker to do very damaging things to our system. The issue of unvalidated input again plays a key part in this security breach, but we also have a new class of exposures that increases the potential for harm based on the violation of the least privilege principle, or granting more authority than necessary.

Although there are several different approaches for identifying the right level of authority for a given application or scenario, they are beyond our scope here. Instead, we will focus on a simple example demonstrating what can happen when we are too generous with the authorization policy. When our web application connects to the DDBE, the DDBE authenticates the Account information that the application is using. Whenever the application attempts to execute a query or command, the DDBE verifies that the account has the authority to perform the operations required for request. For example, the account used by our application must have the ability to read the CustomerLogin table if it is going to verify customer names and passwords, and the ability to update the CustomerLogin table if it is going to change customer passwords.

Suppose this account is authorized to do more than simply read and update a single table. In the previous examples, the attacker tricked our application into executing clever variations of the intended commands. In this scenario, the attacker uses the same security vulnerability (unvalidated input) and the same exploit (SQL injection) but, because we have given a tremendous amount of authority to the underlying DDBE account being used by our application, the unintended commands will be more destructive. For example, suppose our attacker uses the same web-form and the same dynamic SQL scenario as we depicted in Figure 9.5, but now, the values entered are those in Figure 9.10.

Notice that the inputName starts with a single-quote, and then is followed by a semicolon. Recall that the semicolon terminates a SQL command, which means that the remaining text is a new command. The remaining text in the name value is a command to drop the CustomerLogin table. If the account is authorized to do this command, it will destroy the CustomerLogin table structure and content! The second semicolon in this field is followed by a space and two dashes (hyphens, minus signs). The space followed by two dashes is recognized as a "begin comment" command in most SQL parsers. Figure 9.11 shows the SQL command generated for this scenario. Everything after the two dashes is ignored. The fact that the SQL query returns no rows is irrelevant, because after the query executes, the entire table will be dropped.

```
inputName ='; DROP TABLE CustomerLogin; --
inputPass =anything
```

Figure 9.10   Even more malicious input values entered by an attacker.

```
SELECT CustomerId
FROM   CustomerLogin
WHERE  CustomerName = ''; DROP TABLE CustomerLogin; --'
AND    CustomerPassword = 'anything';
```

Figure 9.11   Command built from input values shown in Figure 9.10.

This means that customer login information will be lost, and nobody will be able to log into the system.

9.3.3.4 Preventing SQL Injection

There are several techniques for thwarting this attack. First, we can perform simple input validation, such as ensuring CustomerName values can only contain alphanumeric data (no spaces, punctuation, numbers, etc.). Similarly, verifying that the user-supplied value falls between the minimum and maximum lengths defined for the field can limit the amount of malicious content. Many RDBMS platforms provide a facility known as "prepared SQL," or "parameterized SQL;" facilities like these can use precompiled type checking as a technique to minimize exposure to attacks such as SQL injections. Unfortunately, there is no such thing as a commercial off-the-shelf (COTS) DDBE product. This means that we must manually create the facilities used to parse and execute commands.

SQL injection is just one example of a broad class of software flaws that can compromise security in applications. In order to guard against these attacks, there are many preventative actions that we need to perform, such as ensuring that software memory buffers on stacks and heaps are not overrun in our components, subsystems, and applications, protecting against injection for operating system commands and DBE commands, and properly handling exceptions and return codes. For a good exploration of these application security issues see [Howard05].

9.3.4 Data Inference

Databases can also suffer from a specific security and privacy vulnerability, known as a data inference attack. This attack is extremely difficult to address, and impossible to completely solve as a general case. When we allow certain, individual queries that are by themselves innocuous, we cannot prevent the aggregation of these results, which then exposes confidential information. It is a specific example of a more general problem: when attackers can create data mining results from disparate sources, each of which is authorized, in order to gain confidential results through the aggregate. Suppose we have a relational table named EmpCompensation, containing the columns and data needed to capture employee salary (see Figure 9.12).

Suppose we have three employees named "John," "Mary," and "Karen" (as shown in the figure data), and each employee has an authenticated DDBE account. Employee accounts have the privileges necessary to look up their own salary information, but not the information for other employees. We also allow employees to retrieve statistical information about salaries in the organization (so that they can see where they fall on the salary grid).

EmpName	EmpTitle	EmpSalary
John	Worker	$10,000
Mary	Worker	$20,000
Karen	Manager	$30,000

Figure 9.12 The EmpCompensation table.

```
SELECT EmpSalary
FROM   EmployeeCompensation
WHERE  EmpName='John';
```

Figure 9.13 Employee John's query.

```
SELECT AVG(EmpSalary)
FROM   EmployeeCompensation;
```

```
SELECT COUNT(*)
FROM   EmployeeCompensation;
```

Figure 9.14 Aggregate queries that any employee can execute.

This means that John could execute the query in Figure 9.13, but Mary (or Karen) cannot, but all three employees can execute the query in Figure 9.14. Suppose John uses his query (Fig. 9.13) to retrieve his salary information and Mary uses a similar query to retrieve her salary information. Each of them can execute aggregate queries on the Employee table, such as those shown in Figure 9.14. The first query will return $20,000, while the second query will return three, in this example. Now, if John and Mary collude and share their salaries, the average, and the number of salaries, they can infer their manager Karen's salary. There are some partial (but no complete) solutions to this problem. See [Denning83] for more information on this type of attack.

9.3.5 Data Auditing

Data auditing is an essential component of data security. Often, we cannot detect security breaches when they occur, but examining audit logs for evidence can be a very useful post-attack tool. Audit logs can vary in detail, but they can contain useful information such as the date and time for failed access attempts, successful attempts, important modifications made to the system, and other details. We should try to ensure that the audit log is stored separately from the database so that attackers who compromise the database cannot attempt to hide their tracks by modifying the log as well. One approach to accomplish this is to use a separate audit server that can only receive data in a single direction from the database and uses write-only storage.

9.4 ARCHITECTURAL ISSUES

When designing security architecture for DDBEs, we should consider several issues. We must have a clear understanding of the physical system environments, a clear definition of who the valid and invalid users are, an accurate assessment of the level of sensitivity for the data (from both an eavesdropping and a modification perspective), and an effective plan for operational processes such as enrolling new users, backing up data, and responding to attack incidents. When the requirements are known, we can select the technologies (like those described in the previous sections) that best match the system requirements. In general, the security architecture must address broad issues, including the physical environment security, source code updates, data backup media protection, lost password policies, host operating system maintenance, firewall and intrusion detection system configuration, and user education. Often, database vendors provide technology support and documentation for securing the most common environments and that should be the first source of information and technology. This is usually both the simplest and most secure approach to most security architecture tasks, leaving the more exotic security technologies for unusual requirements.

We can broadly categorize database-based client/server applications by the number of tiers, or major function divisions. In two-tier architectures, the client function is in the first tier and the application logic resides on the same server as the database in the second tier. In three-tier architectures, the client function is in the first tier, an Application server (such as the open source JBOSS or IBM Websphere) resides in the second tier, and the database (or distributed database) resides in the third tier.

For the client tier, there are two major architectural choices: thick client or thin (web) client. In thick client architectures, we can run a stand-alone application that requires preinstallation. This approach can provide a rich GUI platform and potentially better control over security because the application filters and formats user input and controls the information passed to the second tier. However, there are attacks where rogue code eavesdrops on and/or impersonates the first tier, so tier-to-tier communication must be both encrypted and authenticated.

In thin or web-based client architectures, the user interacts with a web browser and leverages scripting languages, such as JavaScript, and active code downloads, such as Java and ActiveX, to validate user input and perform other computation. This opens up a potential entry point for malicious code from a compromised website that can compromise the client system. As in the thick client case, we must encrypt and authenticate the communication between web client and server, often by using TLS.

In three-tier architectures, the application server in the second tier is often given unrestricted access to the database in the third tier because the application server is acting on behalf of all users. This, however, risks database compromise as a consequence of application server compromise. The data security model is often implemented in the application server on individual objects, with the database acting as a general purpose repository for the object persistence.

9.5 A TYPICAL DEPLOYMENT

Let us see how the above concepts and technologies and approaches might be used to secure a typical three-tier distributed database deployment.

A user using a web browser in the first tier connects to an application server in the second tier using the HTTPS protocol, which uses the application server's digital certificate, signed by a certificate authority, to authenticate the server to the client and to encrypt and authenticate the traffic between the first two tiers using the TLS protocol. The application server can then authenticate the user with a user ID and password, securely transmitted on this TLS tunnel, and might leverage an external LDAP server (with its communication also secured via TLS) to provide SSO for user authentication credential checking and application-specific authorization.

The application server code carefully validates any user input to ensure there are no buffer-overruns or SQL injection attacks or other types of accidental or malicious input. Application server objects are retrieved and stored to the third tier distributed network of databases. The communication between the application server and the databases, and between the databases themselves, is also secured with TLS. The application server authenticates itself to the DDBE, typically with a user ID and password that is protected using the application server operating system host security mechanisms, such as a protected registry or keychain.

The database tier uses its SQL security model to ensure that requests are authorized. Each database, if the data is sensitive, might also be encrypted so that theft of hard disks would not result in data compromise. The database backup tapes must also be encrypted so that their storage or disposal will not result in a compromise.

The database tier and application tier execute a strict audit policy and log all significant access attempts, successes, and failures. These audit logs are also protected from modification by leveraging operating system facilities or special purpose, external, one-way, write-only logging servers. Firewalls and intrusion detection systems can be strategically placed across the network to block unwanted traffic and to detect attack attempts.

The security deployment must be validated, usually via a security audit, and all software must be kept up-to-date with patches at all levels. A penetration (PEN) test would further assure the implementation by having an experienced security tester (known as a white hat) try to compromise the system before an attacker (known as a black hat) will. Finally, an organization must have a written set of security processes that implement security policies for system maintenance, testing, incident response, and user and administrator authentication and authorization.

9.6 SUMMARY

Securing computing systems is a very broad topic. The issues we must consider come from several different areas: physical security, host and operating system security, network security, and application security. In order to address the issues in these areas, we must perform many tasks, such as ensuring good coding practices, enforcing good policies and procedures for auditing, and assuring, detecting, and reacting to attacks. Most of the technologies for securing distributed databases focus on the data itself and the communication paths. These protocols are in turn based on cryptographic building blocks and specific implementation algorithms for these blocks. In this chapter, we explored the basic building blocks and associated algorithms. We then looked at some basic protocols for securing communications and data, examined several database-specific security vulnerabilities, examined some broader architectural issues, and looked at a typical deployment. As the amount of online data and the number of people granted access to it (worldwide) continue to increase at a staggering rate, security issues and technologies will only continue to grow in importance.

9.7 GLOSSARY

Advanced Encryption Standard (AES) A conventional symmetric block cipher standard, selected by NIST to replace DES in 2002, based on the Rijndael cipher submission that uses a 128-bit block size with 128-, 192-, or 256-bit key lengths.

Arbitrated Digital Signatures   A family of digital signature protocols that leverage a trusting third party and can help limit the risk of stolen private keys.

Authentication   Any technique used to validate the identity of a source or destination of messages or data.

Authorization   Any technique used to determine whether a particular user, component, or subsystem has sufficient access permissions to perform a desired operation—this is usually checked after the identity has been authenticated.

Block Cipher   A cipher that encrypts and decrypts a group of bits at a time and that does not save state.

Brute Force Attack   An attempt to break encryption by trying all the keys.

Certificate Authority   A company that verifies the identities associated with public keys and then, usually for a fee, signs those keys when they are embedded in digital certificates, to be subsequently verified by the corresponding certificate authority public keys present in browsers and operating systems.

Certificate Revocation List (CRL)   A list of invalid certificate serial numbers maintained by each certificate authority.

Cipher   A form of cryptography that maps symbols (i.e., bytes) to other symbols.

Cipher Block Chaining (CBC)   A cryptographic mode where a given block encryption/decryption depends not only on the current block input but also on the previous block output, forming a dependency chain.

Ciphertext   The message or data after encryption prior to decryption.

Code   A form of cryptography that maps words to other words.

Confidentiality   Any technique that ensures that data is kept private from eavesdroppers, usually by using encryption.

Conventional Cryptography   A cipher that uses a common shared key known only to the sender and receiver.

Cryptanalysis   The science of breaking secrets.

Cryptography   The science of creating secrets.

Data Encryption Standard (DES)   A conventional symmetric block cipher standard selected by NIST in 1976 based on an IBM submission, which uses a 64-bit block size and a 56-bit key.

Decryption   Any technique or operation that recreates plaintext, or the message/data to be communicated, from ciphertext.

Diffie–Hellman   A public key agreement algorithm based on the difficulty of computing discrete logarithms in a finite field.

Digital Certificate   A public key and other identifying information, usually in X.509 format, signed with a certificate authority's private key after the certificate authority verifies the public key identity.

Digital Signature   A cryptographic technique that uses a source private key to sign data such that a destination can use the source public key to authenticate the source with the strength of nonrepudiation.

Electronic Code Book (ECB)   A cryptographic mode where a given block encryption/decryption depends only on the current block input.

Encrypted File System (EFS)   A file system where the disk blocks are encrypted, preventing data compromise if the disk is physically stolen.

Encryption   Any technique or operation that creates ciphertext, which is confidential in the face of eavesdroppers, from plaintext, which is the underlying message/data.

Entropy   A measure of the true information content, in bits, of a password that takes into account the probability of occurrence of each possible password symbol.

Firewall   A network security component that controls access to and from a computing system that can screen out traffic based on network address, port, protocol, or contents.

Hash   Another term for a message digest operation.

Hashed Message Authentication Code   A framework, based on a specific message digest algorithm, for creating a message authentication code.

Initialization Vector (IV)   A nonsecret, never reused, bit string (usually the same length as a cipher block) that starts the chain of encryption and decryption for modes such as cipher block chaining (CBC).

Integrity   A property in security, anything that ensures that a message/set of data is not modified by accident or malicious intent.

Intrusion Detection System (IDS)   A network security component that detects malicious network packet signatures indicating a potential virus, worm, or other attack.

Key   A bit string that controls a cipher's mapping of plaintext to ciphertext for encryption and ciphertext to plaintext for decryption.

Lightweight Directory Access Protocol   An architecture for a read-mostly database, which can contain authentication and authorization data.

Man-in-the-Middle Attack   An attack where an active attacker can read encrypted messages/data only intended for two parties in a manner such that the two parties are unaware of the compromise.

MD5   A message digest algorithm with a 128-bit hash size.

Meet-in-the-Middle Attack   An attack against two successive encryption stages with two distinct keys and a known plaintext/ciphertext pair, where encryption of the plaintext with one key is matched with ciphertext decryption of another key. A match signifies that both keys are now known. This attack reduces Double DES to Single DES strength.

Message Authentication Code   A message digest that also uses a conventional key as part of the fingerprint computation.

Message Digest   A small, fixed sized, digital fingerprint (or hash) for data of arbitrary input size using a one-way algorithm that makes the computation of the message digest fast, but the creation of another input that matches the fingerprint computationally infeasible.

Mode   An algorithm for breaking up plaintext that is larger than the cipher block size in a cryptographically secure manner, usually by making the current block encryption dependent on previous block encryptions.

Nonrepudiation   The inability to deny being the source of a message or data.

One Time Pad (OTP)   A theoretically perfectly secure cipher that uses a perfectly random key that is as long as the plaintext, which the sender XORs to the plaintext to produce the ciphertext. The receiver, who has the same key, XORs the key to the ciphertext to recreate the plaintext.

Padding The addition of bits to fill out a full block size prior to encryption in a cryptographically secure manner.

Plaintext The message/data prior to encryption or after decryption.

Private Key The key from the public key cryptography key pair used for decryption and signing that must be kept secret.

Public Key The key from the public key cryptography key pair used for encryption and signature verification that can be revealed to the public.

Public Key Cryptography A cipher that uses a public/private key pair for encryption or digital signature. For encryption, a source uses the destination public key to encrypt data that the destination can decrypt using its private key.

RC4 A stream cipher, commonly used in TLS/SSL and wireless network encryption, that models a one time pad using a seed as a shared key, which is the input to a pseudorandom number generator.

Rijndael The name of the cipher (now called AES) that won the NIST competition for DES replacement in 2002.

RSA A public key cryptosystem that can be used for encryption and digital signature based on the difficulty of factoring large numbers into component primes.

Secure Shell (SSH) A protocol for secure remote telnet that can also be used for building secure communication channels between two endpoints.

SHA-1, SHA-256 A message digest algorithm with a 160-bit hash size.

Single Sign On (SSO) The concept of consolidating authentication and authorization information in a centrally managed and accessed location.

SQL Injection An attack against a database that typically leverages unvalidated web-form input, which results in malicious SQL statements when these input values are carefully crafted and subsequently concatenated with dynamic SQL statements.

Steganography The science of hiding secrets.

Stream Cipher A cipher that encrypts or decrypts 1–8 bits at a time dependent on input data and previous state.

TLS/SSL A protocol for encrypting communications while providing data integrity, which also authenticates servers to clients (and optionally clients to servers).

Triple DES A cipher composed of three sequential DES ciphers, which offers twice the security as DES and uses a 64-bit block size and 112- or 168-bit keys. Also known as 3DES and DESede.

Virtual Private Network (VPN) A protocol that enables a public, insecure network to be used as if it were private with the use of encryption for confidentiality and digital signature for authentication.

REFERENCES

[Anderson08] Anderson, R. J., *Security Engineering: A Guide to Building Dependable Distributed Systems*, Wiley, Hoboken, NJ, 2008.

[Daemen02] Daemen, J., and Rijmen, V., *The Design of Rijndael: AES—The Advanced Encryption Standard*, Springer, Berlin, 2002.

[Denning83] Denning, D. E., and Schlorer, J., "Inference Controls for Statistical Data Bases," *IEEE Computer* 16, 7 July 1983, 69–82.

[Diffie76] Diffie, W., and Hellman, M., "Multiuser Cryptographic Techniques," in *Proceedings of the AFIPS National Computer Conference*, pp. 109–112, 1976.

[Ferguson03] Ferguson, N., and Schneier, B., *Practical Cryptography*, Wiley, Hoboken, NJ, 2003.

[Howard05] Howard, M., LeBlanc, D., and Viega, J., *19 Deadly Sins of Software Security*, McGraw-Hill Osborne Media, New York, 2005.

[Natan05] Natan, R. B., *Implementing Database Security and Auditing: Includes Examples for Oracle, SQL Server, DB2 UDB, Sybase*, Digital Press, Clifton, NJ, 2005.

[Rivest78] Rivest, R., Shamir, A., and Adleman, L., "A Method for Obtaining Digital Signatures and Public Key Cryptosystems," *Communications of the ACM*, Vol. 21, pp. 120–126, 1978.

[Stallings05] Stallings, W., *Cryptography and Network Security*, 4th edition, Prentice Hall, Englewood Cliffs, NJ, 2005.

EXERCISES

Provide short (but complete) answers to the following questions.

9.1 Suppose Alice and Bob each have a public key pair. Alice sends a signed and encrypted message to Bob, who processes the message. Show the order in which the four keys are used in this scenario.

9.2 Describe at least three reasons why one time pads (OTPs) are impractical.

9.3 Suppose we wanted to go into the certificate authority (CA) business to compete with Verisign. What would we need to do?

9.4 What two functions are performed by the public key cryptographic technology in SSL/ TLS?

9.5 Suppose Alice wants to send a conventionally encrypted message to Bob but they have never met before or agreed on any specifics of the message exchange. Name five things Bob must be told before he can decrypt and interpret the message from Alice.

9.6 Suppose we had a business with an online storefront and our private key corresponding to our SSL/TLS certificate has just been stolen. What actions must we take, and what actions must our customers take?

9.7 Using the same scenario as in Figure 9.5, what would happen if an attacker entered the following values for the web-form fields?

```
InputName = '; DELETE FROM CustomerLogin WHERE ''='

InputPass = ' OR ''='
```

9.8 What is the difference between database authentication and authorization?

9.9 What is the difference between a firewall (FW) and an intrusion detection system (IDS)?

9.10 What role does auditing play in securing databases?

10

DATA MODELING OVERVIEW

This chapter is a brief review of **data modeling languages (MLs), data models (DMs),** and the general process of **data modeling** (writing a DM using a ML)—three things that are all typically covered in much greater detail as part of a traditional **database (DB)** course. For more details about data modeling in general and more examples of data modeling languages, see [Elmasri94], [Sanders95], [Lewis02], and [Kim92]. In Chapter 1, Section 1.1.1, we briefly discussed data modeling languages and data models—and we also mentioned that a ML is the special language or facility that we use to create each DM. But what exactly is a DM?

In some respects, data modeling is similar to construction, and DMs are similar to the blueprints used in construction. Blueprints and DMs are both attempts to capture the intentions of their authors (the architects and data modelers)—but the blueprints are not the physical buildings that they describe and DMs are not the databases that they describe. Even when the authors strive to make their "plans" (the blueprints and DMs) as accurate as possible, these plans are rarely (if ever) 100% complete, 100% accurate, or 100% up-to-date. Some of these discrepancies are necessary because blueprints and DMs are merely abstractions of the things they represent. If the authors of these plans tried to include every detail, these approximations would become too complex and cluttered. If they tried to maintain total accuracy for every detail, it would require an enormous amount of effort (especially if this were done for every draft and revision of their plans).

Distributed Database Management Systems by Saeed K. Rahimi and Frank S. Haug
Copyright © 2010 the IEEE Computer Society

Blueprints and DMs are similar in many respects, and, in particular, both are attempts to capture our intentions. Blueprints capture our intentions for buildings; DMs capture our intentions for data. In other words, the DM is an attempt to represent the structure, shape, or plan for the data; but not the actual data content itself. Therefore, a DM is sometimes referred to as an **intentional model**, an **intentional schema**, or simply as a **schema**. Strictly speaking, English spelling and grammar rules dictate that the plural for schema is schemata, but it is fairly common to see the term **schemas** used for the plural instead. In this book, we will use the term schemas as the plural, and we will also often use the terms schema and model (or any variation of model, such as DM) interchangeably.

Obviously, there are some details that need to be more complete, more accurate, and more up-to-date than other details. For example, when creating the blueprints for a building, all the details about plumbing, electrical wiring, and gas lines should probably be as accurate and complete as possible at all times to avoid problems with safety, health, and building codes. Conversely, even if knowing the precise size, shape, color, style, and location for every door knob is important to the interior designers and decorators, these details are probably not that crucial to the electricians (who would have to wade through a lot of unnecessary details if we included this sort of information in their plans). One solution to this problem is to create separate plans tailored to suit the needs of their intended audience. The same situation occurs with DMs: if we tried to include all the semantic details, all the behavioral rules for interaction among the data, and all the storage details for the data, the complexity would be overwhelming—even for a simple DB. Once again, the complexity can easily be managed, merely by using the right set of plans with the right level of detail for the intended audience. In other words, creating separate DMs of different types (where each type focuses on a different category of details) can be very beneficial for any DB—from the simplest, centralized DBs to the most complex, distributed DBs, and everything in between.

In Section 10.1, we will consider three alternatives for categorizing MLs and the DMs written in these languages. Then, in Section 10.2 and for the rest of the chapter, we will focus on one of those alternatives, namely, the **CLP taxonomy**, and, in particular, the first level in this taxonomy, which is called the **conceptual level**. In Section 10.2.2, we will consider some of the issues, goals, and example MLs within the conceptual level. Finally, we will discuss the model creation process. This discussion will begin in Section 10.4, by first examining the steps needed to create a DM using a particular ML from the conceptual level. Next, we will briefly consider the logical and physical levels. We will conclude this discussion by providing a high-level overview of the issues and activities involved when working with multiple MLs and DMs both within and across multiple levels of this taxonomy. This will also help us to prepare for Chapter 11, which focuses on the logical level MLs and DMs.

10.1 CATEGORIZING MLs AND DMs

As we mentioned in Chapter 1, each DM captures all of the schema details for a particular DB, and each DM is written in a particular ML. When contemplating the creation of a new DM (intended to fulfill a specific set of requirements for a DB), we can decide to write the DM using almost any language. Because each ML has its own set of nomenclature, rules, and representations, using a particular language will affect how the model looks. Nevertheless, we can usually create a sufficient DM in any of the commonly used MLs, with varying degrees of difficulty and elegance. The way that we capture the schema level details in a DM is, of course, dependent on the ML we use, because different languages implicitly emphasize different types of details and usually represent them in different ways.

Earlier, we mentioned that we can categorize the MLs based on the types of details they contain or emphasize. This means that we can even create multiple renditions of the same DM using different MLs (both within the same category and across categories). There are different ways to categorize model details, but in this book, we will usually categorize them using a particular taxonomy that we will call the **CLP taxonomy**—so named because it has three levels in it, which are called the **conceptual level**, the **logical level**, and the **physical level**. This taxonomy (and its levels) can be extremely useful for building centralized DBs. Although the logical and physical levels are not as useful for representing the combined schema in a distributed DB, all three levels are especially useful for implementing **distributed database environments (DDBEs)**. Therefore, this section will review these three levels and focus especially on the conceptual level. Chapter 11 will focus on the logical level and explore some of the logical MLs commonly used in real-world **database environments (DBEs)**.

Data modeling is somewhat similar to application development. Considering all the schema-level details for a DM is analogous to considering all the development details about some component or subsystem, and in both scenarios, we can create models using several different languages to capture these details. We can also categorize these languages based on the types of details that they emphasize for both cases (categories such as requirements, design, and implementation can be used when considering application development). If we are following good software engineering practices, we will create several models to capture these details and use a systematic process to refine the details—perhaps even creating different renditions of the same model (both across categories and within the same categories). For example, a particular algorithm's design could be captured in an object-oriented model (OOM) and then implemented using two different object-oriented programming languages, such as C++ and Java. In other words, this section is merely discussing the data modeling equivalents of these common, application development scenarios.

10.1.1   The CLP Taxonomy

Although the CLP taxonomy is not standardized, it should be fairly familiar to most data modelers, especially if they have ever deployed the same DB schema across several different database platforms. Within each level, there are several different MLs available, and these levels are used to categorize the MLs (and the resulting DMs). Each language is assigned to a level based on the types of schema details emphasized and captured by the ML. DMs belong to the same level as the ML in which they were written. Why do we separate the ML and DMs into levels? If we were to attempt to capture all the schema details for a particular DB by creating only a single, initial model (in other words, if we were skipping over the higher-level DMs by creating our model directly in the physical level as a first step), it would be difficult to manage the complexity. But if we use the levels in this taxonomy appropriately, we can manage this complexity and use a stepwise-refinement approach to create the desired physical-level DM in a more controlled fashion.

Using the taxonomy appropriately means that the first step is using a **conceptual modeling language (CML)** to create a single data model, called a **conceptual data model (CDM)**. We can then use the CDM as the basis for creating one or more data models in the logical level. The DMs we create in the logical level are called **logical data models (LDMs)** and each is written in a **logical modeling language (LML)**. Each LDM can then form the basis for one or more DMs in the physical level. These DMs are called **physical data models (PDMs)**. Obviously, each PDM is written in a **physical modeling language (PML)**.

In Figure 10.1, we consider a situation where we have six data models representing three centralized database deployments (three separate databases on three different platforms) of the same database schema. In the conceptual level, we have a CDM (named "Employee CDM"), which is written in a conceptual modeling language. This CDM forms the basis for two different LDMs in the logical level. The first LDM is named "Hierarchical Employee LDM" and it is written in a logical modeling language representing the **hierarchical data model (HDM)**. The second LDM is named "Relational Employee LDM" and it is written in a different logical modeling language from the first LDM—this logical modeling language represents the **relational data model (RDM)** [Codd70]. The first LDM in this example acts as the basis for a single PDM named "IDS Employee PDM," which is written in a physical modeling language representing a particular centralized database environment (CDBE) platform that implements the HDM. The second LDM in this example acts as the basis for two more PDMs: one named "ORACLE Employee PDM" and one named "DB2 Employee PDM." Each PDM in this example is written in a different physical modeling language. Since the last two PDMs mentioned have a common LDM as a basis, we would expect their

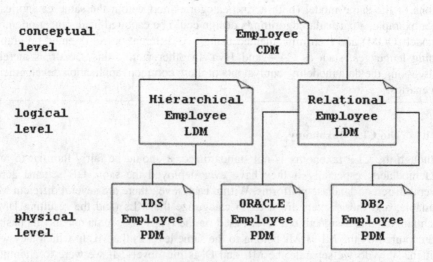

Figure 10.1   Applying the CLP taxonomy to a DM deployed on three CDBEs.

physical modeling languages to represent (different) specific CDBE platforms that both implement the RDM. Obviously, the names used here are contrived, and we would not be able to know these details based solely on the model names in the real world.

Often the data model for a new database is only intended for a single deployment. When that is true, there is only one DM in each level (a single CDM, a single LDM, and a single PDM). Obviously, this is not the case for the scenario shown in Figure 10.1. In this example, we are deploying the same data model across three different centralized database environment platforms (IDS, ORACLE, and DB2). Let's consider how we can follow a stepwise refinement approach to implement one of the PDMs from Figure 10.1. First, we would create the "Employee CDM" using some specific conceptual level modeling language. This model will focus on high-level, abstract concepts. Remember, CDMs focus on the semantic requirements of the database, but not the design or implementation details of the environments that will implement the persistent storage for the database. After we have created and validated the "Employee CDM," we can create one of the LDMs using one of the modeling languages from the logical level. Suppose we create the "Relational Employee LDM" at this point using the RDM as the logical modeling language. Remember that the LDMs can be thought of as different renditions or refinements of the CDM, and in this case, our LDM would include relational data modeling considerations (such as normalization). In other words, the LDM is a translation (or mapping) of the requirements originally captured by the CDM into a particular logical modeling language representing the logical design supported by a particular set of database environments. Although the logical data model refines the high-level details contained in the conceptual data model, it does not create any new high-level details and also will not contain any implementation or deployment details about the target DBE. After we have created and validated our logical data model in this example, we can use it to create one of the PDMs based on this LDM, such as the "ORACLE Employee PDM." A PDM will often reflect many of the high-level details contained in the LDM on which it is based. Often, this is also true for an LDM and the CDM on which it is based. In these situations, the emphasis in the lower-level model is different from the emphasis in the higher-level model, and no new higher-level details are introduced. For example, the "ORACLE Employee PDM" would capture the implementation and deployment details that we excluded from its CDM and LDM (such as the details about data types, indexes, tablespaces, segments, extents, and data files).

There are several advantages to using the CLP taxonomy and this stepwise-refinement based modeling approach. By creating the DMs in this manner, we can validate and verify the details in each level before proceeding to the next. There is a natural, evolutionary order between the categories (moving from a high level of abstraction to a lower level of detail), which guides the data modelers and helps to execute the data modeling tasks in a systematic and managed fashion. Another obvious advantage is the potential for reuse—often, there are techniques (and even tools) that can be used to take an existing DM from one level and generate a new DM in another level. When we generate a DM in a lower level, it is called **forward engineering (FE)**. In most cases, the reverse technique is also possible (albeit with some inaccuracies and omissions). Since we are using a lower-level DM to generate a higher-level DM in this scenario (moving in the reverse direction), this is called **reverse engineering (RE)**. We will discuss forward and reverse engineering again in Sections 10.3 and 10.4, and we will also revisit the topics in Chapter 11.

10.1.2   The 3LM Taxonomy

The CLP taxonomy described in the previous section is just one possible approach we can use to categorize MLs and DMs used to capture the schema details for DBs—there are also other categorizations that can be used. As we mentioned in Chapter 1, the American National Standards Institute's Standards Planning and Requirements Committee (ANSI SPARC) defined an architectural model for databases with three different levels (the **external, conceptual**, and **internal** levels) [SPARC75] [SPARC76] [SPARC77]. For the sake of brevity, we will simply refer to it as the **three-level model (3LM)**. In the 3LM approach, each DM in the external level is a public interface to the data, while each DM in the conceptual level contains all the design details, and each DM in the internal level contains the implementation and deployment details.

Although this sounds similar to the CLP taxonomy, neither the taxonomies nor their levels are equivalent. In order to avoid confusion, we will refer to the DMs for each level in the 3LM taxonomy as schemas in this discussion rather than DMs—but in any other context the terms "model" and "schema" are usually considered to be equivalent. Using the 3LM taxonomy, a single DB can have several **external schemas**, but only a single **conceptual schema** and only a single **internal schema**. This is quite different from the CLP taxonomy, where we explicitly said that one of its advantages was the ability to generate multiple DMs for the lower levels! The 3LM taxonomy allows us to create multiple schemas to capture the requirements for a DB, but all of the higher-level schemas refer to the same physical DB. The 3LM taxonomy focuses on only one particular DB and only one particular DBE. By contrast, the CLP taxonomy focuses on the MLs used to create multiple lower-level DMs. These lower-level DMs are used to design multiple renditions of same DB requirements and to configure the deployment details for each DB instance and each (potentially different) DBE platform managing that instance. Figure 10.2 shows how three different external schemas can be defined for one conceptual schema (and its one internal schema). We could consider the schemas in Figure 10.2 to be a different way to categorize all the schema-level details for one deployment of one DB from Figure 10.1. Let's suppose this figure is

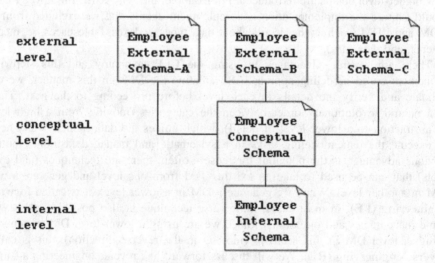

Figure 10.2   Applying the 3LM to a single DM for a single CDBE.

for the DB defined in the "ORACLE Employee PDM"—but the schemas in this figure and the DMs in the other figure would **not** be identical.

There is also another difference between these two taxonomies—the levels in the 3LM taxonomy are not related to each other in quite the same way as the levels in the CLP taxonomy. In particular, because the 3LM focuses on providing multiple external interfaces to the same DB, the 3LM schemas have an implicit requirement that is not necessarily present in the CLP data models—because each external schema is used as the interface to the DB by clients (users or programs), the concepts in its ML **must** be supported by the DBE. The concepts in the ML used for the internal schema **must also** be supported by the DBE, since this is where the all physical implementation and deployment details for the DB schema reside. Often (though not always) the concepts used by the ML for the conceptual schema are also supported by the DBE. Therefore, we will typically use the **same** ML to create the schemas in all three levels of the 3LM taxonomy. By contrast, because the CLP focuses on providing multiple designs for the same concept and multiple implementations for the same design, we often use **different** MLs for different models in the CLP taxonomy. Although we said that DMs could be generated across the levels of the CLP (both forward and reverse), this activity is usually a development process that is not part of the DBE implementation. In other words, when using the CLP taxonomy, the data modeler must generate the LDM and PDM as part of the DB design and implementation process, but the environment used to implement the DB is not necessarily directly involved in the generation process. This means that although each DBE must support the concepts from the physical modeling language that describes it, the DBE is not required to provide direct support for any of the logical or conceptual modeling languages used by the other DMs from which it evolved.

Although we will not discuss the details of these levels further in this chapter, the 3LM is an especially useful point of view to consider for the end user view of both a centralized DB and a distributed DB. The ability to isolate the external user from any changes in the lower-level schemas is particularly useful. These ideas might sound familiar to anyone who is acquainted with the concepts of interface, abstract class, and concrete class from **object-oriented (OO)** techniques—but the ANSI SPARC approach is not the same as OO modeling! Although these concepts are similar and both techniques are examples of encapsulation and information hiding, the techniques are not equivalent.

10.1.3   Other Categorization Approaches

There are many other possible approaches for categorizing the schema details for a DB, but we will not cover them here. Instead, we will merely mention that there is one more informal approach that is commonly used, and it is similar to the CLP taxonomy. Like the CLP taxonomy, this approach has no official name, but it is essentially the same as the taxonomy we presented in Section 10.1.1 with one major difference—it eliminates one level. In this approach, many of the same conceptual-level details and logical-level details are still present, but since there are only two levels in this approach, the details are allocated differently. We can consider the first level in this approach to be a blending of the conceptual and logical levels from the CLP, and the second level in this approach to be a combination of the logical and physical levels from the CLP. Because there is no separate logical level, this approach implicitly assumes that all the physical DBE alternatives are fairly similar with respect to their overall structure, nomenclature, and rules. This means that the nomenclature and notations used in the first level can be closer to the language and notations used in the second level (and the actual implementation systems), and therefore this approach is potentially less ambiguous than the CLP taxonomy. Because there is still a separation between the physical details and the higher-level details, this approach also has some of the same stepwise-refinement aspects and benefits. Obviously, this approach is not appropriate when the DBEs are not based on the same logical design—this approach would not work well for the scenario shown in Figure 10.1 because the DBEs in that example required more than one logical modeling language and more than one LDM. For the remainder of this chapter we will use the CLP taxonomy that we discussed in Section 10.1.1.

10.2   THE CONCEPTUAL LEVEL OF THE CLP

Some issues are common to all MLs and DMs in this level. These issues always need to be handled either by the ML, by the data modeler, or a combination of the two. Similarly, there are some goals that are common to all languages and models in this level. Every DM in this level attempts to achieve these goals regardless of which ML it is written in, or the specific DB requirements it is trying to capture. Therefore, we can consider these issues and goals to be a part of the conceptual level itself rather than a part of a specific language, a specific model, or a specific set of DB requirements—they are something that every CDM must attempt to address in one way or another.

10.2.1   Conceptual-Level Issues

When we say that there are issues common to the conceptual level, we are not referring to issues that data modelers will encounter because of the DB they are attempting to design. These issues are more universal; the authors of the modeling language usually consider these issues more carefully than the data modelers consider them. Depending on the strengths and weaknesses of the conceptual modeling language being used, the data modeler might need to be more or less concerned about these issues. Even if the language being used provides adequate remedies for these issues, the data modelers should at least be aware of these issues—if nothing else, this awareness can be used to select the appropriate conceptual modeling language to use.

We will consider three categories of issues for CMLs and CDMs:

- DBE design and implementation independence issues
- Abstraction issues
- Emphasis issues

10.2.1.1   DBE Design and Implementation Independence Issues   Later in this chapter (in Section 10.3), we will examine three examples of conceptual modeling languages: namely, the **entity relationship model (ERM)**, the **crow's feet notation (CFN)**, and the **Unified Modeling Language (UML)**. At first glance, the ERM and CFN languages might appear to have a slightly relational flavor to them, while the UML has a definite object-oriented flavor. However, all three MLs are actually independent of the DBE storage design and implementation. This means that we can use any DBE to implement a model written in one of these languages—or more specifically, we can use a CDM written in any of these MLs to generate LDMs (and ultimately generate PDMs) for any environment. If the CML is dependent on the design of the DBE, this means that there is a dependency between the conceptual modeling language and a particular physical modeling language—that is, they have some terms, rules, or representations in common. As we mentioned in Section 10.1.3, working with the CDMs, LDMs, and PDMs can become confusing, ambiguous, or even error prone when this happens. Even when the MLs for the different levels are conceptually independent, merely using some of the same vocabulary, nomenclature, or representations can sometimes cause confusion and errors. Theoretically, we can have two extreme scenarios. In the first situation, all of the MLs being used across the levels are either identical, or at least appear to be identical—in other words, they use the same terms, or perhaps different definitions and interpretations for the same terms. The other extreme case would require all three languages to be completely different from each other (sharing no common terms, etc.), which increases the complexity of the data modeling process. Usually, we want to find a balance between the two extreme cases. Although we do not want to use the same ML for all three levels, we also do not want the MLs to be so radically different from each other that we cannot manually recognize the general mappings between the levels and languages.

Because different MLs are used for each of the levels in the taxonomy, we always need to consider how a given construct in one ML will be translated into a different language in a different level. Usually, we are more concerned with the forward direction, which means we are more focused on any issues encountered in the mappings from the conceptual-level ML into the logical-level ML, from the logical-level ML into the physical-level ML, and ultimately from the conceptual level to the DBE implementation. When reverse engineering is also used, we must also consider issues in the reverse mappings (from physical to logical and logical to conceptual). It is not always easy to prevent aspects of a particular data storage design or data storage implementation methodology from creeping into the CML and the CDM. In other words, the same CDM should in theory be compatible with several different logical modeling (data storage design) techniques, and several different physical modeling (data storage implementation) alternatives for each technique, but this is not always easy to ensure. Ignoring the MLs in the other levels for a moment, we could say that the different conceptual modeling languages are merely slightly different representations of the same abstract conceptual modeling process. While there are certainly advantages and disadvantages to the various alternative languages, they are all essentially capturing the same concepts—similar to singing the same song in a different (human) language or in a different (musical) key. Carrying the analogy a bit further, we can also say that depending on the song, the lyrics, the language, and the key being used, the various renditions of this song might be very similar or rather different from each other yet still recognizable as the same tune. What this means is that the same CDM can be captured and represented using different CMLs—although there will be differences between the CDMs themselves, each language should be powerful enough to capture essentially the same details.

Even when the CML authors have considered the issue of independence carefully, there are going to be ramifications for the lower-level models. If the CML is very abstract and independent when compared to the logical and physical modeling languages, we will encounter **semantic impedance** issues. For our purposes here, semantic impedance simply means the degree of difficulty we encounter when trying to translate a concept across different DMs. We will consider some of the semantic impedance issues between logical and conceptual modeling languages in Chapter 11, when we look at forward and reverse engineering. If the CML is not very abstract or independent when compared to the logical and physical modeling languages, we will have lost this independence—this might make it more difficult to generate data models for certain logical and physical approaches. Typically, a CDM will capture a range of interrelated concepts; some concepts will be more complex, more important, more prominent, or simply more emphasized than others. Sometimes the language will influence this emphasis, but as we shall discuss in the next sections, the ML should always provide the necessary support to emphasize or deemphasize the concepts based on the conceptual analysis.

10.2.1.2 Abstraction Issues   Recall that a CDM, which is also called a **conceptual schema**, captures abstract schema details for a DB, in particular, semantic details about the concepts being modeled and their interdependencies. Depending on the language used to capture these details, the CDM might represent these concepts and interdependencies using special ML constructs, textual descriptions, assertions, rules, or some other technique. When we create a CDM, there is always a set of specific requirements for the DB that the model is intended to satisfy. Any single concept taken from these requirements might be included in the CDM or omitted from it. Ideally, when the data modelers are capturing these concepts from the requirements, the conceptual modeling language guides them to consider things at the correct level of abstraction. By using a particular nomenclature, vocabulary, notation, tool, or technique, the CML can nudge the data modeler to capture **metadata** (everything about the data except for the content itself) that is appropriate for this level. For example, most tools used to create CDMs have the ability to capture textual descriptions, definitions, and annotations for almost every construct that the CML is capable of rendering. By providing this ability, the tool encourages the data modeler to consider and document the specific definitions, goals, rationales, and so on for almost anything in the model regardless of the actual construct being used to capture the concept.

Many CMLs provide an abstract (LDM and PDM independent) rendition of some of the lower-level metadata details. Let's look at an example of how a CML can guide the data modeler to the right level of abstraction. Consider how we would store a person's name as an example; we might store this concept using three pieces of interrelated data (the first, middle, and last names). Now consider this simple question (which we could ask about any piece of data that we intend to store in a DB): "Must we always store a nonempty value for this concept?" In this case, we are considering the person's name and wanting to capture whether the value for each piece is mandatory or optional. Notice that when we consider this at the appropriate level of abstraction, we are only focusing on the semantics. In other words, our CML should allow us to consider this question and capture our answer in a manner that is independent of the mechanism used to implement or enforce our decision. Suppose we decided that every person must have a first name and a last name, but the middle name should be considered optional—once we have captured these semantic details in our CDM, suppose we want to generate multiple LDMs and PDMs from this same CDM (similar to the scenario we looked at in Figure 10.1). We might choose to enforce a mandatory first and last name using several different mechanisms in these lower-level MLs and DMs. For example, in a relational ML we could use things such as table constraints, column constraints, and triggers. In other MLs, we might use other techniques, or perhaps we might need to enforce the requirements outside of the data model for those situations where the language cannot enforce our desired semantics. If the CML is careful to use a vocabulary and representation that is at the appropriate abstraction level, then we can easily map this requirement appropriately to many different logical and physical modeling languages. Conversely, if the CML had not captured this requirement in an abstract manner (e.g., if the CML captured this requirement directly as a trigger), it would be difficult to translate the requirement into any language with a different point of view (e.g., the language used to capture a HDM).

10.2.1.3 Emphasis Issues   Whenever we decide to capture a concept in our CDM, we also need to decide how important or complicated the DM representation needs to be for it. Every CML provides various ways to capture a particular concept, ranging from a single language construct to a complex arrangement of several constructs working together in a sophisticated configuration. For example, suppose we have a set of requirements for a database representing a small company. This DB needs to store information about each department within the company and all the employees who work within each department. When we decide to include these concepts in our CDM, we can draw on various sources of information to identify the possible data we could store about this situation. Let's consider what it means to capture "information about each department." At a minimum, we could capture the department name, but we could also capture additional information about each department, such as the yearly budget for the department and the name of the department manager. Similarly, capturing information about "all employees who work within each department" could be as simple as storing a list of employee names for each department or as complicated as storing detailed information (such as the salary, birthday, date of hire, promotion history, list of family members, current home address, hobbies, or favorite color) for each employee. Obviously, some of the details we just mentioned are probably not important (such as favorite color)—in fact, based on the actual requirements, it is possible that we only need to capture employee names! Of course, the actual details required are determined by working through the actual requirements and refining our understanding of the database using these details and feedback from the prospective database users.

Once we understand the requirements, we are ready to start capturing the concepts in our model. Regardless of the conceptual modeling language we use, we need to have the flexibility to model a concept as simply as a single value (like a department name), or as complex as required. By using a simple construct, we place minimal emphasis on a particular concept. Using more complex construct configurations places greater emphasis on the concept. Clearly, data modelers need to be careful about the emphasis they place on each concept they include in their CDMs. In our example, if the DB requirements do not call for detailed information about the department (if we never want to populate, query, or report on these details), then we should not include them in the model. Conversely, if we need to have more complex information captured, then we need to have the ability to model the semantics in the most useful way possible. Ideally, it should be possible to update the model at a later date to increase or decrease the emphasis by changing the parts of the model used to capture a particular concept. Although this is usually possible, it can be very difficult to do once the DB is used in a production environment.

10.2.2   Conceptual-Level Goals

There are three simple goals that apply to the conceptual level as a whole (all the conceptual modeling languages and CDMs have them). Once again, we are not referring to goals or requirements that data modelers will encounter because of the DB they are attempting to design; we are considering goals that are universally shared by the authors of the CMLs as well as all potential data modelers.

Simply put, these three goals are:

- Documenting the DB requirements
- Supporting forward engineering
- Supporting reverse engineering

10.2.2.1   *Documenting the DB Requirements*   There are several reasons why we say that a CDM provides the best documentation for a set of DB requirements, and a CML provides the best format or language for writing that documentation. In particular, each CML is capable of capturing schema details in a much more clear, concise, and unambiguous way than mere textual documentation ever could. Because a CDM only contains high-level details, we do not need to "wade through" all the low-level details. This also means that it is usually easier to change model details in existing CDMs (especially when compared to the task of altering a purely textual description of the DB requirements). Often, the tools used in this level provide facilities for generating reports and diagrams, which can allow us to narrow the focus even further (especially useful for complex models). Assuming that the issues identified in Section 10.2.1 have at least been minimally addressed, the CML will provide better handling of these issues than a typical data modeler using only textual descriptions can ever hope to do—regardless of the actual CML being used. However, this does have one caveat: we need two things to happen in order to achieve this goal. First, the CML authors and tool vendors need to provide useful facilities, and then, the data modelers need to use them appropriately. Unfortunately, data modeling is often like application development—sometimes the comments, annotations, and other tool facilities are not used properly or not even used at all.

10.2.2.2   *Supporting Forward Engineering*   Whether we use tools or manual techniques, a CDM can be employed to generate an initial rendition of the model used for the lower levels. As we mentioned earlier, this is called forward engineering (FE). Using a tool to forward engineer a CDM into an LDM (and later into a PDM) can provide many advantages. Obviously, the tool can automate the same techniques we would manually apply, and perform them in a much more efficient (and presumably much more accurate) fashion. When there are multiple applicable techniques, the tool can allow us to generate multiple renditions and analyze them further. This can be very useful when prototyping a new model, or when analyzing the impact of a proposed feature

enhancement or defect correction in an existing model. Many tools also support the ability to compare different versions of the lower-level models, when they are regenerated from the same high-level model. For example, suppose we use a CDM to generate an LDM and then later modify the CDM and regenerate our LDM (based on this modified CDM). Many tools will provide a merge facility to compare the newly generated LDM with the previously generated version. Such a facility would allow us to identify differences between versions in order to avoid overwriting any additional details added to the first LDM after it was generated. This is important, since there are always additional details needed for the lower-level DMs that are not specified in the higher-level DMs—these details are often manually added after the LDM is generated. Therefore, both automatic forward generation and interactive merge facilities are very useful facilities to have in a modeling tool. Even when manual techniques are used for FE, the ability to generate multiple LDMs and PDMs from the same CDM is a terrific advantage, when compared to generating multiple database models completely from scratch. If the models are intended to be used as different implementations of the same system, then they should capture and represent the same semantic details (even if the implementation and enforcement is different across the different deployed systems). Using a single, consistent CDM as a source provides an easy mechanism for tracing the requirements through the analysis, design, and implementation phases for these environments.

10.2.2.3 Supporting Reverse Engineering

Whenever an existing system needs to be modified, it is useful to isolate the implementation details from the semantic details. This is one way that we can prevent unintentional semantic changes (errors) from being introduced into an existing model. As we mentioned in the previous section, many tools provide regeneration and merging facilities, but before we can use these facilities (assuming we have a tool that provides them) there are two important requirements that need to be met. The first requirement should be obvious—we must have existing CDMs, LDMs, and PDMs for the DB we are trying to modify. There are many reasons why this might not be true: perhaps the DMs were lost, perhaps the tools required to read and modify the DMs are no longer available, or perhaps these DMs were simply never created. Assuming that we have the appropriate DMs, the second requirement is also simple to understand—the DMs must be up-to-date when compared to the actual DB. Once again, there are several reasons why this might not be true. For example, suppose the DB is intended to support one or more applications (which is usually true). It is possible that there were feature enhancements or defect corrections in these applications that required changes to the DB schema, for which the DMs were not necessarily updated. It is also possible for the DMs to be changed without updating the existing DBs—we do not always forward engineer all of the updates to all of our DMs or DBs. Lastly, any of the applications or DBE users with sufficient authorization can change the DB schema using the schema command facilities that many DBEs supply.

When using forward engineering and DM merging is not possible or appropriate, we can use reverse engineering to generate the DMs in the reverse direction. If no DMs exist or the DB is radically different from the PDMs, we can generate the PDM from an existing DB. Similarly, we can pick one PDM to reverse generate the LDM applicable to all PDMs sharing the same logical design—for example, we could use the "ORACLE Employee PDM" from Figure 10.1 to reverse generate an LDM written in the RDM language. We can also choose a particular LDM to reverse generate the

CDM. Once we have all the DMs, we can examine the semantics within an existing system, even if it was created without using the forward engineering approach we just discussed. This can be very useful when moving an existing physical DB system to a new version, new platform, or new release. Again, this can be done manually or automatically—with the obvious advantages for the automated case. It is important to realize that the reverse engineered DMs might not be as unambiguous and precise as we want them to be. Recall that when we are performing the forward technique, sometimes a set of CDM constructs can be mapped into one of several alternatives; this also means that the reverse process is not completely deterministic. Whenever we perform reverse activities, it is important that we manually analyze the new higher-level DMs and correct them before attempting any new forward engineering steps.

10.3   CONCEPTUAL MODELING LANGUAGE EXAMPLES

In this section, we will examine three different conceptual modeling languages (CMLs). Although each CML is unique, and there are always some differences between a specific pair of languages, in some respects, all of these languages are also very similar to each other. Because of this similarity (and the fact that this chapter is only intended to be a brief review), we will cover the first language in greater detail than the other two—but all three MLs mentioned in this chapter, and many other MLs that we do not mention here, can be used effectively to create a DB. First, we will look at the entity relationship model (ERM) language, and then we will briefly look at the crow's feet notation (CFN) language and the Universal Modeling Language (UML).

10.3.1   The Entity Relationship Model

The first example CML we will consider is the **entity relationship model (ERM)** language. Sometimes, the CDMs written in this language are also referred to as ERMs (even though this is actually the name of the CML). It is also fairly common to refer to these CDMs using the name of the most common diagrammatic technique used to display them, namely, the **entity relationship diagram (ERD)**. In order to avoid confusion, we will usually use the term ERD for the CDM and ERM for the conceptual modeling language. Both the ML and the diagram representation were described by Peter Pin-Shan Chen [Chen76]. After Chen introduced the ERM, he extended it (or "enhanced" it) by adding additional constructs to support inheritance. This extended/enhanced version of the ERM is often called the **extended entity relationship model (EER)** or **enhanced entity relationship model (EER)**. Both names are equivalent—they do not refer to different MLs. Although entity relationship modeling and extended entity relationship modeling are often considered to be two separate representations, we will cover them both at the same time. Because EER is simply ERM with the additional techniques of generalization and specialization (inheritance), we can consider them to be one CML sharing one diagrammatic representation—we can simply consider the traditional ERM as an example of EER that chose not to use any inheritance.

10.3.1.1   Construct Review   There are three fundamental constructs in both ERM and EER: the **entity type (ET)**, the **relationship type (RT)**, and the **attribute type (AT)**.

EER has one additional construct, the **inheritance type (IT)**. Since the concept of inheritance is now fairly commonplace, EER might even seem more natural to many modern data modelers. From now on in this chapter, we will use the terms ER and EER interchangeably (we also use them interchangeably in all the other chapters in this book). Chen [Chen76] referred to instances of ETs as entities, RTs as relationships, and ATs as values, while he called the "types" for these things "sets." We will use a slightly different nomenclature and refer to the types explicitly as ETs, RTs, and ATs, while the instances will be referred to as merely entities, relationships, and attributes (or even more explicitly by using the word "instance" or the word "value").

Attribute Types   Each attribute type (AT) is either Singular or Plural, either Identifying or Nonidentifying, and either Atomic or Grouping. This means that there are theoretically eight possible flavors of ATs (see Table 10.1). In a CDM written in this language, we also typically define the set of possible values (called the **domain**) for each AT—perhaps even modeling them as **domain types (DTs)**. But since (at least for our purposes here) this starts to move into the logical and physical levels, we will simply say that our CDM should include some notions about the values that ATs could possibly hold, and depending on the tool used this might be captured in a more or less sophisticated fashion.

In practice, we usually use much fewer than these eight flavors. We almost never use the Plural Identifying (PI) ATs—for example, suppose we created a model with a PIA AT named "EmpNumber" contained within an ET named "Employee." Modeling it this way would mean that each Employee instance has a list of numbers and this entire set of values for a single employee is necessary to identify that person uniquely. Having a Plural Identifying value is not very practical—thus, the PIA and PIG ATs are not really used much. Many data modelers will also avoid using the Singular Identifying Grouping (SIG) AT because using a Grouping AT as an Identifier is also somewhat awkward. In the real world, any CDM written in this language will usually only contain (at most) five of the eight possible flavors for ATs shown in Table 10.1—namely the SIA, SNA, SNG, PNA, and PNG flavors. Data modelers who allow logical or physical considerations to creep into their ER models will also tend to avoid all Plural ATs, meaning that they only use three flavors (SIA, SNA, and SNG) instead of the five we just mentioned (or the eight we listed in Table 10.1). Lastly, data modelers who are heavily influenced by the relational data model (RDM), which is a very popular logical-level ML, will also tend to avoid Grouping ATs—meaning that they only

TABLE 10.1   Possible AT Flavors

Singular or Plural	Identifying or Nonidentifying	Atomic or Grouping	Abbreviation	Typical CDM Usage Frequency
Singular	Identifying	Atomic	SIA	Usually only one per ET
Singular	Identifying	Grouping	SIG	Rarely used, if ever
Singular	Nonidentifying	Atomic	SNA	Several per ET and per RT
Singular	Nonidentifying	Grouping	SNG	Sometimes used
Plural	Identifying	Atomic	PIA	Not really practical
Plural	Identifying	Grouping	PIG	Not really practical
Plural	Nonidentifying	Atomic	PNA	Sometimes used
Plural	Nonidentifying	Grouping	PNG	Sometimes used

use two flavors (SIA and SNA) in the CDMs that they create using this conceptual modeling language. In summary, eight flavors are possible; up to five flavors might be used in practice; but many models use only three of these flavors (or even only two of them) in the real world. Data modelers with different biases or modeling backgrounds might tend to favor different flavors in their conceptual models, and of course reverse engineered data models are always influenced by the physical and logical models (and languages) from which they are generated.

Entity Types   In some respects, entity types (ETs) are the primary construct in the ERM. An ET serves as a container for attribute types (ATs), an endpoint for relationship types (RTs), and the thing being generalized or specialized by an inheritance type (IT). We call an instance of an entity type an **entity** and, similarly, an instance of a relationship type a **relationship**. The ET provides two important qualities to the concept being modeled: existence and identification. Ultimately, the existence of any value for any other construct type depends on the existence of one or more entities. In other words, we cannot have a relationship unless all the entities being connected by it already exist. This is also true for ITs, which we will discuss in the next section. An IT is similar to an RT, it connects two ETs together, with one ET (the Super ET) being a conceptual superset of the other ET (the Sub ET). We cannot have an IT instance (which we call an **inheritance**) without a Super ET instance. Often a Sub ET instance is also required, but as we shall see in the next section, this is not always the case. Since every attribute (AT instance) must be contained in either an entity or a relationship, once again the entity's existence plays a crucial role for attributes. However, merely existing is not enough; we also need to be able to identify a particular instance within an ET. Therefore, we need to consider the identification of a particular entity carefully in any model. Ultimately, an entity's identification comes from the set of Identifying ATs (usually one or more SIA ATs) contained within the ET—this set of attribute types is called an **Identifier**.

Each ET is categorized as either **Strong** or **Weak**. Each Weak ET is partially identified by its Identifier and partially identified by the Identifiers of all the other ETs connected to it via specially flavored RTs (called Identifying RTs). A Strong ET is simply an ET that is not a Weak ET—Strong ETs do not rely on any Identifying RTs. When the ET participates in an IT, we must consider how it participates before we can understand its identification completely. A Strong ET that does not participate in any ITs is completely determined by its own Identifier (which it must contain in this situation). If the ET is a Super ET, then it is possible for it to be either a Weak ET or a Strong ET. If the ET is a Sub ET, then it must not be a Weak ET. In this case, even though the Sub ET is technically a Strong ET, its identification is slightly different. Here, the ET is actually completely identified by the Identifier of the Super ET that it is connected to via the IT. The valid ET flavors are summarized in Table 10.2.

Inheritance Types   Each inheritance type (IT) connects a single entity type (ET) as the Super ET, and one or more other ET as the Sub ET. Each Sub entity instance must have one and only one Super entity instance associated with it via the IT, and these instances are said to represent the same thing. For example, consider a simple case where we have a Super ET named "Person" and two Sub ETs called "Employee" and "Customer." Obviously, each and every Employee (instance) is one and only one Person (instance); similarly, each Customer (instance) is one and only one Person (instance). We do not

TABLE 10.2   Possible ET Flavors

IT Status	Strength	Description
None	Strong	Identification is completely determined by the ET itself.
None	Weak	Identification is partially determined by the ET and partially determined by at least one other ET connected to this one via an Identifying RT.
Super ET	Strong	Same as a Strong ET that does not participate in an IT.
Super ET	Weak	Same as a Weak ET that does not participate in an IT.
Sub ET	Strong	Identification is completely determined by the Super ET.
Sub ET	Weak	This is not possible.

consider a real-world person to be something separate or distinct from a real-world employee or a real-world customer—there is only one person to consider, regardless of whether that person is an employee, a customer, both, or neither! In other words, these distinctions merely focus on more specific (employee, customer) or more general (person) aspects of the same concept! If we want the Person ET to be capable of storing information about a person who is neither an employee nor a customer, then we want to allow a Person Super entity instance to exist when there is no corresponding Employee or Customer Sub entity instance associated with it. This is called **Partial** participation, and it is analogous to the situation in OO modeling where we have a concrete superclass. If we wish to prevent this behavior (in other words, if we want to prohibit Person Super entity instances for people who are neither employees nor customers), then this is called **Total** participation. This is analogous to the situation in OO modeling where we have an abstract superclass. If we want to allow an Employee (instance) to also be a Customer (instance), then we need to allow more than one Sub entity instance to share the same Super entity instance. This is called **Overlapping** participation. If we want to prevent this situation, meaning that each Person instance cannot be associated with more than one Sub entity instance, then we use **Disjoint** participation. This is also called **Mutually Exclusive** participation. In other words, there are four valid flavors of ITs to be considered in the ERM (see Table 10.3), and every IT must have one of these four flavors.

Relationship Types   There are four characteristics we need to consider for each relationship type (RT) in any ERM CDM:

- The degree of the RT
- The minimum and maximum cardinality of the RT
- The ATs in the RT
- The "flavor" of the RT

A relationship type (RT) instance is called a **relationship** and represents a set of connections between entity type (ET) instances. Each connection participating in an RT can specify a **role name**, which is simply a name used to represent what role the ET instance is playing in the relationship. The number of roles (i.e., the number of connections) participating in an RT is called the **degree** of the RT—we can also call this the degree of the relationship. Role names help to disambiguate the

TABLE 10.3   Valid IT Flavors

Super ET to Sub ET	Across Sub ETs	Abbreviation
Total Participation	Disjoint Participation	T-D-P
Total Participation	Overlapping Participation	T-O-P
Partial Participation	Disjoint Participation	P-D-P
Partial Participation	Overlapping Participation	P-O-P

RT and the database requirement that the RT is trying to capture. Data modelers do not always specify the role name for each connection—they will often simply use an abbreviated version of the connected ET name when there is no other obvious role name to use. When no role name is specified, we can pretend that the role name is something like "role-1" or "role-2." However, there is one scenario where role names are extremely useful and therefore usually specified—whenever the RT connects the same ET more than once. This usually only happens with RTs of degree two (which are called **binary relationship types**). A binary relationship type that connects to only one ET is called a **recursive relationship type**, and the role names are vital to understanding the semantics behind the RT in this situation. For example, if we wanted to model the fact that some employees work for other employees, then we would create an RT (perhaps named "WorksFor") that connects to the Employee ET twice. Here, we could use the role name of "manager" for one connection to the Employee ET, and the role name of "subordinate" for the other connection to the Employee ET.

Each connection can also specify the **minimum cardinality** and **maximum cardinality** for the ET instance playing the role that the connection represents. For example, we could set the maximum cardinality to one for the connection with the role name "manager" in the WorksFor RT example we mentioned earlier to indicate that no employee has more than one manager. The maximum cardinality for the other connection (with role name "subordinate") could be set to a specific number (such as 10, 20, etc.) or simply to a value representing "many." A minimum or maximum cardinality of "many" is typically represented as a capital letter "M" or "N." Although specific numeric values can be specified, most data modelers restrict themselves to using only "zero," "one," or "many."

An RT can have attribute types (ATs) contained within it, but usually it cannot have any Identifying ATs (no SIA, SIG, PIA, or PIG ATs). Identifying ATs are normally not allowed in this situation, because the relationship can only exist if all of the entities participating in the relationship already exist. Each relationship instance is uniquely identified by those entity instances. This means that it is not possible for the same entities (playing the same roles) to be related to each other more than once in the same RT. For example, suppose we have two Employee instances representing two employees in our organization (let's call them Alice and Bob). If Alice is Bob's manager, we can populate the WorksFor relationship by connecting the ET instance representing Alice using the connection with the role name "manager" and connecting the ET instance representing Bob using the connection with the role name "subordinate." If Bob is Alice's manager, then we can simply populate this relationship with their roles reversed. The only other scenario to consider is if neither Alice nor Bob works for the other person, in which case, we simply do not populate this relationship or those connections at all. But notice that there is never any situation where it makes sense to populate the same relationship instance more than once! Alice cannot be Bob's manager more than once!

Some data modelers choose to allow Identifying attribute types in RTs but this is really a logical-model-dependent consideration creeping into the conceptual level—which is not necessarily a bad thing, as long as it is understood and translated correctly. In most situations where we would be tempted to use an Identifying AT in an RT, we can use other standard techniques rather than resorting to this situation. For example, suppose we are modeling something that is composed of many parts, such as an engine made from several pistons. Also suppose that we create an Engine ET and a Part ET with a PartType AT defined in it (and, of course, all the other necessary ATs and Identifiers). Now, we create an RT named "EngHasPart" to connect the two ETs. We might think we need an RT Identifier because the same Engine might contain the same Part more than once, for example, a Part instance with PartType equals. "Piston." However, this is a modeling mistake rather than an ML deficiency. There are several ways to capture this situation more correctly such as adding a Quantity AT to the RT and using a single RT instance or modeling Part as a Plural Nonidentifying Grouping attribute type (a PNG AT).

The fourth characteristic to consider for each relationship type is its flavor. We have already informally mentioned the two flavors of RT to consider: namely, Identifying RTs and Nonidentifying RTs. We will use these terms, even though Chen used different terminology in his original paper. An Identifying RT is used to complete the identification for Weak ETs, while a Nonidentifying RT has no impact on the ETs or their identification. One or more Identifying RTs are always used whenever we have a Weak ET, because the Weak ET must be partially identified by some other ET connected to it via an Identifying RT. This also means that it is impossible to have a recursive Identifying RT. Some variations of this conceptual modeling language also allow other flavors to specify additional behavioral constraints in their ERM conceptual data models, but these tend to be logical modeling language concepts that have crept into the conceptual modeling language they are using, and we will not discuss them any further here. See Table 10.4 for a summary of the RT flavors.

ERM Construct Summary   In summary, there are three pairs of options (eight flavors) for attribute types, one pair of options (two flavors) for entity types, two pairs of options (four flavors) for inheritance types, and one pair of options (two flavors) for relationship types. The various flavors for these constructs are summarized in the tables we have already seen (Tables 10.1–10.3, and 10.4, respectively). Although the ERM language is fairly well known, it is not standardized, and thus, there are many different variations or dialects in use. Obviously, the options, flavors, restrictions, and exceptions can vary across these different (but similar) languages—especially when the

TABLE 10.4   Possible RT Flavors

Behavioral Constraint	Description
Identifying	Connects one or more Strong ETs to one or more Weak ETs, causing the Weak ETs to be partially identified by the Strong ETs
Nonidentifying	Connects two or more ETs (Strong or Weak) without changing any identification details for the ETs

conceptual modeling language is implemented by a tool, but the fundamental constructs and concepts remain the same.

Modern hardware and software systems have changed dramatically since the ERM was first introduced in 1976. Software engineering and software development practices have also changed substantially since then. We now recognize that there are many further details that we need to specify and capture in order to improve the quality and maintainability of complex DMs. For example, we usually try to capture some minimal amount of version control information. This might include details such as version, revision or release numbers, dates, times, and authors of various additions and modifications to the model, and other important details such as comments, descriptions, annotations, and definitions. All of these details are called **metadata** (data about the data), and most modern tools support the capture and management of at least some minimal amount of metadata for any DM we create or modify. The original diagram notation introduced by Chen, called the entity relationship diagram (ERD), does not show any of these metadata details. Most diagram notations used today do not show these details either. This is done purposefully—once again, if the diagrams included all the possible details, they would likely become overly cluttered and confusing. Some tools do allow the user to selectively include or exclude some of the details—this enables the user to show important details and hide distracting details while storing all of these important details behind the scenes. Diagram notations also do not usually show any of the rules defining the valid construct combinations and configurations. In other words, although the diagram is the best way to communicate the important details within a particular DM, we should never confuse the diagram with the DM itself or the ML—the diagram is merely one picture containing only some of the details for a given DM.

10.3.1.2 ERM Rules and Guidelines   It is beyond the scope of this chapter to try to describe all the possible details that a good CDM written in the ERM language should have. It is even beyond the scope of this chapter to list all of the rules governing what a valid CDM can or cannot do in this modeling language. We will limit the discussion here to the bare minimum: a few basic naming rules (and even less-restrictive naming guidelines) followed by a few basic rules that control how the constructs can be combined and configured within a data model. Although the rules are stricter than the guidelines, both are actually merely suggestions rather than absolute prohibitions. All data modelers who work together should create their own list of rules and guidelines as they create their DMs. Then, they should try to conform to these rules as much as possible. This means we should consider the ramifications carefully whenever we add, modify, or delete anything from our list.

Naming Rules

- Every ET, RT, IT, and AT must have a name.
- Generally, we try to avoid spaces and punctuation in the names (limit the characters to underscores and alphanumeric characters—some people use dashes in their names but these tend to translate poorly when PDMs are generated later on).
- Different naming conventions and restrictions exist, but generally we try to avoid using the same name across the first three types (ET, RT, and IT), and it is a good idea to avoid duplicate names across all four types.

- A popular exception to the no-duplicate-naming rule just mentioned is to allow multiple ATs with the same name—provided that they are not used within the same containing construct. In other words, when two ATs are not used within the same Grouping AT, not used within the same RT, and not used within the same ET, then they can have the same name.

- Another popular exception to the no-duplicate-naming rule is to allow multiple RTs with the same name—provided that they connect different ETs. For example, the RT name "Has" is often used more than once in a model—there is even one technique that specifies a "Relationship Class Type name" as a way of grouping RTs (using the same name) together, but it is not a very commonly used technique as far as we know.

- While case sensitivity is a personal (or tool-dependent) choice, it is considered bad form to use names that differ only in case to represent different concepts. In other words, if we are being case sensitive, then we should avoid using both "Employee" and "employee" as names within the same model. If we are being case insensitive, then using both "Employee" and "employee" should be considered a duplicate name—and the appropriate "no-duplicate-naming" rule or exception should be applied. While it can be difficult and tedious to maintain consistent case usage, allowing the case to vary randomly can cause confusion and maintenance issues later on.

Now that we have discussed the basic naming rules that most DMs will follow, we will consider some softer conventions or guidelines. These are less restrictive than the previous list and also tend to be more idiosyncratic or personal decisions. These guidelines suggest alternatives that we can choose from when naming the constructs. They merely help to define a naming convention for our DMs. Once a particular naming convention is chosen, it should be used consistently within the DM (and across all DMs if possible)—but we should not be surprised if we see different naming conventions being used in DMs that we did not write ourselves. Naming conventions also tend to change over time based on changes within the corporate culture and tools being used.

Naming Convention Guidelines

- ET names tend to be singular rather than plural. For example, we would usually name an ET "Employee" rather than "Employees."

- ET names tend to be common nouns (not proper nouns, verbs, adjectives, adverbs, etc.) [Chen80] [Chen97].

- AT names can be simple or compound. For example, "Name" is simple, while something like "PrjName," "Project_Name," or "Project_Name" is compound. For large DMs, we prefer compound names using a standard abbreviation of the container type for the first part. This is especially useful if the simple version is likely to be reused across different containing types (e.g., we prefer using "EmpName" and "PrjName" rather than using "Name" and "Name"). While this technique is not necessary, it can improve maintenance by making it clear to which AT (along with its container type) we are referring.

- Plural AT names can themselves use either plural or singular naming conventions, for example, "EmpEmailList," "EmpEmails," and "EmpEmail" are all valid choices for a Plural AT name.

- AT names tend to be common nouns, adjectives, or adverbs [Chen80] [Chen97].
- RT names tend to be verbs (often transitive or linking verbs) [Chen80] [Chen97]. If there are many RTs in the DM, we prefer to include some form of "verb phrase including a standardized abbreviation ET name" as the RT name, but this is merely a suggestion. For example, we would tend to use "EmpWorksForDept" rather than simply using "WorksFor," "Works_For," or "Works" if there were any real potential ambiguity. Another option is to use the full ET names in the RT name, for example, "EmployeeWorksForDepartment," but this can lead to long names and truncation issues later on when the CDM is used to generate LDMs and PDMs.
- IT names almost always begin with "is a" as part of the name. This can be written in different ways, for example, "ISA_Person," "IS_A_Person," "Is_Person," or even "IsPerson." This convention has limited impact since IT names are often unseen in the LDMs and PDMs generated from CDMs—but the naming convention is useful nonetheless.

Lastly, we will consider some of the basic construction rules to follow when writing a CDM using the ERM language. Although these rules might vary depending on the tool being used to write the model, they are more rigid than the naming rules or naming convention guidelines we have just discussed.

Basic Rules of Engagement/Existence for ERM Constructs

- Each AT must exist inside an ET, an RT, or a Grouping AT.
- RTs cannot contain Identifying ATs.
- ITs cannot contain ATs.
- Each RT must connect at least two ETs (with one exception allowed, namely, if there is only one ET connected, but we connect to it twice—this is the recursive RT we discussed earlier).
- Each RT can only connect ETs (RTs cannot connect to other RTs, to ITs, or to ATs—they can contain ATs but cannot connect them).
- Each IT must connect one Super ET to at least one other (different) Sub ET.
- Each IT can only connect to ETs (ITs cannot connect to RTs, ATs, or other ITs—unlike RTs, ITs cannot contain ATs).
- The set of all ETs connected via ITs must be acyclic (in other words, they must form a tree and must not form a graph).
- Each Strong ET must have an Identifier (a set of one or more Identifying ATs).
- Each Weak ET must be connected to at least one Strong ET via an Identifying RT—unless the Identifying RT is one-to-one (which is a bizarre and extremely rare thing to see in a CDM, but possible in a PDM).
- Each Weak ET should have an Identifier contained within it that partially identifies it.
- The set of all Weak ETs connected via Identifying RTs to other ETs must be acyclic. In other words, we cannot have the identification forming an endless loop.

- Each Identifying RT must connect at least one Strong ET and at least one Weak ET. Chaining Weak ETs together via Identifying RTs is probably not valid for most tools, and certainly not necessary.

There are, of course, many more suggestions, conventions, and rules that can be used in addition to those listed here, especially if the CDM is going to be converted into a specific type of LDM or PDM. But again, that is not really important for our purposes in this section. Most of these suggestions and conventions can be either applied to a basic CDM as a postprocess or integrated into the CDM creation process from the start.

10.3.1.3 Traditional Chen ERD Notation   See Figure 10.3 for an example of a CDM using a nonstandardized, but fairly common, representation for a traditional ERM. This diagram uses a representation that is very similar to the notation that Chen introduced in his seminal paper [Chen76], but it is not the notation we would recommend for use in the real world. Having said that, this is the first diagrammatic notation that many data

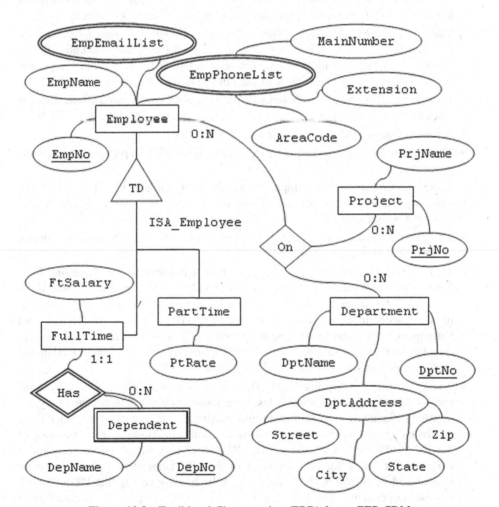

Figure 10.3   Traditional Chen notation (ERD) for an EER CDM.

modelers are introduced to: it is capable of showing all the flavors for all the constructs we discussed in Section 10.3.1.1, and it is very easy to understand. Although we will not exhaustively list everything that this model (or even this diagram) represents, we will point out some examples of the more important notations.

Points of Interest in Figure 10.3

- There are many ATs shown in this diagram. Each AT is represented by a name inside an oval that is connected via a line to the container for that AT.
- There are four SIA ATs (EmpNo, DepNo, PrjNo, and DptNo). We know they are Singular ATs because they are drawn as ovals with a single border. We know they are Identifying ATs because the AT names are underlined. We know they are Atomic ATs because they do not have any other ATs connected to them.
- There is one PNA AT (EmpEmailList) shown as an oval with a double border. We know it is a Plural AT because of the double border. Since there is no underline, we know it is a Nonidentifying AT, and like the previous ATs mentioned, we know that it is an Atomic AT because there are no other ATs connected to it.
- There is one SNG AT (DptAddress). We have already mentioned the notation clues needed to know it is Singular and Nonidentifying, and we know it is a Grouping AT because there is one line connecting it to its container type and another set of lines connecting it to the other ATs that it contains.
- There is one PNG AT (EmpPhoneList). We have already discussed all the notation clues necessary to understand why this is Plural, Nonidentifying, and Grouping.
- All the remaining ATs in the diagram are SNA ATs.
- There are several ETs shown in this diagram. Each ET is represented by a name inside a rectangle.
- There are six Strong ETs (Employee, Department, Project, PartTime, FullTime, and Project). We know they are Strong ETs because they are each drawn as a rectangle with a single border.
- There is one Weak ET (Dependent). We know it is a Weak ET because it is drawn as a rectangle with a double border.
- There is one IT (ISA_Employee), connecting two Sub ETs (PartTime and Full-Time) and one Super ET (Employee). The only way we can know this is by looking at the IT that connects them and noticing which way the arrow with the label inside it points. Because of the label ("TD"), we know this IT has Total Participation ("T") and Disjoint Participation ("D"). If the IT had Partial Participation, the first letter would be different ("P"). Similarly, if the IT had Overlapping Participation the second letter would be different ("O").
- There are two RTs in this ERD. There is a Nonidentifying RT named "On" and an Identifying RT named "Has." We know they are RTs because they are drawn as diamonds. The minimum and maximum cardinalities for each RT are shown using two numbers separated by a colon. For example, each instance of the ET "FullTime" is related via the RT "Has" to a minimum of zero and a maximum of "N" ("Many") instances of the ET "Dependent." This cardinality is indicated by the "0:N" hovering around the line connecting the RT to the ET named "Dependent." The fact that each instance of the ET "Dependent" has a minimum of one and a maximum of one instance of the ET "Employee" related to

it through this RT is indicate by the "1:1" closest to Employee. The Nonidentifying RTs have a single border while the Identifying RTs have a double border, and a different line style on the connection to the Weak ET.

- The RT "On" has degree equal to three (3). In other words, this is a ternary RT. This is something that can happen in the real world and can be represented easily in a conceptual model. In the real world, RTs with degree greater than two are often avoided in the CDM—especially if the planned LDM and PDM do not support nonbinary relationships gracefully or efficiently.

Obviously, this notation has its advantages, but also its disadvantages. In particular, it uses a lot of space but only conveys a limited amount of information. This technique is good for clarity and initial brainstorming. However, once we start doing real analysis or start considering LDM or PDM diagrams, it is not as expressive or concise as we would like. It is also not practical in the real world, where we are likely to have a large number of ATs within each ET. Notice that our diagram here averaged three Atomic ATs per ET; in a real DM, we can easily see hundreds of ETs, hundreds of RTs, and perhaps even thousands of Atomic ATs. So, even though Chen's notation is often the first notation learned by data modelers, we think that the next representation is a better choice for most CDMs.

10.3.1.4 Crow's Foot/Feet Notation There are several alternatives to Chen's ER/EER notation that share a common characteristic known informally as **crow's foot notation** or **crow's feet notation (CFN)** [Everest86]. This notation was invented by Gordon Everest, who originally called it an "inverted arrow" but now calls it a "fork." Each of these names refers to the representation used for RTs (and, in particular, their cardinalities). While Chen's notation could support any value for the minimum and maximum cardinalities of a relationship type (e.g., "4:8" or "5:N"), the strict CFN will limit us to a smaller set of possible cardinalities because it represents the cardinalities graphically rather than textually—we could add the textual cardinalities to the CFN to achieve the same representational power, but then we are no longer simply using the notation (and these numbers can clutter the diagram if the model is complex or simply large).

In CFN, each end of an RT connection can only represent one of four possible cardinality combinations (see Figure 10.4). Although there are several conceptual modeling alternatives that use the CFN, and their actual representations can vary slightly, the notation shown in Figure 10.4 is a reasonably common one. In a CFN

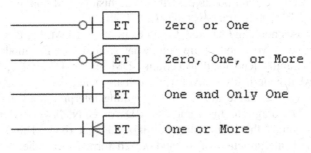

Figure 10.4 Crow's foot notation cardinality summary.

diagram, each RT is shown simply as a line with the RT Name hovering somewhere along it (no diamond). Each end of the line uses two symbols representing the minimum and maximum cardinality with respect to the ET connected at that end. The first symbol (farthest from the ET being connected) uses either a perpendicular line or a circle to represent the minimum cardinality. In other words, this symbol will look like either a one or a zero—which is precisely what the two alternatives represent. The second symbol will look like either a one or a crow's foot (a symbol that sort of looks like a greater than or less than sign with a line bisecting the angle). This is the symbol closest to the ET, and it represents the maximum cardinality—the "like a one" symbol obviously still means "one" and the crow's foot symbol means "many." Since "many" always implies "one," sometimes the crow's foot will also have a one in front of it. When the minimum cardinality is zero, if the maximum is one, we read this as "Zero or One," if the maximum is "many" then we read this as "Zero, One, or More." Figure 10.4 lists the remaining two possibilities and a summary of all the possible symbol combinations for one end of the RT.

ETs in a CFN diagram are drawn as rectangles, with the name of each AT listed inside the rectangle. Some tools put the ET name outside the rectangle at the top. Other tools put it inside the rectangle with a line separating it from the rest of the rectangle contents. Regardless of the ET name location or CFN representation, it is important to recognize that the CFN does not directly represent all of the possible AT variations that EER did. In particular, CFN can only support SIA and SNA attribute types. Another way to explain this limitation is to say that there are no Plural ATs and the only valid container for an AT is an ET, which means that neither Grouping ATs nor RTs can have ATs. CFN has further limitations; in particular, CFN cannot support nonbinary RTs (RTs with a degree greater than two). We mentioned earlier that there are other data modeling categorizations that collapse the conceptual and logical categories into a single category—CFN is often used as the diagram notation when this approach is used, especially for RDMs. But remember that CFN can be used for any DM, so we should not assume that CFN implies any particular categorization or category of DM.

10.3.1.5   *Unified Modeling Language*   Unified Modeling Language (UML) is a standardized format for creating object-oriented models. As object-oriented (OO) techniques began to gain acceptance and become more popular, several competing OO modeling methodologies emerged. As these methodologies evolved, their differences diminished, and eventually the major methodologies merged into a single unified method. One of the results of this merging was the creation of UML, and in the years since the unification, UML has become the de facto standard for OO modeling. There are many articles and books describing the history and continuing evolution of UML; see [Muller97], [Quatrani98], and [Liberty98].

For our purposes here, an OO model is an example of LDM, but this really depends on how it is used. UML models are somewhat similar to CFN models, in that the notation does naturally lend itself to certain LDM biases. Like CFN, UML can still be used somewhat generically (naively) if we really want to use it that way. From a DB perspective, if we ignore the OO programming interpretations and implications, we can treat UML diagrams the same as ERDs or CFN diagrams by using a very naïve interpretation of the UML—but this is somewhat risky. This technique relies on a nonstandard interpretation of a standardized format—in other words, it sort of defeats the primary purpose of UML (capturing concepts using all the nuances that OO modeling has to offer). There are also some concepts that have no concise, direct representation in UML. For example, Identifiers in the ERM have a strict set of rules and interpretations, but UML does not have this same level of enforcement because it uses the concept of a reference or pointer rather than an Identifier. Another example of a feature that can cause confusion is Associations—in UML, Associations represent connections between concepts (like RTs in the ERM do) but Associations can be unidirectional in UML. This is quite different from how RTs behave in ERMs or in CFN diagrams. UML does not directly represent inheritance using the ERM flavors—so it is more difficult to specify these participation details in a UML model of a CDM. In summary, although UML has many facilities for documenting special scenarios (using things like stereotypes), they are not well suited for conceptual data modeling in our opinion: this is because of the emphasis we place on forward and reverse engineering all of the possible LDMs and PDMs that a database environment is capable of using.

Using the naïve interpretation of UML is too fragile—if we accidentally interpret the UML data model using the standard (LDM biased) UML semantics instead of this naive interpretation, there are going to be many problems. For example, an ERM can have a Weak ET participating in two Identifying RTs: if we try to represent this same concept using the UML notation for composition, we would try to model the same class (the Weak ET) as being a private part of two different parent classes at the same time, which is a completely different set of semantics for UML. So, in this extreme scenario, we have a CDM that merely uses UML Classes instead of ETs, UML Member Properties instead of ATs, UML Inheritance instead of ITs, and UML Associations instead of RTs. If we ignore all the other features, nuances, and semantics that UML has to offer, we can create a naïve UML rendition of a CDM. For example, see Figure 10.5, for a naïve UML rendition of the same CDM that we looked at

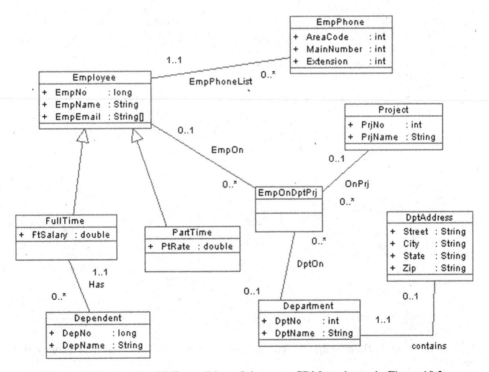

Figure 10.5   A naive UML rendition of the same CDM as shown in Figure 10.3.

previously in Figure 10.3. We strongly recommend using the CFN language instead of this naïve UML approach.

The other extreme scenario is to create a CDM using the UML that is also an OOM (using all the power, flexibility, features, and semantics that the OOM can provide), but sacrificing some logical and physical modeling language independence. When representing a CDM using UML and the standard (as opposed to the naïve) semantics and rules, we create a CDM that is LDM biased. We use the same nomenclature and semantics that we would use for OO programming. By using UML in this fashion, we can represent all the constructs that the ERM language can represent for the same situation, but the notation and nomenclature are somewhat different. Unlike the situation we had when using CFN, there are no obvious shortfalls in what the model can represent when we use UML this way—UML is at least as expressive as the ERM. However, if we create the CDM by following the same steps as we would normally use to create an OO programming model, the resulting DM can be rather different from a traditional CDM. For example, consider the impact of using interfaces, multiple inheritance, accessibility qualifiers (public, private, etc.), other specifiers (virtual, static, abstract), sophisticated associations (aggregations, composition, dependencies), and other UML features on a traditional CDM. This model might be very difficult to translate into multiple LDMs and PDMs later on—especially if the LDMs are not all OO in some respect. Figure 10.6 shows an LDM-biased (OO-biased) rendition of the same DM we used in Figures 10.3 and 10.5. In our opinion, this approach should only be used when it is certain that an incompatible LDM or PDM language will never be

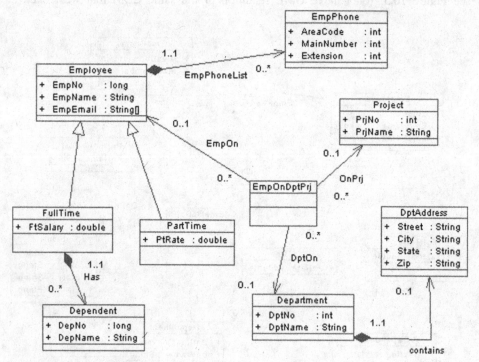

Figure 10.6   An LDM-biased UML rendition of the same CDM as shown in Figures 10.3 and 10.5.

used in the future—realizing that logical-level (and perhaps physical-level) details are creeping into the CDM when we do this.

10.4 WORKING WITH DATA MODELS

We will now explore how we work with conceptual, logical, and physicals data models (CDMs, LDMs, and PDMs). First, we will discuss how CDMs are created. After that, we will briefly discuss how LDMs and PDMs fit into the data modeling process. Finally, we will consider some of the issues we would expect to encounter when working with multiple DMs (and MLs) within the same development environment.

10.4.1 CDMs

In this section (and in most of the book) we will use the CFN for CDMs, since we feel this notation is probably closest to the notation used in the real world (for most scenarios at least). The steps to create a CDM are actually fairly similar regardless of the language used to capture the CDM. There are various techniques described by Chen and by Sanders (see [Chen83] and [Sanders95]). But the overall idea is the same for most techniques. Instead of summarizing one of these techniques, we will simply present a high-level overview of the steps that we have informally followed when creating conceptual level data models.

Steps to Create a CDM

- Capture the requirements.
- Identify concepts in the requirements.
- Group concepts together.
- Remove ambiguities.
- Apply corrections, conventions, and standards.

Let's examine each of these steps briefly.

10.4.1.1 Capture the Requirements In this first step, we attempt to capture the requirements using some standard technique. Typically, we use a series of questions, interviews, facilitated sessions, and so on to build a description of the problem and proposed solution. Often we will use techniques like Structured English, State Diagrams, and Use Cases based on the software development processes followed within our project. While the more sophisticated techniques can be very useful, often the Structured English approach is the easiest to understand and implement. Structured English is merely an attempt to capture requirements in a more formalized and uniform sentence structure and vocabulary. It tends to be very repetitive, unimaginative, and boring to read (and to write), but it has the advantage of removing ambiguity and easily identifying similar patterns within the requirements. Sometimes we will even use high-level ERDs to help capture these details—showing some (not all) of the possible ETs and RTs without all the other details (such as ATs, cardinalities, and role names) that a real ERD would require. These high-level ERDs are merely short-hand notation and not intended to be anything more than simple reminders of the basic structures involved, similar to the way an artist might create a set of rough pencil sketches before painting a detailed portrait.

10.4.1.2 *Identify Concepts in the Requirements*   Once the requirements have been captured, we simply go through the content we captured (usually Structured English and a few simple "sketch" submodels) and try to identify concepts from the problem or solution that seem to be important. For example, if we created a set of Structured English requirements for the Employee CDM examples we used earlier, this set would probably mention some details about our employees, the projects they work on, the departments they work for, and some of the other details like the phone numbers they have, salaries they are paid, and the names for everything. The Structured English would include descriptions for these concepts and also some clues about their interdependencies. For example, is it possible for an employee to work on more than one project at the same time? Can an employee work for more than one department at the same time? These details and others like them will form the foundation of our initial CDM.

10.4.1.3 *Group Concepts Together*   Some concepts will naturally start to group together cohesively based on our understanding of the concepts themselves or the language used to capture the DB requirements. For example, we will know that employees are either full time or part time (but not both), and that this distinction affects how they get paid. Similarly, we will know that departments have names and budgets, employees have phone numbers, and so on. By combining these concepts together, we are starting to form the CDM. As we put ATs together inside container types (ETs, RTs, or Grouping ATs), we start to understand which concepts are more complicated—and then start to ask questions about their existence, identification, and relationships with other concepts. We simply create groups of cohesive concepts using the constructs, rules, and guidelines provided by the conceptual modeling language we have chosen to use.

10.4.1.4 *Remove Ambiguities*   Even if the previous activities were done properly, there will probably be some things that are not completely clear—this is normal. If the requirements were not explicit enough, then either we need to use our own understanding to clarify the missing details, or we need to go back and ask more questions. There are many questions we need to answer here. For example, if we know that an employee can have a phone number, we might need to clarify how many numbers that employee can have. Does every employee have a phone number or do some employees have no phone number? Can an employee have more than one phone number? Can the same phone number be had by more than one employee? What exactly is a phone number? Does it have smaller parts to it? What parts are necessary? What parts are optional? What do we need to keep track of? Do phone numbers exist outside of employees or are they a part of the employee? If we delete an employee does the phone number need to be preserved? Does the phone number need to be deleted when we delete an employee? These are just some of the questions that will help us to choose the appropriate construct type and the appropriate metadata for each concept. Often, these details can be exposed by considering questions similar to those we just mentioned—namely, questions that arise when we start to consider the addition, modification, and deletion of other concepts that are related to the one we are focusing on at the moment.

10.4.1.5 Apply Corrections, Conventions, and Standards   In this last step, we need to review the model and apply any corrections, conventions, or standards as needed. For example, if we are using entity relationship modeling, then each AT must be defined within a container (ultimately an ET or RT); each Weak ET must have at least one Identifying RT connected to it; and so on. Similarly, if we have agreed on any particular naming convention or modeling convention, then we need to ensure that these conventions are being followed correctly and consistently. For example, if we agreed that attribute type names would be all lowercase and begin with an abbreviation of the container type (like "empName" for the AT representing an employee's name within the Employee ET), then these conventions need to be verified and corrected as needed. Lastly, if we have agreed on a particular notation, or modeling technique, we need to verify conformance to the standard and fix any discrepancies. This would also be a good time to verify that we are using the tools we have to the best of our ability—supplying meaningful and accurate comments, descriptions, definitions, and annotations for all the constructs we have defined in our model.

10.4.2   LDMs

Logical data models (LDMs) are similar to CDMs—both capture high-level concepts and their semantic interdependencies. Sometimes, we can even use the same diagrammatic representation for both types of data models. But while the CDM tried to be independent of both the design and implementation for the DM, the LDM is only striving to be independent of the implementation. This means that design details are **supposed to be** captured in the LDM (along with the logical-level translation of the details that were previously captured in the CDM). While we cannot look at all possible LDM languages, we will look at some common examples in the next chapter—so we will not go into great detail about the languages or the data models in this section. Instead, we will provide a quick overview of the purpose of an LDM and then look at a high-level overview of the steps we have followed when creating logical-level data model by forward engineering it from a CDM.

10.4.2.1 Purpose   The LDM is where we capture all the details that are independent of the data storage implementation but dependent on the data storage design. For example, suppose we want to implement our CDM using some relational DB—this means that our logical-level modeling language is equivalent to the RDM. Many of the rules, restrictions, and required details needed to design our relational DB schema are DBMS independent. For example, we need to consider things like Candidate, Alternate, Primary, and Foreign Keys, Functional Dependencies and Normalization, Nullability, and rules to maintain Relational Integrity (things that are often enforced by clauses such as "cascade" or "restrict"). Of course, the actual physical DB used to implement this schema will have a great impact on our model eventually—but not at this stage. If we are using the RDM as our modeling language, then there are many things we can do here without knowing any implementation details—especially if we are only considering ANSI SQL compliant RDBMSs (see [ANSI86a], [ANSI89], and [ANSI92]). If we are considering nonrelational LMLs, we can still have a similar situation—for example, all network DBs behave similar to each other (see [ANSI86b]), all hierarchical DBs behave similar to each other, and all OO DBs behave similar to each other. If we need to support more than one logical modeling language, then we need to use separate LDMs, but often we can generate all of these from the same CDM and then perform additional modifications as necessary.

10.4.2.2 Steps to Create LDMs We will look at some specific details for specific LDM languages in the next chapter, but we can provide a brief, generic overview here. These steps can be used for both automatic and manual forward engineering situations, but the steps are usually easier to follow and the activities are usually easier to perform in the automatic forward engineering scenario.

Steps to Create an LDM

- Create an LDM translation of a CDM.
- Remove ambiguities.
- Apply corrections, conventions, and standards.

Create an LDM Translation of a CDM First of all, we need to capture all the semantic details in our LDM. If we have already created a CDM, then we can translate it into the equivalent LDM representation automatically with some tool or manually if necessary. Depending on the conceptual and logical modeling languages being used, there are different translation rules to apply, but usually there is a straightforward technique that can be applied to each CDM construct in order to generate a corresponding LDM construct or constructs. We will discuss some examples of these translations in Chapter 11, but we will not cover all possible CDM and LDM combinations—only some of the most common ones. If we did not already create a CDM (and do not want to create one), we will still have to perform the equivalent activities. In other words, if we decide to use some other categorization (such as the one with Conceptual and Logical combined), then we can simply repeat all the steps in Section 10.4.1 as the precondition for the activities in this step.

Remove Ambiguities Perhaps because of the translation process, or perhaps for other reasons, there might be some ambiguities in the LDM that need to be resolved—even if the CDM was unambiguous. For example, the naming rules we used for our CDM might be different from those used by our LDM tool or methodology. Usually we can ensure that these rules are followed in the CDM creation process by establishing conventions and standards appropriately (considering all the tools and languages we might want to use ahead of time); but even after we have established these things, we should always check the LDM for potential problems. When logical model constructs are generated from the conceptual model, it is possible that our groupings of constructs might change. For example, concepts that were contained in a single ET in our CDM might be translated into constructs contained in several different relations in our LDM. In general, some constructs that were together in our CDM might be translated into separate constructs in our LDM while other constructs that were separated in our CDM might be translated into the same container within our LDM. Therefore, all the rules and semantics need to be revisited in the new model to ensure that things are still correctly capturing the original requirements. For example, naming rules, existence details, nullability details, and minimum/maximum cardinalities might need to be defined differently in the new model based on these new separations and combinations.

Apply Corrections, Conventions, and Standards   Since the CDM and LDM are **not** identical, we will have to make some corrections, provide nondefault values for some metadata properties, and consider the conventions and standards defined for the LDM. For example, since many of the constructs in the LDM might be automatically generated from the CDM, it is common for new LDM constructs to be created based on the names of existing LDM constructs. This can cause problems if names are too long, or if the same CDM construct is used as the basis for more than one new LDM construct. There are also other things that need to be considered for the LDM—which might not be appropriate or possible in the CDM. For example, if we are using the RDM as our logical modeling language, and we have agreed that our tables should be in third-normal form (3NF) or higher, then we need to examine this and fix it as necessary. A CDM has no notion of normalization, and even if we tried to enforce normalization in the CDM, it would be premature since there are details dependent on the translation technique used for generating the LDM. We will discuss this more in the next chapter.

10.4.3   PDMs

Physical data models (PDMs) are similar to LDMs (and also somewhat similar to CDMs). Once again, all of the details we defined in the LDM (and CDM) need to be reflected in the PDM, but perhaps not in the same way that they were represented before. The format and content of the PDM is highly dependent on the actual implementation and deployment details of a DB. If we deployed the same physical DB on different machines, they could have different PDMs. Although the representation for the PDM can be the same as the LDM, this is a little deceiving because so many of the important details are not shown in any diagram used for the LDM. For example, a diagram of a logical-level, relational data model for a DB shows many (but not all) of the necessary LDM details, but if we wanted to see the important PDM details, we would be better off looking at the Structured Query Language (SQL) for the PDM rather than the PDM diagram. It is also possible for some of the details we captured in the requirements (CDM) or design (LDM) to be absent from the implementation/deployment (PDM). Sometimes this is necessary because of limitations within the physical systems, but sometimes we decide not to implement these details for other reasons—perhaps we do not implement them due to performance considerations, resource requirements, or different priorities. Because the PDM details (other than those that are merely simple translations of their LDM and CDM counterparts) are so proprietary and deployment dependent, it is beyond our scope to discuss them much further here. PDM details include all the tuning details (indexing, storage usage, etc.), which are far beyond what we can cover in this chapter or the next.

10.4.3.1 Purpose   The PDM is where we capture all the details that are dependent on the data storage implementation and deployment. By definition, the PDM also contains details that are dependent on the design of the data storage and the semantics of the model. In other words, the PDM includes all of the CDM and LDM details, but it also includes details that are not in these other categories. These physical details can be vendor specific, platform specific, release specific, or even specific to the DM being created. For example, some details are dependent on which DB vendor we are using, especially the details about proprietary data types, indexing, and storage allocation.

Other details might only make sense when the DB is deployed on certain operating system platforms, especially if they include physical device details, block sizes, and buffer sizes. Even if we consider two deployments that use the same vendor, and are on the same platform, there can be PDM details that are different for the same DB. For example, the PDM might specify some of the details that are new options or obsolete settings depending on what release of the DBMS software, operating system, and so on that we are using. Lastly, some options might be specific to a particular configuration or set of deployment details that simply depend on a particular deployment of the actual DB we are creating with this PDM. For example, a PDM representing a deployment in a production environment might be different from a PDM representing a deployment in a development or test environment.

10.4.3.2 Steps to Create PDMs While it is possible to create the PDM directly (bypassing the CDM and LDM), this is definitely not recommended. If there is no LDM or CDM for a PDM, we would suggest reverse engineering these models before making any serious modifications to the PDM. The steps to create the PDM are similar to those used for the LDM. The only difference is that the "Ambiguities, Corrections, Conventions, and Standards" we consider now include physical implementation and deployment details as well as those we previously included. Therefore, we will simply list the steps here without going into any further details.

Steps to Create a PDM

- Create a PDM translation of an LDM.
- Remove ambiguities.
- Apply corrections, conventions, and standards.

10.5 USING MULTIPLE TYPES OF MODELING

The levels in CLP taxonomy are not only interrelated (as we mentioned at the beginning of this chapter) but they are also, in essence, subsets and supersets of each other. In other words, most of the information contained within a particular CDM is also contained within each LDM generated from it—and most of the information contained within each LDM is also contained within each PDM generated from it. The DMs in these levels form a natural one-to-many, one-to-many dependency chain. This means that if we need to update or change a detail contained in the CDM for some model, then we would also need to change it in all the LDMs generated from that CDM and all the PDMs generated from each of those LDMs. Obviously, if we could actually make the changes in the CDM and then simply regenerate the LDMs and PDMs, we would greatly simplify the maintenance issues and reduce the risk that something would be out of sync or incorrectly modified. Many tools offer the ability to generate LDMs and PDMs automatically, and some also support merging rather than simply overwriting the information. When this is the case, we can preserve modifications specific to the LDM or PDM while propagating modifications based solely on the shared (CDM or LDM) details. Although these automations are never completely foolproof or perfect, and although they can never replace the manual verification steps needed, this automation can greatly streamline the process.

There is also one more level to consider when evaluating these modifications—namely, the actual deployed DB. Recall that even the PDM is still just a model—it is not the actual DB, just a very detailed picture of many important physical (as well as logical and conceptual) details. Once the DB has been created and deployed, the applications, users, development staff, and support staff can (and will) begin using it. This means that some of the physical details might change on the real deployed system. Some changes to the DB will not affect our models in any meaningful way (e.g., selects, inserts, updates, and deletes are all instance-level commands with little or no impact on schema design or implementation details), but it is also possible that other changes will impact the schema. For example, suppose that a programmer adds a column to a table in order to implement some feature request; now the PDM details for that table are out of sync, the LDM details for the LDM construct(s) from which we generated the PDM table are out of sync, and the CDM details for the CDM construct(s) from which we generated the LDM construct(s) are also out of sync. If we did not generate the models automatically from one level to the next, we still have a problem. If we modify the deployed DB, how do we manually update each PDM, LDM, and CDM? If we do not have the "higher-level" models, we might still need to propagate the changes to all the appropriate PDMs. There has to be a better way to handle this situation (and there is)—but it means we need to work with the models and synchronize in the appropriate directions whenever we make meaningful changes.

10.5.1 Conversion to Multiple Models

Using the CLP models can be a great benefit, even for environments where we only have one DB schema to maintain. In the real world, most DBs exist to support one or more applications, and most applications change over time. By separating the DM details across the levels (CDMs, LDMs, and PDMs), we encapsulate the details within the appropriate level and thereby improve reusability. This means that when changes are made for the sake of feature requests, defect removal, or new development, we can manage those changes across the current and future deployments in a much more efficient way. If we clarify conceptual details, they can be propagated and used across all the systems with minimal impact and effort. Similarly, any changes made to the deployed systems can be captured and carried forward in future development. In order to do this properly, we need to be able to generate DMs automatically in both directions: forward from CDM to LDM to PDM to deployed DB and in reverse from deployed DB to PDM to LDM to CDM.

10.5.2 Forward Engineering

We have briefly discussed how the LDM can be generated from the CDM, and how the PDM can be generated from the LDM. Because the PDM details are so proprietary, we won't discuss the actual details here, but most tools do support some mechanism for generating/deploying the schema for the physical DB based on the PDM. Some tools connect directly to the DBMS to do this; other tools generate script files (e.g., SQL files), which can then be batched into the DBMS through some vendor-supplied facility. We will discuss some of the specific mapping rules for generating LDM constructs from CDM construct with specific LDM languages in the next chapter. As we mentioned earlier in this chapter, the term forward engineering

(FE) refers to any tools or techniques that help us to generate, translate, or propagate any details from a higher-level representation to a lower-level one (including the actual deployed DB, which is the lowest level possible).

10.5.3 Reverse Engineering

Similarly, the term **reverse engineering (RE)** refers to any tools or techniques that help us to generate, translate, or propagate any details from a lower-level representation to a higher-level one (including the actual deployed DB, which is the lowest level possible). We mentioned earlier that even when this is possible, there will always be some omissions or minor mistakes made. While we will not discuss this in great detail here, consider the reverse engineering of a PDM from a deployed DB when absolutely no DMs of any kind exist beforehand. Obviously, the names for the constructs will be identical to those in the DB, and all of the metadata (comment, purpose, annotation, definition, goals, and so on) that we would normally define in the CDM will be blank. If the DB naming rules are restrictive, even the names we reverse engineer might be truncated versions of what we would define in the CDM. If we try to reverse engineer this further (to the LDM or CDM categories), there are some mappings that we won't automatically be able to reverse. We will discuss the LDM to CDM issues in the next chapter, but for now, recall the differences we discussed in the sections on CFN and UML. Suppose we wanted to generate an ERD (CDM) from an LDM written in the relational data model. The RDM has no notion of Strong or Weak ETs—there are simply relations and primary keys. We would not always be able to automatically recognize a Strong ET connected to a Weak ET via an Identifying RT—the relation representing the Weak ET would look like all the other relations representing Strong ETs, and we certainly can't automatically infer anything from the construct names! Although reverse engineering is a valuable tool for such an environment, it is better to have all the forward engineered models if possible.

10.6 SUMMARY

DMs are an attempt to capture all schema-level details (metadata) that define and describe the intended plan for the structure and shape of a DB. These details can be split into different categories by various techniques and then represented by creating multiple DMs using different MLs for each category of details. The CLP taxonomy is one such technique. It defines three levels for data models, data modeling languages, and data modeling activities. The taxa (specific groupings) in this taxonomy encapsulate the DM details at the appropriate level, in order to maximize reusability and minimize maintenance issues. Each CDM only contains concepts that are independent of data storage design and implementation. Each LDM includes all the details from the single CDM on which it is based, as well as additional details that are independent of data storage implementation, but dependent on data storage design. Each PDM includes all the details from the single LDM on which it is based, as well as additional details that are dependent on the data storage implementation. Different MLs (approaches combined with nomenclature, rules, and notation details) can be used within each DM category. DMs in each category can be used to forward engineer the next level (including the lowest level, which is an actual deployed DB) or reverse engineer the previous level (up to the CDM which is the highest level). Various tools and techniques can be used to translate between DMs on different levels, both manually and automatically. While forward and reverse engineering are both powerful techniques, they are not a substitute for manual design and analysis—regardless of which direction we are considering. Differences in the purpose of each level, differences in the languages used to represent models in each level, and alternatives provided as part of the generation process can greatly alter the results we generate.

Although a CDM can be represented using any number of tools or notations, we looked briefly at three popular CML diagram notations. When exploring these techniques, we must remember that the tool is not necessarily the same as the technique—sometimes the tool implementers choose to add their own features or restrictions. These enhancements and limitations should not necessarily be ascribed to the particular alternative being used, or to conceptual data modeling as a whole. In general, any CDM representation can be used to capture a CDM, but the limitations of the language might cause the concepts to be captured in different ways—sometimes these differences are equivalent, other times they are not. This does not mean that the CDM is necessarily better or worse in a particular representation. While each technique has its strengths and weaknesses, we did not compare them in that fashion—for example, both the ERM and CFN techniques were recommended for both centralized and distributed database environment development.

When working with DMs from different levels we must be aware of the differences between the levels, MLs, and DMs. We must also consider the mechanisms used to map concepts from DMs in one level or ML into another. Although these differences and mapping techniques are important, we must try to prevent them from creeping into our DMs prematurely—otherwise this will cause difficulties whenever we use more than one ML from any level. When used appropriately, the levels help us to manage the complexity and maximize the reuse between DMs and MLs so that we can gain the most advantage from each.

10.7 GLOSSARY

Atomic AT   A CDM construct that represents an AT that cannot contain other ATs.

Attribute Type (AT)   A CDM construct representing a property that can hold a value. ATs can be one of eight possible flavors due to the three pairs of options possible (Singular or Plural, Identifying or Nonidentifying, Atomic or Grouping).

Cardinality (of an RT)   The explicit specification of the minimum and maximum number of instances on one side of a relationship. For example, if each Employee works for a minimum of zero and a maximum of one Department, then the cardinality for Employee is "0:1."

Conceptual Data Model (CDM)   A high-level DM capturing semantic concepts and their interrelationships/interdependencies for a DB in a way that is independent of both the LDM and PDM (independent of the data storage design or implementation).

Crow's Foot/Feet Notation (CFN)   A diagram notation that is named after the representation used for cardinalities in RTs. This notation is usually used for CDMs, but it is also usable for diagrams in the logical or physical levels.

Degree (of an RT)   The number of roles (separate connections to ETs) participating in an RT.

Disjoint Participation   See **Mutually Exclusive Participation**.

Entity Relationship Diagram (ERD)   A diagram showing all or part of a CDM written in the ERM ML.

Entity Relationship Model (ERM)   A conceptual modeling language (CML) developed by Dr. Peter Pin-Shan Chen in 1976. It captures concepts using ETs, RTs, and ATs. We also use this term to refer to the extended or enhanced ERM, which includes ITs for inheritance.

Entity Type (ET)   A CDM construct used to represent anything for which we want to capture details, relationships, and identity.

Grouping AT   A CDM construct that represents an AT that contains other ATs. This is analogous to a structure or user defined data type in a programming language.

Identifying AT   A CDM construct that represents an AT that is used to help uniquely identify an ET instance.

Identifying RT   A CDM construct used to connect a Weak ET to the one or more Strong ETs that partially identifies it.

Inheritance Type (IT)   A CDM construct that represents a generalization/specialization between two ETs.

Intentional Model   A model that represents the planned structure or shape rather than the actual contents—all the DMs discussed in this chapter are intentional models.

Logical Data Model (LDM)   A middle-level DM that captures details pertinent to the logical design of the data storage for a DB. This model will also usually capture the semantic concepts and their interrelationships/interdependencies in a way that is dependent on the data storage design (but not necessarily dependent on the data storage implementation).

Modeling Language (ML)   A vocabulary and set of rules used to define a model. Typically, there are also hints or suggestions for diagrammatic representations of the model, but this is not strictly speaking a requirement. For example, consider the entity relationship modeling technique described by Dr. Chen, the relational model as formalized by Dr. Codd, and the ANSI standard, or each proprietary Structured Query Language (SQL) defined by a particular RDBMS implementation.

Mutually Exclusive Participation   An option that can be specified for an IT. It indicates that no two Sub Entity instances can be connected to the same Super Entity instance.

Nonidentifying AT   A CDM construct that represents an AT that has no impact on the identification status of an ET instance.

Nonidentifying RT   A CDM concept used to connect two or more ETs, without affecting the identification status of any of the connected ETs.

Overlapping Participation   An option that can be specified for an IT. It indicates that two or more Sub Entity instances can be connected to the same Super Entity instance.

Partial Participation   An option that can be specified for an IT. It indicates that each Super Entity instance does not necessarily need to be connected to any Sub Entity instance.

Physical Data Model (PDM)   A DM that captures details pertinent to the physical implementation of the data storage for a DB. This model will also usually capture the semantic concepts and their interrelationships/interdependencies in a way that is dependent on the data storage design and/or implementation.

Plural AT   A CDM construct that represents an attribute type that contains one or more values. This is analogous to a collection, list, or array in a programming language.

Relationship Type (RT)   A CDM concept used to connect two or more ETs.

Singular AT   A CDM construct that represents an AT that holds a single (Atomic or Grouping) value.

Strong ET   A CDM construct used to represent an ET that contains one or more Identifying ATs that fully identify it.

Total Participation   An option that can be specified for an IT. It indicates that each Super Entity instance must be connected to one or more Sub Entity instances.

Unified Modeling Language   A standardized approach (and representation) for capturing an OOM. While UML can be used for CDM, it is not generally recommended.

Weak ET   A CDM construct used to represent an ET that is partially or fully identified by some other ET connected to it via an Identifying RT.

REFERENCES

[ANSI86a] American National Standards Institute, "The Database Language SQL," Document ANSI X3.135-1986, 1986.

[ANSI86b] American National Standards Institute, "The Database Language NDL," Document ANSI X3.133-1986, 1986.

[ANSI89] American National Standards Institute, "The Database Language SQL," Document X3.135-1989, 1989.

[ANSI92] American National Standards Institute, "The Database Language SQL," Document X3H2, 1992.

[Chen76] Chen, P. P.-S., "The Entity Relationship Model—Toward A Unified View of Data," *ACM Transactions on Database Systems*, Vol. 1, No. 1, pp. 9–36, March 1976.

[Chen80] Chen, P., "Entity-Relationship Diagrams and English Sentence Structure," in *Proceedings of the 1st International Conference on the Entity-Relationship Approach to Systems Analysis and Design*, North-Holland, Amsterdam, 1980, pp. 13–14.

[Chen83] Chen, P., "English Sentence Structure and Entity-Relationship Diagram," *Information Sciences*, Vol. 1, No. 1, pp. 127–149, May 1983.

[Chen97] Chen, P., "English, Chinese and ER Diagrams," *Data Knowledge Engineering*, Vol. 23, No. 1, pp. 5–16, June 1997. DOI = http://dx.doi.org/10.1016/S0169-023X(97)00017-7.

[Codd70] Codd, E., "A Relational Model of Data for Large Shared Data Banks," *Communications of the ACM*, Vol. 13, No. 6, pp. 377–387, June 1970.

[Elmrasi94] Elmrasi, R., and Shamkant, N. B. *Fundamentals of Database Systems*, 2nd edition, Addison-Wesley, Menlo Park, CA, 1994.

[Everest86] Everest, G., *Database Management: Objectives, System Functions, and Administration*, McGraw-Hill, New York, 1986.

[Kim92] Kim, W., *Introduction to Object-Oriented Databases*, The MIT Press, Cambridge, MA, 1992.

[Lewis02] Lewis, P., Bernstein, A., and Kifer, M., *Databases and Transaction Processing an Application-Oriented Approach*, Addison-Wesley, Boston, MA, 2002.

[Liberty98] Liberty, J., *Beginning Object-Oriented Analysis and Design with C + +*, Wrox Press Ltd., Birmingham, UK, 1998.

[Muller97] Miller, P., *Instant UML*, Wrox Press Ltd., Birmingham, UK, 1997.

[Quatrani98] Quatrani, T., *Visual Modeling with Rational Rose and UML*, Addison-Wesley, Reading, MA, 1998.

[Sanders95] Sanders, G., *Data Modeling*, Boyd & Fraser Publishing, Danvers, MA, 1995.

[SPARC75] ANSI/X3/SPARC Study Group on Data Base Management Systems, Interim Report. *FDT, ACM SIGMOD Bulletin*, Vol. 7, No. 2, 1975.

[SPARC76] "The ANSI/SPARC DBMS Model," in *Proceedings of the Second SHARE Working Conference on Data Base Management Systems*, Montreal, Canada, April 26–30, 1976.

[SPARC77] Jardine, D., *The ANSI/SPARC DBMS Model*, North-Holland, Amsterdam, 1977.

EXERCISES

Provide short (but complete) answers to the following questions.

10.1 Suppose we are going to create a new database representing a small university. Our model will capture details about students such as their names, date of birth, current grade point average, declared major and minor fields, the list of classes they are currently taking, as well as the grade they received for each class already completed (or an incomplete for courses that they have taken but not fulfilled all the requirements for). We will also capture details about the classes offered by the university—each class is actually a specific section of a course, which is offered during a specific semester by a specific instructor and department, meeting at specific times on specific days in a specific room of a building on campus. We also need to capture some minimal details about the departments such as the names and standard abbreviations used for them, and about the instructors, such as their names, credentials, and office locations (room and building) on campus.

Create a CDM representing this database schema using the ERM (including EER) language, and any diagramming notation you choose.

10.2 Suppose we are going to create a new database representing a small university, using the same description as provided in Exercise 10.1, but with some additional details. In particular, we must differentiate between graduate and undergraduate students, between graduate and undergraduate courses, and also between full-time and part-time instructors. Each undergraduate student must have a full-time instructor as an advisor, while each undergraduate course taught by a part-time instructor can optionally have one or more graduate students as teaching assistants. Of course, graduate students can only take graduate courses, and undergraduate students can only take undergraduate courses. Each graduate student can optionally be a teaching assistant for at most three classes per semester.

Create another CDM representing this database schema using the ERM (including EER) language, and any diagramming notation you choose—try to capture as many of these new details as unambiguously as possible.

10.3 What is the difference between an IT and an Identifying RT?

10.4 Suppose we captured the details representing the day of the week, time of day, building name, and room number that a particular section of a course meets in the university CDM discussed in Exercises 10.1 and 10.2 by creating one SNA AT for each detail. Would there be any differences between a model that placed these SNA ATs directly inside the ET representing a section and one that placed them in a SNG AT placed inside this ET?

10.5 Consider the same situation as described in Exercise 10.4, but suppose that each section meets multiple times per week (perhaps in different locations). How would we capture this in a CDM written in the ERM language?

10.6 How does the conceptual, logical, physical (CLP) taxonomy differ from the ANSI SPARC three-level model (3LM) categorization?

10.7 Suppose we created a database by following the traditional CLP taxonomy forward engineering (FE) approach—first creating a conceptual data model (CDM) then generating the logical data model (LDM) using the RDM, followed by the physical data model (PDM) for some RDBMS platform, and ultimately creating the database itself. If we reverse engineered a new PDM from the existing database, would it be identical to the PDM we originally used? If not, how would it be different?

10.8 Suppose we reverse engineered a new LDM written in the RDM language from the PDM we reverse engineered in Exercise 10.7. How would this LDM be different from the original LDM?

10.9 Suppose we reverse engineered a new CDM written in the ERM language from the LDM we reverse engineered in Exercise 10.8. How would this CDM be different from the original CDM?

11

LOGICAL DATA MODELS

In Chapter 10, we discussed data modeling in general and the CLP taxonomy for data models (DMs) and modeling languages (MLs). This chapter will focus on four logical modeling languages (LMLs) commonly seen in real database environments (DBEs). In particular, we will look at the **relational data model (RDM)**, the **network data model (NDM)**, the **hierarchical data model (HDM)**, and the **object-oriented data model (OODM)**. For each language, we will briefly review the ML itself, look at its nomenclature and notation, discuss the general rules for forward and reverse engineering, and then examine some of the special cases to consider when forward engineering (FE) and reverse engineering (RE) data models written in these LMLs.

The physical details controlling how a DBE manages the data store behind any database are very dependent on the deployment details for that database. Even if we use the same conceptual data model (CDM) and logical data model (LDM) details as a starting point, the physical data model (PDM) details for two separate deployments can vary greatly across different DBEs due to different DBMS vendors, different operating system (OS) platforms, or even just different versions of the same OS and DBE. This is not surprising because many of the physical details are implementation or deployment dependent details, and the implementation can be very different even when only one of these areas changes (e.g., even when we look at different versions of a DBMS from the same vendor, on the same OS platform, and implementing the same data model). The logical details do not vary quite as much because they are based on design details—in other words these details are related to the public interface that the DBE supports.

Distributed Database Management Systems by Saeed K. Rahimi and Frank S. Haug
Copyright © 2010 the IEEE Computer Society

In software engineering an interface is like a contract—an interface defines "what needs to be done" but not "how to do it." This means that different implementations with the same interface are required to comply with the interface definition, and this definition can only be changed through a very controlled and managed mechanism. Even though there can be changes to the interface over time, any changes are more likely to be gradual when adding new features or restrictions or when altering previous features or restrictions. In addition to the stability that most vendors provide across their different DBMS releases (new versions, new platforms) with respect to the LDM details, there are often industry standards (or simple vendor cooperation) ensuring that the LDM will not radically change.

When new innovations are introduced (new versions, new systems, new platforms, new approaches or techniques), there tends to be some similarities with other LDMs. So even though we are only looking at four examples of logical modeling languages in this chapter, the impact of these four languages goes beyond the systems that physically implement them. For example, even though the NDM and HDM are both primarily used in mainframe based implementations, the OODM actually has some parts that are very similar to these legacy approaches. It is quite possible that we could encounter a database system years from now using some completely new approach, with a completely new logical modeling language—but utilizing pieces that are similar to the pieces in one or more of the languages covered here. Object relational modeling is one such approach that is not really used much now (because it is still evolving and not standardized) but might be popular in the future.

11.1   THE RDM

The relational data model (RDM) is compatible with almost every relational database management system (RDBMS) that we might encounter in the real world. Although there have been many changes in RDBMSs since the RDM was first introduced by E. F. Codd in 1970 [Codd70] (most notably, the impact of the American National Standards Institute standardization efforts [ANSI86a] [ANSI89] [ANSI92]), the RDM itself has actually remained relatively unchanged. We will look briefly at the RDM nomenclature (the terms defined by Codd as well as those more commonly used today) and some common diagram notations for representing LDMs written in the RDM.

11.1.1   Nomenclature

If we are using the strict RDM nomenclature, then we are working with relations. As the RDM gained acceptance and became standardized, the nomenclature shifted slightly, and the terms used were based on an example representation that Codd included as a convenient mental picture, which he called the "array representation for a relation" [Codd70] more commonly known as a "relational table" or simply a "table." Strictly speaking, the RDM deals with **relations, tuples, domains**, and **keys**, while standard SQL uses a more PDM-biased nomenclature. When using the RDM as a language for data modeling in the real world, it is fairly common to use the SQL-flavored nomenclature instead of the original terms that Codd introduced. We will briefly discuss both vocabularies and then look at notations for representing data models written using this logical modeling language.

11.1.1.1 Relations, Tuples, and Domains   The RDM is relational because it is based on the mathematical concept known as a **relation**—not to be confused with the concept of a relationship, which is used in the entity relationship model (ERM) that we discussed in Chapter 10. In order to explain what a relation is, we first need to define two other terms: tuple and domain. A **tuple** is simply an ordered list of component elements, usually represented by a comma separated list enclosed within a set of parentheses. Figure 11.1 shows a tuple with four component elements in it—called a 4-tuple because there are four elements in the list, and also called an **n-tuple** for any generic tuple with n elements (here n equals 4). The elements in the tuple are ordered; this means that the 4-tuple in Figure 11.2 is not the same as the 4-tuple in Figure 11.1. They are different because the first component in Figure 11.1 ('Alice') is not the same as the first component in Figure 11.2 ('100') and the second component in each tuple is also different. A **domain** is defined as a set of possible values. We typically think of the values as being conceptually similar rather than completely random, but this depends on the semantics of the problem being considered. For example, a domain could be all the possible values for an hourly pay rate, all the possible colors of paint used in a manufacturing process, all the possible first and last names for our employees, or even the textual content of all the possible suggestions written on scraps of paper and placed in a suggestion box. Clearly, the last example domain could include almost any value, including well-written suggestions, text with incomplete sentences, text with spelling errors, or even total gibberish.

A relation is a set of n-tuples where each component element comes from a specific domain defined in the model. It acts as a template (called a **relational schema**) that represents all the possible combinations of values taken from the domains included in its definition. We can then say that the **degree of the relation** is n, where n is the number of component elements in each and every n-tuple in the relation. Although the concept of a relation is very useful as a mathematical construct, and completely necessary for serious mathematical arguments or proofs concerning the strengths or weaknesses of the RDM, this concept is not very easy to use in less formal discussions.

Therefore, Codd suggested some other useful, but nonessential ways to think about relations—he called one of these the "array representation of relations" [Codd70]. In this representation, we create a table (not a database table, but a textual one—a rectangle with gridlines dividing it into smaller cells) with each column representing the corresponding domain from the order defined in the relation. Each row in the table represents an n-tuple from the relation, with no duplicate rows allowed. The rows are unordered, but the column order is significant, because it is possible for the same domain to be used more than once in the same relation. In order to make this even

```
( 'Alice', '100', 'blue', '4.5' )
```

Figure 11.1   Example of a 4-tuple.

```
( '100', 'Alice', 'blue', '4.5' )
```

Figure 11.2   Example of a 4-tuple that is different from Figure 11.1.

more useful, we can list the name of the relation as the name of the table, and also include the role-qualified domain names as column headers in the table. Since the same domain can be used more than once, a role-qualified domain name is simply the domain name with additional clues clarifying the meaning or context for the domain when it would otherwise be ambiguous. For example, suppose we defined a domain named "EmpNo" to represent the unique number assigned to each employee in some company, and another domain named "EmpName" to represent each employee's name. We could then create a relation using the EmpName domain once and the EmpNo domain twice—once to represent the employee number for a particular employee and a second time to represent the employee number of that particular employee's manager. This is not a problem for the mathematical definition of the relation, but if we did not qualify the domain name, we would not be able to read the table representation for this relation: How would we know which column was the employee's number and which was the manager's number? If we use EmpNo for the domain representing the employee number of the employee and the role-qualified domain name "MgrEmpNo" for the domain representing the employee number of the manager, the ambiguity disappears. The relational schema for this situation is shown in Figure 11.3.

If we always use role-qualified domains when the same domain is used more than once in the same relation, it makes the table representation more useful, but it is still a little difficult to discuss the particular instances (rows in the table). For example, if we consider the relation instances (n-tuples) from Figures 11.1 and 11.2, it is not clear what each instance is supposed to represent. Codd included another useful (but nonessential) concept called a relationship [Codd70] to address this situation. A **relationship** is a set of (name, value) pairs, where there is one pair listed for each domain in the relation. In other words, we can think of this as the combination of column header and column value for one row in the table. By using this concept of a relationship, the column order in the table or in a relationship instance can safely be ignored, making it much easier to discuss things generically in the RDM, or specifically in any particular LDM written in the RDM. The term **table**, which is used by standard SQL and all the RDBMSs that conform to it, is derived from Codd's array representation for a relation. However, as we mentioned earlier, the term relation in the RDM should not be confused with the term relationship type (RT) in the ERM. Similarly, the term relationship in the RDM should not be confused with the ERM term relationship, which refers to an RT instance in the ERM. This term has a different, unrelated meaning and derivation in the ERM.

11.1.1.2 Keys   For any given relation (table), we can always find at least one subset of domains (columns) that uniquely identifies each instance (row). Any such set is called a **primary key (PK)**. We can always use the full set of domains (i.e., all the columns) as the primary key. However, we usually do not need to include **all** the domains in order to guarantee the unique identification of all rows. This means that there are usually multiple primary keys, since adding any unnecessary domain to such a PK will result in a new PK. When there are multiple PKs, we can arbitrarily pick one of them to be the "official" PK defined for the relation. We can refer to the other

```
Employee( EmpNo, EmpName, MgrEmpNo)
```

Figure 11.3   Relational schema with a role-qualified domain name.

PKs as either candidate keys (CKs) or alternate keys (AKs). When the elements in one relation need to reference other elements (in the same or different relation), we can use the concept of a **foreign key (FK)**. A FK is defined as a set of domains (which is not the PK for this relation) that contains the values of the PK for any relation (including this same relation). This allows us to connect one relation instance to another relation instance (exactly like the concept of an RT instance does in the ERM). If we define an "official" PK for a particular relation, we indicate this by underlining the name of each domain that is part of this PK in the relational schema. If we define any foreign keys, we usually indicate this by drawing a line from the domains in the FK in one relational schema to the relational schema containing the PK to which the FK links (assuming that both relational schemas are being shown). If we are only looking at a single relational schema (only for a single relation), then the FK details might be unclear or hidden.

11.1.2   Rules for Forward Engineering

Although there can be complicated scenarios requiring sophisticated transformations, we will only discuss a few basic rules and techniques to consider when forward generating an LDM written in the RDM from a CDM written in the ERM language. We will consider these rules and techniques for this specific conceptual modeling language (CML) to be a representative (but far from exhaustive) example. In general, we need to consider how we must transform certain configurations and certain constructs in order to generate the equivalent semantics in the LDM—or at least how to transform the constructs into a set of LDM constructs capable of capturing some of the same semantics. In particular, some AT flavors do not translate directly. Similarly, some RT, ET, and IT configurations require special handling. In general, some situations have multiple generation alternatives, with various benefits and disadvantages for each. The rules listed in the following sections describe how to map constructs from the ERM into the RDM—these rules are grouped by the construct type, not the order in which they need to be applied. In practice, the constructs in the ERM are considered one at a time, and the appropriate rule is applied based on the order in which the constructs are considered. In other words, even though we will consider the rules for ATs first in this chapter, attempting to transform all ATs as a first step is not necessary or recommended.

11.1.2.1 Forward Generation of ATs   In the RDM, all domains are atomic, which means that each domain value only holds a single indivisible value. Therefore, only the Singular Identifying Atomic (SIA) and Singular Nonidentifying Atomic (SNA) attribute types will translate directly. Each SIA attribute type and each SNA attribute type becomes a domain in the relation representing the ET. Each domain representing an SIA attribute type becomes part of the "official" PK for the relation. We can ignore the Plural Identifying Atomic (PIA) attribute types and the Plural Identifying Grouping (PIG) attribute types here because these are not really valid flavors in the ERM (as we discussed in Chapter 10). Therefore, in the following sections, we will consider the transformation alternatives for each valid AT flavor and discuss how each must be modeled in the RDM.

Singular Identifying Grouping   The first flavor-based transformation we will consider is the transformation needed for a Singular Identifying Grouping (SIG) attribute type from the ERM. This AT flavor is not used very often, but because it is a valid flavor, we need to consider how to transform these constructs into an RDM. Luckily, this transformation is not too difficult to understand. Although it is possible for the component ATs contained within our Grouping AT to be other flavors, we will only consider the simplest case here—namely, when all the component ATs have the SIA flavor. We will treat this simple case the same way we would treat an ET with multiple SIA attribute types. After we create a relation representing the containing ET, we will add one domain for each component AT and make it part of the PK for this relation. We call this technique **subsuming** the component ATs, because that is what we have done with them. In most cases, the repeated application of the techniques in this section should be sufficient to handle more complicated SIG attribute type configurations and ultimately generate the LDM. When this is not sufficient, we would recommend simplifying the CDM.

Plural Nonidentifying Atomic   The second flavor-based transformation we will consider is the transformation needed for a Plural Nonidentifying Atomic (PNA) attribute type from the ERM. For example, a PNA could represent a list of names, a list of numbers, or a list of dates. Since this is a Nonidentifying AT, we need to transform it into something that can represent an unordered list of possibly duplicated atomic values from some domain. In addition to the relation representing the containing ET, we also need to create a separate, new relation containing a Singular Nonidentifying Atomic (SNA) domain for each Plural Nonidentifying Atomic AT contained in the ET. Each of these new relations must have a PK, and since the PNA attribute type is not guaranteed to be unique, we recommend creating a new domain that will hold a meaningless but unique value to be used as the PK for the new relation. After we have created the new relations and domains for each PNA, we must connect each new relation to the relation representing the container ET. This means that we need to add a new domain to each new "PNA" relation to act as an FK. For example, recall the Employee ET we discussed for the CDM shown in Figure 10.3 in the previous chapter. To generate a relation for this ET, we need to transform the EmpEmailList Plural Nonidentifying Atomic attribute type. Here, the EmpEmailList is intended to represent the set of all email addresses for a particular employee instance (e.g., all of Alice's email account addresses). First, we create a new relation called EmpEmailList and a new domain called "EelAddress" to hold a single email address value from the list. We then create a new domain to use as the PK of the EmpEmailList relation. This can be a simple integer value here, which we will call "EelNo." Finally, we create a new domain to act as the FK in the new EmpEmail relation and connect it to the Employee relation. We will call this FK domain "EmpNo." The relational schema for the new relation is shown in Figure 11.4—here EmpNo is an FK to the Employee relation, even though the relational schema for the Employee relation is not shown here.

Singular Nonidentifying Grouping   The third flavor-based transformation we will consider is the transformation needed for a Singular Nonidentifying Grouping (SNG) attribute type from the ERM. For example, an SNG could represent an address, a multipart name, or anything that has recognizable component ATs. In other words, this

```
EmpEmailList (EelNo, EelAddress, EmpNo)
```

Figure 11.4   Transforming a PNA AT into a new relation.

AT is made up of other ATs (each of which might be either Singular or Plural, either Identifying or Nonidentifying, and either Atomic or Grouping). We will consider the simplest case, namely, when each component is an SNA attribute type. To transform an AT such as this, we have two different alternatives.

The first alternative is similar to the technique we used for the SIG attribute types earlier. In this alternative, we can simply map the component ATs to domains and subsume these component domains into the relation representing the container ET. However, since these are Nonidentifying ATs, we do not make them part of the PK for that relation here. For example, recall the DptAddress AT we discussed for the CDM shown in Figure 10.3 in the previous chapter. To transform it, we would create domains for each of the component ATs contained within the DptAddress AT and then subsume those domains into the Department relation. To do this, we simply place the component domains found inside the DptAddress relation inside the Department relation. Assuming we use the same naming convention for all the domains, the new relational schema generated for the Department relation using this technique is shown in Figure 11.5.

The second alternative is somewhat similar to the approach taken for the PNA attribute types described earlier, but there are some important differences here. When transforming the AT we need to consider how the Grouping AT and the ET interact. For example, let's reconsider the DptAddress AT and the Department ET. Strictly speaking, in the CDM, each Department has one DptAddress and each DptAddress is for only one Department. But because Grouping ATs do not have identifiers unique to the AT, we can have identical values for the ATs across different Department entity instances. Because a Grouping AT will be transformed into a relation in the RDM (somewhat similar to the way that an ET will be), we need to consider the implications of this more carefully. If a DptAddress is intended to represent a United States Postal Service (USPS) mailing address, then we might consider whether there is any advantage to storing this value only once in the database and reusing the instance when it is used by more than one Department instance. In other words, if multiple departments can share the same address, then transforming the SNG AT this way would be equivalent to promoting the AT to an ET and connecting it to its old container via a one-to-many relationship. Modeling it the way we have discussed it so far would mean that many Department instances could be connected to one DptAddress instance. If modeling it this way has benefits, then we can treat this case similar to the PNA situation and create a new relation for DptAddress. We would add a PK to the new relation, add all the component domains to it, and then add an FK domain to the Department relation so that we could refer to the DptAddress instance for a particular Department instance. The relational schema for this situation is shown in Figure 11.6.

However, if we reconsidered the DptAddress AT and the Department ET and decided that we did not want to reuse the new DptAddress instances this way, then we have another option. We can still decide to model the SNG AT as a separate relation, but now we are considering it in a way that is equivalent to promoting the AT to an ET

```
Department (DptNo, DptName, DptStreet, DptCity,
            DptState, DptZip)
```

Figure 11.5 Transforming an SNG AT by subsuming the component ATs.

```
DptAddress (DadNo, DadStreet, DadCity,
            DadState, DadZip)

Department (DptNo, DptName, DadNo)
```

Figure 11.6 Transforming an SNG AT using DptAddress instance reuse.

and connecting it to its old container via a one-to-one relationship. In this case, we could choose to put an FK in the Department relation (as we did in Figure 11.6) or in the DptAddress relation (as shown in Figure 11.7).

Plural Nonidentifying Grouping   The final flavor-based transformation we will consider is the transformation needed for a Plural Nonidentifying Grouping (PNG) attribute type from the ERM. The technique used for this flavor is similar to the one we just looked at in the previous section. We are considering a Plural AT whose elements are made up of other ATs, which, in turn, might be Singular or Plural and Atomic or Grouping. To simplify things in this example, we will consider the simplest case—namely, when each component AT is an SNA attribute type. Now, in order to transform an ET containing this PNG AT configuration, we will essentially follow the second option for the second transformation technique for the SNG attribute types. This means that we will create a new, separate relation, where each instance (row) in the new relation (table) will represent an instance of the Singular Nonidentifying Grouping AT. For example, recall the EmpPhoneList AT we discussed for the CDM shown in Figure 10.3 in the previous chapter. Here we will create a new relation named "EmpPhone" and add all the component domains as well as a PK to it. Although the CDM told us that the same employee can have multiple phone numbers (because it was a Plural AT), it did not tell us if the same phone number can occur in more than one list! Either way, we will use a separate relation, with a new PK and an FK to refer to it but we need to be more explicit when we transform it here. This means we must make a decision before we can transform it into our LDM—depending on what we decide, each decision will require a different transformation into the RDM. If we wish to reuse phone numbers (if the same EmpPhone instance can be used by more than one Employee instance), then we need to use a many-to-many relationship to connect the new EmpPhone relation to the Employee relation. We will discuss that transformation for many-to-many relationships in Section 11.1.2.2 of this chapter. For now, let's assume that the same EmpPhone instance is not used more than once—in other words, even if the same value is used for more than one of the component values, there will be separate instances (rows) and distinct PK values for each instance. Assuming we

```
DptAddress (DadNo, DadStreet, DadCity,
            DadState, DadZip, DptNo)

Department (DptNo, DptName)
```

Figure 11.7 Transforming an SNG AT without using DptAddress instance reuse.

use the same naming convention for all the domains, the new relational schema for the EmpPhone relation is shown in Figure 11.8.

11.1.2.2   *Forward Generation of RTs*   In Section 11.1.2.1, we mentioned that domain values in the RDM are atomic. We also mentioned earlier in this chapter that each relation type (RT) in the ERM is represented in the RDM by adding a new domain (a FK) to a relation that corresponds to one or more domains (PKs) for some relation in the RDM. Because of these two characteristics, an FK value for a particular relation instance (row) is capable of capturing only one PK value and therefore each relation instance (row) can only be connected to (at most) one instance (row) for the RTs represented this way.

This means that transforming any binary RT from the ERM into the RDM is trivial when at least one side has a maximum cardinality of one (we simply add an FK to the relation on the "other" side of the relationship). Similarly, when we transform a one-to-one relationship, we can add the FK to the relation corresponding to the ET on either side (since they are both on the "one" side, putting the FK on the "other" side means that choosing either relation is valid). However, this is not the case for many-to-many RTs. When we transform a many-to-many RT, we need to create a new relation containing a separate FK for each participating role (each connection to an ET). This set of FKs must also be used as the "official" PK for the new relation. This is sometimes done in a CDM using a concept called an associative ET. Similarly, if we want to transform an RT with degree higher than two (a nonbinary RT), we must use this approach—even if the cardinality is one-to-many or one-to-one. In both the many-to-many scenario and the nonbinary scenario, we need to create a new relation and use the FKs as the PK, with each FK connecting to a separate relation representing each participating role. For example, recall the On RT we discussed for the CDM shown in Figure 10.3 in the previous chapter: this is an RT with degree equal to three (3) and therefore a nonbinary RT (it is a ternary RT). Figure 11.9 shows the relational schema for the new relation representing this RT.

11.1.2.3   *Forward Generation of ETs*   The forward generation of a Strong ET is straightforward. Simply create a new relation for each ET and a domain for each of the ATs it contains following the rules in Section 11.1.2.1, as we previously discussed. When the ETs are all Strong ETs that do not participate in any ITs, the process is intuitive and trivial, with only a few special considerations with respect to normalization (see Section 11.1.4). If the Strong ET participates in any ITs, then the additional mapping techniques described in the next section must be applied.

```
EmpPhone (EphNo, EphAreaCode, EphMainNumber,
          EphExtension, EmpNo)
```

Figure 11.8   Transforming a PNG AT without using EmpPhone instance reuse.

```
On (EmpNo, PrjNo, DptNo)
```

Figure 11.9   Transforming an RT with degree greater than two.

When transforming a Weak ET we follow the same approach and then each SIA attribute type contained in a Strong ET connected to this Weak ET through an Identifying RT needs to be propagated into our new relation. This will result in the creation of new domains within this relation that act as part of the PK for the relation. In other words, we first transform the Weak ET the same way that we would a Strong ET. Next, we simply add a new domain for each Identifying AT that is not directly contained in the Weak ET being transformed. Each of these new domains is both an FK to the relations corresponding to the Strong ET from which it came and also part of the "official" PK for the new relation corresponding to the Weak ET. As we discussed in Section 10.3.1.1, Weak ETs usually should not participate in ITs. If they do, then they should only be allowed as Super ETs, and the additional mapping techniques in the next section should be considered and applied—but this scenario is not very common and not recommended.

11.1.2.4 Forward Generation of ITs   The forward generation of ITs is reasonably straightforward. There are three general techniques for mapping a particular IT (including the Super ET and all the Sub ETs that participate in it) into relations in the RDM. Although it is possible to use all three techniques within a single DM, this can be somewhat confusing. This should only be done when there are compelling reasons for doing so—most of the time, the data modelers should choose one technique and overall strategy to use for most (if not all) of the ITs defined in the data model.

In the first IT transformation technique, each ET involved in the IT is mapped to a separate relation, and each IT connection between the Super ET and Sub ETs is mapped as though it were an Identifying RT. This means that the SIA attribute types in the Super ET generate new domains in each of the relations corresponding to each of the Sub ETs. These domains become the PK of the relation for each Sub ET and also act as an FK connecting back to the relation representing the Super ET. In this technique, the SNA attribute types contained in the Super ET can be generated in one of two ways. In the first alternative, we only generate the domains corresponding to these ATs for the relation corresponding to the Super ET. In the other alternative, we also generate new domains corresponding to these ATs for each relation corresponding to a Sub ET. There is no direct enforcement of Total versus Partial participation in the RDM itself, but some physical modeling languages (PMLs) can enforce the participation via mechanisms such as triggers and cascade constraints. Similarly, the Disjoint versus Overlapping participation is not directly enforced in the RDM for this first technique, but some physical modeling languages can enforce these participation flavors using similar mechanisms.

In the second IT transformation technique, there is only a single relation generated for the entire IT configuration. In other words, the collection of Super ET, Sub ETs, and the ITs themselves will result in the generation of a single relation containing domains for all the ATs contained in all the ETs participating in the IT. Here, the values for the domains are present or empty based on the actual type of ET being stored in the relation; therefore, we also require a special AT to be used to specify which ET the information in a particular instance (row) is intended to represent. We call this special AT the specifying AT, and the corresponding domain is called the specifying domain. If any of the Sub ETs require FKs for the RTs in which they participate, these domains are also generated in the new relation. Similar to the first IT transformation technique, there is no direct enforcement of participation flavors. Unlike the first technique, this second technique requires some additional, special considerations for the domains generated on behalf of the mandatory ATs and RTs defined for the Sub ETs. Since there is only a single relation representing the instances for several different ETs, the domains corresponding to the mandatory ATs and RTs are no longer mandatory when a different ET is stored in the relation. For example, if an AT is mandatory for one Sub ET but not defined for another Sub ET, then it cannot be mandatory for the new relation—we would not be able to store instances for any of the other Sub ETs if this were enforced! Therefore, these "mandatory AT and RT" domains lose the ability to simply enforce the desired semantics when this second IT transformation technique is used.

In the third IT transformation technique, we generate one relation for each Sub ET but do not generate a relation for the Super ET. Each AT and RT defined for the Super ET will result in the generation of corresponding domains and FKs in each of the new Sub ET-based relations. Because there is no relation for the Super ET, this third technique only makes sense when the IT uses the Total participation flavor. The RDM cannot directly enforce Disjoint participation, but Total participation is enforced by definition. Any complex constraints or restrictions on the ATs and RTs defined for the Super ET are also not directly enforceable by simple means with this technique—since any checks must now be performed across all the corresponding domains and FKs in all the corresponding relations. Similarly, if any applications wish to perform operations involving the ATs and RTs defined in the Super ET, they must repeat the operations for each of the new Sub ET-based relations.

11.1.3   Rules for Reverse Engineering

When reverse generating a CDM from an LDM written in the RDM language, some constricts will map simply, but some constructs will not be possible to generate automatically. A given relation will reverse generate an ET, or an RT, or combination of several ETs and RTs in the new CDM. Similarly, each domain will reverse generate either an SIA attribute type, an SNA attribute type, or perhaps something more complicated if the domain participates in a PK or in an FK. When the relations being reverse engineered are the result of more complex configurations (such as ITs or Weak ETs with Identifying RTs), the reverse generation process will not be able to capture the semantics automatically. Similarly, participation flavors for ITs will not be recognized in most reverse generation scenarios. If the relations have been further transformed based on the special considerations described in the next section, then the original semantics will not be reversed. For example, the reverse generated rendition of the CDM will not contain any Plural ATs and will also not contain any Grouping ATs. Sometimes these more complex configurations can be added manually to the resulting CDM after it has been reverse generated, but this is not an automatic or trivial process.

11.1.4   Special Considerations

In theory, domains in the RDM can store any kind of value, but this leads to undesirable situations. Therefore, Codd suggested a set of rules that can prevent some of these situations from happening. These rules and the design process we follow to apply them are called **normalization**. A relation that obeys one or more of these rules is said to be in a particular **normal form** (**NF**). The rules are numbered, starting at one, and each successive rule requires conformance with the previous rule. We will not discuss all the details of normalization or look at all the NFs, but we will briefly review the first four forms/rules.

11.1.4.1 Normal Forms A relation is in **first normal form (1NF)** if and only if every domain in the relation contains only simple values—if and only if each domain is equivalent to an SIA attribute type or equivalent to an SNA attribute type. Luckily, there are very simple techniques that we can use to transform a relation that is not already in 1NF into a 1NF relation. If a relation is not in 1NF, then it must have one or more domains that are nonsimple. If we transform every nonsimple domain into a simple domain, then we have achieved 1NF. Sometimes, there will be extremely nonsimple domains, where these techniques need to be applied more than once—we will not discuss those cases, but careful application of these techniques can always (eventually) bring us to a set of one or more relations in 1NF. Merely following the forward generation rules discussed in the previous sections will usually result in 1NF relations.

11.1.4.2 Second Normal Form In order for a relation to be in **second normal form (2NF)**, it must already be in 1NF as a precondition. To determine if a relation that is already in 1NF is also in 2NF, we must explore the dependencies between the domains in the relation and the PK. The concept used for this is called a **functional dependency (FD)**. A domain has an FD upon another domain if the other domain determines the value for it. In order for a relation to be in 2NF, every domain that is not part of the PK must have an FD upon the PK (but not an FD on merely some subset of the PK). If it is dependent on only part of the PK, we say that there is a **partial functional dependency (PFD)**. When the domain is only functionally dependent on the whole PK, we say that there is a **fully functional dependency (FFD)**. In order to be in 2NF, each domain that is not part of the PK must have an FFD upon the PK of the relation.

11.1.4.3 Third Normal Form and Beyond In order for a relation to be in **third normal form (3NF)**, it must already be in 2NF as a precondition. To determine if a relation that is already in 2NF is also in 3NF, we must explore the dependencies further and look for transitive dependencies. A **transitive dependency (TD)** occurs when some domain has an FD upon another domain, which has in turn has an FFD upon the PK. In order to be in 3NF, every domain in the relation that is not part of the PK must have an FFD upon the PK, and no TDs can exist for these domains. The last level of normalization we will discuss is referred to as **Boyce–Codd normal form (BCNF)**. Because 3NF did not consider TDs for domains that are part of the PK, a new normal form called BCNF was defined to address the situation. In order for a relation to be in BCNF, it must first be in 3NF. Additionally, BCNF requires that no TDs exist for the domains that are part of the PK. There are additional normal forms defined, but most relational data models are only concerned with these four forms (1NF, 2NF, 3NF, and BCNF), so we will not discuss the other forms beyond BCNF here.

11.2 THE NETWORK DATA MODEL

The network data model (NDM) was defined by the Conference on Data Systems Languages (CODASYL) committee and later standardized by ANSI's Network Data Language (NDL) [ANSI86b]. Historically, the NDM has been used in many mainframe

DBEs, but it is not typically used for more modern platforms. Having said that, many of the constructs and concepts defined in the NDM are similar to those used in other logical modeling languages and therefore might be applicable for new DBEs in the future. The NDM was developed roughly parallel to the RDM and therefore there are several papers comparing and contrasting the two logical modeling languages [Date75] [Chen84].

11.2.1 Nomenclature

We will not go into exhaustive detail when discussing this language. Instead, we will merely introduce the high-level constructs and concepts. Unlike the RDM, the NDM is not based on tuples, domains, relations, or PK/FK references. Instead, it focuses on **records, data items, record types**, and **set types**.

11.2.1.1 Records, Data Items, and Record Types   A record is somewhat similar to the concept of a tuple, but they are not equivalent—a record is merely a collection of data values. By examining these collections of values, we can define abstract types to define their structure, which we will call record types. Each record type has a name and further details describing the types of data it contains. Again, this is somewhat analogous to relations containing domains in the RDM, or ETs containing ATs in the ERM. Each data item is analogous to an AT in the ERM and capable of storing simple or complex values depending on its data type definition (which is called its **format**). Formats are analogous to the data types commonly used in RDBMSs, but the actual details, features, and restrictions are, of course, dependent on the DBE implementing the NDM, not some other DBE implementing the RDM. The NDM supports plural data items (called **vectors**), grouping data items (called **groups, complex**, or **composite** data items), and plural grouping data items (called **repeating groups**). Each data item has one of two possible flavors—it is either an **actual data item** or a **virtual data item**. Actual data items are analogous to the ATs and domains that we have discussed in other MLs, while virtual data items represent values that are calculated or derived from other data items.

11.2.1.2 Set Types   A set type is used to represent a one-to-many relationship between two record types. Each set type must define the set type name and the names of the record types being connected. We refer to the record type on the one side of the relationship as the owner record type, while the record type on the many side is called the member record type. Since the words "owner" and "one" both start with the letter "o" and the words "member" and "many" both begin with the letter "m," it is easy to remember the corresponding cardinalities for the two record types involved. When NDMs are diagrammed, they usually use a notation called a **Bachman diagram (BD)** [Bachman69]. In this notation, each record type is drawn as a rectangle containing the name of the record type and the names of all the data items contained inside it. Set types are represented as a simple arrow pointing from the owner record type to the member record type with the name of the set type displayed somewhere near the arrow. In Bachman's notation, the set type is also called a **link type (LT)**. A link type cannot connect the same record (instance of a record type) more than once. This means we cannot have the same record as a member of more than one set type instance for the same set type, and can therefore identify a set type instance using either the owner record instance or any of the member record instances. Set types also have another useful characteristic—they define an order for the record instances that they contain. This is very different from the RTs defined in the ERM and the references defined in the RDM.

There are three special types of set types that need to be considered in addition to this generic description. A **system-owned set type** is one where there is no owner record type. This can be thought of as a set being owned by the DBE itself (the system). This is a useful mechanism for navigating the instances of a particular record type as well as a convenient way to define a particular ordering scheme for those instances. A **multimember set type** is a special set type where the member record type allows instances from several different record types rather than restricting the instances to only one record type. Lastly, there are recursive set types which allow the NDM to capture concepts equivalent to the recursive RT scenario for the ERM, which was discussed in Chapter 10. However, recursive set types are somewhat cumbersome to use and therefore recursive relationships are often implemented using special techniques (such as the technique we will discuss in Section 11.2.2).

11.2.1.3 Data Storage and Navigation   Unlike the RDM, which uses domains containing values that reference other domains (FKs referencing PKs), the NDM uses pointers to uniquely identify and relate record type instances. Therefore, the concept of a PK does not really exist in the NDM. We can define complex rules and restrictions for the data item formats, including rules that enforce uniqueness, rules that define the optional or mandatory nature of a data item, rules that define which data items are used to order the instances within a set type, and even rules that control the semantics for deletion.

11.2.2 Rules for Forward Engineering

Similar to the situation discussed for the RDM, we will only consider a few basic rules and techniques for the forward generation of an NDM from a CDM. Once again, we will consider a CDM written in the ERM language, but similar rules and techniques can be defined for any conceptual modeling language.

11.2.2.1 Forward Generation of ATs   Because the data items defined in an NDM can be quite complex, we can directly translate the various AT flavors directly into their NDM counterpart most of the time. In particular, all of the Nonidentifying ATs have no significant issues to consider. However, since the concept of a PK does not really exist in the NDM, we need to consider Identifiers differently. It is, of course, possible to simply create a data item corresponding to the Identifying ATs—essentially treating them the same as Nonidentifying ATs. We can also consider whether they are still necessary. If the ATs were defined merely to support the unique identification of ET instances and connectivity within relationships, then we can choose to not generate a corresponding data item for these ATs. However, if the ATs also have some semantic value, then we should treat them the same as Nonidentifying ATs and generate the data item in the corresponding record type.

11.2.2.2 Forward Generation of RTs   The ERM can support several RT configurations that the NDM does not directly support. For example, we must use special techniques to represent many-to-many RTs and RTs with degree greater than two (non-binary RTs) in the NDM. This is essentially the same situation that the RDM had to handle. Here, we would create a new record type with multiple set types rather than creating a separate relation with multiple FKs, but otherwise the technique is essentially the same. However, there is an addition RT configuration that we must consider for the NDM, which the RDM did not need to consider. This is the recursive RT we mentioned earlier. In this situation, we might be able to use the special recursive set type, but usually we will model this using a technique similar to the many-to-many RT. Here, we will create a new record type representing the RT and then create two set types to connect the two roles within the RT. The first set type specifies the original record type as the owner member and the new record type as the member, while the second set type reverses these roles. This new record type will often contain no data items—it merely exists to link the records to each other. Therefore, this record type is often referred to as either a **linking member** (emphasizing its role) or a **dummy member** (emphasizing the fact that it contains no data items). Because identification is different in the NDM, Identifying and Nonidentifying RTs are handled identically and the PK issues discussed for the RDM forward engineering do not apply.

11.2.2.3 Forward Generation of ETs Like the case for the RDM, the forward generation of the ET is straightforward. Simply create a new record type for the ET and a new data item for each AT contained within the ET. Because of the differences in identification (as we discussed in Section 11.2.2.1), Weak and Strong ETs are typically handled identically and the PK issues discussed for the RDM forward engineering do not apply.

11.2.2.4 Forward Generation of ITs Similar to the RDM, we have three alternatives to consider for the ETs participating in ITs. Once again, it is possible to use multiple techniques but probably unwise. Identifying ATs would be treated like Nonidentifying ATs (as we discussed in Section 11.2.2.1) and RTs would be handled (as discussed in Section 11.2.2.2) by creating set types as needed without any data item corresponding to an FK being generated.

In the first alternative, we generate a new record type for the Super ET and a new record type for each of the Sub ETs. We then create a separate set type for each IT connection, with the record type corresponding to the Super ET acting as the owner record type and each ET corresponding to the Sub ET acting as the member record type of its corresponding set type. Using the constraints available to the NDM, we can enforce the Total participation flavor directly in this alternative and also enforce the Disjoint flavor directly. Once again, we can choose to generate the data items corresponding to the ATs defined in the Super ET only once or to generate them once for each record type corresponding to a Sub ET.

In the second alternative, we generate a single record type and then create all the necessary data items to correspond to all the ATs defined in the Super ET and its Sub ETs. Again, we would make sure to have a specifying data item so that we could distinguish the actual ET being represented in a particular instance. In this alternative, the Total and Disjoint are not directly enforceable, and the same precautions with respect to AT and RT rules and restrictions that we discussed in Section 11.1.2.4 still apply.

In the third alternative, we generate one record type for each Sub ET but do not generate any record type for the Super ET. The ATs and RTs involving the Super ET will cause data items and set types to be generated for each record type corresponding to a Sub ET. As discussed in Section 11.1.2.4, this alternative only makes sense when the IT has the Total participation flavor. In this alternative, the NDM can only directly enforce the Disjoint participation flavor if we generate a data item corresponding to the PK.

11.2.3 Rules for Reverse Engineering

Similar to the reverse engineering scenario discussed in Section 11.1.3, we will be able to reverse generate some constructs more directly than others when we attempt to create a CDM from an NDM. We will again consider the CDM to be written in the ERM language, but we could use other conceptual modeling languages instead with slightly different rules and techniques. Each record type will reverse generate an ET, or an RT, or combination of several ETs and RTs in the new CDM. Because the NDM does not capture PKs, we will not be able to automatically generate an Identifying AT based on an existing data item, but we can simply generate a surrogate identifier (a new Identifying AT that is not based on any existing data item or AT). This also means that Identifying RTs will not be part of the reverse generated CDM. Similar to the situation for the RDM, we will not be able to automatically reverse generate any ITs from the NDM. It is also unlikely that the reverse generation will automatically recognize the set types used to represent recursive relationships or many-to-many relationships. If we use other set type flavors such as the system-owned, multimember, or recursive set types in our NDM, we cannot capture the semantics correctly in the CDM because there are no equivalent constructs to generate. Similarly, the rules and restrictions (e.g., the defined orders for record type instances and the enforcement of various things such as Disjoint or Total participation) will not be automatically recognized or reverse generated. In summary, the CDM that we reverse generate from an NDM will most likely require manual engineering in order to make it accurate or usable for any future activities.

11.2.4 Special Considerations

The NDM supports record type, data item, and set type definitions that are fairly similar to the complexity supported by the ERM, but it also has some restrictions that the ERM does not. Constructs such as pointers, virtual data items, and special set type flavors combined with the NDM's facility for defining rules and restrictions makes it a powerful LDM, but these constructs also make it difficult to directly translate DMs written in this logical modeling language into a CDM or into an LDM written in another language. Although simple DMs can be translated in and out of a DM written in this LML in a relatively straightforward fashion, intermediate to advanced DMs will require knowledge of both the NDM language and the other MLs in order to ensure that semantics are not lost or incorrectly translated.

11.3 THE HIERARCHICAL DATA MODEL

The hierarchical data model (HDM) is another logical modeling language commonly used in mainframe environments, but seldom seen in other places. This is not a standardized ML in the same way that the RDM, NDM, and OODM are—instead, this is the language used by several different DBE implementations all of which are based on hierarchical data storage structures. In some respects, there are parallels between the HDM and the object-oriented data model (OODM), which is not surprising since the OODM often uses inheritance hierarchies. However, the HDM was not created for OO purposes. The HDM was developed to represent the hierarchical relationships between data that occur naturally in the real world without the additional considerations that the OODM defines. For example, the HDM is well suited to capture data representing corporate structures (who works for whom) and taxonomic classification schemes (class, species, subspecies, etc.).

11.3.1   Nomenclature

The HDM uses some of the same terms as other logical modeling languages, but the definitions and restrictions are not the same. In particular, the HDM defines **records, fields, record types, parent–child record types**, and **hierarchies**.

11.3.1.1   Records, Fields, and Record Types   Similar to the nomenclature used by the NDM, the HDM uses the term **record** to refer to a collection of values. Each of these values is called a **field value**, while the definition of their structural details is called a **field** (or sometimes called a **data item**). Once again, the term **record type** refers to the structural definition of a record, which includes the name for the record type as well as all the fields defined within it.

11.3.1.2   Parent–Child Association and Link Types   In the HDM, a link type (LT) represents a one-to-many relationship between two record types. The record type on the one side of the LT is called the **parent record type**, while the record type on the many side of the LT is called the **child record type**. Similar to the NDM, the HDM link type indicates a one-to-many association. Here, the LT associates a parent record with its children, resulting in a hierarchy of records in the database.

11.3.1.3   Hierarchies   A **hierarchy** is a collection of record types connected by LTs. This is not merely a collection—each hierarchy must also conform to a strict set of rules. One record type in the hierarchy must be designated as the **root** of the hierarchy. This record type must not be the child record type in any LT. Every other record type in the hierarchy must be a child record type in exactly one LT. In short, the LTs are used to construct a tree using all record types contained in the hierarchy. An LDM written in the HDM language is simply a collection of these hierarchies (separate trees of record types connected via LTs). Each record type must belong to only one hierarchy.

11.3.1.4   Virtual Record Types and Virtual Link Types   In order to capture nonhierarchical associations, the HDM uses the concept of a **virtual record type**, which is merely a record type containing pointers to other records rather than the actual field values themselves. Virtual record types are used to support many-to-many relationships, to effectively allow the same record type to be a child record type in more than one LT, and to support a situation equivalent to an RT defined in a CDM written in the ERM with degree greater than two (a nonbinary RT). Similarly, a **virtual LT (VLT)** refers to a construct similar to an LT that uses a virtual record type rather than the actual record types. A VLT connects a virtual parent record type to a virtual child record type by using pointers to the actual record types involved.

11.3.2   Rules for Forward Engineering

The HDM has some fairly strict restrictions that make it difficult to automatically generate LDMs in some situations, but the fundamental mappings are not that complicated. Because many of the issues and alternatives are similar to those mentioned for other logical modeling languages, we will focus on the aspects unique to the HDM and refer to the other sections for those aspects shared with other LMLs. Again, we will consider a CDM written in the ERM language here, but we could have chosen to use a CDM written in any other conceptual modeling language.

11.3.2.1   Forward Generation of ATs
Each AT defined in the CDM written in the ERM language will result in a new field being defined inside a record type. The HDM uses pointers rather than PKs and FKs; therefore, it is quite similar to the NDM for many of the AT mapping issues and considerations. The rules and restrictions available to the HDM are as complete as those in the NDM, but otherwise the NDM data item and HDM field are fairly similar.

11.3.2.2   Forward Generation of RTs
Only one-to-many RTs can be directly represented in the HDM, and these must form a tree in order to make a hierarchy. When the data being captured by the CDM is not particularly hierarchical, we will be forced to generate several hierarchies and use VLTs to connect the record types found in different hierarchies. Similarly, VLTs must be used for all nonbinary or many-to-many RTs.

11.3.2.3   Forward Generation of ETs
Each ET in the CDM will result in a new record type in the HDM with new fields defined for each AT contained in the ET. Otherwise, the situation is very similar to that considered in the NDM with respect to the identification issues and ET flavors, except that the location of the record type in the hierarchy affects the existence and lifetime. In other words, whenever a parent record type instance is deleted, all of its associated child record type instances are also deleted. VLTs reduce the impact of this situation, but this restriction greatly affects the decision process for determining which ET should be generated as the parent record type of another. In some cases, this restriction is compatible with the definition of Weak ETs, but that is not always the case.

11.3.2.4   Forward Generation of ITs
ITs defined in the CDM written in the ERM language can be used to define the hierarchies of record types and link types in the HDM. The generation is straightforward, with only a single technique—namely, generating a record type for the Super ET and each Sub ET and then generating one link type for each IT connection between Super ET and Sub ET. Fields are generated in the corresponding record types. Both the Total and Partial participation flavors are supported, as well as the Disjoint and Overlapping participation flavors—but no direct support for enforcing these flavors is provided. Similar to the NDM, the lack of a PK concept makes this mapping use slightly different semantics than the RDM did.

11.3.3   Rules for Reverse Engineering

The reverse generation is fairly straightforward. Each field becomes an AT. Each record type will generate an ET or an RT. Similarly, each LT will "reverse generate" an RT.

However, there is no automatic support for reverse generating ITs. Because most relationships are stored in the HDM using the hierarchy, we certainly cannot assume that the hierarchy is the basis for any ITs! Therefore, manual inspection and analysis is the only way we can recognize when a particular LT represents an inheritance (compatible with the concept of an IT) versus when that LT represents a simple relationship (more compatible with the concept of an RT). Similar to the NDM, the reverse engineering of the HDM equivalent of many-to-many RTs and nonbinary RTs might also require manual analysis. VLTs and virtual record types will also not always reverse generate the constructs we would expect to see.

11.3.4   Special Considerations

Because the HDM cannot capture nonhierarchical data elegantly, any attempt to bring DMs capturing nonhierarchical data into or out of an LDM written in the HDM language will result in a DM with issues. These issues need to be addressed manually by somebody who understands the data being captured as well as the nuances of the HDM. In summary, using the HDM when there are no naturally occurring hierarchies is not recommended.

11.4   THE OODM

Loosely speaking, the OODM can refer to any DBE using an OO approach for persisting data. This does not mean that there have not been efforts to standardize the OODM; in particular, the Object Database Management Group (OODMG) created three versions of its standard before disbanding in 2001. The third version of the standard ("The Object Data Standard 3.0") defined programming language specific bindings as well as language independent concepts. This effort has been revived by the Object Management Group (OMG), which has set up the Object Database Technology Working Group (ODBTWG) and obtained the rights to continue developing the OODMG's now-defunct standard. Regardless of the efforts to standardize the model, the overall concepts can be considered, and that is the purpose of this section.

11.4.1   Nomenclature

Some of the terms used for the other concepts in this logical modeling language might be influenced by a particular vendor or a particular OO language. If we ignore those biases, we can focus on the overall concepts and rules used to capture data in an OO fashion. In particular, we will consider **properties, methods, classes, class inheritance, objects, object identifiers, navigation**, and **extents**.

11.4.1.1   Properties and Methods   In the OODM, we can model data as well as the operations that surround that data. **Methods** are essentially functions, subroutines, or routines that surround the object. These methods can be used to include code along with the data that provides operations and behavior for the object. The data is captured using **properties**. A **property** is essentially the same as the other concepts with the same purpose that we have already discussed for other logical modeling languages. Properties have some OO specific characteristics, such as the allowable data types including the use of classes as data types (classes are defined in the next section). Each property definition can also include qualifiers or specifiers to control its scope, lifetime, persistence, and accessibility characteristics. Similar to data items in the NDM and ATs in the ERM, properties can be defined to store plural or singular values. They can also be defined to use primitive data types (atomic values) or classes. When the property is using a class as its data type, it can also be thought of as implementing a relationship between the instances of the container class and the class used as the data type for the property.

11.4.1.2 Classes and Class Inheritance   Similar to the way that an ET is an abstraction of an entity, a **class** is an abstraction of an object. The class defines the methods and properties for the object, as well as its inheritance details. Often, we say that there is some ultimate class from which all other classes inherit. This ultimate class often has a simple name, such as "Object," and provides the fundamental properties, operations, or behavior required by the system. Different physical modeling languages might have different rules and restrictions, especially with respect to **class inheritance**. In particular, the question of multiple inheritance (allowing the same subclass to have more than one superclass) and its nuances is a very implementation dependent consideration. Regardless of whether multiple inheritance is allowed or prohibited, inheritance is a fundamental part of the OODM.

11.4.1.3 Objects and Object Identifiers   In the OODM, every instance is called an **object**, and every instance must be uniquely identifiable by an **object identifier (OID)**. This is a system maintained property that is usually assigned a globally unique identifier (GUID) or some other system dependent value. Often, this is a property (and perhaps some methods implementing the desired behavior surrounding this property) defined in the ultimate superclass we discussed in the previous section.

11.4.1.4 Navigation and Extents   Each object is accessible by navigation. This means that we find an object instance by following a chain of pointers or references (properties). But how do we add the first object or navigate to it once it has been created? The answer is a concept known as an **extent**. A class captures the intentional view of the objects (the structure) while an extent captures the extensional view of the object (the instances). An extent is very similar to the system-owned record set concept we discussed (in Section 11.2.1.2) for the NDM language. It provides us with a (possibly sorted) list of objects.

11.4.2 Rules for Forward Engineering

Similar to the situation discussed for the RDM, we will only consider a few basic rules and techniques for the forward generation of an OODM from a CDM. Once again, we will consider a CDM written in the ERM language, but similar rules and techniques can be defined for any conceptual modeling language.

11.4.2.1 Forward Generation of ATs   Each AT defined in a CDM written in the ERM language will generate a property. Similar to the NDM and HDM, the OODM has no construct equivalent to the PK. Therefore, ATs that are used merely to provide a PK for the ET might be omitted if they have no semantic purpose, and the Identifying

AT flavor is essentially ignored. Similar to the RDM, we will generate classes for any Grouping ATs defined, but unlike the RDM, we do not need to be concerned about Plural ATs because the OODM supports them directly. Atomic ATs will generate properties using either primitive data types or perhaps using system supplied **wrapper classes** that provide additional behavior.

11.4.2.2   Forward Generation of RTs   Each RT defined in the CDM written in the ERM language will result in the generation of properties in the OODM. Because RTs in the ERM are bidirectional, we need to create a separate property for each direction if we want to support navigation for both directions in the OODM rendition of the DM. Each many-to-many RT will result in the generation of at least one plural property (two of them if the bidirectional navigation is desired). Although there are several techniques for generating the equivalent of an RT with degree greater than two, avoiding them in the CDM is probably a wiser choice. Similar to the NDM, the Identifying RT flavor is not directly generated in the DM using this logical modeling language, because PKs and FKs are not used.

11.4.2.3   Forward Generation of ETs   Each ET defined in a CDM written in the ERM language will result in the generation of a new class in the OODM. The OODM is similar to the NDM and HDM, with respect to the handling of Weak ETs—in other words, it is essentially ignored most of the time. Each AT defined in the ET will result in the generation of a property in the new class.

11.4.2.4   Forward Generation of ITs   Each IT defined in the CDM written in the ERM language will generate an inheritance relationship in the OODM. The classes corresponding to Super ET and Sub ETs will be used as the superclass and subclasses in the OODM. ITs in the ERM usually use single inheritance, but if multiple inheritance is used, then there might be some issues when generating the OODM inheritance relationships. If an IT uses the Total participation flavor, the superclass in the OODM will be declared as abstract (or virtual) to enforce this. Otherwise, if the IT uses Partial participation, then a concrete superclass will be used. There is no direct support for the Overlapping IT flavor—all inheritance in the OODM is Disjoint, but techniques similar to those used in the RDM can be used to capture this flavor indirectly if necessary.

11.4.3   Rules for Reverse Engineering

Each class in the OODM will generate a new ET in the CDM written in the ERM language. Each property using a primitive data type will generate an SNA attribute type except for the OID, which will require an SIA attribute type. Properties using classes for their data type will generate a new ET for the property along with an RT connecting the new ET to the ET corresponding to the container class. Each superclass and its associated subclasses will generate ITs connecting the corresponding ETs.

11.4.4   Special Considerations

When reverse engineering, many details may be lost. In particular, the specifiers and qualifiers used for properties will not be captured by the new ERM. Similarly, methods are not represented in an ERM. This means that methods will not be reverse engineered in an ERM and it also means that an OODM generated from an ERM will not have any methods defined in it. Unidirectional associations and references used by the OODM are not the same as the bidirectional RTs used in the ERM: ambiguities and errors may occur when reverse engineering an OODM into a CDM. If the OODM does use extra properties to implement a bidirectional relationship, the CDM will contain duplicate RTs.

11.5 SUMMARY

The LDM is written using a logical modeling language (LML) that is intended to capture the semantics defined in the CDM along with additional details that are important to the data storage design (but not its implementation or deployment). Different LMLs correspond to the different classes of existing DBEs and the physical modeling languages/PDMs on which they rely. We examined four LMLs: the RDM, the NDM, the HDM, and the OODM. Each language has its own nomenclature, features, and restrictions. When generating an LDM written in one of these languages from a CDM, many of the conceptual constructs have a simple and direct mapping, some conceptual constructs have several techniques to choose from in lieu of a direct mapping, and some conceptual constructs have no generation option. When considering the reverse process, we will usually encounter some ambiguities or problems—in particular, we often cannot reverse generate the original conceptual construct when there are multiple alternatives for the forward generation activities. Although all of the LMLs we considered here were quite different from each other, they also had quite a few similarities. Depending on the actual constructs defined in a DM, the forward engineering and reverse engineering activates might be easier or more difficult than first suspected.

11.6 GLOSSARY

Bachman Diagram (BD)   A diagrammatic notation developed by Charles Bachman for capturing the structure of data—especially when using the network data model (NDM).

Boyce–Codd Normal Form (BCNF)   A normal form higher than third normal form (3NF)—a relation is in BCNF if it is already in 3NF and also has no transitive dependencies for any of the domains in the relation that are part of the primary key (PK).

Child Record Type   The record type connected to the many side of a parent–child record type (LT) in the hierarchical data model (HDM).

Class   A class is an abstraction of an object in the object-oriented data model (OODM) in the same way that a relational schema is an abstraction for a tuple in the relational data model (RDM).

Class Inheritance   The rules and nomenclature used to define how classes inherit from one another in the object-oriented data model (OODM).

Data Item   A term that is used in both the network data model (NDM) and hierarchical data model (HDM) to refer to a construct that is analogous to an attribute type (AT) in the relational data model (RDM).

Degree (of a Relation)   The number of (possible role-qualified) domains in a relation in the relational data model (RDM)—it is analogous to the number of columns in the "table" representation for a relation.

Domain   A set of possible values in the relational data model (RDM)—it is analogous to a column in the "table" representation for a relation.

Dummy Member   The name given to a record that is created simply to be the member of a special purpose set type used in the network data model (NDM). Because it typically contains no data items, it is called a "dummy" and is used to model situations that are not directly supported by the NDM, like many-to-many relationships. It is also sometimes called a linking member.

Extent   A construct that contains all the instances for a particular class or interface type in the object-oriented data model (OODM)—this is somewhat analogous to the system-owned set type used in the network data model (NDM) and the relation in the relational data model (RDM).

Field   An alias for "data item" in the hierarchical data model (HDM).

First Normal Form (1NF)   A relation in the relational data model (RDM) is said to be in first normal form (1NF) if all of its domains are single valued and atomic—this is often claimed to be guaranteed by the RDM.

Foreign Key (FK)   A set of domains, in the relational data model (RDM) (which is not the PK for the relation containing it), that must contain the values of the domains in the PK for any relation (including the PK for this same relation in the case of a recursive relationship).

Functional Dependency (FD)   A domain is functionally dependent on another domain if the other domain determines the value for it.

Group   A compound or complex data item in the network data model (NDM)—analogous to a Grouping AT in the entity relationship model (ERM).

Hierarchical Data Model (HDM)   A logical modeling language (LML) commonly used in mainframe DBEs. It captures concepts using record types, parent–child record types, and hierarchies.

Link Type (LT)   A record type that is used to connect two record types in a one-to-many relationship within the hierarchical data model (HDM). The record type on the one side is called the parent record type, while the record type on the many side is called the child record type, and the parent–child record type (LT) is used to connect the two.

Linking Member   An alias for "dummy member." The name linking emphasizes the role that the record plays in the set.

Logical Data Model (LDM)   A middle-level DM that captures details pertinent to the logical design of the data storage for a DB. This model will also usually capture the semantic concepts and their interrelationships/interdependencies in a way that is dependent on the data storage design (but not necessarily dependent on the data storage implementation).

Method   A method is essentially a function, subroutine, or routine that surrounds an object in the object-oriented data model (OODM). Methods can be used to include code along with the data and typically provide operations and behavior for the object.

Modeling Language (ML)   A vocabulary and set of rules used to define a model. Typically, there are also hints or suggestions for diagrammatic representations of the model, but this is not strictly speaking a requirement. For example, consider the entity relationship modeling technique described by Dr. Chen, the relational model as formalized by Dr. Codd, and the ANSI standard, or each proprietary Structured Query Language (SQL) defined by a particular RDBMS implementation.

Navigation   The mechanism used in the object-oriented data model (OODM) to find an object instance by following a chain of pointers or references (properties) from one object to another.

Network Data Model (NDM)   A logical modeling language (LML) commonly used in mainframe DBEs. It was defined by the Conference on Data Systems Languages (CODASYL) committee and later standardized by ANSI's Network Data Language (NDL) and captures concepts using records, data items, record types, and set types.

Normalization   A set of rules defined by E. F. Codd and others to transform logical data models (LDMs) written in the relational data model (RDM) language in order to prevent some undesirable situations with regard to functional dependencies.

Object   An instance of a class in the object-oriented data model (OODM)—this is analogous to a tuple in the relational data model (RDM) or a record in the network data model (NDM) or hierarchical data model (HDM).

Object-Oriented Data Model (OODM)   A logical modeling language (LML) commonly used in object-oriented DBEs. Although there is no single standard, there are several attempts at standardization such as those performed by the Object Database Management Group (OODMG) and the Object Management Group (OMG). It captures concepts using properties, methods, classes, class inheritance, objects, object identifiers, navigation, and extents.

Parent Record Type   The record type connected to the one side of a parent–child record type (LT) in the hierarchical data model (HDM).

Parent–Child Record Type   See **Link Type**.

Primary Key (PK)   A subset of the domains (columns) defined within a relation (table) that uniquely identifies all the instances (rows) within the relational data model (RDM).

Property   A term used in the object-oriented data model (OODM) to refer to a construct that is analogous to an attribute type (AT) in the relational data model (RDM).

Record   An instance of a record type in the network data model (NDM) or hierarchical data model (HDM)—this is analogous to a tuple in the relational data model (RDM) or an object in the object-oriented data model (OODM).

Record Type   An abstraction of a record in the network data model (NDM) or hierarchical data model (HDM) in the same way that a relational schema is an abstraction for a tuple in the relational data model (RDM) and a class is an abstraction of an object in the object-oriented data model (OODM).

Relation   A construct that contains all the tuples for a particular relational schema in the relational data model (RDM)—this is somewhat analogous to the system-owned set type used in the network data model (NDM) and the extent in the object-oriented data model (OODM).

Relational Data Model (RDM)   A logical modeling language (LML) commonly used in RDBMSs. It was defined by E. F. Codd and captures concepts using relations, tuples, domains, primary keys, and foreign keys.

Relational Schema   An abstraction for a tuple in the relational data model (RDM) in the same way that a record type is an abstraction for a record in the network data model (NDM) or hierarchical data model (HDM) and a class is an abstraction of an object in the object-oriented data model (OODM).

Repeating Group   A plural compound or plural complex data item in the network data model (NDM)—analogous to a Plural Grouping AT in the entity relationship model (ERM).

Second Normal Form (2NF)   A normal form higher than first normal form (1NF)—a relation in the relational data model (RDM) is said to be in second normal form (2NF) if it is already in 1NF and it is also true that every domain contained in it that is not part of the PK has FD upon the PK (but does not have FD on merely some subset of the PK).

Set Type   A construct that is used to represent a one-to-many relationship between two record types in the network data model (NDM).

System-Owned Set Type   A construct in the network data model (NDM) that represents a set of records that is not owned by any record type (it is owned by the DBE system itself). This is somewhat analogous to the extent in the object-oriented data model (OODM) and the relational schema in the relational data model (RDM).

Third Normal Form (3NF)   A normal form higher than second normal form (2NF)—a relation is in 3NF if it is already in 2NF and it is also true that every domain in the relation that is not part of the PK has FFD upon the PK, with no TDs existing for these domains.

Tuple/n-Tuple   An instance of a relational schema in the relational data model (RDM)—this is analogous to a record in the network data model (NDM) or hierarchical data model (HDM) or an object in the object-oriented data model (OODM).

Vector   One name used for a plural data item in the network data model (NDM)—analogous to a Plural AT in the entity relationship model (ERM).

Virtual Link Type (VLT)   A construct in the hierarchical data model (HDM) that is similar to an LT but uses virtual record types rather than actual record types in order to capture nonhierarchical associations between record types.

Virtual Parent–Child Record Type   See **Virtual Link Type**.

Virtual Record Type   A record type in the hierarchical data model (HDM) that contains pointers to other records rather than the actual field values themselves. It is used in conjunction with virtual parent–child record types (VLTs) to capture nonhierarchical associations between record types.

REFERENCES

[ANSI86a]American National Standards Institute, "The Database Language SQL," Document ANSI X3.135-1986, 1986.

[ANSI86b]American National Standards Institute, "The Database Language NDL," Document ANSI X3.133-1986, 1986.

[ANSI89]American National Standards Institute, "The Database Language SQL," Document X3.135–1989, 1989.

[ANSI92]American National Standards Institute, "The Database Language SQL," Document X3H2, 1992.

[Bachman69]Bachman, C., "Data Structure Diagrams," *SIGMIS Database*, Vol. 1, No. 2, pp. 4–10, July 1969.

[Chen84] Chen, H., and Kuck, S., "Combining Relational and Network Retrieval Methods," in *Proceedings of the ACM SIGMOD International Conference on Management of Data* Boston, MA, June 1984.

[Codd70]Codd, E., "A Relational Model of Data for Large Shared Data Banks," *Communications of the ACM*, Vol. 13, No. 6, pp. 377–387, June 1970.

[Date75]Date, C., and Codd, E., "The Relational and Network Approaches: Comparison of the Application Programming Interfaces," in *Proceedings of the 1974 ACM SIGFIDET (Now Sigmod) Workshop on Data Description, Access and Control—Data Models: Data-Structure-Set Versus Relational*, Ann Arbor, Michigan, May 1974. FIDET'74. ACM, New York, 1974, pp. 83–113.

EXERCISES

Provide short (but complete) answers to the following questions.

11.1   What is the difference between the degree of a relation in the relational data model (RDM) and the degree of a relationship type (RT) in the ERM?

11.2   What is the difference between a relation and a relationship in the RDM?

11.3   Why do we need role-qualified domains in the RDM?

11.4   What are the benefits and disadvantages for each of the two forward engineering alternatives we discussed for translating a Singular Nonidentifying Grouping (SNG) AT from a CDM written in the entity relationship model into an LDM written in the relational data model (RDM)?

11.5   How is the "data item" construct in the network data model (NDM) different from the "domain" concept in the relational data model (RDM)?

11.6   The relational data model (RDM) needs to use keys, but the network data model (NDM) and hierarchical data model (HDM) do not use keys. Why?

11.7   Why does the network data model (NDM) need to use dummy/linking members?

11.8   How is a virtual link type (VLT) in the hierarchical data model (HDM) different from a link type or a virtual record type in the HDM?

11.9   What is the most obvious difference between a class in the object-oriented data model (OODM) and a relation in the relational data model (RDM)?

12

TRADITIONAL DDBE ARCHITECTURES

In most large organizations, information that is vital to business operations does not reside on a single computer system; instead, this information is scattered across many diverse systems. This distribution of information is more the result of mergers and acquisitions than any corporate strategy or plan. When a large company subsumes several smaller companies, it also inherits the information systems that these smaller companies own. In most cases, these systems do not fit neatly together—often, the database systems are incompatible, the same information is stored in multiple places using different representations, and the level of quality across these systems is inconsistent. The larger company, therefore, is faced with the challenge of application and information integration across these preexisting, incompatible systems that are expected to have inconsistent and duplicated data. If the company in this scenario decides to build a new system in an attempt to address the integration challenges we just described, what kind of system should the company build? This chapter provides some insight into the traditional, architectural alternatives suitable for this task.

As we discussed in Chapters 10 and 11, there are several ways to categorize data modeling and data storage techniques. Similarly, there are multiple ways to categorize **database management systems (DBMSs)**. There are even different techniques for categorizing the different infrastructures and architectures on which these **database environments (DBEs)** are built. In Section 12.1, we will present one such technique, based on the taxonomy we introduced in Section 1.4 of Chapter 1. Before we do that, however, it would be useful to revisit why we prefer to use the term "DBE" in this book, rather than the term "DBMS." In Section 1.1.4, we introduced the concept of a DBE as a way to focus on the similarities between different database implementations, while ignoring any potential differences in their requirements, abilities, or limitations. For example, we said that even though a DBMS is a useful tool, there are times when we do not need all of its power or complexity. Therefore, we developed our own

Distributed Database Management Systems by Saeed K. Rahimi and Frank S. Haug
Copyright © 2010 the IEEE Computer Society

vocabulary. This new term can now safely be used to identify a subsystem within our architecture that would be satisfied by a DBMS, but could also be satisfied by something much less powerful than a DBMS or by something much greater than a mere DBMS. In other words, we introduced this term because the traditional term had too many nonstandard usages and unintended implications and ambiguities.

We introduce our taxonomy-based categorization technique for similar reasons—we think that the nomenclature used by other categorization techniques is unintentionally laden with implications and ambiguities, due in part to the lack of standard definitions for the fundamental terms being used. For example, the term "distributed database management system" has traditionally been used in two distinctly different ways. In the first usage, the term "DDBMS" refers generically to any architecture that supports distributed data. Therefore, it is valid to say that "a federated database system is one example of a DDBMS, and a multidatabase system is another example of a DDBMS." However, in its second (and still traditional) usage, the term "DDBMS" is interpreted as the name of a specific architectural approach for implementing a distributed database. The architecture to which this second usage refers is radically different from, and incompatible with, many of the other architectural alternatives. Therefore, it is also valid to say that "the architecture for a federated database system is completely inappropriate and incompatible with any implementation of a DDBMS." It is difficult to discuss the generic architectural issues across these two architectures when both interpretations of "DDBMS" are being used. Similarly, it is potentially confusing to explain how a system with multiple databases is not necessarily the same as a multidatabase system because the former does not meet all of the necessary architectural requirements. Therefore, as discussed in Chapter 1, we will use the term **DDBE**, rather than the generic usage of "DDBMS," to encompass all architectures that support distributed data—we will try to use only the second interpretation of "DDBMS." We believe that this will make it less confusing to discuss DDBE architectural issues.

In Section 12.1, we will apply our taxonomy-based categorization technique to the traditional DDBE architectures. In Section 12.2, we will consider a different, more traditional categorization technique, apply it to the same traditional architectures we considered in Section 12.1, and discuss how these two techniques compare with each other. In Section 12.3, we will discuss DDBE development alternatives for the traditional architectures that we have now categorized. Next, we will focus on the deployment considerations and integration challenges for these architectures. The remainder of the chapter will focus on examples and experiments that demonstrate many of the concepts covered in the other sections.

12.1 APPLYING OUR TAXONOMY TO TRADITIONAL DDBE ARCHITECTURES

For all of the architectures discussed in this chapter (and most of the book), we are looking at distributed DBEs (DDBEs). Often, we will compare them to a centralized DBE (CDBE) in order to highlight the similarities while recognizing the differences. A DDBE does not necessarily require more than one machine—the distinction is that the components or subsystems (COSs), including the databases (DBs), are capable of being deployed across multiple systems. In our classification, we use the term "DDBE" to refer to any system implementing a distributed database, including all of the systems traditionally known as DDBMSs, multidatabases (MDBs), and federated databases (FDBs). Examples of MDB and FDB experimental systems include DDTS [Devor82][Dwyer87], Mermaid [Templeton86], SDD-1 [Bernstein80], and Multibase ([Landers82], [Landers86]). Without further qualification, the terms "DBE," "CDBE," and "DDBE" do not imply anything specific about the architecture or implementation. Similarly, we cannot determine to which taxonomic group (taxon) the system belongs from just these abstract terms. In the next sections, we will apply our taxonomy to three specific, traditional architectures: the DDBMS architecture, the MDBs architecture, and the FDBs architecture.

12.1.1 Classifying the Traditional DDBMS Architecture

The DDBMS architecture (meaning the second, traditional interpretation) can be classified in many ways, but we will look at how it fits within our taxonomy first, before we discuss any of the other classification methods. In this architecture, the DDBE consists of several Sub-DBEs (S-DBEs) networked together. The S-DBE's only purpose in this architecture is to serve the DDBE as a whole. In other words, the S-DBEs do not allow independent access from outside the DDBE. For this reason, it could be argued that the S-DBEs are quite different from local database management systems (LDBMSs). Instead, the S-DBEs act more like the **Data Accessors** or the **Data Getters** we discussed in Chapter 1 (without any application processor to support outside requests). For example, even if the S-DBEs provided a query processor and a command processor, it would not be LDBMSs. Typically, LDBMSs would provide one or more interfaces to allow both users and applications direct access to the data contained in their databases.

12.1.1.1 The COS-DAD Level The first level in the taxonomy is the COS-DAD level. Here, we group all the components and subsystems together (ignoring the differences between them) and focus on how distributed the deployment **can be** within the architecture. For the traditional DDBMS architecture, we have several databases and several S-DBEs. Each S-DBE is typically deployed at the same site as the database or databases that it manages, but otherwise, all the COSs can be deployed in a highly distributed fashion. The data stored inside the DBE can also be highly distributed (fragmented, replicated, or merely located on different S-DBEs).

12.1.1.2 The COS-COO Level The second level in the taxonomy is the COS-COO level. Here, we look at how closed or open the various components and subsystems are. For the traditional DDBMS architecture, we have essentially implemented the system from scratch. Therefore, this architecture is completely open. This is a great advantage, since it means that we can always view and modify the implementation and interface details for any COS in the architecture. However, it also means that in order to implement this architecture, we probably need to write everything ourselves—which can be a monumental task unless we limit the functionality that we will support. For example, we might have restrictions on replication, fragmentation, or even the transactions and write operations—all in an attempt to make the implementation more practical (and possible).

12.1.1.3 The SAD-VIS Level The third level in the taxonomy is the SAD-VIS level. Here, we focus on the schema and the data for all things stored in the DDBE—in particular, we will focus on the **visibility** (ability to access). Since the DBs in this architecture (and S-DBEs) are only used to support the DDBMS as a whole, we can have total visibility (TV). If we have TV, then we have both total schema visibility (TSV) and total data visibility (TDV). In other words, there are no hidden data structures and no hidden data content in this architecture. Every data structure stored in the database must be visible to the distributed database administrator (DDBA), because it is impossible to define any data structures from outside the DDBMS—those operations are not allowed in this architecture. Similarly, all data content must be accessible by the DDBA, because it is impossible to load any data content without using the DDBMS. We mentioned in Chapter 1 that we can artificially mandate partial visibility (PV), which means either partial schema visibility (PSV), partial data visibility (PDV), or both PSV and PDV. This is a common practice, especially in relational DBMS environments—in fact, this is one of the primary purposes of the SQL view, namely, to limit the schema and data visible to particular users or applications. Again, this can be artificially mandated (for several good reasons) for the non-DDBA accounts, but strictly speaking, the architecture requires TV for the DDBA.

12.1.1.4 The SAD-CON Level   The fourth, and final, level in the taxonomy is the SAD-CON level. Here, we focus on the visible schema and the visible data for all things stored in the DDBE, and we are mainly concerned with the **degree of control** that the DDBA can exercise. In other words, if the DDBA can perform all possible (valid) schema operations on the visible schema, then we have total schema control (TSC), if the DDBA can do the same for the visible data, then we have total data Control (TDC) and the combination is total control (TC). The partial schema control (PSC), partial data control (PDC), and partial control (PC) are analogous to the previous level's "partial" scenarios. In the traditional DDBMS architecture, we have TC—since partial control would imply that some other environment had control over some piece of schema or data and that is not possible in this architecture. Once again, we could artificially mandate PC for non-DDBA accounts, but the DDBE requires TC for the DDBA.

12.1.1.5 DDBMS Architectural Summary   The schema for the DDBMS is designed top–down in this architecture and components and subsystems are designed and implemented from scratch. The databases, components, and subsystems can be completely distributed within the environment. Because we write the COSs ourselves, and only access the databases through the DDBMS environment, the system is completely open, and the data and schema are completely visible and under the system's control. We can always artificially impose limits or restrictions on the distribution, visibility, or control—but these are not required by the architecture itself.

12.1.2   Classifying the Federated Database Architecture

Another popular architecture is called the federated databases architecture. In this architecture, the DDBE also consists of several Sub-DBEs (S-DBEs) networked together—but unlike the traditional DDBMS architecture, each S-DBE is also an independent (autonomous) DBMS in its own right. Here, each S-DBE **completely supports** independent access from outside the DDBE. Each S-DBE consists of a data processor (DP), and each DP leverages the functionality provided by a local DBMS rather than implementing all of the functionality directly by itself. We can use different DBMSs at different sites, and these DBMSs can use different physical and logical data modeling languages. For example, we can create a federated database by combining relational, network, and hierarchical databases.

12.1.2.1 The COS-DAD Level   The first level in the taxonomy is the COS-DAD level. When we focus on the set of components and subsystems that make up this DDBE and consider how distributed the deployment **can be** within the architecture, we see that the system supports a high degree of distribution. Of course, the COSs contained within the LDBMSs themselves are limited by the LDBMSs architectural requirements and restrictions. Aside from this limitation, the components, subsystems, schema, and data can be widely distributed throughout the environment.

12.1.2.2 The COS-COO Level   The second level in the taxonomy is the COS-COO level. The degree to which a LDBMS is closed or open depends on the actual LDBMSs being used (see Section 1.4.2 in Chapter 1 for further details). The other components are most likely written by us and therefore they are open. Thus, this architecture is at least partially open. If the LDBMSs are not open to us, then we are only partially open—but if the LDBMSs are open to us, then we are completely open. When we are only partially open, it will be difficult for us to implement complex control mechanisms such as new locking or transaction management techniques. However, using existing LDBMSs also means that we do not need to implement the low-level data services (like the Drd-S) or the higher-level services (like the Qry-S) from scratch.

12.1.2.3 The SAD-VIS Level   The third level in the taxonomy is the SAD-VIS level. Because the data stored in each database can be defined and modified by users and applications outside the DDBE, we are more likely to have only partial visibility. Typically, the DDBE will only see some of the schema and only some of the data. In other words, there will probably be hidden data structures and hidden data content in this architecture that even the DDBA cannot access through the DDBE. While it is possible to create a federated database with total visibility, that is not a very common or realistic scenario—usually there are existing applications that control and use the data outside the DDBE, and these applications usually do not want to relinquish their data or schema completely.

12.1.2.4 The SAD-CON Level   The fourth, and final, level in the taxonomy is the SAD-CON level. Recall that we focus on **only** the visible schema and the visible data for all things stored in the DDBE here. Because we have partial visibility in the previous level, due to other applications using and controlling much of the data in the local databases, the DDBA will probably also have limited control over the visible schema and data. Often, the non-DDBE applications will be the only place where some of the semantic rules protecting the data's integrity are implemented, which means that the data in the federated database is often read-only from the DDBE perspective. Similarly, any attempts to modify the schema through the DDBE could have direct repercussions for these applications. Therefore, in the traditional federated database architecture, we usually have PC—for both the schema and the data.

12.1.2.5 Federated Database Architectural Summary   The schema for the federated database is designed bottom–up and S-DBEs are implemented using local DBMSs that are integrated into a larger distributed environment. The DDBE can support a wide range of distribution options, with the exception of the components and subsystems contained in the LDBMSs themselves. The higher level COSs are completely open while the openness of the lower-level COSs depends on the openness of the LDBMSs being used. These LDBMSs usually share only some of their schema and only some of their data—while retaining their autonomy and their ability to provide access to their own non-DDBE users and applications. Because of this, the visibility and control given to the DDBE is often limited and frequently does not include the ability to insert, update, or delete data. Similarly, the DDBE is often prevented from altering schema within the S-DBEs. Schema changes in the DDBE itself are allowed for the global constructs only, allowing the creation, modification, and deletion of the mapping details between global constructs and the local constructs that implement them.

12.1.3 Classifying the Nonfederated Database Architecture

Another popular architecture is called the nonfederated database architecture. This architecture is similar to both the federated database architecture and the DDBMS architecture, but, of course, it is also different from both of them as well. In this architecture, the DDBE also consists of several Sub-DBEs (S-DBEs) networked together. Like the DDBMS architecture, each S-DBE is not an independent (autonomous) DBMS—the S-DBE's sole purpose here is to serve the DDBE. As a result, each S-DBE does not support independent access from outside the DDBE. Each S-DBE consists of a data processor (DP), and like the federated database architecture, each DP leverages the functionality provided by a local DBMS rather than implementing all of the functionality directly by itself. We can create a nonfederated database by combining relational, network, and hierarchical databases. Similar to federated databases, the global schema for a nonfederated database is created bottom–up.

12.1.3.1 The COS-DAD Level   For nonfederated databases, the COS-DAD level is exactly the same as COS-DAD for federated databases. Components distribution and deployment are only limited by the LDBMSs within the architecture and restrictions that local systems impose. Once again, the COSs implemented by each LDBMS are not under our control, and therefore their distribution and deployment alternatives are limited by the LDBMS vendor, rather than the architecture itself. For example, we cannot choose to relocate the subsystems implemented within a particular LDBMS (like the query optimization service), unless the vendor provides this ability. Similarly, if a particular LDBMS vendor does not support deployment on the UNIX operating system, then our DDBE cannot have an S-DBE using that LDBMS deployed on the UNIX operating system either.

12.1.3.2 The COS-COO Level   The second level in the taxonomy is the COS-COO level. Again, since a nonfederated database is created from a set of S-DBES implemented on top of LDBMSs, the degree to which an S-DBE is closed or open (as discussed in Section 1.4.2 in Chapter 1) depends on the actual LDBMSs being used. As a result, this architecture is at least partially open. If the LDBMSs are open to us, then the S-DBEs and the DDBE itself are completely open. When we are only partially open, it will be difficult for us to implement complex control mechanisms such as new locking or transaction management techniques. Similar to federated databases, using existing LDBMSs means that we do not need to implement the low-level data services (like the Drd-S) or the higher-level services (like the Qry-S) from scratch.

12.1.3.3 The SAD-VIS Level   The third level in the taxonomy is the SAD-VIS level. In nonfederated databases, because the data stored in each database cannot be defined or modified by users and applications outside the DDBE, we can choose to have total visibility. Typically, the DDBE limits what a DDBE user sees in a local DBE by using views. Therefore, users typically only see some of the schema and only some of the data. In other words, we will probably choose to hide some data structures and data content from the end-users, giving them only PV—but this is not a strict, architectural requirement in the way that it was for the federated database architecture. The DDBA, on the other hand, can access the entire schema and data content of each S-DBE through the DDBE, and therefore we have TV for the DDBA.

12.1.3.4 The SAD-CON Level   The final level in the taxonomy is the SAD-CON level. Recall that we focus on **only** the visible schema and the visible data for all things stored in the DDBE at this level. As mentioned in Section 12.1.3.3, we could have total visibility to the schema and data. That is because in a nonfederated database the local DBEs do not serve applications outside the DDBE environment. This also means that we can have total control of local schema and data. Once again, in reality, the DDBA may limit what each global user sees and controls by imposing views (and granting or revoking access to individual users or to groups of users) that hide portions of schema and data from these global users. Therefore, any attempts to modify the schema through the limited view of a DDBE user or application might fail for the same reasons that access to nonvisible contents through a local view might fail, but as an administrator, the DDBA would have TC.

12.1.3.5 Nonfederated Database Architectural Summary   The schema for the non-federated database is designed bottom–up and local DBMSs used by each S-DBE are integrated into a larger distributed environment. The DDBE can support wide distribution options, with the exception of the components and subsystems contained in the LDBMSs themselves. The higher-level COSs are completely open and the openness of the lower-level COSs depends on the openness of the LDBMSs. In a nonfederated database, these LDBMSs only serve the overall DBE, and not any other applications or users outside the DDBE. As a result, while the local DBEs retain their autonomy, they usually provide total visibility and control to both the schema and the data content. Because of this, the visibility and control given to the DDBE is not limited; But the ability to insert, update, or delete data may be limited in some situations where the local DBE imposes some restriction and does not provide a totally open interface.

12.2 THE MDBS ARCHITECTURE CLASSIFICATIONS

A good representative of other classification techniques for DDBE architectures can be found in a survey by Sheth and Larson [Sheth90]. What we call a DDBE in our taxonomy is called a multidatabase system (MDBS) in their classification system. In a MDBS, each S-DBE is called an LDBMS and is actually limited to being a CDBE. This is different from our nomenclature and taxonomy—although all the traditional architectures we have considered so far also have this limitation; the architectures we will discuss in Chapter 13 will use other DDBEs as their S-DBEs. According to Sheth and Larson, a MDBS can be either a nonfederated database (NFDB) system or a federated database (FDB) system. There are several differences between these two subcategories, but the primary distinction is whether the component database systems (S-DBEs) can be used outside the MDBS. In an FDB, the components can freely be used outside the FDB, while component database systems participating in an NFDB cannot be used in this way. This distinction makes the component LDBMS systems in an FDB autonomous while they are nonautonomous in an NFDB. Therefore, the FDB architecture provides partial visibility and partial control while the NFDB MDBS architecture allows total visibility and total control. An example of an NFDB is the UNIBASE architecture [Brzezinski84]. The COSs within FDBs can be coupled to each other loosely or tightly, Sheth and Larson [Sheth90] define a loosely coupled FDB as one that provides its users with an imported, global view of the schemas defined by the local systems; while a tightly coupled FDB provides its users access to an integrated, global schema. The difference in coupling is essentially the distinction between an imported view and an integrated view. An example of a loosely coupled FDB is the MRDSM architecture [Litwin87]. Tightly coupled FDBs are further divided into single-federation systems, such as DDTS [Dwyer87], versus systems with multiple federations, for example, Mermaid [Templeton86]. In a single–federation system, all of the DDBE users have access to a single, integrated schema. In a multiple-federation FDB, there are multiple, integrated schemas. How do these classifications map to our taxonomy? Table 12.1 illustrates the mapping for the high-level categories. Other classifications have also been proposed that focus on whether or not database systems and data models are homogeneous or heterogeneous. Yet others focus on degree of distribution. Interested readers are referred to ([Özsu99], [Litwin87]), and [Ram89].

TABLE 12.1 Mapping the MDBS Classifications into Our Taxonomy

MDBS Category Name	Example Architectures	Mapping to Our Taxonomy
MDBS	Any generic DDBMS architecture	A DDBE (no further classification)
DDBMS	The traditional DDBMS architecture	A DDBE that is fully distributed and completely open, with total visibility (TV) and total control (TC)
FDB	The MRDSM architecture, the DDTS architecture, and the Mermaid architecture	A DDBE that is fully distributed and partially open, with partial visibility (PSV and PDV) and partial control (PSC and PDC)
NFDB	The UNIBASE architecture	A DDBE that is fully distributed and partially open, with total visibility (TV) and total control (TC)

12.3 APPROACHES FOR DEVELOPING A DDBE

There are two main approaches for developing a DDBE—the first approach uses a top–down methodology to create the entire system from scratch, while the second uses a bottom–up methodology to integrate the DDBE from its component S-DBEs. The top–down or bottom–up approaches apply to both software and database schema creation.

Before delving into the details of the top–down and bottom–up alternatives, we will review the architecture of a DDBE.

12.3.1 The Top–Down Methodology

In the top–down approach, we develop the entire set of DDBE software components from scratch. In this approach, we design, develop, test, and deploy all required software components such as the user interface, transaction management, recovery and fault tolerance, and optimization services. We can choose to use any programming languages or development environments we like for these tasks. In effect, we act as the DDBE software vendor. Taken in the extreme, this is not a good idea. In practice, we feel that this approach is only acceptable for experimental or research-oriented DDBE projects. This approach is simple to implement in the sense that it avoids the headaches normally associated with integrating new software with existing DBMS software. However, we must be willing to invest the time and money necessary to develop all the required software components, and we must have the necessary skills and experience to implement this DDBE project by ourselves.

12.3.1.1 Creating the GCS Top–Down When a DDBE is created top–down, the global conceptual schema (GCS) is created first. Next, the requirements for local conceptual schemas (LCSs) are determined, and the global constructs are distributed and deployed into LCSs as needed. Information is loaded into the local databases as specified by the local system's LCS. Therefore, the DDBE has total visibility and total ownership and control over the information in the system. Distribution and fragmentation design decisions we discussed in Chapter 2 will be used to create the LCS for each local system. Figure 12.1 depicts creation of a set of local conceptual schemas from a global conceptual schema.

12.3.1.2 Developing the Software Top–Down In a top–down approach, we develop all the necessary software components according to a predetermined set of requirements. The top–down strategy is typically used for experimental and research situations where total control is necessary.

12.3.2 Bottom–Up Methodology

In addition to inherent philosophical differences between top–down and bottom–up methodologies, it is important to mention that in a top–down implementation the DDBE ends up with only one GCS—the original GCS that we started with. By contrast, in the bottom–up implementation, the GCS is created by integrating portions of participating LCSs, and, as a result, we have the option of creating more than one GCS. We can create multiple GCSs to satisfy the needs of different groups of users and different applications.

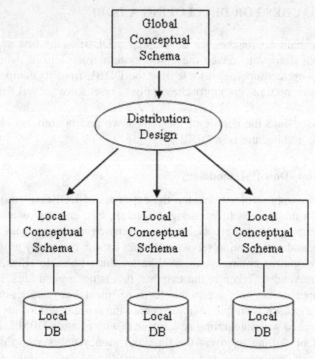

Figure 12.1 Top–down information architecture design.

12.3.2.1 Creating the GCS Bottom–Up When we use the bottom–up approach to implement a GCS, each local **database administrator (DBA)** decides what degree of visibility and control to allow the DDBE to have. Each DBA defines a subschema for each local database. Each subschema identifies which parts of the schema and data will be made visible to the DDBE. Each subschema (called an **export** schema [Sheth90]) is then integrated with the other relevant subschemas from the other local databases in the environment. This integration results in the creation of a single integrated GCS (called the **unified** schema) as implemented in DDTS [Dwyer87] or the creation of multiple unified schemas as implemented in Mermaid [Templeton86]. See Figure 12.2 for an example of a DDBE with multiple unified schemas.

12.3.2.2 Developing the Software Bottom–Up In the bottom–up software development approach, we utilize the database management system functionality of the underlying S-DBEs (usually CDBEs) to develop software capabilities for distributed concurrency control, distributed fault tolerance, distributed commit, distributed query optimization, and distributed semantic integrity control. Any additional software functionality that we need to develop must use, or at least interface with, the capabilities that the underlying S-DBEs provide. In order to accommodate this, the bottom–up architecture typically uses the local DBMS software to manage the local data. The DP for each S-DBE interfaces with the LDBMS software to run the local transactions that were delegated to it by the AP. Figure 12.3 depicts the software architecture for this approach.

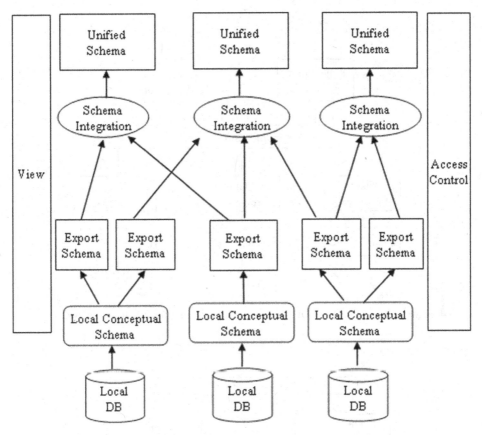

Figure 12.2   Bottom–up information architecture design.

12.4   DEPLOYMENT OF DDBE SOFTWARE

Once written, the software components of a DDBE need to be deployed across the different computer systems within our environment. These computer systems may run different operating systems and support different DBMS software. In order to deploy a software component on one of these target computer systems, we must compile, link, and install it using the facilities provided by the underlying platform (the facilities satisfying the fundamental DDBE Platform requirements, which we will discuss in Section 14.2). In a well-designed architecture, we can reuse the same source code for several different component implementations and deployments (ideally, across the entire set of target operating systems and DBMSs in our environment). In other words, the design and implementation of the components have been done with portability to different systems in mind, as we will discuss in Section 14.2.1.3. Figure 12.4 depicts an example deployment, where a CP and an AP have been deployed to both a Windows system and a UNIX-based system. In this example, since the CP has been deployed on both systems, users on either system can access the information contained within the other system (from both the Oracle and SQL Server databases collectively).

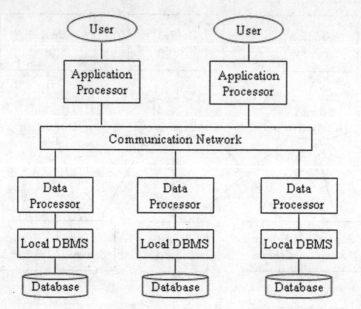

Figure 12.3   High-level DDBE software architecture for a bottom−up system.

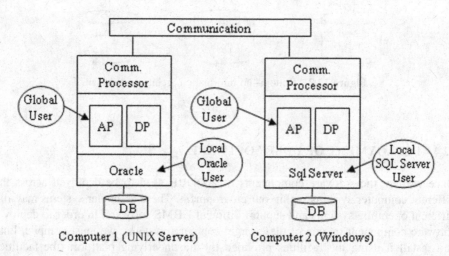

Figure 12.4   Example of packaging software.

Figure 12.5 depicts a different deployment, for a different environment, where a DP has been deployed to a mainframe system, but there is no AP deployed within that system. In this case, the users who login to the mainframe do not have access to the data in the Oracle database, but users on the UNIX machine do have access to both the local data within the Oracle database and the data within the DB2 database deployed on the mainframe.

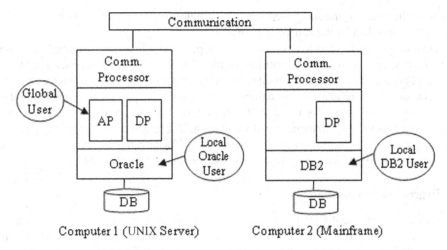

Figure 12.5   Another example of packaging software.

12.5   INTEGRATION CHALLENGES

Integration and control of existing information systems brings up a new set of challenges. There are several traditional DDBE architectural alternatives that run on top of a set of existing information systems. These systems are collectively known as multidatabases (MDBs). The DDTS architecture [Devor82], Multibase architecture [Landers82], Mermaid architecture [Templeton86], and SDD-1 architecture [Bernstein80] are all examples of experimental multidatabase systems.

There are three fundamental, yet conflicting, requirements that make the development of a MDB system more difficult.

1. *Transparency.* An MDB needs to provide the illusion that all data in the environment is integrated and controlled by one DBMS. It must be able to provide for location, replication, fragmentation, network, hardware, software, and DBMS transparencies.

2. *Heterogeneity.* Local DBMSs use different approaches to handling the databases they control. For example, one DBMS may use locking for concurrency control while another system may utilize timestamping; one DBMS may use the immediate commit approach while another system may use the deferred commit approach; and so on.

3. *DBMS Autonomy.* Local DBMSs need to work autonomously. It is not feasible to change the characteristics of the underlying DBMSs to facilitate integration, and the autonomy of these systems must be preserved.

A DDBE runs distributed transactions against the collection of data sources, each of which is controlled by a CDBE. The first challenge in developing a DDBE system is the creation of an integrated global conceptual schema (GCS) based on the underlying local conceptual schemas (LCSs). Once we have created the GCS, we need to address the end-user, access-related issues. For example, we need to answer questions such as,

"Should the users of the integrated schema be able to not only query but also modify the underlying data in the source systems?"

Therefore, a DDBE has to overcome three types of challenges—schema integration, data access, and software integration/interface issues. We group schema integration and data access under information integration challenges and discuss software interface issues under software integration challenges. Since software and information integration pose a lot of challenges for the developers of a DDBE, the right level of integration that fits the users' requirements must be chosen. There are many levels (or degrees) of integration for existing database applications. These range from a nonintegrated system, to a fully integrated system, and systems that are in between.

Degrees of Integration

- In a nonintegrated DDBE, existing systems are not integrated. These stand-alone systems have been designed and developed in isolation from the other systems in the environment and have possibly been acquired by the organization as a result of mergers and acquisitions. Data redundancies, data inconsistencies, and the lack of an integrated view of the data and applications in the environment are all major headaches for the organizations attempting to integrate these systems. There are some systems that cannot (or should not) be integrated: for example, legacy systems that use data storage mechanisms that are not, per se, a database, or systems implemented using languages that do not interface well with the newer languages used in application development today.

- When an organization's systems do not inherently lend themselves to integration, total integration is required. Doing a total integration requires the organization to invest the money to redevelop the functionality. This means redesigning and reimplementing the organization's applications (and their required databases) from scratch, in a totally integrated DDBE, using the top–down methodology we discussed earlier. The existing systems are used while the new integrated DDBE is being developed. To test the new system, both the legacy and new development are run in parallel to make sure the results from the new system are correct during a trial period. The roll over from the legacy systems to the new integrated system can be attempted only after the new system passes all such tests. The main issue with total integration is the cost. Companies have invested huge amounts of resources in developing the applications and collecting information for their mission critical systems. Therefore, most of the time, an organization will attempt to develop a partially integrated DDBE before attempting the totally integrated solution.

- In a partially integrated DDBE, some, but not all, of the applications' functionality and data are integrated. Partial integration attempts to streamline inefficient functions in existing systems and/or create new functionality that does not exist in the current systems. In this case, existing systems continue to remain in production while the new functionality is being developed. The underlying databases are kept intact to allow the existing applications to operate correctly. An integrated view of the information contained in existing databases is created as a GCS. Then new functionality is developed against the GCS. If the functions that are developed are to replace existing functions, a crossover procedure, as explained in the previous paragraph, is used. The new functionalities are put in production after process testing and verification. A benefit of using partial integration to replace existing functionality is the smaller cost of development since existing data is used as the base. Also, partial integration can provide a path to total integration by replacing the older systems' functionality over time.

12.5.1 Software Integration Issues

Integration between the DDBE software layer and the component DBMSs that make up the environment is a difficult task. The reasons, as discussed earlier, are the heterogeneity, incompatibility, and autonomy of the local systems. As an example, consider a Microsoft Excel spreadsheet as a data source for a DDBE. Now assume that the DDBE software architecture intends to implement distributed concurrency control using locking. There are two types of challenges that the architect has to address. The first challenge is mapping the spreadsheet rows and columns to similar rows and columns within a relational view, assuming that the end-user of the DDBE is using the relational data model (which we discussed in Section 11.1) as the canonical data model for all the underlying information sources. The second challenge is locking the right granule of the spreadsheet data when it is required by the distributed concurrency control service.

The first challenge is not as difficult to satisfy (see Section 12.5.2.2 on schema mapping later in this chapter). The latter challenge, however, is more problematic. As discussed in Chapter 5, row-level locking is the desired granularity for concurrency control. This requires that a row in the Excel spreadsheet be locked before it is read or written and unlocked only when the transaction is ready to commit. In Microsoft Excel, access to the contents of a spreadsheet can be controlled programmatically using Visual Basic for Applications (VBA). Using VBA, the DDBE programmer can lock and unlock a desired number of cells within a sheet for as long as required. The programmer also needs to add capabilities to add, read, and modify the cell contents. Once such functionality is developed, the VBA program can be integrated with the software of the local DDBE agent at the site where the file is deployed.

As another example, let's now consider implementing the three-phase commit protocol in a DDBE where all underlying data is controlled by commercial off-the-shelf (COTS) relational DBMS products. In this case, we need to be able to control (and to some degree modify) the way the commit protocol of the underlying commercial DBMSs work. As far as controlling the underlying commit functionality of the local systems is concerned, these systems are mostly closed. Unless the DBMS vendor has made provisions for supporting a distributed transaction commit operation, there is no way that this commercial DBMS can be told to put a transaction in the pre-commit state (since this state does not exist within its centralized commit protocol). Even implementing the two-phase commit protocol can cause issues for some DBMSs. Suppose that the DBMS we are using does not support the concept of deferred commit; that is, the DBMS commits a transaction as soon as it finishes executing it. In these types of systems, it is not possible to implement two-phase commit, since delaying the commitment of a transaction in a local system (until the global transaction wants to commit it) is not possible.

Where do restrictions and limitations like these leave the developers of the DDBE software? One thing is very clear—in most cases, disregarding the accessibility of these required functions at the local level when designing a DDBE system does not work. Some requirements must be lessened, compromises must be made, and simplifying assumptions are necessary. However, these concessions lead to the development of DDBE systems that may not necessarily provide all the "bells and whistles" that a fully integrated DDBE would provide.

The software integration challenges stem from the following facts:

- Local DBMSs are heterogeneous—they differ in their data model, their data storage methodology, their support for transaction processing, their support for concurrency control, and their fault tolerance support.

- Local DBMS systems are autonomous—they do not necessarily support the concept of integration since they are rigid functionally; that is, it is difficult, if not impossible, to change the local DBMS support functions to suit the distributed DDBE's desired functionality.

- Not all local DBMSs support standards suggested for integration such as XA (see Chapters 14–19) for externalization of transaction support, for example.

- A truly heterogeneous DDBE system incorporates three levels of control over global transactions. At the highest level of the hierarchy, the Global Transaction Manager (GTM) decides on how a transaction must be divided to run on multiple sites. Within each site, the Local Transaction Manager (LTM) decides on how to run the transaction on multiple DBMSs that it supports locally. Within each DBMS, at the lowest level of control, transactions are processed as if they were local. Coordinating the activities of these three layers of software requires well-defined and accepted protocols that guarantee the consistency of the database with or without failures.

12.5.2   Schema Integration Issues

As mentioned earlier, the GCS is the main component of the GDD. It provides for an integrated view of all the data in the local systems' conceptual views. There are two issues with GCS in a bottom–up design approach. The first deals with the creation of the GCS from component LCSs. The second issue is with the maintenance of the GCS once it has been created. We will address the maintenance issue first in Section 12.5.2.1. The creation issue, which is more involved, is discussed in Section 12.5.2.2.

12.5.2.1   GCS Maintenance Issues   When maintaining a GCS, our primary concern is to making sure that its contents are synchronized with the local conceptual schemas. This requirement does not pose a major concern if we assume that underlying local database conceptual schemas do not change. In real life, however, this is not an acceptable assumption. New structures are added to existing local databases; existing structures are modified; and existing structures are deleted from the local database schemas on an ongoing basis. Each of these schema changes needs to be reflected in the GCS to make sure that a distributed user's view of the underlying local systems is accurate. For example, let's assume that a distributed user's view includes a table called EMP with columns ID, FNAME, MI, LNAME, ADDRESS, and SAL. If the column ADDRESS is removed from the underlying local database's schema, the GCS must be updated to reflect the fact that ADDRESS no longer exists in the global view for this user. How do we maintain this synchronicity? The answer depends on how the GCS is implemented.

Logical Implementation of GCS   We can implement the GCS as a logical view of information in the local conceptual schemas. In this implementation, the GCS does not physically exist. A global view of the information is created from the LCSs as needed. This approach is similar to the bootstrap approach that a computer operating system takes. When the computer is first started, it loads a small program from the disk (boot sector) into the main memory. This program then loads the rest of operating system and other necessary programs to bring the computer to full functionality. In a logical implementation of the GCS, we load a small amount of information such as site names, IP addresses, and number of tables into the GCS at each site that participates in the distribution. In this case, the first step when executing a distributed user's query against the DDBE is to retrieve the local conceptual schema information for those constructs accessible to the user. After this discovery step, the user can employ this schema information to actually submit the request to the DDBE. Since no physical copy of the GCS is maintained in this approach, there is no need to synchronize its contents with the local conceptual schemas at the local sites.

Physical Implementation of GCS   We can also implement the GCS physically. In this approach, the GCS contents are maintained physically and are accessible to the GTM for lookup when a global query is processed. Maintaining a physical GCS brings up a new set of issues. The main issue with a physical implementation of the GCS is its currency.

MAINTAINING CURRENCY FOR A PHYSICAL GCS   This copy of the GCS is kept in sync with the local sites' LCSs either manually or automatically. In manual synchronization, the DBA will update the GCS when the underlying LCS information is changed. The issue with this approach is the fact that the GCS may contain outdated information if manual updates are not done frequently enough for systems with many changes to their local conceptual schemas. The DBA could set up batch-updates for synchronizing the GCS contents as well. These jobs run periodically and compare the contents of the GCS with the information from the local systems and update the GCS as needed. Depending on the frequency of schema changes to the local systems, the sync job can run daily, weekly, or less frequently.

There are two extreme deployment alternatives for implementing a physical GCS. At one end of the spectrum, the GCS is implemented completely at one site. At the other end of the spectrum, the GCS is implemented as multiple copies—perhaps some copies are merely subsets of the GCS—at multiple sites. We refer to the first implementation as a centralized implementation and the second as a distributed implementation.

Centralized Implementation of a Physical GCS   In a centralized implementation of a GCS, a single copy of the GCS is physically maintained at one site. The DBA has to decide where the single copy of the GCS is stored. Like any other centralized implementation of control, this implementation of the GCS has advantages and disadvantages. Updating the single copy of the GCS is most efficient since all GCS information is local to one site. On the other hand, since the entire GCS is stored at one site, the site becomes a bottleneck for network traffic from all sites requiring GCS access at runtime. This approach is also less resilient to failures since the failure of the site will cause complete loss of access to the GCS contents. Figure 12.6a illustrates the centralized implementation of the GCS in a three-site system.

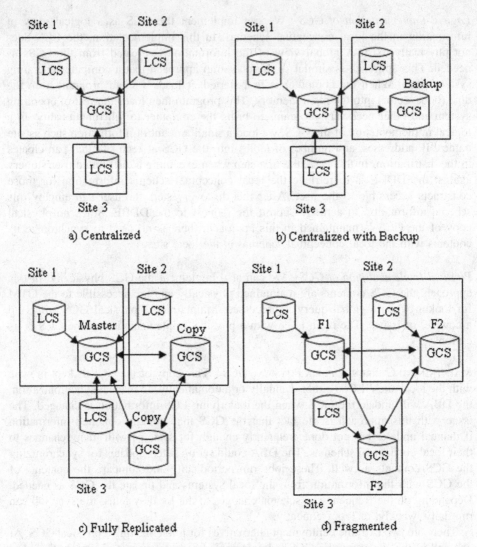

Figure 12.6 Physical GCS implementation alternatives.

Distributed Implementation of a Physical GCS   In a distributed implementation of a GCS, either multiple copies of the entire GCS are created or multiple copies of subsets (fragments) of GCS are created (see Figure 12.6b–d). The simplest form of implementing a distributed GCS is to have a backup copy of the GCS that is kept in sync with the GCS all the time. This copy acts as a "hot" standby copy and can act as the GCS if the main copy fails. To protect against loss of the GCS when a site fails, the standby should be kept at a site different from the main site. We can also create multiple copies of the entire GCS and keep one copy at each site that participates in the DDBE. This approach is called a replicated GCS implementation. Finally, a GCS can be partitioned, with each partition stored at a separate site. Ideally, the GCS partition that pertains to the information on a local site is stored at that site. This implementation of the GCS is called a fragmented GCS. Although there are multiple variations to implementing a distributed GCS, a careful reader realizes that the more distributed the GCS, the more difficult it is to query its contents. As a matter of fact, the distributed implementation of the GCS presents all the problems that we are trying to solve for distributed data access. In other words, when a GCS is distributed, we need to formulate a distributed query that can find the location, replication, and fragmentation information about the underlying data items in the environment prior to processing the actual query. It is therefore questionable that such a complicated distribution approach for the GCS is worth the overhead that the approach puts on the system.

12.5.2.2 GCS Creation Issues   In this section, we explain the issues related to the generation of the GCS. Recall that in the bottom–up approach, the local conceptual schema information from the local databases is used and integrated into a cohesive global conceptual schema. There are many references in the literature that talk about schema integration challenges and provide methodologies for addressing those challenges. Sheth and Larson [Sheth90] and Özsu and Valduriez [Özsu99] have formalized the steps in GCS integration. The steps in these formalisms outline the details for creating a GCS from a set of local conceptual schemas. We encourage interested readers to review these sources. We will merely summarize these steps here for completeness. Then we will use an example to explain the proposed process in the next section. There are three main steps in the process, with Step 3 being further divided into four substeps as outlined below.

Step 1: Translation to a Common Data Model   The DBMS components that make up a DDBE can be homogeneous or heterogeneous. The "homogeneity or heterogeneity" between any two DBMSs depends more on the database's logical data model than the differences in how the DBMSs are implemented or deployed. For example, we consider a DDBE to be homogeneous if, although from different vendors, all the underlying DBMSs use the relational data model. In a heterogeneous environment, the challenge is to translate all the logical data model constructs used into a neutral (common) format before integration. In a homogeneous environment, on the other hand, since all data models are of the same type, the challenge is only in integration.

The relational data model (RDM) and the entity relationship model (ERM) have both been proposed as candidates for the common model. The ERM has been chosen over the RDM by many. The reasons for selecting to use the ERM as the common model are: (1) the ERM is a graphical representation of the schema that is the de-facto standard in database modeling and design; (2) ERM concepts are understood by many database users and designers; (3) the rules for translating relational, network, and hierarchical data models to the ERM and vice versa (see Chapter 11) are well understood; (4) the ERM can better model the real world than the RDM; and (5) translation to the ERM and vice versa can be automated, that is, programmed. Note that we need to write one translator program for each database model that we intend to support as part of the DDBE.

Figure 12.7 depicts the relational schema for a relational database and its translation into the ERM. Note that in this database, although an employee can work only for one department at any given point in time, the employees can work for multiple departments during their tenure. Of course, this model does not capture the situation where the same employee worked for the same department on-again-and-off-again several different

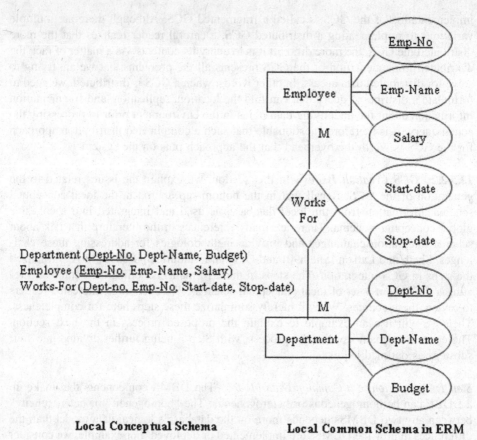

Department (<u>Dept-No</u>, Dept-Name, Budget)
Employee (<u>Emp-No</u>, Emp-Name, Salary)
Works-For (<u>Dept-no, Emp-No</u>, Start-date, Stop-date)

Local Conceptual Schema   **Local Common Schema in ERM**

Figure 12.7   Example of relational to ER translation.

times. The database keeps track of the tenure details by using two date columns that indicate the duration of the time a given employee has been working for a given department. This information in the relational schema is kept in the Works For table. In the ERM, the same information is mapped to the attribute types contained within the relationship type that connects the Employee entity type to the Department entity type. As a result, although we start with three tables in the relational model, we end up with two entity types in the ERM. In addition to mappings of the table names to entity type names and column names to attribute type names, the additional fact that the Works For relationship type is mapped to the Works For table needs to be maintained. An auxiliary database is used for this purpose (see later discussion)

Step 2: Export Schema Generation   Local DBAs have control over the local schema and data. They may or may not wish to share all of the information under the control of the local schema with the DDBE users. The data that a local DBA is willing to share with the DDBE users is typically a subset of the locally stored data. This subset schema is called the export schema. Designers of a DDBE negotiate with local DBAs to define the structures that will be included in any export schema. A DBA may generate one or more export schemas. When multiple export schemas are generated from the same site, they may be disjoint or they may overlap in their contents. In most cases, the export schemas have a limited scope as compared to the local conceptual schema. The limited view of an export schema creates challenges with respect to transaction management. For instance, if all mandatory ("NOT NULL") columns of a given table are not included in the exported schema, users may not be able to update, delete, or insert information at the global level.

The limited view of an export schema may invalidate modifications to the entire row, due to invalidation of the consistency constraints attached to the columns that are not part of the export schema or constraints that are associated with the primary key or referential integrity of a foreign key. We referred to this type of visibility as partial (PV). Even if all columns of the tables are included in the view that a DBA shares, the DBA may still decide to limit the access to only query and not allow modifications. This gives the DDBE users limited ownership, which we categorized under POC. Export schema generation is the second step in GCS integration. Note that export schema generation is done after all source data models have been translated into the ERM. This allows us to write the schema generation tool once and use it regardless of the source data model.

Figure 12.8 illustrates how the example ER schema in Figure 12.7 is used in generating a component export schema in the ERM. In this example, the DBA does not want to share the entire local database with the DDBE users. The DBA would use a tool to graphically pick and choose which entity types and which attribute types contained within those entity types should be part of the export schema. In this case, the DBA restricts access to sensitive information such as salary and department budget. Also, the primary key of the Department entity type is not included in the export schema. The elimination of the primary key from an entity type in the export schema raises issues with respect to updating the database through the view that is based on this export schema, as explained above. Additionally, the elimination of the primary key from the Department entity type causes the generator to combine the information into a single entity type called "Employee." Generation information such as this is kept in the auxiliary database.

Figure 12.9 depicts the fact that our export schema does not contain all of the attributes in the original local schema. The empty ovals in the export indicate what attributes are missing from the original schema.

Each local component database's conceptual schema will be put through the same process until all component export schemas have been generated. Figure 12.10 depicts these two steps combined. As shown in this figure, translation to the ERM and export schema generation steps are not 100% automatic and need interaction from the DBA.

Step 3: Schema Integration   Schema integration is the last step in the generation of the GCS from its component export schemas. The challenges in this step are due to overlaps, similarities, differences, conflicts, inconsistencies, and interpretations of each export schema that is to be integrated. This is the most time-consuming and error-prone step in the process. The difficulty of this step does not have a technical source but stems from not understanding the contents, the intentions, and the semantics of structures contained in each export schema. That is why this step cannot be completely automated. Stepwise refinement of the GCS is required with the DBAs and the DDBE designers working together to make sure that the outcome is correct. The integration step is divided into four substeps.

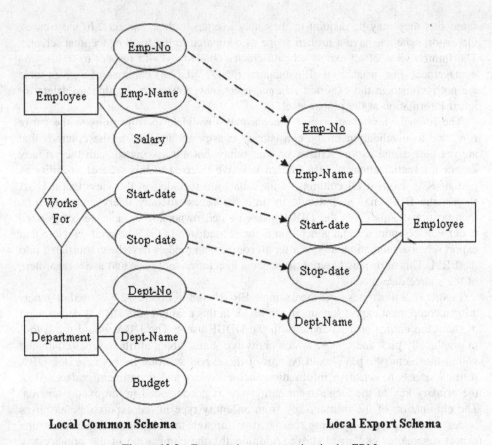

Local Common Schema   **Local Export Schema**

Figure 12.8   Export schema generation in the ERM.

STEP 3.1: PREINTEGRATION   In this step, a designer decides on the order and nature of integration of export schemas. The most common approach for integration is the ladder approach. In this approach, the designer starts with the first export schema as the GCS. Other export schemas are integrated one at a time to complete the process. Figure 12.11 shows the use of ladder integration. The current integrated schema (the first schema when we start) is integrated with a new export schema and generates the revised integrated schema. When we need to integrate another schema, we use the revised integrated schema as the current schema and create a new integrated schema. This process is repeated until all schemas have been integrated.

STEP 3.2: DISCOVERY   In this step, the designer looks for similarities, differences, conflicts, and overlap in the two export schemas being analyzed.
   In this step, the goal is to identify:

- Overlap—where a structure in one schema is a subset of a structure in the second schema
- Naming conflicts—where two objects are synonyms or homonyms
- Structural conflicts—where two constructs have incompatible mappings: for example, this occurs when the same entity type has a primary key in one schema

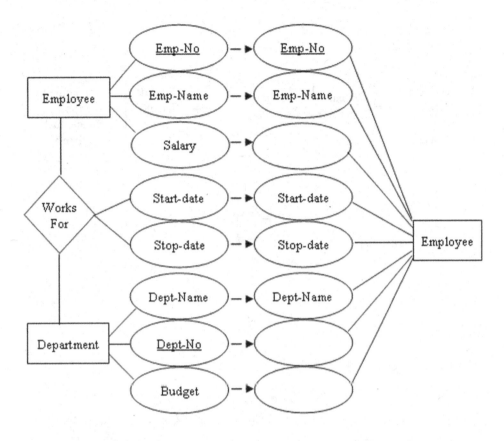

Figure 12.9   The export schema as compared to the original schema.

but does not have that primary key in the other schema, or when a concept is mapped to an attribute type in one schema but it is mapped to an entity type in the other schema

- Constraint conflicts—where the same construct has different, incompatible requirements: for example, this occurs when the same attribute is optional (nullable) in one schema but is mandatory (not null) in the other schema

STEP 3.3: RESOLUTION   In this step, the designer resolves the conflicts identified in Step 3.2.

The following techniques can be used to resolve the conflicts found in Step 3.2:

- Inheritance types are used to embed the concepts from one overlapped schema into the other.
- Aliases are used for synonyms and schema names are used as prefixes to make the homonyms map to different names.
- Mapping of attributes to entities is used as a way of resolving structural conflicts.

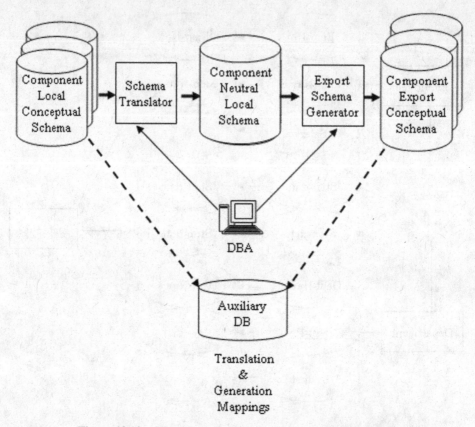

Figure 12.10   Schema translation and export schema generation.

- Conflicting constraints are recorded in an auxiliary database for use in query processing later.

We will use these techniques in an example in Section 12.6 to integrate schemas from three different databases.

STEP 3.4: MERGING   In this step, the designer constructs the integrated schema. Note that we use the term assembly since by the time Step 3.4 starts all inconsistencies between the two schemas have been resolved.

The integrated schema satisfies the following three requirements:

- No structure from component schemas is lost in the integrated schema. This requirement is known as the completeness of the integrated schema.
- The integrated schema must not have any duplicate information. This requirement is known as the minimality of the integrated schema.
- The integrated schema must be easily understood.

Figure 12.12 depicts how two example schemas have been integrated.
We have summarized all the substeps in schema integration in Figure 12.13.

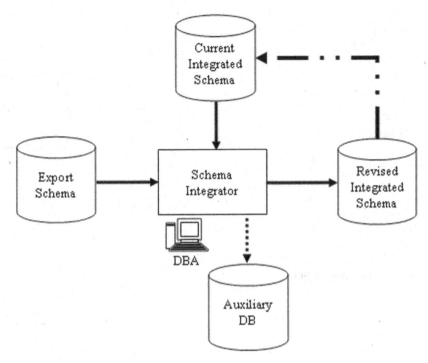

Figure 12.11   Integrated schema generation process.

Auxiliary Database   As discussed earlier (see Chapter 1, Figure 1.9), the information architecture for a DDBE consists of four levels of abstraction—the local internal schema, the local conceptual schema, the global conceptual schema, and the user schemas. The integration process requires an auxiliary database with its own schema to keep track of the translations, mappings, and integration decisions. The DDBE users work with their integrated view at the highest level of the abstraction. Their queries will need to be decomposed into a set of subqueries that run against the local databases. One auxiliary database, stored at each site, enables the processing of the local subqueries against the local database. Figure 12.14 illustrates the information architecture for the DDBE including the auxiliary database and its schema. The contents of the local conceptual schemas and the GCS have been discussed in detail up to this point. We will describe the contents of the auxiliary database in the next section.

An auxiliary database is a repository of supporting information for schema integration. The information in this repository is not part of the GCS but it is part of the global data dictionary and it is necessary for processing queries and transactions running against the integrated DDBE's distributed database. Information about data model translations, export schema generations, and schema integration are stored in the auxiliary schema. A designer's assumptions and assertions during the integration process are also kept in the auxiliary schema.

The information in the auxiliary database can be categorized as follows:

- Location information such as server name, site ID, and site IP address.
- Database information such as database name, logical data model, and schema name.

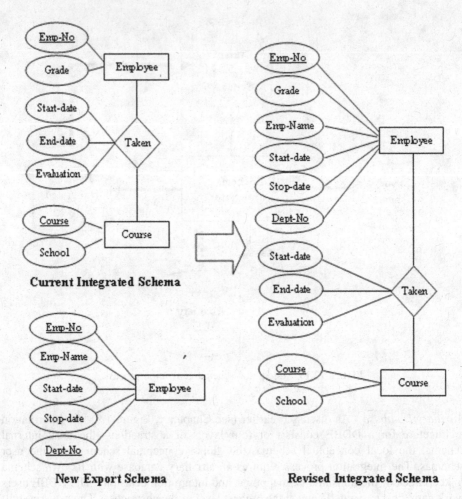

Figure 12.12   Integration of two export schemas.

- Translation information such as mapping type from original objects and associations to ERM. Assume we are mapping the schema of a relational database to ERM. The mapping type is Relational-ER. We also track the original database or schema name, the original table name and its name as an ER entity type, original column name and its name as an ER attribute type, and so on.
- Constraint information such as capturing that an item must be positive, an item has to have a value in a given range, and so on.

Figure 12.15 represents a subset of the conceptual model of the auxiliary database (please refer to Chapter 10 for information on the diagram notation used). We have eliminated data types for attributes and other details so as not to clutter the diagram. We will show more of the details in our example in the next section.

In Figure 12.15, the generic term Object refers to Table in relational and Record Type in network and hierarchical data models. Similarly, we have also used the term Property to refer to Column in relational and Field in network and hierarchical data

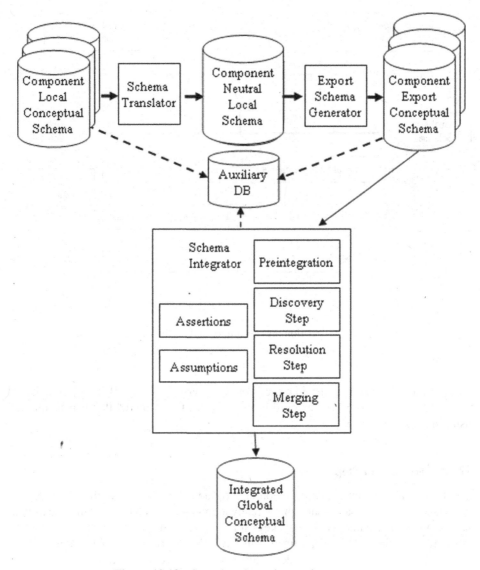

Figure 12.13   Steps in schema integration process.

models. Note that server and database information are already part of the GDD. We have shown these entity types here again for clarity.

12.6   SCHEMA INTEGRATION EXAMPLE

This example integrates three export schemas from three local systems. The first database is a hierarchical database (IBM IMS), the second database is a relational database, and the third database is a network (CODASYL) database. All three databases pertain to different aspects of a university environment. For this example, we assume

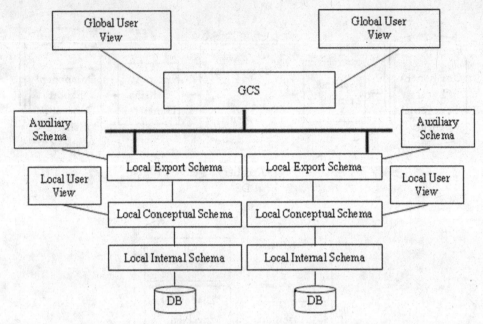

Figure 12.14   Information architecture including the auxiliary database.

that the ERM is used as the interface for the users of the DDBE. This requires a graphical query interface as opposed to use of a relational model that can be queried using the language SQL.

12.6.1   Translation Step

The Db1 database contains information about graduate students working for a department (see Figure 12.16a). Although not really a good idea, we have used the department name and student name as primary keys for simplicity in this example—the primary keys are underlined. Each department can have one or more graduate students working for it. A single graduate student can work for more than one department (they really need the money to pay those high graduate tuition fees). Different departments pay different students different amounts. This is clearly a many-to-many relationship between the graduate student and the department entity types.

In the hierarchical model, the database schema is a tree consisting of two subtrees, one to show the students hired by a given department (the right subtree) and one to show which departments a given graduate student works for (the left subtree). Although the tree shows two copies of each record type, in reality each copy is a virtual record type. Each subtree has three record types—the department, the graduate student, and the support. The department and graduate student record types are self-explanatory. The support record type has one field that tracks the amount of support a department pays for a graduate student. This information is kept in a separate record type since it is not a property of the graduate student or the department but a property of their association.

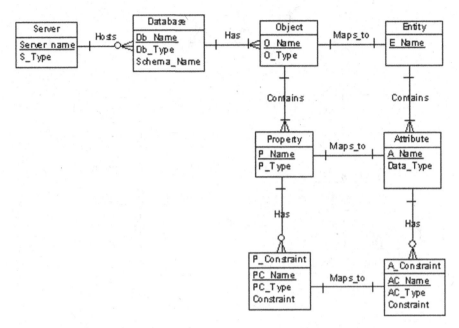

Figure 12.15 Conceptual model of the auxiliary database.

In translating this database to the ERM, the graduate student and the department record types are mapped to two entity types with the same name. The fields within these record types are mapped to attributes in the corresponding entity types. The amount of money (Amt) that each department pays each specific graduate student is kept with the relationship between the two entities (see Figure 12.16b).

The second database is a CODASYL (network) database (see Figure 12.17a). This database contains information about classes that students take. A student is either a graduate student or undergrad student. The schema has three record types—Student, Class, and Takes. Both Student and Class own the Takes record type. The Takes record type has only one field (called "Grade"), which records the grade that is given to a specific student for a specific class. This indicates a many-to-many association between student and class. The equivalent schema for this database in the ERM contains two entity types. One entity type is mapped from the Student record type and the other from the Class record type. The Takes record type is mapped to a relationship type connecting the Student and Class entity types. The Grade attribute type is contained within this relationship type (see Figure 12.17b).

The third database is a relational database and maintains information about the university's departments and departments' faculty. A faculty member works for only one department while a department can have one or more faculty members. This represents a one-to-many association between the Faculty and the Department entity types. Since a faculty member can only work for one department at a time, the primary key of the Department table is used as a foreign key of the Faculty table to show the association. A faculty member also teaches one or more sections of one or more courses. A specific section of a course is keyed by the course name and a section number, requiring the combination of the columns "CName" and "Sec#" to be included

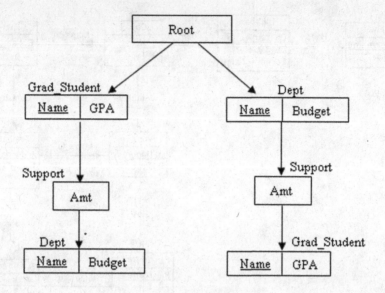

(a) Hierarchical Model

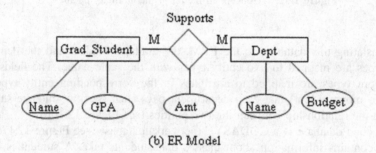

(b) ER Model

Figure 12.16 Hierarchical database schema—mapping details for Db1.

in the primary key for Course. Different sections of a course are taught by one or more faculty members, making the association between Faculty and Course many-to-many. This is shown as a separate table, called "Teaches," in the database. The tables in this database are defined as follows:

DP(Name)

Faculty(FName, Rank, Salary, Dname)

Teaches(FName, CName, Sec#)

Course(CName, Sec#)

The ER equivalent schema for this database is depicted in Figure 12.18. This figure should be self-explanatory.

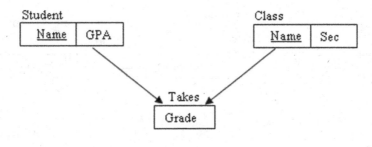

(a) CODASYL Model

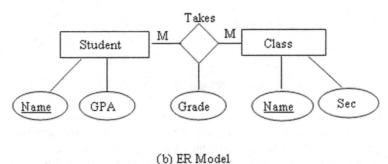

(b) ER Model

Figure 12.17   Network database schema—mapping details for Db2.

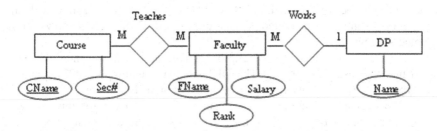

Figure 12.18   Relational database schema—mapping details for Db3.

12.6.2   Export Schema Generation

For this example, we assume that each database's entire contents are shared. As a result, there is no export schema generation step.

12.6.3   Discovery and Resolution Steps

In this step, we analyze the component export schemas for conflicts, similarities, and overlaps. We also resolve issues we find by entering the decisions made to resolve them in the auxiliary database. We have chosen to use the ladder approach for integration. We start by integrating the Db1 schema with the Db3 schema. Analysis of the two schemas reveals that "Dept" and "DP" are aliases used for the Department object. We

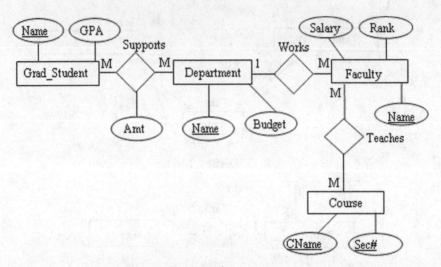

Figure 12.19   Integration of Db1 and Db3.

choose "Department" as the name of the object in the integrated schema. The two entity types that represent the Department entity type have different attribute types defined in each schema as well. In Db1, the entity type has two attribute types while in Db3 the entity type has only one attribute type. The Department entity type in the integrated schema will, therefore, have two attribute types. We have chosen "Name" and "Budget" as the names for these attribute types. Our schemas do not capture any interdependencies between Course in Db3 and Grad_Student in Db1, so we will simply carry them over into the integrated schema unchanged. Figure 12.19 shows the latest integrated schema.

Once we have completed the integration of Db1 and Db3, we integrate the Db2 schema into the resulting schema. The Db2 schema contains the Student and Class entity types. The Class entity type in Db2 is a synonym for Course in the integrated schema. We decide to continue to use "Course" as the name for this entity type. Although our schemas do not reflect it, we know that the Student entity type in Db2 is a supertype of Grad_Student in Db1 (and the latest version of the integrated schema). However, since Student does not exist in the integrated schema, it is therefore carried over "as is," without conflicts. The result of this integration is depicted in Figure 12.20.

12.6.4   Restructuring Step

Once the analysis step has been completed, we are ready to restructure the results to remove redundancies and make sure the schema is complete and minimal. There are no redundancies in our integrated schema so far, but there are structures that can be combined into hierarchies. As mentioned before, Grad_Student is a subtype of Student. Although each student takes classes, only graduate students can work and get support from a department. This supertype/subtype structure is shown as a thick double-lined arrow from the subtype to the supertype in Figure 12.21. Since each subtype inherits all the attributes and relationships of its supertype, the Name attribute type only needs to be associated with Student and not directly defined for the Grad_Student. Similarly,

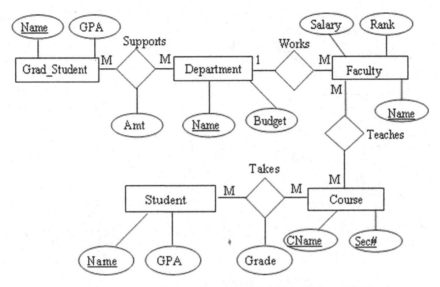

Figure 12.20   Final integration result for Db1, Db2, and Db3.

both Student and Faculty are subtypes of an entity type that we call "Person." As a result, we need to show this inheritance type in the final schema as well. Again, Name is contained within the Person entity type making it possible to be inherited by all its immediate subtypes (Faculty and Student) and also lower-level subtypes (Grad_Student). The complete and minimal integrated schema for these three databases is shown in Figure 12.21.

12.7   EXAMPLE OF EXISTING COMMERCIAL DDBEs

Commercially available DDBEs from IBM, Oracle, and Microsoft are all bottom–up implementations. They integrate information from existing database systems into a virtual database that users can query and, with some limitations, modify. In order to be able to perform their intended tasks, these products have to address the schema translation/integration and software integration challenges as we discussed earlier in this chapter. In this section, we provide an overview of the capabilities of some of these products. We encourage interested readers to review the product literature from these companies for more information.

Commercially available products provide an integrated view of the information in heterogeneous multidatabases and allow the users to query and update the information regardless of where it is stored and how it is controlled. None of the commercial products we have reviewed are able to achieve this goal completely. The difficulty they each have is the ability to support schema and data modifications within the local databases performed by a global user. The issues they encounter are the issues we outlined in Section 12.5.1. The overall goal of the software and schema integration process is to create an environment like the one depicted in Figure 12.22.

The commercial products, however, do not provide a single schema translation/integration and a software integration layer. Instead, these products offer software

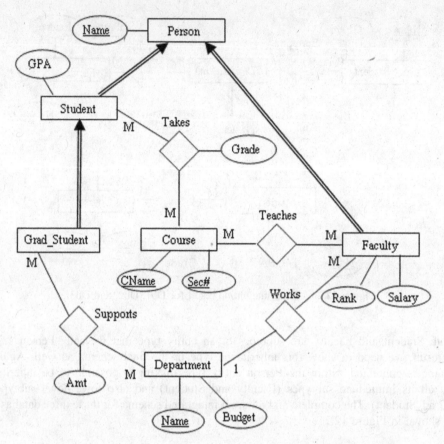

Figure 12.21 Complete and minimal integrated schema for our example.

wrappers or gateways that are designed and developed to work with specific data source types. Figure 12.22 contains an integrated schema for the six databases shown. In this figure, the integrated schema is shown in the oval at the center of the diagram surrounded by the software layers we just mentioned. The various deployed DDBMS environments are shown in orbit as different geometric shapes—emphasizing the heterogeneous nature of the DDBMSs. Within each DDBMS, there is an export schema (ES) containing a single letter representing the local constructs contained within it. These export schemas are linked to an integrated construct within the integrated schema (named with an uppercase version of the same letter). Let us suppose the user wants to query the F global table, which is defined in the integrated schema, by issuing a query written in SQL. Also assume that the target local system is a hierarchical database such as IBM IMS. We, therefore, know that F is mapped from the F record type. We also know that SQL, which is a 'table–oriented' language, is quite different from the record-oriented language used by this hierarchical system. Even though the user thinks that the SQL query runs against F, in reality the query must run against the F record type in the IMS system. The SQL query must be mapped to an equivalent set of IMS operations—typically a loop structure with all

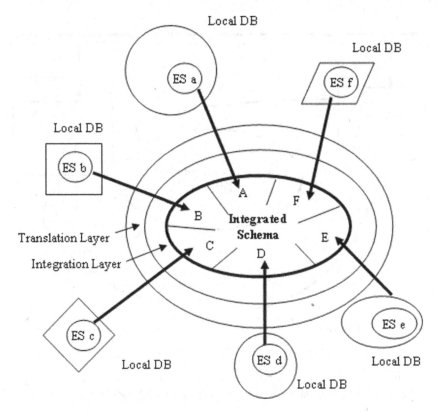

Figure 12.22   The schema integration goal for commercial DDBE products.

records within the F record type being examined. These IMS commands will run against the F record type and a set of records that satisfy the query conditions will be returned by the IMS DBMS. The client software does not understand records and needs to receive a set of rows instead. This necessitates another translation of the results from the record set to the row set for presentation and processing in the client application. The software that achieves this is specific to IMS and is different from the other software that works with other DBMSs (perhaps even using different logical data models, such as the network data model or the object-oriented data model). The DBMS vendor, who supports a specific logical data model, offers the packaged software as a gateway or wrapper. Figure 12.23 depicts the gateway necessary for working with the IMS hierarchical system.

12.7.1   Schema Integration in Commercial Systems

Commercial products do not use the theoretical approach for schema integration that we discussed in this chapter. That is because, as we outlined earlier in this chapter, although the theoretical approach is doable, commercial products have to operate within the limitations and restrictions that the DDBMS vendors put on the interface to their products.

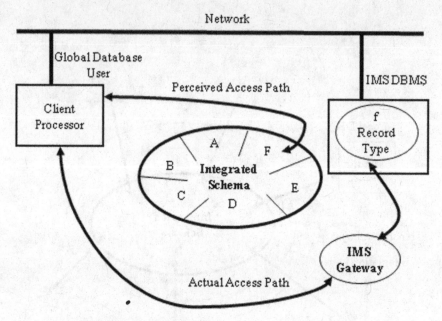

Figure 12.23   Use of gateway or wrapper in integration.

The differences between the theoretical approach and the commercial product approach for schema translation and integration are as follows:

1. The target data model is the relational data model instead of the ER model that we used in our discussion and examples, because these products use SQL as their interface language.

2. Since the interface is SQL, the target of any mapping is a relational table.

3. The mapping of the source constructs (such as relational system tables and views, Excel spreadsheets, comma or tab delimited files, and other data sources) to target constructs is done on a per-construct basis. In other words, the entire schema (or a subset of it) is not handled as a unit of integration. Instead, the DBA must choose which individual construct of the source schema to use as part of the integrated schema.

4. Mapping software does not support many constraint types including referential integrity. For example, if the user chooses two tables from a local database to use as part of the global schema, the tables are mapped to two tables in the target database. The table and column constraints are not mapped over. In addition, if the two tables have a referential integrity between them, this constraint is not visible in the target database either.

12.7.2   Software Integration in Existing Products

As mentioned at the beginning of Section 12.7, existing products use the concept of a gateway or wrapper software to interface local existing databases into the DDBE.

The gateway software utilizes open standards for communicating with the underlying DBMS software whenever possible. The most commonly used standard interface is the open database connectivity (ODBC) standard and its related technologies (OLEDB, ADO, DotNet, etc.) The ODBC interface has been widely used to provide access to many data sources used in the market today. Many relational databases, flat files (comma and tab delimited files), Excel spreadsheets, and other data sources provide an ODBC public interface. This interface software, called an ODBC driver, is supported either by the original "data source vendor" or by a third party.

When an ODBC driver is not available to interface to a particular local system, we have to develop an interface on top of the publicly available interface from the vendor. This interface is not necessarily well suited for our purpose, and there is a danger that if the "data source vendor" changes the interface, our interface will not work. This situation can be considered both a challenge and an opportunity. The challenge is in upgrading our interface software to work with the new interface that the "data source vendor" provides. The opportunity is for third-party software vendors whose existence depends on maintaining the software that fills this gap.

In the following two sections, we review two existing commercial products that provide for DDBE implementation. The two products we have analyzed are Microsoft Access and IBM InfoSphere Federation Server. The reason for choosing these two products is the fact that these two represent two extremes in integration. We first summarize each of the two products. Then, we will provide the details of database setup and the experiments we have run.

12.7.3 Microsoft Access

We choose Access for two reasons: first, Access is a database integration environment that can easily support a DDBE implementation, and second, Access is a widely used, single-user DBMS software package and many people are familiar with it. The capabilities that Access provides to integrate different data sources are easy to understand, but at the same time Access only provides for limited functionality. The version of Access used in our experiment is Access 2003, SP3. Access is a relational based DBMS in which the entire database is stored as a flat file. This file has the file extension. MBD under the Microsoft Windows operating systems. Although the graphical user interface is probably the most popular interface to Access, the system also supports SQL and an application programming interface as well. The basic unit of storage in Access, like any other relational DBMS, is a table. Queries are run against one or more of the tables available within the system (using joins) and the results are displayed on the screen as a table or printed as a report.

Access can also work with information stored outside its databases, such as information that is stored in other relational DBMSs, flat files, or Excel spreadsheets. This ability makes Access a multidatabase (with some limitations). To work with information stored outside Access, the system can either import a snapshot of the information (as a table) or link to it. An import is a disconnected copy of the source, while a link provides live connection to the source. Access uses ODBC, similar related interfaces, or the native interface provided by the "data source vendor" to connect to data that is stored outside the Access databases. Access can also interface with information in XML files, Microsoft Outlook, Microsoft Exchange, Paradox, Microsoft Sharepoint, HTML documents, dBase databases, flat files, other Microsoft Access databases, and any data source that supports an ODBC interface. Regardless of the data source and its format, inside Access information is treated as a relational table.

12.7.3.1 Differences Between Importing and Linking in Access   A table that is accessible inside Access is either a native table, an imported table, or a linked table. Tables that have been created inside Access give the creator complete visibility, ownership, and control. Imported tables that are accessible inside Access are snapshots of the source data. They are disconnected from the source and therefore do not reflect the changes made to the source after the snapshot has been taken. This can be a useful feature because it allows us to copy a table from outside Access and then work with it as if it were created by Access. The schema details for the imported tables can be changed by Access users inside the system. The users can also modify the contents as needed without having to worry about the source. A table that is linked to Access can dynamically be modified by the users of the Access database. It is not a copy of the original data source but is instead the actual data. In other words, what users see in Access is the live data as it appears within the data source, which is actually outside Access.

In our experiments, we only used linked tables since we were interested in seeing how Access dynamically works with other DBMS products and non-DBMS data sources such as spreadsheets and flat files. Access did not have any problem with linking in our experiments.

12.7.4   InfoSphere Federation Server

The second product we reviewed is from IBM, and it is called "InfoSphere Federation Server 9.5." This product was chosen since it is exactly the opposite of Access in functionality and scalability. IBM has allowed us to use the software free of charge as part of the IBM Academic Initiative in our Distributed Database class. To provide enhanced performance and functionality, instead of ODBC, the Federation Server uses the native client for most of the data sources that it accesses. For example, Federation Server uses Net8 client for Oracle and CTLIB for Sybase. ODBC is used as a catch-all for these data sources for which there is no specific wrapper/connector ([Nelson03], [Roth97]). The specific wrapper/connector is always customized for a particular data source. A wrapper is a software package that specifically targets a type of data source. For example, a wrapper for Oracle allows Federation Server to see and work with data in Oracle, while a wrapper for XML allows the Federation Server to work with XML data. To be able to do this, a wrapper must map SQL queries to the query dialect language that the target data source understands when processing requests, and perform data format mapping when results are sent back.

IBM provides wrappers for most of today's DBMS products including SQL Server, Oracle, Sybase, and Teradata. There are also wrappers provided for working with flat files, such as comma/string delimited files, tab delimited files, XML, and spreadsheets. In addition, users can write their own wrappers for custom databases and applications using the Java or C++ programming languages. Once a user has a wrapper for the data source, the IBM Federation Server can map the data source objects (e.g., tables, views, files) as if they were tables inside DB2. The IBM Federation Server refers to the data source objects that are mapped into DB2 as "nicknames." Think of a nickname as an alias or synonym for a remote data source object. Once the nickname for a remote data source is defined in the Federation Server, the nickname can be used as if it was a local DB2 table. In other words, the nickname can be referenced in an SQL statement the same way that a table can be (e.g., it can be referenced in the "FROM list" for an SQL select statement). User applications can also use these nicknames in conjunction with other nicknames and DB2 tables and can view remote data regardless of where the data resides. A nickname in DB2 and a linked table in Access are similar concepts; however, there are differences with respect to the flexibilities and limitations for these concepts with the two systems.

12.8   THE EXPERIMENT

This section covers the experiment we ran using Microsoft Access and InfoSphere Federation Server. We will discuss the sample database we used, how the database was distributed, where each component of the data was stored, and what queries and transactions we ran.

12.8.1   The Example Database

The conceptual model of the database is depicted in Figure 12.24. In this example, we keep track of the employees (Emp), the grants they supervise (Grant), and the children they have (Child). Since an employee can supervise one or more grants and can have one or more children, the relationship type connecting the Emp entity type to the Grant entity type has one-to-many cardinality and so does the relationship type connecting Emp to Child.

12.8.2   Database Distribution

We decided to use a hybrid fragmentation for this database. The Emp table is vertically distributed into two fragments: "Emp_Name(EmpID, Ename)" and "Emp_Sal(EmpID, Sal)." The Emp_Name table is replicated into two copies. These copies are called "Emp_Name_Access," which is under the control of the Access database, and "Emp_-Name_DB2," which is controlled by DB2. The Emp_Sal table is further fragmented horizontally based on salary—one fragment holds the employees who make less than or equal to $5000 and the other holds those who make more than $5000. These fragments are called "Emp_Sal_LE5K" and "Emp_Sal_GT5K." The other tables are not fragmented and are stored as a whole. Since the Emp and Emp_Sal tables are fragmented they do not physically exist. These are called logical/virtual tables, as we discussed in Chapter 2. Note that even though we have intentionally used unique names for these table fragments, in reality, that is not required. We have used unique names to make it easy to know which table we are talking about in this chapter.

The tables and fragments are deployed based on the following criteria:

- There are four computers utilized in this experiment: Computer 1 (C1) runs Access 2003, Computer 2 (C2) runs Oracle, Computer 3 (C3) runs InfoSphere and DB2, and Computer 4 (C4) runs Microsoft Access and Excel 2003. All computers run Microsoft Windows XP Professional Edition operating system. The four computers are networked together using TCP/IP over Ethernet for communications.
- Table "Emp_Name_Access" is stored on C1 under the control of Access.

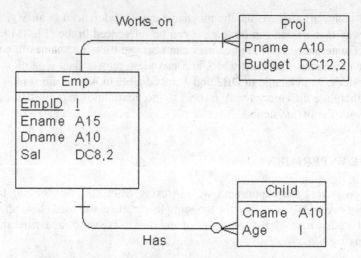

Figure 12.24   Conceptual model of the sample database.

- Table "Emp_Name_DB2" is stored in DB2 on C3.
- Tables "Emp_Sal_GT5K" and "Child" are stored under the control of Oracle on C2.
- Table "Emp_Sal_LE5K" and the Grant spreadsheet are stored on C4.
- Table "Child(Cname, EmpID, Budget)" is stored in an Oracle 10g database on C2.

Figure 12.25 illustrates the data deployment across the four computers.

Tables 12.2, 12.3, and 12.4 provide a conceptual view of the data stored in this distributed database environment. Note that, although we have shown the contents of the Emp table as one table for simplicity's sake here, in reality, the table is fragmented and its physical components are stored across computers C1, C2, C3, and C4. Also note that we are assuming the first row in the spreadsheet has the column names (as headings).

12.8.3   The Setup

In order to be able to compare the functionality of Access and InfoSphere Federation Server, we ran the same set of queries and modifications in SQL across both systems. The following subsections outline how the two systems were prepared for the experiment and then discuss the experiment's results for both systems.

TABLE 12.2   The Emp Table

EmpID	Ename	Sal
1	Rahimi	7500
2	Haug	4800
3	Jones	5000
4	Paul	8100

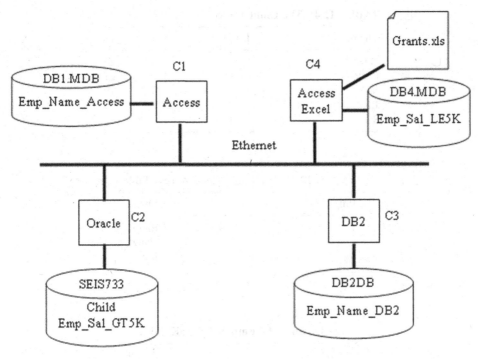

Figure 12.25 Data deployment across computers in our experiment.

We assume the following has already been done by the user:

1. Both Microsoft Office 2003 and InfoSphere 9.5 are installed and the supporting ODBC drivers for Oracle and DB2 are in place in appropriate computers. Oracle 10 and SQL Server 2005 server and client software are installed where necessary. For example, since Federation Server needs access to Oracle client, the software must be installed on C3.

2. There is a spreadsheet called Grant loaded with the information from Table 12.3 stored in C4. This sheet is called "Grant.xls."

TABLE 12.3 The Grant Spreadsheet

Gname	EmpID	Budget
DD_Design	1	1000
Fed. Database	1	2000
Online teaching	3	3000
Grid Technology	3	4000
XML in databases	4	5000
Distributed System Development	2	6000

TABLE 12.4   The Child Table

Cname	EmpID	Age
Omeed	1	23
Leela	1	21
Jack	3	19
Jill	3	20
Sam	4	15

TABLE 12.5   The Emp_Name_Access Table

EmpID	Ename
1	Rahimi
2	Haug
3	Jones
4	Paul

TABLE 12.6   The Emp_Sal_GT5K Table

EmpID	Sal
1	7500
4	8100

3. There is an Oracle database on C2 called "SEIS733." This database has a table called "Child" populated with the information from Table 12.4. This database also has a table called "Emp_Sal_GT5K" loaded with information from Table 12.6.

4. There is an Access database on C1 called "DB1.MDB." This database has a table called "Emp_Name_Access" properly loaded with data from Table 12.5.

5. There is a DB2 database called "DB2DB" running in C3. This database has a table called "Emp_Name_DB2" also loaded with the information from Table 12.5. Based on this distribution, the DB2 table (Emp_Name_DB2) and the Access table (Emp_Name_Access) are copies of each other.

6. There is also an Access database in C4 called "DB4.MDB." This database has a table called "Emp_Sal_LE5K" loaded with data shown in Table 12.7.

12.8.4   Setting Up Data Source Names

Both Microsoft Access and InfoSphere Federation Server have the capability to use the native data source client interface when it is available. For example, Federation Server can use Net8 to connect to an Oracle database and DBLib to connect to an SQL Server database. Similarly, Microsoft Access can connect directly to another Access database or to information stored in Microsoft Exchange Server. In the absence of such a native

TABLE 12.7   The Emp_Sal_LE5K Table

EmpID	Sal
2	4800
3	5000

interface, the ODBC interface can be used. In this section, we will create the data sources required for the experiment. Note that all these data sources are machine data sources and not user data sources. This allows any user who logs into the computer to run the experiments. Each data source is identified by a data source name (DSN), which is specified as part of the data source configuration steps that follow.

Define the DSN for the Emp_Name_Access Table in the "DB1.MDB" Access Database

- Open Start → Settings → Control Panel → Administrative Tools → Data Sources (ODBC).
- Make sure you click on the "System DSN" tab.
- Click on the "Add" button.
- Choose Microsoft Access Driver (*.mdb).
- Click on the "Finish" button.
- In the "Data Source Name" field, type "Emp_Name_Access_DNS" (without the quotes).
- Click on the "Select" button.
- Traverse to the directory where the "DB1.MDB" file is located and select it.
- Click on the "OK" button in the file browser dialog.
- Click on the "OK" button in the other dialog.
- The DSN is now added. Click on the "OK" button to close the ODBC dialog.

Define the DSN for the Emp_Sal_LE5K Table in the Access DB4.MDB Database

- Open Start → Settings → Control Panel → Administrative Tools → Data Sources (ODBC).
- Make sure you click on the "System DSN" tab.
- Click on the "Add" button.
- Choose Microsoft Access Driver (*.mdb).
- Click on the "Finish" button.
- In the "Data Source Name" field, type "Emp_Sal_LE5K_DNS" (without the quotes).
- Click on the "Select" button.
- Traverse to the directory where the "DB4.MDB" file is located and select it.
- Click on the "OK" button.
- Click on the "OK" button again.
- The DSN is now added. Click on the "OK" button to close the ODBC dialog.

Define the DSN for the Child Table in the Oracle SEIS733 Database

- Open Start → Settings → Control Panel → Administrative Tools → Data Sources (ODBC).
- Make sure you click on the "System DSN" tab.
- Click on the "Add" button.
- Choose Oracle—OraDb110g_home1 and click on the "Finish" button.
- In the dialog that opens, fill in the following:

    For the Name of the data source, type "Child_DNS" (without the quotes).

    Under the TNS Service Name, choose SEIS733 (in our case, the service name is also SEIS733).

    Under the user ID, type the name of the user you used to create the table Child (SKR in my case).
- Click on the "Test connection" button.
- Enter the password for the user and then click on the "Test" button.
- Make sure it worked!
- Click on the "OK" button.

Define the DSN for the Emp_Sal_GT5K Table in the Oracle SEIS733 Database

- Open Start → Settings → Control Panel → Administrative Tools → Data Sources (ODBC).
- Make sure you click on the "System DSN" tab.
- Click on the "Add" button.
- Choose Oracle—OraDb110g_home1 and click on the "Finish" button.
- In the dialog that opens, fill in the following:

    For the Name of the data source, type "Emp_Sal_GT5K" (without the quotes).

    Under the TNS Service Name, choose SEIS733 (in our case, the service name is also SEIS733).

    Under the user ID, type the name of the user you used to create the table Child (SKR in my case).
- Click on the "Test connection" button.
- Enter the password for the user and then click on the "Test" button.
- Make sure it worked!
- Click on the "OK" button.

Define the DSN for the Emp_Name_DB2 Table in the DB2 Database

- Open Start → Settings → Control Panel → Administrative Tools → Data Sources (ODBC).
- Make sure you click on the "System DSN" tab.
- Click on the "Add" button.
- Choose IBM DB2 ODBC DRIVER—DB2COPY1.
- Click on the "Finish" button.

- Type "Emp_Name_DB2_DNS" (without the quotes) for the data source name.
- Under Database Alias choose DB2DB.
- Click on the "OK" button.

Define the DSN for the "Grant" Excel Spreadsheet in Computer 4

- Open Start → Settings → Control Panel → Administrative Tools → Data Sources (ODBC).
- Make sure you click on the "System DSN" tab.
- Click on the "Add" button.
- Choose Microsoft Excel Driver (*.xls).
- Click on the "Finish" button.
- Type "Grants_DNS" (without the quotes) for the data source name.
- Click on the "OK" button.
- Click on the "OK" button again.

12.8.4.1 Linking Data Sources into Access   This step is required to link the tables and Excel spreadsheet outside Access (DB1 on C1).

Linking to the Grant Excel Spreadsheet on C4

- Linking an Access database to an Excel spreadsheet that resides on a different machine requires setting up a mapped network drive on the remote system. In our setup, we need to link the Excel spreadsheet named "Grant.xls," which is located on C4, to the Access database named "DB1.MDB," which is located on C1. We assume there is a mapped drive on C1 called "C4Drive" that points to the directory with this sheet in it. Linking Access to an Excel spreadsheet cannot be done via ODBC and must be done using the native interface to Excel.
- Open up the Access database "DB1.MDB" (if it is not open already).
- Choose File →Get External Data→ Link Tables.
- In the "Look in" field, type "C4Drive:\ Grants.xls" (without the quotes) or browse to the directory and choose the file.
- For "Files of Type," scroll down and choose Microsoft Excel (*.xls)—you cannot use ODBC here.
- Click on the "Link" button.
- Make sure that the checkbox for "First row contains column headings" is checked.
- Click on the "Next" button.
- For the name of linked table type "Grants_Sheet" (without the quotes).
- Click on the "Finish" button.
- The "Grant" spreadsheet is now linked as a table called "Grants_Sheet" (without the quotes).
- Double click on this table to see its contents.

Linking to the Emp_Sal_LE5K Table in Access on C4

- Open up the Access database if not open already.

- Choose File → Get External Data → Link Tables.
- Scroll all the way down in the "Files of Type:" and choose ODBC Databases().
- Click on the "Machine Data Source" tab.
- Choose "Emp_Sal_LE5K_DSN."
- Click on the "OK" button.
- The "Emp_Sal_LE5K" table from Access is now linked.
- Double click on it to see its contents.

Linking to Child Table in Oracle on C2

- Open up the Access database if not open already.
- Choose File → Get External Data → Link Tables.
- Scroll all the way down in the "Files of Type:" and choose ODBC Databases().
- Click on the "Machine Data Source" tab.
- Choose "Child_DNS."
- Type in your Oracle user_name and password and click on the "OK" button.
- Choose the "**UserName.**Child" table (in our case "skr.Child").
- Click on the "OK" button.
- The table with the name "SKR_Child" in Access is now linked to the Child table in Oracle.
- Right click on it and rename it Child.
- Double click on it to see its contents (when asked, put in your Oracle credentials).

Linking to the Emp_Sal_GT5K Table in Oracle on C2

- Open up the Access database if not open already.
- Choose File → Get External Data → Link Tables.
- Scroll all the way down in the "Files of Type:" and choose ODBC Databases().
- Click on the "Machine Data Source" tab.
- Choose "Emp_Sal_GT5K_DSN."
- Put in your Oracle user_name and password and click on the "OK" button.
- Choose the "**UserName.Emp**_Sal_GT5K" table (in our case "skr.Emp_Sal_GT5K").
- Click on the "OK" button.
- The "Emp_Sal_GT5K" table from Oracle is now linked to Access as the "SKR_Emp_Sal_GT5K" table.
- Right click on it and rename it "Emp_Sal_GT5K."
- Double click on it to see its contents (when asked, put in your Oracle credentials).

Linking to the Emp_Name_DB2 Table in DB2 on C3

- This is not really required since we have a copy of the same table in Access. We outline the steps here for completeness.
- Open up the Access database if not open already.
- Choose File → Get External Data → Link Tables.

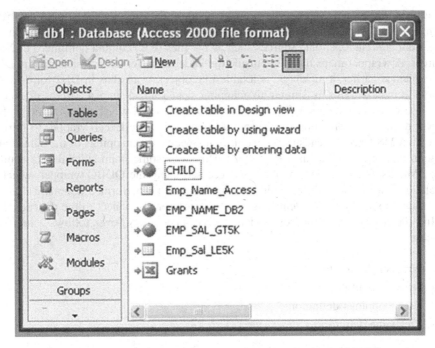

Figure 12.26   The contents of the Access database "DB1.MDB."

- Scroll all the way down in the "Files of Type:" and choose ODBC Databases().
- Click on the "Machine Data Source" tab.
- Choose "Emp_Name_DB2_DNS."
- Provide your DB2 user name and password and click on the "OK" button.
- Choose the "UserName.Emp_Name_DB2" table (in our case "SAEED.Emp_Name_DB2").
- Click on the "OK" button.
- The table is linked as "SAEED_Emp_Name_DB2."
- Since we are going to use the table "Emp_Name_DB2" in our queries, right click on the "SAEED_Emp_Name_DB2" table and choose Rename.
- Change the name to "Emp_Name_DB2."
- Double click on it to see its contents (when asked, put in your DB2 credentials).

When all the steps listed above have been successfully completed, the Access database "DB1.MDB" will have all the tables shown in Figure 12.26 in it. As seen from this figure, only table "Emp_Name_Access" is a local table. All other tables are linked from outside Access, as was expected. This fact is indicated by an arrow next to the table name that is linked from outside Access.

12.8.5   Linking Data Sources into Federation Server

The InfoSphere Federation Server uses wrapping technology to connect to different data sources. A wrapper allows you to connect to different types of data sources. The Federation Server provides two types of wrappers: **relational wrappers** and **nonrelational**

wrappers. Relational wrappers let you manipulate data in other relational databases such as DB2, Oracle, or Microsoft Access. Nonrelational wrappers support retrieving data from nonrelational data sources such as flat files (e.g., comma-delimited) or XML sources. A wrapper maps the data outside the Federation Server to a nickname in DB2. As explained earlier, a nickname is a table-like object or an alias in DB2 for data that resides remotely. This is similar to mapping data sources into a Microsoft Access database with one exception. When using the nonrelational wrappers in the Federation Server to access nonrelational data sources (e.g., using the Excel wrapper to retrieve data from MS Excel spreadsheets), we have to specify the mappings of the data source column names to our nickname columns. However, some nonrelational data sources (e.g., Microsoft Excel, flat files) can be accessed using the ODBC wrapper, which is a relational wrapper, and thus column mapping will be performed automatically. We also have to specify the credential for the remote user to connect to the data source.

In order to retrieve data from a data source, Federation Sever follows a four-step process:

- Wrapper definition
- Server definition
- User mappings definition
- Nickname definition

We will first retrieve data from the Excel spreadsheet to get the Grant information.

12.8.5.1 Creating the Nickname for the Excel Spreadsheet on C4   InfoSphere Federation Server provides two mechanisms for accessing an Excel spreadsheet. One is based on the ODBC interface and uses the ODBC wrapper (relational wrapper). The other is based on the Microsoft Excel application interface and uses the Excel wrapper (nonrelational wrapper). We will use the Excel wrapper here.

Steps to Create a Nickname for an Excel Spreadsheet

- Launch the Federation Server administration conceal (DB2 Control Center).
- In the "All Databases" expand the database "DB2DB."
- Right click on the "Nicknames" button and select "Create."
- After the "Create Nicknames" wizard comes up, click on the "Next" button.
- In the "Specify the data source and the wrapper" panel, select the "Microsoft Excel" data source type from the drop down and click on the "Create" button.
- For wrapper name type in "Excel" and click on the "OK" button.
- In the "Specify the data source and the wrapper" panel, highlight the wrapper name we just created and click on the "Next" button.
- In the "Specify the Server Definition for the data source" panel, click on the "Create" button.
- Specify the server name where our Excel spreadsheet is located. Since the sheet in on C4 and IBM Federation Server is on C3, we assume there is a mapped drive on the system where the Excel spreadsheet is located that refers to the Federation Server machine. Here, we'll assume the mapped drive for C4 is named "C4Drive." In this case, we will use the name of the local server as the server name (in our

case, "gateway"). Note that the server name specified in this step is a logical name and can have any value regardless of the actual machine name.

- Click the "OK" button.
- In the "Specify the Server Definition for the data source" panel, highlight the server we just created and click on the "Next" button.
- In the "Define Nicknames" panel, click on the "Add" button and type "Grant_NN" for the nickname.
- Click on the "Add" button in the "Add Nickname" dialog box and specify the columns names and their data types, the same as we specified in the Excel data.
- In the "Add Nickname" dialog box, click on the "Settings" tab.
- For the "FILE_PATH" option, type "C4Drive:\Grants.xls" in the value field.
- Leave the "Range" option unchecked.
- Click on the "OK" button.
- In the "Define Nicknames" panel, click on the "Next" button.
- Click on the "Finish" button.
- The nickname "grant_nn" in Federation Server database (i.e., the DB2 database) now refers to the Excel spreadsheet on Computer 4. To test it out, right click on the nickname and choose "Open" from the context menu. We should have a table with six (6) rows and three (3) columns. If there are any errors, go back and check what was done for each step.

12.8.5.2 Creating the Nickname for the "Empl_Sal_LE5K" Table For interfacing to Microsoft Access databases, Federation Server uses ODBC. In this example, we will take a different route from the one we used for Excel to create the mapping. Instead of using the "Create Nickname" Wizard, which guides us through the steps to retrieve data from a data source, we will perform these steps one-by-one: first, we define an ODBC wrapper to the Federation Server; second, we add a server definition for our ODBC data source (which is the Microsoft Access database "DB4.MDB"); third, we define a user mapping from the local user to the remote user; and lastly, we define a nickname.

Registering the ODBC Wrapper

- **Note**: If we have already created an ODBC wrapper, we can skip this part.
- Launch the DB2 Control Center if it is not open already.
- In the "All Databases" expand the database named "DB2DB."
- Traverse to the "Federated Database Objects" entry.
- Right click on this entry and then choose the "Create Wrapper" button.
- In the dialog that opens, under the data source field, choose "ODBC."
- Click on the "OK" button.

Registering a Server Definition for the ODBC Wrapper

- Expand the ODBC wrapper we just created.
- Right click on the "Server Definitions" folder and choose the "Create" menu item.
- In the dialog that opens, click on the "Discover" button.

- Click on the "Uncheck All" button.
- Find the DSN called "Emp_Sal_LE5K."
- Put a check mark on the check box under the "Create" field for this data source.
- Click on the "OK" button.

Creating User Mapping and Nickname for This Server Definition

- Expand the server definition you just created; it should be named "Emp_Sal_LE5K."
- Right click on the "User Mappings" folder and choose "Create."
- In the dialog that opens, select your Federation Server user name and click on the ">" button.
- Click on the "Settings" tab.
- Type in your Microsoft Access user name and password.
- Click on the "OK" button. User mapping is now added.
- Right click on the "Nicknames" folder and choose "Create."
- In the dialog box "Create Nicknames," click on the "Add" button.
- For nickname type "Emp_Sal_LE5K_NN," leave Remote schema name blank.
- For Remote table name, type "Emp_Sal_LE5K."
- Click on the "OK" button.
- The nickname "Emp_Sal_LE5K_NN" in DB2 database now refers to the table "Emp_Sal_LE5K" in the "DB4.MDB" Access database on Computer 4. To test it out, right click on it and choose Open. We should have a table with two rows and two columns. If there are any errors, go back and check your steps.

12.8.5.3 *Creating the Nicknames for Emp_Sal_GT5K and Child* InfoSphere Federation Server provides a specific wrapper for Oracle that is customized for accessing Oracle databases. The wrapper is referred to as the Oracle wrapper and uses Oracle native client protocol (i.e., Oracle OCI) when accessing Oracle databases. Another alternative to accessing Oracle databases is to use the ODBC wrapper, which relies on Oracle's ODBC interface. Since the ODBC wrapper is a generic wrapper that is not customized for a specific type of data source, we will use the Oracle wrapper instead. The following steps are based on the Oracle wrapper, which requires the installation of an Oracle client on the Federation Server machine (on C3).

Registering the ODBC Wrapper

- Launch the DB2 Control Center if not open already.
- In the "All Databases" expand the database "DB2DB."
- Traverse to "Federated Database Objects."
- Right click on it and then choose "Create Wrapper."
- In the dialog box that opens, under data source field, choose "Oracle using OCI 8."
- Click on the "OK" button.
- **Note**: The wrapper is now created for working with Oracle using the Oracle OCI (also known as Net8) communication interface. When creating the wrapper, Federation Server needs to know where Oracle is installed—what is known as

"Oracle Home." If this environment variable is set in your computer, it will be used automatically. To see this, right click on the Net8 wrapper and then choose "Alter." In the dialog, click on "Set variables." The "Set environment variables" dialog comes up. If the checked box with the variable name "Oracle Home" in it appears, we are done. Otherwise, enter the full path to where Oracle client is installed in the Federation Server machine. As mentioned earlier, the Oracle client has to be installed on the computer where the Federation Server is installed.

Registering a Server Definition for the Net8 Wrapper

- Expand the Net8 wrapper you just created.
- Right click on the "Server Definitions" folder and choose "Create."
- In the dialog that opens, click on the "Discover" button.
- Click on the "Uncheck all" button.
- Find the TNSName for the Oracle database where the "Emp_Sal_GT5K" is (in our case, SEIS733).
- Put a check mark on the check box under the "Create" file for this database.
- Under the Version field, click on the "Select" button, and then choose the version of Oracle being used (in our case, 10g).
- Click on the "OK" button.

Creating User Mapping and Nickname for This Server Definition

- Expand the server definition you just created; in our case, it is named SEIS733.
- There should be four folders: User mappings, Nicknames, Federated stored procedures, and Remote table.
- Right click on the "User mappings" folder and choose "Create."
- In the dialog that opens, select the Federation Server user name and click on the ">" button.
- Click on the "Settings" tab.
- Type in your Oracle user name and password as values for "REMOTE_AUTHID" and "REMOTE_PASSWORD" fields.
- Click on the "OK" button. The user mapping is now added.

Once the user mappings for the "Emp_Sal_GT5K" and the "Child" tables are created, the following steps are used to create nicknames for them in the Federation Server.

Creating the Nickname for the Emp_Sal_GT5K Table

- Right click on the "Nicknames" folder and choose "Create."
- In the dialog "Create Nicknames," click on the "Add" button. (For an alternative approach, see the note at the end of these steps.)
- For the "Nickname," type "Emp_Sal_GT5K_NN" (without the quotes).
- For "Remote schema," enter the schema name in the Oracle database where the tables "Emp_Sal_GT5K" and "Child" reside (note that the remote schema name is in all uppercase, SKR in our case).

- Enter "EMP_SAL_GT5K" (in all uppercase without the quotes) as the "Remote table name."
- Click on the "OK" button.
- The nickname "Emp_Sal_GT5K_NN" in the Federation Server database now refers to table "Emp_Sal_GT5K" in the Oracle database on Computer C2. To test it out, right click on it and choose "Open." You should have a table with two rows and two columns. If there are any errors, go back and check your steps.
- **Note:** Instead of creating nicknames individually (by using the "Add" button) or when the remote schema and table names are unknown, one can use the "Discover" button in the "Create Nicknames" dialog to browse through tables and views that reside in the Oracle database. This option is convenient when creating multiple nicknames.

Creating the Nickname for the Child Table

- Right click on the "Nicknames" folder and choose "Create."
- In the dialog "Create Nicknames," click on the "Add" button.
- For "Nickname," type "Child_NN"(without the quotes).
- For "Remote schema," enter the Oracle schema name where the "Child" table resides (note that the name is in all uppercase, SKR in our case).
- Enter "CHILD" (in all uppercase without the quotes) as the "Remote table name."
- Click on the "OK" button. If your schema and table name are correct, the Federation Server finds the table in the proper schema and displays it. If not, go back and enter the correct information.
- Click on the "OK" button.
- The nickname "Child_NN" in the Federation Server database now refers to the table "Child" in the Oracle database on Computer C2. To test it out, right click on it and choose "Open." You should have a table with two rows and two columns. If there are any errors, go back and check your steps.

Although we used DB2's Control Center to create the wrapper definitions, the server definitions, and the nicknames interactively using the GUI interface, the process is a lot more straightforward using the Command Window interface for DB2. We urge readers interested in using the command line interface to consult the Federation Server manuals. Once we have successfully completed the above steps, we have a native DB2 table called "Emp_Name_DB2" and the four nicknames as shown in Figure 12.27. At this point, both the Microsoft Access and IBM Federation Server environments are ready for starting the experiments.

12.8.6   The Experiments

Our experiments consisted of a set of queries and a set of modification statements (update, insert, and delete), which we ran against the distributed database. The same commands were run in Access and in Federation Server and the results were compared. The first set of queries used a single table on a computer (either remote or local). The second set of queries used fragments of a table stored at different computers. The modification statements were also run against the same type of tables (nondistributed and

Figure 12.27   DB2 database contents.

distributed). We used the "Command Editor" in the DB2 Control Center for working with the objects in the Federation Server and used the query interface for working with objects in Access.

12.8.7   Querying the Database from Access and Federation Server

The following are queries for the experiment:

Query 1: Print the names of all employees in the database. Figure 12.28a shows the results for Federation Server and Figure 12.28b shows the results for Access. The queries in this case are local queries against a single table.

Query 2: Print the names of all employees and the names of their children. This is a two-site query against two nonfragmented tables. Figures 12.29a and 12.29b show the results from Federation Server and Access, respectively.

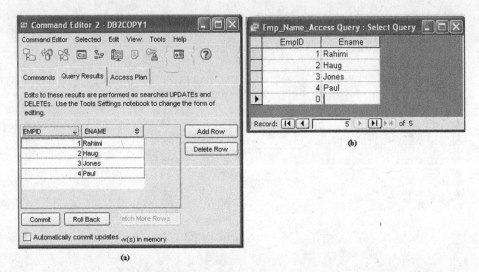

Figure 12.28   Single-site queries.

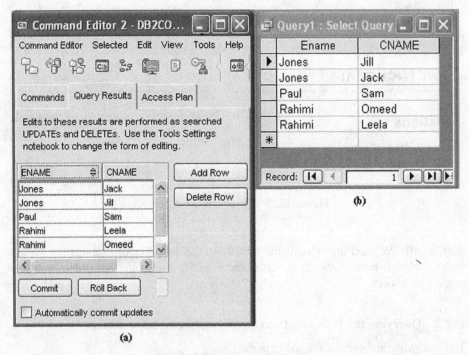

Figure 12.29   Two-site queries.

Query 3: Print the names of all employees, the grants they work on, the names of their children and their salaries. This is a four-site query that uses all the tables and fragments in the system. This can be done in a couple of different ways. For Federation Server, we used an inline view to union the rows from the two vertical tables that hold the salaries for the employees and then joined all the

```
select E. Ename, G.Gname, C.Cname, S.Sal
from Emp_Name_DB2 E, Child_NN C, Grant_NN G,
((select sal, EmpID from emp_sal_le5k_NN)
union
(select sal, EmpID from emp_sal_gt5k_NN)) as s
where E.EmpID = C.Empid and E.EmpID = G.Empid
AND E.EmpID = S.EmpID
order by E.Ename;
```
(a)

```
Emp_Sal Query:
((select sal, EmpID from emp_sal_le5k)
union
(select sal, EmpID from emp_sal_gt5k));
```
(b)

```
SELECT E.Ename, G.Gname, C.CNAME, S.sal
FROM Emp_Name_Access AS E, Child AS C, Grants AS G, Emp_Sal AS S
WHERE (((E.EmpID)=[C].[Empid] And (E.EmpID)=[G].[EmpID]
And (E.EmpID)=[S].[EmpID]))
ORDER BY E.Ename;
```
(c)

Figure 12.30 Federation Server and Access multisite queries.

fragments together to arrive at the answer. The query for Federation Server is shown in Figure 12.30a. For Access, on the other hand, the inline view concept causes problems. We chose to create a query called "Emp_Sal"—in Access views are called "queries"—and then used this query to get the results as shown in Figures 12.30b and 12.30c. The results are displayed in Figure 12.31.

12.8.8 Modifying the Database from Access and Federation Server

We also ran a set of single-site and multisite modification statements from Access and Federation Server. The modifications included update, insert, and delete. We ran the commands first from Access and then from Federation Server. To make sure the database was restored to the original state, after running a command from Access, we compensated for it before we ran the same commands from Federation Server. For example, after inserting a row from Access, we deleted it to be able to reinsert it from DB2.

The following are modification statements for the experiment:

1. In this experiment, we try to update a single remote Access table and then a remote Oracle table. Table 12.8 shows the commands and the results for this experiment. Both Access and Federation Server handle this case easily.

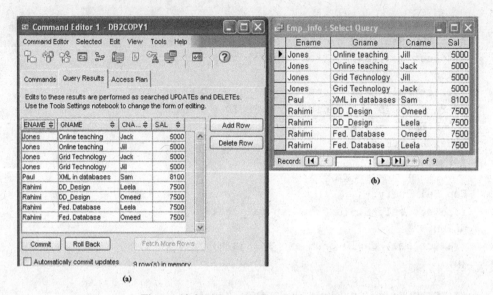

Figure 12.31   Results of multisite queries.

TABLE 12.8   Single Remote Table Update

Target Table	Command Ran	Results

Target is a remote Access table	Update issued from Access
	
	`update Emp_Sal_LE5K`
	`set sal = 4850`
	`where EmpID = 2;`
		Succeeded

	Update issued from DB2
	
	`Update Emp_Sal_LE5K_NN`
	`set sal = 4850`
	`where EmpID = 2;`
		DB20000I, the SQL command, completed successfully

Target is a remote Oracle table	Update issued from Access
	
	`update Emp_Sal_GT5K set`
	`sal = 8000`
	`where EmpID = 1;`
		Succeeded

	Update issued from DB2
	
	`Update mp_Sal_GT5K_NN`
	`set sal = 8000`
	`where EmpID = 1;`
		DB20000I, the SQL command, completed successfully

2. In this experiment, we try to run an update against a remote Excel spreadsheet. Table 12.9 shows the commands and the results for this experiment. Both Access and Federation Server fail to support this. According to Microsoft, the capability to modify linked Excel spreadsheets has been disabled in Access for legal reasons. This applies to Access 2002, Access 2003, and Access 2007 (see article

TABLE 12.9   Update Against a Remote Excel Spreadsheet

Target Table	Command Ran	Results

Target is a remote Excel spreadsheet	Update issued from Access
	
	`update Grants`
	`set Budget = 5500`
	`where EmpID = 4;`
		Not allowed

	Update issued from DB2
	
	`update Grant_NN`
	`set Budget = 5500`
	`where EmpID = 4;`
		No updates were allowed to Excel spreadsheet rows

number 904953, September 17, 2007, Revision 7.1 on the Microsoft web site). In Federation Server, inserts and updates are allowed against the target sheet when the wrapper is based on ODBC. No modifications are allowed when Federation Server uses a native Excel wrapper, which is what we used.

3. In the third experiment, we try to insert a new row into a remote Access table and then into a remote Oracle table. Table 12.10 shows the commands and results

TABLE 12.10   Single Remote Table Insert

Target Table	Command Ran	Results

Target is a remote Access table	Insert issued from Access
	
	`Insert into Emp_Sal_LE5K`
	`values (5, 3000);`
	
	`Delete from Emp_Sal_LE5K`
	`where EmpID = 5;`
		Succeeded

	Insert issued from DB2
	
	`Insert into`
	`Emp_Sal_LE5k_NN values`
	`(5, 3000);`
		DB20000I, the SQL command, completed successfully

Target is a remote Oracle table	Update issued from Access
	
	`Insert into Emp_Sal_GT5K`
	`values (6, 6000);`
	
	`Delete from Emp_Sal_GT5K`
	`where EmpID = 6;`
		Succeeded

	Update issued from DB2
	
	`Insert into`
	`Emp_Sal_GT5k_NN values`
	`(6, 6000)`
		DB20000I, the SQL command, completed successfully

TABLE 12.11   Single Remote Table Delete

Target Table	Command Ran	Results

Target is a remote Access table	Delete issued from Access
	
	`delete from Emp_Sal_LE5K`
	`where EmpID = 5;`
	`Insert into Emp_Sal_LE5K`
	`values (5, 3000);`
		Succeeded

	Delete issued from DB2
	
	`delete from`
	`Emp_Sal_LE5K_NN where`
	`EmpID = 5;`
		DB20000I, the SQL command, completed successfully

Target is a remote Oracle table	Delete issued from Access
	
	`delete from Emp_Sal_GT5K`
	`where EmpID = 6;`
	
	`Insert into Emp_Sal_GT5K`
	`values (6, 6000);`
		Succeeded

	Delete issued from DB2
	
	`delete from`
	`Emp_Sal_GT5K_NN where`
	`EmpID = 6;`
		DB20000I, the SQL command, completed successfully

for this experiment. Note that we delete the row we added from Access before we try to add it again from DB2.

4. Now we try to delete the Salary row we added for employees 5 and 6. Table 12.11 shows the commands and the results. Again, to make sure we undo the delete we performed from Access, we reinsert the row before deleting it from Federation Server. Both Access and Federation Server handle the single table delete easily.

5. Multitable modification statements in SQL are not allowed. Instead, we have to create a view that uses unions, joins, or both to bring the tables together and then apply update, insert, and delete to it. Creating a complete view of employee information requires using all tables we have. We are going to use an inner join and therefore will be leaving out those employees who do not have children. Also, since we know that modifications to the Excel spreadsheet are not allowed by Access linked tables and via the Excel wrapper by Federation Server, we will not include the Grants sheet in this experiment. The view that we need to create is the one we used previously for Query 3, except that we need to leave out grant information as shown below. Neither Federation Server nor Access allows update, delete, or insert statements against multiple table views.

```
Access View:
Emp_Sal Query:
((select sal, EmpID from emp_sal_le5k)
union
(select sal, EmpID from emp_sal_gt5k));

SELECT E.Ename, C.CNAME, S.sal
FROM Emp_Name_Access AS E, Child AS C, Emp_Sal AS S
WHERE (((E.EmpID)=C.Empid  And (E.EmpID)=S.EmpID));

Federation Server View:
create view EMP(EmpID, Ename, Cname, sal) as
select E.EmpID, E.Ename, C.Cname, S.Sal
from Emp_Name_DB2 E, Child_NN C,
((select sal, EmpID from emp_sal_le5k_NN)
union
(select sal, EmpID from emp_sal_gt5k_NN)) as s
where E.EmpID = C.Empid AND E.EmpID = S.EmpID;
```

12.9   SUMMARY

In this chapter, we reviewed architectures for managing distributed databases. We categorized these systems, which we generically called DDBEs, as DDBMSs—systems that are designed and developed top–down and provide total visibility and controls—and MDBSs—systems that are designed and developed bottom–up and provide partial visibility and control. We further classified MDBSs into two groups called federated databases (FDBs) and nonfederated databases (NFDBs). We discussed issues in designing and developing the top–down and bottom–up systems. Challenges in software and schema integrations for MDBSs were also pointed out. In the last section of this chapter, we introduced two commercial products that help in integrating heterogeneous database systems and compared their functionality.

12.10   GLOSSARY

Auxiliary Database   A database that contains translation, mapping, and integration information for a federated database.

Bottom–Up   A methodology that creates a complex system by integrating system components.

CODASYL   A DBMS standard that uses a network data model.

Commercial Off-the-Shelf (COTS)   Any piece of commercially available software.

Data Accessor (DA)   A service in a DBE that enables a user to access information under the control of the DBE.

Data Getter (DG)   A service in a DBE that enables a user to read information under the control of the DBE.

Data Source Name (DSN)   An alias given to a data source using the open database connectivity (ODBC).

Database Environment (DBE)   A collection of one or more DBs along with any software providing at least the minimum set of required data operations and management facilities.

Distributed Database Environment (DDBE)   A collection of one or more DBs along with any software providing at least the minimum set of required data operations and management facilities capable of supporting distributed data. A DDBE can also be a collection of dispersed software services or components that control access to, and modification of, data in a database.

Distributed Database Management System (DDBMS)   A term with two interpretations: it either refers to a specific DDBE environment that is built top–down, or to a generic environment we will refer to as a "DDBE" instead.

Export Schema   A portion of a database schema that a DBA shares with the systems outside the DBA's control.

Federated Database (FDB)   A specific DDBE that is built bottom–up.

Global Conceptual Schema (GCS)   An integration of schemas from two or more databases' local conceptual schemas.

Global Data Dictionary (GDD)   The portion of global conceptual schema that contains dictionary information such as table name, column names, or view names.

Global Transaction Manager (GTM)   A service or component that handles transactions that need to access data on multiple data sources.

Linked Table   A table that resides outside the Microsoft Access DBMS and is accessible from within Access.

Local Conceptual Schema   The conceptual schema of a system that pertains to the data inside the local system.

Local Transaction Manager (LTM)   A transaction manager that only handles a local transaction.

Multidatabase (MDB)   A DDBE that consists of a number of existing and possibly heterogeneous DBEs.

Nonfederated Database (NFDB)   A federated database in which the local DBEs do not support any request from outside the federation.

Nickname   An alias given to a data source outside IBM's InfoSphere Federation Server.

ODBC   The open database connectivity standard that enables creation of uniform code across different data sources and types.

Schema Integration   The act of integrating local conceptual schemas of the component database systems into a cohesive global conceptual schema.

Schema Translation   The act of translating the conceptual schemas of heterogeneous databases into a uniform model such as ER or relational.

Top–Down   A database design methodology that starts with the requirements of a distributed system (the global conceptual schema) and creates its local conceptual schemas.

Unified Schema   An integrated, nonredundant, and consistent schema for a set of local database systems.

Wrapper A software component that wraps a data source and provides a uniform interface to the outside world by hiding the specifics of its representation and command interface.

REFERENCES

[Bernstein80] Bernstein, P., and Shipman, D., "The Correctness of Concurrency Control Mechanisms in a System for Distributed Databases (SOD-1)," *ACM Transactions on Database Systems*, Vol. 5, No. 1, pp. 52–68, March 1980.

[Brzezinski84] Brzezinski, Z., Getta, J. R., Rybnik, J., and Stepniewski, W., "UNIBASE—An Integrated Access to Databases," in *Proceedings of the 10th International Conference on VLDB*, August 27–31, 1984 (U. Dayal, G. Schlageter, and L. H. Seng, Eds.), Morgan Kaufmann Publishers, San Francisco, CA, 1984, pp. 388–396.

[Devor82] Devor, C., Elmasri, R., and Rahimi, S., "The Design of DDTS: A Testbed for Reliable Distributed Database Management", Technical Report HP-82-273:17–38, Honeywell Computer Sciences Center, Camden, MN, 1982.

[Dwyer 87] Dwyer, P., and Larson, J., "Some Experiences with a Distributed Database Testbed System," *Proceedings of the IEEE*, Vol. 75, No. 5, pp. 633–647, 1987.

[Landers82] Landers, T., and Rosenberg, R., "An Overview of Multibase," in *Distributed Databases*, North-Holland, Amsterdam, 1982, pp. 153–184.

[Landers86] Landers, T., and Rosenberg, R., "An Overview of Multibase," in *Distributed Databases*, Vol. II, Artech House, Norwood, MA, 1986, pp. 391–421.

[Larson85] Larson, J., and Rahimi, S., *Tutorial. Distributed Database Management*, IEEE Computer Society Press, Silver Spring, MD, 1985.

[Litwin87] Litwin, W., and Vigier, P. "New Capabilities of the Multidatabase System MRDSM," in *HLSUA Forum XLV Proceedings*, New Orleans, October 1987.

[Nelson03] Nelson Mendonça, M., "Integrating Information for On Demand Computing," in *Proceedings of the 29th VLDB Conference*, Berlin, Germany, 2003.

[Özsu99] Özsu, M., and Valduriez, P., *Principles of Distributed Database Systems*, Prentice Hall, Englewood Cliffs, NJ, 1999.

[Ram89] Ram, S., and Chastain, C., "Architecture of Distributed Data Base Systems," *Journal of System Software*, Vol. 10, No. 2, pp. 77–95, 1989.

[Roth97] Roth, M., and Schwarz, P., "Don't Scrap It, Wrap It! A Wrapper Architecture for Legacy Data Sources," in *Proceedings of the 23rd Conference on Very Large Data Bases*, Athens, Greece, August 26–29, 1997.

[Sheth88] Sheth, A., Larson, J., Cornelio, A., and Navathe, S., "A Tool for Integrating Conceptual Schemas and User Views," in *Proceedings of the Fourth IEEE International Conference on Data Engineering*, Los Angeles, CA, pp. 176–183, February 1988.

[Sheth89] Sheth, A., "Heterogeneous Distributed Databases: Issues in Integration," Tutorial Notes, in *Proceedings of the Fifth International Conference on Data Engineering*, 1989.

[Sheth90] Sheth, A., and Larson, J., "Federated Database Systems for Managing Distributed, Heterogeneous and Autonomous Databases," *Computing Surveys*, Vol. 22, No. 3, pp. 183–236, September 1990.

[Templeton86] Templeton, M., Brill, D., Chen, A., Dao, S., and Lund, E., "Mermaid: Experiences with Network Operation," in *Proceedings of the 2nd International Conference on Data Engineering*, 1986.

EXERCISE

Provide short (but complete) answers to the following question.

12.1 Map each of the following three schemas (shown in Figure 12.32) to ER and then integrate them into a minimal and complete integrated database.

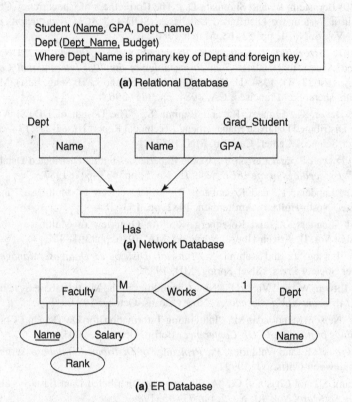

Student (<u>Name</u>, GPA, Dept_name)
Dept (<u>Dept_Name</u>, Budget)
Where Dept_Name is primary key of Dept and foreign key.

(a) Relational Database

(a) Network Database

(a) ER Database

Figure 12.32   Example databases to be integrated for Exercise 12.1.

13

NEW DDBE ARCHITECTURES

In this chapter, we will discuss two new architectural alternatives for implementing a **distributed database environment (DDBE)**. When these architectures were first introduced, their names used the traditional nomenclature (DDBMS); in this book, the term "DDBE" is used instead. These two alternatives have several things in common with each other. In particular, both are attempts to implement an environment that is more dynamic (with respect to deployment details) than the traditional DDBE alternatives we discussed in Chapter 12. The first architecture is called the **cooperative distributed database environment (COOP)** [Rahimi07a] and the second is called the **peer to peer distributed database environment (P2P)** [Rahimi07b]. After we have discussed each of these architectures, we will explore the similarities and differences between them and then discuss the similarities and differences between these two architectures and the traditional architectures discussed in Chapter 12.

13.1 COOPERATIVE DDBEs

The first approach we are going to explore in this chapter is the **cooperative distributed database environment (COOP)**. The primary motivation for this architecture came from various cooperative systems that started to gain popularity in the late 1990s and early 2000s. Although cooperative systems can be used for various tasks, and all cooperative systems will have some aspects in common, the primary motivation for the COOP is in the similarities that exist between a set of cooperative DDBE subsystems and a set of cooperative systems designed to share content. These content-sharing systems typically share streams of music or some other type of electronic file content over a loosely controlled and extremely dynamic system environment [Ripeanu01]. Each of these environments consists of a set of systems, which in turn combine to

---

Distributed Database Management Systems by Saeed K. Rahimi and Frank S. Haug
Copyright © 2010 the IEEE Computer Society

form a loosely coupled network. Often, one or more **components or subsystems (COSs)** will act as a directory or communication switchboard for the loosely affiliated network nodes currently connected to a particular environment. Some of these nodes will provide content, while others will be seeking to consume content. The nodes in these networks can operate over an extremely dynamic environment (i.e., an intranet or even the Internet/World Wide Web). These systems also provide a very resilient and efficient distribution mechanism for the content being shared.

If we consider the environment from the content consumer node's point of view, it begins its participation with the system by sending out a request message to the environment. This request message typically contains query criteria for a particular piece of desired content. Each provider node that is capable of supplying the content responds to the request—if it is connected to the environment at that time and available. Often, there are multiple provider nodes available and even multiple renditions or versions of the same content available at the same time in the environment. When this situation occurs, the consumer node can select the provider node it wishes to use.

If we consider the environment from the content provider node's point of view, participation in one of these networks of content-sharing systems is usually a relatively simple and easy process. Although there is some communication overhead (perhaps registering with or connecting to the switchboard system), there is usually not a rigid control structure or an overly complex protocol to follow in order to join the environment. Each provider node can freely enroll in the network, provide its content to any consumers in the environment that wish to receive it, and then exit the network gracefully whenever the provider decides that it no longer wishes to participate in the network. These enrollment and exit activities can occur frequently and haphazardly based on the idiosyncratic whims of the provider nodes and consumer nodes without any complicated reconfiguration or shutdown/restart process required. Obviously, exit activities should attempt to be graceful whenever possible, but otherwise the exit process can be very simple and hassle-free. In a graceful exit for a provider node, the exiting provider node should deny requests for future connections and wait for existing connections to complete before exiting. In a graceful exit for a consumer node, the exiting consumer node should close all the connections to its providers before exiting the network.

In some implementations, each provider includes self-ranking metadata in the response it provides to the initial request. This metadata can describe conditions at the provider (such as the current number of transfers, the current number of connections available, etc.) and can also include details that describe the content being provided (such as the file size, creation date, modification date, and other similar details about the data content and data quality). Additional metadata can be calculated from these details, such as the estimated transfer rate and the relative distance between the consumer node and the provider node. All of this metadata is intended to help the client choose from the list of currently active providers for a given set of content. In most cases, the consumer node is able to build a prioritized list of providers for the desired content. This list is built using the provider-supplied self-ranking metadata and a flexible combination of both automatic and user-influenced strategies. This also allows the client to automatically switch to the next most desirable provider if it is unable to complete the transfer with a particular provider for any reason.

The COOP system is an attempt to provide the same sense of loosely coupled cooperation that other non-DBE systems have demonstrated—but rather than forming

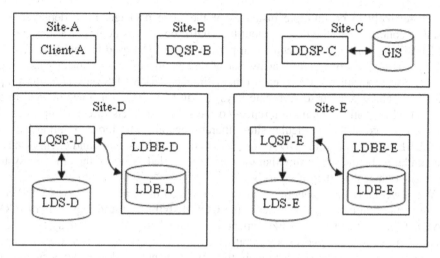

Figure 13.1   A typical COOP deployment.

environments using networks of cooperating systems in order to provide the functionality of a file server or web server, the COOP architecture is intended to provide the functionality of a DBE. Historically, the components in a DDBE are rather tightly coupled; altering the deployment details for any particular COS is not a trivial task in these traditional environments. In order to achieve the desired level of decoupling, the components and subsystems in the COOP need to be designed differently. For simplicity, we will refer to these parts of the COOP environment as subsystems—even though some subsystems are often implemented as a single component.

13.1.1   Subsystems Overview

Figure 13.1 shows a typical deployment of the COOP environment. In this example, there is a single client subsystem instance ("Client-A") deployed at Site A, a single **distributed query service provider (DQSP)** subsystem instance ("DQSP-B") deployed at Site B, and a single **data dictionary service provider (DDSP)** subsystem instance ("DDSP-C") with its associated **global interface schema (GIS)** instance deployed at Site C. Sites D and E are identical with respect to the number of component and subsystem instances deployed at each site—at each site there is a single **local query service provider (LQSP)** subsystem instance deployed along with a single instance of a **local deployment schema (LDS)** for that site. At each site, there is also a single instance of a **Sub-DBE (S-DBE)**, which we refer to as a **local database environment (LDBE)**, deployed along with the **local databases (LDBs)** that it contains and controls. This is merely a simple example deployment: an actual deployment in the real world could have many more clients, service providers, and DBEs, but this diagram should be sufficient for our discussions in this chapter.

The subsystem instances in the COOP database environment can be heterogeneous or homogenous. For example, LDBE-D might be a **relational database management system (RDBMS)** while LDBE-E could be either the same RDBMS package, a different RDBMS package, or a non-RDBMS based DBE. Usually, the DBEs will depend on existing system deployment details while the various service provider subsystems are more likely to be multiple instances of the same package. Each deployed LDS instance contains only the details about the DDBE constructs deployed at that particular LDBE site, and only the details that pertain to the LDB used to deploy it. Because the LDS is focused on such a narrow set of details, the LDBE instances can be very loosely coupled with respect to each other. Similarly, each LDS only contains simple reference values (similar to surrogate keys) linking it to the constructs defined in the GIS. The LDS only contains references to the GIS constructs directly impacting the pieces deployed at that particular site—thereby enabling the loose coupling between the LDBE instances and the DDSP instances. The DQSP instances and client instances use similar techniques to ensure that they are not coupled to any of the other subsystem instances tighter than they need to be.

When we apply the taxonomy that was introduced in Chapter 1 to the COOP environment, the first taxon we consider is the **COS distribution and deployment (COS-DAD)**. Clearly, the COOP environment is a completely distributed system—each subsystem can be deployed on a separate machine. The next level considers the openness or closedness of the subsystems in the environment. The lowest level subsystems (the LDBEs) might be implemented by **commercial off-the-shelf (COTS)** components, by open source components, or potentially by components that we developed from the ground up. Regardless of the decision made for the LDBEs, all the other components are written by us. Therefore, the COOP environment is either a completely open system or a mostly open system depending on the details for the LDBEs. The next level of the taxonomy considers the schema and data visibility at each local database environment. Although there is some flexibility within this level, most COOP environments will consist of LQSP instances that provide only a small subset of the GIS. The COOP environment is similar to the federated DDBEs discussed in Chapter 12—its LDBEs can operate outside the DDBE and can contain data that is not part of the LDS or the GIS. It is even possible for the deployed data to be implemented by a partial subset of an existing table in the LDB. Therefore, the visibility for both schema and data is probably partial visibility in most scenarios. Because of the dynamic nature of the environment, updates are not really a practical consideration in the COOP environment. In other words, because the LQSP instances can dynamically join and exit the environment frequently and haphazardly, there is no practical way to enforce the synchronization required for all of the replicas when insert, update, and delete operations are allowed. While it is possible to use some external mechanism (outside of the COOP DBE) to enforce synchronization, it is not necessarily a requirement. Each LDBE can instead supply details about the most recent modifications and allow the clients to determine whether the data is out-of-date or not (from the client's point of view). The final level of the taxonomy considers the schema and data control, which is also quite limited in this environment. For the reasons we just mentioned, data modification is not supported through the DQSP interface for extremely dynamic, ad hoc environments. Similarly, schema modifications in the COOP DBE are somewhat complex and therefore not supported through the DQSP interface in this extreme scenario.

However, we can consider deploying the COOP environment in a more restricted set of circumstances—we do not have to configure our DDBE deployment as a completely ad hoc environment just because the architecture can support it. Instead, we can use this loose coupling to minimize the impact of deployment changes, while still retaining enough static characteristics to support data modification or even schema modification. It should be noted that this is not the primary goal of this architecture and therefore the controls and facilities for these operations are not as simple, efficient, or powerful as other alternatives. In other words, if our goal is to deploy a DDBE with a high volume of data modification or a high volume of schema modification operations, then a different architecture would probably be a better solution.

In summary, the COOP DBE is typically a completely distributed, mostly open (or perhaps completely open), partially visible, partially controlled DBE. It works best for mostly read-only environments where the goal is to support dynamic, ad hoc providers of (mostly) read-only content whose structure does not need to be changed dynamically within the environment. This architecture is well suited for supplying multiple deployment plans for the same data and dynamically changing those deployment details. In the next sections, we will briefly describe each of the subsystems in the environment. After that, we will examine the interactions between the subsystem instances in this deployment example.

13.1.1.1   Client   Each client subsystem is a user-written program or end-user application implemented using web services or similar-minded approaches. Approaches such as web services [Singh04] are intended to be platform independent (as much as possible), which is implicitly part of the COOP environment's primary goal. In reality, most clients are written on top of a simple framework that provides the necessary communication details—allowing the client code to focus on its intended operations instead of the underlying communication details. This also means that clients can easily be implemented as small, lightweight, and multithreaded applications. Although the framework provides the necessary functionality, it is important to keep the overhead low and the logic simple—otherwise, it would be difficult for users to create the client programs that they need. Each client subsystem instance sends requests to a single instance of the distributed query service provider. Theoretically, this request could be implemented using any interface we choose to use. In practice, however, we chose to use a subset of the ANSI standard Structured Query Language (SQL) or a programmatic interface that mirrors the select statement defined within the standard.

13.1.1.2   Distributed Query Service Provider   The **distributed query service provider** (DQSP) subsystem is reasonably lightweight. The DQSP subsystem can be deployed as several instances within the intranet and can be pooled within an application server. For example, it can be deployed using a managed assembly within the Microsoft .NET Framework or it can be deployed as an EJB within a J2EE application server such as JBOSS [Fleury03]. It can also be deployed as a web service and registered dynamically by using the **web services description language (WSDL)** and the **universal description, discovery, and integration (UDDI)** facility. The DQSP is merely an encapsulation and decoupling of the communication complexities and potentially complex threading required for processing query requests and results correctly and efficiently in the network of cooperating subsystem instances. The DQSP verifies that the client (SQL) request uses valid syntax and parses it into a more efficient format. The DQSP requires no access to the GIS or LDS because it does not validate the names of the global tables and columns used in the request. The DQSP does not verify that the request is unambiguous either—this would require access to the GIS in order to determine the global column names defined for the global tables involved. Instead, the DQSP sends the more efficient format of the query to the DDSP subsystem for verification with respect to the GIS and disambiguation.

13.1.1.3 Data Dictionary Service Provider The **data dictionary service provider** (DDSP) subsystem has a very specific role in the environment—it acts as the dynamic registry for all the constructs, components, and subsystems active in the environment at the present moment. This means that the DDSP needs to know how to look up information about the global constructs defined within the environment and the LDBEs active within the environment.

The DDSP subsystem provides two important services to the COOP DDBE:

- It provides access to the GIS.
- It monitors and tracks the LQSP subsystem instances registered in its network.

First and foremost, the DDSP subsystem is the only subsystem in the environment that directly accesses the GIS. It does this on behalf of the DQSP in order to validate and disambiguate the global schema constructs referenced in the client SQL. The DDSP uses the GIS to look up the fully qualified names for all the global constructs referenced in the SQL—using the additional user-supplied qualification details when they are present. When the qualification details (container names or aliases) are not present, the DDSP attempts to determine the fully qualified name without them. This is only an issue if there is more than one possible container name referenced in the (SQL) request. If there is more than one possible name, the (SQL) request is ambiguous—a fatal error for the query. Similarly, if any of the construct names referenced in the query are not defined in the GIS (regardless of whether they are qualified or not in the query), the (SQL) request is invalid—another fatal error. If there are any fatal errors with the request, the DDSP returns an appropriate error message to the DQSP. Otherwise, the DDSP uses the information it retrieves from the GIS along with other details to locate potential LQSP instances in the environment at the time of the request.

Keeping track of the details used to locate potential LQSP instances is the other, equally important service provided by the DDSP. These location details are not contained in the GIS—instead each DDSP instance dynamically keeps track of the subsystems currently registered within its environment. Each LQSP instance registers itself with the environment (and with the DDSP in that environment) when it joins the environment. Similarly, each LQSP deregisters itself from the environment (and DDSP) before leaving the COOP environment. There are several alternatives that could be used for this registration process, but if we are using web services, then using a standard approach (like WSDL and UDDI) makes the most sense.

This registration information is usually simply cached in memory, but it is possible to persist it in some database (DB) if necessary. The basic registration mechanism must include the necessary communication details (protocol and port details) for the subsystem instance being registered. More advanced registration mechanisms could also be used to improve performance and reduce communication overhead—for example, each LQSP subsystem instance could include details about the GIS constructs it provides when it registers with the environment. These details could then be used to narrow the list of potential LQSPs available for a distributed query request. When the DDSP disambiguates and validates all the global constructs referenced in a particular (SQL) request, it might use those details to filter the list of currently registered LQSP instances. Regardless of whether the DDSP filters the list or simply uses the unfiltered list, the list of LQSP instances is returned to the DQSP component along with a status message indicating that there were no errors with the request, as well as all the qualification details for the constructs in the original request.

13.1.1.4 Global Interface Schema   The **global interface schema** (GIS) replaces the traditional **global data dictionary (GDD)**, which is discussed in Section 2.4 of Chapter 2 and Section 12.5 in Chapter 12. Like a GDD, a GIS is a special purpose database that contains all the global table names, global column names, and global data types/nullability details in the environment. However, unlike a GDD, a GIS does not contain any fragmentation, replication, or location details. All of those deployment details are relegated to the LDS instances. Instead, a GIS model focuses on the conceptual definition of the global tables and columns, along with the constraints that apply to them.

The GIS provides a virtual namespace for global constructs by defining global databases, schemas, and tables. The GIS also supports the definition of global users and groups along with the population of relationships between these security constructs and the global databases, schemas, tables, and columns. These details enable security details to be queried from the GIS. Obviously, the actual enforcement of these details can rely on more secure mechanisms such as those discussed in Chapter 9. However, when it is deemed appropriate, these policies can be reflected in the GIS model in order to provide metadata about the GIS to tools. When security needs to be more tightly enforced, and schema details need to be more closely guarded, these policy details can be omitted. But the dynamic nature of the COOP architecture probably lends itself to a somewhat loose security policy. In other words, a dynamic environment consisting of several loosely coupled data providers only makes sense when the data is not highly confidential and proprietary, or when all participants are guaranteed to be secure by virtue of stronger circumstances: for example, if the COOP environment is deployed on an isolated network of machines within a locked room and/or using advanced techniques in order to provide the necessary security (i.e., functions like confidentiality, authentication, and nonrepudiation—which are all discussed in Section 9.1).

Another important difference between the GIS and a traditional GDD is the level of completeness for an individual instance and the degree of synchronization required when multiple instances exist for the same DDBE. Traditionally, the GDD is a bottleneck for traditional DDBE architectures that disallow multiple GDD instances. In these architectures, there is a single, centralized GDD that must be consulted whenever global constructs are translated into their physical deployed counterparts. Although the contents of the GDD are usually small compared to the contents of the global tables they represent, this restriction requires all components to have access to a central server and central database. To remove this bottleneck, some other traditional DDBE architectures permit multiple copies of the GDD to be deployed in the environment as long as all GDD instances have identical structure and content. This works well in environments with minimal deployment changes and minimal schematic changes, but can be cumbersome for more dynamic environments.

The COOP DDBE permits either a single GIS instance or multiple GIS instances—even when there are multiple DDSP instances in the environment. When we consider multiple GIS instances that are deployed in the same environment, the instances do not need to be identical with respect to their content (or even their structure). When we consider each GIS instance with respect to the LDS instances deployed within the same environment, once again, the content and structure do not need to be identical. However, we will only be able to use LQSP instances whose LDS corresponds to the desired GIS construct.

In order to support these independencies, the GIS model needs to differ significantly from the GDD in three key respects:

- Focus on the interface
- Support for multiple deployment plans
- Use of unique identifiers for both plans and constructs

The first difference between the GIS and GDD is the concept of an **interface**. We could characterize a traditional GDD as considering each global construct to be a virtual construct. A virtual construct is merely a convenient mapping mechanism for dealing with the real tables—that is, the physical fragments and replicas (or the simple physical table stored at a particular location in the case of a nonfragmented and nonreplicated global table). By contrast, the GIS considers the global table and column definitions to be an interface to the deployed content in the same way that object-oriented programming (OOP) techniques consider an interface and the concrete classes that implement it. All of the deployment details are unimportant to the GIS as long as they are consistent with respect to the global interface represented by the virtual table and its columns.

The second difference between the GIS and the GDD is the GIS's support for multiple deployment plans for the same global construct. This support is only possible because of the first difference—that is, it is precisely because the global tables and columns act like an interface, that we can support multiple deployment plans for the same global table and its global columns. Again, this is analogous to using different concrete classes that implement the same interface in OOP. The details for each deployment plan are stored in the LDS instances where that plan is implemented, but not in the GIS. This means that even when multiple plans for the same global construct exist in the same environment, the GIS is unaffected—as long as the plans conform to the GIS information.

The third difference between the GIS and the GDD is the GIS's reliance on unique identifiers for constructs and plans. These identifiers are crucial to supporting the loosely coupled situation we desire. The GIS requires the use of unique identifier values to enable the easy identification of specific constructs or plans with minimal overhead and minimal synchronization. These unique identifiers can be implemented using any reasonable technique, but the most obvious choice is to use the same mechanism used in many interface implementations for program environments—namely, **globally unique identifiers (GUIDs)**. A GUID uses a unique combination of system details (network card unique addresses, date and timestamps, and other details) to ensure that a value generated on a particular machine, at a particular date and time, cannot also be generated by another computer anywhere else. This is true even though the computers never communicate with each other. When a global construct is defined, it is assigned a GUID, which is stored with the construct definition in the GIS. If the same definition for the same construct needs to be shared across multiple systems (such as different GIS instances or the LDS instances that implement a deployment plan for the construct), this same GUID value must be copied to the other systems—but we do not need to copy all the constructs! Each LDS must be synchronized with the GIS for only those constructs deployed at the LDBE where the LDS resides. When the DDSP queries the

GIS, it retrieves the GUID for each global table and column referenced in the query as part of its validation and disambiguation process. These GUIDs are then added to the fully qualified version of the query (along with the other qualification details).

Using a GUID value as a unique identifier for GIS constructs (and LDS constructs) is not a new idea—it is somewhat analogous to the version identifier ("serialVersionUID") used by Serializable classes in Java, and also similar to the various identifiers stored in the registry by the Microsoft Common Object Model (COM)—the ancestor of Microsoft .NET Framework. While those two environments were initially implemented as centralized programming environments, many distributed computing mechanisms also use GUID values for this same purpose—namely, identifying when a deployed or distributed version of something matches the expected version. There are many examples of environments using this approach, such as the **Common Object Resource Broker Architecture (CORBA)**, Microsoft .NET Framework, and Java's Remote Method Invocation. This enables components that are disconnected from each other most of the time to verify that they are synchronized each time they dynamically connect to each other.

13.1.1.5 Local Deployment Schema   Each **local deployment schema** (LDS) instance contains the deployment details for the global constructs defined in the GIS that are deployed (in whole or in part) at the site where that LDS instance is deployed. In particular, the LDS must store the GUID values for these global constructs. The LDS must also store mapping details for each local construct deployed in the local database environment at the site (the local tables representing the whole tables, table fragments, or replicas). These mappings connect each local construct to the global construct (or fragment of a global construct) that it represents. When a global table is deployed, it must define a deployment plan (which can also be considered a reconstruction plan).

For example, suppose we have an Employee table (represented by the first relational schema in Fig. 13.2) that is fragmented vertically into two fragments (represented by the second and third relational schemas in Fig. 13.2). In this example, the MgrEmpNo and DptNo columns reside in one vertical fragment (EmpVf1) and the EmpName and EmpTitle columns reside in a second vertical fragment (EmpVf2). Because the EmpNo column is the primary key for the global table, it must appear in both fragments (it is used to join the fragments back together in reconstruction). The LDS would need to define the fragmentation plan for this table. This plan would include information about

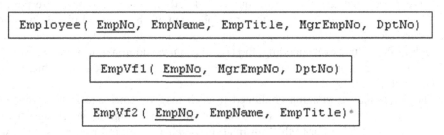

Figure 13.2 A global relation and its two vertical fragments.

the type of fragmentation, the number of fragments, and also the mappings for each global column defined in the table. This plan would also be assigned a GUID when it was first defined, so that all of the LDS instances containing a fragment for this plan can be synchronized without being connected to each other—having the same GUID value for the plan means that they are the same plan. Similarly, a simple method using bitmask values allows us to easily determine when all the required plan fragments are present. For example, suppose the EmpVf1 fragment has a bitmask value of "0x01" and the EmpVf2 fragment has a bitmask value of "0x02." In this scenario, the plan would store a bitmask value of "0x03" for the completed table—now we simply use the binary OR operation to combine the bitmask values for each fragment and compare this result with the desired value for the whole table. This same technique can be used for hybrid fragmentation to determine when all of the subfragments are present to reconstruct a larger fragment.

The GIS and LDS can support multiple plans for the same global construct by simply storing different plans with different GUIDs. All of the LDS instances participating in a particular plan would use the GIS GUID value for the global construct and the LDS GUID plan value for its fragments. Meanwhile, all the LDS instances participating in a different deployment plan for the same global construct would still use the same GIS GUID value, but they would use a different LDS GUID plan value for the fragments of this different plan.

13.1.1.6 *Local Query Service Provider*   The **local query service provider** (LQSP) subsystem is responsible for all the local query processing. It connects to the LDBE and executes the necessary commands for a global request. Each LQSP instance registers itself with the environment, which allows the DDSP to know about its availability. As we mentioned earlier, this registration can be very simple or it can include further details to help reduce the communication overhead when queries are being processed after the registration has completed. The details included in the latter scenario would provide hints (perhaps using the GUIDs for global constructs or deployment plans) to aid in the LQSP election process.

When the environment processes a query, each LQSP instance registered in the environment at that time and containing a deployed part of a construct (a local table, fragment, or replica) referenced in the query is a candidate for being a content provider to the query. When the DDSP returns a fully qualified version of the query to the DQSP (including the necessary GUIDs), it also includes a list of LQSP instances that might be used to answer the query. The DQSP then passes this information on to the LQSP instances in the list and waits for feedback from them. If there are not enough LQSP participants capable of providing the content, or if they do not respond within a configurable time limit, then the query will fail. If there are enough responding LQSP instances (and if they have the same plan and all the required pieces for all the necessary global constructs), then we can process the query. If there are more than enough LQSP instances responding, the DQSP can use additional information included in each of the responses (one response from each LQSP) to determine which LQSP instances the query should use.

The additional information contained in each response message is determined by each LQSP instance itself and is based on statistics and configuration settings that are under its control. We refer to this information as self-ranking information—because it contains values, used to rank how efficient or suitable a particular LQSP instance is for a given part of a given query, that were generated by the instance itself. Each LDBE in the environment stores metadata about the data it stores—this is also a common practice for many traditional, centralized RDBMSs [Elmrasi94]. In addition to this traditional metadata (which typically captures details about the size and shape of the centralized data such as the estimated selectivity for columns, details about the row size and index utilization, etc.), the LQSP and LDBE also store metadata relevant to the DDBE in which they participate, including deployment details. For example, the self-ranking information for LQSP-D could include the date and time its data was last updated, the average response time for the server, the number of queries currently being processed, load factor details, and estimated latency times. This information is crucial to the distributed query plan creation, which is discussed in the next section.

13.1.2 Implementation Specifics

In this section, we will briefly consider the registration/deregistration process and then we will look at a query processing example to demonstrate how the subsystems cooperate within the environment to satisfy a client request (SQL query).

13.1.2.1 DQSP/LQSP Registration and Deregistration Each DQSP instance can support several client instances at the same time. Although it is theoretically possible for each DQSP instance to register and deregister with several DDSP instances for the same set of clients, this is not the intended deployment architecture. Each LQSP instance can support several DDSP instances at the same time. These registration (and deregistration) activities are typically implemented as part of a Directory Service, which is discussed in Chapter 14, Section 14.3.2. Each DQSP instance is intended to serve as the query service provider for a set of loosely affiliated LQSP instances—namely, those that have registered with the same DDSP instance where the DQSP is registered. Although the DQSP instances could register with multiple DDSP instances (and therefore connect to multiple sets of LQSPs), this can complicate the DQSP processing unnecessarily. Because LQSP instances can dynamically register and deregister with different DDSP instances, there is usually no need for the DQSP to register with multiple DDSP instances. As a fallback strategy, the DQSP could be asked to connect to other DDSP instances when no provider for a global table or column can be found. However, it would probably be better for the client to implement this strategy instead, since this would have a smaller impact on the other deployed clients and services. After the DDSP performs its tasks, it will return a message to the DQSP instance. This returned message will contain either error information or details used to communicate with the LQSP providers in the environment.

13.1.2.2 The Client Sends a Query to the DQSP The COOP environment uses a generic form of structured query language (SQL)—actually it is a subset of the American National Standards Institute (ANSI) standard SQL, to communicate requests from the client subsystems to other parts of the environment. For example, suppose we have two global tables named "Employee" and "Department" defined by the relational schemas shown in Figure 13.3. If a client needs to retrieve the names of all the engineers as well as the name of the department for which each engineer works, it can send a query like the one shown in Figure 13.4 to any DQSP in the DDBE.

```
Employee( EmpNo, EmpName, EmpTitle, MgrEmpNo, DptNo)
```

```
Department (DptNo, DptName, DptStreet, DptCity,
            DptState, DptZip)
```

Figure 13.3   Two relational schemas for two global relational tables.

```
SELECT  EmpName, DptName
FROM    Employee E, Department D
WHERE   E.DptNo  = D.DptNo
AND     EmpTitle = 'Engineer';
```

Figure 13.4   A global query written in SQL requiring the use of table aliases.

Because the COOP DDBE provides complete distribution transparency (as discussed in Chapter 2), the SQL commands sent by the client do not need to include any table fragmentation, location, or replication details. The only requirement for the client SQL is that it be written using the accepted syntax (a subset of ANSI SQL excluding DDL, DML, and overly complex queries) and be unambiguous and correct with respect to that syntax. The syntax requirements for the global SQL are a subset of the requirements we would expect to see for any DBE supporting ANSI SQL. Because the syntax must be validated for every query before it can be processed by the DDBE, we perform syntax validations in the subsystem responsible for providing the query service (the DQSP). Only syntactically correct queries need to be checked for ambiguity (because queries with syntax errors will not be processed).

13.1.2.3   The DQSP Sends a Query to the DDSP   After the DQSP has validated the syntax for a given query, it is possible to check if all the global tables and global columns referenced by the query are valid and unambiguous. This is done by checking the global definition of the DDBE and the contents of the query. Because the global definitions are contained in the GIS, which is usually not deployed on the same site as the client or the DQSP, neither the client nor the DQSP can directly implement this type of validation. Instead, the DQSP passes the syntactically correct query to the DDSP for validation and disambiguation.

The queries sent by the client nodes to the DDBE are intended to be written by (and readable by) the client application authors and users. In this sense, the client is the only external subsystem in the environment. Therefore, its queries are written in a well-known, standardized language—namely, SQL. Other messages, sent and received among the other subsystems, are internal to the DDBE and can therefore use a more programmatically efficient format. These internal formats are implemented in XML. Figure 13.5 shows a brief example of one of these XML formats—here only the top-level elements are shown, with ellipses taking the place of additional subelements that define the clauses more completely.

The contents of these subelements are highly dependent on the actual content being represented. For example, Figure 13.6 shows the SelectExpressionList contents for the SQL query we discussed for Figure 13.4. This is the list of expressions being returned to

```
<Query>
   <SelectExpressionList>...</SelectExpressionList>
   <FromExpresionList>...</FromExpressionList>
   <JoinConditionList>...</JoinConditionList>
   <NonJoinConditionList>...</NonJoinConditionList>
</Query>
```

Figure 13.5 Internal XML format (showing only top-level elements).

```
<SelectExpressionList>
   <SelectExpression>
     <SelectColumnExpression>
        <SelectColumnName>EmpName</SelectColumnName>
     </SelectColumnExpression>
   </SelectExpression>
   <SelectExpression>
     <SelectColumnExpression>
        <SelectColumnName>DptName</SelectColumnName>
     </SelectColumnExpression>
   </SelectExpression>
</SelectExpressionList>
```

Figure 13.6 SelectExpressionList for global query in Figure 13.4.

the client. In this example, they are simple columns, but more complicated queries could perform other operations, including functions or mathematical operations. Figure 13.7 shows the FromExpressionList for this same query—notice that since the user query included table aliases, they are also included here. Figures 13.8 and 13.9 show the JoinConditionList and NonJoinConditionList contents for this query, respectively.

The ambiguity concerns in the global query are analogous to the concerns found in any traditional RDBMS—we must qualify the global table names and global column names whenever the unqualified name could refer to more than one concept in the query. For example, we must qualify the global column names by adding the global table name or a table alias as a prefix to the column name if the same column appears in more than one table referenced in the query. We must also qualify the global column names if the query references the same global table more than once within the same context. The query shown in Figure 13.4 is written against two global tables, which are named "Employee" and "Department" (their relational schemas are shown in Figure 13.3). This query is an example of an unambiguous query performing a natural join (the join coloums have the same name). In order to ensure that this query is not ambiguous, we defined two table aliases ("E" and "D"), and also used each alias to identify the table containing each join column in the join condition.

13.1.2.4 The DDSP Sends a Fully Qualified Query to the DQSP Once the query has been disambiguated, the DDSP sends a message back to the DQSP. This message

```
<FromExpressionList>
  <FromExpression>
    <FromTableExpression>
      <FromTableName>Employee</FromTableName>
      <FromTableAlias>E</FromTableAlias>
    </FromTableExpression>
  </FromExpression>
  <FromExpression>
    <FromTableExpression>
      <FromTableName>Department</FromTableName>
      <FromTableAlias>D</FromTableAlias>
    </FromTableExpression>
  </FromExpression>
</FromExpressionList>
```

Figure 13.7   FromExpressionList for global query in Figure 13.4.

```
<JoinConditionList>
  <JoinCondition isEquiJoin='True'>
    <JcLeftColumn>
      <JcLeftTableAlias>E</JcLeftTableAlias>
      <JcLeftColumnName>DptNo</JcLeftColumnName>
    </JcLeftColumn>
    <JcRightColumn>
      <JcRightTableAlias>D</JcRightTableAlias>
      <JcRightColumnName>DptNo</JcRightColumnName>
    </JcRightColumn>
  </JoinCondition>
</JoinConditionList>
```

Figure 13.8   JoinConditonList for global query in Figure 13.4.

contains the fully qualified XML version of the query, which is similar to the examples we have seen, but with even more information included for each subelement. This message also contains a list of candidate LQSP instances.

13.1.2.5 The Election Process   After receiving the message from the DDSP containing the fully qualified query and candidate list details, the DQSP sends a message to each of the candidate LQSP instances. Each LQSP instance in this list will consider the information in the query message, the information in the LDS deployed at its site, and other site metadata (such as the current load factor and number of requests being processed). If a particular LQSP instance decides to participate in the query, it will form a rough execution plan for the parts of the query that it can provide. By doing this, the participating LQSP instance calculates an estimate for the self-ranking metadata that we discussed in Section 13.1.1.6. This self-ranking information is then returned to the DQSP.

```
<NonJoinConditionList>
  <NonJoinCondition Type='Equals'>
    <NjcLeftExpression>
      <NjcColumnExpression>
        <ColumnName>EmpTitle</ColumnName>
      </NjcColumnExpression>
    </NjcLeftExpression>
    <NjcRightExpression>
      <NjcLiteralExpression>
        <StringValue>Enginner</StringValue>
      </NjcLiteralExpression>
    </NjcRightExpression>
  </NonJoinCondition>
</NonJoinConditionList>
```

Figure 13.9   NonJoinConditonList for global query in Figure 13.4.

The DQSP waits until it hears from all the candidate LQSP instances or until a specified timeout limit has expired. If there are multiple candidates for any part of the query, then the DQSP uses the self-ranking information to pick the best candidate. When there is only one candidate capable of providing a part of the content, this candidate is elected by default. If each part of the query has elected an LQSP instance, then the DQSP sends out a message to all the candidates identifying the elected instances. If we do not have adequate coverage in the environment at this time, then the DQSP sends a message (to the candidates and to the client) indicating that the query has failed because of insufficient provider availability.

When there is adequate coverage, each elected LQSP instance uses the plan calculated in the previous step to process its part of the query. All LQSP instances use the same logic for deciding the control logic (which partial results are sent to which instance) in a manner similar to those discussed in Chapter 4. This means that no further coordination is required unless there are timeouts or errors.

The query results are returned using data types native to the programming languages that the clients are written in or using another simple XML format. The COOP DDBE uses the **relational data model (RDM)** as its **logical level modeling language (LLML)**, which we discussed in Chapter 11. Therefore, the external query format, internal query formats, and query result format all have a relational flavor. Like most DDBEs, each database cooperating in the COOP environment must translate its **physical level modeling language (PLML)** constructs into the appropriate logical level modeling language constructs in order to participate in the COOP DDBE. Obviously, this is easier to implement when all of the DBs use the same LLML as the DDBE, but this is not a strict requirement of the system. As we discussed in Chapter 12, other LDMs can be used if the appropriate translations are implemented. We simply translate the requests and results from the low-level subsystems (Query Processors, Command Processors, or Data Processors) into the canonical format for the DDBE (and here, it is the RDM). This means that subsystems within the environment can pass the internal queries and query results to each other without knowing the PLML (or even the LLML) used by each DB in the environment.

13.2 PEER-TO-PEER DDBEs

The second approach we are going to explore in this chapter is the **peer-to-peer distributed database environment (P2P)**. It is based on many of the same concepts as the COOP environment. However, in the P2P environment, additional emphasis is placed on the idea of service providers being peers—that is, equal members of the environment. In the P2P environment, each peer is a query service provider—we do not consider the clients to be peers because they usually do not have a local database environment. In many respects, the P2P environment is an evolution of the COOP environment, sharing many of the same characteristics. Therefore, we will limit the discussion in this section to aspects that are different from the COOP environment. The subsystems defined within each of these architectures are not identical—there are some subtle, but important, differences across the architectures (even for subsystems with identical names).

13.2.1 P2P Overview

Figure 13.10 shows a typical deployment of the P2P environment. In this example, there is a single client subsystem instance ("Client-A") deployed at Site A, and three **query service provider (QSP)** subsystem instances ("QSP-B," "QSP-C," and "QSP-D"). There are two GIS instances: one deployed at Site B ("GIS-B") and one deployed at Site C ("GIS-C"). The QSP at Site D uses the GIS deployed at Site C. Each QSP instance is deployed with a single instance of its LDS, local database environment, and the (one or more) associated LDBs that it contains and controls. This is merely a simple example deployment: an actual deployment in the real world could have many more clients, service providers, and DBEs but this diagram should be sufficient for our discussions in this chapter.

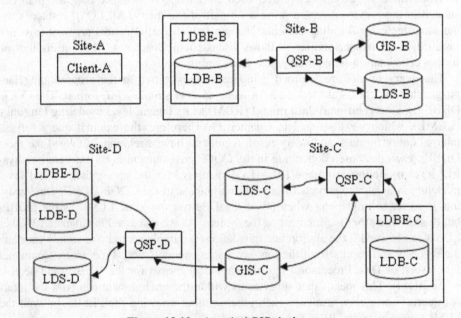

Figure 13.10   A typical P2P deployment.

The client subsystem is essentially equivalent to the client in the COOP—except that it talks to a peer-to-peer QSP instance instead of a cooperative DQSP instance. The GIS and LDS we discussed in the COOP environment are also present in this environment and behave in essentially the same way as before, but because of the emphasis on query provider subsystems behaving as peers, there is only one programmatic nonclient subsystem—the query service provider.

13.2.1.1 Client   Once again, each client subsystem is a small, lightweight, multi-threaded, user-written application written on top of a framework and implemented using web services or similar-minded approaches. This allows the client code to largely ignore the underlying communication details. Clients will again communicate with the DDBE using the same subset of ANSI SQL that the COOP clients used. Similarly, the clients will again retrieve the results as program-dependent data structures or as XML streams. A client in this DDBE connects to a QSP instance, which means that in the deployment shown in Figure 13.10, the client can connect to any QSP instance (QSP-B, QSP-C, or QSP-D).

13.2.1.2 Global Interface Schema   The global interface schema (GIS) subsystem is almost the same as the GIS subsystem we defined for the COOP environment. It also uses GUIDs for the global constructs and contains no deployment details. Once again, it does not need to be **completely** synchronized across the various subsystem instances in the environment. Each subsystem instance only needs to be synchronized for the actual constructs being used by that instance in the environment. Total synchronization is not discouraged, but it is also not required. However, there is an important difference in the P2P environment: each QSP instance will directly connect to a GIS instance. When it is feasible, multiple QSP instances can share a common GIS instance, but this is merely an option and not a requirement. Notice that this sharing is demonstrated by QSP-C, QSP-D, and GIS-C in Figure 13.10, while QSP-B uses its own separate (GIS-B) instance.

13.2.1.3 Local Deployment Schema   The local deployment schema (LDS) subsystem is essentially identical to the LDS defined in the COOP environment. It still uses deployment plan GUIDs to link deployed plans together across multiple LDBEs. Once again, the GUIDs from the GIS are used to tie the local constructs to their global counterparts. Each LDS instance is still deployed with a single LDBE, and each instance is only required to be synchronized with respect to the contents deployed at that site. Further synchronization is not forbidden but not required. The LDS also uses the same bitmask-based technique to determine coverage and completeness for the fragments within a particular deployment plan.

13.2.1.4 Query Service Provider   The query service provider (QSP) subsystem is quite different from the other components (DQSP, DDSP, and LQSP) defined in the COOP environment. It is somewhat correct to say that the QSP is the combination of the DDSP, DQSP, and LQSP subsystems from the COOP environment, but this is also somewhat inaccurate and misleading. Each QSP subsystem connects to a GIS instance and to an LDS instance. The GIS instance and LDS instance could be deployed in the same DBE or even the same DB but that is not a requirement. Alternatively, several QSP instances can share a common GIS instance.

Each QSP instance in the environment must register with the environment before it can begin providing content. Once again, there are several options for this registration process. Because there is no single subsystem instance responsible for registration, the process is somewhat different for the P2P environment than it is in the COOP environment. Although we can still use some of the same mechanisms (WSDL, UDDI, etc.), each QSP instance is responsible for keeping track of the currently active nodes. Therefore, it is more reasonable to use a messaging facility to accomplish this task. QSP instances can use broadcast messages or any form of message propagation to ensure that all of the nodes in the environment keep track of the currently available nodes. These functions are discussed in Chapter 14, Section 14.3.2.

13.2.2 Implementation Specifics

Each QSP instance in the environment is capable of receiving client (SQL) requests. Once the QSP receives a request, it connects directly to a GIS instance and performs the necessary verification and disambiguation activities. If there are any errors, the QSP instance returns an error message to the client (exactly like we did in the COOP environment), and if there are no errors, then the actual processing can begin.

The QSP instance that received the initial client request will use the registration information to build a list of candidate QSP instances (exactly like the DDSP did for candidate LQSP instances in the COOP environment). The verified and unambiguous version of the request will then be sent to all the candidate (QSP) sites. Each (QSP) instance capable of providing part of the query processing will then build a rough plan and respond with its self-ranking metadata used to elect the actual providers. This is similar to the election process in the COOP environment, but it is not quite the same since we have no LQSP/DQSP separation.

The QSP subsystem will use the same criteria that the DQSP used in the COOP environment to determine when an election is over and whether there is adequate coverage or insufficient provider availability. When the query can be processed, the QSP will notify all the candidates and each candidate will use the information contained in the previously generated plan and the common query strategy information to determine which partial results are sent to which QSP instance. The result format is the same as used by the COOP. Ultimately, the results are returned to the client.

13.3 COMPARING COOP AND P2P

In this section we will briefly compare and contrast some of the different distributed database environment architectures we have just discussed in this chapter and the previous chapter. First, we will compare the two new alternative architectures (COOP and P2P) to each other. Next, we will group these two architectures together and compare them with the traditional architectures we discussed in Chapter 12. Lastly, we will consider how the COOP and P2P architectures compare to other alternative distributed database environment approaches.

13.3.1 COOP Versus P2P

The fundamental difference between these environments is the number of primary subsystem types and the separation of query processing and registration functionality. In the COOP environment, each subsystem has a specific role to play in the environment. Each DQSP subsystem instance receives the query request, manages the LQSP election process, and ultimately returns the query results to the client instance. Each LQSP instance only processes the part of the query that it can, using the LDS at its site. In the P2P environment, each nonclient subsystem is truly a peer—providing equal functionality (albeit with different data deployment details and content). Each QSP instance is both a distributed query request coordinator and a local query processor.

The DDSP and DQSP in the COOP environment can potentially create bottlenecks because of the way communications are forced into a "narrow channel"—all requests move through a single point for the disambiguation, for the client query request, and for the ultimate results. However, this can be alleviated by deploying additional instances and distributing the load across them evenly. This narrow channel has some additional benefits from a security viewpoint—limited access requirements require simple firewall rules and also make it easier to ensure proper security is implemented on "external" channels (connections between the client and the DQSP).

In the P2P environment, we can support a more flexible arrangement of query provider (QSP) nodes than we can in the COOP environment. However, along with this added flexibility, we also get the issue of added complexity with the registration process and the load-balancing process. Luckily, there are various techniques available for us to use when addressing these concerns in a particular implementation of the P2P environment. For example, we can use COS pooling (as will be discussed in Section 14.2.2.1). We can also use a more sophisticated Directory Service implementation to provide support for better COS naming and versioning policies. We can even choose to add "special" QSP instances to our deployment plan that essentially act like DQSP instances. These instances can be used to make the environment more manageable from a security or load-balancing perspective. Each of these "special" QSP instances responds to distributed query requests but has no deployed content at its site. All of these techniques can help to alleviate these issues in our P2P implementation.

13.3.2   COOP/P2P Versus Traditional DDBEs

Both the COOP and P2P environments are well suited for DDBEs that focus on read operations. This is fairly similar for many traditional DDBEs as well, particularly federated DDBEs, which are discussed in Chapter 12, Section 12.1.2. Both the COOP and P2P environments can support CRUD (create, retrieve, update, delete) operations, but only if we use additional constraints not defined by the architecture. For example, we can support CRUD operations if we require all potential instances and sites to be registered in the environment before allowing any write operations to be performed, or if we implement additional services such as the replication control service discussed in Chapter 7.

Unlike the traditional DDBEs, the COOP and P2P environments can support multiple deployment plans for the same construct to coexist at the same time. They can also support multiple versions of the same GIS construct to exist within the environment. Most importantly, these environments do not require total synchronization of all global/distributed schema and deployment details. Instead, they support database environments where partial synchronization is sufficient, and deployment details can change dynamically in between query processing requests.

13.3.3   COOP/P2P Versus Other DDBEs

There are, of course, other DDBE alternatives than those mentioned in Chapter 12 and this chapter. For example, there is one approach that uses a bidding algorithm to allow the providers to process queries in a manner similar to our self-ranking-based election approach [Pentaris06]. This approach uses e-commerce as its motivation—consumers and providers engage in various types of trading (bidding, auctions, etc.) using the cost estimates as the perceived values. There are also variations within this "bidding" approach that differ in how the providers compete or cooperate as well as the protocols used to control the trading. However, this particular approach still relies on total synchronization of the GDD information. As far as we know, there is no support in this approach for multiple versions of global constructs, multiple deployment plans for the same global construct, or dynamic registration/deregistration of content providers. Most DDBE alternatives that we know of require this GDD synchronization—and many would consider the dynamic registration and deregistration operations as only appropriate in the face of system errors.

13.4   SUMMARY

The COOP and the P2P distributed database environments are two new DDBE alternatives. Both of them support dynamic content-provider deployment and participation (registration and deregistration) as the primary goal. Because they both share some common architectural subsystems (namely, the GIS and the LDS), they both allow multiple versions of global constructs and multiple deployment plans for the same global construct to coexist within the environment at the same time. These environments work best for read operations, because they provide no architectural mechanism for enforcing data synchronization of offline content (content deployed at LDBEs that are unregistered at the time of modification). Although they do not prohibit CRUD operations, the implementation of non-read operations is more complex than read-only operations.

The COOP environment uses separate components and/or subsystems for the major functions used in implementing a distributed query: the parsing, disambiguation, and processing of the smaller parts of the query based on deployment details. The P2P uses a single component or subsystem for all query processing steps (parsing, disambiguation, and processing of parts). Both environments use a separate client subsystem, a separate GIS subsystem, and separate LDS subsystem. Clients connect to the DQSP component or subsystem in the COOP environment or the QSP component or subsystem in the P2P environment. Both environments rely on the Directory Services (especially the Registration Service) provided by the underlying DDBE Platform.

The dynamic registration and lack of total synchronization are the primary differences between these environments and traditional DDBEs. These are also the primary differences between these environments and other DDBE alternatives. However, the COOP and P2P environments both share some characteristics in common with federated DDBEs. There are also other DDBE alternatives that use a similar (but not identical) approach for query plan creation and optimization.

13.5 GLOSSARY

Client A COS in the COOP or P2P environment that sends queries from the user to the DDBE.

Commercial Off-the-Shelf (COTS) Any piece of commercially available software.

Cooperative DDBE (COOP) The first DDBE we discussed in this chapter, which supports dynamic registration, partial synchronization of global constructs, multiple versions of global constructs, and multiple deployment plans for the same global construct.

Data Dictionary Service Provider (DDSP) The COS in the COOP environment responsible for query disambiguation and also responsible for monitoring the registration/deregistration.

Distributed Query Service Provider (DQSP) The COS in the COOP environment responsible for coordinating the communication necessary for distributed query processing.

Global Data Dictionary (GDD) A COS in a traditional DDBE responsible for storing global construct information and deployment details.

Global Interface Schema (GIS) The COS in the COOP and P2P environments that stores a subset of all the global construct information in the environment but no deployment details.

Globally Unique Identifier (GUID) A value generated in a way that is guaranteed to be unique without synchronization

Local Database Environment (LDBE) The DBE (a CDBE) responsible for an LDB.

Local Database (LDB) The DB where the deployed part of a global construct is stored and controlled.

Local Deployment Schema (LDS) The COS in the COOP and P2P environments that stores the deployment details for all global construct pieces deployed at a particular (single) site.

Local Query Service Provider (LQSP) The COS in the COOP environment that communicates directly with the LDBE in order to process part of the global query.

Peer-to-Peer DDBE (P2P) The second DDBE we discussed in this chapter, which supports dynamic registration, partial synchronization of global constructs, multiple versions of global constructs, each non-client COS acting and multiple deployment plans for the same global construct—with noncontent COS acting as a peer within the environment.

Universal Description, Discovery, and Integration (UDDI) A facility that implements Directory Services for web services, providing an XML-based registry service suitable for finding web service instances deployed within the environment and defined using WSDL.

Web Service A component or subsystem that provides some service that conforms to the web services specification, usually implemented using SOAP, UDDI, WSDL, and XML.

Web Services Description Language (WSDL) An XML-based description of the services and service providers implemented as web services within an environment.

REFERENCES

[Elmrasi94] Elmrasi, R., and Navathe S., *Fundamentals of Database Systems*, 2nd edition, Addison-Wesley, Reading, MA, 1994, pp. 479–489.

[Fleury03] Fleury, M., and Reverbel, F., "The JBoss Extensible Server," in *Proceedings of the ACM/IFIP/USENIX International Middleware Conference*, pp. 344–373, 2003.

[Pentaris06] Pentaris, F., and Ioannidis, Y., "Query Optimization in Distributed Networks of Autonomous Database Systems," *ACM Transactions on Database Systems*, Vol. 31, No. 2, pp. 537–583, June 2006.

[Rahimi07a] Rahimi, S., and Haug, F., "A Cooperative Distributed Query-Processing Approach," in *Proceedings of the European Computer Conference*, Athens, Greece September 2007.

[Rahimi07b] Rahimi, S., and Haug, F., "A Distributed Query-Processing Approach for Peer-to-Peer (P2P) Databases," *International Conference on Parallel and Distributed Processing Techniques and Applications*, Las Vegas, NV, June 2007.

[Ripeanu01] Ripeanu, M., "Peer-to-Peer Architecture Case Study: Gnutella Network," in *Proceedings of the International Conference on Peer-to-Peer Computing*, Linkopings, Sweden, pp. 99–100, 2001.

[Singh04] Singh, I., Brydon, S., Murray, G., Ramachandran, V., Violleau, T., and Sterns, B., *Designing Web Services with the J2EE 1.4 Platform: JAX-RPC, SOAP, and XML Technologies*, Addison-Wesley, Reading, MA, June 2004.

EXERCISES

Provide short (but complete) answers to the following questions.

13.1 How is the global interface schema (GIS) similar to the traditional global data dictionary (GDD)?

13.2 How is the global interface schema (GIS) different from the traditional global data dictionary (GDD)?

13.3 How is the local deployment schema (LDS) similar to the traditional global data dictionary (GDD)?

13.4 How is the local deployment schema (LDS) different from the traditional global data dictionary (GDD)?

14

DDBE PLATFORM REQUIREMENTS

Even in the best implementations, a **distributed database environment (DDBE)** is a complicated, distributed computer application. In theory, it is possible for each piece of software in the architecture to be deployed on a different, separate machine. Obviously, in practice, this is most likely not the case—it is doubtful that there is a significant advantage to implementing the architecture with **that** much distribution. Nobody would choose to deploy the software with that degree of distribution just because it **should be** possible. However, the fact that we **could** implement the environment this way should act as a significant motivator in determining the underlying requirements for the machines and software we use to implement our DDBE. In an attempt to prevent bias toward a particular hardware system, operating system, local database environment (DBMS vendor, version, etc.), programming language, or other technology, we will call the combination of the aforementioned our **DDBE Platform**.

Enumerating all the possible hardware platforms, operating systems, local database environment (LDBE) platforms, programming languages, networking technologies, and so on that we can choose from when considering which ones to include in our DDBE Platform can be a daunting task. We can choose to make our environment as homogeneous or heterogeneous as we need it to be, as long as we ensure that all our selections can be integrated into our environment and can communicate effectively with each other. In the past, this was a more difficult problem than it is today. Technological advances in computing power, networking technologies, and programming languages have made distributed computing reasonably easy, efficient, and almost ubiquitous (at least compared to the way things were 10 or 20 years ago!). Similarly, we now have a variety of different software packages including both **commercial off-the-shelf (COTS)** and **free or open-source software (FOSS)** to choose from when attempting to provide portability and interoperability for the pieces of our architecture that we

Distributed Database Management Systems by Saeed K. Rahimi and Frank S. Haug
Copyright © 2010 the IEEE Computer Society

deploy across different hardware systems, operating systems, programming languages, and LDBEs within our environment.

> There are several different types of "free" software. The primary distinction between the various types of "free" software has more to do with the licensing details than any other detail. For example, the GNU project provides "copylefted" software that caries with it the GNU Public License (GPL), while the Apache Software Foundation has its own license (actually there are several versions of the Apache License and the GPL), and projects like Perl allow the user to choose from the GNU Public License, the Apache License, or its own "Artistic License." There are also other licenses (including public domain) and other sources of open software that we will not discuss any further in this book (see [Scacchi07] and [Michaelson04] for further details). For our purposes, we are lumping all of these various "free" software flavors and licenses together and referring to this collection of software (and licensing details) as FOSS or simply "open." Other terms that might fit our very loose criteria include "Libre," "FLOSS," "F/OSS," and "open source"—even though these terms are not strictly speaking identical in other respects.

Listing all of the alternatives currently available for our DDBE Platform (or even attempting to create a reasonably complete taxonomy for the alternatives) is out of the scope for this chapter and this book. If we were to attempt such a listing, it is likely that some of the alternatives mentioned would already have new releases and different versions before this book left the publisher. Similarly, after this book has been published, there will likely be some new alternatives available that did not exist at the time this book was written, while some existing (or even popular) alternatives might become obsolete or inactive. Therefore, it is more practical and pragmatic to define our essential requirements for a DDBE Platform in this chapter and then consider some of the historical alternatives rather than jumping directly into a discussion about how a specific platform alternative fulfills our requirements. In Chapters 15–19, we will discuss those details for the specific platforms we will be using to implement the Starter Kits (SKITs) provided with this book.

In the first section of this chapter, we will briefly introduce some architectural vocabulary—some of these terms have been discussed in other chapters while some have not. Next, we will consider the functionality necessary to implement any DDBE. When considering all the DDBE architectural alternatives (such as those discussed in Chapters 12 and 13), and all the possible implementation alternatives that we might want or need in our particular situation, there are several underlying features that we need. These features can be grouped into cohesive categories of functionality. We will refer to each of these categories as a set of **Platform Requirements**.

We will divide the set of all Platform Requirements into three high-level categories. The first category will focus on the requirements that should be considered for any application architecture. These requirements should be considered regardless of whether we are building a centralized environment or a distributed environment—even if there are no databases within the environment. We will therefore call this category the **Fundamental Platform Requirements**. Next, we will focus on the requirements crucial to any distributed system. Although these requirements can be either considered or ignored for many centralized environments, we feel that they are necessary for any distributed environment (even systems without databases). Therefore, we will call this category the **Distributed Process Platform Requirements**. Lastly, we will consider the requirements that are crucial for any environments working with distributed data—we will call this last category the **Distributed Data Platform Requirements**.

Because new implementations are often based on previous implementations, we will also present a brief history of implementation alternatives. The "historic" implementations we will discuss can provide **some** of the features we need. However, this list is not complete, and no implementation is the "ideal solution." Because there is no single, perfect set of implementation alternatives, we will not attempt to identify any particular implementation alternative as being part of the "definitive implementation platform."

14.1 DDBE ARCHITECTURAL VOCABULARY

Before we discuss DDBE Platform Requirements, it is useful to formalize the terminology used when discussing the architecture as a whole and the smaller architectural components inside it. Some of the concepts we discuss in this section will be used later in this chapter and in Chapters 15–19. First, we will review some architectural concepts that we introduced in Chapter 1 (in Section 1.2). Next, we will look at how we can group these architectural constructs into logical categories (called **tiers**) and discuss how they interact with each other. We will also identify a special category of software known as **middleware** and discuss its role within the architecture.

14.1.1 Components and Subsystems

As we mentioned in Chapter 1, a **component** is simply a deployable bundle that provides a reasonably cohesive set of functionality. This can take many forms, can be implemented using several different technologies, and can include code, data, and configuration details. A **subsystem** is a collection of one or more components (and perhaps one or more other subsystems) that works toward a common goal. A subsystem is a part of the total architecture (the system) but it is also a system in and of itself (hence the name subsystem). In theory, some subsystems might consist of a single component, but it is more likely the case that a subsystem will include several components. Components and subsystems are similar in many respects—the primary difference between them is merely a matter of scope and scale. A more formal definition of these concepts can/be found in [Booch07]. Usually, we will ignore these distinctions and simply refer to these things as **components or subsystems (COSs)**.

14.1.2 Service Consumers and Service Providers

In Chapter 1, we also discussed some terminology associated with services. Recall that a **service** is a cohesive collection of well-defined functionality. A COS that uses a service is called a **service consumer**. A COS that implements a service is called a **service provider**. There is only one other detail that we need to know about service providers and consumers within our architecture. It is possible for the same COS to be both a service provider for one set of functionality and a service consumer for another set of functionality. It is even possible for a COS to be both a consumer and provider for the same set of functionality. In fact, this is a fairly common scenario. For a nondatabase environment example, consider the domain name service (DNS). DNS servers frequently use other domain name servers in order to translate a domain name into an Internet protocol (IP) address. We can also see an example of this in a DDBE—recall the Semantic Integrity Service (Semi-S), which we discussed in Chapter 1. The Semi-S is responsible for verifying semantic integrity constraints—in a relational system this would include enforcing constraints such as referential integrity constraints (foreign-key to primary-key references) or entity integrity constraints (table or column check constraints). Typically, the Semi-S service provider will be used by anything that needs to check database consistency. For example, both the Replication Service (Repl-S) and the Transaction Management Service (Tran-S) might need to use the Semi-S for this purpose. Here the Repl-S and Tran-S are service providers themselves (providing replication and transaction management services, respectively), but they are also service consumers with respect to the Semi-S.

14.1.3   Architectural Visualizations

There are several different approaches we can choose from when trying to capture the way pieces within our architecture fit together to create an environment. While there are many approaches compatible with our usage in this book, we will merely discuss two examples very briefly here: namely, the **three-tier model (3TM)** and the **service-oriented architecture (SOA)** approaches.

14.1.3.1   The Three-Tier Model   The **three-tier model (3TM)** is a useful technique for visualizing and discussing distributed application architectures. This visualization approach was popular with many implementation alternatives in the 1990s, and, in particular, it was often used for describing distributed applications written using the Microsoft Common Object Model (COM) and later implementation alternatives that evolved from COM. In the 3TM, we partition the architecture into three different levels (called tiers). Each component or subsystem (COS) that contains executable code is allocated to one of the tiers based on the primary function being performed. Interaction between COSs is very controlled within the 3TM tiers. Each COS is assigned to **one and only one tier**. The COSs within the **same tier** can communicate with each other freely, but the COSs on different tiers can only communicate with each other **if the tiers are adjacent**.

Figure 14.1 shows a 3TM view for a traditional (centralized) database application. In this example, we see five COSs: the "Sales Report" and the "Print Service" COSs are allocated to the first tier, the "Overdue Accounts" COS is allocated to the second tier, and the "Sales Record" COS is allocated to the third tier. The "Sales" database is also a COS—if we consider the database to be a "black box" that does not contain any code written by us for this application, then it is not allocated to one of the tiers. Alternatively, even if there is code within the database (stored procedures, triggers, etc.), we can consider the "Sales" database to be a black box that is part of the third tier—in which case, the arrow connecting the "Sales Record" COS and the DB would be connecting two COSs in the same tier. In this diagram, we draw an arrow from each COS acting as a consumer to the COS acting as the provider for some service. Notice that the "Sales Report" COS connects to providers in both the first and second tiers in this example. If we follow the strict 3TM view of the architecture, then the interactions

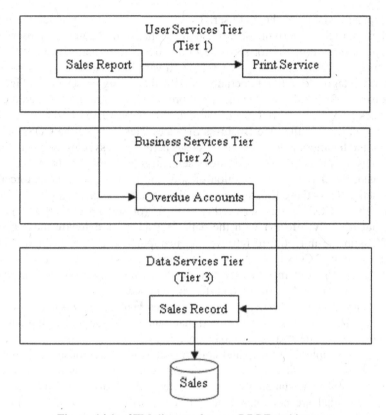

Figure 14.1 3TM diagram for non-DDBE architecture.

are even more rigidly defined—a COS can only provide services to another COS if the consumer is either in the same tier or in the tier immediately above the provider. This means that service consumers in the first tier can only connect to service providers in the first or second tier. Similarly, service consumers in the second tier can only connect to service providers in the second or third tier, and service consumers in the third tier can only connect to service providers in the third tier. This is sometimes informally referred to as "over and down" invocation because the diagrams like Figure 14.1 will always contain arrows that are drawn "over" (within the same tier) or "down" (to the tier immediately below). Notice that the arrows are never drawn "up" (from the third tier to the second tier or from the second tier to the first tier). These arrows are also never drawn "across" the tiers (they are never drawn from the first tier to the third tier, skipping over the second tier).

The three tiers in the 3TM are called

- The User Services Tier
- The Business Services Tier
- The Data Services Tier

The **User Services Tier** is the first tier in the 3TM. Sometimes, this tier is also referred to as the **User Presentation Tier**. Both names are accurate, because COSs in the first tier are typically visible to the end-user. These COSs ultimately provide the user with some interface to the underlying data—usually in the form of a graphical user interface (GUI). The primary function for software in this tier is information presentation rather than information verification or processing. Software in the first tier does not directly perform any integrity or CRUD operations on the data being presented. In Figure 14.1, we have two COSs in this tier: the first COS provides a GUI to the data and the second COS creates a hard copy (printout) of the data that is processed in the lower tiers.

The second tier is called the **Business Services Tier** because the COSs in this tier implement the **business rules**. For our purposes here, business rules are validation rules based on business logic and other business semantics pertaining to the underlying data being considered. The primary function of software in this tier is the enforcement of business semantics—these COSs prevent or detect semantic errors and rule violations. Even though the COSs in this tier need to evaluate (or perhaps even modify) the data, they do **not directly interact** with the data. Instead, they **delegate** those operations to the COSs in the third tier to retrieve and manipulate the data. In Figure 14.1, the "Overdue Accounts" COS in this tier contains the business logic necessary to determine which data records contain accounts that are "overdue" based on the business rules and semantic understanding of the data for this application.

The third and final tier is called the **Data Services Tier**. The COSs in this tier provide routines that handle storage, retrieval, and manipulation of the underlying data, which is contained within the "Sales" database in our example. They treat the information at this level as simple data types and content—devoid of any business semantics. In Figure 14.1, the "Sales Record" COS represents one or more sales records, but it is devoid of any real understanding of the data contained within it—all of the logic and semantics rules that are not implemented directly within the "Sales" database itself must be implemented in the second tier not the Data Services Tier.

Putting it all together, we can see that the User would connect to the "Sales Report" subsystem via its GUI. This GUI might include several options including information that can be passed to the lower tiers as additional selection or filtering criteria—but not the actual logic used to determine when an account is overdue. The "Overdue Accounts" subsystem uses its internal logic and rules to process the data fetched via the "Sales Record" subsystem. The final results are passed back to the "Sales Report" subsystem. If a printed version of the report is desired by the end-user, then the final results are passed to the "Sales Report" subsystem.

14.1.3.2 Service-Oriented Architecture   The **service-oriented architecture (SOA)** is another useful technique for visualizing and discussing application architectures—but it is very different from the 3TM technique. The SOA has received a lot of attention lately because of its applicability to more modern technologies such as XML Web-Services [Nagappan03], and the benefits it has for distributed applications. Rather than focusing on tiers, the SOA is concerned with interaction between the services in a distributed architecture. Proponents of SOA argue that it provides a more practical solution to managing the complexities involved when deploying and maintaining services in a real-world distributed environment. A service in SOA is compatible with our simplified definitions, but the SOA places additional emphasis and architectural constraints on the connections between service providers and service consumers. Because the interactions between service consumers and providers can be quite complicated, the SOA constraints help to simplify things and remove some potential issues.

For our purposes here, there are only two high-level constraints to consider. The first constraint that the SOA requires is for each service provider to agree to support a contract (a small set of ubiquitous interfaces available to **all service consumers and providers**). These interfaces are devoid of any service-specific semantics. Because of this constraint, any additional information needed by the service provider or consumer must be communicated using some other mechanism. This is addressed by the second constraint, which has two parts. The first part states that all service-specific semantic details must be communicated using descriptive messages and the second part states that these messages must be defined using an extensible message schema. An extensible message schema refers to a set of message types that can be expanded in a backward-compatible fashion using techniques like inheritance, rather than replacements to refine later versions of the messages. So the second constraint states that all service-specific semantic details are communicated via descriptive messages, which are defined by an extensible message schema.

By using a contract that is devoid of semantic details, changes in the service definition or service semantics do not break the interfaces defined in older versions of the consumer or provider for the service. Similarly, by using an extensible message schema we can ensure that any changes in the messages being used will not break the older versions of the service. While these constraints may seem overly restrictive, they are an attempt to address a very important issue in distributed application architecture. Services tend to evolve over time and, therefore, the semantic details required by different versions of the same service are also likely to change over time. Because the COSs are tightly coupled to the interfaces they use and support, any changes to a shared interface result in a ripple effect of required changes. Each COS that supports or uses a particular interface needs to have the same definition for that interface. If the interfaces were not identical, then the connection between the COSs would be broken. In order to fix this broken connection, both COSs using the interface would need to be redesigned, recompiled, reinterpreted, or redeployed to ensure that they are using the same version of the same interface.

By constraining the interfaces (excluding the semantic details), the only changes required to the interfaces are those that result from a systemwide version update. When a systemwide version does change, breaking all COSs that are not using the correct version of the interface is an acceptable outcome. Similarly, by defining the messages using an extensible schema, we ensure that newer versions of the message definition will not break our existing COSs. Even though the newer messages might not take advantage of any new details contained in the new message format, the connection between the COSs will not be broken. These two constraints help us to ensure that the COSs are loosely coupled, and this helps us to avoid the undesirable ripple effect.

The SOA also emphasizes the value of descriptive communication between components and subsystems. Notice that the messages are **descriptive**, meaning that they do not include any instructions about **how** the service should process the information. In other words the messages contain **descriptive requests** (details specifying "what" things need to be done) rather than **prescriptive requests** (details specifying "how" things should be done). Therefore, within an SOA-based project, we must have some mechanism that enables service consumers to discover the available service providers for a given service. There are several mechanisms that are compatible with this requirement, and many of these mechanisms are also compatible with our definition of a Directory Service (which is discussed in Section 14.3.2). By using descriptive communication, the COSs in the environment are able to tell each other which version of a service they support or desire. Ideally, these messages should also be based on an extensible schema. Once again, this will loosen the coupling between service consumers and providers and also loosen the coupling between different versions of the same service consumer or provider.

There are several different interpretations of the SOA, with slightly different nuances. Discussing all the specific techniques and requirements for SOA is beyond our scope here, but the basic idea is to ensure that multiple versions of the service can coexist without any issues. See [Bieberstein05] and [Josuttis07] for further details about SOA.

14.1.4   Middleware

Every COS in our environment that contains executable code needs to communicate with at least one other COS in the environment. Any COS that did not do so would serve no purpose since it would either be a service provider with no clients or a service consumer with no provider. Recall that the different COSs in our environment can be as homogeneous or heterogeneous as we want or need them to be. This means that the communication between our COSs might need to overcome several issues depending on the degree of distribution and heterogeneity. For example, suppose we have two COSs that need to communicate with each other. Perhaps they are on different machines, perhaps they are written in different languages, and perhaps they even use completely different instruction sets and character sets. It is even possible that the underlying network communication mechanism they use is different from the COSs themselves in these respects. We can overcome all of these differences by providing (writing) additional code to interpret and translate the requests and responses for the COSs wherever these differences arise. However, some of the COSs will be similar to each other, even if they do not communicate with each other.

This implies that there is an opportunity for reuse—it is not necessary to rewrite this translation code completely from scratch for each COS. At the very least, we can probably factor out the code that implements the communication mechanisms. Perhaps we can even factor out some of the logic (the application-defined protocol) needed to control the conversation between the COSs involved. After we have factored out this code, we can bundle it into a separate COS and then deploy in such a way that it is available to any components or subsystems that need it. While this refactoring would be useful, it is a bit impractical. In essence, if we try to refactor the code in this way, we are really trying to analyze the code's structure after-the-fact. In other words, we are trying to discover structure and order within the end-product, even though we did not consciously put any structure or order into its initial design or construction.

It makes more sense to consider the communication requirements **before** we implement the COSs. By looking across the different COSs in the architecture and considering the reasonable degree of distribution and deployment needed, we can address these requirements architecturally. In particular, when we design our COSs, we can attempt to encapsulate the communication details to a small set of low-level components and then focus on making them as reusable as possible in order to achieve a greater benefit throughout the architecture. For example, consider the query processor (QP) subsystem and the command processor (CP) subsystem in a typical DDBE as we discussed in Chapter 1. Each subsystem (which could be deployed separately on different machines) needs to talk to the local data processor (DP) subsystem (which could also be deployed on another, separate machine at the same site). The QP and CP also need to participate in distributed transactions for the sake of the environment as a whole, and work invisibly behind the scenes when a client requests a distributed CRUD (create, retrieve, update, or delete) operation. Therefore, it makes sense to attempt to reuse the code connecting these COSs. Similarly, there might be an opportunity to reuse the code used by the DP when it accesses the LDBE—even if we are using different **database management system (DBMS)** vendors or different versions of the DDBE from the same vendor.

There are many obstacles to overcome when attempting to integrate COSs in a larger system. If the COSs are significantly different from each other, it is likely that they will not fit together seamlessly. This can be true for many reasons, such as different vendors, different underlying technologies, or even different purposes and goals. Even when interoperability is a goal, COSs from different vendors might not support the same interfaces. Integrating software developed using different computer languages often requires some translation of the data types, stack frames, exceptions, function invocation requests, and results.

Often in cases like those we just discussed, we can use an additional piece of software to bridge the gap between the COSs. Generally, any piece of software that does this for us is called **middleware**. Middleware can have various vendors, versions, flavors, and goals, but for our purposes all middleware acts as the "glue" that attaches our components and subsystems together. Middleware can be implemented using an approach (technique and language) that is either object-oriented or non-object-oriented, but in Chapters 15–19, we are primarily going to focus on object-oriented middleware that implements features required by a DDBE.

Our definition for middleware is very informal, namely, the "glue" that attaches our components and subsystems together. This is a common understanding of the term, but there is also an alternate definition that considers middleware to be a layer of software that sits on top of the operating system and beneath the COSs, in effect attaching the higher-level code that we write to the lower-level code provided by the operating system, networking system, or DBMS. This alternate definition is not really incompatible with the first definition; it merely places different emphasis on the role played by the middleware. As Daniel Yellin states in [Yellin01], the first definition can be thought of as gluing the components together "horizontally" while the second definition can be viewed as gluing components to the underlying services "vertically." Both definitions imply that the middleware factors out the "glue" details, enabling the code we write to focus on its own goals rather than the details needed to enable communication and interaction with other components or the environment. This also makes it easier to replace those "glue" details at a later time with a different flavor or type of "glue" with minimal impact to the code we wrote.

Middleware is usually written at the "lower levels" necessary to allow us to reuse it effectively in our architecture. Middleware can be used within COSs, and we can use multiple flavors within the same environment at the same time. When thinking about the environment using the 3TM, we can say that middleware can be used within any of the tiers, and it can also be very useful in spanning the tiers. Different pieces of middleware can be used at the same time (and even by the same COS at the same time, but it is probably better to try not to overcomplicate things). In general, we should attempt to use as few middleware flavors, vendors, and packages as possible within the DDBE Platform without negatively impacting the performance and maintenance of the COSs.

14.2 FUNDAMENTAL PLATFORM REQUIREMENTS

In this section, we will look at the DDBE Platform Requirements that are equally relevant for any architecture—even centralized environments that do not involve any databases. We will call these requirements **Fundamental Platform Requirements** to emphasize this fact, but remember that all of these requirements are also DDBE Platform Requirements! In Chapter 12, we looked at several traditional DDBE architectures and in Chapter 13, we looked at two new DDBE architectures. All of the architectural alternatives in these chapters were designed by combining smaller pieces of software (the COSs) and deploying them across multiple machines. When considering the (non-database related) requirements for these COSs, it is useful to think about their life cycle. For our purposes here, we can consider each COS to move through three different life-cycle phases: **development, deployment**, and **execution**. The **development** phase refers to all the activities necessary to create the implementation (compilation, linking, bundling, etc.); the **deployment** phase refers to all the activities required to install the software on the target machine after it has been developed; and **execution** refers to all the activities required to run the software within the environment once it has been deployed. We will use these life-cycle phases to categorize the requirements further, by considering the requirements for each phase. There will be some overlap and interdependencies between the requirements and life-cycle phases but that is not important since this grouping is merely a convenient way to organize the requirements—it has no direct or indirect impact on the DDBE Platform itself. For example, the development details for a particular COS (such as whether the COS is statically linked or dynamically linked) will have a direct impact on the actual deployment and execution details for that COS, but we are considering these requirements for the architecture as a whole and not for a particular COS in this section.

14.2.1 Development Requirements

The Fundamental Platform Requirements in this section are strongly related to the activities performed in the **development** life-cycle phase. This means that we are considering the development activities and issues involved for each requirement. We are looking at issues related to compilation, interpretation, byte compilation, linking, and so on. In this section, we will not focus on any particular programming language or development environment, but will instead try to consider the abstract requirements. Of course, when considering these requirements for a specific environment, we would consider all the specific details that were involved—but this is not our goal in this chapter.

There are three subcategories within the Development Requirements:

- Integration Requirements

- Extensibility Requirements (frameworks)
- Portability Requirements

14.2.1.1 Integration Requirements   The Integration Requirements consider the ability of our COSs to work with each other during the development life-cycle phase. How do two different COSs connect to one another? The answer is highly dependent on the programming language we use to implement each COS, the operating system on which we deploy and execute them, and whether or not the two COSs need to be able to support nonlocal communication between them. In some cases, COSs implemented in different programming languages can interact directly. For example, Java provides a mechanism to execute code written in C, and all of the languages in the Microsoft .NET Framework-based DDBE Platform are capable of integrating with each other through well-defined mechanisms (see Chapter 18 for more details). When it is possible to use a more direct approach, we usually can obtain better performance and less complicated code. Often, when we do not use a direct mechanism, the alternatives we have to choose from are similar to the alternatives we would consider in the cases involving different operating systems or remote communication. For example, COSs can use Web Services written in different programming languages and deployed on different operating systems. Of course, Web Services can also be used to connect COSs written in the same programming language and deployed on the same machine under the same operating system. We can often use middleware like Web Services and SOAP for **both situations**, but the middleware solution will usually perform worse than the native approach due to the internal overhead and complexities being addressed. Regardless of the mechanism we use to connect the COSs, there are three main areas we are focused on with respect to our Integration Requirements:

- The Namespace Requirements
- The Reference Requirements
- The Binding Requirements

Namespace Requirements   Most programming languages allow us to name the various constructs they contain, such as variables, functions, constants, modules, classes, and interfaces. We will call this our **Namespace Requirements**, and it is our first area within the Integration Requirements. Most programming languages also ensure that we do not have duplicate, ambiguous names within the same program. This can usually be done by enforcing specific syntax rules for the language. Whenever one COS needs to connect directly to some piece of code defined in another COS, it must have some way of indicating the name that exists in the other program. This is true whenever one COS connects directly to another COS or directly to a piece of middleware. If all of the names defined in each piece of code were visible to all of the other pieces of code, it would be impossible for the programming language to prevent duplicate, ambiguous names. Luckily, most languages have a way of limiting the visibility of names (private scope) or a way of qualifying names using a **namespace**. This is identical to the way that traditional relational DBMSs use namespaces to prevent duplicate ambiguous names for the tables and columns defined within them. Regardless of how this facility is implemented, we need to have some way of disambiguating names in our DDBE Platform.

Reference Requirements   Similar to the Namespace Requirements, whenever we reference some programming construct that is not defined within our COS itself, we need to have a way to specify where the construct we want to reference is defined. We will call this our **Reference Requirements**, and it is our second area within the Integration Requirements. Having an unambiguous name for a particular code construct is not sufficient; we also need to have some way of referring to the code or library that contains the definition or declaration so that we can use it correctly within the code. Different programming languages and development environments have different ways of implementing this. Regardless of how this facility is implemented, we need to have some method for identifying that a set of unambiguous names is actually referring to code constructs that are defined and implemented in some other set of code in our DDBE Platform.

Binding Requirements   Any piece of unambiguously named code that is defined outside our program eventually needs to be connected to our implementation. We refer to this "connection" as binding—and it can happen at different phases of the life cycle. It can also happen in different ways, depending on the programming language, development environment, and intentions of the developer. For example, sometimes the code is compiled and linked into a single executable—we call this "static binding" or "static linking." Other times, we might use a mechanism that verifies the information at development time but leaves the code in separate deployment bundles—we sometimes call this "late," "dynamic," or "deferred" binding. We refer to the ability to specify these binding characteristics as the **Binding Requirements**, which is our third main area within the Integration Requirements. For example, Java classes can be bundled into a single Java Archive File (JAR) or can be bundled into separate files. Similarly, many systems and languages support so-called shared libraries or dynamic link libraries (DLLs) that also postpone binding until a later time. Ultimately, we need to have some form of binding available to us in the DDBE Platform, and ideally we have multiple options for defining the binding.

14.2.1.2 Extensibility Requirements (Frameworks)   The previous set of requirements focused on the Development Requirements that help us to integrate our physical pieces of code. In this section, we will consider the Development Requirements that focus on the logical relationships between our pieces of code. How can we maximize the reusable code while minimizing the amount of implementation-specific code? By using a technique known as a **framework**, we can define the boundary between "more-reusable code" and "less-reusable code." This technique uses a concept known as extensibility (which we discussed briefly in Section 14.1.3.2). This is why we refer to these Development Requirements as the **Extensibility Requirements**. Adding implementation-specific code by building on a framework is referred to as "extending" the framework. We call the "less-reusable code" that we create by extending the framework the **extension**. Although frameworks are traditionally discussed in an object-oriented context, they can be implemented using an approach (technique and language) that is either object-oriented or non-object-oriented. Using an object-oriented approach is more natural and more common. Even if a non-object-oriented approach is used, the object-oriented terminology is a useful way to describe the framework.

The framework typically consists of a set of public interfaces, public extendable classes, and perhaps some private concrete or abstract classes. The public interfaces define a contract between all classes that implement them. For each method (a.k.a. function, routine, procedure), the interface defines the method name, the return type (if there is any), the exceptions (errors) that can be raised by the method, and parameter details. When a method in the interface uses formal parameters, the interface defines the name, data type, and order for all parameters in the method. Extendable classes are classes that can be extended by using inheritance. Each extendable class can be either abstract or concrete. Abstract classes cannot be directly instantiated. This means that we cannot create a new object as an instance of that class. To create an instance when the extendable class is abstract, we must define our own concrete class as an extension of the framework class and then create an object as an instance of this new subclass. Concrete classes can be directly instantiated. This means that we can create a new object as an instance of the framework class directly or we can once again create our own concrete class as an extension of the framework class and create an instance of the subclass directly. When a framework provides a public extendable (abstract or concrete) class, it can choose to implement the code for this class invisibly or visibly. Being "public and extendable" means that we can inherit directly from the class and invoke directly its methods. "Invisible implementation" means that we cannot see the implementation source code, while visible means that we can see it. However, even a visible implementation might delegate important details to other private classes and interfaces that we cannot see or invoke directly.

Using frameworks to create extensions can be a very efficient way to replace one implementation with another implementation within the DDBE with minimal impact and effort. While the extensions we write can (and should) be reused within **our** architecture, they are "less reusable" than the framework because they are less "general purpose" and most likely written to suit the implementation details in our architecture. So while our extension is reusable within our architecture, the framework can be reusable within **any architecture**. This is why middleware is often implemented as a framework, while our COSs are more likely to be implemented as an extension of a framework.

14.2.1.3 *Portability Requirements*

The Portability Requirements are those Development Requirements that refer to the simple idea that the code for our COSs should be as portable as possible. The **Portability Requirements** include all aspects necessary to run our code across all of the platforms contained within our environment without separate redevelopment. This means that the same code should be able to run across different operating systems, different versions of the same operating system, different hardware systems, and so on with little or no modification. The example platforms we use in Chapters 15–19 (JMS, J2EE, and the Microsoft .NET Framework) all support portable code—but in different ways. Both JMS and J2EE are implemented using Java, which is portable to any platform supporting the **Java Virtual Machine (JVM)**. This is one of Java's primary goals—enabling the same byte-compiled code to run on different platforms without modification or even recompilation. However, each platform must have a different JVM, which means that there are potential caveats, omissions, or delays in support for all features on all platforms. Similarly, the Microsoft .NET Framework-based platform supports portability for its components across all the operating systems that support the platform. However, realistically, this is primarily the Microsoft Windows-based operating systems, and again there are potential caveats, omissions, or delays in support for all features on all these potential platforms.

The degree of portability we require for our DDBE is highly dependent on the specific details for the environment we are trying to create. The more homogeneous our environment is, the easier it is to run the same COS code on all our systems, or to simply reinterpret/recompile the same code on each system. However, the more heterogeneous our environment is, the more difficult it will be to do these things. When we cannot reuse our existing code, our only alternative is to redevelop the code separately for each incompatible platform. Different programming languages and development environments can provide some support for these redevelopment activities, but ultimately we would like to reduce the amount of code that is nonreusable within our environment.

14.2.2 Deployment Requirements

In the previous sections, we considered the development life-cycle-based Fundamental Platform Requirements. Once we have developed the code for our COSs, we need to deploy the COS instances at the appropriate sites within our environment. The Fundamental Platform Requirements that focus on the deployment life-cycle phase are called the **Deployment Requirements**. The deployment life-cycle activities include the physical transfer of code and data for each COS (installing the programs, libraries, configuration files, etc.) as well as performing any steps necessary to make the environment aware of the new instances. For example, we might need to populate registry entries when a COS instance is installed at a site running one of Microsoft's operating systems. Alternatively, when a COS is installed at a site running a Java-based platform, we might need to install deployment descriptors and perform some other related activities.

Potentially, we have multiple instances of multiple versions of multiple COSs deployed (installed) throughout the machines within our DDBE. We will discuss the functionality required to manage this complex situation in this section. As we will discuss in Section 14.3.2, there are several different scenarios to consider when we look at how our deployed COS instances are used within our DDBE. Sometimes, we will accept any COS instance that provides any version of some desired service—this is one extreme scenario. At other times, we might need to connect to a particular instance of a particular version of a particular COS deployed on a particular machine—this is the other extreme scenario. Of course, there are other situations that might require something in between these two extremes. Therefore, our Deployment Requirements must consider several different types of functionality in order to ensure adequate support for all these situations.

There are four subcategories of Deployment Requirements:

- COS Pooling Requirements
- COS Versioning Requirements
- COS Configuration Requirements
- COS Deployment Requirements

In order to support the first "extreme" scenario, we need to consider **COS Pooling Requirements**. For the other "extreme" scenario, we need to consider **COS Versioning Requirements**. In all possible scenarios, we need to consider theses two subcategories as well as the **COS Configuration Requirements** and the **COS Deployment Requirements**.

14.2.2.1   COS Pooling Requirements   We strive to design our COSs for reusability. This means that we want each COS to be reused by as many other COSs as possible. For some COSs (especially those that wrap network, database, or messaging connections), the startup and shutdown activities are the most expensive activities performed as part of the execution process. If we can make our COS instances stateless, or enable them to switch contexts efficiently, then we can place them in a **pool**. A pool is merely a way to identify those COS instances that do not need to be shut down and restarted between uses across different callers. The **COS Pooling Requirements** address the Deployment Requirements that relate to pools and pooling. By pooling COS instances, we can reuse the pooled instances among different callers—without performing the expensive shutdown and startup activities in between the task swapping. The potential savings are similar to those we experience when we choose to use the standby/hibernation features on a computer (letting it go to sleep when it is not being used) rather than performing a hard shutdown and cold reboot.

Many different platforms provide support for pooling. Both J2EE Application Servers (like JBOSS) and the Microsoft .NET Framework have support for pooling. However, merely using a platform that has this support available is not sufficient. We must also be careful when we design and implement the COSs themselves to ensure that they can be pooled (reused in this way). In particular, we must be sure to make our COSs thread-safe and we must avoid using global variables within the code as much as possible. We also need to avoid performing any operations that implicitly depend on the state of the COS instance after returning from a procedure or method call. For example, database connections and transactions are two very important considerations for any pooled COS instances. We would not implement a method in our COS that opened a database connection, began a database transaction, and then did not commit or abort the transaction before returning from the call. If we want our COS instances to be pooled, we either need to make sure that our COSs do not do things like those we just mentioned, or we need to use more sophisticated techniques to address these situations. Many platforms support sophisticated options such as nested transactions and container managed transactions for precisely this reason.

It is beyond our scope here to discuss all the possible features or pitfalls for pooled COS instances. Therefore, we will simply mention that pooling is a powerful feature that we can use in many scenarios with minimal restrictions. Having sophisticated facilities can make pooling an attainable goal for many COSs, but merely having these facilities available within the platform does not ensure that it is always possible to convert an existing COS into a pooled COS without redesign or reimplementation. In some cases, it might not be possible to convert the COS without a complete redevelopment regardless of level of support found within the deployment platform.

14.2.2.2   COS Versioning Requirements   Ensuring that multiple versions of the same COS can coexist within the system without causing errors or issues is a difficult goal, but it is crucial to the development and maintenance of the DDBE. The **COS Versioning Requirements** refer to the Deployment Requirements that address this area. In particular, we need to define how versions will be managed within the DDBE Platform, and which specific features are most important. These requirements can make use of several facilities found within the programming languages, protocols, and platforms used to implement the DDBE. Often, versioning considerations are addressed by the facilities used to fulfill the Remote-Code Execution and Directory Service Requirements. In other scenarios, simple naming conventions can be used to identify the desired COS version and the available COS version. Ideally, the version information is separate from the naming information. This allows more flexibility when a client is looking for a particular service. In all cases, the version information should be different whenever any significant change (to either the publicly visible interface or the private, hidden implementation) has been made. The environment should also support requests for a specific version as well as requests for "any version." This can also be implemented by having version numbers that have multiple parts; for example, if the version number is indicated by a major version number and a minor version number. The specific implementation details are often very dependent on the programming language and other similar specific environmental details, but there are several different alternatives that we can use to satisfy this requirement.

14.2.2.3 *COS Configuration Requirements*   The ability to reconfigure our components and subsystems on a per-deployed-instance basis is crucial to maximizing their reusability. The **COS Configuration Requirements** refer to the Deployment Requirements that address this ability. They define how COSs are configured within the DDBE Platform and identify how this can be decoupled from COS compilation and linking. Many programming languages and application execution environments support simple property files, which can be used for this purpose. More sophisticated environments also support more complex methods for specifying deployment-specific details independent of the executable code. For example, J2EE uses a special XML file, called a **deployment descriptor**, to store both system-defined and programmer-defined deployment-specific details. Similarly, the Microsoft .NET Framework platform supports configuration files (which are also implemented as XML files) to provide the same functionality.

14.2.2.4 *COS Deployment Requirements*   The DDBE Platform needs to be able to adapt to user and system needs if it is to be a scalable solution. This means that we need to be able to change deployment details dynamically with minimal impact to the overall system. Therefore, we need to define how COSs are dynamically deployed within the DDBE Platform. We also need to identify how consumers of these newly deployed services can react to these changes without requiring additional design or configuration changes to the service consumers. We refer to the Deployment Requirements that focus specifically on the act of dynamically deploying a COS instance as the **COS Deployment Requirements**.

The most fundamental COS Deployment Requirement is the ability to create and deploy dynamically linked COSs. If two COSs are dynamically linked, the code for each COS can be compiled into a separate file. This means that the COSs can call methods or procedures in each other without being linked as a single program or library. Most modern operating systems and application environments support several flavors of dynamic linking—but this does not make it an automatic situation. The COS author must deliberately design the COS to identify which modules are (statically) part of the COS and which parts are external—then the author must use the appropriate language and environment-specific facilities to ensure that the external components are dynamically linked.

When the environment stores deployment/configuration details in a separate file (as discussed in the previous section), changing the deployment can be done without requiring recompilation or relinking. Often, a COS instance will require several files. This can make it very complicated to install new COSs and uninstall old COSs. Luckily, many environments provide a mechanism for packaging these files into a single bundle. For example, J2EE has several different archive files such as **Enterprise Archive (EAR)** files, **Web Archive (WAR)** files, and **Java Archive (JAR)** files. The Microsoft .NET Framework supplies **assemblies**, which serve the same purpose.

14.2.3 Execution Requirements

In the previous sections, we considered the Fundamental Platform Requirements that reflected our development and deployment life-cycle activities. In this section, we will consider the requirements that address the execution life-cycle phase—the Execution Requirements. Most modern operating systems (or at least most of the modern operating systems we are likely to use to implement a DDBE) have very powerful options for controlling program execution. The execution of a program is usually called a process, but there are other ways that code can be executed. We will refer to any mechanism that executes a piece of code as a task, and the Execution Requirements will focus on the various task execution details we need to consider. Because all of our COSs are either service consumers, service providers, or both, we will almost always have multiple tasks executing in our environment. These tasks might be on the same machine or on different machines. Since we are focusing on the Fundamental Platform Requirements in this section, we will limit ourselves to the single machine scenario (execution on different machines will be discussed in Section 14.3). We will split the Execution Requirements into two areas. The first area will focus on what we need to have in order to execute multiple tasks on the same machine within the environment—the Multitasking Requirements. Whenever we have multiple tasks executing at the same time and interacting with each other, we also need to consider how these tasks address process concurrency issues. Therefore, the second area we will consider for Execution Requirements will focus on the Concurrent Execution Requirements. The concept of execution concurrency should not to be confused with the concept of database concurrency (which we discussed in Chapter 5), even though there are some similarities between the two concepts. In the following subsections, we will highlight some of the concepts and issues to consider for these two areas (multitasking and concurrency). However, we will not discuss any specific issues or remedies—since these details are very DDBE Platform dependent.

14.2.3.1 Multitasking Requirements For our purposes, a **task** is merely a generic name for something that is running on the computer. This can be a complete program, or it can be something that is more lightweight. Most single processor computers cannot actually execute more than one task at the same time—instead, they provide the illusion of multiple executions by switching back and forth between multiple tasks very quickly. This is called task switching or task swapping. Some systems have more than one central processing unit (CPU) and can literally execute multiple tasks at the same time. Many modern processors actually contain multiple CPU cores, which is analogous to multiple processors. Even on these more sophisticated systems, however, it is fairly common to use task switching—otherwise the number of active tasks would be limited by the number of CPUs or the number of CPU cores. Regardless of how the system supports multiple task execution, there are three distinct alternatives that we want to consider in this set of execution life-cycle-based Platform Requirements. These alternatives are somewhat interrelated, and therefore, we will consider them based on their relative power and complexity. First, we will consider **multitasking via multiple threads**; next, we will consider **multitasking via multiple processes**; and lastly, we will consider **multitasking via multiple users**.

Multitasking Via Multiple Threads   Whenever we write code in a traditional programming language (Java, C#, C++, Visual Basic, etc.), we create statements that define the logical control flow for the code. When the code executes, the system creates an execution of the program code; this execution is called a process. The CPU follows the instructions the program provides, in the specified order, obeying any control flow statements (conditional branching, iteration, etc.) as necessary. We can call this execution a "thread of control." When there are multiple "threads of control" within the same process, we say that the process (or program) is **multithreaded**. In a multithreaded process, even though there are not multiple instances of the same program executing at the same time, the code gives the appearance of doing more than one task at the same time. This is called multithreading.

While multithreaded programming is a powerful technique, it also requires careful programming practices. Because multiple threads are executing within the same process, they share the same data and same system resources. When we choose to write a multithreaded program, we must ensure that none of our threads conflict with each other to corrupt the data or resources they share. In some respects this is similar to the way a DBMS must ensure that multiple transactions, cursors, and user connections preserve the integrity of the database while avoiding dirty-reads and dirty-writes. We will discuss the concurrent execution requirements further in Section 14.2.3.2.

When we use multiple threads within a single process, the threads share the data and resources allocated to the process. If we were to execute the program separately for each thread, these processes would not share anything and therefore would require more overhead to accomplish the same effect. For this reason, threads are sometimes referred to as "lightweight" processes. While using multiple threads has some definite advantages, there are also some potential disadvantages to this situation. For example, suppose we have a process with multiple threads. If this process encounters any serious problems, failures, or errors, then all of the threads within that process will also be adversely affected. If the error is severe enough, or if it is not handled properly, then the entire process and all of its threads might be terminated (killed).

Multitasking Via Multiple Processes   Some systems do not allow more than one program to execute at the same time—even via task swapping. But most modern operating systems that we are likely to use to implement a DDBE do not have this limitation. When multiple processes run, they are similar to multiple threads except that each process has its own data and resources. This means that each process can have a different state (different values for its variables, etc.), but it also means that more resources are required. Although there are no concerns about shared variables, we still have to worry about conflicts for resources (files, network connections, etc.). We will discuss these concerns further in Section 14.2.3.2. In many **multiprocessing** systems, each process must be executed by some other process (called the parent process). In these systems, there are usually several different execution alternatives (such as spawn, fork, etc.) as well as mechanisms that allow the parent process to pass configuration details to the child process and also control its execution. We will not discuss these details further here, but it is important to consider the specific details for each platform within our environment before choosing a particular approach for deploying and executing the COS instances that comprise our DDBE.

Multitasking Via Multiple Users   Many systems support the concept of a user and allow multiple users to be defined. Each user can then be configured with different preferences, rights, privileges, and restrictions. If a system supports multiple users being connected at the same time (and implicitly multiple processes executing at the same time), we call it a **multi-user system**. Not all multiprocessing systems are multi-user systems. For example, Microsoft Windows NT® and Linux® are multi-user (and multiprocessing) systems. However, Version 1.0 of OS/2 was not a multi-user system (although it was a multiprocessing system) and neither was MS DOS® (in any version). Multi-user systems share the same benefits and disadvantages as multiprocessing systems but also provide a richer mechanism for customizing the process executions because different users can have different privileges and different configuration details.

14.2.3.2 Concurrent Execution Requirements   Whenever two or more tasks interact with each other (via shared data, shared resources, or actual interaction), we need to ensure that the tasks do not unintentionally interfere with each other. Sometimes the tasks need to cooperate with each other to achieve some larger goal; sometimes the tasks are in competition with each other. There are several issues to consider when implementing concurrent execution on the same platform—and several alternatives for resolving those issues. In this section we will look at some of the alternatives that might be provided by the DDBE Platform. The actual alternatives available are highly dependent on the actual DDBE architecture, implementation, and deployment details. The best approach to use for a particular situation is dependent not only on all these details but also on the type of conflict we need to prevent and the type of multitasking being used. In general, there are five techniques we can choose from to help us avoid conflicts within our code.

These techniques for avoiding conflicts in the face of concurrent task execution are as follows:

- Reentrancy
- Thread safety
- Synchronization
- Semaphores
- Message passing

Reentrancy   A section of code is **reentrant** if it can be safely suspended and reentered by multiple threads at the same time. Suppose that thread "A" was suspended while executing a piece of reentrant code. If thread "B" begins to execute that same code, we would expect thread "A" and thread "B" to be able to continue their executions successfully without any interference or unintentional interaction between the threads. Writing reentrant code is certainly possible to do, but it is not always easy to do or practical to attempt for all scenarios. Implicitly, reentrant code cannot use any static or global variables (constants are allowed, but not variables). This also means that reentrant code cannot obtain any locks or use any singleton resources (e.g., it cannot write to the same, specific file). Lastly, for obvious reasons, reentrant code cannot call any nonreentrant code. We must be very careful whenever we modify a piece of reentrant code—adding a single call to a nonreentrant method can destroy our reentrancy! Therefore, when working with reentrant code, it is very important to maintain a list of all the COSs and methods that it calls. It is equally important to maintain a list of all the callers for a particular piece of reentrant code. This can often be done automatically by the development tools and integrated development environment (IDE).

Thread Safety   A section of code is **thread-safe** if it functions correctly with no side effects when multiple threads of control are executing the code at the same time. Thread-safe code has fewer restrictions than reentrant code. In particular, multiple threads are allowed to access the same piece of data as long as they do so one-at-a-time and do not cause any unexpected or unintended side effects. This is analogous to the concept of serializability, which we discussed in Chapter 5—but here we are looking at shared variables and resources not database values. One way to achieve thread safety is also analogous to a database solution (transactions and locking): we can use some technique (such as synchronization, semaphores, or messaging) to ensure that only one thread enters the section of code where a conflict can occur. Each section of code that is controlled like this is called a **critical section** or a **guarded section** (the names are equivalent). There are also various other techniques that can be used to ensure the necessary behavior. For example, Java code can use **synchronized** methods to achieve this goal. Once again, we need to be careful when calling other code from within our critical section, or else we might destroy the thread safety of our code!

Synchronization   There are two types of synchronization possible between two potentially conflicting threads: competitive synchronization and cooperative synchronization. **Competitive synchronization** is precisely the situation we just discussed in the previous section—two threads compete over a shared piece of data or a shared resource. Often, we can use critical sections or any similar techniques to handle competitive synchronization conflicts. However, just like the similar scenario for databases, we need to be careful to avoid deadlocks, starvation, and livelock scenarios. In the case of cooperative synchronization, the threads are intentionally working together and therefore must find some way to communicate with each other. This can be via shared variables (protected by critical sections), semaphores, or message passing. In **cooperative synchronization**, it is very important for the threads to notify each other and then to wait for each other at the appropriate points in the code. Once again, just like the situation with competitive synchronization, there are still potential problems with timeouts, deadlocks, starvation, and so on, when cooperative synchronization uses these techniques.

Semaphores   A **semaphore** is a piece of atomic data. This means that operations (read, write, etc.) performed on it cannot be interrupted, just like the atomic property for transactions. Even though it looks simple, the programmatic statement that reads or assigns a variable's value is actually much more complicated than it seems. When a computer accesses a variable (or any value stored in memory), there are actually several low-level (machine language) instructions being performed. For example, first, the computer may need to load a base address into one hardware register. Next, it might load an offset value into another hardware register. It might then add the two registers together and place the result in a third hardware register. The computer might even need to perform other operations to dereference the register (look at the value stored in the location to which it points). Unlike the operations performed on a normal variable, operations performed on semaphores cannot permit multiple processes or multiple threads to interleave their execution of these low-level operations. In particular, semaphores are often used to implement synchronization and protect critical sections by creating **mutually exclusive objects (mutexs)**. Only one thread of control can obtain a particular semaphore at a given time; any other threads attempting to read or modify it will be forced to wait for it to be released. In this respect, semaphores are analogous to exclusive locks in databases, but semaphores are implemented as part of the operating system or program execution environment (independent of any database or database management system).

Message Passing Many operating systems provide facilities for passing messages between local processes running on the same system. This is sometimes referred to as **interprocess communication (IPC)**. When this facility is present, it can be used to coordinate between different threads of control while they are executing the same section of code. This can be used to support both competitive and cooperative synchronization as long as the message passing facility is reliable. If it is possible for messages to be lost or to arrive in a different order from that in which they were sent, then message passing will not be an ideal solution for resolving potential conflicts or providing either type of synchronization. The message passing solution and its potential issues are similar to those we will disuses in Section 14.3.1.2. However, because the sender and receiver are both on the same machine for the message passing scenarios we are considering here, there are no network operations required. Therefore, the performance will probably be much better for the message passing alternatives than it will be for the remote messaging alternatives.

14.3 DISTRIBUTED PROCESS PLATFORM REQUIREMENTS

In the previous sections, we considered the Fundamental DDBE Platform Requirements—the Development, Deployment, and Execution Requirements that we feel should be considered for every project (even centralized, nondatabase applications). In this section, we will consider the subset of DDBE Platform Requirements necessary to implement any distributed environment (even when there is no database involved). We call these requirements the Distributed Process Requirements, and we will focus on two subcategories within this subset. The first subcategory is called the Remoteability Requirements, while the second subcategory is called the Directory Services Requirements. **Remoteability** is defined as the ability to connect different COS instances to each other (either directly or indirectly) when they are deployed on different machines within the same environment. While the

Remoteability Requirements consider how we implement communication between COS instances deployed on different machines, the Directory Services Requirements consider how we manage the availability status of all the COS instances currently deployed within our environment. In Section 14.3.1, we will consider two alternatives for implementing our Remoteability Requirements. We can choose to use both of the two Remoteability alternatives within the same environment at the same time, or we can choose to use either one of them as the only Remoteability alternative implemented within our environment. In Section 14.3.2, we will consider the implementation alternatives for our Directory Services Requirements.

14.3.1 Remoteability Requirements

Remoteability is the ability to connect a particular COS instance that is deployed on one machine to another COS instance that is (potentially) deployed on some other (remote) machine. Because every component and subsystem in the DDBE can in theory be on a different computer system, almost any interaction between COS instances might potentially be considered a conversation between distributed (remote) applications. As we mentioned before, this extreme scenario is not very likely. However, because some level of distribution must exist within the DDBE, we would like to make the architecture as flexible as possible with respect to the ability to change the location for almost any COS instance. If we focus on a particular COS, and its point of view of the architecture, it will be involved in several conversations over the course of its execution. Some conversations will be initiated by this COS instance itself, but other conversations will have been initiated by some other COS instance. Similarly, sometimes the COS instances involved will be deployed on the same machine, while at other times the instances will not be deployed on the same machine. When the instances are on the same machine, we consider them to both be **Local COSs**. When the COS instances are not deployed on the same machine, each instance considers the other instance to be a **Remote COS**.

Conversations between Local COSs can use any valid mechanism provided by the underlying DDBE Platform, including all the traditional mechanisms for interprocess communication (IPC) that we mentioned in Section 14.2.3.2. We can also use simple function/method calls implemented in the native programming language/operating system. Choosing the mechanism for remote conversations is a far more interesting and challenging decision, and ultimately necessary for at least some COS instances. In most scenarios, the remote communication mechanism will be less efficient than the local mechanism, but most remote mechanisms can also be used to connect to Local COSs with only a slight overhead penalty. The flexibility with respect to deployment opportunities often outweighs the penalty incurred by implementing the remote mechanism—but we can always choose to reimplement the COS using local mechanisms if the performance becomes unacceptable.

Code that is implemented within the same COS will be the most efficient (with the least communication overhead), but it will be tightly bound to a single COS instance. This means that it cannot be split into (or shared among) multiple COSs very easily. Code that is implemented in two, separate, Local COSs and implemented using traditional IPC mechanisms will be slightly less efficient (with more communication overhead than code within the same COS). However, this approach will have the advantage of being more independent and modular than the previous approach. This code can be split into or shared among multiple COSs easily. Code that is implemented in two, separate, Local COSs and implemented using some remote conversation mechanism will have even greater overhead than the COSs implemented with a traditional, local IPC mechanism. When these COSs are both local, the communication will be less efficient than traditional IPC communication, but more efficient than remote communication. This code can not only be split into and shared by multiple COSs easily, but it can also be deployed on different machines and moved to other machines very easily.

The mechanism being used for this remote conversation can be either general purpose or task specific. **General-purpose mechanisms** do not specify any restrictions or details about the content of the conversation—this is compatible with the SOA point of view (see Section 14.1.3.2). General-purpose mechanisms can be used for any purpose, but offer no additional benefit for any conversations specific to a particular task. By contrast, **task-specific mechanisms** are very detailed about the conversation content, restrictions, and protocols. Task-specific mechanisms usually use one or more general-purpose mechanisms behind the scenes. There are two primary flavors of general-purpose mechanisms: **Remote-Code Execution** and **Remote Messaging**. There can be as many task-specific mechanisms as there are implementations of COSs that execute specific tasks. Most task-specific mechanisms are flavored by the underlying general-purpose mechanism being used. Attempting to identify all the possible task-specific mechanisms is far beyond our scope here. Therefore, we will look at the two flavors of general-purpose mechanisms in greater detail, with the understanding that any task-specific mechanism would be somewhat analogous to the general purpose flavors we discuss.

14.3.1.1 Remote-Code Execution

Remote-Code Execution is the first general-purpose Remoteability mechanism that we will consider. It allows one COS instance (the caller) to call functions, procedures, routines, or methods that are implemented in another COS instance (the callee)—even when the caller and callee are deployed on different machines. Usually, we want to try to make this remote execution call look as similar as possible to a local execution call in the programming language. Depending on the particular implementation mechanism chosen for Remote-Code Execution, there will be varying levels of support for heterogeneity across the components. Some implementations are programming language specific but support multiple operating systems and hardware configurations. Other implementations can support multiple programming languages but only work on a single operating system or a single hardware configuration. Obviously, it is not likely that a single approach will cover all possible programming languages, hardware configurations, and operating systems seamlessly. Remote-Code Execution alternatives can be implemented using either a non-object-oriented approach or an object-oriented approach. In the next few paragraphs we will describe the non-object-oriented approach and the object-oriented approach. Then we will compare these alternatives. Because there are many issues common to both alternatives, we will consider how values are passed between the Local and Remote COSs. Similarly, we will consider how the control flow in the calling program works for a multitasking caller and callee. Lastly, we will consider how errors and exceptions are handled in both Remote-Code Execution alternatives.

Remote Procedure Calls   When a non-object-oriented programming language is used, we can call the remote "function, routine, subroutine, or procedure" a **Remote Procedure**. In most non-object-oriented programming languages (like C, Pascal, FORTRAN, and Basic), Remote-Code Execution usually requires using a preprocessor to generate code. This preprocessor replaces the local procedure calls with calls to the Remote Procedure. In effect, each call spanning the components is actually using additional library routes to perform a corresponding call on the remote machine. This is why we refer to this technique as a **Remote Procedure Call (RPC)**. Usually, the preprocessor is bundled with a set of third-party tools and libraries that implements the remote execution. This third-party code is necessary to achieve the remote communication.

Remote Method Invocation   When Remote-Code Execution is implemented using an object-oriented approach, we can call the remote "function, routine, subroutine, or procedure" a **Remote Method**. The object that implements these Remote Methods is called a **Remote Object**. Because we are using object-oriented terminology, we do not say that a method is "called"; instead, we say that the method is "invoked." This is why we refer to this technique as a **Remote Method Invocation (RMI)**. While object-oriented programming languages (like Java, Visual C#, Visual Basic, and Visual C++) can choose to use a preprocessor and set of third-party tools and libraries to implement the remote communication code (the same as most RPC implementations often do), these languages can alternatively choose to use frameworks and extensions to include the desired functionality as part of the development and runtime environment.

RPC Versus RMI   There are a few significant differences between a Remote Procedure and a Remote Method. When using Remote Procedures in our code, there are typically some library-specific startup procedures that must be called before the remote calls can be made. After the conversation is finished, there are usually some library-specific procedures to be called to close the network connections and release the resources. Failure to call these startup and shutdown procedures properly can result in errors or resource (memory, network connections, etc.) leaks. Remote Methods essentially have the same concerns, but because of the object-oriented nature of the implementation, we can handle them differently. Typically, our Remote Methods would be organized (and refactored as needed) into cohesive collections of classes, interfaces, and methods. The required startup and shutdown code can be encapsulated into the class that implements the Remote Methods or invokes them. While it is probably not a good idea to implement the startup and shutdown code inside constructor/initializer and destructor/finalizer methods, that is also one possibility. While memory/resource leaks are still a concern, they are somewhat more manageable because of the garbage collection facilities provided within the object-oriented programming languages themselves. It is possible for us to pool the Remote COSs—however, to do this we must ensure that they implement the COS Pooling Requirements correctly. We usually need to consider thread safety and reentrancy issues for the callee (and perhaps for the caller) when pooling is used here.

Marshalling and Unmarshalling Parameters   Regardless of whether Remote Procedures or Remote Methods are used, we need to consider how data is sent and received between the local and remote code. There are several issues to be considered here. Both approaches communicate via a "stream of data." This "stream" needs to contain information identifying which procedure/method is being executed, as well as the parameters/return values involved in the call. As part of the call, the list of parameters needs to be converted into a single "stream" of data and then sent over the network to the callee. The callee must then convert the "stream" back into individual parameters again. We call the initial conversion process (from the parameters into the data stream) **Marshalling Parameters** and the corresponding conversion process (from the data stream back into parameters) **Unmarshalling Parameters**.

At first glance, Marshalling and Unmarshalling might seem to be relatively simple operations, but this is not necessarily the case. Each parameter being sent needs to be converted into a format that is compatible with the underlying network protocol used to connect the two processes. Obviously each parameter received on the other side must also be converted from this network compatible format into the format used by the remote program. If there are any values modified by or returned from the remote code, these also need to be translated into the network compatible format and then translated into the format compatible with the original calling program.

Different programming languages, operating systems, and network protocols can store data in different ways. Even simple integer values stored using two's-complement binary representations (the most common representation format on most PCs) can be stored differently in each of these places—for example, one place might choose use Big-Endian representations while the other might use Little-Endian representations. If the parameters or values being passed back and forth are implemented using complex data types, then we need to convert all the fields contained inside the parameters/returned values. For example, we need to perform this more complex conversion if any parameters or returned values are implemented using structures or unions in a traditional programming language. This "complex conversion" is also used whenever the parameters or return values are implemented using objects in an object-oriented programming language. Similarly, if any of the fields within these complex data types are themselves implemented using complex data types, then we need to do this conversion process recursively for all such fields.

Because an object is essentially "data plus code," passing objects as parameters has an additional level of complexity to consider. Both the Local COS and the Remote COS must have the ability to load all the classes and interfaces needed to define the object being passed. Recall the Development Requirements that we discussed in Section 14.2.1, especially the Integration Requirements we discussed in Section 14.2.1.1. Implicitly, we must have the same version of these classes available to both COSs (as we discussed in Section 14.2.2). Methods called on the object will execute where the object is, unless the object passed as a parameter is itself a Remote Object. If the object passed as a parameter is a Remote Object, any methods implemented by this object and invoked by this Remote COS are themselves Remote Methods that might be executing within yet another Remote COS (possibly on yet another machine!). Similarly, if the object passed as a parameter contains any Remote Objects inside it, things can become quite complicated from both a communication perspective and potentially from a concurrent execution perspective. Obviously, the communication overhead can also be greatly increased in scenarios like this.

The Marshalling and Unmarshalling operations must ensure that both the number and the order of parameters being sent match the corresponding number and order of parameters being received. Remember that the format used to send these values over the network is ultimately just a stream of data. This means that we need to include some information about the number, size, and data types used for each parameter in this block of data, and the code on both sides of the stream must agree on the format used for representing this information. In order to handle network issues and failures properly, the code on both sides must also verify the data inside each block, using some form of checksum or some other similar techniques.

Blocking and Nonblocking Calls   If the thread of control in the calling process (the caller) waits for the Remote Method or Remote Procedure to return before it continues processing, this is known as a **Blocking Call**. It is named this way because the thread is blocked from further execution while the remote program (the callee) processes the call. If the caller process is a single-tasking process, then the whole caller process is blocked. If the caller process is multithreaded, then the other threads of control can continue to execute in the caller process, even though this particular thread in the caller process is blocked. If the callee process is a single-tasking process, then it will only be able to handle one caller at a time! If the callee process is multithreaded, then each call will be run as a separate thread.

However, if the thread of control in the caller continues immediately after the call is made, without waiting for a response from the callee, then this is known as a **Nonblocking Call**. The real distinction between these two types of calls is the expected behavior when the callee does not immediately respond. In other words, if the callee was always available and always returned quickly, then we would not notice any real difference between the two call types. However, since most calls actually need time to respond, and time to perform whatever action the call is supposed to implement, there is usually a big difference between these call types. Typically, Nonblocking Calls do not return any real information, since any variables receiving the return value of the remote call are undefined until the call actually returns successfully. Therefore, we usually expect remote calls to be Blocking Calls, but it does not necessarily need to be this way in all implementations. When Nonblocking Calls are used, many of the same issues we discussed in Section 14.2.3.1 (Multitasking Requirements) need to be considered, even if the calling process is single-threaded. Also, when Nonblocking Calls are used, the issues and considerations are somewhat similar to those we encounter with Nonblocking Messaging, which we will discuss in Section 14.3.1.2.

Communication Errors and Exceptions   All Remote-Code Execution calls need to consider how errors in the network communication will be returned and handled. Typically, a local procedure call might include some error conditions as part of its logic. All caller code (both remote and local) should include the task-specific logic we wrote inside the call to handle the expected errors for the action itself. With Remote-Code Execution calls, we usually need to add special return codes to the callee and special error handling logic to the caller representing any errors that might result from network-related issues. In the very least, we must handle the case when a call does not return after some configurable timeout period. This is necessary because the remote program might not be executing any longer, there might be some other networking problem preventing communication, or the remote program might simply be taking too long. These error codes and the associated special handling also need to be tested!

14.3.1.2 Remote Messaging

Remote Messaging is the other general-purpose Remoteability mechanism that we will consider. Remote Messaging is similar to Remote-Code Execution, but it is not identical. Once again, there are object-oriented approaches and non-object-oriented approaches from which to choose—but here, this distinction is not as important as it was in the Remote-Code Execution alternative. In Remote Messaging, the caller code passes its data in the form of a Message parameter to a generic "send message" method, procedure, function, or routine. The code on the callee side will either make a generic "check for message" call and a generic "retrieve message" call or it will use a special piece of code that acts as a message event handler/listener. Instead of using multiple methods or procedures with parameters specific to the task being performed, we will use specific messages. Remote Messaging is often implemented using an extensible framework. This description is potentially compatible with the SOA view of messaging, which we discussed earlier. Of course, we would still need to follow the other restrictions we discussed in Section 14.1.3.2 for this to be truly compatible with that view. In other words, Remote Messaging can be compatible with SOA messaging, but this is not always the case.

In Remote Messaging, we need to consider the Messages themselves, as well as the impact of Message-Oriented Programming. There are some issues that are unique to messaging, such as the role of Message Timeouts, Ordering, and Durability. Other issues are similar (but not identical) to those we discussed for Remote-Code Execution, such as Blocking versus Nonblocking communication and the handling of Communication Errors and Exceptions. We will discuss each of these briefly in the following sections.

Messages   A message is usually implemented as a single data structure or a single object. In object-oriented approaches, we create classes that inherit from a Message class or implement a Message interface. Non-object-oriented approaches typically have a common structure at the start of the message (a message header) that specifies message type and length information. In this way, we can create as many different messages as desired with virtually unlimited possibilities for the content.

When a framework provides the basic messaging functionality, we implement the actual messages and the COSs that send and receive the messages as an extension. The data passed inside each message must also be translated into and out of the "data stream" (similar to Marshalling Parameters and Unmarshalling Parameters). Each data structure or object representing a message needs to be converted into a single "stream" of data sent over the network and then converted back into individual data fields, structures, or objects again. Because messages are like complex parameters (they are data structures or objects), this is once again a recursive process that needs to be applied to each field in the message. Each field sent needs to be converted into a format that is compatible with the underlying network protocol used to connect the two processes, and converted from this network compatible format into the format used by the remote program. For example, Big-Endian and Little-Endian conversions (and other similar considerations) are still important, but there is no need to worry about the number of parameters or the order/sequencing of parameter values within the call. The message usually contains all the details needed about the size of all fields and details about all the data types being used. Similar to the case when objects were passed as parameters in RMI, both sides must agree on the definition of the format. This is true even for non-object-oriented implementations of Remote Messaging, which means we usually have some form of version or revision embedded in the message to catch the case where they are not using the same message structure definitions.

We mentioned the terms "Big Endian" and "Little Endian" once before when we discussed Marshalling and Unmarshalling, and they refer to the same concepts here. In particular, the terms "Big Endian" and "Little Endian" are derived from the novel *Gulliver's Travels*, written by Jonathan Swift. Here, however, these terms refer to the order in which the bytes making up a multibyte word are stored. Big Endian formats store the most significant byte first, while little Endian formats store the least significant byte first. If we considered the two different representations for a single multibyte word value, the representations look almost like mirror images of each other (but at the byte level not the bit level). For example, consider the 16-bit value 0x1234 (this is hexadecimal notation, for the decimal value 4660). This value would be stored in Big Endian format using the byte value 0x12 first, followed by the byte value 0x34. This value would be stored in Little Endian format using the byte value 0x34 first, followed by the byte value 0x12. In binary representation, the Big Endian representation would consist of the following sequence of bits: 0001001000110100; while the Little Endian representation would consist of the bits 0011010000010010. Clearly, it is very important to know which representation should be used at each step involved in the communication process.

Message Oriented Programming   Consider a typical conversation between two or more components. One of the components will begin the conversation by making a request. Each of the other components in the conversation will react to the request in one of three ways: respond to the request, ignore the request, or begin a new conversation. When the requests and replies are implemented using Remote-Code Execution, the conversation is more restricted—in effect, the request and response are implemented by making separate Remote Procedure Calls or Remote Method Invocations between each pair of components involved. In this case, the reaction is implemented using the return value or the output parameters available after the call/invocation completes. In other words, from the requesting component's point of view, the "reaction details" are "immediately available" after the procedure call/method invocation completes.

By contrast, when the same conversation is implemented using Remote Messaging, we do not immediately see the "reaction details" as part of the messaging operation. Instead, we must use separate operations (involving separate messages) to implement the requests and the reactions. This is not difficult to implement: we simply send another message, but this time the reacting component sends the message and the requesting component receives the message. This subtle change has some radical implications for the way we write the code in these COSs. Our code becomes focused on the messages rather than the procedure calls and method invocations. We can say that the COSs using Remote-Code Execution are somewhat process oriented (focusing on procedure calls or method invocations), while the COSs using Remote Messaging are message oriented (focusing on the messages used to implement requests and reactions/responses to those requests). There is another subtle difference between Remote Messaging and Remote-Code Execution—Remote Messages can be sent to multiple places with a single call. This also means that sending a single message might result in multiple response messages being returned.

TIMEOUTS, DURABILITY, AND ORDERING   The remote calls used to implement a process-oriented COS look like traditional method or procedure calls. By contrast, however, the code used to implement a message-oriented COS looks more like event-driven programming. Message-oriented code uses techniques similar to those found in many graphical user interface (GUI) programming scenarios. Typically, after the Local COS sends a request message, it must do one of two things—it goes to sleep, or it goes off to perform some other activity while it waits for one or more Remote COS instances to send back a "reaction-details message."

Messages can arrive at any COS that uses Remote Messaging, at almost any time. These messages can be from almost any other COS in the architecture. These messages can have different message types and can arrive in almost any order. It is also possible for our code to be "hung" while waiting for a message that will never come (perhaps the COS instance that was supposed to send it failed). In these cases, we cannot tell the difference between a message that has been delayed due to a busy message sender, a message that will never be sent due to a crashed message sender, and a message that somehow got lost in transmission. In these situations, we usually specify some duration (timeout period) to wait for a response before we consider the sender to be unavailable and the conversation to be over due to some sort of failure. Often, the Messaging Subsystem or Messaging Middleware will provide a message queue or similar construct to allow the receiving program to continue to receive messages even when the receiving program is not actively looking for them. Usually messages need to be processed in the order that they are queued, but sometimes the Messaging Subsystem or Messaging Middleware provides techniques to look ahead or filter the queue for more efficient processing. Some Messaging Subsystems include a message priority flag inside the message to ensure that higher priority messages are queued ahead of lower priority messages. We will discuss some specific messaging implementations in Chapter 15.

Blocking and Nonblocking Messaging   Remote Messaging can be implemented using either **Blocking Message Operations** or **Nonblocking Message Operations**. These operation types are not quite the same as their Remote-Code Execution counterparts (Blocking Calls and Nonblocking Calls), but we can draw some parallels between them. Typically, the code containing our send message operations will be implemented using **Nonblocking Messaging**. This means that the sending COS can continue execution immediately after the message has started its journey out of the Local COS. The typical situation for the code implementing the receive message operations is not as straightforward. When we explicitly use Nonblocking Message Operations (such as the "check for message" or "retrieve message" operations), we refer to this as **Nonblocking Messaging**. Similarly, we explicitly use Blocking Messaging Operations; we refer to this as **Blocking Messaging**.

We can choose to use either form of messaging, assuming that the Messaging Subsystem or Messaging Middleware provides both types of operation. Using Blocking Messaging means that the thread executing in the receiving COS instance will not return from the call to "check for message" or "retrieve message" unless a message is actually available, or a timeout period has expired. When there is no Blocking Messaging form of a particular operation provided, it is easy to write the equivalent code by placing the corresponding Nonblocking operation inside a "while loop," a "for loop," or similar programming language control flow construct. When a Blocking Messaging form is supplied, it typically uses a configurable timeout period to prevent the operation from waiting forever when network (or other) errors prevent communication from continuing.

Typically, Remote Messaging is implemented in multithreaded environments, but this is not a requirement. Using multithreaded code can be a great advantage in this situation, because this means that the Local COS instance and Remote COS instance can continue processing during the lag time in communication. But this also means that both the local and remote programs we must write will be more complicated. When we use Blocking Messaging in a multithreaded program, only the thread making the Blocking call will be suspended (the **other threads in the program will not be blocked**). While this is a powerful technique, it also requires careful programming. The issues we raised in the Multitasking Requirements (see Section 14.2.3.1) need to be carefully considered in this scenario.

Communication Errors and Exceptions   Each call used to send or receive a message needs to consider how network communication errors will be returned and then handled. Typically, the Messaging Subsystem will return error codes, throw exceptions, or raise signals when a network error occurs. When messages are used to implement more complex conversations, we usually define a protocol (an application-defined protocol) to include error-status messages and handshake messages. This means that we need to define specific positive acknowledgment (ACK) or negative acknowledgment (NACK) message types and write our code to send and receive them at critical points in the conversation. We also need to add code to respond appropriately when the expected message is not received or a messaging exception is raised.

14.3.2 Directory Service Requirements

As we discussed in Section 14.1, we implement our DDBE architecture by creating several COSs to provide (and consume) the various services we need. In Section 14.2, we mentioned that in addition to having several different COS types we also may have multiple instances of the same COS deployed across several machines in our network—and we may even have multiple instances of multiple versions of our COSs. Each of our COSs must communicate with at least one other COS (using Remote-Code Execution or Remote Messaging as discussed in Section 14.3.1). When one COS instance needs to communicate with another COS instance, how does it specify which COS instance it is looking for? How does this COS instance let the other COS instances know how to communicate with it? For that matter, once it has specified which COS instance it needs, how does it locate that COS instance on the network? These functions are often referred to as Naming, Registration, and Lookup services, respectively. If we bundle these three subservices together into one service, we can refer to this as a **Directory Service**. We can use several different implementations and approaches for this service, even within the same DDBE architecture. Often, there are even mechanisms or techniques for bridging across different Directory Service implementations. In a distributed processing environment, the DDBE Platform must provide these functions, and therefore we call the second subcategory of DDBE Distributed Processing Requirements the Directory Service Requirements. This subcategory is split into three areas based on the subservices we just mentioned—which we will discuss in the following sections.

The three areas of the Directory Service Requirements are

- Naming Service Requirements

- Registration Service Requirements
- Lookup Service Requirements

14.3.2.1 Naming Service Requirements   The **Naming Service** is the service (or sub-service) responsible for managing all the possible naming issues. For example, in order to find a particular instance of a particular version of a particular COS, we need to have a unique name for that instance. Often, a "human readable" name is clumsy for this purpose. How would we distinguish between two different versions of the same COS? What about two different instances? If we simply attempted to append a version number or instance number to the name, this would become cryptic and difficult to maintain. Therefore, we need to have a more sophisticated naming system.

Using the phonebook as an analogy, we need to have the ability to handle COSs with names that are only slightly different from each other (similar to people with the same last name but different first name). We also need to support COSs with identical names but different connection details (similar to multiple phone numbers for the same person). There must be some way to manage the namespace, so that we can narrow the scope when we use a COS name (similar to the way we can use country, city, and street address information to restrict the names considered in a phonebook). A DDBE Platform that satisfies our Naming Service Requirements needs to support multipart names. Some parts of the name will be the same across all possible versions of a COS. Some parts of the name will be specific to a particular version of the COS. Some parts of the name might be specific to a particular instance (e.g., used in a particular subsystem or on a particular machine). We also want to have some way of assigning a unique name or unique number to this multipart name to improve the performance and overall usability of the name. Lastly, we need to have some way of associating additional information about the COS once we are using the full name or unique name/number.

14.3.2.2 Registration Service Requirements   We need to have some way for a particular instance of a particular version of a particular COS to indicate that it is ready to have the other COS instances in the environment communicate with it. There are several mechanisms that can be used for this process, but generically we can refer to this COS instance as **registering** itself with the DDBE architecture. The **Registration Service** is the service (or subservice) responsible for managing all COS registration issues. As part of this registration process, the COS instance needs to provide its Naming details, Service details, Version details, and also some information about where the COS instance is located. Therefore, our Registration Service Requirements are highly dependent on other DDBE Platform Requirements.

After a particular instance of some service provider is deployed and ready to be used, it registers itself with the DDBE architecture. This is analogous to what happens when a person moves into a new neighborhood and gets a listed phone number. This person must provide information (including their name, phone number, and some notion of where they live or at least what state and city they are to be listed in) to the phone company, and ultimately to the phonebook publishers. In the DDBE, we also have to consider what happens when a particular instance of a COS is no longer available. It makes sense to provide a **deregistration** function, allowing a COS to remove its registration information when it is no longer valid (such as when a COS is being shut down). Obviously, this is analogous to what happens when a person moves out of a neighborhood and makes a request for the phone company to disconnect the phone service and remove the listing the next time the phonebooks are updated.

Registration and deregistration can be done in many different ways. They can use a centralized service running on a single machine, they can involve several services deployed throughout the architecture, or they can even be done with broadcast messages to all COS instances currently running in the environment. Obviously, each of these approaches has advantages and disadvantages. A centralized approach could become a bottleneck for communication and could be costly for COS instances deployed on far-away machines. This mechanism is also somewhat wasteful, since each COS instance probably does not need to communicate with every other COS instance in the architecture. The broadcast mechanism is similarly wasteful and costly with respect to bandwidth and potential timeouts in communication. Using some form of Registration Service deployed for a local region of the network is the more typical implementation, because it can provide a reasonable amount of control, with minimal overhead. These local registries can communicate with each other to synchronize information on a regularly scheduled or need-to-know basis, similar to how Domain Name Servers (DNS) work in a TCP/IP network.

14.3.2.3 *Lookup Service Requirements*   The **Lookup Service** is responsible for managing all service provider lookup issues. Assuming we have provided some form of a Naming Service and also provided some form of a Registration Service, we still need to have some way of querying the names of all registered COSs—otherwise a service consumer would not be able to locate the service provider with which it needs to communicate. The Lookup Service Requirements define how this location process (the Lookup Service) works. This service is analogous to the 411 service that the phone companies provide. Again, there are several mechanisms that can be used for this function, but generically we can refer to this as a **Lookup** function. The Lookup Service implementation depends heavily on the implementation details for the Naming Service Requirements and Registration Service Requirements, which in turn depend on other DDBE Platform Requirements.

Sometimes, we want to look up a particular COS instance deployed at a particular location/machine. Other times we might want a particular version of a particular COS, deployed at a particular location/machine. In other scenarios, we might accept a particular version of the COS if it is deployed anywhere within the "local" area of the network. Perhaps, in some situations, we might accept any version of the COS that is actively deployed anywhere within the "local" area of the network. We might even have some cases where we would accept any COS that provides a particular service regardless of the specific COS name, version, or deployment details. In some rare circumstances, it is even conceivable that we might want to look up a specific instance of a particular COS, but most of the time we are not that specific. We always care about actual service being provided and the version of that service (mainly for compatibility concerns). We sometimes care about the location details (usually for communication cost and efficiency concerns). But we rarely need to be more specific than that.

The lookup function will typically either return a single COS name, a list of potential COSs, or an error/exception indicating that no such COS can be found at the moment. If there is an error, we can go to sleep and try to look it up again later, or we can handle the error in some appropriate fashion. If we obtain a list of potential COSs, we can somehow select a single COS to communicate with (e.g., using additional registration information as filtering criteria, or simply picking the first COS that responds). Once we have selected a COS instance, we attempt to communicate with it using Remote-Code Execution or Remote Messaging as described in Section 14.3.1.

14.4 DISTRIBUTED DATA PLATFORM REQUIREMENTS

In the previous sections, we discussed the DDBE Platform Requirements for "any" environment and "any distributed processing" environment. In this section, we will briefly discuss the remaining DDBE Platform Requirements—some of which we will discuss again in Chapters 15–19. The remaining DDBE Platform Requirements consider requirements that are especially important for distributed processing environments with distributed data. Once again, the Platform Requirements discussed in this section are not irrelevant to other environments, but they are also somewhat less important when there is no data in the environment. In Section 14.4.1 we consider the Architectural Security Requirements—treating security as a DDBE architectural issue. Then, in Section 14.4.2, we will discuss the Database Connectivity Requirements—here we will consider how the COSs in our environment connect to the local databases and other similar issues. Lastly, in Section 14.4.3, we will consider the Transaction Management Requirements—these requirements focus on things like the level of distributed transaction support supplied by the DDBE Platform.

14.4.1 Architectural Security Requirements

Security is an important and complex concept in any database system. This is especially true for a distributed database system. DDBE Security concepts and details about the available mechanisms and techniques that can be used to enforce it are discussed in greater detail in Chapter 9. Our purpose here is merely to identify the Architectural Security Requirements for our DDBE Platform. When implementing Architectural Security for a DDBE, we first define a Security Policy, and then use the facilities provided by the DDBE Platform to implement and enforce our Security Policy. There are several facilities to choose from, and several security-related functions that we can perform in most environments. In particular, we are usually concerned with authentication and authorization. When the data is sufficiently confidential or sensitive, we also need to consider encryption. Ultimately, Architectural Security is an attempt to provide the right level of protection based on the specific data and the specific environment involved. We will briefly consider each of these points in the following sections.

14.4.1.1 Security Policies Within the DDBE, an **identity** is a user, a group of users, a user role, or any system COS instance. A **security target** can be almost any DDBE Platform construct, including DDBE and LDBE structures like tables or columns and even the DDBE components and subsystems. Depending on the type of security target, there are various possible **Operations** that can be performed on the security target. A **Security Policy** is essentially a list of all the permitted and prohibited operations between all identities and security targets.

We can specify further details about the identity, security target, and operation to achieve a fairly fine level of granularity of control. For example, we can specify that a particular user is permitted to select, insert, update, and delete column contents for a particular column in a particular table. We can also specify structural operations.

For example, we can specify that a particular user is permitted to add, drop, rename, or modify column definitions, constraints, or indexes for a particular table. We can even be more specific, perhaps limiting the dates and/or the times when an operation is allowed or denied. We might even specify which machines the request must come from in order to permit the operation. For example, a particular user can only select from the Employee table if the query is being run from the same machine as the LDBE containing the table.

All of these Security Policy details are **not** part of our Architectural Security concerns, but without proper Architectural Security, our Security Policies cannot be effectively enforced. Without architectural support, what is to prevent a user or program from circumventing our Security Policy? **Architectural Security** refers to the mechanisms and techniques we can use to ensure that our COSs acting on behalf of the DDBE users and subsystems are working within the defined Security Policy for the DDBE. We need to ensure that COSs do not grant access to things that they should not and do not prevent access when it has been granted. In order to ensure this, our DDBE Platform needs to have architectural support for authentication, authorization, and encryption. This means that our COSs can use these services correctly, and as needed within the DDBE.

14.4.1.2 Authentication   The first step in Security Policy enforcement is authentication. **Authentication** is the process by which we establish and verify the identity involved. In other words, we need to find out "who" is trying to do something. The identity in question can refer to the subsystem or component directly making a request or it can refer to the ultimate user on whose behalf the request is being made. Regardless of which type of identity we are attempting to authenticate, it is vital for us to establish who the requestor is before we allow any specific type of access to any specific target. There are several different authentication mechanisms and technologies discussed in Chapter 9. Our requirement here is merely to have the ability to use one or more of these mechanisms easily, efficiently, and effectively in the DDBE Platform. Ideally, we should be able to "wrap" our COSs inside an authentication technology. Wrapping the COS means that we can add authentication support to an existing COS using only a minimal amount of additional code or configuration. Architecturally, we are primarily concerned about preventing "imposters," meaning that we want to make it difficult for COSs to lie about the identity they are representing to the DDBE architecture.

14.4.1.3 Authorization   **Authorization** is the process used to determine if an operation is permitted or prohibited. There are several different authorization mechanisms and technologies discussed in Chapter 9. For our purposes here, authorization merely involves reading the Security Policy and obeying or enforcing it. This means that when a COS instance requests a particular type of operation against a particular security target on behalf of a particular (and authenticated) identity, we want the architecture to prevent the operation when it is not permitted. It would be relatively easy to circumvent our Security Policy decisions if we allowed the COS instance to be responsible for enforcement by itself. By moving the enforcement into the architecture, we can make our DDBE much more secure.

14.4.1.4 Encryption   **Encryption** is a set of techniques used to protect the contents of any information that is stored or transmitted in the DDBE architecture. There are several different encryption mechanisms and technologies discussed in Chapter 9, and our

DDBE Platform will probably use more than one encryption mechanism. Encryption is vital to many areas within the DDBE. Obviously, we must use encryption to protect confidential information like passwords. But it is also vital to the authentication and authorization processes. Ideally, our DDBE Platform will include the ability to "wrap" COSs inside an encryption mechanism, thereby creating a "secure" version of the COS. "Wrapping the COS" means that communications to and from the COS become secure (encrypted) communication, merely by changing some configuration or deployment details. We should not need to change a lot of code inside the COS to achieve this, and might not have to change any code at all!

14.4.1.5 Final Thoughts on Security Ultimately, the level of security required depends on the sensitivity of the area within the environment we are attempting to protect, the risk of accidental or malicious security violations, and the ultimate cost of such a violation. Even when the environment is nonsensitive, there is little justification for making the system completely insecure. In particular, we should always attempt to use the existing facilities within our environment to the best of our abilities. For example, there is no excuse for making the Security Policy editable by the public, or allowing nonadministrator users to edit, delete, or reconfigure our deployed COS instances.

14.4.2 Database Connectivity Requirements

The Database Connectivity Requirements consider the underlying Sub-Database Environments (S-DBEs), especially the local database environments (LDBEs) that share the same logical data modeling language. Whenever we can reuse the same COS to access these environments without a significant performance or development cost, we should. Most modern platforms provide some support for database connectivity across different vendors and versions. In particular, Microsoft has a long successful history of providing this type of access—via Open Database Connectivity (ODBC), Object Linking and Embedding Database (OLEDB), Active Template Libraries (ATL), Active Data Objects (ADO), and the Microsoft .NET Framework Data Providers. Similarly, Java provides Java Database Connectivity (JDBC) as well as other mechanisms for connecting to several different database platforms. Both of these platforms support an impressive variety of COTS and FOSS database vendors and versions, as well as many advanced features such as support for connection pooling. When there is no suitable driver or connector available, we should attempt to implement our own driver/connector if possible or, at the very least, we should attempt to create a COS that encapsulates the proprietary details and behaves similar to one of the more standard environments.

Some environments are more interoperable than others are, but this is also highly dependent on configuration details, the features being used, and the way in which they are used. For example, many relational database management systems (RDBMSs) support the American National Standards Institute (ANSI) Structured Query Language (SQL)—but the level of support is typically not the same across all vendors or even across all versions from the same vendor. Similarly, almost all RDBMSs provide nonstandard features that are not portable by definition. Even when the same standards are used across different platforms, there can be different versions of the standard or different levels of compliance supported by the platforms. These differences could be insignificant, a minor issue, or a fatal issue (depending on the standards involved, the actual platforms, the user-designed COSs, and the specific implementation details for these COSs).

14.4.3   Transaction Management Requirements

Transaction Management is a very important consideration for most DDBEs. Of course, it is more important for DDBEs where there are CRUD operations (as discussed in Chapter 1). Even if the DDBE does not support CRUD operations (perhaps it is a read-only distributed system with partial visibility and partial control), Distributed Transaction Management can prevent undesirable scenarios (dirty reads, isolation issues) in the face of the CRUD operations being performed directly against the LDBEs by legacy clients outside the DDBE. Transaction Management in the DDBE is typically implemented by leveraging the underlying Transaction Management facilities in the DDBE Platform and the LDBEs. By using the underlying features provided by the platform as well as those provided by each LDBE in order to implement distributed transaction processing (as discussed in Chapters 3 and 5), we can greatly improve the performance and reliability of the DDBE. Although the underlying features are not sufficient in and of themselves, since they usually do not contain any of the necessary distributed semantic integrity control, we can use them to implement our own transaction processing, whether that is using two-phase commit, three-phase commit, or any of the other techniques discussed in Chapters 3 and 8.

There are several alternatives to choose from when looking for implementation alternatives for this functionality, such as the X/Open XA interface for distributed transactions. In Chapters 15–19, we will look at two specific implementations of the **Distributed Transaction Service (DTS)**. In Section 16.3.3, we will look at the DTS as specified by the **Java Transaction API (JTA)** and **Java Transaction Services (JTS)**—these are defined as part of the J2EE specification and the example implementation we will consider is part of the J2EE platform. In Section 18.3.3, we will look at the Microsoft .NET Framework-based platform and, in particular, at the COM+ and Enterprise Services subplatform support for this service. Although it should be possible to combine COSs written across these different platforms in the same distributed transaction, there are many caveats and potential issues—beyond the scope of this book—that we will not discuss. Our intention here is merely to introduce the topics and some of the facilities available for future exploration and experimentation.

14.5   PREVIEW OF THE DDBE PLATFORMS USED IN CHAPTERS 15–19

In this chapter, we tried to identify the broad categories of functionality that need to be present in the underlying platform (operating system, programming language, database systems, development, deployment, execution environments, etc.) in order to make the implementation of a DDBE feasible. In this section we will briefly preview the three DDBE Platforms we will use to implement the starter kits for making DDBE implementation easier. In Chapters 15–19, each of these platforms will be discussed in greater detail before each starter kit is presented. This discussion will not contain all possible details (there are many books devoted to each of these platforms, so we certainly cannot cover all the details for all of them), but will highlight the implementation alternatives chosen to implement the starter kit for each platform. Each starter kit is intended to provide a jumpstart for implementing DDBEs like those discussed in Chapters 12 and 13 or for implementing new architectural alternatives that nobody else has thought of before.

Chapters 15–19 will use the Java Message Services platform, Java 2 Enterprise Edition platform, and the Microsoft .NET Framework-based platform to implement these starter kits. Therefore, we will briefly preview those platforms in this section and also consider some of the other implementation alternatives that influenced these platforms. Although we will not go into excessive detail for any of these implementation milestones, it is important to recognize that even though some of these alternatives are now antiquated or obsolete, many of their fundamental concepts are still relevant for today's DDBE Platform alternatives.

14.5.1 The Java Message Service (JMS) Platform

The Java Message Service (JMS) is a standard mechanism for providing Remote Messaging as we discussed in Section 14.3.1.2; in particular, it provides **reliable messaging**. Reliable messaging means Remote Messaging with some important, additional features. Reliable Messaging guarantees that each message we send will either be received or an exception will be raised—no exception means that the message was definitely received. Each message that is received is also guaranteed to be sent and received only once (no lost messages and no duplicate messages). Another important feature of reliable messaging is the guaranteed order between the same sender and receiver. This means that if we send three messages from a particular sender to a particular receiver, we know that the messages will be processed in the order that they were sent—it is possible that other messages sent by some other sender might be interpolated within this sequence, but the order is guaranteed with respect to the same sender and receiver.

The JMS is a standard specification, which defines the necessary Java interfaces but does not define the classes that provide the implementation. There are several standards-compliant implementations to choose from, including ApacheMQ, Open-JMS, and others. The JMS uses another standard mechanism called the Java Naming and Directory Interface (JNDI) to provide Directory Services that satisfy our DDBE Platform Requirements. The JMS specification and the service it describes are also part of the Java 2 Enterprises Edition (J2EE) platform. We implicitly have all of the JMS features and functionality available within the J2EE platform. Conversely, we often have J2EE's features available to us when we use the JMS—although it is possible to use the JMS as an independent platform. The JMS is influenced by many other implementation alternatives including the Enterprise Java Beans (EJB) and the Java Transaction API (JTA) specifications, which were defined in 2001. The JMS also evolved from the Java Remote Method Invocation (RMI) specifications in 2001 (and before that in 1998). These specifications were, in turn, based on the work done in Remote Procedure Calls (RPCs) by Sun and many others.

14.5.2 The Java 2 Enterprise Edition (J2EE) Platform

The Java 2 Enterprise Edition platform is a standard platform for developing, deploying, and executing enterprise applications. It consists of a specification for an application server, development APIs, and various file formats used by deployable components that run within the application server. It also includes a family of related standards including the JMS, JTA, and J2SE standards as well as many more specifications that define the mechanisms suitable for providing for all the DDBE Platform Services we discussed in this chapter. Components and subsystems are deployed within the application server using archive files that contain the necessary code and deployment details—with many of the actual binding details being defined in special files contained in the archives (called deployment descriptors).

The J2EE specification is a family of standardized specifications, which defines all the necessary classes and interfaces required to implement an enterprise application server. This includes several implementation alternatives for all of the DDBE Platform Requirements we discussed in this chapter and many additional facilities which we did not discuss. Although there is a reference implementation available, there are also several other standards-compliant implementations to choose from, including Apache Geronimo, JBOSS, JONAS, Websphere, and others. The J2EE platform and specifications have evolved from many other implementations, including all of those mentioned for JMS as well as the Common Object Resource Broker Architecture (CORBA) defined by the Object Management Group (OMG) and the X/Open XA specification for Distributed Transactions Processing defined by the Open Group.

14.5.3 The Microsoft .NET Framework-Based Platform

The Microsoft .NET Framework-based platform is a "mostly proprietary" platform used to develop enterprise distributed applications that run "mostly" on Microsoft Windows-based operating systems. We mention the qualifier "mostly" here because there are specifications for the .NET Framework, as well as some "non-Microsoft" implementations of the platform, and even some implementations for "non-Windows" operating systems. However, most .NET discussions are usually focused on Microsoft's implementations and Microsoft's operating systems. The .NET Framework has actually evolved from facilities provided within Microsoft's earlier platforms and operating systems. It incorporated many of the standards found in other environments, such as the Simple Object Access Protocol (SOAP), the Extensible Markup Language (XML), and XML Web Services. The .NET Framework has also incorporated facilities provided by earlier releases of .NET itself. At its core, we find the Common Language Runtime (CLR). Components and subsystems are bundled as deployable packages called assemblies and written in any of the programming languages directly supported by .NET (C#, C++, Visual Basic, etc.) and its Common Language Specification (CLS). Like the J2EE platform, .NET provides implementation alternatives for all of the Platform Requirements discussed in this chapter.

The .NET Framework is a platform that supports distributed applications (primarily) on Microsoft's operating systems. There have been several different releases of .NET, and multiple versions of this platform can coexist on the same machine at the same time. The most relevant implementation milestones are those technologies previously created by Microsoft: Object Linking and Embedding (OLE), Common Object Model (COM), Distributed Common Object Model (DCOM), Active-X, Common Object Model Plus (COM+), and previous releases of .NET itself. This platform also evolved from Microsoft's implementation of Remote Procedure Calls (RPCs), which in turn was based on the RPC implementation found within the Distributed Computing Environment (DCE). The DCE was defined by the Open Software Foundation (OSF). Although the DCE was an important precursor of many of the modern distributed computing platforms used today, it is not nearly as popular as the other platforms we just discussed. The .NET platform supports several standards including the X/Open XA specification for Distributed Transactions Processing defined by the Open Group, and those we already mentioned throughout this chapter (such as XML).

14.6 SUMMARY

Implementing a DDBE architecture is complex and fraught with many potential problems. Distributed applications are complex on their own, but implementing a DDBE includes many additional considerations. Heterogeneity is one of the greatest strengths of a distributed database, but it is also one of the most difficult factors to manage within an environment. By clarifying the DDBE architecture and identifying the DDBE Platform Requirements, we can make the attempt to address some of the most important issues in a mostly implementation-independent way. Even a DDBE with minimal functionality can use a variety of facilities to satisfy the DDBE Platform Requirements. There are many decisions to make when designing a particular DDBE architecture and additional decisions about the design, implementation, and deployment of each COS in the environment.

In order to implement a DDBE, the underlying platform (the set of all hardware platforms, operating systems, local database environment platforms, programming languages, networking technologies, and middleware) must provide us with some minimal sets of functionality. We call this set of functionality the DDBE Platform Requirements. The actual requirements for a given environment depend on the idiosyncratic details of the DDBE we are trying to build and the constraints placed on us at that time. For example, a read-only DDBE that does not support nonrelational LDBEs will have different requirements than a DDBE that must support full replication, fragmentation, and location transparency for both read and write operations across relational, network, and hierarchical LDBEs.

In an effort to manage the complexity within this potentially large set of required functionality, we can identify three categories of DDBE Platform Requirements: the Fundamental Data Platform Requirements, the Distributed Process Data Platform Requirements, and the Distributed Data Platform Requirements. These categories build on one another with the first category focusing on the minimal requirements for development, execution, and deployment of components or subsystems (COSs) in the environment without any emphasis on distribution issues. The functionality contained within the second category relies heavily on the first category, but considers the minimal requirements for building an application that supports distributed processing—while ignoring distributed data related issues. In particular, this second category considers the minimal requirements necessary to enable local COS instances to locate and communicate with remote COS instances. The final category relies heavily on the previous two categories (building on them) but focuses on the minimal requirements for building an application capable of supporting both distributed processing and distributed data. These requirements include security considerations for the environment as a whole, local database environment connectivity, and global transaction processing across the whole environment. Within each category, there are several smaller groupings to be considered. There are also several possible implementation alternatives capable of satisfying many of these requirements. By using middleware and frameworks to satisfy these requirements, we can maximize reusability and provide loose coupling for the COS instances within the environment.

Any DDBE Platform used should provide some minimal services. In the very least, a distributed environment must support some form of Remoteability—such as a Remote-Code Execution facility or Remote Messaging facility. Often we will use a Directory Service to encapsulate many of the communication details for our remote COS instances. We must also consider security issues from an architectural standpoint—even if the actual enforcement is delegated to underlying facilities within the operating system or network. Ideally, we should also have sophisticated facilities for managing all the deployment details efficiently and effectively within the environment. These facilities should address issues such as pooling and versioning as well as the actual installation and configuration of the COS instance itself. Depending on how heterogeneous or homogeneous our environment is, we may need sophisticated or more simplistic support for portability and interoperability with our architecture. Because our environment is not only a distributed one but also a database environment, we also would expect to have some database-specific facilities available to us such as some form of database connectivity and transaction management.

14.7   GLOSSARY

Application-Defined Protocol   An application-specific definition of all the expected sequences of messages used and the operations that we want to perform when those messages are produced and consumed.

Architectural Security   The overall plan for security within the DDBE—identifying the important security functions and which COSs are responsible for implementing them.

Authentication   Any technique used to validate the identity of a source or destination of messages or data.

Authorization   Any technique used to determine whether a particular user, component, or subsystem has sufficient access permissions to perform a desired operation—this is usually checked after the identity has been authenticated.

Blocking   A message transfer, method call, or procedure call that will not allow any further communication until after the current operation completes.

Business Services Tier   The middle tier in the three tier model (3TM).

Callee   A piece of code that is called (invoked) by another piece of code—this can refer to any level of scope within the code itself from the actual method (or function, routine, procedure) being called, to any container of that method. For example, the callee can refer to the method, the module (class), or the component or subsystem containing the code being invoked.

Caller   A piece of code that calls (invokes) another piece of code—this can refer to any level of scope within the code itself from the actual method (or function, routine, procedure) containing the call, to any container of that method. For example, the caller can refer to the method, the module (class), or the component or subsystem containing the code that invokes some callee.

Commercial Off-the-Shelf (COTS)   Any piece of commercially available software.

Competitive Synchronization   A situation where two or more threads compete over a shared piece of data or a shared resource.

Component   A deployable bundle that provides a reasonably cohesive set of functionality.

Component or Subsystem (COS)   A term that refers to a component or subsystem, ignoring any differences between the two concepts.

Cooperative Synchronization   A situation where two or more threads are intentionally working together and therefore must find some way to communicate with each other.

Data Services Tier   The third tier in the three-tier model (3TM).

DDBE Platform   A set of hardware systems, operating systems, local database environments, programming languages, and other technologies used to implement a distributed database environment (DDBE).

DDBE Platform Requirement   A set of cohesive functionality provided by the DDBE Platform in order to support the implementation of a DDBE.

Deployment   Any features, issues, concepts, or considerations related to how a COS instance is installed on a particular machine at a particular site.

Deregistration   The act of removing information from a directory service listing, typically done when a COS is no longer available within an environment—the opposite of registration.

Distributed Data Platform Requirements   The third grouping of DDBE Platform Requirements that focus on Security, Database Connectivity, and Distributed Transaction activities.

Directory Service   A service that provides several important functions such as naming, registration, lookup, and possibly security.

Distributed Process Platform Requirements   The second grouping of DDBE Platform Requirements that focus on Remoteability and Directory Services activities.

Encryption   Any technique or operation that creates ciphertext, which is confidential in the face of eavesdroppers, from plaintext, which is the underlying message/ data.

Extension   The "less-reusable," user-written code that extends a framework.

Framework   The "more-reusable," framework-author-written code on which an extension is based.

Free or Open Source Software (FOSS)   A category of software that is available through a license that permits its use and redistribution without any additional cost to the user.

Fundamental Platform Requirements   The first grouping of DDBE Platform Requirements that focus on Development, Deployment, and Execution activities.

Identity   A user, group of users, user role, or COS that can be authenticated or authorized.

Lookup Service   A service that is used to locate a particular COS instance within an environment.

Marshalling   The collection of techniques capable of converting parameters into a data stream, usually to support RMI, RPC, or Messaging—the opposite of Unmarshalling.

Message   A data structure or textual stream representing content sent from one COS instance to another.

Message Oriented Middleware (MOM)   Any piece of middleware that uses messaging for remote communication.

Middleware   Any additional software used to "bridge the gap" (translate or hide differences) between COSs.

Multiprocessing System   Any system that allows two or more processes to appear to be running at the same time.

Multitasking System   Any system that allows two or more tasks to appear to be running at the same time.

Multithreaded Programming   A programming technique that uses multiple threads of control to give the illusion that multiple things are being done at the same time.

Multi-user System   Any multiprocessing system that allows multiple users to be logged in at the same time.

Naming Service   A facility that is responsible for managing all naming issues and providing all the necessary naming functions.

Nonblocking   The opposite of blocking—it refers to a message transfer, method call, or procedure call that allows other communications to occur while the current operation is still executing.

Pooling   A technique that groups multiple instances of the same COS to be reused instead of being shutdown/unloaded and restarted/reloaded in between calls by different COSs.

Reentrant Code   Any section of code that can be safely suspended and reentered by multiple threads of control at the same time.

Registration   The act of adding information to a directory service listing, typically done when a COS becomes available within an environment—the opposite of deregistration.

Registration Service   The service responsible for registration and deregistration operations.

Remote Method Invocation (RMI)   A remote execution technique based on object-oriented method invocation (calls).

Remote Procedure Call (RPC)   A remote execution technique based on traditional, third generation (non-object-oriented) procedure calls (invocations).

Remoting   The collection of techniques used to perform any remote functions including remote execution and messaging.

Security Policy   The collection containing all authorization definitions for an environment.

Security Target   The object being acted on by an authorized identity.

Semaphore   A piece of atomic data (a variable) used analogous to a lock.

Service   A logical collection (specification/design) of well-defined, cohesively related functionality or a software instance (physical collection) that implements this functionality.

Service Consumer   A component or subsystem that uses a set of functionality implemented by some other component or subsystem (consumes a service implemented by some service provider).

Service Oriented Architecture (SOA)   A specific architectural design technique that is focused on interactions between services. It is especially useful for visualizing and discussing distributed application architectures.

Service Provider   A component or subsystem that implements a set of functionality and makes it available to other components and subsystems (provides a service to be used by some service consumer).

Subsystem   A collection of components and/or subsystems that is part of a larger system but also a system in its own right.

Synchronization   See competitive synchronization or cooperative synchronization.

Thread   A "thread of control," which is analogous to a separate execution of a program.

Thread-Safe   Any section of code that supports multithreading (multiple threads within the same program) without data corruption or other issues.

Three-Tier Model (3TM)   A technique for visualizing and discussing distributed application architectures consisting of the user services tier, the business services tier, and the data services tier.

Unmarshalling   The collection of techniques capable of converting a data stream into one or more parameters, usually to support RMI, RPC, or Messaging—the opposite of Marshalling.

User Presentation Tier   Another name for the user services tier in the three-tier model (3TM).

User Services Tier   The third tier in the three-tier model (3TM).

REFERENCES

[Bieberstein05]   Bieberstein, N., Shah, R., Jones, K., Bose, S., and Fiammante, M., *Service-Oriented Architecture (SOA) COMPASS: Business Value, Planning, and Enterprise Roadmap*, Pearson Education, Upper Saddle River, NJ, 2005.

[Booch07]   Booch, G., Maksimchuk, R. A., Engle, M. W., Young, B. J., Conallen, J., and Houston, K. A., *Object-Oriented Analysis and Design with Applications*, 3rd edition, Addison-Wesley, Reading, MA, 2007.

[Josuttis07]   Josuttis, N., *SOA in Practice: The Art of Distributed System Design*, O'Reilly Media, Sebastopol, CA 2007.

[Michaelson04]   Michaelson, J., "There's No Such Thing as a Free (Software) Lunch," *Queue*, Vol. 2, No. 3, pp. 40–47, 2004.

[Nagappan03]   Nagappan, R., Skoczylas, R., and Sriganesh, R. P., *Developing Java Web Services: Architecting and Developing Secure Web Services Using Java*, John Wiley & Sons, Hoboken, NJ, 2003, p. 22.

[Scacchi07]   Scacchi, W., "Free/Open Source Software Development," *Proceedings of the 6th Joint Meeting of the European Software Engineering Conference and the ACM SIGSOFT Symposium on the Foundations of Software Engineering*, Dubrovnik, Croatia, September 3–7, 2007. ESEC-FSE '07. ACM, New York, 2007, pp. 459–468.

[Yellin01]   Yellin, D. M., "Stuck in the Middle: Challenges and Trends in Optimizing Middleware," *SIGPLAN Notes*, Vol. 36, No. 8, pp. 175–180, 2001.

EXERCISES

Provide short (but complete) answers to the following questions.

14.1   What is the fundamental principle used to determine in which tier of the three-tier model a component or subsystem belongs?

14.2 How is the service oriented architecture's focus different from the three-tier model's focus?

14.3 How are Remote Messaging and Remote-Code Execution different?

14.4 How are the concepts of "thread safety" and "pooling" related to each other?

14.5 How are the concepts of thread safety and reentrancy related?

15

THE JMS STARTER KIT

We refer to the combination of a framework and a sample extension (of that framework) as a **starter kit (SKIT)** because we intend to use this combination of software as a toolkit that will help us to start developing software projects. SKITs are not intended to be complete solutions, or production-ready code, but the starter kits provided with this book should be useful when learning about **distributed database environment (DDBE)** concepts, and helpful when creating academic, research, prototype, or proof-of-concept projects. Starter kits like this one can also help us to improve our understanding of the specific DDBE architecture that we are attempting to develop, as well as the underlying technical facilities we can use, and the technical issues we need to address.

In this chapter, we are considering the starter kit that we call the JMS-SKIT. The JMS-SKIT is available for download via the official website for this book (see the Preface for further details). We named the starter kit this way because both the framework and the extension contained within it rely on the **Java Message Service (JMS)** as defined by the **Java Message Service Specification (JMS-SPEC)** [Java02], which is also available for download via http://java.sun.com/products/jms/.

This chapter is intended to be a high-level overview of the starter kit, but it is not intended to be a detailed description of the implementation details. The bundle downloaded from the website contains all the source code, Java documentation, and example configuration files for the JMS-SKIT. It also contains a "cookbook" (a document containing a collection of "recipes") that describes how to use the starter kit in some common JMS Provider implementation alternatives and offers hints for how to customize the starter kit to work in other scenarios and implementation alternatives.

We intend this starter kit to be used primarily for **component or subsystem (COS)** software development, and especially within the context of a **distributed database environment (DDBE)**. Before we can discuss the JMS-SKIT further,

Distributed Database Management Systems by Saeed K. Rahimi and Frank S. Haug
Copyright © 2010 the IEEE Computer Society

we need to understand more about the JMS, and the JMS-SPEC. The specification defines a standard mechanism for implementing Remote Messaging (as we discussed in Section 14.3.1.2). As the name implies, the specification defines the requirements for a particular (remote) messaging service. Our goal in this chapter is to demonstrate how we can use the JMS platform (the combination of the specification and a particular implementation of it) to meet the DDBE Platform Requirements for Remote Messaging. The JMS-SPEC primarily applies to code written in the Java programming language. Although it is possible for programs written in other programming languages to use the JMS facilities, we will focus on the Java programming language in this chapter and, more particularly, the **Java 2 Standard Edition (J2SE)** platform. Aside from being compatible with some non-Java languages, the JMS is also compatible with other Java platforms, such as the **Java 2 Enterprise Edition (J2EE)** platform, which we will discuss in Chapters 16 and 17. In addition to the Remote Messaging facilities provided by the JMS, we can also use any of the facilities provided by the J2SE Platform to satisfy our other DDBE Platform Requirements, which we discussed in Chapter 14. For example, the J2SE platform has support for some of the Fundamental Platform Requirements (for development and execution). It also has support for many of the Distributed Processing Requirements and many of the Distributed Data Requirements. Similarly, we are also able to include other middleware in our DDBE Platform if we wish to do so (in fact, that is precisely what J2EE is—a specific set of several, standardized specifications intended to provide the facilities needed for enterprise applications). However, in this chapter, we are only going to focus on the JMS facilities, and largely ignore those other possibilities.

If we were to implement our DDBE software without using the JMS or a similar piece of middleware, such an implementation would need to implement all the required communication details directly. While it is certainly possible to implement a DDBE in this way, it is somewhat complicated and fraught with potential problems. This is especially true when we consider the ambitious goals we discussed in Sections 14.2, 14.3, and 14.4 (including Extensibility, Pooling, Multitasking, Concurrent Execution, etc.). Because these goals can be especially challenging to achieve when we design and implement all of the code completely from scratch, it is reasonable to pursue less challenging alternatives. Therefore, this chapter will demonstrate how we can use the JMS middleware to help us manage the Remote Messaging Requirements much more effectively. In Section 15.1 of this chapter, we will discuss the JMS concepts defined by the specification that are relevant to our goals. Because we are focusing on the specification rather than any particular implementation, we can choose from several different implementation alternatives. In Section 15.2, we will highlight the bare-minimum configuration details needed to deploy two specific JMS Provider implementation alternatives for the sake of supporting the code discussed in this chapter. Even when we decide to use the JMS instead of directly implementing all of the code ourselves, we have an additional layer of complexity in our code because of this decision. As designers and developers, we still have to consider all the JMS concepts and issues. Luckily, we can create an extensible framework (as we discussed in Section 14.2.1.2) to encapsulate many of these concerns. We will present an overview of the simple JMS-SKIT framework in Section 15.3. In Section 15.4, we look at several ways we can use the JMS-SKIT. In Section 15.4.1, we will look at the sample extension included in the JMS-SKIT. Next, we will discuss how we can use the framework to create new extensions in Section 15.4.2, and, finally, in Section 15.4.3, we discuss how to enhance the JMS-SKIT framework and how to create other, new and different frameworks on top of the Java Message Service.

15.1   JAVA MESSAGE SERVICE OVERVIEW

In this section, we will cover the concepts relevant to the implementation and use of the JMS-SKIT framework. While the level of detail at which we consider the JMS concepts in this section should be sufficient for most readers, anyone who wants to create a more powerful JMS-based framework (or anyone who merely wants to understand the JMS concepts and issues more completely) has a whole world of additional resources to explore. In addition to reading the specification itself, we can choose to read any of the numerous books, articles, forums, and websites that discuss the JMS concepts and issues. If we want to find places like these on the Web, we can simply enter "JMS specification" or "JMS" into our favorite Internet search engine—several examples should usually appear. Similarly, most JMS Provider implementations (and the JMS specification itself) have dedicated websites, mailing lists, web forums, or Internet relay chat rooms filled with links to other sources in the JMS community. For example, there are forums available via http://java.sun.com/javaee/community/forums/index.jsp for the JMS specification itself, and other forums available via http://activemq.apache.org/discussion-forums.html for the ActiveMQ JMS platform implementation. All of these locations are potential sources of more detailed information about the JMS. The best way to find information on the Web is to start from places like these.

In essence, the JMS specification defines an architectural point of view and set of Java language constructs that provide the **application–programming interface (API)** for the Java Message Service. Some parts of the specification and API are necessary for the JMS platform vendors, some parts are necessary for the JMS application developers, and, of course, some parts are used by both. We will only focus on the concepts relevant to the JMS application developers, because our framework will be implementing **JMS Clients**—we are not creating our own implementation of the JMS platform itself. Before we can discuss the actual JMS API constructs, we need to clarify some messaging issues and discuss how the JMS specification addresses them. The JMS platform can be implemented as a thin layer of middleware on top of existing (legacy) messaging systems, or it can be implemented completely from scratch. Similarly, the platform can be implemented in any programming language. Using Java certainly has some distinct advantages, most notably the improved portability and interoperability with other code written in Java. Ideally, the implementation and deployment details should be mostly irrelevant to JMS application developers. More importantly, these details should be almost completely irrelevant to the users of the applications running on top of the JMS platform. There will always be some important and potentially visible, proprietary aspects that need to be managed, but if we plan the implementation and deployment properly, many of these details can be handled behind the scenes.

15.1.1   Architectural Overview

Suppose we have created the simple JMS application depicted in Figure 15.1. In this example, we have three top-level subsystems. We have one **JMS Provider** instance (named "JMS Provider-A") and two **JMS Client** instances (named "JMS Client-B"

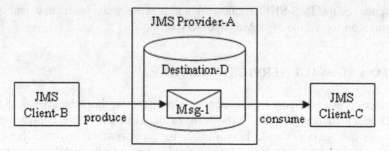

Figure 15.1   JMS Client-B produces a message for JMS Client-C to consume.

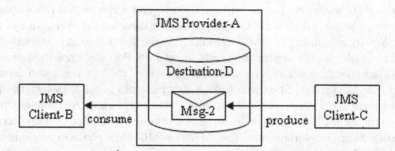

Figure 15.2   JMS Client-C produces a message for JMS Client-B to consume.

and "JMS Client-C"). The deployment details are not particularly relevant to this discussion—but for the sake of completeness, we can consider each COS to be deployed on a separate machine. It would be equally possible for us to deploy all the COSs on the same machine, or any other possible variation. In this example, we have configured a destination within the JMS Provider (named "Destination-D"), and we can also see that JMS Client-B has produced a message (Msg-1), which JMS Client-C will consume. Notice that the destination is both the target of the production operation and the source of the consumption operation.

Presumably, the two clients are cooperating in some respect to fulfill a distributed activity, and therefore we would expect some form of communication moving in the other direction as some point in the future. This might look something like the situation show in Figure 15.2. Notice that the two diagrams are very similar to each other. We could have configured a new destination within JMS Provider-A, but this is not necessary here. We could also have shown many more messages, destinations, and clients (in a real environment there certainly would be more), but these simple scenarios are sufficient for our discussion in the next section.

15.1.1.1   Service Terminology Review   As we discussed in Chapter 1 (in Section 1.2.1), any piece of software implementing a service is called a **service provider**, which is precisely why the JMS specification refers to such an implementation as the **JMS Provider** (the Java Message Service Provider). The JMS Provider is implemented by the JMS platform vendor. In Chapter 1, we also said that any piece of software that uses a service is called a **service consumer**; however, the JMS specification will use the term **JMS Client** for this purpose instead. Generically, each service has at

least one "contractual agreement" that defines the inputs, outputs, and protocols used by the service consumers and providers—in Section 1.2.1 we called this an interface. Although the Java programming language also has a specific construct called an interface, these are not equivalent terms. We should always be able to determine which type ofinterface we mean (the "contract" or the "construct") from the context in which it is being discussed. The JMS specification defines this "contract" between service consumers (JMS Client instances) and service providers (JMS Provider instances) for the JMS platform, including the definition for many of the Java constructs (Java classes, interfaces, etc.) being used. There is one more potentially confusing situation in the JMS specification that we should point out. In the JMS specification, the terms "produce" and "producer" refer to the originator of a message, while the terms "consume" and "consumer" refer to the recipient of a message. The specification uses these terms to avoid the messaging-domain bias implied by other more common words like "send" and "receive" (we will discuss messaging domains in Section 15.1.3). Therefore, it is important to remember this: the JMS Provider is a service provider and the JMS Client is a service consumer—but whenever the JMS specification mentions a "consumer" it is not talking about a service consumer, it is talking about the recipient of a message.

The JMS Client instances produce and consume messages as part of the conversations that they have with each other, while the JMS Provider merely acts as the facilitator for these conversations. The JMS Provider does not directly participate in the conversations. In this respect, the JMS Provider is analogous to many messaging services used to facilitate communication between people in the real world. For example, when we read email, we use an email client application to connect to an email server, then send and receive email messages with other email clients. Notice that even though our email client connects to an email server, we are really (ultimately) communicating with the other email clients. Actually, we are really communicating with the people who are running those other email clients. We do not have a conversation with our email server or anyone else's email server. The email servers are merely facilitators (service providers) in the same way that the JMS Provider is merely a service provider for the JMS Client instances.

15.1.1.2 Administered Objects   The JMS platform contains some concepts (which we will loosely refer to as objects) that the JMS API represents using Java interfaces and classes. Although the specification completely defines the behavior for some of these concepts, there are also some concepts mentioned in the specification that are not completely controlled by it. Some of the details controlling these "partially defined" objects are left as implementation-dependent and proprietary details. These objects are called **administered objects** in the specification, because they refer to things that need to be administered (defined, monitored, and managed) by the JMS Provider. Because the specification does not define all the specific details for these administered objects, each JMS Provider vendor can choose how to implement those "undefined" portions of the objects without any restrictions. This enables a JMS Provider to be implemented on top of an existing messaging system that does not directly conform to the JMS specification. Some implementations provide (proprietary, nonstandard) programmatic interfaces for administering these objects while others use (proprietary, nonstandard)

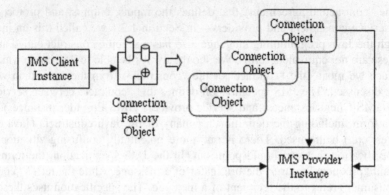

Figure 15.3   Creating Connection objects.

configuration files or even separate administrative applications or facilities for this purpose. We will discuss some of the relevant proprietary administration details for two specific JMS Provider implementations in Section 15.2. The two types of administered objects defined in the specification are called the **Connection Factory object** (which we will discuss in the next section) and the **Destination object** (which we will discuss in Section 15.1.1.5). The specification also defines many other **nonadministered** objects, some of which we will discuss in the following sections as needed.

15.1.1.3 Connection Factories and Connections   Each JMS Client instance uses a **Connection Factory object** to create one or more **Connection objects** (each of which represents an actual connection to a specific JMS Provider instance). While it is possible for a JMS Client to create several Connection objects to the same JMS Provider instance by using the same Connection Factory object (as shown in Figure 15.3), this is not necessary since the Connection object is thread-safe (as we discussed in Section 14.2.3). Because the Connection Factory object is also thread-safe, we are free to reuse the same factory object or to create new Connection Factory objects as needed. If a JMS Client instance wishes to connect to more than one JMS Provider instance, it will usually create a separate Connection object for each connection. Once a Connection Factory object has been created, we can configure it with the details necessary to perform the lookup operation for a specific JMS Provider instance, and then connect to the instance once it has been located. The JMS specification does include any standard syntax or format definition for the name criteria used in the lookup operation. Typically, this lookup will be performed with the Java Naming and Directory Interface (JNDI) facilities. This is the standard mechanism for .implementing the Directory Service Requirements (as we discussed in Section 14.3.2) for a Java-based platform.

15.1.1.4 Thread-Safety Considerations   Each Connection object is used to create one or more **Session objects** within the JMS Client. Unlike the Connection Factory object and Connection object, the Session object is **not thread-safe**. Therefore, each Session object we create represents the connection between a single thread of control within the JMS Client instance and the JMS Provider instance specified in the Connection object. While it is possible for one thread of control to create several different Session objects (see Figure 15.4), we can only use one session at a time within the same thread (by definition, we can only do one thing at a time within a single thread). This also

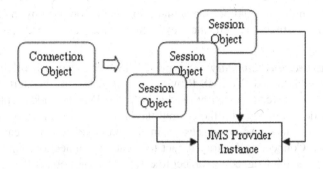

Figure 15.4 Creating several Session objects for the same JMS Provider instance.

means that it is not possible for the same Session object to be used by more than one thread of control at the same time.

Session objects provide several crucial functions to our JMS Client. Most importantly, they perform the actual operations necessary to enable the JMS Client to produce and consume messages via a particular JMS Provider instance. If we want to be more specific, we should say that we use each Session object to create one or more **Message Producer objects, Message Consumer objects**, and **Message objects**. The Message Producer objects are used to produce ("send") a Message object, while the Message Consumer objects are used to consume ("receive") a Message object. Like the Session objects, both the Message Producer objects and Message Consumer objects are **not thread-safe**. The Message objects represent the actual message content (including some of the necessary technical details controlling how the messages are processed and managed). JMS Client instances pass messages back and forth among themselves by producing and consuming these Message objects. The specification does not require many methods for the Message objects because these details are determined by the JMS Client designers and developers. Therefore, the thread safety of the Message objects depends on the methods we create within them. We will consider Message objects again in Section 15.1.4.7.

15.1.1.5 Destination Objects The JMS specification defines one more important concept that we need to consider in this architectural overview: namely, the second administered object, which is called the **Destination object**. When a JMS Client instance wants to send a message to another JMS Client instance, it follows the steps we just outlined to create a Message Producer object and a Message object. The JMS Client uses the Destination object to indicate the intended destination for the Message object being produced. As we shall see in the next section, there are several different destination flavors to choose from, but generically, we can consider each of these flavors to be represented by different Destination objects. When clients communicate with each other within the JMS platform, they always use the JMS Provider instance as an intermediary—they never connect to each other directly. Therefore, each Destination object actually represents the details needed by the JMS Provider to ensure message delivery. Typically, these details will include some hints or configuration settings concerning the message storage within the JMS Provider as well as the "proprietary address details" needed to ensure that the intended recipient (or recipients) can consume the messages. Because the Destination objects are merely the client's representation of the actual destination details, and not the actual implementation used by the JMS Provider instance for the destination itself, the Destination objects are thread-safe.

15.1.1.6 *Architectural Summary*

15.1.1.6 Architectural Summary   A typical JMS conversation involves at least two JMS Client instances and one JMS Provider instance. Before the start of the conversation, we use whatever proprietary mechanisms the JMS Provider supplies to create the necessary destinations (with the desired flavor and other characteristics) within the JMS Provider instance. As we discussed in the previous sections, each JMS Client instance uses a Connection Factory object to create a Connection object. Each client instance then uses that Connection object to create a Session object to establish the link between one thread of control in the client and the JMS Provider instance. After that, each client uses a Destination object to specify the details necessary to identify the destination within the JMS Provider instance. Next, each client uses its Session object to create whatever Message Producer objects and Message Consumer objects it needs in order to use that destination. When a client instance wants to produce a message, it uses the same Session object that it used to create the Message Producer object to create a new Message object. The client then uses the methods of its Message Producer object to produce (actually "send") the message. This passes the information contained within the Message object to the destination defined within the JMS Provider instance. At some point after the message has been produced (which can be almost immediately after the message has been produced, or much later than that), the message is available and can be consumed. Now, the JMS Client instance that we intended to receive the message can use the methods of its Message Consumer object to consume (actually "receive") the Message object from the destination. Notice that the destination is both the target of the produce operation and the source of the consume operation. In addition, it should be noted that the client instance producing the message needed to create the Message object **explicitly** before performing the produce operation. However, the client instance consuming the message did not need to explicitly create the message before performing the consume operation. Instead, the Message object was **implicitly** created by the underlying JMS middleware. Lastly, we should recognize that all JMS Client instances involved must contain the same (application defined) definition for the Message objects and the same (JMS specification defined) definition for the JMS Provider supplied JMS objects involved.

15.1.2 Messaging Overview

Distributed communication is a complex concept. There are a number of situations to be considered and there are often a number of alternative solutions to choose from when issues arise. For our purposes here, we will try to consider some of the fundamental concepts involved, but we will certainly not attempt to address all possible scenarios—even the JMS specification itself does not attempt to do that! To illustrate the concepts and issues involved, we will look at a few more example scenarios.

In Figure 15.5, we see a simple, multimessage conversation between two JMS Client instances. The two clients are named "JMS Client-B" and "JMS Client-C." Even though it is not shown in the diagram, suppose that each client instance has used a Connection Factory object to create a Connection object. We can also assume that these Connection objects have connected to the JMS Provider instance shown here (JMS Provider-A), and

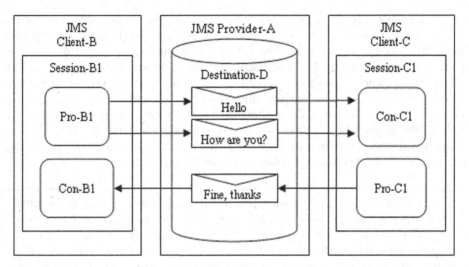

Figure 15.5   A simple, multimessage conversation between two JMS Client instances.

ultimately, each client instance has created a single Session object (named "Session-B1" and "Session-C1," respectively). Each client instance then used its Session object to create its own Message Producer object (Pro-B1 and Pro-C1) and its own Message Consumer object (Con-B1 and Con-C2). We can also see three Message objects (shown as envelopes containing "Hello," "How are you?," and "Fine, thanks") being produced and consumed in this example. The arrows indicate production and consumption operations, while the Message objects themselves are shown inside the destination (Destination-D), which is itself contained within the JMS Provider-A instance.

It is important to notice that this example is not equivalent to a sequence diagram—it does not tell us any details about the order in which the messages are produced or consumed. Even though the deployment details are somewhat irrelevant to this example, we can consider the client instances and the provider instance to be deployed on separate sites. Each Message Producer object and Message Consumer object must be deployed at the same site as the Session object that created it. Similarly, each Session object is deployed at the same site as the JMS Client instance that created it. Meanwhile, the destination can be deployed at the same site as the JMS Provider instance or possibly at a different site if it is implemented using a database for the message storage. Again, these deployment details do not have a big impact on our considerations in this section—they are merely mentioned here for the sake of completeness.

15.1.2.1 Application-Defined Protocols   If we want our JMS application (the collection of all the cooperating JMS Client instances) to accomplish any useful task, we need to consider the types of conversations our JMS Client instances participate in and the general rules (or grammar) that these conversations should follow. In other words, we are defining the expected sequence of messages and the operations that we want to perform when those messages are produced and consumed. We loosely refer to these rules as a **communication protocol**, and since it is defined by our application, we can call this an **application-defined protocol**. In Figure 15.5, we see a conversation, but unless we know the application-defined protocol for this situation, we cannot understand what is really happening. For example, suppose our protocol indicated that every valid conversation must begin with the "first client" producing a greeting message ("Hello") that is then immediately followed by an inquiry message ("How are you?"), both produced by the same client, and then followed by an answer message ("Fine, thanks") produced by the "second client" instance. If this was our application-defined protocol, there could be variations within the content, such as other greeting messages ("Good morning," "Good afternoon," etc.) and other answer messages ("Terrific!," "Not so good," etc.). However, we would always know that the "second client" would not produce an answer message until after it had consumed a greeting message followed by an inquiry message, both sent from the same "first client" instance.

If we had considered a different application-defined protocol (and, in particular, if we had considered a more meaningful and realistic one), we could understand our JMS Client conversation example even more completely. Of course, to do this properly, we would need to define all the possible variations in message content as well as all the possible variations in conversation structure. In order to do this, we would need to define a list of all the valid message types and another list of all the possible conversations (all the valid and invalid sequences of message types). Each conversation in this list might represent radically different underlying semantics and expected consequences. For example, consider how our DDBE might implement an application-defined protocol like the two-phase commit protocol or the three-phase commit protocol (which we discussed in Sections 8.8.4 and 8.8.5 in Chapter 8). Protocols like these are much more representative of the conversations we need to implement in our DDBE; however, they are also very complicated to define and understand. Luckily, we do not need to worry about complex or meaningful protocols like these in order to understand the issues that are important to this section. Therefore, we will use the simplistic examples presented here instead of any real DDBE application-defined protocols.

15.1.2.2 Synchronous Versus Asynchronous Messaging   Suppose we want to implement the conversation shown in Figure 15.5 using the simplistic "greeting, inquiry, answer" application-defined protocol we discussed in the previous section. Also suppose that Pro-B1 produces the greeting message and then, shortly afterward, produces the inquiry message. When will these messages be consumed by Con-C1? Even though we have an application-defined protocol, we cannot answer this question without first considering two other messaging concepts known as **synchronous messaging** and **asynchronous messaging**.

Synchronous messaging means that messages are only consumed when the consumer **explicitly requests** the message. In other words, if Pro-B1 produces a message, but JMS Client-C is busy doing other things, then the message will not be consumed at that time. Asynchronous messaging is the name for the opposite situation. In asynchronous messaging, some (short) time after Pro-B1 produces the message, the code in JMS Client-C will attempt to consume the message—even if it was busy doing other things. Of course, there will be a small latency time between the message production and consumption, based on how busy the systems are, the speed of the network, and so on—but the message consumption will essentially happen at the same time as the message production when the conditions are ideal. This is asynchronous messaging because the message reception does not occur at fixed or specific times. Whenever the message is produced, the consumer will be interrupted, and the message will be consumed. By contrast, in synchronous messaging we consume messages at a fixed place in the algorithm or based on a fixed time schedule—regardless of when the messages were actually produced. Asynchronous messaging is similar to event-driven programming, if we consider the sending of a message to be an event. Therefore, asynchronous messaging is sometimes referred to as message-driven programming. In fact, J2EE has a special type of Java Bean called a Message Driven Bean (MDB), which is usually implemented using the JMS facilities (we will discuss MDBs in Chapter 16). Generically, asynchronous messaging can be implemented using either multithreading techniques or single-threaded techniques, but in both cases, we must process the messages carefully from a multitasking perspective. The multithreaded implementation is the most common (and straightforward) way to implement asynchronous messaging.

The JMS provides support for both synchronous and asynchronous messaging. When asynchronous messaging is used, it typically uses multithreading in the JMS Client software, and therefore as application developers, we must be sure to use the JMS API calls carefully—remember that the Session objects and all the other objects that are ultimately created from them are not thread-safe! It is also important to recognize that both synchronous and asynchronous messaging can use either blocking or nonblocking calls—these concepts are not equivalent to each other. For example, suppose JMS Client-C implements asynchronous messaging by using a separate thread of control to consume the messages. If it is possible for this thread to be blocked while waiting for the message, then we are using asynchronous, blocking messaging. However, if it is not possible for this thread to be blocked while it is waiting to consume the messages, then we are using asynchronous, nonblocking messaging. In the first case, the thread executes and when the blocking call is reached, the thread is suspended until a message is available for consumption and the call returns with the message. In the second case, the thread executes and when the nonblocking call is reached, it will return regardless of whether there is a message available for consumption or not. In both scenarios, if there are many messages being produced and the consuming client needs to perform some actions for each message it consumes, then it is possible that the messages will start to "pile up"—similar to the way items can "pile up" in our in-box while we are working on other things in the real world. This is one of the primary reasons for using a JMS Provider, namely, its ability to manage these "piles" of messages. In the next section, we will consider some alternatives for how the provider can manage these messages that are waiting to be consumed.

15.1.2.3 Message Persistence   Even in our simple messaging example, there are many unexpected complex situations that could happen. What happens to the messages that "pile up" while JMS Client-C is busy processing other requests? What happens if JMS Client-C never receives one of the messages that JMS Client-B sent to it? What if JMS Client-C shuts down and exits before it consumes all the messages that JMS Client-B produced for it? Recall that the JMS Client instances are actually communicating directly with a JMS Provider instance, and not directly with each other. This means that it is possible for JMS Client-B to produce its messages successfully, without any errors or issues, even when it is not possible for JMS Client-C to consume the messages.

We can consider many scenarios in which the potential for lost messages is high. For example, this can happen if the network is very congested, or the participants are prone to network failures due to the time or distance between them on the network. Similarly, if the participant machines or processes are very busy or working under a heavy load, then the potential for lost messages increases. However, when we are using a JMS Provider, we can also configure the JMS Provider instance to minimize the potential communication losses. What happens if there is a network error between JMS Client-C and JMS Provider-A that has no impact on the connection between the JMS Provider-A and JMS Client-B? Suppose the machine on which the JMS Client-C instance is running has some failure or the JMS Client-C application is not running for some reason: What happens then?

Because messages are actually transferred through a destination contained within the JMS Provider instance, we have several options available to us. After a Message Producer object has produced a Message object, the Message object is placed inside the destination, which is defined and administered within the JMS Provider instance. The JMS Provider instance can "hold onto" several Message objects while waiting for the Message Consumer object to consume them. It does not matter how the Message objects are being held, unless there is a failure with the JMS Provider instance. For example, the Message objects being held could be stored in memory, or some form of secondary storage (e.g., a hard disk or database) could be used. The Message objects can be stored within the JMS Provider while they "pile up," and we can specify many details controlling how the provider will administer the Message objects it is holding.

From the Message Producer object's point of view, when we create the Message objects and produce them, we can specify several details about how the messages should be handled by the JMS Provider instance. In particular, we can specify a **time-to-live (TTL)** value in each message that indicates how long the JMS Provider instance must "hold onto" a message before discarding it (assuming that it has not been consumed before the timeout has been reached). We can also specify whether a message should use **persistent** delivery or **nonpersistent** delivery as part of the produce operation. Messages that are produced using nonpersistent delivery must be sent **at-most-once**, which means that there will never be a duplicate message sent; but if there are errors, then the message might (possibly) be lost and therefore never sent at all. Persistent message delivery ensures that the message will be delivered **once-and-only-once**. This not only prevents duplicate messages, but it also ensures that the messages will not be lost once they have successfully been produced—even if there are JMS Provider failures or failures in the JMS Client containing the intended JMS Consumer object. Note that these considerations only affect the producer side of the conversation—it is still possible for messages produced with either delivery mechanism to be lost on the consumer side (not consumed) due to the TTL value timing out or other causes.

From the JMS Consumer object's point of view, how can we ensure that messages are not lost when the JMS Consumer object is not actively connected to the JMS Provider? Recall that this situation can be caused by a network error, system error, or application error on the JMS Consumer object's site. This situation, therefore, cannot be addressed by merely specifying some detail in the JMS Consumer object's container-application. Instead, the JMS specification addresses this situation via the Destination object. When we create a destination within the JMS Provider instance via the proprietary mechanisms it supplies, we can specify whether the destination should retain messages for inactive consumers or whether the messages should be thrown away when no active JMS Client instance consumes the message before the TTL value expires. The specification refers to destinations in the former case as **durable destinations** while the destinations in the latter case ("nondurable" destinations) are called **temporary destinations**. We will consider how message persistence influences our communication issues when we discuss **message reliability** in Section 15.1.2.5 and again when we discuss messaging domains in Section 15.1.3.

15.1.2.4 Message Acknowledgment

In Section 14.3, we discussed how Remote Messaging is different from Remote-Code Execution. In particular, we said that, unlike a function call or method invocation that can immediately return a result, there is no returned value when a message is sent. This is true even when we use blocking messaging calls. Instead of relying on return values, an application-defined protocol (the expected sequence of message types and operations) must be used to supply any desired return values from the other participant in the conversation in the form of one or more expected messages. In Figure 15.5, JMS Client-B sends two messages and then at some point in the future it receives one message back. If JMS Client-C does not respond, then JMS Client-B has no way of knowing whether the messages it produced ("Hello" and "How are you?") were consumed. If there is a failure when Pro-B1 attempts to send the message, a special type of error used within the Java programming language (an Exception) will be raised in JMS Client-B. Similarly, if Con-C1 is unable to consume a message due to a JMS Provider or network failure, then an Exception will be raised in JMS Client-C. However, when errors make communication between the two clients impossible, there is no way for one JMS Client instance on the "successful" side of the conversation to know about any Exceptions raised by any of the other JMS Client instances on the "unsuccessful" side of the conversation.

In the previous section, we mentioned that a durable destination could be used to ensure that the JMS Provider instance retains the Message objects when a JMS Consumer object is not able to consume the messages. The JMS Consumer object could be unavailable (inactive) for any reason, including a failure in the JMS Provider instance itself at some point after the message has been produced. Assuming that the JMS Client instance containing the "inactive" JMS Consumer object is able to reconnect to the JMS Provider instance at some later point in time, how does the JMS Consumer object know which Message objects it needs to process? Suppose that the JMS Client-C instance in Figure 15.5 had failed and restarted at some point during the conversation. What should it do if the first message ("Hello") has been consumed successfully, but the second message ("How are you?") was not consumed prior to the failure? What if the "Hello" message was consumed before the failure but the actions necessary to process it completely within JMS Client-C had not completed before the failure occurred? How would the JMS Client instances and JMS Provider instance know the state of these messages?

The JMS specification uses a concept called **message acknowledgment** to control the message state from the JMS Consumer object's point of view. The JMS specification can also use the concept of **messaging transactions** to control the acknowledgment and recovery alternatives available for the consumer. The transactions involved here are analogous to database transactions; in fact, they can be managed using the Java Transaction Service (JTS) and Java Transaction Application Program Interface (JTA) facilities. However, the JMS specification does not require the JMS Provider implementation to use database transactions to implement these messaging transactions, even if the JMS Provider uses a database for the message storage mechanism. When we use a Connection object to create a Session object, we can specify the transaction details for that session. The session's transaction details are then used by the Message Producer objects and Message Consumer objects created by that Session object. These details are used to control the acknowledgment and recovery for all the messages produced and consumed within the session. When messages are consumed within a transaction, the acknowledgment is handled automatically by the transaction's commit operation and the recovery is handled automatically by the transaction's rollback operation. When a session does not have a transaction, all the recovery operations must be handled manually (programmatically in the JMS Client), while the acknowledgment can be handled in one of three different mechanisms.

Acknowledgment is somewhat analogous to the way many email clients can be configured to consider each email marked as "read" to be suitable for automatic deletion. When such an email client instance connects to an email server, it can see all the message headers and even download the message content, but none of the messages are marked as read until after the user actually opens the message.

If we carry the analogy further, the first acknowledgment mechanism would be similar to an email client that only deletes "read" email on logout. In this scenario, if the email server or the email client crashed, or if the communication link between them were lost for some other reason, then the messages marked as "read" would not be deleted—the next time we log in, we might accidentally read the same email again. The second acknowledgment mechanism would be similar to an email client configured to delete each email message immediately after we closed the message (immediately after we mark the message as being "read"). The third acknowledgment mechanism would be similar to an email client that was not configured to delete our email automatically for us. In this scenario, we would need to delete the messages manually after we have read them in order to avoid accidentally reading the same email more than once.

For the sake of completeness, we can consider the transaction mechanism to be equivalent to the first or second email scenario we just mentioned, but with a "trash can" or "recycling bin" that holds the deleted email message for us: the email client automatically "empties the garbage" on successful exit (analogous to a commit operation) and restores all items "still in the trash bin" on restart (analogous to a rollback operation). Of course, JMS messages are not the same as emails, and JMS Client instances are not the same as people or email client instances—but the behavior is similar, nonetheless.

The first acknowledgment mechanism uses automatic, "lazy" acknowledgment. This means that each message will automatically be acknowledged when it is consumed by the JMS Message Consumer object, but this acknowledgment might not be reflected in the JMS Provider instance immediately. Therefore, if a failure occurs, it is possible that some messages will not to be acknowledged within the JMS Provider instance, even though we have processed and acknowledged them within the JMS Client instance. This mechanism has lower overhead because it can "group" the acknowledgments together rather than updating the JMS Provider instance immediately, but it might result in duplicate message processing when failures occur because the "restarted" consumer will not see these messages as being acknowledged.

The second mechanism uses automatic, "nonlazy" acknowledgment. With this mechanism, each message once again is automatically acknowledged when the message is consumed, but unlike the first mechanism, this acknowledgment is immediately communicated to JMS Provider instance and the status is immediately reflected there. This mechanism has greater overhead than the first mechanism, but it prevents duplicate message processing.

The third mechanism uses manual acknowledgment, which means that the client application must explicitly invoke an acknowledge method for each message it has consumed. When this method is invoked, the acknowledgment is immediately communicated to JMS Provider instance and the status is immediately reflected there. The application developer is responsible for ensuring that messages are acknowledged correctly and for controlling how often the JMS Provider instance's "acknowledgment" state is updated.

15.1.2.5 Message Reliability   Most DDBE subsystems will have strict Remote Messaging Requirements. Although there may be some scenarios where duplicate or lost messages within our DDBE conversations are not a critical issue, there is never a scenario where duplicate messages or lost messages would be considered desirable. When our messaging middleware can prevent (or at least greatly minimize the chance of) these undesirable message types, we call the mechanism being used an example of **reliable messaging**. By using the appropriate JMS Provider configurations and programming calls, we can use the JMS to fulfill these **message reliability requirements**. In particular, we can use the combination of **persistent delivery** mechanisms in our producers and **durable destinations** to handle a majority of the concerns from the Message Producer object's point of view. We can then choose our preferred acknowledgment mechanism (transactions, automatic-lazy, automatic-nonlazy, or manual) and implement the message consumer code to suit our needs from the Message Consumer's point of view. Of course, it is still possible through coding errors or poor design to cause messaging issues, but from a DDBE Platform perspective, we have leveraged as much functionality as we can by using the options we discussed in the previous sections.

15.1.2.6 Message Errors and Exceptions   In some respects, we can consider all failures within our JMS-based DDBE to belong to one of three categories. The first category includes all the failures directly related to the JMS Provider instances, JMS Client instances, or the JMS specification. When these types of failures occur, JMS Exceptions will be thrown by the underlying JMS calls. The code that we write should catch these exceptions and handle them as gracefully as possible. This usually involves logging the Exception and its surrounding details or wrapping the Exception within another Exception defined by us. The second category of failures would be those Exceptions thrown by any non-JMS code we are using, but did not write ourselves. For example, the Java runtime can throw Exceptions, as can any other middleware we might be using. When these Exceptions are thrown, we should again catch the Exception, but now we might choose to ignore the Exception, to log the Exception, to wrap the Exception, or perhaps even to send some messages to other JMS Client instances. This last option would use special messages reflecting the application-specific interpretation of the failure. For example, we might produce a message indicating that there was a syntax error in an SQL statement or a semantic integrity violation in a distributed transaction-processing step. The last category of failures to consider would be those based on the logic within the code we write. We might use Exceptions to address these situations, we might use special return values, or we might use special "Error" messages. We must remember that the only way to convey information across COSs that are deployed on different sites is to use some form of Remoting, and in this case, we are using Remote Messaging as the primary mechanism for that functionality. However, whenever we use a message to convey other error information, it is important to ensure that the code involving our JMS Producer objects and JMS Consumer objects correctly handle both these new "Error" messages and the potential issues from the other two categories of failures we just discussed.

15.1.2.7 *Message Ordering*

Whenever we design an application that uses Remote Messaging, we need to consider how to handle messages that arrive in an unintended or inappropriate order. There is always potential for unexpected ordering behavior when messages are sent from one COS instance to another COS instance. For example, when there are several COS instances deployed across several sites, there is always the likelihood that some conversations will become interleaved. Even when we only have two COS instances in the environment, each message production and consumption operation is a unique situation. For example, it is possible for messages to travel by different paths due to the constantly changing network topography and routing details. Perhaps some messages will have a longer path to travel due to routing decisions and bandwidth usage. Perhaps other idiosyncratic details (such as the number of open connections active on a particular machine, intermittent hardware failures, available memory and resources, number of executing processes, and length of message content) will effect the delivery time. Of course, the messaging mechanisms and configuration details being used also have a great impact on the delivery and retrieval times. Even when we attempt to use the same mechanism and configuration details, it is possible for delivery and retrieval times to vary.

Using a JMS Provider can help to manage this situation but cannot completely control all the message ordering issues. JMS Message objects can specify a priority, which will influence the order in which messages are produced and the order in which they are consumed. Similarly, JMS Message Consumer objects can use sophisticated mechanisms to delay the consumption for some messages or to select specific messages for consumption sooner. The JMS specification will provide some delivery-order guarantees if we use persistent messaging with durable destinations and send messages with identical (and normal) priority levels. If we do not use any filtering or selection criteria to alter the order, the JMS specification will also provide some guarantees with respect to the order in which messages are consumed. However, these guarantees only apply to a specific scenario. From the JMS Producer object's point of view, this only applies to messages that are sent from the same JMS Session object, to the same JMS destination, using the same underlying communication mechanism. From the JMS Consumer object's point of view, we must again limit ourselves to a single session and mechanism. Because a JMS Session is not thread-safe, neither it nor the JMS Message Consumer objects it creates can be used for both synchronous and asynchronous consumption at exactly the same time. Similarly, it is not possible for a JMS Producer object to use both synchronous and asynchronous production at exactly the same time. Therefore, it is possible to control message consumption order to a reasonably high degree, but not completely. For example, suppose we are using persistent delivery, durable destinations, and normal priority for all the messages in Figure 15.5. Furthermore, suppose that we are using synchronous messaging, and that we are not using any sophisticated filtering or selection operations. Now we can say that the JMS specification will ensure that the first message ("Hello") will always be consumed before the second message ("How are you?"), as long as the first message is always produced before the second message.

Recall that when we used this example earlier, we said we would use the application-defined protocol to prevent JMS Client-C from sending its message ("Fine, thanks") until after it had processed both of the messages from JMS Client-B—but this was only enforced by the logic that we put into the code we wrote. If we were to implement this logic differently, or if we were to fail to handle all of the possible situations correctly, then we would have no control over the order of messages across these two different conversation paths. It would be possible for the messages to be produced and consumed in any order as long as the first message ("Hello") was sent and consumed before the second message ("How are you?"). This would mean that the production and consumption operations for the third message ("Fine, thanks") could occur before, after, or in between the operations for the first two messages. This is analogous to the way statements in different database transactions can interleave in any order as long as they do not interfere with each other (see Figure 5.7 in Section 5.2.3 of Chapter 5).

By using the appropriate JMS constructs, configuration settings, and coding techniques, we can reduce the chances of unexpected message ordering between the two COSs in Figure 15.5. However, JMS has no mechanisms to control the delivery order for messages produced across different JMS Session objects, even when the messages are being consumed by the same JMS Message Consumer object. For example, suppose some other JMS Client wanted to talk to JMS Client-C in the same way that JMS Client-B does in Figure 15.5. In fact, we can even consider the situation where JMS Client-B has another JMS Session object configured identical to Session-B1. In both of these situations, we have more than one JMS Session object sending messages to the same destination. JMS can only guarantee that the "Hello" message produced by Session-B1 will be consumed before the "How are you?" message produced by Session-B1 is consumed. It is possible for the greeting and inquiry messages produced by different sessions to be interleaved in several different ways. The answer messages produced by JMS Client-C will be consumed in the order they were produced, but this is highly dependent on the order in which the first two messages were consumed.

15.1.3 Messaging Domains

The JMS specification identifies two different messaging styles, which are sometimes referred to as two different **messaging domains**. The first messaging domain is called **point-to-point (PTP)** messaging. The second messaging domain is called **publish-and-subscribe (Pub/Sub)** messaging. Both messaging domains provide sophisticated operations for filtering and selecting messages, and both domains support both manual and automatic acknowledgment mechanisms. The specification includes both a messaging domain-specific interface and a messaging domain-independent version of the interfaces we discussed in Section 15.1.1. We will identify the mapping from the messaging domain-specific interface name to a messaging domain-independent interface name in each of the sections that follow this one, but we will not describe all of the nuances necessary to use the messaging domain-independent interfaces correctly within a specific domain. In other words, both messaging domains can use the same Java interface, but it is possible for the program to attempt to perform some operations that are defined in the interface, which are not appropriate for the specific messaging domain currently being used at runtime. If this does occur, then an Exception will be raised from the JMS middleware. Typically, our JMS Client instances will choose one messaging domain or the other when the Connection Factory object is created, and then all of the subsequently created JMS objects will conform to this decision. As we mentioned earlier, we can use multiple Connection Factory objects, but this is usually not necessary. Each JMS destination is created using one flavor or the other (not both) via the proprietary JMS Provider supplied administration facilities. The messaging domain decision made in the code must match the messaging domain flavor of the JMS destination being used; for example, we would not try to use the Pub/Sub messaging domain to connect to a JMS destination created using the PTP messaging domain.

It is possible to use both of the JMS messaging domains within the same application, and even within the same JMS Client. Because the JMS messaging domains use different JMS Session objects and different JMS destinations, conversations that attempt to use more than one messaging domain have very little control over the order in which messages are consumed. Therefore, we should usually avoid using multiple domains (or even multiple destinations) when the messages are intended to be part of a single conversation. Although we can safely use both messaging domains in the same application, it is not necessary for us to do so. It is possible, and not that difficult, to write code that uses only one of the two messaging domains. We can even write code using one messaging domain that "emulates" the default behavior for the other messaging domain (albeit with processing that is probably less efficient than it would be if it had been written to use the other messaging domain code directly). The JMS specification does not require all JMS Provider implementations to support both JMS messaging domains—it is permissible for the implementation to support PTP only, Pub/Sub only, or both the PTP and Pub/Sub messaging domains.

15.1.3.1 *Point-to-Point (PTP) Messaging*

When PTP messaging is used, each JMS Message object is produced into a specific type of JMS Destination object, called a **Queue**. The produce operation is often referred to as a "send" operation and the consume operation is often referred to as either a "read" or "receive" operation when this messaging domain is being used. The name "Queue" is appropriate for the JMS Destination object using this messaging domain because the JMS destination essentially behaves like a traditional queue. A queue is a double-ended list structure that supports insertion operations at one end and removal operations at the other. When a message is produced, it arrives at the rear of the queue. After the message has been consumed and acknowledged, it is removed from the front of the queue. Messages are consumed in the order in which they arrived with the caveats we discussed in the previous section. The defining characteristic for a JMS Queue is the simple fact that only one Message Consumer object is intended to consume each Message object in the Queue. Once a Message object has been consumed and acknowledged, it is expected to be removed from the Queue, and then to be no longer available. If we wanted to emulate the behavior of the Pub/Sub messaging domain using a Queue, we would simply produce multiple messages (one for each recipient) and use filtering to ensure that the messages are not consumed more than once by each message recipient. This is somewhat analogous to the way messages and mailboxes work when we use email for human-to-human communication.

Traditional queues are sometimes called FIFOs because of the order in which elements in the queue are processed (FIFO stands for first-in, first-out). This processing is common in the real world and occurs whenever we wait in line for a single resource, such as a single bank teller. A JMS Queue is not quite the same thing as a traditional queue, however, because we can perform much more sophisticated operations on a JMS Queue than we can on a traditional queue. For example, JMS Client instances can use selection and filtering operations to skip over messages in the queue, and they can also use other operations to "peek ahead" and see items in the queue without removing them, or even push items back into the front of the Queue as part of recovery operations. These operations are not usually allowed with a traditional queue, but they are quite useful and necessary for a JMS Queue. This is somewhat analogous to allowing the people waiting in line to "skip ahead" or reorder themselves based on the preferences or whims of our solitary bank-teller—not the sort of behavior that most bank customers waiting in line would appreciate!

The mapping between the JMS messaging domain-specific names and the independent names is reasonably intuitive. The Connection Factory, Connection, and Session objects are simply prefixed by the word "Queue" for the PTP messaging domain-specific name. For the other three names, we simply replace the independent name with the messaging domain-specific name: Destination is replaced by Queue, Message Producer is replaced by Queue Sender, and Message Consumer is replaced by Queue Receiver.

15.1.3.2 Publish-and-Subscribe (Pub/Sub) Messaging   When Pub/Sub messaging is used, each JMS Message object is produced into a specific type of JMS Destination object, called a **Topic**. When this messaging domain is being used, the produce operation is often referred to as either a "publish" operation or a "publication" and the consume operation is often referred to as either a "subscribe" operation or a "subscription." JMS Client instances publish Message objects to a specific Topic. Topics have names (perhaps even hierarchies of names) used to organize the Message objects that they contain. JMS Client instances can also subscribe to a specific Topic and then consume all the Message objects contained within their subscription. When we produce JMS Message objects and place them in a Topic, it is because these messages are intended to be consumed by at least one Message Consumer object. Unlike the messages in a Queue, these messages are intended to be available for multiple consumers. Many aspects within this messaging domain are left as implementation-defined behavior (such as the syntax for Topic names, and mechanisms for administering Topics). The combination of these implementation-defined aspects and the possibility of having multiple consumers can make the message acknowledgment, removal, and recovery processing more complicated than the situation for JMS Queues. However, we will not discuss those details further in this chapter. This is somewhat analogous to the way newsgroups and web-forums work when we use them for human-to-human communication.

In some respects, the messages produced in this messaging domain are similar to those used in traditional broadcast messaging, but the two concepts are not quite equivalent. In order to consume the messages contained within the Topic, each Topic Subscriber must connect to the JMS Provider instance and to the JMS destination representing the Topic itself. JMS Message objects within this messaging domain can use all of the features we discussed previously (persistent delivery, durable subscriptions, and all the acknowledgment alternatives). These features are not present for most messages used within a traditional broadcast messaging technique.

Once again, the mapping between the JMS messaging domain-specific names and the independent names is reasonably intuitive. The Connection Factory, Connection, and Session objects are simply prefixed by the word "Topic" for the Pub/Sub messaging domain-specific name, and for the other three names, we simply replace the independent name with the messaging domain-specific name: Destination is replaced by Topic, Message Producer is replaced by Topic Publisher, and Message Consumer is replaced by Topic Subscriber.

15.1.4 JMS API Constructs

In this section, we will provide a brief summary of the high-level concepts defined in the JMS specification that are represented in the JMS application–programming interface (API). The information provided by the JMS specification and the Java documentation (Javadoc) included with the API is far more complete than the details provided here—this section is merely intended to serve as a quick reference.

15.1.4.1 Connection Factory   The Connection Factory objects are represented by the "javax.jms.ConnectionFactory" Java interface. These objects are thread-safe and usually obtained by using Java Naming and Directory Interface (JNDI) calls. Numerous mechanisms can be used to obtain the Connection Factory object. Figure 15.6 shows two generic examples. The first method assumes that the system properties have been configured to the correct default values, and that "ConnectionFactory" is the name to lookup once the JNDI initial context has been obtained. The second method allows the caller to specify the class name for the initial context factory, the Uniform Resource Locator (URL) for the Naming Service provider, and the class name used to implement the connection factory. The details specified within the parameters (especially the "url" parameter) are highly dependent on the JMS Provider implementation, but the syntax of the call is reasonably portable and the parameter contents can be configured via the Java Properties facilities (as opposed to being hard-coded). The JNDI lookup call returns an object implementing the "javax.jms.ConnectionFactory" Java interface, which means that the object itself might be implemented using any JMS Provider supplied class as long as it implements this JMS specification-defined interface. Actually, the object returned will also implement one of the two JMS messaging domain-specific Java interfaces that extend the "javax.jms.ConnectionFactory" Java interface. PTP messaging uses the "javax.jms.QueueConnectionFactory" Java interface and Pub/Sub messaging uses the "javax.jms.TopicConnectionFactory" Java interface.

15.1.4.2 Connection   Connection objects are represented by the "javax.jms. Connection" Java interface. A Connection object is a thread-safe connection to a particular JMS Provider instance. Even though "javax.jms.Connection" is the

```
import  java.util.HashTable;
import  javax.naming.*;
import  javax.jms.*;

ConnectionFactory getFactory()
{
  Context           ctx;
  ConnectionFactory cf;

  ctx = new InitialContext();
  cf  = (ConnectionFactory)ctx.lookup("ConnectionFactory");
  return  cf;
}

ConnectionFactory getFactory(String iCtx,String url,String fN)
{
  Context           ctx;
  ConnectionFactory cf;
  Hashtable         env = new Hashtable();

  env.put(Context.INITIAL_CONTEXT_FACTORY,iCtx);
  env.put(Context.PROVIDER_URL,url);
  ctx = new InitialContext(env);

  cf  = (ConnectionFactory)ctx.lookup(fN);
  return  cf;
}
```

Figure 15.6 Generic code to lookup a Connection Factory object.

messaging domain-independent name, we will automatically obtain the correct messaging domain-specific object based on the actual Connection Factory object we obtained in the previous step. The Connection object is created using the "createConnection" method defined in the "ConnectionFactory" interface. There are two forms for this call: one with no parameters and one that specifies a username and password value. Authentication and Authorization are considered JMS platform implementation-dependent behavior, so the second form of the call is not always supported. The generic-example code to create a Connection object is shown in Figure 15.7.

15.1.4.3 Session Session objects are represented by the "javax.jms.Session" Java interface. A Session object is not thread-safe, so we must be careful how we use it. Once again, even though "javax.jms.Session" is the messaging domain-independent name, we will automatically obtain the correct messaging domain-specific object based on the actual Connection object we obtained in the previous step. The Session is created using the "createSession" method defined in the "javax.jms.Connection" interface. This method has two parameters. The first parameter is a Boolean value indicating the transactional state for the session. A "true" value means that the session uses a transaction while a "false" value means that there is no transaction used for the session. The second parameter can be set to one of three constants, representing the acknowledgment mechanisms we discussed in Section 15.1.2.4. The

```
        import  javax.naming.*;
        import  javax.jms.*;

        Connection  newConn(ConnectionFactory cf)
        {
          Connection  conn;
          conn  = cf.createConnection();
          return  conn;
        }
```

Figure 15.7   Generic code to create a Connection object.

```
import  javax.naming.*;
import  javax.jms.*;

Session newSess(Connection conn)
{
  Session sess;
  sess  = conn.createSession(false, Session.AUTO_ACKNOWLEDGE);
  return  sess;
}
```

Figure 15.8   Generic code to create a Session object.

"Session.DUPS_OK_ACKNOWLEDGE" constant represents automatic-lazy acknowl-edgment, the "Session.AUTO_ACKNOWLEDGE" constant represents the automatic-nonlazy acknowledgment, and the "Session.CLIENT_ACKNOWLEDGE"constant rep-resents manual acknowledgment. The generic-example code to create a Session object is shown in Figure 15.8. Notice that we are not using transactions and we are using the automatic-nonlazy acknowledgment mechanism.

15.1.4.4 Destination JMS   Destination   objects   are   represented   by   the "javax.jms.Destination" Java interface. Each JMS messaging domain has two Java interfaces that inherit from this independent interface (one for a "temporary" destination and one for a "nontemporary" destination). A temporary destination only exists for the lifetime of the session that creates it. Therefore, this package contains four names, representing the four possible subtypes: Queue, TemporaryQueue, Topic, and TemporaryTopic. Even though there are several methods for obtaining a Destination object, we will only consider how we would lookup a nontemporary Destination in Figure 15.9. This can essentially be done in the same way that we obtained the Connection Factory object, except that in this code, we would specify the destination (Topic or Queue) name using the proprietary JMS Provider defined syntax. The generic-example code to create a Destination object is shown in Figure 15.9. Note that this is not the proprietary mechanism for actually defining and creating a destination within the JMS Provider instance. Instead, this is the mechanism we use to specify the details for the administered object, so that we can create Message Producer objects and Message Consumer objects that connect to the destination within the JMS Provider instance.

```
import  javax.naming.*;
import  javax.jms.*;

Destination newDst(Context ctx, String dstName)
{
  Destination dst;
  dst = (Destination)ctx.lookup(dstName);
  return  dst;
}
```

Figure 15.9 Generic example code to create a Destination object.

```
import  javax.naming.*;
import  javax.jms.*;

MessageProducer newProd(Session sess, Destination dst)
{
  MessageProducer mp;
  mp  = sess.createProducer(dst);
  return mp;
}
```

Figure 15.10 Generic code to create a Message Producer object.

15.1.4.5 Message Producer   JMS Message Producer objects are represented by the "javax.jms.MessageProducer" Java interface. Each JMS messaging domain has its own Java interface ("javax.jms.QueueSender" or "javax.jms.TopicPublisher") that inherits from this independent interface. If we need to invoke any method calls that are specific to one interface or the other, we need to downcast the object into the appropriate interface before we invoke the method. We should always perform type checking before downcasting, and include code to catch any Exceptions, just in case something unexpected occurs. The generic-example code to create a Message Producer object is shown in Figure 15.10.

15.1.4.6 Message Consumer   JMS Message Consumer objects are represented by the "javax.jms.MessageConsumer" Java interface. Once again, each JMS messaging domain has its own Java interface ("javax.jms.QueueReceiver" or "javax.jms.TopicSubscriber") that inherits from this independent interface. Just like the situation for the Message Provider object, if we need to invoke any method calls that are specific to one interface or the other, then we need to downcast the object into the appropriate interface before we invoke the method. There are several different mechanisms for creating a Message Consumer object. This range of mechanisms covers all the possible scenarios (there are several valid combinations of messaging domain types, selectors, filters, and durability details to choose from). We will not address all of those variations here. The generic-example code to create a Message Consumer object is shown in Figure 15.11.

15.1.4.7 Message   JMS Message objects are represented by the "javax.jms.Message" Java interface. This interface contains the methods that apply to all JMS Message

```
import javax.naming.*;
import javax.jms.*;

MessageConsumer newConsumer(Session sess, Destination dst)
{
  MessageConsumer mc;
  mc = sess.createConsumer(dst);
  return mp;
}
```

Figure 15.11 Generic code to create a Message Consumer object.

TABLE 15.1 The Five Java Interfaces Used to Represent JMS Message Objects

Interface Name	Description
BytesMessage	The message content is raw binary data (bytes).
MapMessage	The message content uses name-value pairs (like a java.util.Map).
ObjectMessage	The message content is an application-defined class.
StreamMessage	The message content is Stream (like file input and output operations).
TextMessage	The message content is a single text string (a java.lang.String).

objects. The JMS specification defines a JMS Message as an object that consists of some "message header" information, a set of properties (some of which are defined by the specification, some by the JMS Provider implementers, and some by the JMS Application developers), and the actual message content itself. The JMS specification also defines five specific types of JMS Message objects, each represented by a separate Java interface within the "javax.jms" package. These JMS interfaces are summarized in Table 15.1. There are methods on some of the other interfaces we mentioned in previous sections that create and manipulate the JMS Message objects implementing these interfaces. Similarly, there are many important methods defined in these interfaces, but we will not cover those details here. Instead, we recommend reading the JMS specification, the JMS API Javadocs, and the JMS Provider-specific documentation for more details.

15.2 JMS PROVIDER IMPLEMENTATION ALTERNATIVES

If we decide to use a JMS Provider instance within our DDBE, we can choose from several different JMS Provider vendor and implementation alternatives. Sometimes the implementation is bundled as part of another software package (e.g., the JMS platform is usually bundled within a J2EE platform), sometimes the JMS platform is implemented as a thin layer on top of some existing messaging system, and sometimes it is a separate stand-alone package. This section is not intended to provide a list of the best implementations (although we like all the implementations discussed here), and it is not intended to replace the detailed and useful documentation provided with these implementations. Instead, this section is merely intended to provide a high-level overview of the steps necessary to deploy these environments for experimenting with the JMS starter kit we will be discussing for the rest of the chapter. Many JMS implementations allow us to specify how we want the message data storage to be implemented. In particular, they often support using a relational database management system (RDBMS) or proprietary flat files. The starter kit includes several command scripts, configuration file excerpts, suggestions, and hints to make it easier to run the sample extension in these environments with some common configurations.

15.2.1   Apache ActiveMQ

ActiveMQ (Apache Active Message Queue) is the name of the JMS Provider created and maintained by the Apache Software Foundation. It is licensed under the standard Apache License, which means that, for our purposes, we consider it an example of **free or open source software (FOSS)**. At this time, the current, stable release is Version 5.3.0. Because ActiveMQ is written in Java, it is very portable. It can be configured to use either files or databases as the message data storage mechanism. If databases are used, then the Java Database Connectivity (JDBC) facility is used as middleware between the JMS Provider and the DBMS containing the message data store. ActiveMQ can use several different underlying network communication mechanisms to connect JMS Provider instances and JMS Client instances. The installation software and further information about how to use it can be found at the Apache ActiveMQ website (http://activemq.apache.org). Obviously, the installation instructions and release notes provided by the website (as well as the license agreement and other details) should be consulted before installing the software in any environment to ensure that it is the appropriate implementation to be used.

15.2.1.1   Software Installation   We can simply download the latest stable release appropriate for the desired operating system (a zip file or a tar.gz file) and extract the software to the installation directory. When we extract the files, we will create a single directory named something like "apache-activemq-5.3.0" containing all the files and subdirectories within it. We do not need to execute any separate installation script or execute any separate "setup" application. After extracting the software, we should now have several files and subdirectories (named "bin," "conf," "data," etc.) within the "single" installation directory. Within the starter kit files and documentation, we will refer to this installation directory (i.e., the one named similar to "apache-activemq-5.3.0") as the ACTIVEMQ_HOME directory.

15.2.1.2   Configuration   We can create destinations in the JMS Provider instance by editing the ActiveMQ configuration file (named "activemq.xml" and located in the "conf" subdirectory under the ACTIVEMQ_HOME directory). This file is read during the startup processing for the service. We can also dynamically create destinations by calling the "createTopic" and "createQueue" methods in the "Session" interface once the JMS Provider instance has been started. Although both of these mechanisms are possible, they are admittedly somewhat nontrivial. Therefore, we recommend using one of the proprietary administration facilities for this task instead. At this time, the default configuration does not require any additional database configuration; it uses the "data" subdirectory to store messages. We can change this configuration file to use a Java Database Connectivity (JDBC) connection to a database, but this requires some additional configuration steps. Since this change is not crucial to the starter kit, we will not discuss the details further here. There are comments in the configuration files and the pages on the vendor website covering most of the popular

JDBC configuration details, as well as further details described in the JMS-SKIT files. If we want to make any changes to the default configuration that can survive a JMS Provider instance shutdown/restart operation, then the configuration file is the best approach for specifying those details; however, in a development and testing environment it is actually quite useful to have an easy method for resetting the JMS platform to a clean state. A simple compromise solution is to implement the necessary configuration details first in a separate utility that is executed as needed during development activities, and then later to deploy these details as configuration file modifications for nondevelopment scenarios as needed.

15.2.1.3 Startup and Shutdown To start the JMS Provider instance, we simply execute a command script that came bundled inside the bin subdirectory of the ACTIVEMQ_HOME directory. Usually, we will want to open a command shell and change directory into the bin directory before running the script (named "activemq.bat" on Microsoft Windows platforms). We might also want to modify the properties for the shell window to increase the screen buffer size (width and number of lines in the scroll back buffer); while this is not necessary, it can be especially useful during software development. Running the startup script will cause the provider instance to be executed within the command shell. To shut down this instance, we can simply type control-c (holding the "ctrl" key down while pressing the "c" key) in this shell window. We can also open another command shell and use the "activemq-admin.bat" script from the "bin" subdirectory, passing the word "stop" as the only parameter to the call.

15.2.1.4 Administration Facilities When we start the JMS Provider instance as we discussed in the previous section, the command shell in which we ran the startup script will become the output console for this execution. Depending on the configuration details and the state of the system, there can be many different details displayed here. When the default configuration is used, there are a few values of particular interest to us in this section. There should be several output lines starting with the word "INFO," and one of them will indicate how to access the ActiveMQ Console. This line will include text similar to "ActiveMQ Console at http://0.0.0.0:8161/admin." This is one of the proprietary administration facilities provided, and it is a web-based interface. In reality, we usually do not connect to this URL as it is displayed in this line; we need to specify the hostname or IP address of this machine instead of the "0.0.0.0" value in the URL.

If we open a web browser and type in the URL "http://localhost:8161/admin" (without the quotes), we should see a web page with several details about ActiveMQ and the instance running on this machine. If we type the IP address or hostname into the URL instead of "localhost," we should see the same web page as before—but now we can do this from a web browser running on some other machine if we wish. At the top of the page, there is a menu bar containing items named "Home," "Queues," "Topics," "Subscribers," and "Send." "Home" is the default page, and it shows Broker information, including details about how much space is used/available in the data storage areas used for messages. The "Queues" page lists management details (including the names) for all the existing queue (PTP) destinations. It also provides facilities for creating new queues and looking at the messages inside the queues (by simply clicking on the name of the queue). The "Topics" page has similar details and facilities for managing topic (Pub/Sub) destinations. The "Subscribers" page can be used to create (and delete) durable topic subscribers. The "Send" page is essentially a web-form interface to produce a message into a particular destination (queue or topic). There are also some other facilities we can access (such as some web-application demonstrations, and a Java Management Extensions (JMX) administration facility); see the documentation and website for further details.

15.2.2 OpenJMS

OpenJMS is the name of another FOSS JMS Provider implementation. OpenJMS is an open source implementation of the JMS 1.1 specification (hence its name). At this time, the current, stable release is Version 0.7.6_rc3, but there is also a later version (0.7.7-beta-1) available for download at the official website. The same portability and interoperability benefits we discussed for ActiveMQ can be found with OpenJMS, because it is also written in Java. Similarly, it can be configured to use JDBC databases for its data storage mechanism. Although earlier releases supported nondatabase message storage, all of the recent releases require a database for this purpose. The latest version available at this time has the Derby database environment included with it and it is configured to use this mechanism by default. Either way, the result is the same: we can either alter the default configuration to use a different database or use the default configuration without modification and without installing any additional database management software. The installation software and further information about how to use it can be found at the OpenJMS website (http://openjms.sourceforge.net).

15.2.2.1 Software Installation Similar to ActiveMQ, we simply download the desired release in the appropriate format and extract it into the installation location. Once again, there is no separate install script or setup application to run, and once again, all the files and subdirectories will be placed in a single directory (named something like "openjms-0.7.6_rc3" or "openjms-0.7.7-beta-1"). We will refer to this directory as the OPENJMS_HOME directory, and we recommend setting two environment variables if this JMS provider is going to be used. The first environment variable should be named "JAVA_HOME" and it should be set to the full pathname of the directory containing the J2SE's bin directory (this can be the parent directory of the bin directory within either the JDK or the JRE, but we recommend using the JDK directory if both are present on the system). The second environment variable is named "OPENJMS_HOME," and it should point to the OPENJMS_HOME directory we just described (i.e., the one named similar to "openjms-0.7.6-rc3" or "openjms-0.7.7-beta-1").

15.2.2.2 Configuration Before we can use the software, we need to configure it. If we are using the latest release with the default configuration and using Derby as the database, then there is no real work to be done. If we are going to use a different database for the backend, then we first need to edit the script file that sets up the classpath used by the OpenJMS tools ("setenv.bat" or "setenv.sh" in the "bin" subdirectory under the OPENJMS_HOME directory). Next, we need to edit the configuration file ("openjms.xml" in the "config" subdirectory under the OPENJMS_HOME directory) to include the JDBC connection details (user name, password, connection URL, etc.)

Before we can run the software, we need to create the database schema used for message storage. Again, if we are using the Derby backend as it is configured by default,

```
%OPENJMS_HOME%\bin\dbtool.bat
 -recreate
 -config %OPENJMS_HOME%\config\openjms.xml
```

Figure 15.12   Command to recreate the OpenJMS schema for the Derby database.

we do not need to do anything. For other databases, we need to run the "dbtool" application after we edit the other files. This tool can be used to set up the initial database
schema or to recreate the schema for an existing configuration (including the default
Derby scenario). We simply execute the "dbtool" script ("dbtool.bat" or "dbtool.sh")
and pass arguments necessary for it to find the "openjms.xml" configuration file and
the desired operation. Figure 15.12 shows the command we would type on Microsoft
Windows-based platforms if we wanted to drop all the OpenJMS data and recreate the
Derby database (note that this would all be typed on a single line, and it assumes that
the OPENJMS_HOME environment variable is set correctly to a directory pathname
that does not contain any spaces).

15.2.2.3   *Startup and Shutdown*   When we want to start the OpenJMS Provider
instance, we simply execute the script ("startup.bat" or "startup.sh") that came bundled
within the bin subdirectory under the OPENJMS_HOME directory. This will cause
another shell window to open and the provider instance to be executed within the
new command shell. To shut down the instance, either we can type control-c in the
shell window where it is running, or we can execute another script ("shutdown.bat" or
"shutdown.sh") from another command shell. We can also use the administration tool,
which we will discuss in the next section, to start and stop the JMS Provider instance.

15.2.2.4   *Administration Facilities*   We can run the administration tool by executing
the appropriate script ("admin.bat" or "admin.sh"). The admin tool is a graphical user
interface (GUI) that can be used to start, stop, or connect to the OpenJMS Provider
instance. When we connect to an instance (by selecting the "Actions" menu, followed
by the "Connections" subwindow, and the "Online" menu item found there), we can
see the destinations (queues and topics) defined in the JMS Provider instance as well
as details about them. We can use this tool to do many things, aside from viewing the
various destinations and subscribers; we can right-click on the various items shown to
perform additional operations. For example, we can add topics, create consumers, and
perform other administration tasks. However, any changes made with the tool will not
be reflected in the configuration file. Some administrative changes might be "undone"
or "lost" when the JMS Provider instance is restarted and the configuration file is reread.
Other changes will survive the restart. For example, if the configuration file defined a
destination, but the admin tool dropped the destination, then it would be recreated on
the restart. However, if, instead, we had used the administration tool merely to delete
all the messages in the destination (but not to remove the destination itself), then the
message objects would still be deleted after a restart (they would not reappear).

15.3   JMS STARTER KIT (JMS-SKIT) FRAMEWORK OVERVIEW

In this section, we present a simple framework that we can use to satisfy the Remote
Messaging Requirements within a DDBE. All of the source code for the framework

presented in this chapter (as well as the example code and some additional documentation for using the framework and sample application) is available for download via the official website for this book (see the Preface for further details). We do not bundle any JMS Provider implementation software with the JMS-SKIT, because there is no "official" JMS Provider for the starter kit. The SKIT will work with any JMS Provider that complies with the JMS specification once the deployment details are configured properly. Also, we should always go to the official homepage (like those we mentioned in the previous section) for any piece of "third-party" software that we install so that we can check for the latest updates. We should always remember that the official homepage is not only the source for the software, but also the best source for important support information, including known issues, available patches and work-around advice, and other important details. As we mentioned earlier, the framework in the JMS-SKIT is implemented on top of JMS, but it is not intended to provide all the flexibility or functionality that JMS supplies. Our framework is not intended to replace JMS! In order to understand how to use the framework and the other code found in the starter kit, first we need to discuss the framework's primary goals. Then, we will examine how the framework is designed and implemented. Lastly, in Section 15.4, we will explore how the starter kit can be used.

15.3.1 Framework Goals

The framework included in the JMS-SKIT has several primary goals. Ultimately, this framework is intended to support the minimal Remote Messaging Requirements desired to implement DDBE software for research and educational purposes. When we were first designing the JMS-SKIT, after we decided to focus on Remote Messaging as the underlying Remoting mechanism, we tried to identify the messaging aspects that we felt were necessary for most scenarios (special scenarios usually require additional, custom development, and so they were not the primary focus).

Although there are many lesser goals to be considered for a framework such as this, we focused on four primary-goal areas:

- Message reliability
- Communication topography
- Deployment topography
- Software complexity

15.3.1.1 Message Reliability Goals Message reliability (which we discussed in Section 15.1.2.5) is crucial when attempting to understand and implement a system that has distributed data. When message reliability is not present, other issues and concepts might be obscured. For example, it is very difficult to research, understand, or merely implement complex distributed algorithms when the messages being exchanged can be randomly lost, duplicated, and reordered. Therefore, we decided that providing support for reliable messaging was one of the most important goals this framework should have. In fact, this was one of the primary reasons for selecting the JMS as the underlying middleware to be used. We also wanted this reliable messaging mechanism to support several different possible applications easily. We recognized the need to create an extensible framework that provided some level of reliable messaging—our goal was not merely to implement reliable messaging directly for a specific distributed application. We needed reliable messaging that supported extensible application code and extensible communication data (similar to SOA's goal of using message calls that were devoid of semantics and an extensible message schema, as we discussed in Section 14.1.3.2). Leveraging the reliable messaging abilities present in the underlying JMS middleware is therefore a primary goal for the framework in this starter kit.

15.3.1.2 Communication Topography Goals   When experimenting with distributed algorithms, we must consider several different communication topographies. For example, COSs developed using this starter kit should be able to communicate with each other in any of the patterns required by the traditional algorithms commonly found in DDBE research. Nevertheless, this starter kit must also have the potential to support new algorithms. In particular, we identified three basic communication topographies: **Sequential Messaging, Broadcast Messaging**, and **Ad Hoc Messaging**. Sequential Messaging refers to messages that are passed from one node to another (like a daisy chain) until the message reaches its ultimate destination. Broadcast Messaging refers to messages that are sent from a single node to several other nodes at the same time. Ad Hoc Messaging refers to messages that are sent to specific nodes on an idiosyncratic basis. Therefore, we decided that the starter kit should be capable of supporting these types of communication topographies in both a direct and extensible fashion.

15.3.1.3 Deployment Topography Goals   Because students and researchers are a very visible and important part of the intended audience for this starter kit, the framework must be able to support software experiments for both new and existing architecture, deployment, and algorithmic scenarios. Therefore, the framework needs to be very flexible with respect to deployment details. In particular, we did not want to place too many restrictions on the possible development environment. Because of this, we focused on JMS platform implementations that supported multiple operating systems and multiple message storage mechanisms. We also considered the JMS Provider instance deployment details—wanting to be able to support multiple provider instances in the same conversation (assuming that the provider implementations support this).

15.3.1.4 Software Complexity Goals   This framework is intended to aid students, researchers, and first-time implementers. Members of this audience (like most readers of this book) should be focused on understanding the distributed database algorithms and concepts. Although the underlying technology used to implement a DDBE project is important, the technology used is not the primary focus. In other words, we considered users of this framework to be DDBE developers who happened to be using JMS rather than JMS developers who happened to be working on a piece of DDBE software. Therefore, we also had a goal of encapsulating the underlying messaging design and implementation details as much as possible. This means that the framework should prevent potential technical issues by using information-hiding techniques appropriately. We believe that the framework should shield the developer from any details that are not directly relevant to the DDBE areas being focused upon. Advanced developers (and others who are interested in the underlying technology) are free to expand the framework, to explore its inner workings, or to use the underlying JMS platform directly. We made a conscious decision to prefer external simplicity to many other benefits that a less abstract, more implementation-dependent approach might obtain (such as providing better performance or more advanced functionality).

15.3.2   Framework Package Overview

The JMS-SKIT framework consists of two packages. Each of these packages is a sub-package within the same container-package namespace ("com.srdbsoft.ddbe.jms.skit"). The first subpackage ("com.srdbsoft.ddbe.jms.skit.itf") contains all the public classes and interfaces defined for the framework—its parts make up the "official contract" between the framework and any software that uses the framework. The second subpackage ("com.srdbsoft.ddbe.jms.skit.imp") contains a specific implementation for the framework.

By separating the framework code in this way, we hope to achieve some of the same separation that the JMS specification achieved with respect to the different JMS Provider implementations. Even though we did not do this for the other platforms used in this chapter and Chapters 16–19, it should be possible to reimplement this frame-work, perhaps using some other Remote Messaging platform, with minimal impact to any code written on top of the framework. This separation can also potentially reduce the dependency requirements for applications written on top of the framework. For example, applications written on top of the framework do not need to import the pro-prietary JMS Provider classes or interfaces directly—as long as we keep those details isolated in the second subpackage.

15.3.2.1   Framework Interface Package Overview   The first subpackage ("com. srdbsoft.ddbe.jms.skit.itf") is our "interface package." There are several Java Exception classes in this package; they represent the errors that might be encountered when using the framework (all of the Java class names defined in the framework for these Excep-tions start with the prefix "Ex"). This package also contains some other Java constructs that provide useful operations and default implementation details for these concepts. The framework uses its own vocabulary terms to describe its solution for Remote Messaging. These terms might sound similar to terms used in other Remote Messaging environments, but any similarities are purely coincidental—these names were chosen in an attempt to prevent unintentional biases toward one specific implementation approach. There are six fundamental terms defined in this new vocabulary: **Msg, Node, NodeFactory, Hub, HubFactory**, and **ChatRoom**. This package defines three Java interface and two Java classes to represent the first five concepts—the ChatRoom concept is so simplistic that it is not directly represented as a separate construct.

Msg   All messages used by the framework are represented by the "com.srdbsoft.ddbe. jms.skit.itf.Msg" interface—because all of the framework interfaces we will be dis-cussing here are in this namespace, we will usually not mention the fully qualified name for the rest of this section. The actual Java class used to implement the Msg interface can contain any Serializable content (content conforming to the "java.io.Serializable" Java interface) deemed necessary. This Java interface does not have any direct con-nection to Java classes or interfaces used to represent a JMS Message object. Because the Msg interface does not depend on the JMS Message interfaces, there is no need for other code using the framework to know about JMS Message objects directly.

A Msg in the framework must have one and only one Source ("From:") and one or more Destinations ("To:"). The term "Destination" in the framework has nothing to do with the concept of a JMS Destination object; instead, it refers to the name of a particular intended recipient. Although this is potentially confusing for anyone looking at both the framework details and the JMS details, remember that framework users are mostly shielded from those details. Each Msg object instance has one subject string and one sequence number, both of which are used to help control message processing order (implemented using JMS production and consumption calls). Each Msg instance also has a message topography type that corresponds to one of the communication topography types (Ad Hoc, Broadcast, or Sequential, as we discussed in Section 15.3.1.2). The primary difference between these topography types is demonstrated when we consider how they handle Msg object instances that specify more than one destination. If an Ad Hoc Msg has multiple Destinations, then the framework will create a separate Ad Hoc message for each destination and send each message as a separate operation. By contrast, a Broadcast Msg that has multiple Destinations will send one message to each "group" of Destinations that are capable of seeing the message (we will discuss this further later).

We can consider sending Broadcast messages to be similar to sending a single letter to each household in a family. For example, we might send one letter to the house where our Aunt and Uncle live and another copy of the same letter to the house where both our Grandparents live. Similarly, we can consider sending Ad Hoc messages to be similar to sending a separate copy of the letter to each family member (even when all the family members live in the same house). In this case, we would send one copy of the letter to our Aunt, another copy of the letter to our Uncle, another copy to our Grandmother, and yet another copy to our Grandfather, even if we know that some of them live in the same house and most of them talk to each other on a regular basis. Sending Sequential messages would be similar to a single "chain letter" or a single memo with a "routing list" that we send to only one person, who is then expected to forward the message to the next person on the list.

There are two classes (AdHocMessage and BroadcastMessage) provided in the framework, that we use (inherit from) to create specialized classes for a messaging implementation. The SequentialMessage type is intended to behave as we discussed in Section 15.3.1.2, but we have purposely not provided any design or implementation details for its behavior in the framework (no interfaces are defined and no abstract or concrete classes are implemented). This way, enhancing the framework can be assigned as an exercise for students to consider.

Node   In the framework, Node is the name of another Java interface. We use this interface to represent each piece of software that can directly participate in a conversation. Although we should officially avoid using JMS terms to define framework terms, we can consider the implementation details a useful example for explaining the concept for us here—a Java class that implements the Node interface uses both a JMS Producer object and a JMS Consumer object. Java classes implementing this Java interface are capable of communicating directly with other Node instances via the framework's Remote Messaging facilities. Each Node instance must have a unique, logical, case-sensitive name (a "NodeName") used to identify it inside the system (e.g., "AP_New_York," "DP_MN," and "Client-1" are all good choices for "NodeName" values).

NodeFactory   NodeFactory is the name of a Java class in the framework. A NodeFactory is responsible for creating objects that support the Node interface. Once we have created a NodeFactory object, it can choose one of two mechanisms for determining the class names to use when creating Node instances. The NodeFactory object can lookup a system property or it can use a hard-coded default class name. It is necessary to have two mechanisms because some environments (e.g., Applets) cannot read system properties without special security policy changes. When a NodeFactory object is created, it defaults to using the hard-coded value. If the NodeFactory instance is created with the "doLookupProperty" parameter set to true, then it will use the system property approach.

Hub   Hub is the name for the Java interface that represents a centralized communication point—a physical or virtual place where multiple pieces of software (Nodes) connect to exchange messages (Msgs) with each other. We can think of a Hub as a virtual building used for meetings, like a convention center, where the Node instances can come to communicate with each other. Each Hub instance must have a unique, case-sensitive, logical name (a "HubName"), which is used to identify it inside the system. For example, "HUB_MN," "Hub-1," and "Primary_Hub" are good choices for "HubName" values. Each Hub instance must also specify some location information which will be used to connect to the correct physical Hub deployment. This location information is stored as a URL. The URL consists of a protocol, machine name (or IP address), port number, and (optionally) the rest of the URL (the URL suffix). For example, we would interpret a URL with the value "http://myHost:1234/SomeImplementationDetail" to mean that we should use the "http" protocol to connect to a certain machine ("myHost") using a particular port ("1234") with the specified suffix ("/SomeImplementationDetail"). It is possible that some pieces within the URL will be missing (this is implementation dependent).

HubFactory   HubFactory is the name of a Java class in the framework. This is another factory class (like the NodeFactory) but this class is responsible for creating objects that support the Hub interface rather than the Node interface. Other than this difference, it uses the same techniques as the NodeFactory—HubFactory can select either of the two mechanisms we discussed for NodeFactory, and then proceed to use the class name returned by the chosen mechanism to create a new Hub instance.

ChatRoom   We said that a Hub instance could be thought of as a building containing multiple meeting rooms where Nodes can come to communicate. The ChatRoom is the name we use to represent this concept of a "meeting place." Each Node instance in the system can only be in one ChatRoom and each Node can only be on one Hub. Each ChatRoom must have a case-sensitive, logical name (a "ChatRoomName"), used to identify it inside a given Hub (unique within a particular Hub instance).

We can think of the ChatRooms as being analogous to Video Conference rooms with cameras, microphones, and video screens linking all ChatRooms that have the same "ChatRoomName" together across all the different Hubs in the environment. Nodes in the same ChatRoom can communicate with each other even if they are on different Hubs; but they cannot communicate with Node instances in other ChatRooms, regardless of which Hub they are on. Each DDBE COS instance can contain multiple Node instances to communicate using different Hubs and different ChatRooms. Similar to the way that a company can send multiple people to attend different presentations in different conference rooms at the same time—regardless of whether the presentations are being given at the same convention center or not.

15.3.2.2 Framework Implementation Package Overview The second subpackage ("com.srdbsoft.ddbe.jms.skit.imp") is our "implementation package." At first glance, the "implementation package" appears to be simpler than the "interface package," because the former contains fewer Java classes (and not all of them are public scope). This first impression is somewhat misleading, however. The "interface package" had more Java classes and interfaces, but most of these are very simplistic. The classes in the "implementation package" are not as simplistic, but they are also not too difficult to understand. There is a nonpublic class ("com.srdbsoft.ddbe.jms.skit.imp. JMSConfiguration"), which is merely used to hold some default JMS configuration values. Once again, since all the classes and interfaces we focus on in this section are in the same package, we will not mention the fully qualified names for the rest of this section. As we mentioned earlier, there are some environments where it is not easy to read property files and therefore the "JMSConfiguration" class provides a convenient mechanism to handle the situation. There are two public classes in this package ("JmsHubImpl" and "JmsNodeImpl") that provide the implementation for the Hub and Node interfaces using a JMS Provider as the underlying messaging middleware. The JmsHubImpl class is a very simple class; it merely represents the "translation" between the abstract Hub concepts and the equivalent JMS Provider concepts. In other words, it is primarily used to create the appropriate URL value to send to the InitialContext lookup call prior to obtaining the Connection Factory object, and to associate that URL value with the appropriate framework-defined Hub concepts.

The JmsNodeImpl class is really the heart of this framework implementation. This class represents the JMS implementation of a Node—an object that is capable of communication within the environment (implemented using a JMS Producer object and a JMS Consumer object). All of the JMS communication details are implemented inside this class. The implementation provided in the starter kit uses the Pub/Sub messaging domain to implement all of the message production and consumption activities. It also uses persistent delivery and durable consumers to ensure reliable messaging.

Each Node instance has a unique logical node name and reads from a single chat room name located on a single hub. Each Node instance can only read messages that are sent to the node (by specifying the node name in the destination list for the message), posted to that node's "readFrom" hub, and posted to the chat room name from which the node instance reads. When a message is posted by a Node, it is sent to all the Nodes specified in the list of destination node-names for the Msg. This means that the Msg will be sent to one or more Hubs. The Msg is sent to a given Hub only if that Hub is the one and only hub for one of the nodes in the list of destination node-names. The code creates one JMS Producer object for each hub to which the message is being sent. Each Msg posted by a Node is then implemented by creating one or more JMS Message objects, which are produced using the JMS Producer object for the appropriate hub. When a Node consumes a message, it is implemented by using the one and only JMS Consumer object contained in the Node. The JMS Consumer object uses a JMS selector to filter out any messages (permanently) that the node should not see. This includes messages that are not sent to this node or messages that are sent from this node itself. Note that a node cannot send messages to itself. This filtering is permanent for all current or future instances of a given Node (it is enforcing the definition of the Node concept). After a JMS Consumer object acknowledges a particular JMS Message object, that JMS Message object becomes invisible to that JMS Consumer object. Unfortunately, whenever a JMS Object message is acknowledged, all the other JMS Message objects that were produced prior to this acknowledgment are also acknowledged—whether those messages were processed or not. This means that the acknowledge mechanism cannot be used to mark a message as being "already processed" without causing some other complications. To handle this situation, the class implementing the Node interface needs to keep a list of IDs that track the messages that have been "returned" to the caller. We use this mechanism in conjunction with the manual acknowledge mechanism to prevent processing the same message more than once. This serves two purposes: it ensures that "already processed" messages will not be re-read if the node is restarted, and it flushes the list of "already processed" messages to improve performance.

15.4 USING THE JMS-SKIT FRAMEWORK

Three different scenarios represent the typical use cases for the JMS-SKIT. In the first scenario, we are simply trying to run the sample extension (which is included as part of the starter kit along with the framework). We will discuss this scenario in Section 15.4.1. In the second scenario, which we will discuss in Section 15.4.2, we are attempting to create a new extension (this is the primary purpose for the starter kit). The last scenario is more advanced; in this scenario, we are attempting to improve the framework. We will discuss this scenario in Section 15.4.3.

15.4.1 Sample Extension Overview

We will briefly discuss the starter kit's sample extension in this section. This extension demonstrates how the framework can be used to create a simple DDBE. In Section 15.4.1.1, we will consider the architectural view of the sample extension (ignoring the framework and JMS platform details). In Section 15.4.1.2, we will consider the overall design aspects demonstrated in the sample. Section 15.4.1.3 will discuss implementation aspects. Finally, in Section 15.4.1.4 we will look at some of the deployment details. We will only discuss the sample extension briefly and at a high level, because the starter kit includes a full set of documentation for all the code constructs (Javadocs) and a "cookbook" document that describes (step-by-step) all the actions required to compile, deploy, and execute the sample application.

15.4.1.1 Sample Extension Architectural Overview   The sample architecture defines three subsystems: the client, the application processor, and the data processor. Although the implementations for these subsystems in this example are far from complete, each subsystem in this architecture is compatible with the subsystem of the same name that we discussed in Chapter 1.

The client represents a DDBE client application. In this sample, it is a simple console application, with a very limited user interface. The client takes a command line argument (either "-commit" or "-abort") which it uses to run one of two simple test scenarios. Each scenario sends messages to the other components to simulate a distributed transaction execution, followed by either a distributed commit or a distributed rollback operation.

The application processor communicates with the client and the data processor. It also communicates directly with a simple global data dictionary database via JDBC. The application processor is a simple, single-threaded application that merely waits in a loop for messages from the client or the data processor, and then processes the messages appropriately, as they are consumed. Messages from the data processor represent the results from operations requested by the application processor on behalf of the client.

The data processor application is an even simpler, single-threaded application that merely waits in a loop for the messages it expects to receive from the application processor. When a message arrives, the data processor performs a naive conversion into a local database operation, which it then performs. Once the operation completes (succeeds or fails) the data processor sends a message back to the sender. This message contains the execution status and the results of the operation if there were any to be returned.

15.4.1.2 Sample Extension Design Overview   Even though there are only three subsystems, there are five packages in the sample extension. In addition to the three subsystem-specific packages, there are two "shared" packages. These shared packages are intended to be referenced and reused by more than one subsystem. These classes perform common essential functions, such as JDBC database access, framework tasks, and the application-specific message classes. These message classes are placed in a separate package from the other shared classes. There are several reasons for separating them this way. One reason is simply that the message classes might need to be shared across many components that do not need the other functionality. Another reason is that it provides a convenient grouping of the message class types, which is useful from a deployment, maintenance, and documentation perspective. Even though there are several other benefits, we will only mention one more advantage that this separation provides: namespace conflict resolution. In this example, the names for all of the message classes begin with a prefix ("Msg"), but that is merely a convention—by using a separate package we can ensure that the class names used for message classes and the class names used for other classes do not conflict. For example, it is possible that we will want to create a class called "MsgError" to represent an error message, while some other package might create a class with the same name that is used for a different purpose. We can always specify the fully qualified name, but the separate package allows us to use Java import statements to control which name we mean when it is not fully qualified.

The application processor contains several classes, with each one responsible for a separate aspect of the distributed database operations being performed. The client only has two classes: one class encapsulating the communication to the application processor, and the other representing the main class for the client. The data processor consists of a single class. All of the other functionality is implemented by the shared classes.

15.4.1.3 *Sample Extension Implementation Overview*

The framework hides many of the underlying details, including all the JMS details including message acknowledgment. The shared package hides many of the framework usage details and provides reusable implementations for commonly shared concepts such as transactions, requests, and catalogs of the subject strings used by different messages. The catalogs are useful when building filters to manage the message processing logic.

Each subsystem ultimately has a single framework Node, which it uses for all communication. The JMS Message objects use the ObjectMessage message type to pass the "application-defined" message classes (contained in the shared package) for all conversations. There is only a single ChatRoom used for this DDBE. When each application starts, it uses an application-defined protocol to control how conversations are processed. In particular, the application processor fetches information about which nodes are defined in the environment and the hubs that they are located at from the GDD. The other applications wait for a special message (a node-directory-info message), which broadcasts this information to all the nodes in the environment.

15.4.1.4 *Sample Extension Deployment Overview*

Each application automatically loads a properties file. This file contains the details necessary to locate the (one and only) hub that "contains" the (one and only) node in the application. The application processor uses a simple but effective global data dictionary, which is stored in a DBE (RDBMS). The properties file for each application can contain many other details, including the JDBC connection details and actual SQL statements used by a particular deployed instance of an application.

The databases used by the application processor and each data processor need to be created before these applications can be run. All of the runtime details can be specified in the properties files for each subsystem. The default deployment configuration specifies that all of the subsystems be deployed on a single machine. If we want to move a subsystem to a different machine, or deploy a new subsystem instance, we simply need to update the table found in the GDD database. Similarly, if we want to add another Hub to the environment, we simply deploy the JMS Provider instance and update the data in the GDD database to reflect the nodes that are located in that Hub.

15.4.2 Creating New Extensions

The sample extension is a reasonably flexible application. Although it does not handle all possible DDBE scenarios, it is not supposed to—it is merely an attempt to demonstrate the potential that the framework and the JMS platform both have with respect to DDBE development activities. Whenever we encounter some DDBE scenario that the sample cannot address, we can use the sample as the basis for new software development focused on that aspect. There are several techniques available for creating these new extensions: we can copy the sample extension code and modify it to suit our needs, we can start completely from scratch, or we can selectively copy portions of the sample extension into a new software project. For example, we could consider whether the framework would be useful in implementing any of the services we discussed in the other chapters. We cannot know if an extension would be useful for implementing services like replication control, distributed query processing, or distributed query optimization unless we perform some analysis and design activities. If we determine that a new extension would still be insufficient for a particular scenario, we have one more strategy we can try before we abandon the framework: we can attempt to improve the framework itself.

15.4.3   Improving the JMS-Based Framework

Because we have the source code for the framework, we can also use the framework as the basis for creating new frameworks. Once again, there are several approaches we can take when attempting to improve the framework. We can attempt to add new functionality to the existing framework, to modify the existing functionality, or simply to use the framework as inspiration to create an entirely new framework for DDBE development. The framework is flexible and reasonably powerful, but it also has several areas that could be improved upon. This is especially true if we have different goals or priorities for the new and improved framework. When we modify the framework, we need to be careful not to break any existing code that uses the original framework. Several software engineering practices can help us with this task, such as simple version control, configuration management, issue tracking, and regression testing techniques. At the very least, we can use a few simple techniques such as incrementing the "serialVersionUID" value in the code or changing the name of the constructs when behavior is radically different from previous versions.

15.5   SUMMARY

The JMS specification defines a powerful platform that supports many different messaging scenarios. While the specification ensures a set of minimum requirements for implementation behavior and a certain degree of portability and interoperability, vendors are free to support a wide variety of situations effectively by creating as many specific implementation alternatives as they need to. Similarly, we are free to pick the best JMS platform vendor and implementation for the specific environment we are trying to build. There are several important messaging issues to consider and address in any distributed messaging platform, and a JMS Provider has several standard features that we can use to address many of them (at least partially). Although there is no single, simple approach or technique that can automatically address all the issues, we can use a combination of features such as persistent messaging and durable messaging to provide an adequate degree of message reliability.

The JMS specification defines many concepts that are directly applicable to implementing code that satisfies the Remote Messaging DDBE Platform Requirements. We can implement complex messaging scenarios by leveraging the JMS messaging domains provided by a given JMS Provider implementation. We can also choose from several different JMS Provider implementations—even running the same code across different implementations with only minimal changes (if our code is careful to avoid the proprietary facilities). We looked briefly at two different JMS Provider implementations—but we certainly did not discuss all of the possible alternatives here!

For these reasons (and those we discussed in this chapter), we can see that both the JMS specification and the JMS platform have great potential for application development in general and for DDBE software development in particular. However, we also recognize the potential complexity inherent in any attempt to implement distributed communication. This is especially true when complex application-defined protocols (like those we discussed in Chapters 1–9) are required. Therefore, we discussed the JMS Starter Kit (JMS-SKIT) that is available with this book—a simple framework and an example extension of that framework focused on the distributed communication needs for a DDBE software development project. By leveraging the functionality that the JMS specification and JMS Provider implementations supply (and hiding some of the inherent complexities from the application developer), we can use the framework to implement several important DDBE scenarios. The framework should be useful for building new DDBE projects, while the example extension should help to demonstrate how the framework could be used to improve DDBE development activities. Therefore, we feel that the starter kit also provides us with a launch pad for building more powerful extensions and frameworks in the future.

15.6 GLOSSARY

Administered Object A JMS specification concept representing both the specification defined and the JMS Provider's proprietary details necessary to administer a deployed instance of a particular JMS Provider implementation.

Application-Defined Protocol An application-specific definition of all the expected sequences of messages used and the operations that we want to perform when those messages are produced and consumed.

Asynchronous Messaging A technique used for messaging that delivers the message at the time it was sent rather than waiting for the consumer to explicitly request the message retrieval.

Authentication Any technique used to validate the identity of a source or destination of messages or data.

Authorization Any technique used to determine whether a particular user, component, or subsystem has sufficient access permissions to perform a desired operation—this is usually checked after the identity has been authenticated.

Blocking A message transfer, method call, or procedure call that will not allow any further communication until after the current operation completes.

Component A deployable bundle that provides a reasonably cohesive set of functionality.

Component or Subsystem (COS) A term that refers to a component or subsystem, ignoring any differences between the two concepts.

Connection Object A JMS specification defined object representing a thread-safe connection to a particular deployed JMS Provider instance.

Connection Factory Object A JMS specification defined administrated object capable of creating a Connection object.

DDBE Platform A set of hardware systems, operating systems, local database environments, programming languages, and other technologies used to implement a distributed database environment (DDBE).

DDBE Platform Requirements   A set of cohesive functionality provided by the DDBE Platform in order to support the implementation of a DDBE.

Deployment   Any features, issues, concepts, or considerations related to how a COS instance is installed on a particular machine at a particular site.

Destination Object   A JMS specification defined administrated object representing the message storage area for a JMS messaging domain.

Directory Service   A service that provides several important functions such as naming, registration, lookup, and possibly security.

Distributed Data Platform Requirements   The third grouping of DDBE Platform Requirements that focus on Security, Database Connectivity, and Distributed Transaction activities.

Distributed Process Platform Requirements   The second grouping of DDBE Platform Requirements that focus on Remoteability and Directory Services activities.

Durable Subscriber   A JMS message consumer object used to retrieve messages from a JMS destination using persistent messaging.

Extension   The "less-reusable," user-written code that extends a framework.

Framework   The "more-reusable," framework-author-written code on which an extension is based.

Fundamental Platform Requirements   The first grouping of DDBE Platform Requirements that focus on Development, Deployment, and Execution activities.

JMS Message Consumer Object   A JMS specification defined object representing a specific connection between a particular thread of control within a particular deployed instance of a JMS Client that is used to retrieve JMS Message objects from a particular JMS destination contained within a particular deployed JMS Provider instance.

JMS Message Object   A JMS specification defined object representing a message.

JMS Message Producer Object   A JMS specification defined object representing a specific connection between a particular thread of control within a particular deployed instance of a JMS Client that is used to send JMS Message objects through a particular JMS destination contained within a particular deployed JMS Provider instance.

Lookup Service   A service that is used to locate a particular COS instance within an environment.

Marshalling   The collection of techniques capable of converting parameters into a data stream, usually to support RMI, RPC, or Messaging—the opposite of Unmarshalling.

Message   A data structure or textual stream representing content sent from one COS instance to another.

Message Oriented Middleware (MOM)   Any piece of middleware that uses messaging for remote communication.

Middleware   Any additional software used to "bridge the gap" (translate or hide differences) between COSs.

Nonblocking   The opposite of blocking—it refers to a message transfer, method call, or procedure call that allows other communication to occur while the current operation is still executing.

Nonpersistent Messaging   A messaging technique that does not ensure the messages will survive the failure (shutdown and restart) of the JMS Provider.

Persistent Messaging   A messaging technique used to ensure that messages survive the failure (shutdown and restart) of the JMS Provider.

Queue   A JMS destination that is used for the point-to-point messaging domain.

Remoting   The collection of techniques used to perform any remote functions including remote execution and messaging.

Service   A logical collection (specification/design) of well-defined, cohesively related functionality or a software instance (physical collection) that implements this functionality.

Service Consumer   A component or subsystem that uses a set of functionality implemented by some other component or subsystem (consumes a service implemented by some service provider).

Service Provider   A component or subsystem that implements a set of functionality and makes it available to other components and subsystems (provides a service to be used by some service consumer).

Session Object   A JMS specification defined object that represents a single-threaded session between a JMS Client and a JMS Provider so that it can create JMS Message Producer Objects, JMS Message Consumer Objects, and JMS Message Objects.

Subsystem   A collection of components and/or subsystems that is part of a larger system but also a system in its own right.

Synchronous Messaging   A technique used for messaging that delivers the message only when the consumer explicitly requests the message retrieval, rather than delivering it at the time it was sent.

Temporary Queue   A JMS Queue that is created, available, and then destroyed within the scope of a session.

Temporary Topic   A JMS Topic that is created, available, and then destroyed within the scope of a session.

Thread   A "thread of control," which is analogous to a separate execution of a program.

Thread-Safe   Any section of code that supports multithreading (multiple threads within the same program) without data corruption or other issues.

Time-to-Live (TTL)   A field in a JMS message that controls the minimum duration that an unconsumed message must remain available before it can be removed from the destination.

Topic   A JMS destination that is used for the publish-and-subscribe messaging domain.

REFERENCE

[Java02] Java Message Service: Version 1.1, Sun Microsystems, Palo Alto, CA, 2002.

EXERCISES

Provide short (but complete) answers to the following questions.

15.1 Suppose we have implemented some DDBE service using the JMS-SKIT framework and a new extension based on it. Now suppose that we need to add some new functionality to our code.

(A) What are the ramifications for adding the functionality to the framework?

(B) What are the ramifications for adding the functionality to the extension?

15.2 Is it possible to implement/emulate point-to-point messaging using the publish-and-subscribe messaging domain? If it is possible, how would we do it; if it is not possible, why is it impossible?

15.3 Is it possible to implement/emulate publish-and-subscribe messaging using the point-to-point messaging domain? If it is possible, how would we do it; if it is not possible, why is it impossible?

15.4 Look at the source code for the JMS-SKIT (framework and sample). Does it use the point-to-point messaging domain, the publish-and-subscribe messaging domain, neither domain, or both domains? How can we tell?

15.5 Attempt to extend the framework to support the SequentialMessage type.

16

THE J2EE PLATFORM

The **Java 2 Enterprise Edition (J2EE) platform** is a powerful platform for enterprise application development. In this context, enterprise applications are applications intended to support the needs of a large organization. More specifically, each enterprise application consists of multiple **components or subsystems (COSs)**, which are deployed across several different sites. These COSs (and the enterprise application itself) work toward a common goal and thereby integrate several different systems. We can view this integration as a by-product of the platform (by definition we need to integrate the COSs in our application in order to build the application). However, we can also view this integration as a goal in and of itself. For example, integrating all of the database systems within our environment is the primary goal behind a **distributed database environment (DDBE)**. The J2EE platform can be used to implement several different enterprise applications at the same time. It effectively acts like a virtual operating system for our distributed environment by leveraging the services provided by each of the actual operating system platforms installed on the sites where the J2EE platform is deployed within our environment. This is analogous to the way that a DDBE is intended to act as a virtual database by leveraging the services provided by the Sub-DBEs deployed within our environment.

While we cannot describe all the nuances of the J2EE platform completely in a single chapter, we will attempt to provide the details necessary to enable us to use the J2EE platform for DDBE software development activities. In Section 16.1, we will provide a high-level overview of the J2EE platform. First, we will focus on some of the prominent vocabulary terms. Next, we will discuss the overall J2EE architecture, the relevant J2EE architectural concepts and deployment considerations, and a subset of the many J2EE application–programming interface (API) constructs that we will need to consider in order to discuss the **J2EE Starter Kit (SKIT)**, which we will present in Chapter 17. We have already discussed some of the supporting details for this

Distributed Database Management Systems by Saeed K. Rahimi and Frank S. Haug
Copyright © 2010 the IEEE Computer Society

material in earlier chapters. For example, we considered DDBE Platform Requirements in Chapter 14. In Chapter 15, we discussed how some of these requirements might be satisfied by the **Java 2 Standard Edition (J2SE)** platform when it is augmented by the Java Message Service (JMS) platform. Because both of these platforms are contained within the J2EE platform, we will not revisit those areas in this chapter. Instead, we will focus on how the J2EE platform can fulfill our DDBE Platform Requirements in three areas that we did not focus on in Chapter 15—namely, the Remote-Code Execution Requirements, the Database Connectivity Requirements, and the Transaction Management Requirements. Our primary purpose in this chapter is to provide background details in support of the starter kit implemented using the J2EE platform (J2EE-SKIT), which we will discuss in Chapter 17. In Section 16.4, we will highlight some of the implementation alternatives available.

16.1   JAVA 2 ENTERPRISE EDITION (J2EE) OVERVIEW

Like the **JMS** platform, which we discussed in Chapter 15, the J2EE platform is more than merely a single software implementation: the J2EE platform consists of a specification and an implementation. Actually, within the J2EE platform, we could say that there are many smaller subplatforms. Each of these subplatforms is part of the J2EE platform as a whole, but they are also potentially useful outside the J2EE platform as independent platforms in their own right. This situation is analogous to the way that we can divide a system into subsystems, and then choose to consider the subsystems independently, or as pieces of the "big picture." Here, the "big picture" specification is called the **J2EE specification (J2EE-SPEC)**. This specification defines the contract between the J2EE platform and all the software that interacts with the platform (including the subplatforms as well as all of the applications, components, and subsystems found within our environment). Similar to the situation we discussed for the JMS platform in Chapter 15, we can choose from several different alternatives that implement the J2EE-SPEC and provide us with this "big picture" platform. In addition to defining the platform as a whole, the J2EE-SPEC also references other specifications, each of which, in turn, defines one or more of the subplatforms. These subplatform specifications can then be implemented by choosing from the different alternatives available for each of them. After we have chosen a particular J2EE platform implementation alternative, which we will discuss in Section 16.4, we can choose to alter our platform by switching the implementation alternative for any of the subplatforms within our chosen J2EE platform implementation. In fact, the JMS platform is an example of one such subplatform. This means that we could (in theory at least) choose from any of the alternatives we discussed in Section 15.2. In practice, some alternatives work with each other better than others do. A specific J2EE platform implementation might impose further restrictions or have additional requirements for its subplatforms that are not defined by the specifications.

16.1.1   Fundamental J2EE Vocabulary Terms

In this section, we will briefly consider some of the vocabulary terms needed to discuss the J2EE platform, the J2EE platform implementation alternatives, and the J2EE-SKIT. In addition to the specification (http://java.sun.com/javaee/5/javatech.html), there are also several other good sources of information to which we can turn, such as the Java blueprints [Singh02] and the J2EE tutorial [Bodoff02]. There are several books written about the J2EE platform itself (see [Farley06] and [Roman04]) or about a particular implementation alternative (see [Fleury03] and [Genender06]). We can also find entire books focusing on a single subplatform or subplatform implementation alternative [Java02] and [Singh04]. However, we are focusing at a very high level of abstraction in this section, and we are narrowing our focus so that only a very small subset of terms is considered here. We need to restrict our focus because the overall collection of documentation, including all of the platform and subplatform specifications as well as the documentation provided with each implementation alternative, is quite large, and the total number of relevant terms is very daunting.

16.1.1.1 Java 2 Standard Edition   Whenever we see the term "Java," our first instinct is to assume it means the Java 2 Standard Edition (J2SE) platform. Although we often think of this platform as a common, ubiquitous, and relatively simple facility, it is really much more than that. Aside from being an impressive tool for creating and executing programs written in the Java programming language, this platform contains many subplatforms, subsystems, and facilities. For example, it not only contains both the J2SE Development Kit (JDK) and the Java Runtime Environment (JRE), which we will discuss in the next two sections, but it also contains some of the subplatforms we discussed in Chapter 15. There are also tools for compiling, archiving, documenting, monitoring, securing, and troubleshooting our Java software projects.

16.1.1.2 J2SE Development Kit   The J2SE Development Kit (JDK) contains development tools such as the Java compiler, the Java archive (JAR) tool, and a large set of library functions and documentation. There are many subsystems represented in the standard JDK libraries, such as Remote Method Invocation (RMI) and Java Database Connectivity (JDBC), as well as support for security, regular expressions, logging, graphical user interface development, and different deployment mechanisms (such as Java Web Start). The JDK is essentially the set of all programmatic interfaces (and programmatic tools) necessary to access the underlying features of the J2SE platform. Java source code can be compiled directly, but typically, it is byte-compiled into a tokenized format that is then processed (interpreted) by the Java Virtual Machine when the code is actually executed. The tokenized format is portable to any operating system that contains the same version of the J2SE on it. This means that Java code is very portable, which is why Java code is sometimes said to be "write once, run anywhere" code.

16.1.1.3 Java Runtime Environment   While the JDK contains the documentation and programmatic access to the facilities and features of the J2SE platform, the Java Runtime Environment (JRE) contains the actual code and underlying software that implements those facilities and features. At its core, the JRE provides the Java Virtual Machine (JVM), which acts as the host environment for all the code that executes within the J2SE platform. There are two different flavors of JVM provided in the J2SE: one for client systems and one for server systems. The primary distinction between them involves how they choose to optimize and execute code. There can be several different JVMs active on the same machine at the same time, and communication between different JVM instances is treated somewhat more like Remote-Code Execution rather than interprocess communication. The JRE and JVM are somewhat analogous to the

Common Language Runtime (CLR) and Application Domains in .NET, which we will discuss in Chapter 18.

16.1.1.4 Java 2 Enterprise Edition   The J2EE platform is built on top of the J2SE platform and therefore we can say that the J2SE is a subplatform of the J2EE platform. We will be discussing the J2EE platform throughout the rest of this chapter, and in fact, the J2EE platform contains all of the details we have discussed in the previous sections as well as all of the details in the sections that follow this one.

16.1.1.5 J2EE Application Servers   A particular installation of a particular J2EE platform implementation alternative is referred to as a J2EE Application Server, or simply an **Application Server (AS)**. The term is somewhat misleading, in the sense that it is possible for each of the subplatforms to be implemented as independent programs, and these programs can be packaged and installed independently from each other. Even though there is not necessarily a single process (instance of a software program that is currently running) representing the J2EE platform implementation, we can think of the collection of all these subplatform processes that are running as the AS.

16.1.1.6 Containers   In Chapter 14, we developed a list of DDBE Platform Requirements in an attempt to categorize the operations, features, and facilities necessary to implement a DDBE. This categorization was based on the DDBE COS developer's point of view. However, if we consider the operations, features, and facilities provided by the J2EE platform from the J2EE platform's point of view, we might create different categories. We might use different criteria and focus on operations, features, and facilities that do not pertain to DDBEs. This is essentially what the J2EE-SPEC does—it considers COS deployment and development details and then focuses on identifying the specific subsystems necessary to provide the specific subsets of functionality it has identified as being important. The runtime environments implemented by these systems are called **Containers**. Because we consider the COS instances that we develop, deploy, and execute to be contained by the subsystem providing this support, the COSs contained within a particular Container can then be used by other COSs within the environment, even if they are not within the same Container or within the same type of Container. For example, we can say that web-based COSs are contained, deployed, and executed within the Web Container.

16.1.1.7 Java Beans   A **Java Bean** is a module (a Java class) written in the Java programming language that conforms to a set of naming conventions and rules of behavior in order to allow other tools to manipulate instances of the class visually. These conventions and rules are not very difficult to follow—the class merely needs to have a no argument constructor, use getter and setter methods for its properties, and be Serializable (it must conform to the "java.io.Serializable" Jave interface). Java Beans are used in many software development areas—not just J2EE applications.

16.1.1.8 Enterprise Java Beans   The JMS-SPEC defines all of the necessary development, deployment, and execution details for server-side components that implement the business logic for a J2EE application. These components are called **Enterprise Java Beans (EJBs)** because they are used by the enterprise application and implemented as Java Beans with some very specific, additional requirements. EJBs are contained within the EJB Container, which provides all the necessary support facilities that the EJBs require. The EJBs are bundled within **EJB Archive (EJB-JAR)** files that contain the Java class files as well as the necessary resource files such as the **deployment descriptor**. The descriptor allows the EJB to configure the EJB Container-supplied facilities at deployment time rather than hard coding the details. For example, the EJB Container can manage transactions for the EJB, provide security functions like Authentication and Authorization (which we discussed in Chapter 9), and automatically provide the Remote-Code Execution operations needed to connect EJBs to their clients and to each other.

16.1.1.9 Application Clients Application Clients are stand-alone applications that run on the client (not the server). They are essentially the same as their Java 2 Standard Edition (J2SE) counterparts except that they are J2EE aware, and contained within the Application Client Container. This means that they can use the J2EE facilities, including the operations necessary to access remote EJBs. Application clients are bundled within **Enterprise Archive (EAR)** files that contain all the client-side Java class files and optionally resource files such as the Application Client **deployment descriptor**. This is similar to the EJB deployment descriptor file, except that it allows the Application Client to configure the Application Client Container-supplied facilities at deployment time rather than hard coding the details in the Application Client.

16.1.2 Architectural Overview

The J2EE platform can be viewed as several Containers running on several sites within the environment. Each client machine can host an Application Client Container where the Application Clients are deployed and executed. The users of these client machines might also be executing Web Browsers that contain J2EE thin-clients such as dynamic web pages or Applets. Each server machine might include a Web Container where **Java Server Pages (JSPs)** and Servlets can act as intermediaries between the EJBs and clients that are web-aware but not J2EE-aware. The JSPs and Servlets allow simple Web Browsers that do not contain any Applets or Dynamic HTML to interface (indirectly) with the J2EE platform. Applets are defined as part of the J2SE specification. Java Server Pages and Servlets are defined within a separate specification and implemented as a subplatform within the J2EE platform. This means that there are also several implementation alternatives for the Web Container. Many J2EE implementations include the same Web Container implementation alternatives. In particular, Apache Tomcat (http://tomcat.apache.org) and the open source Jetty (http://www.mortbay.org/jetty/) are two popular alternatives. Both are freely available, and both are licensed using the Apache License 2.0. Each server machine can also optionally contain an EJB Container where the EJBs can be deployed and executed.

16.1.3 Development Overview

The J2EE-SPEC defines all of the application–programming interface (API) details specific to each of the different types of clients and components discussed in the previous section. In particular, the "javax.ejb" and "javax.persistence" packages contain the necessary EJB API details. **Java Message Service (JMS)** details are contained within the "javax.jms" packages. Java Web Services (JWS) use the API details within the "javax.jws" package as well as calls from the other Java packages (XML API details, EJB details, etc.) as necessary, depending on functionality implemented by the web services. The J2EE API details for database operations are primarily addressed by the "javax.resource" package, the "javax.transaction" package and the "javax.sql" package. Our COSs implement the interfaces and use the classes defined by these packages to connect to the underlying J2EE platform services.

Both the J2SE and the J2EE platforms support the development construct known as an Annotation. **Annotations** are a special syntax used to represent metadata within the source code. These annotations can be accessed at runtime via a technique known as reflection, as well as by the compiler when it translates source code into byte-compiled code. This provides the Java development environment with the opportunity to inject code. For example, we can use annotations to specify the type of Enterprise Java Bean (EJB) that a particular class implements (which we will discuss in Section 16.2) or to specify the desired Container Managed Transaction (CMT) attribute (which we will discuss in Section 16.3.3) used by a given method. Annotations provide a simple mechanism for indicating places in the code where some relatively fixed strategy should be automatically applied on our behalf by some tool or special facility, including the JVM.

16.1.4 Deployment Overview

Once we have developed our client, component, or subsystem code, we need to bundle the class files into the appropriate **Java Archive (JAR)** file format. As we mentioned earlier, there are special archive formats appropriate to the different Container types. Code that is deployed within a Web Container uses a **Java Web Archive (WAR)** file for the Servlets, Java Server Pages, HTML pages, and class files that implement the COS, as well as the resource, configuration, and class files used by the implementation code. Application Clients deployed within an Application Client Container are bundled into EAR files. Similarly, our EJBs are bundled into EJB-JARs. These are not different file formats (they are all JAR files after all), but each of these archive files contains a set of files and a directory structure that is suited to (and defined by) the specific Container in which the code will be deployed.

Strictly speaking, we can also deploy the same files and directory structure that is normally found inside a JAR file by creating a directory image of the JAR and referencing this directory image instead of the JAR. There are some minor differences and some restrictions depending on the Container type and specific implementation of the J2EE platform, but this is usually an option. This is quite often useful when testing or developing software components. In order for this to work, we must pay special attention to the "CLASSPATH" value used by the executing Container and the directory details involved.

16.2 J2EE SUPPORT FOR DISTRIBUTED PROCESS PLATFORM REQUIREMENTS

The J2EE platform includes several alternatives for implementing the Distributed Process Platform Requirements we discussed in Chapter 14 (Section 14.3). In this section, we will provide an overview of the J2EE facilities provided. These facilities are part of the J2EE specification and therefore we would expect to find them in any J2EE platform implementation alternative. There might also be nonstandard facilities provided by a particular implementation, or nonstandard extensions to the standard facilities considered here. Similarly, we also have the ability to include other software packages that are not defined in the J2EE-SPEC—including packages that are not part of any J2EE platform implementation alternative. For example, we can always select additional middleware packages (our J2EE-SKIT is a simplistic example of this). However, with the exception of the J2EE-SKIT, we will not discuss these "other" nonstandard facilities further.

16.2.1   J2EE Remote-Code Execution

There are several facilities for Remote-Code Execution available to us within the J2EE platform. In particular, we can choose from Java **Remote Method Invocation (RMI)**, XML Web Services implemented using the **Simple Object Access Protocol (SOAP)**, or Enterprise Java Beans (EJBS). EJBs are usually our preferred facility—but the other approaches can be more appropriate for certain scenarios. We will briefly discuss each of these facilities in the following sections.

16.2.1.1   Remote Method Invocation   Because the J2EE platform is built on top of the J2SE platform, we always have Java Remote Method Invocation (RMI) available to us as an option for Remote-Code Execution. However, this is a relatively low-level approach and therefore we have better options to choose from within the J2EE platform. Because this facility is part of the underlying J2SE environment, it is often used by the J2EE platform implementers to provide the higher-level facilities—in other words, this facility is always present in a J2EE platform implementation for several fundamental reasons. RMI uses a special piece of code (called a proxy) to represent the remote code to the local code and to perform the necessary marshalling and unmarshalling activities behind the scenes. Entity Java Beans are often implemented "behind-the-scenes" using a special flavor of RMI called RMI-IIOP (which is short for "Remote Method Invocation interface over Internet Inter-Orb Protocol"). EJBs often use RMI or RMI-IIOP to marshall the parameters between two different J2EE Application Server Instances. Typically, our J2EE code will use EJBs rather than direct RMI calls for Remote-Code Execution—but the RMI calls are often used indirectly when we use EJBs.

16.2.1.2   XML Web Services and SOAP   Unlike the EJBs that use RMI, Web Services use another set of related standards, specifications, and facilities to implement Remote-Code Execution. Sometimes, we will refer to Web Services more explicitly as XML Web Services because they use the extensible markup language (XML) to encode and decode the parameters and return values used for Remote-Code Execution. Web Services implement the marshalling and unmarshalling operations that we discussed in Section 14.3.1.1, by generating XML content representing the parameter and return values. The XML content is then sent back and forth between the components. This XML content is defined by the SOAP specification.

Originally, "SOAP" was an acronym for "Simple Object Access Protocol," but strictly speaking, this is no longer true. Even though earlier versions of the specification used the longer form of the name, the latest version uses "SOAP" without any expansion or explanations for the letters. This change does not have any impact on the way things actually work or on any of the technical details contained within the specification. Therefore, this change is probably only relevant when we are using a search engine or similar facility. If we search for the older name ("Simple Object Access Protocol"), then it is likely that we will find older information—since the newer information might not bother to contain this expanded text. On the other hand, if we search for the newer name ("SOAP"), then we are more likely to find the newer information—but we are also more likely to find information about detergents or television melodramas.

16.2.1.3 Session Beans   There are two "high-level" types of Enterprise Java Beans: Session Beans and Message Driven Beans. A **Session Bean** is an EJB used to implement a special Remote-Code Execution scenario. In this scenario, the code being executed (the callee) is implemented within the Session Bean while the code requesting the execution (the caller) might be located anywhere. The Session Bean acts as an intermediary between the caller and the callee. From the caller's point of view, the Session Bean provides the interface to the operations we want to execute. For example, we could use a Session Bean to contain the "interface/contract" for one of our DDBE service providers. From the Application Server's point of view, the Session Bean represents a session between the caller's code and the callee's code that is deployed within this Application Server instance. In other words, the caller's code wishes to invoke the methods contained within an EJB. The EJB is contained within the EJB Container, which, in turn, is contained within the Application Server, but the caller's code can have several possible deployments. For example, the caller's code might be located inside a J2EE Client that is contained within the Application Client Container. Similarly, the caller's code could be deployed as another EJB within the EJB Container. It is also possible for the caller's code to be deployed inside any of the other valid Container types, even within Containers and Application Servers that are deployed on other sites. The deployment details needed to connect a caller to a particular Session Bean can be defined within the caller's code, or within the appropriate deployment descriptor for the caller's Container type. The deployment details for the Session Bean will be defined within the EJB deployment descriptor and deployed with the Bean instance itself. There are two types of Session Beans: Stateful Session Beans and Stateless Session Beans. We will briefly discuss each of these Session Bean types in the following sections.

Stateless Session Beans   Stateless Session Beans do not retain their conversation state between method invocations. This is equivalent to saying that all of the instance variables defined within the Bean instance are zeroed out once the Bean method returns its response details to the caller that invoked it. The term "conversation state" also includes other details that are indirectly reflected inside the Bean instance's variables. For example, if all of the instance variables are zeroed out in between method invocations, then it is impossible for the Bean to have any unique files open or any unique database connections. This also means that it is possible for different instances of the same type of Session Bean to be used for subsequent calls. It is very easy for an EJB Container to pool Stateless Session Beans (as we discussed in Section 14.2.2.1) because there is no difference between the Bean instances. We can still use database connections, transactions, and so on within the Bean instance's method, but the state cannot be remembered by the Bean across different invocations of that method. Instead of trying to remember the state for these things, we can use more sophisticated techniques (such as connection pooling and managed transactions) to allow the Stateless Session Beans to be pooled when database operations are being performed by the Bean.

Stateful Session Beans   Stateful Session Beans are EJBs that remember the conversation state across method invocations. This means that the Stateful Session Bean represents a unique session between a particular caller instance and a particular callee (Bean) instance. This does not mean that the Beans cannot be shared or pooled—it merely means that the EJB Container must preserve the conversation state. For example, perhaps the Container saves the conversation state before allowing a different client to reuse the Bean and restores the conversation state afterwards. This technique works well for simple instance variables, but does not work for things like file handles or network connections. If we need to preserve these more complicated conversation state details, then we need to consider implementing a more sophisticated mechanism within the Bean itself to address the situation.

16.2.2   J2EE Remote Messaging

The Java Message Service is a subplatform within the J2EE platform, and therefore we can use it to implement Remote Messaging within the J2EE platform. There are two different approaches we can choose from when using this subplatform. In the first approach, we use the second type of Enterprise Java Bean (the Message Driven Bean). In the other approach, we write code that directly invokes the JMS operations (just as the JMS-SKIT did in Chapter 15).

16.2.2.1   *Message Driven Beans*   A Message Driven Bean (MDB) is an EJB that listens for JMS Messages. Clients do not directly perform any Remote-Code Execution with this type of Bean. Instead, each Client instance communicates with the MDB instance by sending messages to one or more destinations (Topics or Queues) located within the JMS Provider instance. The MDB instance needs to listen to these destinations and process the messages accordingly. Our MDB instances are always invoked via asynchronous messaging. Like the Stateless Session Bean instances, our MDB instances do NOT retain their conversation state between the messages that they receive. Therefore, we can only use them in scenarios where this type of messaging is appropriate.

16.2.2.2   *Java Message Service*   We will not discuss using Java Message Service (JMS) operations directly in detail here, because we would essentially use the same techniques and encounter the same issues as those we considered in Chapter 15. In that chapter, our goal was to implement a particular form of communication—building the JMS-SKIT. Therefore, we rejected many of the messaging alternatives (such as Queues or nondurable consumers) that were available to us within the JMS platform. We could

choose to use any of those alternatives here if we wanted to, but we would still need to consider whether a given alternative was appropriate for our particular implementation.

We need to use the JMS operations directly in any client (caller) code that wishes to communicate with the MDB instances. Therefore, we will always use some JMS operations directly whenever we choose to use the Remote Messaging facilities provided by the JMS platform. This is true regardless of whether we choose to use MDBs or a more direct JMS implementation approach within the callee's code. Although we can choose to implement the listener code directly in the callee, it is not recommended when the full J2EE platform is available for us to use. For this reason, our J2EE-SKIT implementation (which we will discuss in Chapter 17) does not use JMS calls. Also, because our JMS-SKIT does use the JMS operations, we choose to focus on the Remote-Code Execution in the J2EE-SKIT—the J2EE-SKIT does not use MDBs. However, using JMS operations or MDBs in future projects based on the J2EE-SKIT is not forbidden or discouraged.

16.2.3   J2EE Directory Services

In Section 14.3.2, we discussed the Directory Service Requirements, which contained three subrequirements inside of it. We mentioned that these subrequirements were based on (and often fulfilled by) three subservices: the Naming, Registration, and Lookup services. Within the J2EE platform, there are several implementation alternatives for these services. Many of the operations defined in these services are performed automatically for us by the various J2EE Containers within the Application Server. Each Container provides these services for the COS instances it contains, using the details specified within the deployment descriptors that we bundle with our J2EE code. We will briefly mention three additional facilities available to us within the J2EE platform that are capable of satisfying these requirements in the following sections.

The three J2EE platform supplied facilities we will consider are the following:

- The Java Naming and Directory Interface (JNDI) facility
- The RMI Registry facility
- The Universal Description, Discovery, and Integration (UDDI) facility

However, most of the time, we can simply use the automatic support provided by the Container facilities. This is the preferred approach, especially when we can achieve the desired deployment configuration by making minor modifications to the deployment descriptor details.

16.2.3.1   The Java Naming and Directory Interface Facility   The Java Naming and Directory Interface (JNDI) facility is actually not a service itself. Instead, it is a general-purpose interface to many different service implementation alternatives. We can use the JNDI API to perform lookup and registration operations against the J2EE Containers or against external services. For example, we can use JNDI to connect to the **Lightweight Directory Access Protocol (LDAP)** service, which we discussed briefly in Chapter 9. Of course, we must specify different details to the API calls when we use different implementation alternatives for this service. For example, in Chapter 15, we mentioned that we needed to use different classes for the InitialContext when we switched between the OpenJMS Provider and the ActiveMQ provider. We might also need to use different lookup and registration naming conventions depending on the actual implementation being used. However, most of these changes do not have any direct impact on our code because they are specified within the deployment details rather than being hard coded in the COS itself.

16.2.3.2   The RMI Registry Facility   The RMI registry facility is used by the Remote Method Invocation subsystem to keep track of the communication details for RMI Servers. An RMI Server is any COS instance that contains the remote code. An RMI Server is merely a COS instance that provides a callee that directly uses the RMI mechanism for Remote-Code Execution. Similar to the situation for JMS, code deployed within the J2EE platform can use RMI directly or indirectly. For example, the J2EE platform implementation can use RMI to implement the connection between EJB instances and their callers. Therefore, the RMI registry can be used by both the Containers within the J2EE platform and the code we write. In some circumstances, this code can also be implemented directly or even indirectly via the JNDI interface.

16.2.3.3   The Universal Description, Discovery, and Integration Facility   The Universal Description, Discovery, and Integration (UDDI) facility essentially provides a Directory Service for XML Web Services. It maintains a registry of Web Service Description Language (WSDL) details for the Web Services that are currently active within the environment. This service can be very useful wherever Web Services are used. For example, in Chapter 13 we mentioned how useful this service could be when implementing the two new DBE architectural alternatives (COOP and P2P) that we presented in that chapter. The Cooperative DBE (COOP) recommended using UDDI for managing its Distributed Query Service Provider COS instances, and likewise, the Peer-to-Peer DBE (P2P) recommended using UDDI for managing its Query Service Provider COS instances.

16.3   J2EE SUPPORT FOR DISTRIBUTED DATA PLATFORM REQUIREMENTS

The J2EE platform also includes several alternatives for implementing the Distributed Data Platform Requirements we discussed in Chapter 14 (Section 14.4). In this section, we will briefly provide an overview of the facilities provided by the J2EE platform that are capable of satisfying these requirements. These facilities are defined as part of the J2EE specification and therefore we would expect to find them in any J2EE platform implementation alternative. However, once again, a particular J2EE platform implementation might provide some nonstandard facilities or some nonstandard extensions to the standard facilities that we will consider here. We will not discuss any of these facilities in detail here, because those details would vary depending on which implementation alternative is used and how it is configured and deployed. It is more important to recognize how well the J2EE platform provides us with an enormous amount of freedom when choosing the implementation and configuration alternatives for these facilities, than it is to discuss any implementation-specific or installation-specific details.

16.3.1   J2EE Security

The J2EE platform supports several different security-related APIs and services—we discussed many of the underlying concepts used by these facilities in Chapter 9. We can use the Java Authentication and Authorization Service (JAAS) to implement authentication and authorization operations. The Java Generic Security Service (Java GSS) provides the Java GSS-API, which allows us to implement a token-based approach for secure messaging. The Java Cryptography Extension (JCE) provides us with a starter kit for working with encryption, security key management, and Message Authentication Code (MAC) algorithms. It also supports symmetric, asymmetric, block, and stream ciphers. The Java Secure Sockets Extension (JSSE) is a starter kit for working with the SSL and TLS protocols. The J2SE platform also provides support for security policy definition and enforcement, while the J2EE platform allows us to configure security details as part of the deployment process and within the deployment descriptor details for each COS instance we deploy.

COS instances that are deployed within the J2EE platform specify their security details in their deployment descriptor or leverage the security details configured within the existing security functionality present in the J2SE Security Policy and Security Management facilities. These (J2EE-defined and J2SE-defined) facilities allow us to textually declare the permitted and disallowed actions we desire a given class, package, or deployed bundle to possess. The fact that the policy is defined within the deployment bundle allows us to modify the policy details without needing to recompile the code. While it might seem risky to have this defined in a plaintext file, the file is intended to be protected by the same security that protects the actual code. If the code can be overwritten by those who should not have this type of access, then the policy is already worthless—but if both the code and the policy are safe from this unwanted access, then the fact that the policy is declared as plaintext is not really an issue.

We also have the option of using the cryptographic functions present in the J2EE platform to sign or encrypt our files and communications if necessary. We will not discuss the details further here, but these considerations become much more important once we deploy our J2EE projects in a production environment. When our projects are only deployed within simple academic or research environments, these facilities are not necessarily as important.

16.3.2   Java Database Connectivity

The Java Database Connectivity (JDBC) API provides a single, uniform interface to many different database management systems. From the database client's perspective, these details can also be specified as part of the deployment process and deployment descriptor details. Different database vendors can provide JDBC Drivers that implement the database-specific operations necessary to perform the operations defined in the JDBC API's "official contract" with the database clients. Although the syntax of the actual database statements will still be database dependent, it is possible to isolate or even avoid many of these differences. For example, many relational databases support ANSI Standard Structured Query Language (SQL) syntax for SQL queries and Data Control Language (DCL), Data Definition Language (DDL), and Data Manipulation Language (DML) commands. The J2EE platform also provides connection-pooling capabilities for many of these database management systems by leveraging the functionality accessible via the JDBC API and the JNDI API.

16.3.3 J2EE Transactions

Transactions in the J2EE platform can be controlled in several different ways. The Java Transaction API (JTA) provides several mechanisms for transaction demarcation. Transaction demarcation refers to the act of specifying the beginning and end for a transaction. Essentially, this means we are defining which operations are included in the transaction, and which operations are not included. When we specify the end of a transaction, we also specify how the transaction has ended. In other words, we indicate whether the transaction is committed or rolled back. A JTA Transaction has one of two distinct flavors, based on where the transaction demarcation is implemented—a JTA transaction can be either a Container Managed Transaction (CMT) or a Bean Managed Transaction.

Bean Managed Transactions implement the transaction demarcation within an EJB itself. This means that the code for the EJB includes calls to the JTA that connect to the Java Transaction Service (JTS) provided by the J2EE platform implementation. To implement a BMT flavored EJB, we simply add code to our EJB method implementation that explicitly invokes the "begin()" method and either the "commit()" method or the "rollback()" method, all of which are provided by the "javax.transaction.UserTransaction" interface. Even though this flavor seems familiar and comfortable for most database-application developers, we recommend using the CMT flavored approach instead.

Container Managed Transactions implement the transaction demarcation using declarative transaction demarcation. This means that the EJB Container will automatically invoke the "begin()" method and either the "commit()" method or the "rollback()" method (as appropriate) on behalf of the Bean instance. The EJB container will use default policies and the transaction details declared in the EJB instance's deployment descriptor to decide when and how the transaction should be started and ended. These details are controlled by specifying values to the Transaction Attributes for each method exposed by the Bean to its clients. These attribute values specify the appropriate strategy for various transaction scenarios. For example, what should the EJB Container do if a CMT EJB method is invoked but no transaction has been begun yet? What should the Container do if there is already an active transaction? Table 16.1 provides a summary of the possible JTA Transaction Attribute Values and the corresponding actions that will automatically be performed by the EJB Container on behalf of the CMT EJB for these two scenarios. By default, the Container will begin a transaction before the method invocation has begun and commit the transaction immediately after a successful return from the Bean's method. Transactions will automatically be rolled back if the Bean's method raises an Exception, or if the code for the Bean's method explicitly invokes the "setRollBackOnly" method provided programmatically by the JTA.

16.4 J2EE PLATFORM IMPLEMENTATION ALTERNATIVES

There are several different J2EE platform implementation alternatives to choose from, even when we limit our choices to those alternatives that supply a complete J2EE Application Server and all of the possible J2EE Container types. In this section, we provide a brief description for some of the popular J2EE vendors and implementations. Even within the small list provided here, there are often several different editions and versions to choose from within each alternative. Some alternatives are examples of

TABLE 16.1 JTA Container Managed Transaction Attribute Summary

JTA Attribute Value	Action Taken when There Is a Preexisting Transaction	Action Taken when There Is No Preexisting Transaction
NotSupported	Suspend, Execute, Resume	Execute
Required	Join, Execute	Start New, Execute, Commit, or Rollback
Supports	Join, Execute	Execute
RequiresNew	Suspend, Start New, Commit, or Rollback, Resume	Start New, Execute, Commit, or Rollback
Mandatory	Join, Execute	Throw Exception
Never	Throw Exception	Execute

commercial off-the-shelf (COTS) software packages while others are examples of **free or open-source software (FOSS)** packages. In some cases, there are separate editions for the same implementation, where one edition is a COTS product and the other is a FOSS product.

16.4.1 JBoss

JBoss is the name of a J2EE platform implementation alternative and it is also the name of the J2EE Application Server included in that implementation. JBoss has two different technical support mechanisms, based on which edition we choose to use. The community edition is found at one website (http://www.jboss.org/) and it is an example of a FOSS product. There is also subscription-based support available via another website (http://www.jboss.com/), which is provided by the JBoss Company, a division of Red Hat. This other edition is essentially a COTS product.

JBoss provides several releases of its implementation on its website, including older revisions, the current revision, and even releases that are new, experimental, or still in the process of being developed and finalized. Because the software is "open," we can choose to download the source code or choose a binary release. Since the source code is written in Java, the binary release means the JAR files, classes, configuration files, and so on are arranged in the appropriate installation layout. With the binary release, we can simply download and install the release, while the source release requires additional building and installation activities. Some older releases of the software support older editions of the J2EE specifications. Different releases may also include different JBoss-proprietary facilities—the JBoss architecture evolves over time as new features and facilities are added, modified, or phased out.

JBoss provides a web-based interface to administer and monitor the platform configurations, execution, and deployment details. It also supports several different configurations within a single installation, including five default installation types. Each installation type is encapsulated within a separate subdirectory located within the "server" subdirectory under the installation directory. Each installation type has a separate configuration, deployment, and work environment—all changes, including actual software deployments, are unique to the installation type and not shared between them.

16.4.2   Apache Geronimo

Apache Geronimo is the name of the J2EE platform implementation and Application Server provided by the Apache Software Foundation. Its official website (http:// geronimo.apache.org/) has many details about it. This is a FOSS implementation, covered by the Apache License. Similar to JBoss, the official website contains several different releases: past, present, and future. The configuration and deployment details for the Apache implementation alternative are slightly different from those used by JBoss, but there are some similarities between the two alternatives. Both support web-based administration facilities (listening to port 8080 by default) and file-copy ("drag-and-drop") deployment mechanisms. Geronimo also provides command-line tools for performing some common activities such as deployment, startup, and shutdown.

16.4.3   JOnAS

JOnAS is another FOSS (in this case open source) J2EE platform implementation alternative and Application Server. It is provided by the OW2 Consortium. Like the other alternatives, it also has an official website (http://wiki.jonas.objectweb.org/xwiki/ bin/view/Main/WebHome). There are several different releases, with different standard and proprietary features—just like the previous implementation alternatives. There are also multiple download editions available, each including a different set of subplatform implementations within the same release. For example, we can choose to download an edition containing the Apache Tomcat Web Container, the Jetty Web Container, or no Web Container. Since this is an open source project, we can always download the source and modify it to use these different subplatforms ourselves, but the different editions provide a quick and easy mechanism for downloading a preconfigured installation.

The basic setup is trivial, but we should always check the release notes for further details regardless of how simple it is, of course. To use this alternative, we simply download the release, unbundle the files, set a single environment variable to the location where we unbundled the files (the "JONAS_ROOT"), and add the "bin" subdirectory found underneath this directory to the execution path for our operating system. Similar to JBoss, JOnAS provides several standard configurations, but we can also create our own. JOnAS also provides a web-based interface for administration and monitoring, listening on port 9000, by default. This port is different from the port used by default for the other alternatives, but it is also reconfigurable.

16.4.4   Other J2EE Platform Implementation Alternatives

There are many other J2EE platform implementation alternatives to choose from—far too many for us to list exhaustively. Instead, we will merely mention two more alternatives here, along with their website information. Glassfish is an open source J2EE implementation and Application Server provided by Sun Microsystems. Its main website (https://glassfish.dev.java.net) has many details about it. IBM Websphere is a COTS implementation alternative and Application Server provided by International Business Machines (IBM). Once again, we can find many details about the various products, services, and support options available for it at its main website (http://www-01.ibm.com /software/websphere/).

16.5 SUMMARY

The J2EE platform is a combination of many subplatforms. Each platform, including the J2EE platform itself, is defined by a standard specification. There are several different implementation alternatives to choose from for this platform. These alternatives include several different possible installation packages that are implemented by several different vendors, released as several different editions and, of course, with several different versions. The specifications, and the fact that these platforms are all implemented on top of the Java 2 Standard Edition (J2SE) platform and programming language, provide an enormous degree of support for portability and interoperability. There are also several alternatives available for many of the subplatforms defined within the J2EE platform. These subplatforms can often be interchanged within a given J2EE platform implementation. Also, the code developed for a particular platform implementation can often be ported to another platform with minimal effort and minimal changes.

When considering how to provide the necessary or desired Distributed Database Environment Platform Requirements (which we discussed in Chapter 14) using the J2EE specification and a particular J2EE platform implementation alternative, there are several paths we can take. Each of these paths has some trade-offs to consider, but the flexibility offered by the platform is a far more important consideration. The Java language and J2EE platform provide a rich set of facilities for providing the Fundamental Platform Requirements. Similarly, the J2EE platform offers several options for each of the functional areas we considered for providing the Distributed Process Platform Requirements. The J2EE specification can support multiple approaches and implementations for Remote-Code Execution, Remote Messaging, and Directory Services. The Distributed Data Platform Requirements are fulfilled by the J2EE platform with an equal degree of support and flexibility. Security policy details are managed as deployment considerations (with only minimal implementation impact). The level of security complexity (and strength) can easily be controlled and configured for different deployments of the same component or subsystem, even within the same environment. Database access and Transaction operations are also largely addressed as deployment considerations. Overall, the facilities used to implement all the Distributed Database Environment Platform Requirements fit together in a loosely coupled but cohesive platform. Often there are several different approaches, several different implementations, and several different configurations available. These approaches and their implementations are very flexible because they are also defined by a standard specification and implemented by several, different, mostly interchangeable software alternatives.

The J2EE-specific approaches for implementing our DDBE Platform Requirements are all centered on the concept of Java Beans and, more specifically, centered on the concept of Enterprise Java Beans. These concepts and the facilities that the J2EE platform provides for their development, deployment, and execution enable the J2EE developer to alter many of the necessary deployment and execution details without resorting to any code changes or recompilation activities. These alterations are handled by default policies, customized deployment descriptors, and declarative deployment attributes. This also improves the reusability of the components and subsystems implemented on top of the J2EE platform. This provides us with a great potential for simplicity in homogeneous environments and reuse in heterogeneous ones.

16.6 GLOSSARY

Applet   A web-based client that is downloaded into a web browser and executed on the client.

Application Client   A stand-alone, J2EE-aware application that runs on the client and is contained, deployed, and executed within an Application Client Container.

Application Client Container   A Container type that supplies all the J2EE platform-defined operations, features, and facilities necessary to deploy and execute the Application Clients contained within it.

Application Sever   A particular installation of a particular J2EE platform implementation alternative.

Bean Managed Transaction (BMT)   A flavor of EJB where the Bean's implementation code must explicitly call the "begin()" method and either the "commit()" method or the "rollback()" method (all of which are provided by the JTA and implemented by the JTS) in order to manage the JTA Transaction actions for the Bean.

Callee   A piece of code that is called (invoked) by another piece of code—this can refer to any level of scope within the code itself from the actual method (or function, routine, procedure) being called, to any container of that method. For example, the callee can refer to the method, the module (class), or the component or subsystem containing the code being invoked.

Caller   A piece of code that calls (invoke) another piece of code—this can refer to any level of scope within the code itself from the actual method (or function, routine, procedure) containing the call, to any container of that method. For example, the caller can refer to the method, the module (class), or the component or subsystem containing the code that invokes some callee.

Component   A deployable bundle that provides a reasonably cohesive set of functionality.

Component or Subsystem (COS)   A term that refers to a component or subsystem, ignoring any differences between the two concepts.

Container Managed Transaction   A flavor of EJB where the EJB Container manages the JTA Transaction actions based on the current transactional state and the Transaction attributes declared for the EJB.

Deployment   Any features, issues, concepts, or considerations related to how a COS instance is installed on a particular machine at a particular site.

Deployment Descriptor   A file (usually an XML file that conforms to a particular Document Type Definition format) that contains the deployment-specific details for software deployed within the J2EE platform.

Directory Service   A service that provides several important functions such as naming, registration, lookup, and possibly security.

Enterprise Archive File (EAR)   A JAR file that contains the files needed for a J2EE application that is contained, deployed, and executed within an Application Server.

Enterprise Java Bean   A Java Bean implementing the business logic for a J2EE application that is J2EE-aware and deployable within an EJB Container.

Enterprise Java Bean Archive File (EJB-JAR)   A JAR file that contains the files needed for an EJB that is contained, deployed, and executed within an EJB Container.

Enterprise Java Bean Container (EJB Container)   A Container type that supplies all the J2EE platform-defined operations, features, and facilities necessary to deploy and execute the EJBs contained within it.

Extensible Markup Language   See **XML**.

Java Archive File (JAR)   A single file created using the JAR tool that contains one or more other files and directories used by the Java Virtual Machine—this is a convenient mechanism for bundling several files together within the Java development and execution runtime environments.

Java Bean   A Java class that conforms to a set of naming conventions and rules of behavior in order to allow other tools to manipulate instances of the class visually.

Java Server Page   A special file, contained within a Web Container, that is used to generate a servlet dynamically.

Lightweight Directory Access Protocol   An architecture for a read-mostly database, which can contain authentication and authorization data.

Marshalling   The collection of techniques capable of converting parameters into a data stream, usually to support RMI, RPC, or Messaging—the opposite of unmarshalling.

Message   A data structure or textual stream representing content sent from one COS instance to another.

Middleware   Any additional software used to "bridge the gap" (translate or hide differences) between COSs.

Platform   A set of software that provides a well-defined set of operations, facilities, and functionality that serves as the foundation for components, subsystems, and other software that runs on top of the platform.

Remote Method Invocation (RMI)   A remote execution technique based on object-oriented method invocation (calls).

Remoting   The collection of techniques used to perform any remote functions including remote execution and messaging.

Servlet   A piece of software contained, deployed, and executed within the Web Container that can act as an intermediary between the EJBs and clients that are web-aware but not J2EE-aware.

Session Bean   An Enterprise Java Bean that represents a client within the Application Server. Session Beans are useful because EJBs are contained within the EJB Container, which, in turn, is contained within the Application Server. The actual client itself is contained within the Application Client Container—not the Application Server, and most likely not even on the same machine as the Application Server.

Simple Object Access Protocol (SOAP)   A mechanism for implementing remote method invocation using XML to marshal and unmarshall the parameters and return values.

Stateful Session Bean   A Session Bean that represents a unique conversation between a particular client instance and a particular Session Bean instance. Stateful Session Beans need to preserve the conversational state—the Bean's instance variable values must be remembered by the Bean after the Bean method invocation returns its results to the caller.

Stateless Session Bean   A Session Bean that represents a conversation between a particular client instance and a particular Session Bean instance. Stateless Session Beans do not preserve the conversational state—the Bean's instance variable values are effectively zeroed out after the Bean method invocation returns its results to the caller.

Subplatform   A platform that is also a smaller piece of another platform.

Subsystem   A collection of components and/or subsystems that is part of a larger system but also a system in its own right.

Transaction Attribute   A method of controlling the JTA Transaction actions for a BMT EJB by specifying one of six possible values for the attribute using a Java annotation or EJB deployment descriptor.

Universal Description, Discovery, and Integration (UDDI)   A facility that implements Directory Services for web services, providing an XML-based registry service suitable for finding web service instances deployed within the environment and defined using WSDL.

Unmarshalling   The collection of techniques capable of converting a data stream into one or more parameters, usually to support RMI, RPC, or Messaging—the opposite of marshalling.

Web Archive File (WAR)   A JAR file that contains the files needed for a web-aware application, component, or subsystem that is contained, deployed, and executed within a Web Container.

Web Container   A Container type that supplies all the J2EE platform defined operations, features, and facilities necessary to deploy and execute the web-based J2EE-aware software contained within it.

Web Service   A component or subsystem that provides some service that conforms to the Web Services specification, usually implemented using SOAP, UDDI, WSDL, and XML.

Web Services Description Language (WSDL)   An XML-based description of the services and service providers implemented as web services within an environment.

XML   A markup language that uses tagging to indicate semantic details or logical structure for a set of data content.

REFERENCES

[Bodoff02]   Bodoff, S., Green, D., Haase, K., Jendrock, E., Pawlan, M., and Stearns, B., *The J2EE Tutorial*, Addison-Wesley, Reading, MA, 2002.

[Farley06]   Farley, J., Crawford, W., Malani, P., Norman, J., and Gehtland, J., *Java Enterprise in a Nutshell*, *3rd edition*, O'Reilly, Sebastopol, CA, 2006.

[Fleury03]   Fleury, M., and Reverbel, F., "The JBoss Extensible Server," in *Proceedings of the 2003 ACM/IFIP/USENIX International Middleware Conference*, pp. 344–373, 2003.

[Genender06]   Genender, J. M., Snyder, B., and Sing, L., *Professional Apache Geronimo*, John Wiley & Sons, Hoboken, NJ, 2006.

[Java02]   Java Message Service: Version 1.1, Sun Microsystems, Palo Alto, CA, 2002.

[Roman04]   Roman, E., Brose, G., and Sriganesh, R. P., *Mastering Enterprise JavaBeans*, 3rd edition, John Wiley & Sons, Hoboken, NJ, 2004.

[Singh02] Singh, I., Johnson, M., and Stearns, B., *Designing Enterprise Applications with the J2EE Platform*, 2nd edition, Addison-Wesley, Reading, MA, 2002.

[Singh04] Singh, I., Brydon, S., Murray, G., Ramachandran, V., Violleau, T., and Sterns, B., *Designing Web Services with the J2EE(TM) 1.4 Platform: JAX-RPC, SOAP, and XML Technologies*, Addison-Wesley, Reading, MA, 2004.

EXERCISES

Provide short (but complete) answers to the following questions.

16.1   How are Stateful Session Beans and Stateless Session Beans different?

16.2   How are Stateful Session Beans and Stateless Session Beans alike?

16.3   How are Message Driven Beans and Stateless Session Beans different?

16.4   How are Message Driven Beans and Stateless Session Beans alike?

16.5   Which JTA Transaction Attribute Value (listed in Table 16.1) is equivalent to the default behavior for the Container Managed Transactions flavor Enterprise Java Beans?

16.6   Why would we ever use both the Required and NotSupported JTA Transaction Attribute Values for different methods in the same Enterprise Java Bean?

17

THE J2EE STARTER KIT

We refer to the combination of a framework and a sample extension (of that framework) as a **starter kit (SKIT)** because we intend to use this combination of software as a toolkit that will help us to start developing software projects. SKITs are not intended to be complete solutions, or production-ready code, but the starter kits provided with this book should be useful when learning about **distributed database environment (DDBE)** concepts, and helpful when creating academic, research, prototype, or proof-of-concept projects. Starter kits like this one can also help us to improve our understanding of the specific DDBE architecture that we are attempting to develop, as well as the underlying technical facilities we can use, and the technical issues we need to address.

In this chapter, we are considering the starter kit that we call the J2EE-SKIT. The J2EE-SKIT is available for download via the official website for this book (see the Preface for further details). We named the starter kit this way because both the framework and the extension contained within it rely on the **Java 2 Enterprise Edition (J2EE)** platform. As we discussed in Chapter 16, the J2EE platform is defined by the **Java 2 Enterprise Edition Specification (J2EE-SPEC)**, which is available for download via http://java.sun.com/javaee/technologies/javaee5.jsp.

This chapter is intended to be a high-level overview of the starter kit, but it is not intended to be a detailed description of the implementation details. The bundle downloaded from the website contains all the source code, Java documentation, and example configuration files for the J2EE-SKIT. It also contains a "cookbook" (a document containing a collection of "recipes") that describes how to use the starter kit in some common J2EE implementation alternatives and offers hints for how to customize the starter kit to work in other scenarios and implementation alternatives.

In Section 17.1, we discuss the high-level considerations for the starter kit. First, we will discuss the starter kit's goals and its architecture. Next, we will provide separate architectural overviews for the framework and extension, which are contained

Distributed Database Management Systems by Saeed K. Rahimi and Frank S. Haug
Copyright © 2010 the IEEE Computer Society

within the starter kit. In Section 17.2, we will focus first on the design details for the starter kit as a whole, and then on the design details for the framework and extension individually. In Section 17.3, we will summarize how the starter kit can be used to create DDBE projects that reuse, modify, extend, or replace the code provided by the J2EE-SKIT, and provide a description of how to use the J2EE specification, J2EE vendor-specific documentation, and J2EE-SKIT documentation to successfully build and deploy a DDBE project.

17.1   JAVA 2 ENTERPRISE EDITION STARTER KIT (J2EE-SKIT) OVERVIEW

The primary purpose of this starter kit is **component or subsystem (COS)** software development, especially within the context of a **distributed database environment (DDBE)**. There is quite a broad range of topics that we need to have some knowledge about before we can use this starter kit effectively. First, we need to have a good understanding of distributed database concepts and issues: in other words, all of the things we need to know about in order to design or implement a DDBE architecture. This book helps to address some of those topics. Next, we need to have a basic understanding of the Java programming language. Obviously, this is necessary since this is the implementation language for our project. Lastly, we must have at least some familiarity with the concepts and issues related to the J2EE platform. However, most of the gory details are hidden behind the starter kit and underneath the J2EE platform itself. Because of this, we should be able to use this starter kit effectively even if we only have a minimal understanding of the J2EE concepts. See Chapter 16 for a high-level summary of the J2EE concepts involved.

There are several different J2EE platform implementation alternatives to choose from, but we should try to use the same alternative for all our development, deployment, and execution activities within a DDBE project. The files included with this starter kit are designed to work with almost any implementation alternative that is compliant with the current specification (Version 5.0). The starter kit has been tested with the JBoss platform implementation alternative and, more specifically, with the 5.1.0.GA (General Availability) release. It should be relatively simple to use this starter kit with other implementation alternatives (only minor modifications should be required). This is especially true for new, "stable" JBoss releases once they become officially available, but it is also true for non-JBoss implementations. For example, when a new "GA" release or new "Milestone" release (like the current JBoss 6.0.0.M2 release) is officially listed as available for download and then installed locally, the Java classpath values and Java Archive (JAR) file names probably need to be modified in order to match the specific configuration in our J2EE platform installation. In some cases, the steps necessary to compile, deploy, or execute the code might be slightly different across these different alternatives. The current version of the starter kit bundle will contain details for using the SKIT with some of the different alternatives, and the documentation files included with the bundle also contain further hints on modifying these setting appropriately.

17.1.1   J2EE-SKIT Goals

If we were to implement our DDBE software project without using the J2EE platform, our project would need to implement all the required communication, coordination, execution, and deployment details directly. While it is certainly possible to implement a DDBE in this way, it is somewhat complicated and fraught with potential problems. If we decided, instead, to use multiple pieces of middleware to implement these operations and facilities, it is possible that the integration effort would be almost as bad as the decision to implement everything from scratch. The J2EE platform provides us with a convenient, standards-based, bundling of services that can easily supply the Distributed Database Environment Platform Requirements we identified in Chapter 14. Even when we develop our DDBE project on top of the J2EE platform, there are many concepts and issues for us to consider if we want to implement our code successfully, some of which we discussed in Chapter 16. In addition to these considerations, we also have to think about how we will design our project. This is especially true if we want to be able to reuse some of the software that we develop in future DDBE projects.

All of these things can distract us from our primary focus—namely, the distributed database environment we are trying to develop! Therefore, our starter kit, which is also built on top of the J2EE platform, provides us with a better starting point. From here, we can concentrate more on the DDBE-specific concerns and less on the DDBE Platform Requirements. Both the framework and extension contained within the starter kit can be used, modified, and extended as necessary to suit our new DDBE software development projects. This means that we can choose how to use the starter kit based on our specific goals, experience, and DDBE project details. For example, we might choose to expand the starter kit to focus on leveraging as much functionality as possible from the underlying J2EE platform. Alternatively, we might choose simply to use the existing starter kit implementation and ignore as many of the underlying platform details as possible. Obviously, we can choose to apply any other degree of J2EE-awareness and J2EE-obliviousness we desire for our particular DDBE project development activities.

We intend the framework and extension bundled within the J2EE-SKIT to be used as the basis for building the skeleton of one or more DDBE architectures. For example, we want the starter kit to be useful for implementing distributed database environments compatible with architectures we discussed in Chapter 12. We should also find it useful when implementing new architectures such as the cooperative DDBE (COOP) and peer-to-peer DDBE (P2P) architectures that we discussed in Chapter 13. We chose the J2EE platform as the underlying DDBE Platform for this starter kit because of its abilities to provide both powerful facilities and multiple implementation alternatives across a wide range of hardware and software platforms.

17.1.2 J2EE-SKIT Architectural Overview

The J2EE starter kit represents the fundamental infrastructure of a generic DDBE. We use a separate Java package for each subsystem in this infrastructure. This makes it easier to isolate those portions of the architecture and code that we need to modify or extend. The main component in each subsystem is implemented using a **Stateful Session Bean** (see Section 16.2.1.3). While these components could also be implemented using other types of **Enterprise Java Beans (EJBs)**, Stateful Session Beans have fewer restrictions from an interface (the "contract" they support) standpoint. For example, with a Stateful Bean, we do not need to pass all of the "conversation state" details as parameters to all of the methods. We also chose to use Declarative Transaction Demarcation and Container Managed Transactions (see Section 16.3.3) for all the subsystems that directly connect to real databases (i.e., the Dem and Lem subsystems). We chose this approach because these components need to manage the underlying database transaction operations appropriately for distributed query and distributed execution. This is true even when our DDBE project is not focusing on distributed transaction management topics. The subsystems that do not directly access any databases (the Parser and Qualifier) are also implemented using these techniques, but since they do not actually use any database (or JMS) transactions, this has only a limited impact on them. We include the Parser and Qualifier in this decision merely to enable the transaction semantics to be implemented as simply as possible for future modifications and extensions. This is done to provide support for most of the potential implementation and design scenarios we can easily anticipate. Perhaps there is a new implementation or architecture where it would be useful or necessary for these components to use distributed transactions.

There are seven subsystems included in the starter kit. Each is classified as being part of the framework or part of the extension. This distinction is based on the location of the implementation within the starter kit. Because we have access to the source code for both of these packages, it is not too difficult to refractor the code and relocate these subsystems if desired. However, these locations were chosen in an attempt to anticipate the structure of most typical academic projects, such as those assigned within a course in distributed database management systems. The extension portion of the starter kit can easily be modified, extended, or replaced based on the actual scenario in which the starter kit is being used. Although we can also do these things within the framework code, it is not always as simple or straightforward, and therefore it might not be a suitable task for beginners.

17.1.2.1   *J2EE-SKIT Subsystem Identification*   Table 17.1 contains a brief overview of each of the seven major subsystems defined within the starter kit. The starter kit provides a simple implementation for each of these subsystems. This table lists the name, the implementation location, and a brief description for each subsystem. Regardless of where they are implemented, each of these subsystems (except for the DdbmsClient) is represented by interfaces defined within the framework. These interfaces and implementations are merely starting points for the final implementations in a particular DDBE project. This way, on a project-by-project basis, we can choose to reuse the simple implementations for those areas that we are not focused on in the project and choose to create our own more detailed designs and implementations for those areas that we are focused on in the project. These implementations also allow us to develop simple prototypes and proof-of-concept projects quickly.

The subsystems in the starter kit provide a minimal implementation for the fundamental operations necessary in a generic DDBE architecture. In particular, as a whole, they act as a design pattern—namely, a Template Method [Gamma95]. We use this pattern to connect the subsystems together in a reasonable (but modifiable and extensible) configuration. For example, suppose we wanted to focus on query optimization. Using the starter kit, we have a sufficient implementation for the Parser and Qualifier subsystems. Now, we can focus on the Planner subsystem, and perhaps the Dem and Lem subsystems as well. However, what would we do if we wanted to focus on some other aspect of a DDBE in some other project instead? In this scenario, we can reuse the original Planner subsystem, which was implemented in the starter kit, as the Planner for our new project. In the very least, we can use it as the starting point. Assuming that our focus is on some other DDBE area, many of the starter kit implementations should

TABLE 17.1 Summary of the Primary Subsystems Defined Within the SKIT

Subsystem Name	Implementation Location	Subsystem Description
DdbmsClient	Extension	This subsystem represents the client application or user interface to the DDBE that we are implementing. Because it is not invoked by the other subsystems, it does not have an interface, only an implementation.
Ddbms	Framework	This subsystem is the facade to the DDBE project that we are implementing.
Parser	Framework	This subsystem is a simple SQL parser implementing a subset of ANSI SQL. It also provides a simplistic interface inspired by relational algebra.
Qualifier	Extension	This subsystem ensures that all the table names and column names identified by the Parser are fully qualified.
Planner	Extension	This subsystem builds the distributed execution plan for the DdbmsClient request being processed.
Dem	Extension	This subsystem acts as a Distributed Execution Manager and executes the plan generated by the Planner subsystem.
Lem	Extension	This subsystem acts as a Local Execution Manager, executing the localized portions of the plan on behalf of the Dem subsystem.

be sufficient for our new project's purposes. If any of them are not, we can always choose to use the implementations from one of our other projects instead. Similarly, we can always create a new implementation within the new project itself. If our focus is narrow enough, we might simply modify a small portion of the code within the starter kit-supplied subsystem implementations rather than replacing them completely. Moving forward, we can also choose to use any of these new implementations as well as the original starter kit versions as a starting point for new projects. Perhaps we might use them in new projects that focus on the applications and clients that use a DDBE rather than projects that focus on the back-end subsystems.

In Figure 17.1, we illustrate a "reasonable configuration" for some hypothetical, new project. Here, we see that the subsystems are implemented in different places. Some subsystems are implemented in the SKIT framework. Others are implemented in the SKIT extension. There are also two other subsystems that are implemented in a new, custom extension. In this example, we have created our own new Planner and Lem subsystems; perhaps we are focusing on query optimization in this project. We have reused the other subsystem implementations from the SKIT framework and extension.

17.1.2.2 J2EE-SKIT Subsystem Interaction Overview We will largely ignore the DdbmsClient subsystem, because it is not really part of the back-end implementation. The Ddbms subsystem acts as a facade. This is another design pattern, namely, the Facade [Gamma95]. A Facade acts as the public interface—in this case the public

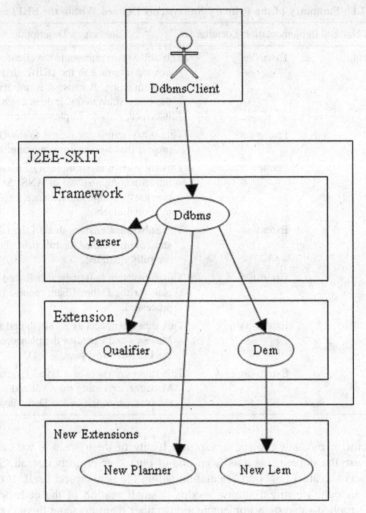

Figure 17.1   Example usage of the J2EE-SKIT.

interface to the whole DDBE project. Ideally, our DDBE project will provide one or more of the various types of transparencies we discussed in Chapters 1–9. If the Ddbms subsystem's programmatic interface looks as close to a traditional DBMS interface as possible (in form if not in scope), this would help to achieve that goal. The Ddbms subsystem fulfills client requests by delegating them to the other subsystems. It does not actually do any of the real work itself. The DdbmsClient can connect to the Ddbms subsystem and pass a request as an SQL string, or use a parameterized call representing the statement type and major operands. If an SQL string is passed from the client, then the Parser is used to parse the SQL and capture the appropriate information about the SQL request. If the parameterized call is passed from the client instead, then a different method within the Parser is called to capture the appropriate information.

The best way to understand how the subsystems interact with each other is to consider a typical scenario. For example, suppose some client application (the DdbmsClient or an equivalent application) has connected to our Ddbms subsystem and asked it to process an SQL SELECT query against the DDBE project that we have implemented. Our DDBE project will perform the following steps, in the order listed here.

1. The DdbmsClient (or equivalent COS) makes a query request of the Ddbms subsystem by sending it an SQL string or the equivalent set of relational algebra-based details. In the steps that follow, the Ddbms subsystem will call the other subsystems to satisfy this client's request. First, the Ddbms calls the Parser. Next, it calls the Qualifier. Then, it calls the Planner. Finally, it calls the Dem, which will presumably call the Lem subsystems. However, since the Dem and Lem subsystems are implemented within an extension (outside the framework, but perhaps still inside the SKIT), those details are likely to be more project dependent.

2. Once the Ddbms has received the request, it passes the request to the Parser. The Parser takes the request as an SQL string or as a set of lists representing the operands for the clauses normally seen in an SQL query. The Parser then checks that the request is supported. When the SQL string parameter is used, the Parser will verify that the syntax is valid with respect to the grammar that the Parser implementation understands. If the syntax is valid, the Parser transforms the request into a structure that is represented by an interface defined within the framework (named "ParsedSQL"). When the "set of lists" form of the request is used, the same result is obtained, but no actual parsing is required—the Parser only performs minimal parameter validation. In either scenario, the interface representing the parsed form of the request ("ParsedSQL") provides implementation-independent access to the semantic information determined by the Parser implementation. The parsed form of the request (the ParsedSQL) is then returned to the Ddbms.

3. The Ddbms passes the ParsedSQL, which it just obtained from the Parser, to the Qualifier. The Qualifier then uses this information in combination with other information to transform the request further. Presumably, the other necessary details are contained in a global data dictionary (GDD) or obtained using some similar mechanism. The "transformed" request is stored in another class/structure, which is represented by another framework-defined interface (named "QualifiedSQL"). Now, we can use this interface to access the physical data-mapping information outside of the Qualifier implementation. The qualified form of the request (the QualifiedSQL) is then returned to the Ddbms.

4. Next, the Ddbms passes the QualifiedSQL to the Planner. QualifiedSQL provides access to the type of request it represents, as well as identity and location details for all physical constructs into which all of the global constructs mentioned in the original SQL request were mapped. The Planner uses QualifiedSQL to satisfy all of its information needs. It then uses its own algorithms to create the execution plan. This plan is stored as a third class/structure and represented by another framework-defined interface (named "DET"). The interface name (an acronym for "Distributed Execution Tree"), reflects the external view of the execution plan, but not necessarily its implementation. The distributed execution plan (the DET) is then returned to the Ddbms.

5. Lastly, the Ddbms passes the DET to the Dem, which is responsible for overseeing the execution of the request. Actually, the SKIT implementation for the Dem merely reads the subrequests from the DET and delegates most of the work to the

Lems. If the request was a query, the Dem collects and formats the results (if any) before returning the results to the Ddbms. These results are stored using a fourth class/structure and represented by another framework-defined interface (named "QueryResultSet"). Finally, the Ddbms returns the results (the QueryResultSet, the request's execution status, or any Java Exceptions raised) to the DdbmsClient (or equivalent COS) that invoked the Ddbms method for the original request.

These steps describe how the example implementation provided with the starter kit would satisfy a query request. We can modify the example to do any or all of these things differently if we choose. For example, we could implement triangular control or other alternatives within the Dem. However, this example illustrates the fundamental interactions between the subsystems that are likely to be used for most DDBE projects.

17.1.3   J2EE-SKIT Framework Architectural Overview

In this section, we will briefly discuss the subsystems implemented within the SKIT framework. These implementations should be reusable by most new projects with little or no modifications. Typically, the only modifications required are limited to editing the deployment descriptors, which are simple XML files. In fact, most of these edits will primarily be cutting and pasting different deployment details.

17.1.3.1   The Ddbms Subsystem   This is the external application–programming interface (API) for our DDBE project. As we mentioned earlier, it acts as a Facade [Gamma95] for the DDBE as a whole. It provides the end user applications with the publicly available methods for using the DDBE and acts as a single access point for the end user applications. By using this subsystem, we can simplify our client Remote-Code Execution operations. The clients connect to this subsystem rather than connecting to each of the other subsystems directly. This subsystem is responsible for communicating most of the information used in the DDBE processing of requests and provides most of the coordination details used by the other subsystems. Each DDBE project implementation will most likely edit the deployment details for this subsystem to ensure that each subsystem being used is the correct instance. We need to ensure that the new project is using the expected implementation for each subsystem, rather than accidentally using some other (older) implementation that was also deployed within the same J2EE environment. Aside from these changes, this subsystem should be reusable by most new projects without any modification or recompilation required.

17.1.3.2   The Parser Subsystem   The Parser subsystem is responsible for recognizing valid SQL statements, rejecting malformed or unsupported SQL statements, and producing a data structure that captures the semantic information for the valid SQL statements it can recognize. Since this subsystem is only invoked by the Ddbms subsystem, and only communicates to the other subsystems indirectly, it is also probably reusable for many new projects without any code modifications. It returns an object to the calling subsystem (Ddbms) that is accessed via a framework-defined Java interface. This object is then used to pass this semantic information to the other subsystems as needed. Therefore, we usually will not need to perform any deployment edits, code modification, or recompilation for this subsystem. If there is a need to change the supported syntax for a specific project, then this subsystem will need to be modified.

However, if this is not the case, then the same subsystem instance can often be reused in many DDBE projects without any additional deployment or configuration required.

17.1.4   J2EE-SKIT Extension Architectural Overview

The remaining subsystems are all implemented in the extensions rather than in the framework. These subsystems will always be implemented outside the framework. Either these subsystems are implemented in the SKIT-provided extension or they are implemented in a new extension that we create for a new project. To a certain extent, we are free to make design/implementation decisions that differ from the SKIT implementation, as long as the implementation still fulfills the requirements set forth by the framework-defined interfaces. Actually, we always have the option of modifying the framework-defined interfaces too, but that decision should not be made too hastily. Usually we will not need (or want) to modify the framework. Even when we do need to modify the framework, we will usually be making a change to the existing implementation or creating a new framework-defined interface. Hopefully, we will rarely need to modify one of the existing framework-defined interfaces. The SKIT-provided extension contains a reasonable implementation for each subsystem, but these implementations are not necessarily the best possible implementation with respect to features, performance, or flexibility. The goal of the SKIT extension is merely to provide a sufficiently complex example implementation that verifies the operation of the framework as a whole, demonstrates the feasibility of a typical DDBE project implementation, and provides a quick start for new DDBE project development.

17.1.4.1 The Qualifier Subsystem   The Qualifier subsystem is responsible for translating the Tokenized Statement (produced by the Parser) into a format suitable for use by the Planner subsystem. In other words, after the Qualifier examines the Tokenized Statement, it determines the mapping information needed to translate the global constructs into the physical constructs. This is done for each Global Conceptual Table and each Global Conceptual Column contained within the Tokenized Statement. These activities include determining the necessary information to support Location Transparency and Distribution Transparency. This means we first need to determine which physical database tables and columns are needed for our global constructs. Later, we must determine which Local Execution Managers are capable of accessing those physical constructs. Ultimately, we should try to determine the information necessary to support other transparency types. For example, we should try to support Fragmentation Transparency and Replication Transparency in our DDBE project. We can also choose to implement (full or partial) support for these transparency types in the other subsystems.

We suggest that the Qualifier should execute queries against a global data dictionary (or use a similar technique) to determine qualification details it needs. However, since this subsystem is part of the extension, we are always free to implement this subsystem differently for different projects. For example, we might choose to use the **Java Database Connectivity (JDBC)** API to access a relational database containing these GDD details. Alternatively, we might use some other mechanism to access a nonrelational database. Perhaps we might even access an object-oriented database or use an object persistence engine. We could even implement these details by developing new Entity Java Beans that use either Bean Managed Persistence or Container Managed

Persistence—using the J2EE platform and EJBs to store the transparency-mapping details directly.

17.1.4.2 *The Planner Subsystem*

The Planner subsystem uses the information produced by the Qualifier to build a Distributed Execution Tree (DET). The DET represents the physical operations and statements required in order to carry out the Global Statement. The DET is based on a tree structure where each node represents a Union, Join, or Concatenation operator or a leaf node. Typically, this tree represents the request as a set of relational algebra Project, Join, and Select operations, along with the Lem identification information for each node. In other words, the DET provides an interface to a tree-like structure that is compatible with the representations we discussed for query optimization in Chapter 4—for example, the DET could represent the plans for Figures 4.21 and 4.22 among many other possible plans. The Planner is responsible for describing what commands are to be executed and which Lem instances are responsible for executing them. Typically, the leaf-node commands will be performed at specific Lem sites, while the interior-node commands (Union, Join, and Concatenation) are most likely performed in some Dem instance at some Dem site. We are free to experiment with different techniques for execution control, such as those shown in Chapter 4, Figure 4.18. The Planner does not perform any of these operations itself, however; it merely creates the execution plan and stores it as a DET. We can choose to implement simple query optimization, advanced query optimization, or no query optimization in this subsystem. Regardless of which optimization strategy and control strategy we choose to implement, we should try to ensure that this subsystem always creates a correct plan. This is true even when the plan is not optimized.

17.1.4.3 *The Dem Subsystem*

The Dem subsystem is responsible for reading the plan created by the Planner. The DET is a parameter passed to one or more methods in the Dem. Typically, the Dem executes the plan by delegating the operations to one or more Lem subsystem instances as needed. In the SKIT-provided implementation, the DET will conform to one of two general plan categories based on the shapes of the tree that the DET represents. Here, the DET will conform to either a Concatenated Tree or a Query Tree.

The Concatenated Tree is used to represent Data Manipulation Language (DML) statements. A Concatenated tree is used to represent a global INSERT, global UPDATE, or global DELETE statement. The node operator will always be set to "Concatenate" for DETs whose trees conform to a Concatenated Tree shape. Each "Concatenate" node can be interpreted as saying, "First process the left leaf, and then process the right leaf." The leaf nodes in this type of tree will all contain commands that are of the same type. For example, every leaf node in the tree might represent an INSERT operation. Alternatively, every leaf node could represent an UPDATE operation. The only other possibility would be a tree where every leaf node represents a DELETE operation. Presumably, these operations would usually be executed at different Lem sites. In the degenerate case where a single Lem can perform the entire statement, the tree will contain a single "Concatenate" node and a single (left) leaf node.

The Query Tree will never contain a "Concatenate" node. The node operator will always be either "Join" or "Union" for this type of tree. Union is used primarily when working with horizontal fragmentation, while Join is used for most other situations. In the degenerate case where a single Lem can perform the entire statement, the tree will use a "Union" node operator with a single (left) leaf node. Query results must be returned to the Ddbms and ultimately its client. Therefore, we must use another data structure to return these results. This structure must be able to store the number of columns and the number of rows in the result. It must also be able to store details for each column, such as the column name, and details for each row, such as the value for each column in that row. This will be accomplished by using a class that implements an interface with the needed functionality (called "QueryResults"). When we create new projects, we are free to implement the QueryResults interface any way that we want to, or to use the implementation provided within the starter kit.

17.1.4.4   The Lem Subsystem   The Lem subsystem is responsible for carrying out the pieces of the global statement at a particular Lem instance. Each Lem instance executes part of the global plan for a local database at a particular site. The global statement will be broken into pieces by the Planner subsystem and delegated to a particular Lem instance by the Dem subsystem. The pieces of this global statement will typically be of the same type. A global query will usually result in one or more local queries; a global INSERT will usually result in one or more local INSERTS; and so on. The Lem subsystem can implement its operations in any way that it needs to, but typically, we would expect the Lem to leverage the facilities implemented by a local database management system (LDBMS). When this is the case, we would also expect the Lem to access the LDBMS via the Java Database Connectivity (JDBC) API. Although this is the technique used within the SKIT-provided implementation, new projects can also choose to implement the operations in radically different ways. The Lem is essentially a data processor (DP), which means we can implement it in any of the ways we discussed in Chapter 1. In particular, we can use any of the alternatives we discussed in Section 1.3 and summarized in Figure 1.6.

17.2   J2EE-SKIT DESIGN OVERVIEW

In this section, we will highlight some of the design details for each subsystem, and, in particular, we will identify the primary interfaces being used. This section will serve as a high-level roadmap for the code contained in the starter kit. The low-level documentation is provided with the code and generated from it using Javadocs. From this high-level vantage point, we can consider the code to be divided into four separate areas: the framework, the extension, the parameter types, and the Exception types. In some respects, the last two areas span the framework and the extension. The parameter types are the interfaces used to send information between the subsystems while the Exception types are used to send error information between the subsystems. Most of the interface and superclass code for these last two areas is actually implemented within the framework, but these interfaces and classes are used by both the framework and the extension. We also can define subtypes of the interfaces and classes within the extension code. Therefore, these areas are not strictly contained within the framework or the extension.

17.2.1   J2EE-SKIT Framework Design Overview

Each SKIT subsystem in the framework is implemented using a separate EJB. Each of these EJBs follows the Business Methods Interface Design Pattern [Johnson02]. This pattern is also loosely referred to as the "business interface" design pattern. Essentially, this means that there are three Java interfaces and one Java class defined for each of our subsystem EJBs. We use the term, "Bean Class" to refer to the class in this pattern. Similarly, we use a separate term for each of the three interfaces in the pattern.

The first interface (the "Home Interface") extends the "javax.ejb.EJBHome" interface, which is defined in the J2EE-SPEC. The Home Interface is used to represent how the EJB Container should initialize our EJB instance whenever it is created. The second interface in the pattern (the "Business Methods Interface" or "Business Interface") is used to define all the methods that we want our EJB's callers to be able to use. In other words, it contains the methods that perform our Bean-specific business logic and operations. The last interface in the pattern (the "Remote Interface") extends the "java.ejb.EJBObject" interface, which is defined in the J2EE-SPEC. The Remote Interface also extends the Business Methods Interface. The Remote Interface is used by the EJB Container to implement Remote-Code Execution for our EJB instances—supplying all the necessary generic EJBObject functionality and all the necessary Bean-specific functionality. The Bean Class is the implementation class for the EJB—it implements the "javax.ejb.SessionBean" interface, which is defined in the J2EE-SPEC. It also implements the Business Methods Interface. It does not implement the Remote Interface or the Home Interface—the EJB Container will use these interfaces behind the scenes to connect the remote callers and the local callee instance.

In the following sections, we will briefly consider the design details for each subsystem implemented as an EJB. For each subsystem, we will provide a short design overview followed by a table that summarizes the design using the design pattern details we just discussed. In these tables, we will identify the design pattern-based type names (the name of the Bean Class and the names of each of the three interfaces). The tables will also provide a brief summary of the general purpose for each of these types.

Many J2EE implementation alternatives support the latest J2EE specification, which allows us to use annotations (see Section 16.1.3) in our EJB source code as hints for generating the Home Interface and Remote Interface automatically. Because annotation support is a newer feature of the J2EE-SPEC, some implementation alternatives might not support these annotations yet. Regardless of whether the annotation support is present, the functionality represented by the design pattern and these interfaces is still present—even if the details are hidden by automatic generation facilities. Therefore, we have listed all three interfaces as well as the Bean Class for each subsystem.

17.2.1.1 The Ddbms Subsystem   In Table 17.2, we list the type names used by this subsystem. The code written in the SKIT-provided extension (or in the new extensions we create for new projects) will use these interfaces whenever a client application needs to connect to the DDBE. New projects can directly use the DdbmsBean class and these interfaces. The DdbmsHome interface most likely contains a single create method

TABLE 17.2   Type Names for Ddbms Subsystem

Type	Name
Bean Class	com.srdbsoft.ddbe.j2ee.skit.framework.ddbms.imp.DdbmsBean
Home Interface	com.srdbsoft.ddbe.j2ee.skit.framework.itf.ejb.DdbmsHome
Remote Interface	com.srdbsoft.ddbe.j2ee.skit.framework.itf.ejb.Ddbms
Business Methods Interface	com.srdbsoft.ddbe.j2ee.skit.framework.itf.ejb.DdbmsBmi

with no parameters, while the DdbmsBmi contains one or more simple methods for performing distributed queries (SELECT) and distributed DML commands (INSERT, UPDATE, DELETE).

The packages used within the SKITs are named using the typical package naming convention, which is designed to avoid naming conflicts. In particular, the class, interface, enumeration, and subpackage names only need to be unique within the scope of their immediate parent package (the name that is immediately in front of the rightmost period in the name). This is analogous to the way Internet host, domain, and subdomain names work. For example, suppose we had two fully qualified hostnames representing our sales ("www.sales.srdbsoft.com") and marketing ("www.marketing.srdbsoft.com") departments. On the World Wide Web, it is OK to reuse the host name "www" across the two different subdomains. It is even OK for some other company to reuse the subdomain names ("sales" and "marketing"), but no other site under the ".com" root domain can use the same name as we did for the last part ("srdbsoft"). If such duplication were allowed, it would cause problems for our domain name servers! For the Web, the individual pieces within a fully qualified domain name move from the most-specific name to the most-generic name. However, in Java, package names work in the opposite direction. Therefore, this naming convention uses the same technique but after the initial two name parts ("com.srdbsoft") we use package names that represent architecture, deployment, or other software development concepts. Even though the package names used in our SKITS are similar to DNS names, the Java package names do not necessarily correspond to any network-specific or network-based details—using the inverted DNS name for the first two parts of the package name is merely a convenient naming convention used by many organizations.

17.2.1.2   The Parser Subsystem   In Table 17.3, we list the type names for the Parser subsystem. While it is possible that some other subsystems will use some of these types, the DdbmsBean is the only subsystem that is explicitly intended to use this subsystem directly. Most new projects will only use this subsystem indirectly—we must specify the type names in the deployment descriptor. The ParserHome interface will usually remain as it is defined in the framework—simply containing a single create method with no parameters. The ParserBmi interface will contain methods for parsing an SQL statement, most likely just a single method. It will also contain a few methods for the commands based on relational algebra. The Ddbms subsystem will use this Bean to validate an SQL statement and add semantic information. The Parser only needs to handle a single SQL statement at a time. The syntax supported

TABLE 17.3   Type Names for Parser Subsystem

Type	Name
Bean Class	com.srdbsoft.ddbe.j2ee.skit.framework.parser.imp.ParserBean
Home Interface	com.srdbsoft.ddbe.j2ee.skit.framework.itf.ejb.ParserHome
Remote Interface	com.srdbsoft.ddbe.j2ee.skit.framework.itf.ejb.Parser
Business Methods Interface	com.srdbsoft.ddbe.j2ee.skit.framework.itf.ejb.ParserBmi

is a subset of the ANSI-92 syntax for SELECT, INSERT, UPDATE, and DELETE. There is not much (if any) support for functions or complex subclauses (subqueries, aggregate queries, order by clauses, having clauses, etc.), and there is no support for vendor-specific syntax or features. Of course, we can always modify or expand this in the new DDBE projects we create using this SKIT.

17.2.2   J2EE-SKIT Extension Design Overview

Most of the interfaces that are implemented in an extension specify the contract between the facade (Ddbms) and these other subsystems. In order for the Ddbms subsystem, which is implemented in the framework, to use any subsystem that is implemented in an extension, the Ddbms subsystem must know how to create and use these extension-defined implementations. These interfaces form the "contract" between our subsystems and, in particular, the "contract" between our framework and our extensions. Therefore, these interfaces must be defined in the framework—even though the extension-defined implementation classes must be defined in the extension. The loose coupling between implementation classes is accomplished by specifying the implementation class names within the appropriate deployment descriptors. This enables the implementation details to be changed (replaced by different implementations) at deployment time. By contrast, the interfaces must be referenced directly in the framework and extension implementation code—in addition to being specified in the deployment descriptors.

The starter kit provides implementations that use a simple "subsystem interaction strategy" (as we discussed in Section 17.1). In this strategy, most of the subsystems are service providers to the other subsystems in the framework—but the Ddbms subsystem is the primary service consumer for these services. The Ddbms is the only subsystem that needs to connect to the Parser, Qualifier, Planner, and Dem subsystems. Although this strategy is somewhat simplistic, it should be useful for many typical DDBE project scenarios. The Lem subsystem is a special case—the Lem subsystem is only used directly by the Dem subsystem and both of these subsystems are actually implemented completely within an extension. Because of this, the interfaces for the Lem subsystem are directly used by the Dem subsystem. Therefore, all the type name details and other restrictions mentioned for the Lem subsystem in this chapter and in the documentation provided with the starter kit should be considered to be more of a suggestion than a firm requirement. We assume that many DDBE projects will choose to use these suggestions, and be similar to the implementation provided in the SKIT, but that is not necessarily true for all DDBE projects.

Aside from the caveat we just mentioned for the Lem, almost all extension implementations will implement the same interfaces—namely, the interfaces defined in the framework and identified in this chapter. Even when our DDBE project chooses to implement the code behind one of these interfaces using a different class name, a different package name, or different implementation details—these interfaces will probably not change. The Bean Class name will usually be different for each particular DBE project implementation but the interface names will usually be the same as those listed here. Therefore, the rest of this section will list the type names for each of the subsystems that are implemented in an extension and identify the Bean Class names defined by the SKIT-provided extension implementation.

It is important to recognize that we can choose to modify the framework, if we need to. In general, we can add, modify, or delete any of the interfaces, classes, or

TABLE 17.4   Type Names for Qualifier Subsystem

Type	Name
Bean Class	com.srdbsoft.ddbe.j2ee.skit.extension.qualifier.QualifierBean
Home Interface	com.srdbsoft.ddbe.j2ee.skit.framework.itf.ejb.QualifierHome
Remote Interface	com.srdbsoft.ddbe.j2ee.skit.framework.itf.ejb.Qualifier
Business Methods Interface	com.srdbsoft.ddbe.j2ee.skit.framework.itf.ejb.QualifierBmi

TABLE 17.5   Type Names for Planner Subsystem

Type	Name
Bean Class	com.srdbsoft.ddbe.j2ee.skit.extension.planner.PlannerBean
Home Interface	com.srdbsoft.ddbe.j2ee.skit.framework.itf.ejb.PlannerHome
Remote Interface	com.srdbsoft.ddbe.j2ee.skit.framework.itf.ejb.Planner
Business Methods Interface	com.srdbsoft.ddbe.j2ee.skit.framework.itf.ejb.PlannerBmi

methods defined within the framework. This is not usually necessary or recommended, however, because the other code (framework and extensions) must also be modified to reflect these changes. For the remainder of this chapter, we will assume that no changes to the framework are required. Obviously, changing the framework might potentially change some of the restrictions and suggestions described in this chapter and in the documentation provided with the starter kit files.

17.2.2.1   The Qualifier Subsystem   The Home Interface for the Qualifier will (most likely) always have a single create method that takes no parameters. The QualifierBmi interface will probably have a single method that takes the output of the Parser as an argument and returns a qualified structure as the result. (See Table 17.4.)

17.2.2.2   The Planner Subsystem   The Home Interface for the Planner will most likely have a single create method that takes no parameters. The PlannerBmi interface will probably have a single method that takes the output of the Qualifier as an argument and returns a DET as the result. (See Table 17.5.)

17.2.2.3   The Dem Subsystem   The Home Interface for the Dem will most likely have a single create method that takes no parameters. The DemBmi interface will have two methods: one method for query and one for executing a distributed DML statement (INSERT, UPDATE, or DELETE). Both methods will take an object implementing the DET interface as an argument. The query method will return a type storing the query results. The DML method will most likely return nothing. It will throw Exceptions for errors rather than using a return value. It is possible that a DDBE project will choose to redefine this interface to include the number of rows affected or similar status information. However, we think that this is probably project-dependent behavior with no applicable, universal semantics. For example, if there are three replicas for a given row and we modify this "global row," did we modify one row or three? Therefore, we have left method signatures representing this type of status information out of the SKIT (for now). (See Table 17.6.)

TABLE 17.6   Type Names for Dem Subsystem

Type	Name
Bean Class	com.srdbsoft.ddbe.j2ee.skit.extension.dem.DemBean
Home Interface	com.srdbsoft.ddbe.j2ee.skit.framework.itf.ejb.DemHome
Remote Interface	com.srdbsoft.ddbe.j2ee.skit.framework.itf.ejb.Dem
Business Methods Interface	com.srdbsoft.ddbe.j2ee.skit.framework.itf.ejb.DemBmi

17.2.2.4   The Lem Subsystem   The Lem subsystem is implemented entirely inside an extension, so the details listed here are merely suggestions. However, we should usually follow this restriction—the Home Interface should only define a single method for creation. The LemBmi interface can have a greater degree of freedom with respect to the methods it defines. Typically, it should have one method for executing queries, and one or more methods for executing DML statements.

We can choose to implement separate methods for each type of DML, or we can choose to implement a single method that handles all DML statement execution. We can also implement other methods for working with connection information for our data sources. These details are better handled by the EJB Container—provided we are using container managed data sources or connection pooling. We can also choose to define other methods that are specific to our DDBE project here. For example, we might define different methods for different Lem implementations when they use different execution control strategies. Consider how the interface might need to be different when implementing a "master–slave" control strategy versus a "triangular" control strategy—see Section 1.7 of Chapter 1 for an example of these strategies.

We can also choose to define our methods differently depending on the types of parameters we want to use. If we want to pass the local SQL commands and queries into the Lem subsystem as strings, then our method would need to have a String (the SQL statement) as a parameter. Suppose we decided to use a more relational algebra-flavored approach instead. What types should we use for the parameters now? We could still use a String parameter here, but now it would contain a relational algebra statement instead of an SQL statement. This is not the only possible implementation for this approach, however, and therefore other method signatures might be more appropriate. For example, we might use several parameters representing the individual "pieces" required for the specific relational algebra operation. We typically translate an SQL SELECT statement into a relational algebra command that uses several specific arguments. In this scenario, we might define our method parameters to represent a list of columns to be projected, a list of tables to be joined, a list of the join conditions to be applied, and a list of non-join conditions to be selected. We might choose from several other approaches as well: we could use a tree structure containing those operators and operations. Supporting this kind of flexibility is precisely why the Business Methods Interface for this subsystem is defined within an extension rather than inside the framework. (See Table 17.7.)

17.2.3   Parameter Type Interfaces

We define a separate package (and namespace) for all the Java interfaces used to represent the parameter types in the SKIT framework. These interfaces are used to

TABLE 17.7   Suggested Type Names for Lem Subsystem

Type	Name
Bean Class	com.srdbsoft.ddbe.j2ee.skit.extension.lem.LemBean
Home Interface	com.srdbsoft.ddbe.j2ee.skit.extension.itf.ejb.LemHome
Remote Interface	com.srdbsoft.ddbe.j2ee.skit.extension.itf.ejb.Lem
Business Methods Interface	com.srdbsoft.ddbe.j2ee.skit.extension.itf.ejb.LemBmi

represent the parameters that we pass between the subsystems in the framework. We can also use them in an extension. Most of these interfaces are actually implemented by classes that we define within an extension. This package is named "com.srdbsoft.ddbe.j2ee.skit.framework.itf.parameters" and the interfaces it contains are designed as generically as possible. We have done this in an attempt to balance the required functionality with the ability to implement innovative approaches in our new DDBE projects and in our new extension implementations. This section lists the (unqualified) names for the interfaces contained in this framework-defined package.

17.2.3.1   ParsedSQL   The class that implements this interface is part of the Parser subsystem. This interface is used as output by the Parser subsystem and as input by the Qualifier subsystem. This interface provides access to the Parser output for the rest of the DDBE in general and especially the Qualifier subsystem, but we must be careful when we modify or extend this interface. In particular, we should never expose any of the implementation details and therefore should ensure that this interface provides read-only access to the contents. Otherwise, we might introduce implementation dependencies that make it very difficult to use a different implementation for the subsystems in other projects. In other words, if we are not careful we can damage our reusability.

17.2.3.2   QualifiedSQL   The class that implements this interface is part of the Qualifier subsystem. This interface is used as output by the Qualifier subsystem and as input by the Planner subsystem. Like the previous example, this interface should be used to provide one subsystem with read-only access to the output generated by another subsystem. Once again, we are concerned about implementation details and read-only access. We are also a little more concerned about supporting multiple implementation alternatives for this interface because the Qualifier subsystem is implemented in an extension.

17.2.3.3   DET   The class that implements this interface is part of the Planner subsystem. This interface is used as output by the Planner subsystem and as input by the Dem subsystem. Although this is also a read-only, implementation-independent interface, we do have some design details exposed though this interface—namely, the fact that this interface is intended to represent a tree. This will place some limitations and restrictions on the implementation alternatives for the Planner subsystem, but we can always modify the framework if necessary.

17.2.3.4   QueryResultSet   The class that implements this interface is part of the Dem subsystems. This interface is used as output by the Dem subsystem, and as input by the Ddbms subsystem. In the SKIT-provided extension, this same interface is used to represent the output of the Lem subsystem. Therefore, the implementation can be thought of as a shared implementation in this case. In a given DDBE project, we might choose to implement this interface using several different classes or we might choose to use a different interface (and therefore a different class) for the Lem subsystem's output. We can also choose to implement different classes supporting this interface across different Lem implementations within the same project. For example, this might be necessary or at least recommended when we are using heterogeneous DBMSs for our local database management systems in our DBE project.

17.2.4 Exception Type Classes

Even though we should always try to use meaningful Exception classes to represent all the possible, expected problems that our DDBE project might encounter, we also want to be able to create reusable code that is easy to use for prototype and proof-of-concept implementation projects. One way to achieve this is to use a common superclass for our Exceptions. This makes it easier to wrap the derived classes and handle the Exceptions by sacrificing some of the ability to ensure more detailed exception handling within the code. This section briefly identifies the base classes provided within the starter kit for this purpose.

17.2.4.1 Framework and Extension Exception Base Classes All Exceptions thrown from the framework, or thrown from any extension of the framework, should be one of the following: an EJB expected Exception, a System Exception, or a subclass of the ExFramework class defined in the framework. The EJB expected Exceptions are the Exceptions defined as part of the J2EE specification, such as CreateException, EJBException, or RemoteException. The System Exceptions are those Exceptions that are defined by the J2SE runtime, or the J2EE platform and subplatforms. Obviously, the last category (the Exceptions based on ExFramework) covers all other scenarios. In an effort to enable better exception handling, we actually provide some standard subclasses of this Exception that should be used to form a hierarchy of Exceptions. This allows the developer of the calling code to choose whether the code should react to the specific type of Exception involved or if the calling code should create a "catch all" situation that handles it in a relatively safe manner (making it easier to prototype things rapidly).

Framework Exception Base Classes All generic framework Extensions and extension Exceptions should inherit from the "com.srdbsoft.ddbe.j2ee.skit.framework.itf. exceptions.ExFramework" class. Although Hungarian notation has somewhat fallen out of favor, we use a simple form of it in the starter kit. All our Exception classes in the framework are named with a prefix ("Ex"). We feel this does not damage readability, and actually has some nice benefits with respect to the understandability of the code. We would not recommend taking this technique further than this, however.

Extension Exception Base Classes The "com.srdbsoft.ddbe.j2ee.skit.framework.itf. exceptions.ExExtension" class is a subclass of the "com.srdbsoft.ddbe.j2ee.skit. framework.itf.exceptions.ExFramework" class. All extension Exceptions should inherit from this class to make it easier to distinguish between extension and framework Exceptions. We think this is potentially useful when debugging and testing, even though the former is a subset of the latter.

TABLE 17.8   Subsystem-Specific Exception Base-Class Summary

Subsystem	Unqualified Exception Base-Class Name
Ddbms	ExDdbms
Parser	ExParser
Qualifier	ExQualifier
Planner	ExPlanner
Dem	ExDem
Lem	ExLem

17.2.4.2 Subsystem-Specific Exception Base Classes Each subsystem can also have an Exception base class: this is the technique used in the SKIT framework and extension. If these base classes are used, they do not necessarily need to inherit from the previous classes. It is more important to identify the subsystem than it is to identify the implementation location for that subsystem. Table 17.8 identifies the Exception base classes provided with the starter kit. All of these Exceptions are contained within a framework package (named "com.srdbsoft.ddbe.j2ee.skit.framework.itf.exceptions"). The Business Methods Interface for each subsystem, which we discussed in Section 17.2.1, uses the appropriate Exception base class for the throws clause on the methods it defines. Table 17.8 provides a summary of these classes for each subsystem. It lists the name of each subsystem and the unqualified class name for the Exception class that acts as the base class, or perhaps the actual implementation class for all the subsystem Exceptions. The Business Method Interface for the Ddbms subsystem is slightly different from the others because it is the Facade. Therefore, it also declares the appropriate subsystem-specific Exception base class as being potentially thrown from its methods. This is useful, because it enables client applications to react to subsystem-specific Exceptions. For example, a client can catch the ExParser Exception and then attempt to handle or at least report it more appropriately because it knows where the Exception occurred. It might even use the instanceof operator to downcast the Exception into an even more specific exception handling strategy.

17.3 SUMMARY

Our J2EE-SKIT consists of many classes and interfaces, which are in turn factored into several different packages. These packages can be compiled and bundled into Java Archive (JAR) files and then reused within the J2EE development and deployment environments. A subset of the packages (meaning the classes and interfaces that they contain) form a framework representing the fundamental subsystems within a typical DDBE project. The framework provides an overall infrastructure and implements some of the foundations for building a DDBE project. Although the framework can also be directly modified, we intend the framework to be extended through inheritance rather than reimplemented whenever it is not able to satisfy the needs of a particular set of project requirements. The other packages (that are not part of the framework) are part of an example extension that is also included within the starter kit. We would expect these interfaces and classes to be usable as they are, or to be extended through inheritance to satisfy the requirements for some projects. We would also expect some projects to completely ignore the extension packages and directly implement all of the code necessary for their extension. The SKIT extension and any other extensions implemented in new DDBE projects can then serve as a basis for new implementations, or merely as examples, in addition to fulfilling their own project requirements.

In general, all executable content deployed within the J2EE platform has a physical directory structure and associated set of configuration details, which are bundled together into a specific type of Java Archive file based on the type of deployment container (see Section 16.1.4) being used. All of the subsystems defined within the SKIT framework are implemented as Enterprise Java Beans (EJBs) and deployed as EJB JAR files. Similarly, the subsystems implemented in the SKIT-provided extension are also deployed as EJB JAR files. Clients connecting to any DDBE project implementation that is based on the J2EE-SKIT (including the SKIT-provided example extension) can choose the deployment format that they need from any of the available options provided by the J2EE platform implementation being used. This includes Java Server Pages (JSPs), Servlets, Applets, or J2EE Applications. Each of these deployment types has a specific set of deployment requirements, which are defined by the J2EE Specification and documented by the J2EE platform implementation vendor. Many development environments also provide support for building and maintaining these various deployment files and their associated requirements. Ultimately, all deployment mechanisms use some form of directory structure or JAR file with special deployment descriptor or configuration file.

We should always consult the vendor-specific documentation for the J2EE platform installation we are using for our DDBE project's development and deployment activities. This documentation should always be consulted **first**, because it is always the most relevant to the activities we are attempting. The J2EE specification should be consulted whenever we require a better understanding of the concepts, issues, or other details surrounding the vendor-specific or J2EE-SKIT provided information. The J2EE specification should also be consulted to clarify any concepts presented in this book about the J2EE platform.

The J2EE-SKIT includes further details, recipes, and suggestions for building, deploying, and executing our DDBE projects based on the framework provided. However, these details cannot cover all the specific details for all possible J2EE platform installations. Instead, these documents provide an example of how we can compile, deploy, and execute the SKIT extension in a typical installation. There are also recipes for modifying the deployment details once we have successfully built and deployed the example extension within an environment. Although these recipes might not be identical to the steps required for a particular installation, they should provide sufficient details to enable us to translate the steps into the appropriate actions based on the vendor-specific documentation and installation-specific configuration details. Once we have succeeded in deploying the example, it should be reasonably simple to create a new project that modifies or extends the starter kit, and then to redeploy the resulting code.

17.4 GLOSSARY

Application Client   A stand-alone, J2EE-aware application that runs on the client and is contained, deployed, and executed within an Application Client Container.

Application Client Container   A Container type that supplies all the J2EE platform-defined operations, features, and facilities necessary to deploy and execute the Application Clients contained within it.

Application Sever   A particular installation of a particular J2EE platform implementation alternative.

Bean Managed Transaction (BMT)   A flavor of EJB where the Bean's implementation code must explicitly call the "begin()" method and either the "commit()" method or the "rollback" method (all of which are provided by the JTA and implemented by the JTS) in order to manage the JTA Transaction actions for the Bean.

Component   A deployable bundle that provides a reasonably cohesive set of functionality.

Component or Subsystem (COS)   A term that refers to a component or subsystem, ignoring any differences between the two concepts.

Container Managed Transactions   A flavor of EJB where the EJB Container manages the JTA Transaction actions based on the current transactional state and the Transaction attributes declared for the EJB.

Deployment   Any features, issues, concepts, or considerations related to how a COS instance is installed on a particular machine at a particular site.

Deployment Descriptor   A file (usually an XML file that conforms to a particular Document Type Definition format) that contains the deployment-specific details for software deployed within the J2EE platform.

Enterprise Archive File (EAR)   A JAR file that contains the files needed for a J2EE application that is contained, deployed, and executed within an Application Server.

Enterprise Java Bean   A Java Bean implementing the business logic for a J2EE application that is J2EE-aware and deployable within an EJB Container.

Enterprise Java Bean Archive File (EJB-JAR)   A JAR file that contains the files needed for an EJB that is contained, deployed, and executed within an EJB Container.

Enterprise Java Bean Container (EJB Container)   A Container type that supplies all the J2EE platform-defined operations, features, and facilities necessary to deploy and execute the EJBs contained within it.

Extensible Markup Language   See **XML**.

Java Archive File (JAR)   A single file created using the JAR tool that contains one or more other files and directories used by the Java Virtual Machine—this is a convenient mechanism for bundling several files together within the Java development and execution runtime environments.

Platform   A set of software that provides a well-defined set of operations, facilities, and functionality that serves as the foundation for components, subsystems, and other software that runs on top of the platform.

Session Bean   An Enterprise Java Bean that represents a client within the Application Server. Session Beans are useful because EJBs are contained within the EJB container, which, in turn, is contained within the Application Server. The actual client itself is contained within the Application Client Container—not the Application Server, and most likely not even on the same machine as the Application Server.

Stateful Session Bean   A Session Bean that represents a unique conversation between a particular client instance and a particular Session Bean instance. Stateful Session Beans need to preserve the conversational state—the Bean's instance variable values must be remembered by the Bean after the Bean method invocation returns its results to the caller.

Stateless Session Bean A Session Bean that represents a conversation between a particular client instance and a particular Session Bean instance. Stateless Session Beans do not preserve the conversational state—the Bean's instance variable values are effectively zeroed out after the Bean method invocation returns its results to the caller.

Subsystem A collection of components and/or subsystems that is part of a larger system but also a system in its own right.

Transaction Attribute A method of controlling the JTA Transaction actions for a BMT EJB by specifying one of six possible values for the attribute using a Java annotation or EJB deployment descriptor.

XML A markup language that uses tagging to indicate semantic details or logical structure for a set of data content.

REFERENCES

[Bodoff02] Bodoff, S., Green, D., Haase, K., Jendrock, E., Pawlan, M., and Stearns, B., *The J2EE Tutorial*, Addison-Wesley, Reading, MA, 2002.

[Gamma95] Gamma, E., Helm, R., Johnson, R., and Vlissides, J., *Design Patterns Elements of Reusable Object-Oriented Software*, Addison-Wesley, Reading, MA, 1995.

[Johnson02] Johnson, R., *Expert One-on-One J2EE Design and Development: J2EE Design and Development*, John Wiley & Sons, Hoboken, NJ, 2002.

EXERCISES

Complete the following programming exercises.

17.1 Download the J2EE-SKIT and compile, deploy, and execute the example extension.

17.2 After consulting the vendor-specific documentation and the recipes supplied with the J2EE-SKIT, modify the deployment details for the example extension to use different database vendors for each of the Lem databases.

17.3 After consulting the vendor-specific documentation and the recipes supplied with the J2EE-SKIT, modify the example extension, and deploy the Ddbms subsystem on a different J2EE platform installation (preferably on a different machine). Next, move one of the Lem subsystems to another machine.

17.4 Section 4.5.1 discussed query execution strategies, including a triangular control strategy, as shown in Figures 4.18 (b) and (c). Create a new DDBE project based on the J2EE-SKIT that implements this triangular strategy for query execution—this does not need to be based on query optimization details, but can be either hard-coded to use a particular pattern or controlled by deployment-specific settings (settings specified in the GDD or in the deployment descriptors).

18

THE MICROSOFT .NET PLATFORM

Microsoft .NET is software for connecting people, information, systems, and devices. The **Microsoft .NET ("Dot Net") Framework** is an application development, deployment, and execution environment that is useful for building distributed database environment projects—that is, a powerful DDBE Platform. Although its official name uses the term "Framework," we will usually refer to it as a "platform." In part, we do this to avoid confusion with the framework we include inside the Microsoft .NET Framework-based starter kit (the **DNET-SKIT**), which we will discuss in Chapter 19. Also, calling the Microsoft .NET Framework a platform is simply more appropriate for our purposes—after all, it is a DDBE Platform. Using this nomenclature will make it easier to compare and contrast Chapters 15–19 with each other and to apply the concepts from Chapter 14 to this environment.

We will not be making any "blow-by-blow" comparisons between the JMS platform, the J2EE platform, and the Microsoft .NET Framework-based platform—but we will mention that these three platforms do share some common aspects. For example, this DDBE Platform is also defined by specification. Like the other two platforms we just mentioned, this platform also has multiple implementations including some that are not implemented by Microsoft. We can even run these platform implementation alternatives on several different operating systems, including some operating systems that are not implemented by Microsoft. Our focus here, however, will be limited to the Microsoft implementations for both this platform and the operating systems on which it runs.

We should also mention that all three DDBE Platforms (including this one) support messaging services. Of course, even if we did not read Chapter 15, we would suspect that the JMS platform supported messaging, simply because of how it is named. If we recognize that the JMS platform is a subplatform of the J2EE platform, then we should also realize that the J2EE platform supports messaging services—this would be obvious even if we had not read about Message Driven Beans in the previous chapters.

Distributed Database Management Systems by Saeed K. Rahimi and Frank S. Haug
Copyright © 2010 the IEEE Computer Society

Like the J2EE platform, the Microsoft .NET Framework-based platform can be viewed as having subplatforms contained within it—including one subplatform that supports Remote Messaging. However, since our purpose in this chapter is to highlight how this Microsoft .NET Framework-based DDBE Platform can support the DNET-SKIT, which we will present in Chapter 19, we will not focus on any facilities that are not directly related to our starter kit. Because this starter kit is similar to the J2EE-SKIT we discussed in the previous chapter, we will be focusing on Remote-Code Execution more than Remote Messaging. Similarly, there are many other facilities provided by this DDBE Platform that we will not address here.

Even with this narrow view of the facilities provided by this platform, the platform is quite impressive. Perhaps the most impressive aspect of this platform is its simple ubiquitous nature. The Microsoft .NET Framework and its supporting runtime environment are present (at least in one form or another) on most systems running a reasonably recent Microsoft Windows-based operating system. Of course, it is possible that some of the more advanced platform facilities will not be present or configured for all these deployed environments. Nevertheless, this fact does not diminish the potential opportunities that this "preexisting" DDBE Platform deployment brings us.

In spite of the near-universal availability that this platform has, there are many reasons why two different deployments (machines) might have different platform facilities and services available on them—even when they both have the Microsoft .NET Framework installed. For example, there might be differences in the operating systems deployed on the two machines in question. Even when both operating systems are Microsoft Windows-based operating systems, they might not be identical operating systems. We must remember that there are many different variations within the set of all available Microsoft Windows-based operating systems. For example, we could be running operating systems from different product families, such as the Windows NT operating system, the Windows 2000 operating system, the Windows XP operating system, the Windows Vista operating system, or the Windows 7 operating system. Within each family, there are also different editions from which to choose. For example, the Windows NT operating system had both "Server" and "Workstation" editions and the Widows 2000 operating system had separate editions as well (the Windows 2000 Professional operating system, the Windows 2000 Advanced Server operating system, and the Windows 2000 Datacenter Server operating system). It is also possible for the operating systems to be from different generations, which is only natural as operating systems evolve and change to meet new consumer demands. These systems are always changing over time, but not all systems are updated at the same time. Therefore, we might need to consider the differences between the latest Windows-based operating system and the previous one (e.g., the differences between the Windows 7 operating system and the Windows Vista operating system, or the differences between the Windows XP operating system and the Windows 2000 operating system). It is even possible for the systems to have different hardware-targeted flavors for some of these operating systems, including any differences from the CPU manufacturer to hardware details such as the difference between 32-bit and 64-bit operating systems. Even when we consider machines that are running the exact same operating system, there might be differences between the machines due to the specific deployment details for each. For example, they may have different service pack levels installed or perhaps they have different additional third-party software installed. It is even possible that these machines have simply been configured differently—having different services installed, enabled, or disabled and different options chosen within their system configuration details.

Because the Microsoft .NET Framework is useful and powerful, it is often required by other, third-party software products. Therefore, our DDBE Platform is often automatically installed as part of the deployment process for those third-party packages. In spite of this, we might still encounter systems that do not have the platform installed, or systems where the version of the desired platform facility is not as current as we need it to be. In these scenarios, we can always connect to Microsoft's website and download the latest version that is supported by our Microsoft operating system. We can also connect to this website and find the latest service packs and hot fixes for the platform.

We cannot possibly cover all the variations and nuances for all the alternative environments that the previous paragraphs describe. Instead, in this chapter, we will start our platform discussion by providing a brief overview of the Microsoft .NET Framework-based DDBE Platform in isolation from most of these considerations. This overview will focus on the platform architecture and its primary uses rather than any actual deployment or configuration details. For our purposes, this description will be sufficient to get the starter kit that we introduce in Chapter 19 to work in our environment. After the overview, we will consider how this "vanilla" view of the platform can be used to fulfill the DDBE Platform Requirements we identified in Chapter 14.

18.1 PLATFORM OVERVIEW

There are several different releases of our DDBE Platform (the Microsoft .NET Framework) currently available and actively being used, just like there are several different releases of the Windows-based operating systems available and in use. Not all Microsoft .NET Framework releases will work on all versions of the operating system, however. The latest release of the platform at this time is Version 3.5, with Service Pack 1 (3.5 SP1), but Version 4.0 is already in the Release Candidate stage, and will soon become the latest offical release. Version 3.5 (and Version 4.0) will work on the Windows XP operating system and the Windows Vista operating system, but it will not work on any older-generation operating systems (such as the Windows 2000 operating system). The latest release that works on the Windows 2000 operating system is Microsoft .NET Framework 2.0, which is still available. There is also another release of this platform available (Microsoft .NET Framework 1.1), but this is a very old version of the platform.

These different platform releases share a somewhat complicated deployment relationship with each other. The earlier releases (1.0, 1.1, and 2.0) were separate bundles that could be installed side-by-side, independently from each other. For example, it was possible to have both release 1.0 and release 1.1 deployed on the same system at the same time without any conflicts. This also meant that removing one release would not affect the other. The later releases are related as subsets and supersets of each other. For example, the 3.0 release includes the 2.0 release inside it and the 3.5 release includes both the 3.0 and the 2.0 releases inside of it. For our purposes, we will mainly be leveraging the functionality and facilities that were first provided by the 2.0 platform, which are also still supported by later releases of this platform. We recommend using the latest release available for the operating systems deployed within our environment. The fact that we mainly use features provided in the 2.0 release of the platform does not mean that we cannot benefit from the most current implementation of those features. These facilities were defined in earlier versions of the platform because they are so fundamentally useful—often used to support the newer facilities included in later generations of the platform.

Each new release of the platform is, in many respects, an evolutionary change, rather than a complete replacement. After all, both portability and interoperability are two important features of this platform. It would be extremely shortsighted to break backward compatibility completely with each new release! Often, there are minor releases within the major releases. These are typically "hidden" improvements—improvements that, for the most part, do not affect the existing development, deployment, or execution environment in any visible way. The major releases have historically involved highly visible changes, as well as new and improved facilities and features (i.e., new or improved "subplatforms" for our purposes). We should always check the documentation provided with each new release for the actual details about what has changed, what is new, and what might no longer work the same as before.

Our DDBE Platform consists of several different services, subsystems, and facilities. This is a logical view of the platform—not a physical one. We will not focus on enumerating or examining all the logical or physical platform details here. Instead, we will only focus on those logical subplatforms related to the DNET-SKIT and the custom development that we might do within our DDBE projects deployed on this platform. Before we can discuss these details further, however, we need to define some new (and important) terms. Therefore, in Section 18.1.1, we will look at some of the vocabulary necessary to understand this platform better. Next, in Section 18.1.2, we will look at the architectural view of the platform. In Section 18.1.3, we will focus on the development view of this platform. We will finish our platform overview in Section 18.1.4 when we discuss the deployment details for this platform.

18.1.1 Fundamental Platform-Specific Vocabulary Terms

There are many new terms used in this platform that we have not discussed elsewhere in the book. However, we will focus on only a small subset of these terms, which are relevant to our other discussions in Chapters 15–19. In particular, before we can discuss the architecture in Section 18.1.2, we need to understand some of the terms that describe the fundamental subplatforms, subsystems, and components within the architecture. Note that we will ignore the distinctions between these three different architectural categorizations. Although there are many other terms we need to learn and understand when working in this platform on a day-to-day basis, we will restrict ourselves to nine fundamental vocabulary terms (with a few additional terms included as part of the discussion for each). We strongly recommend reading the online help for further clarification of these terms and concepts.

The nine fundamental terms we will consider are the following:

- Common Language Runtime (CLR)
- Base Class Library (BCL)
- Common Language Specification (CLS)
- Common Type System (CTS)
- Intermediate Language (IL)
- Managed/Unmanaged Components
- Assemblies

- Global Assembly Cache
- Application Domains

18.1.1.1 Common Language Runtime The **Common Language Runtime (CLR)** is really the heart of the platform in many respects. The CLR manages the runtime aspects for all software running on top of the platform. In comparison to the other two platforms we considered, the CLR is analogous to the Java Virtual Machine or one of the various J2EE Containers in the J2EE platform. When Microsoft .NET Framework-based code executes, the CLR can manage many important aspects for it, such as memory management, resource management, and security management. In a nutshell, the CLR provides deployment and execution services to the components and subsystems we develop.

18.1.1.2 Base Class Library The **Base Class Library (BCL)** is a set of application–programming interfaces (APIs) used to connect the programs that we develop to the underlying services and subsystems contained in the platform. The classes and interfaces defined within the BCL can be used to create service providers as well as service consumers. Note that when we use these terms here, they are compatible with the concepts of the same name that we reviewed in Section 14.1.2, and originally introduced in Chapter 1. The BCL provides access to the Common Language Runtime (CLR), uses the Common Type System (CTS), which we will discuss in Section 18.1.1.4, and is often used by many of the other subplatforms that we will not discuss here. In general, the BCL is a set of programmatic constructs that are bundled into different namespaces (analogous to packages in the Java world). These constructs conform to the CTS, and the Common Language Specification (CLS), which we will discuss next. The namespaces used by the BCL all follow an easy to understand naming convention—we can be confident that any construct in the "System" namespace (or one of its sub-namespaces) is part of the BCL, or at least similar to the BCL with respect to its purpose and role within our DDBE projects.

18.1.1.3 Common Language Specification The **Common Language Specification (CLS)** is a set of programming language features and rules designed to ensure cross-language (and, to a certain extent, cross-platform) interoperability. This means that the code we develop on top of this platform can be implemented in any of several different CLS-compliant programming languages. For example, we can choose to use Visual C++, Visual C#, Visual Basic, or any of several other languages—as long as the language conforms to the CLS. Visual C# is a relatively new language, which is somewhat similar to C++ and somewhat similar to Java, but different from both [Chandra05]. Most of the time, we will use a language that is supported by Microsoft Visual Studio. Microsoft Visual Studio is an integrated development environment (IDE) that can be used for software development, deployment, testing, and debugging activities. Many of the details defined for the CLS are important to programming language implementers and designers. However, many of these details can be safely ignored by those of us who are mere users of the programming languages. In other words, as we simply write a program in one of these languages for this platform, there are sophisticated techniques being used and important actions being performed on our behalf by the platform and our development tools. Even though these things are all necessary and vital to the programs we are developing and the particular programming language we are using, many of them occur "behind the scenes" and "under the covers" from our perspective.

18.1.1.4   Common Type System   The **Common Type System (CTS)** is vital to the interoperability between the programming languages that conform to the Common Language Specification (CLS). In essence, the CTS eliminates many of the data type representation and implementation differences that normally exist between different programming languages. There are two different general categories for data types in the Microsoft .NET Framework: the **value types** and the **reference types**. Value types include the "simple" data types that directly contain their values—such as integers, characters, bytes, and floating-point numbers. Reference types are data types that store a reference to the memory location where the value is ultimately stored. References are similar to pointers, but the concepts are not equivalent. While pointers are essentially mere-memory addresses, references are a much more sophisticated concept in any language, and in the CTS. Reference types include self-describing types, pointer types, and interface types. Self-describing types are types that can be used to determine their own reference type information (e.g., both arrays and classes are self-describing types).

The primary distinction between value types and reference types is demonstrated by considering how we compare the two different variables defined using these types. Suppose we have two variables (A and B) that are defined using a **value type**. If we compare these variables and find that they both contain an integer value of zero (A = 0 and B = 0), then we consider the variables to be equal and interpret this by saying that we have one value (the same value) stored in two different variables. Now, suppose we have two more variables (C and D) that are defined using a **reference type**. We can compare these variables using one of two different mechanisms. The first mechanism considers the location that each variables references. If this location is the same for both variables, then the variables are both referring to the same thing and the variables are therefore identical. For example, if both C and D referred to our variable A, then they would both refer to the same location (our A variable). The second mechanism considers the content stored at the location that each variable references. Obviously, if both variables refer to the same location, then the content stored there will once again be equal. For example, if both C and D referred to our variable A, then the content they both refer to would be the value stored in the A variable. Since the content stored in the A variable is equal to the content stored in the A variable, this second mechanism would consider C and D to be identical for both the first mechanism and the second mechanism in this scenario. What happens if our reference type variables refer to different locations? Suppose C referred to the A variable but D referred to the B variable. Now, when we perform the first comparison mechanism, because the variables refer to different locations, the first comparison mechanism considers them to be different from each other. If our A and B variables both contain the same value (e.g., if A = 0 and B = 0), then the second comparison mechanism will consider the two variables (C and D) to be identical to each other because their contents are identical. This is far more complicated than the simple value type scenario—depending on which mechanism we are using, we can consider two reference type variables to be identical to each other and different from each other at the same time!

The CTS specifies many other details that ultimately enable powerful interoperability for the data types defined in different programming languages. For example, a class implemented in Visual Basic can inherit from another class that was implemented in Visual C#. All types in the CTS inherit from (extend) the "System.Object" class. The CTS also provides a programming language independent understanding of namespaces. This is not necessarily the same as the programming language's understanding of the namespace concept, but is implemented in such a way that each programming language vendor can translate between the native programming language namespace concept and the CLS/CTS understanding of namespaces. Implicitly, because the types in the CTS are programming language neutral and programming language independent, they cannot be stored in a programming language specific format. Instead, we use a new format, called the Intermediate Language to represent these types, which is the vocabulary term we will consider next.

18.1.1.5   Intermediate Language   The source code we write for this platform must be written using a programming language that conforms to the Common Language Specification (CLS) and Common Type System (CTS). This source code is not compiled directly into machine code the way our "traditional" programs are usually compiled on other platforms. Instead, the code is compiled into a special format called the **Microsoft Intermediate Language (MSIL)**, the **Common Intermediate Language (CIL),** or simply the **Intermediate Language (IL)** [Costa05]. Regardless of which name we choose to use for this format, it is the final format generated during our development activities. Just before the Common Language Runtime (CLR) is ready to execute our code, it uses another subplatform, the Just-in-Time (JIT) compiler. The JIT compiler translates the IL format into a natively executable format. Figure 18.1 depicts how the IL code uses the CLS/CTS to interface with the Base Class Library (BCL) and access the functionality contained within the platform. The outer layer shown in this diagram represents our code that is written in a programming language and compiled into the Intermediate Language. The IL sits on top of/works through the CLS and CTS to access the BCL. The BCL, in turn, wraps the CLR services and facilities, effectively wrapping access to all the underlying services provided by this DDBE Platform inside the BCL.

18.1.1.6   Managed/Unmanaged Components   Once our source code has been compiled, we can refer to it as a **module**. A collection of one or more modules can be considered as a single unit, and referred to as a **component**. This term is compatible with our definition of a **component or subsystem (COS)** from Chapter 1, but it also contains some platform-specific details. In particular, the Microsoft .NET Framework considers all components to be **managed components** or **unmanaged components**. Managed components are compiled into the Intermediate Language (IL) format and execute within the Common Language Runtime (CLR) using the Common Language Specification (CLS), Common Type System (CTS), and Base Class Library (BCL) as we discussed in the previous sections. Unmanaged components are not compiled into the IL format. Each of the "traditional" programs we alluded to in Section 18.1.1.5 is considered as an unmanaged component. All code that is not based on the Microsoft .NET Framework is considered "traditional" in this respect. It is also possible to create unmanaged components that are based on the Microsoft .NET Framework—even though they are not managed themselves, they can optionally load the CLR and

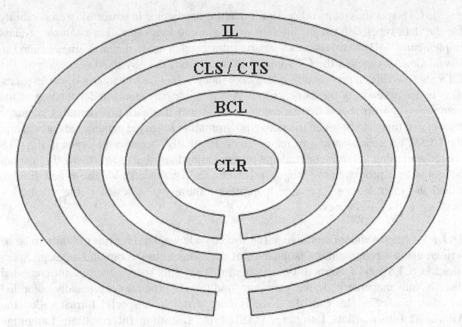

Figure 18.1 The IL, CLS/CTS, BCL, and CLR

use it to execute managed components on their behalf. This technique provides us with a useful bridging mechanism that has many practical applications within the platform.

Version 6.0 of the Microsoft Internet Explorer is an example of an unmanaged component that uses the bridging mechanism we just discussed. Even though this component is not compiled into the IL format, it can host the Common Language Runtime (CLR). This hosted instance of the CLR can then execute Microsoft .NET Framework-based components on behalf of Microsoft Internet Explorer. This is very useful when connecting to web pages that contain or use managed components. Other versions of Microsoft Internet Explorer might be implemented as a managed component (rather than as an unmanaged component)—which is why we explicitly mentioned Version 6.0 here. We knew that this version was not implemented as a managed component, and think that this version will probably never be reimplemented as a managed component in the future, since it is no longer the most recent version commonly in use.

It is also possible to use a technique known as a wrapper to allow managed components to invoke unmanaged components, and vice versa. This is different from the CLR-hosting option we discuss in the box. We mention this detail here for the sake of completeness, as well as in recognition of the fact that wrappers might be employed within our DDBE projects even when we do not use them directly ourselves.

For example, if we needed to connect to a database environment that did not have a Microsoft .NET Framework-based database driver available for it, we might employ a wrapper to enable our managed components to use an unmanaged database connectivity component. Similarly, the database vendor might choose to implement their "official" Microsoft .NET Framework-based connectivity component by using a wrapper "behind the scenes." Having said that, we think that most of the DDBE projects we will develop have very little need for explicitly avoiding managed components. Even if some component in our DDBE project did not **need** to be implemented as a managed component, there are very few circumstances in which such a component **could not** be implemented that way.

18.1.1.7 Assemblies   When a file containing some of the source code for a managed component is compiled into the Intermediate Language and saved into a new file, we call this new file a module. However, this is not the primary deployment bundle within the platform. That deployment bundle is called an assembly, and it is written in a file format called the Portable Executable (PE) format. Although there are a few different deployment alternatives available for us to choose from, an **assembly** is usually created as a single file that contains several important things. Obviously, it contains all the Intermediate Language modules compiled from the source code for the component or subsystem that this assembly is supposed to deploy. The assembly also contains the necessary metadata (including version, security, and deployment details) for the code. In addition to the resource details for the assembly (such as database connectivity details and application-specific properties), this metadata includes the assembly's name (different from its file name) and the version information for the "assembly as a whole."

Optionally, we can assign a "strong name" to the assembly. The **strong name** for an assembly consists of the textual name and version number we just mentioned, combined with optional culture information, a required public key, and a required digital signature. The strong name serves two fundamental purposes within the platform. First, the Common Language Runtime (CLR) can use the strong name to uniquely identify the assembly, and even use it to compare two assemblies claiming to be the same thing. Second, the strong name provides the CLR with a mechanism for verifying the assembly contents and identifying if/when the assembly has been tampered with. The underlying techniques used by the platform to implement this concept are largely hidden from us developers, aside from a few addition development activities that we must perform and a few restrictions we must obey when strongly named, managed components are used in our projects. Even though the developer must consider the ramifications of using assemblies with strong names (and act accordingly), the developer does not need to know any public key implementation details. Similarly, these implementation details are largely unnoticed by the average (computer/application/component/subsystem) user.

Although strong names are useful with respect to the identification and integrity issues concerning an assembly, strong names do not include details necessary to ensure trust. We can address this issue by signing our strongly named assemblies using a Digital Certificate. By signing an assembly that has a strong name, we can leverage the Authentication and Nonrepudiation cryptographic functions that the underlying public-key-based platform facilities implement on our behalf. Although we do not have access to the implementation details for these facilities, we can be certain that they are implemented using mechanisms and techniques similar to those we discussed (Digital Certificates, Digital Signatures, etc.) in Section 9.1 of Chapter 9.

18.1.1.8 Global Assembly Cache

The **Global Assembly Cache (GAC)** acts as a machinewide container for shared assemblies. There is only one GAC on each computer where the CLR is installed. Usually the GAC is located in a directory that is contained within the "Windows directory." The "Windows directory" is often reflected in the "WinDir" and "SystemRoot" environment variables. Its precise location is a deployment-dependent value that can vary based on the specific Microsoft Windows-based operating system that is installed and the details that were specified when the operating system was installed. Usually, we can determine this location in the command shell, by simply typing "echo %SystemRoot%" or "echo %WinDir%" without the quotes. This command will print the name of the "Windows directory." Under the "Windows directory," we should find a subdirectory named "assembly"; this is the GAC directory. The GAC directory and the assemblies it contains are subject to the access control list (ACL) restrictions implemented by the operating system (file permissions). There are also security metadata details deployed within each assembly and Microsoft .NET Framework security settings for the whole machine that control the access to the assemblies deployed via the GAC. The GAC provides a convenient location for deploying assemblies that are used systemwide or at least shared by many different programs, components, and subsystems.

This is somewhat analogous to the way dynamic link libraries (DLLs) and executables (EXEs) are deployed in the "system" and "system32" directories, which are also found under the Windows directory—but the GAC is a much more sophisticated and powerful deployment mechanism than that scenario. As we mentioned before, assemblies can optionally have a strong name—those in the GAC are required to have a strong name. We also mentioned that the metadata contained within an assembly includes many important deployment details, including the assembly name and version details.

The combination of the strong name and these deployment details can prevent many of the headaches that the older mechanism caused. In the old technique, if a shared DLL or EXE was updated by some new application installation/deployment, there was a potential risk that other existing applications might be broken by the act of replacing the old, shared files. With the GAC, however, we do not need to replace the old files; instead, we install a new assembly "side-by-side" with the old one. The decision to continue using the old assembly or to switch to the new assembly is controlled by the deployment and configuration details for each application, as well as the machinewide defaults for these settings. The traditional approach did not offer such flexibility.

18.1.1.9 Application Domains

Whenever a managed component is executed, the component runs inside a logical process called an **Application Domain**. This is true regardless of the specific deployment alternative we choose when we deploy the managed assembly (GAC versus non-GAC deployment, signed versus unsigned assemblies, assemblies with or without strong names). Each Application Domain acts like a virtual machine, allowing the components inside the Application Domain to interact directly with each other but preventing unwanted interaction between the components that are inside different Application Domains. Within the same Application Domain, components and assemblies can incur less overhead when they interact with each other, but they can also potentially have a direct impact on each other. For example, if one component fails (crashes) it can cause the other components within the same domain to fail as well. Components that are in separate Application Domains can also interact; however, they might incur more overhead when they do. This overhead should be less than the overhead we encounter when remote execution is used. The lowest overhead possible occurs whenever the components are in the same Application Domain. Separate Application Domains can be started and stopped independently from each other—provided we write our code correctly. This also means that a failure in one Application Domain does not necessarily cause a crash in the other Application Domain, or a crash at the system level. Each assembly must be loaded into an Application Domain before it can be executed. If the caller code does not do this before the call is made, then the Common Language Runtime (CLR) will load the other assembly into the caller's Application Domain by default. When an assembly is used by more than one other Application Domain, the assembly's code (but not its data) can be shared by all the other Application Domains.

18.1.2 Architectural Overview

Within the architecture for this DDBE Platform, there are several subsystems, which we have already briefly discussed in the process of defining the necessary vocabulary terms. At the core of the platform's architecture, the Common Language Runtime (CLR) manages the execution for all the managed components. These components are deployed within assemblies, which are stored as files implementing the PE format. These PE files are located either in the GAC or in any of the normal locations we would expect to find executables on the computer—in other words, they can also be stored in any folder/directory, just like the "traditional" applications and DLLs.

We can categorize Microsoft .NET Framework-based applications as being either client applications or server applications. Client applications are similar to "traditional" applications and can use any of the normal user interface mechanisms, including graphical user interface (GUI) techniques or console interfaces (using command-line arguments and output to a command shell). Client applications can also include ActiveX controls (or their Microsoft .NET Framework-based replacements, which are called Windows Form Controls). In addition to the "traditional" deployment and execution mechanisms available on the client machine, client applications can be deployed on a web page. Server applications can be accessed as XML web services, ASP.NET services, or using any of the other "traditional" execution mechanisms available on the server machine.

There are several facilities (some of which could be considered subplatforms for our purposes at least) that are used by the Microsoft .NET Framework behind the scenes. As we already discussed, the CLR manages the execution for all managed components. We also mentioned another facility, the JIT compiler, which converts Intermediate Language (IL) into native code prior to execution. Similarly, we discussed how the Base Class Library (BCL) is essentially the API for the CLR and the platform as a whole. There are also some additional facilities, which we can consider to be sitting on top of the BCL. These facilities can optionally be used by the components deployed on this platform, depending on their specific purpose and deployment details. For example, the Winforms, ASP.NET, and ADO.NET facilities provide APIs to GUI controls, web-related controls, and database controls, respectively.

Additional services can optionally be present in our DDBE Platform depending on the requirements for the machine within our environment. For example, most client machines will not need many additional services, but a web server will most likely have the Internet Information Services (IIS) installed. It is also possible that one or more machines in our environment will have the Exchange Mail Service installed. Obviously, our database servers would have some form of database management system (DBMS) installed—Microsoft SQL Server is an example of one type of DBMS commonly found in such an environment. Such a machine might also include several other services such as the database engine service, analytical processing service, reporting service, integration service, and other related facilities. Another service that is commonly found on machines that act as database servers is the COM+ subplatform. Such a machine would probably have the Microsoft .NET Framework-based components for COM+ access (found in the "System.EnterpriseServices" namespace) installed as well. By using the BCL supplied "System.EnterpriseServices" namespace and more specifically the "ServicedComponent" class, we can use the COM+ subplatform to create components that access the distributed transaction processing facilities available within the platform.

All of these services and subplatforms are either accessible through native interfaces and through the basic Microsoft .NET Framework-based BCL facilities, or through some other higher-level facilities/subplatforms. There are several such higher-level facilities included in the later versions of the platform that were not present in earlier releases. For example, Version 3.0 of the Microsoft .NET Framework includes three "foundations" that were not present in Version 2.0. These "foundations" are the Windows Presentation Foundation (WPF), the Windows Communications Foundation (WCF), and the Windows Workflow Foundation (WF). Similarly, Version 3.5 of the platform includes two new subplatforms that were not present in Version 3.0: namely, the ASP.NET AJAX subplatform and the Language Integrated Query (LINQ) subplatform.

18.1.3   Development Overview

When we develop Microsoft .NET Framework-based components and applications, we can choose any programming language that conforms to the Common Language Specification (CLS) and Common Type System (CTS). The Intermediate Language (IL), Common Language Runtime (CLR), Base Class Library (BCL), CLS, and CTS even allow us to mix and match different programming languages within the same subsystem or component. Having said that, we think it best not to make the code development process more complicated than necessary. While certain components, applications, or developers might have a clear preference for one language or another, we should consider the software maintenance issues carefully before we introduce new languages into our projects. While it is true that the platform and the development environment can easily handle multilanguage development, deployment, and execution scenarios, it can be confusing and frustrating for the people involved. This is especially true when we are debugging our DDBE project code.

There are several rules and suggestions to consider when developing code for this multilanguage environment. Although we will not attempt to present any such details here, we will say that the online documentation, dedicated websites, user forums, and books should be consulted before we embark on any serious development project.

Many of the guidelines are really common sense—except that we normally would not consider them necessary in a mixed-language environment. For example, because we now have to consider how other components will interact with our component even when they are developed in different languages, we should try to avoid using more global/publicly visible constructs than necessary. Similarly, we should place even more emphasis on "programming to interface," which is the informal name for the general technique of exporting public interfaces and using them rather than directly referencing the class that implements a particular publicly accessible method. In this case, using the interface makes it easier to reimplement the code later on using a different programming language or to support multiple implementations at the same time. Although both of these examples are good practices to follow in any environment, we would usually not apply them across code written in different programming languages because different programming languages do not typically interoperate this way outside this platform.

When we create our Microsoft .NET Framework-based components, we should be aware of the execution issues we discussed in Section 14.2.3, particularly the multi-tasking considerations. Earlier, we mentioned that the Application Domain acts like a virtual machine for the components executing within it; now we can also emphasize that a given thread of control is active within only one Application Domain at a time. As a component executes, a given thread of control can "travel" across domains, and a given domain can have multiple threads. While those details sound like they should be discussed in the next section, which considers deployment details, we mention these facts here to emphasize that the threading model is somewhat different from most "traditional" scenarios, and therefore must be addressed very carefully during the software design and implementation processes.

18.1.4 Assembly Deployment Overview

An assembly is somewhat similar to a dynamic link library (DLL) or executable (EXE) file used by the older, "traditional" applications that are not based on the Microsoft .NET Framework. In many respects, the assembly represents the "unit of work" for deployment considerations in this platform. For example, security permissions are defined for an assembly (applicable to all modules contained within it as a whole). Similarly, the assembly acts as the boundary between these security settings—we can consider different assemblies to represent deployments with potentially different "security clearance levels" within our environment. Assemblies also act as a scoping mechanism, allowing us to reuse the same type names for different types across different assemblies—if we want to, we can also share types across them.

Assemblies can be private or shared, and the shared assemblies can be deployed using several different alternatives. It is beyond the scope of this section (and this chapter) to discuss all the alternatives or all the deployment issues and settings necessary to implement them. Instead, we will merely provide a brief overview here. Shared components can be pooled, deployed "side-by-side" with other versions of themselves, and involved in transactions (either manually or automatically). They can be referenced by both local and remote callers (in various ways) and can be configured either to use the default deployment behaviors for the machine or to use deployment behaviors that are specific to a particular deployment of a particular instance of the assembly. For example, by default, each of our assemblies will be deployed with a versioning policy that only allows them to use a specific version of another assembly (as configured within its metadata). By altering the appropriate configuration details, we can change or override this default versioning policy to allow the assembly to use a newer version, an older version, or simply a different, specific version of another assembly.

Each assembly deployed within the platform can specify a version identifier as part of its deployment. This version identifier can be thought of as a string of the form "<major>.<minor>.<build>.<revision>"; for example, we can release an assembly as version "1.0.0.0," "1.1.0.0," or even "1.2.345.6789." The values stored for each placeholder in this version "string" are under our complete control.

Often, the changes in the value of "<major>" are used to indicate a visible (and perhaps incompatible) change in the assembly. Changes in "<minor>" typically represent a visible change that is not radically different from (or breaking compatibility with) the existing behavior of a previous version sharing the same "<major>" version. These are merely conventions, however, not strictly enforced rules. The "<build>" and "<revision>" places are often used to represent new releases or updates that may or may not contain any visible changes at all. These last two places can even be managed automatically within the development process by specifying the "AssemblyVersion" value as "<major>.<minor>.*"; for example, using a value of "1.0.*" will automatically use the default build and revision numbers.

18.1.4.1   Configuration   We can control many deployment details using the Microsoft .NET Framework configuration facilities. For example, as we discussed earlier, we consider versioning to occur at the assembly level of detail. This enables the "side-by-side" execution of different versions of the same assembly on the same computer at the same time. This is very different from the deployment and execution scenarios that we used for "traditional" applications in a Windows-based operating system environment. When our managed components are deployed, they can specify rules controlling which version of an assembly should be used. In fact, we can also specify which version of the Common Language Runtime (CLR) should be used. These details are not hard-coded into the application, and they are not stored systemwide in the window registry. Instead, these details are specified within one of the standard configuration files.

For our purposes here, we are focusing on three standard types of configuration files used within the platform:

- Machine configuration file
- Application configuration file
- Security configuration

The machine configuration file is named "machine.config" (not the machine's host-name but the literal word "machine"). It is deployed within the "config" subdirectory of the CLR installation path. Typically, the installation path points to a subdirectory under the "%SystemRoot%" directory we mentioned earlier, that is, inside the "Windows directory." Within the "Windows directory," we will see another directory named "Microsoft.NET," which in turn will contain a directory named "Framework." In this "Framework" directory, we will possibly see several subdirectories for the various versions of the platform that we have installed on this machine (each subdirectory is named something like "v2.x.y," where the "2" reflects the major release number of the platform and the "x" and "y" reflect the minor release numbers). Finally, within this version-specific directory, we will find the machine configuration file ("machine.config"). This file specifies details for machinewide assembly building, "builtin" remoting channels, and ASP.NET. When an assembly is run, this file is consulted first, looking for the appropriate "<appSettings>" section; then any user-defined locations are consulted; and lastly, the application configuration file (if there is one) is consulted.

The application configuration file is named differently depending on the host type where the application is deployed. If the assembly is hosted within an executable program (a file with the ".exe" extension), then assembly is "exe hosted," and the application configuration file is named the same as the executable file but with the ".exe.config" extension. If the application is hosted by ASP.NET, then the application configuration file is named "web.config" and its location is inherited from the URL for the web application (analogous to being in the same directory as the assembly, it is in the same "URL directory"). If the assembly is hosted within a browser (like Microsoft Internet Explorer), then a special element within the file launching the assembly will point to the configuration file. Once again, this file must be in the same location as the assembly.

The security configuration details are controlled at the machine, user, and enterprise levels by using the "Code Access Security Policy Tool" (implemented in an executable named "caspol.exe"). The directory containing this tool is not necessarily found within our "PATH" environmental variable. This tool is located within the same subdirectory as the "machine.config" file we discussed earlier. We can also use the ".NET Framework Configuration Tool" (found in the same directory as "caspol.exe"), but this tool is usually accessed via the icon in the "Administrative Tools" area found underneath the "Control Panel" (or similar facility). While the security settings (and other configuration details) are very important to a real-world deployment, we will not discuss any of the security or other configuration specifics here. Instead, we recommend using the online help as a primary source for further details.

18.1.4.2 Assembly Deployment Alternatives   There are many deployment alternatives available to us within the platform—far too many for us to cover completely here. In the previous section, we mentioned that an assembly can be "hosted" within the Common Language Runtime (CLR). We also said that an assembly could be hosted within an instance of the CLR that is itself being "hosted" by another application such as a web browser. An assembly can also be hosted by ASP.NET. In Section 18.1.1.1, we mentioned that the CLR acts as the ultimate container for our deployed assemblies, even when the CLR is hosted by another application, such as the web browser scenario we just considered. Aside from the container alternatives we just mentioned, there are also many different configuration options that can control our assembly's deployment and execution. Because the issues, details, and trade-offs for these considerations are beyond our scope here, we will focus on only one important aspect, which we first mentioned in Section 18.1.1.7—namely, strong names.

As we discussed earlier, an assembly with a strong name has many desirable qualities: it can be uniquely identified by the CLR, it can be deployed side-by-side with different versions of the same component without any unpredictable side effects, it can be verified (checked for tampering), and optionally it can even be signed. However, there are some drawbacks to consider before we decide to use a strong name for all our assemblies. We will look at three different aspects of these considerations in this section. In particular, we will focus on these considerations, based on three different deployment alternatives. Although this does not encompass all possible scenarios or all possible issues, it serves as a good introduction to the concepts and covers many of the situations we are likely to encounter in a typical academic research DDBE project.

The three deployment alternatives we will consider in the subsequent sections are the following:

- Deploying a GAC, strongly named assembly
- Deploying a COM+, strongly named assembly
- Deploying a private, strongly named assembly

18.1.4.3 *Deploying Shared Assembly*   Shared assemblies must have strong names. Shared assemblies cannot load types from private assemblies—this would cause a shared construct to depend on a private construct. This is forbidden because it would also potentially circumvent the verification (and optional signing) by essentially injecting private code into the shared code. Shared assemblies can be deployed in the same manner as a private assembly. Although the Microsoft .NET Framework does not prevent this, the normal deployment mechanism for a shared assembly is different from the mechanism used for a private assembly. In particular, shared assemblies are typically deployed using the GAC. If the shared assembly contains a class inheriting from (extending) the "ServicedComponent" class, as we discussed in Section 18.1.2, then it is deployed differently because it is a component leveraging functionality from the COM+ subplatform. We will briefly consider these two alternatives in the next two subsections.

Deploying a GAC, Strongly Named Assembly   In general, most of our assemblies will not be deployed in the GAC. The GAC should be used only for those components that are truly shared by many different projects. We should not deploy assemblies in the GAC when they are merely used by multiple components within the same project. Assemblies can be installed into the GAC via custom installation or setup programs, using the "Global Assembly Cache Tool" (gacutil.exe) or by simple file copy/drag and drop actions where the GAC directory is the destination directory/folder.

Deploying a COM+, Strongly Named Assembly   Serviced Components (the classes in assemblies that inherit from the "ServicedComponent" class) can leverage the COM+ facilities like object pooling and distributed transaction management. These assemblies are shared assemblies, but they are not always deployed in the GAC. When the assembly is hosted by the Enterprise Services facility (DLLhost.exe), it can be deployed in the GAC, and usually should be. If the assembly is actually a server application, then it should be installed into the COM+ applications. This means that it can be managed via the "ComponentServices" icon inside the "Administrative Tools" area underneath the "Control Panel." If the assembly acts as a "Library Application," then it does not need to be deployed using either the COM+ applications area or the GAC.

18.1.4.4 *Deploying a Private Assembly*   The term "private assembly" is used to refer to any assembly that is not deployed in any of the "special" ways we just discussed. In other words, a private assembly is deployed in a manner that is similar to the more "traditional" deployment mechanisms used on the Microsoft Windows-based operating systems, but it is not quite the same deployment mechanism. In particular, since we are still working with an assembly, and we are still deploying the assembly within the Microsoft .NET Framework, there is no need for the registry activities that usually accompany "traditional" deployments. These assemblies can be deployed as DLLs or EXEs and copied into application-specific directories. The term "private" does not mean that the assembly cannot be referenced and used by other assemblies (a DLL that could not be referenced by any other assembly would be completely worthless). Instead, the term "private" refers to the fact that the assembly is not deployed using any deployment mechanism that explicitly allows other projects to easily share it. In other words, it is used privately by the application (typically an EXE) with which it was deployed, but easily not used by any other applications. Private assemblies can optionally have a strong name, but they do not need to have one. We will consider both of these cases in the next two sections.

Deploying a Private Assembly with a Strong Name   There are several reasons why we would choose to use a strong name with our private assembly. For example, we might use a strong name for our private assembly if we think that the assembly might be used as a shared assembly at some point in the future. However, the real reason for using a strong name with a private assembly is to take advantage of the benefits that can only be provided by a strongly named assembly. In particular, we would want to use a strong name with our private assembly to make the assembly more tamperproof and to establish trust with the assembly. Using a strong name will enable verification, which essentially depends on the notion of identity. If we also want to establish trust and nonrepudiation for this assembly, we must also use signing, and we cannot sign an assembly unless the assembly already has a strong name. Therefore, using a strong name is the first step toward a more secure assembly.

Deploying a Private Assembly Without a Strong Name   Private assemblies can also choose not to have a strong name, in which case they do not have the benefits we have already discussed. When our private assemblies do not have a strong name, they do not require additional development and deployment steps (such as generating the strong name). If the assembly will never be shared and does not need the added security we mentioned in the previous section, then we can forgo the strong name option. Arguably, even though working with strong names is not that difficult or cumbersome, it would be somewhat foolish (and certainly unnecessary) to require strong names for all our assemblies. This is precisely why we might choose to use this option for at least some (if not all) of our DDBE project assemblies. This deployment option is certainly acceptable for those assemblies that we intend to use only in proof-of-concept, prototype, academic, research-only, or simply "nonproduction" projects.

18.2 SUPPORT FOR DISTRIBUTED PROCESS PLATFORM REQUIREMENTS

The Microsoft .NET Framework-based DDBE Platform includes several alternatives for implementing the Distributed Process Platform Requirements we discussed in Chapter 14 (Section 14.3). In this section, we will provide a brief overview of the facilities it provides. Because we can also use third-party middleware, as well as "traditional" facilities, the actual alternatives for each of these requirements includes many options that we do not even mention here. Recall that the requirements in this category are focused on distributed processing, and, in particular, we will consider the platform options for satisfying the Remote-Code Execution Requirements, Remote Messaging Requirements, and Directory Services Requirements.

18.2.1   Remote-Code Execution Requirements

Recall that Remote-Code Execution is a set of features and functionalities that enable one component or subsystem (COS) instance (the caller) to call procedures or invoke methods that are implemented within another COS instance that is deployed on a different machine (the callee). We refer to the COS making the calls as the Local COS. We refer to the COS that is being called as the Remote COS. The relationship is not necessarily symmetrical. Although our Local COS can call methods within our Remote COS, the Remote COS does not necessarily have the ability to invoke methods within our Local COS. This means that the caller can always invoke messages in the callee, but the callee usually does not invoke methods in the caller.

In this platform, there are several implementation alternatives to choose from for satisfying the Remote-Code Execution Requirements. In particular, we can use ASP.NET (for web-based components) or a particular flavor of ".NET Remoting" such as HTTP, or TCP. The term ".NET Remoting" is the official term for these protocol-flavored approaches. We can also implement Remote-Code Execution within this platform via XML web services using SOAP. Since our starter kit will not be implemented as web-based components, and since we have already discussed SOAP, in Section 16.2.1.2, we will only consider .NET Remoting in this section.

18.2.1.1   .NET Remoting   When we use .NET Remoting, the caller (Local COS) is usually referred to as a client, while the callee (Remote COS) is referred to as the server. When the caller requests a remote object, the platform provides two different mechanisms for satisfying the request. The object returned to the request can be a copy of the server object or it can be a reference to the server object. If a copy of the server object is used, then the server object is merely sent to the caller (marshalled by value), which means that the methods invoked on the callee are actually executed on the client machine (the machine where the Local COS is deployed). If a reference to the server object is returned (marshalled by reference), then the methods invoked on the callee will be executed on the server object's machine (the machine where the Remote COS is deployed). We discussed marshalling and unmarshalling in Section 14.3.1.1, and we discussed reference types within the Common Type System (CTS) in Section 18.1.1.4. The two scenarios we just discussed are essentially the combination of those two concepts with additional functionality being provided by the .NET Remoting subplatform facilities. The second scenario is the situation we are most interested in for DDBE development, at least most of the time. There are many options to choose from and restrictions to follow when creating a Remote COS using .NET Remoting.

While the detailed discussion is beyond the scope of this chapter, many of the relevant details are described very clearly in the online documentation for the Microsoft .NET Framework-based platform. We will briefly summarize the basic concepts here. We say that a server (remote) object is "consumed" by a client and "exposed" by a server. The server object can be client activated (referred to as **activated**) or server activated (referred to as **wellknown**). The lifetime of an activated server object is determined by the client. The lifetime of a wellknown server object is classified as being either a **singleton** or **singlecall**. A singleton server object will use a single instance for all client requests, while a singlecall server object will use a separate instance for each request.

18.2.2 Remote Messaging Requirements

As we mentioned earlier, the platform provides several facilities and subplatforms. One of these facilities is the Microsoft Message Queuing (MSMQ) service. This facility can be used for Remote Messaging and in many respects is similar to the Java Message Service (JMS), which we discussed in Chapter 15. The platform also provides access to lower-level networking constructs and facilities, including sockets and channels. We can also use the .NET Remoting and marshalled by value server objects we discussed in the previous section to implement Remote Messaging. However, since the DNET-SKIT (like the J2EE-SKIT) is not focused on Remote Messaging, we will not discuss any of these facilities further.

18.2.3 Directory Services Requirements

As we discussed in Section 14.3.2, the Directory Services Requirements encompass three important subservice-based requirements: the Naming Service Requirements, the Registration Service Requirements, and the Lookup Service Requirements. The platform provides all of these services, although they are not necessarily referred to in this manner. For example, the Global Assembly Cache (GAC) provides a convenient container for shared assemblies, and the assemblies within the GAC must have strong names. Recall that strong names uniquely identify an assembly to the Common Language Runtime (CLR). Therefore, these two subplatforms are one example of how the platform provides Naming, Registration, and Lookup services to local components or subsystems. Similarly, the .NET Remoting facilities we discussed in Section 18.2.1 can use Uniform Resource Locators (URLs) to connect client objects to server objects deployed on other machines. When the server objects are implemented to allow this access, the platform can use these three concepts together to provide a powerful implementation that satisfies the Directory Service Requirements, including the support for remote components and subsystems.

There are other subplatforms and facilities available that can satisfy this DDBE Platform Requirement. We will not discuss them in detail here, but we will mention some of them briefly. The web services support within the platform includes support for **Universal Description, Discovery, and Integration (UDDI)** and **Web Services Description Language (WSDL)**, both of which we have discussed previously. Other examples of facilities that satisfy these requirements include the Enterprise Services facility we mentioned in Section 18.1.2 and the Service Components (leveraging COM+ functionality) facility, which we mentioned in Section 18.1.4.3.

18.3 DISTRIBUTED DATA PLATFORM REQUIREMENTS

The platform also includes several alternatives for implementing the Distributed Data Platform Requirements we discussed in Chapter 14 (Section 14.4). In this section, we will briefly provide an overview of the platform provided facilities. The platform can leverage functionality from "external" environments and facilities that are not part of the Microsoft .NET Framework-based platform per se, including the underlying Microsoft Windows-based operating system facilities and other, nonoperating system facilities as well as other sophisticated systems. For example, the platform can leverage external systems such as those compatible with the **Lightweight Directory Access Protocol (LDAP)** service, which we have briefly mentioned before in both Chapters 9 and 16. We will not discuss any of these "external" facilities in detail here because those details would vary depending on which implementation alternative was used as well as how it was configured and deployed. Nevertheless, it is important to recognize that the platform can be integrated into these environments in addition to the facilities it natively provides.

18.3.1 .NET Security

We have already mentioned security concepts both implicitly and explicitly throughout this chapter. For example, we discussed the security configuration facilities in Section 18.1.4.1. We also implied that there were powerful cryptography, authentication, and authorization facilities being used through the combination of the configuration tools and the underlying support for strong names and certificates within the platform. At several points, we discussed some aspect of the platform that relied on underlying security facilities, such as the existing operating system security facilities for logins and account management. We also mentioned how other operating system facilities, such as access control lists (ACLs), interact with platform facilities such as the GAC, to provide security to the platform. Although we will not discuss the security details further, there is also support for other security constructs found in the "System.Security" namespace of the Base Class Library (BCL).

18.3.2 ADO.NET Database Connectivity

In addition to the "traditional" database connectivity options usually found within a Microsoft Windows-based operating system, the platform also provides its own database connectivity subplatform. The Active Data Objects .NET (ADO.NET) subplatform provides database connectivity to managed components. Strictly speaking, the actual database access might be implemented using unmanaged components that are wrapped inside a managed component, or they could be implemented directly as true managed components. From our perspective, these differences are not particularly relevant most of the time. The more important consideration is the simple ease with which we can access databases from different vendors through a common interface, namely, the ADO.NET types and methods exposed via the Base Class Library (BCL).

18.3.3 .NET Transactions

Database transactions within the platform can be implemented using several different alternatives. The transactions can be managed manually or automatically. Here, manual means via explicit calls to the ADO.NET transaction methods, or to a special class called the "ContextUtil" class. Automatic transactions are controlled via transaction attributes defined within the metadata for a class. The automatic transaction attribute values and their interpretation are summarized in Table 18.1.

TABLE 18.1 Enterprise Services Transaction Attribute Summary

Attribute Value	Action Taken when There Is a Preexisting Transaction	Action Taken when There Is No Preexisting Transaction
Disabled	Ignore the transaction	Ignore the lack of a transaction
NotSupported	Create a new context without a transaction	Create a new context without a transaction
Required	Share the current transaction	Create a new transaction
RequiresNew	Create a new transaction	Create a new transaction
Supported	Share the current transaction	Ignore the lack of a transaction

If we compare this table to Table 16.1, there are some striking similarities, but the values and their interpretations are not identical across these two platforms. In particular, the J2EE platform includes situations where exceptions are thrown due to a mismatch between the code's transaction expectations and the actual environment's transaction status. The Microsoft .NET Framework-based platform does not have this behavior. There are also subtle differences between the behaviors in these two environments for seemingly similar transaction attribute names. There is, however, one more similarity between this platform's transaction management and the J2EE platform's transaction management—they both manage transactions differently based on the deployment type for the COS and the subplatform responsible for managing that deployment container. Although this platform does not refer to the automatic transactions as being container managed, they are handled differently for web-based deployments, Enterprise Service-based deployments, and basic deployments. Similarly, although the J2EE platform does not call the Bean Managed Transactions "manual" or the Container Managed Transactions "automatic," both of these terms are appropriate in these situations (respectively). However, one major difference is the restrictions placed on the transaction attributes in this platform—a single attribute applies to an entire class, and that class must inherit from the "ServicedComponent" class that we mentioned earlier.

18.4 SUMMARY

The Microsoft .NET Framework is a powerful, ubiquitous platform consisting of many subplatforms. There are several different versions of the platform, with additional facilities and subplatforms being added to the later releases. The variety of facilities supplied directly by this platform combined with this platform's ability to leverage the existing operating system and third-party facilities make this a very powerful platform with a large number of potential deployment targets.

The Microsoft .NET Framework provides an architectural solution to many of the issues we need to resolve when considering the development of a DDBE project. The platform contains several subplatforms, such as the Common Language Runtime (CLR), Base Class Library (BCL), Common Language Specification (CLS), and Common Type System (CTS). The platform and its subplatforms provide several alternatives for satisfying the Distributed Database Environment Platform Requirements (as discussed in Chapter 14). The architecture addresses many of the Fundamental

Platform Requirements directly, while the subplatforms offer several options for each of the function areas we considered for providing the Distributed Process Platform Requirements and the Distributed Data Platform Requirements. Overall, the facilities used to implement all the Distributed Database Environment Platform Requirements fit together in a single, consistent platform, with a uniform interface and philosophy.

The platform-specific approaches for implementing our DDBE project requirements are all centered on the concepts of assemblies, the underlying CLR subplatform, and the other areas of the platform that support the CLR. These concepts and the facilities within the platform provide the DDBE developer with a powerful set of tools for component and subsystem development, deployment, and execution. The developer can configure the deployment details flexibly and pick the best implementation from several different alternatives within the same environment, including the ability to deploy multiple versions of a COS at the same time without conflict, and to use different programming languages with almost no interoperability concerns.

18.5   GLOSSARY

Application Domain   The logical process that contains a managed component whenever it is being executed.

Assembly   The fundamental unit of work for any deployment considerations in the Microsoft .NET Framework. Although assemblies can consist of multiple files, we usually bundle all the modules into a single file written in the Portable Executable (PE) format and save it as either a DLL or an EXE.

Base Class Library (BCL)   The set of application–programming interfaces (APIs) used to connect managed components to the underlying services and subsystems provided by the Microsoft .NET Framework-based platform.

Client Activated Server Object   A remote object whose lifetime is controlled by the client. This means that it is created and destroyed on the server by the code executing on the client in order to support .NET Remoting.

Common Intermediate Language (CIL)   See **Intermediate Language**.

Common Language Runtime (CLR)   The core subplatform within the Microsoft .NET Framework-based platform that manages all runtime aspects for managed components executing within the platform.

Common Language Specification (CLS)   A set of programming language features and rules designed to ensure cross-language interoperability among managed components.

Common Type System (CTS)   A subset of the CLS that defines data/class/interface types in a programming language independent way. This can also refer to the subset of the CLR/Microsoft .NET Framework-based platform that implements the CTS.

Component   A deployable bundle that provides a reasonably cohesive set of functionality.

Component or Subsystem (COS)   A term that refers to a component or subsystem, ignoring any differences between the two concepts.

Deployment   Any features, issues, concepts, or considerations related to how a COS instance is installed on a particular machine at a particular site.

Digital Certificate   A public key and other identifying information, usually in X.509 format, signed with a certificate authority's private key after the certificate authority verifies the public key identity.

Digital Signature   A cryptographic technique that uses a source private key to sign data such that a destination can use the source public key to authenticate the source with the strength of nonrepudiation.

Directory Service   A service that provides several important functions such as naming, registration, lookup, and possibly security.

Global Assembly Cache (GAC)   The machinewide container for shared assemblies.

Intermediate Language (IL)   A file format used to represent compiled modules in a programming language independent way.

Managed Component   A piece of software that is designed, implemented, and deployed in such a way that it can execute inside the Microsoft .NET Framework-based platform, with the CLR managing its runtime environment.

Marshalling   The collection of techniques capable of converting parameters into a data stream, usually to support RMI, RPC, or Messaging—the opposite of unmarshalling.

Message   A data structure or textual stream representing content sent from one COS instance to another.

Microsoft Intermediate Language (MSIL)   See **Intermediate Language**.

Middleware   Any additional software used to "bridge the gap" (translate or hide differences) between COSs.

Nonrepudiation   The inability to deny being the source of a message or data.

Platform   A set of software that provides a well-defined set of operations, facilities, and functionality that serves as the foundation for components, subsystems, and other software that runs on top of the platform.

Portable Executable (PE) Format   The programming language independent and platform independent file format in which assemblies are written.

Private Key   The key from the public key cryptography key pair used for decryption and signing that must be kept secret.

Public Key   The key from the public key cryptography key pair used for encryption and signature verification that can be revealed to the public.

Public Key Cryptography   A cipher that uses a public/private key pair for encryption or digital signature. For encryption, a source uses the destination public key to encrypt data that the destination can decrypt using its private key.

Remoting   The collection of techniques used to perform any remote functions including remote execution and messaging.

Simple Object Access Protocol   See **SOAP**.

Singlecall   A mode used for wellknown server activated objects, indicating that each method call will receive a new instance of the server object. This also implies that the server object is Stateless since it is recreated (without any parameters passed to its constructor) just before each method invocation.

Singleton   A mode used for wellknown server activated objects, indicating that all clients and all method calls will share a single instance of the server object. This also implies that the server object is Stateful since it is not disposed of or recreated in between method invocations.

SOAP A mechanism for implementing remote method invocation using XML to marshall and unmarshall the parameters and return values. Previous releases considered this an acronym but now it is the official name of the specification itself rather than an acronym or abbreviation.

Subsystem A collection of components and/or subsystems that is part of a larger system but also a system in its own right.

Transaction Attribute A method of controlling the JTA Transaction actions for BMT EJB by specifying one of six possible values for the attribute using a Java annotation or EJB deployment descriptor.

Universal Description, Discovery, and Integration (UDDI) A facility that implements Directory Services for web services, providing an XML-based registry service suitable for finding web service instances deployed within the environment and defined using WSDL.

Unmanaged Component The opposite of a managed component, a piece of software that does not use the CLR to manage its runtime environment, and therefore does not run inside the Microsoft .NET Framework-based platform—although it can still coexist and interact with managed components that do run that way.

Unmarshalling The collection of techniques capable of converting a data stream into one or more parameters, usually to support RMI, RPC, or Messaging—the opposite of marshalling.

Web Service A component or subsystem that provides some service that conforms to the web services specification, usually implemented using SOAP, UDDI, WSDL, and XML.

Web Services Description Language (WSDL) An XML-based description of the services and service providers implemented as web services within an environment.

Wellknown Server Activated Object A remote object whose lifetime is controlled by the server. This means that it is created and destroyed on the server (by the code that is also executing on the server) in order to support .NET Remoting. It can have one of two possible modes: singleton or singlecall.

XML A markup language that uses tagging to indicate semantic details or logical structure for a set of data content.

REFERENCES

[Chandra05]   Chandra, S. S., and Chandra, K., "A Comparison of Java and C#," *Journal of Computing Sciences in Colleges*, Vol. 20, No. 3, pp. 238254, 2005.

[Costa05]   Costa, R., and Rohou, E., "Comparing the Size of .NET Applications with Native Code," in *Proceedings of the 3rd IEEE/ACM/IFIP International Conference on Hardware/Software Codesign and System Synthesis*, Jersey City, NJ, September 19–21. CODES+ISSS '05. ACM, New York, 2005, pp. 99104.

EXERCISES

Provide short (but complete) answers to the following questions.

18.1 What is the difference between managed and unmanaged components?

18.2 What is the difference between an assembly and a module?

18.3 What is the difference between an Application Domain and the CLR?

18.4 Why do signed assemblies need to have a strong name?

18.5 Since the Global Assembly Cache (GAC) is such a powerful deployment facility, should we use it to deploy all of our assemblies? Why or why not?

18.6 Suppose we have two variables containing two different instances of the same class type, but one was marshalled by value and the other was marshalled by reference (let's call them "objByVal" and "objByRef," respectively). Name three ways in which these two variables might behave differently in the same piece of code, based solely on their marshalling differences. (*Hint*: Consider both the local and remote object scenarios for these objects.)

19

THE DNET STARTER KIT

We refer to the combination of a framework and a sample extension (of that framework) as a **starter kit (SKIT)** because we intend to use this combination of software as a toolkit that will help us to start developing software projects. SKITs are not intended to be complete solutions, or production ready code, but the starter kits provided with this book should be useful when learning about **distributed database environment (DDBE)** concepts, and helpful when creating academic, research, prototype, or proof-of-concept projects. Starter kits like this one can also help us to improve our understanding of the specific DDBE architecture that we are attempting to develop, as well as the underlying technical facilities we can use, and the technical issues we need to address.

In this chapter, we are considering the starter kit that we call the DNET-SKIT. The DNET-SKIT is available for download via the official website for this book (see the Preface for further details). We named the starter kit this way because both the framework and the extension contained within it rely on the **Microsoft .NET ("Dot Net") Framework**, which is a platform provided by Microsoft (and others) for several flavors of operating systems, especially Microsoft Windows-based operating systems.

This chapter is intended to be a high-level overview of the starter kit, but it is not intended to be a detailed description of the implementation details. The bundle downloaded from the website contains all the source code, documentation, and example configuration files for the DNET-SKIT. It also contains a "cookbook" (a document containing a collection of "recipes") that describes how to use the starter kit in some common Microsoft Windows-based operating systems and offers hints for how to customize the starter kit to work in other scenarios and platform implementation alternatives.

In Section 19.1, we will discuss the high-level considerations for the DNET-SKIT, beginning with a description of the starter kit's goals and its architecture. Next, we will provide separate architectural overviews for the starter kit as a whole and the

Distributed Database Management Systems by Saeed K. Rahimi and Frank S. Haug
Copyright © 2010 the IEEE Computer Society

subsystems that are all implemented within the extension. In Section 19.2, we will focus on the design details for the starter kit as a whole, and then focus on the design details for the framework and extension individually. Lastly, in Section 19.3, we will summarize how the starter kit can be used to create DDBE projects that reuse, modify, extend, or replace the code provided by the DNET-SKIT.

19.1   DNET-SKIT OVERVIEW

The primary purpose of this starter kit is **component or subsystem (COS)** software development, especially within the context of a distributed database environment. Obviously, if we want to do this sort of development, we need to understand distributed database concepts and issues. This book helps to address some of those topics. In addition to understanding what a distributed database environment is, we need to have a basic understanding of at least one of the many programming languages supported in the Microsoft .NET Framework-based environment. After all, we cannot write DDBE programs without a programming language! Lastly, we must have at least some familiarity with the fundamental concepts and issues related to the Microsoft .NET Framework-based platform and its underlying subplatforms, features, and facilities. Ideally, many of the underlying details and issues should be hidden behind (and handled by) the starter kit. Because of this, we should be able to use this starter kit effectively even if we only have a minimal understanding of the platform concepts (see Chapter 18 for a high-level summary of the platform concepts involved).

When considering which release of the Microsoft .NET Framework-based platform we should choose as the target for all our development, deployment, and execution activities within a DDBE project, there are several different implementation alternatives available. The files included with this starter kit are designed to work with the Microsoft .NET Framework release 2.0 or later, and they have been configured for this implementation alternative by default. It should be possible (and relatively simple) to use the files contained within this starter kit with any of the later releases, provided we follow the instructions in the release notes appropriately. Most of the time, the new releases of the Microsoft .NET Framework platform should maintain backwards compatibility. As we mentioned in Chapter 18, the newer releases of the platform should also always contain the older releases as a subset. This combined with the ability to configure the precise version of the CLR used by each assembly we deploy should cover most cases. Now that we have considered all these caveats, we can also recognize the fact that the code we are implementing for the DNET-SKIT and our custom DDBE project extensions will typically be using only the fundamental services that should have no update issues. Therefore, our code should be able to port to multiple releases with little or no issues—except for those DDBE projects where we used more complex, sophisticated, or release-dependent functionality.

Once we have developed and/or deployed some of our DDBE projects, we need to consider the act of applying new updates to our systems carefully. Whenever we update the operating system or platform software installed on the machines within our environment, we should choose a single test machine before we update all of our other machines. Using this test machine, we should try to recompile the existing code, deploy it locally, and perform regression tests. Ideally, if this first test succeeds, we should test the newly compiled code across at least two test machines, before we officially change the configuration for all the machines we use to develop, deploy, and execute our DDBE projects.

19.1.1 DNET-SKIT Goals

If we decided to implement a new DDBE project directly on top of the Microsoft .NET Framework-based platform, it would certainly be doable. As we discussed in Chapter 18, the platform provides several alternatives for many of our DDBE Platform Requirements. Therefore, we could certainly start a project this way. At some later point, we could then move on to another project, and perhaps later still we would move on to yet another project after that, and so on. However, if we want to reuse our code between multiple projects, we need to take some steps to ensure that we plan for this reuse. We are not referring to the concept of a shared assembly (see Section 18.1.4)—that is a deployment consideration while this is a design consideration. Instead, we are referring to the more general concept of purposely designing code for reusability. Similarly, if we wanted to implement some portion of an existing project differently, or if we wanted to try some new technique for an existing subsystem, we would need to refactor our code if we had not planned for this ahead of time. In essence, using the DDBE Platform **directly** is not our ideal solution—our ideal solution in these scenarios involves creating DDBE components and subsystems that are reusable and extensible, which just happen to use the DDBE Platform directly.

We intend the framework and extension bundled within the DNET-SKIT to be used as the basis for building the skeleton of one or more DDBE architectures, precisely so that we can create projects in the manner we just identified as our ideal solution. Our goals with this starter kit are similar to the goals we identified for the J2EE-SKIT: namely, we wish to encapsulate and leverage the underlying DDBE Platform capabilities with only a minimal amount of implementation-specific (Microsoft .NET Framework-specific) concepts being visible or required in the extension code. If our DDBE developers are Microsoft .NET Framework experts, our starter kit will not prevent them from using advanced concepts—in fact, they should be able to do this more easily than nonexperts could. Contrariwise, if our DDBE developers are not Microsoft .NET Framework experts, then our starter kit should help get things started much more quickly than they would if we were using the platform directly without the starter kit.

The example extension included within the SKIT is intended to be usable for the widest set of DDBE projects, rather than the most powerful or sophisticated subset of DDBE projects. This should enable novices to implement simple projects easily. At the same time, advanced users should not find it too difficult to extend the example or the framework to address the more complicated distributed database environment scenarios. Because we have the source code for all framework and extension code, we can even selectively choose which portions to reuse and which portions to replace within a given project.

19.1.2 DNET-SKIT Architectural Overview

At first glance, the DNET-SKIT looks very similar to the J2EE-SKIT. This should not be surprising, since they are both attempts to implement an extensible framework for distributed database environment component and subsystem development! However, even at the architectural level, there are some subtle differences—we will not perform a "blow-by-blow" comparison of the two starter kits because that would not serve any purpose, but we will highlight some differences throughout our discussion in both chapters. The DNET-SKIT represents the fundamental infrastructure of a generic distributed database environment, using the same essential subsystem names and functions as the J2EE-SKIT did in Chapter 17. We use a separate Microsoft .NET Framework namespace for each subsystem in this infrastructure to make it easier to isolate those portions of the architecture and code, which we need to modify or extend. The main component in each subsystem is represented by two interfaces. There are also several other interfaces used within each subsystem, since each of them shares information with at least one other subsystem.

There are two interfaces for each service-provider subsystem in the starter kit. This is because we are using a special design pattern, the **Abstract Factory** [Gamma95]. In this pattern, the term "abstract" refers to the technique of "programming to interface." When a caller needs to reference an object or invoke a method, it uses the interface rather than the class. Because interfaces do not contain any implementation details, they are "abstract." Here, we have two interfaces: one for a factory and one for a product. This means that the caller uses an abstract factory to create an abstract product. In our case, each factory will create one of our service-provider subsystems. We will use an interface to access the factory and an interface to access the subsystem instance it returns. The caller obtains the factory object through other means, in this case .NET Remoting. As shown in Figure 19.1, the caller uses the factory interface (IDdbmsFactory) to access the factory object. The caller invokes a method defined within the factory interface to create the product, which is then returned using the product's interface (IDdbms).

This has several important advantages, especially within our distributed database environment and starter kit. In particular, the caller code does not need to have access to the implementation classes for the factory or the product—only the interfaces are required. Since we are using .NET Remoting, this is an ideal design pattern for us. Without this pattern, our caller would be tightly coupled to the concrete implementation

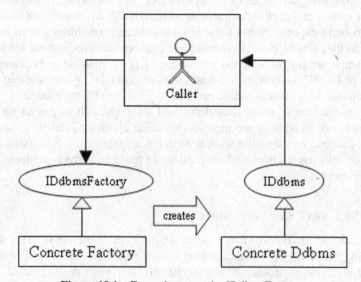

Figure 19.1   Example usage the IDdbmsFactory.

of the factory and/or product. In other words, without this pattern, it would be very difficult to redefine or replace the "Concrete Factory" or "Concrete Ddbms" shown in Figure 19.1 without recompiling our caller. With the pattern, we have no such issue. By using this pattern, we do not need to deploy the assembly containing the "Concrete Factory" or "Concrete Ddbms" on the caller machine. The caller can also be locally deployed or remotely deployed.

Since we are usually using remote callers and .NET Remoting, the two solid arrows in the diagram are actually the marshalling and unmarshalling of parameters and results for Remote-Code Execution. This means that another design pattern is being used, the **Proxy** [Gamma95]. The objects used by the caller are not merely a different interface to the real implementation—they are proxies. They simply forward the requests to the real object, and similarly forward real object's responses back to the caller. See Figure 19.2. This means that none of the implementation-specific code (and none of

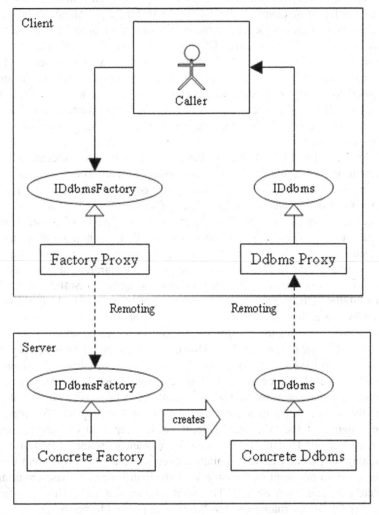

Figure 19.2   The IDdbmsFactory showing proxies.

the other code that it needs to reference) needs to be sent back and forth. When we execute a method in the Ddbms object, we want that method to execute remotely (not on the caller's machine) and therefore the proxy is crucial to this process.

In this starter kit, the framework provides implementation classes for very few constructs—the framework portion is mostly interfaces. However, the example extension bundled with the starter kit includes implementations for the subsystems. These classes can be modified directly, or extended via inheritance within new DDBE projects, but they are not the only possible implementation. There are seven subsystems included in the starter kit, and each one is represented by two interfaces (one abstract factory and one abstract product) in the framework. There are also two classes in the extension for each (the concrete factory and concrete product). The interfaces are defined in the framework, while the classes are implemented in the extension.

Because we have access to the source code for both the framework and the extension, we could refactor the code and relocate these subsystems if desired. However, we purposely chose these locations. In our DDBE project implementation, we can choose from several different mechanisms for DDBE Platform Requirements implementation. In particular, we can choose several different flavors of Remote-Code Execution. We can use ASP .NET, .NET Remoting, COM+, web services, or DCOM, just to name a few examples. We chose to use .NET Remoting for the example extension provided with the starter kit, but that is not the only possible choice. Because the interfaces can be reused for many of these other alternatives, it makes sense to define them in the framework. However, because the .NET Remoting implementation for the service providers is only one possible implementation, it makes sense to define these classes within the extension.

Recall from Section 18.2.1.1 that, within this implementation alternative, there are three different options available. In .NET Remoting, we can choose from two forms of server activated objects or one form of client-activated objects. In all three cases, we are working with a remote object—the distinction focuses on the activation and lifetime controls for the object. Server activated objects are called "wellknown" server activated objects, and they can be either **singleton** or **singlecall**. The singleton approach creates a single instance that serves all possible clients. The singlecall approach creates a new object every time a method is invoked via the proxy—regardless of how many or few callers are present. In effect, this also means that the singleton is **Stateful**, while the singlecall is **Stateless**. Client-activated server objects are simply called "activated." They are created by the caller using the normal constructor and disposed of by the caller. Even though the caller uses the constructor, the object is created remotely and its methods are executed on the remote machine. However, using a client-activated server object forces the caller to have access to the implementation classes (assemblies) locally on the same machine as the caller, and to be tightly coupled with the implementation class.

Therefore, we did not want to use the client-activated server objects alternative. However, the wellknown objects are also somewhat inappropriate for our purpose. Since the instance of the "Concrete Ddbms" object represents a single connection, or session within our DDBE project, we do not want to share a single object (singleton) among all DdbmsClients! Similarly, even if we do not implement distributed transactions, we do not want our session with the distributed database environment to be completely Stateless (singlecall). This would mean that all session-specific details (including the DDBE username and password) would need to be passed as parameters to each DDBE method call!

Using the Abstract Factory and Proxy design patterns together allows us to avoid many of these potential issues. Therefore, we can use either the singleton or singlecall to create our concrete factory and return the abstract factory interface to the concrete factory's proxy object. We then use the create product method defined in the abstract factory to connect to the remote concrete factory and create the concrete product on the remote machine. The abstract product interface representing the concrete product's proxy object is then returned to the caller. Since the factory is only used to create the product, it can be either Stateful or Stateless—once the product has been returned, we do not use the factory again until we need another product. Because the concrete factory is created by the client, it is like the client-activated server object, except that we do not have the tight coupling or the need to deploy the implementation assembly on the caller's machine.

The other .NET Remote-Code Execution alternatives we mentioned have more complex deployment and development considerations than the .NET Remoting approach. Therefore, we did not choose to implement the example with any of those approaches. However, by implementing the subsystems in the extension, rather than in the framework, we have made it easier to change these alternatives on a per-project basis, or even a per-subsystem basis. The alternative we chose as our default (.NET Remoting) should be suitable for most typical academic projects for a course in distributed database management systems. It should also be appropriate for most DDBE projects that are not primarily focused on deployment and remote execution considerations.

19.1.2.1 *DNET-SKIT Component Identification*

Table 19.1 contains a brief summary for each of the seven major subsystems defined within the starter kit. The starter kit provides a simple implementation for each of these subsystems in the extension. However, as we discussed in the previous section, each service-provider subsystem is accessed via two interfaces, which are defined in the framework. Table 19.1 lists the subsystem name, abstract factory interface name, abstract product interface name, and a brief description of the subsystem.

Although the implementations are not intended to be complete, they do illustrate some of the common mechanisms available for configuration, deployment, and execution. We should recognize that these are merely starting points for the final implementations. This way, on a project-by-project basis, we can chose to reuse the simple implementations for those areas that we are not focused on in the project and create our own more detailed designs and implementations for those areas that we are focused on. These example implementations also allow us to develop simple prototypes and proof-of-concept projects quickly.

The subsystems in the extension provided with the starter kit provide a minimal implementation for the fundamental operations necessary in a generic DDBE architecture. In particular, they act as yet another design pattern, namely, the Template Method [Gamma95], connecting the subsystems together in a reasonable (but modifiable and extensible) configuration. This is almost identical to the way the subsystems in the J2EE-SKITs work. However, here the design pattern is implemented in the extension instead of the framework. We will not repeat the discussion from Chapter 17 here, but if we consider the DNET-SKIT extension code as well as the framework code, then the points raised in Section 17.1.2.1 are equally relevant here.

TABLE 19.1   Summary of the Primary Subsystems Defined Within the SKIT

Subsystem Name	Abstract Factory Interface Name	Abstract Product Interface Name	Subsystem Description
DdbmsClient	N/A	N/A	This subsystem represents the client application or user interface to the distributed database environment we are implementing. Because it is not a service provider, it does not have any Abstract Factory pattern interfaces, only an implementation.
Ddbms	IDdbmsFactory	IDdbms	This is the "facade" to the distributed database environment that we create.
Parser	IParserFactory	IParser	This subsystem is a simple SQL parser implementing a subset of the ANSI standard SQL language. It also provides a simplistic interface inspired by relational algebra.
Qualifier	IQualifierFactory	IQualifier	This subsystem ensures that all the table names and column names identified by the parser are fully qualified.
Planner	IPlannerFactory	IPlanner	This subsystem builds the distributed execution plan for the statement being processed.
Dem	IDemFactory	IDem	This subsystem acts as a Distributed Execution Manager and executes the plan generated by the Planner subsystem.
Lem	ILemFactory	ILem	This subsystem acts as a Local Execution Manager executing the localized portions of the plan on behalf of the Dem subsystem.

19.1.2.2   DNET-SKIT Subsystem Interaction Overview   The Ddbms subsystem acts as a "facade," the public interface, to the whole DDBE project. The various types of transparencies implemented in the project are achieved by ensuring that this subsystem's interface looks as close to a traditional DBMS interface as possible (in form if not in scope). The Ddbms subsystem fulfills client requests by delegating the requests to the other subsystems. The Ddbms subsystem does not actually do any of the real work itself. The client can connect to the distributed database environment and pass a request as an SQL string, or use a parameterized call representing the statement type and major operands. If an SQL string is passed from the client, then the parser is used to parse the SQL. If the parameterized call is used instead, then a different method within the Parser is called to load the appropriate information.

Let's consider a typical scenario, where some client application has connected to the Ddbms subsystem and asked it to process an SQL SELECT query against the distributed database environment. Suppose that the abstract factories have already been set up and the abstract products and proxies are already created and returned to the caller before we begin our scenario.

Our DDBE project will perform the following steps, in the order listed here:

1. The DdbmsClient (or a similar component or subsystem) makes a query request of the Ddbms subsystem sending it an SQL string or the equivalent set of relational algebra-based details. This is done via a method invocation through the abstract product interface (IDdbms) for the Ddbms subsystem. Within the next steps, the Ddbms subsystem will call the other subsystems to satisfy the client's request. First, it calls the Parser, using its abstract product interface (IParser). Next, it calls the Qualifier (using IQualifier). Then, it calls the Planner (using IPlanner). Finally, it calls the Dem (using IDem), which presumably calls the Lem subsystems, but those details are probably project dependent.

2. The Parser (like all the subsystems in this SKIT) is an extension subsystem. We emphasize the point here because this is in contrast to the Parser subsystem for the J2EE-SKIT. If the call accepting an SQL string is implemented, it takes a request as an SQL string and checks that the request is supported and that the syntax is valid with respect to the grammar that the parser implementation understands. If the syntax is valid, the Parser transforms the request into a structure containing the necessary details before returning it to the caller. If the other methods are called, then the same result is obtained, but no actual parsing is required.

3. The Ddbms passes the information, which it just obtained from the Parser, to the Qualifier via the IQualifier interface. The Qualifier then uses this information in combination with other information (presumably described within a global data dictionary or obtained using some similar mechanism) to further transform the request. It augments the parser information with the physical data-mapping details it has been able to determine.

4. Next, the Ddbms passes the information returned by the Qualifier to the Planner via the IPlanner interface. The Planner uses this information to satisfy all of its information needs, and then uses its own algorithms to create the execution plan.

5. Lastly, the Ddbms passes the Planner's results to the Dem, which is responsible for overseeing the execution of the request. The starter kit implementation for the Dem is invoked via the IDem interface. Once it has been invoked, it merely reads the plan information and uses the ILem interface to pass most of the work details to the Lems. If the request was a query, the Dem collects and formats the results (if any) before returning the results to the Ddbms. Finally, the Ddbms returns the results, execution status, or exceptions to the client application that invoked the original request.

19.1.3   DNET-SKIT Extension Architectural Overview

All of the subsystems are implemented in the extensions, either in the starter-kit-supplied extension or in a new extension that we create for our new DDBE project implementation. In some respects, we are free to make design/implementation decisions that differ from the starter kit implementation, as long as the implementation still fulfills the requirements set forth by the framework-defined interfaces. The starter kit extension provides a reasonable implementation for each subsystem, but these are not necessarily the best implementation alternatives with respect to features, performance, or flexibility. The goal of the starter kit extensions is merely to support sufficient complexity to verify the operation of the framework or DDBE project as a whole and to demonstrate the feasibility of a typical DDBE project implementation.

As part of the deployment process for each subsystem, we must edit the deployment details. This is necessary to ensure that our newly deployed subsystem instance is connecting to the correct platform services (databases, etc.) and the correct instances for the other subsystems in the project. In particular, the remoting details need to be changed to ensure that the channels, ports, and Uniform Resource Locators (URLs) used to connect the proxy objects to the abstract factory interfaces and concrete factory objects are not in conflict with other subsystems deployed within our environment. When multiple subsystems are deployed on the same machine, we must ensure that the configuration details for the wellknown and activated server objects match the configuration details used by each client attempting to connect to them. In a typical DNET-SKIT deployment, the server details need to be checked for all subsystems, but the client details only need to be checked for the DdbmsClient, Ddbms, and Dem subsystems.

19.1.3.1 *The Ddbms Subsystem*

This is the external application–programming interface (API) for our DDBE project. As we mentioned earlier it acts as a "facade" to the DDBE project. More precisely, it acts as a Facade design pattern [Gamma95] for the distributed database environment as a whole. It provides the end-user applications with the publicly available methods for using the distributed database environment and acts as a single access point for the end-user applications. By using this subsystem, we can simplify our client Remote-Code Execution operations. Our clients connect to this subsystem rather than connecting to each of the other subsystems directly. Since this subsystem provides most of the communication to the other subsystems, it must be deployed as a separate instance for each new DDBE project. However, aside from the configuration file changes needed in redeployment, this subsystem should be reusable by most new projects with minimal (if any) code modification or recompilation required.

19.1.3.2 *The Parser Subsystem*

The Parser subsystem is responsible for recognizing valid SQL statements, rejecting malformed or unsupported SQL statements, and producing a data structure that captures the semantic information for the valid SQL statements it can recognize. Since this subsystem is only invoked by the Ddbms subsystem, and only communicates to the other subsystems indirectly, it is probably reusable for many new projects without any code modifications. It returns an object that is accessed via an interface to the calling subsystem (Ddbms), which then passes the information to the other subsystems as needed. Therefore, we usually will not need to perform any deployment edits, code modification, or recompilation for this subsystem.

We can even use the same deployed instance of this subsystem across several different DDBE projects that are deployed within the same environment. Alternatively, we can replace or modify this subsystem as necessary to add support for new commands or to support new syntax. If we need to support more complex clauses but are not very proficient with respect to parsing techniques, we can simply implement traditional method calls instead. For example, we can include special methods to implement explicit transaction control, locking requests, or whatever functionality we need to add to our project. We can also choose to add methods such as these to the IDdbms interface instead, or to add them in both places.

19.1.3.3 The Qualifier Subsystem The Qualifier subsystem is responsible for translating the information produced by the Parser subsystem into a format suitable for use by the Planner subsystem. Because the Qualifier identifies the Global Conceptual Tables and Global Conceptual Columns referenced in a distributed command request, it is a project-dependent subsystem. Like the DDbms subsystem, the deployment-specific details are probably relegated to the database containing the GDD and the configuration file that points this subsystem at the right GDD. However, this does make the subsystem instance somewhat less reusable. This means that we will probably need to redeploy the subsystem for new projects in order to change the configuration details—even though the code can be reused in most cases. Of course, if a DDBE project requires a different degree of transparency, or supports more sophisticated transparency alternatives (fragmentation, replication, or location details), then we may need to implement custom code for this subsystem in addition to deploying a project-specific GDD.

19.1.3.4 The Planner Subsystem The Planner subsystem uses the information produced by the Qualifier subsystem to build a distributed plan. This subsystem shares a strong dependency relationship with the Qualifier and the Dem subsystems. Because the Qualifier details depend on the transparency design and implementation details for the project, and the Planner subsystem shares this dependency as well, these subsystems seem to be coupled more tightly than the others we have discussed so far. For example, if the Qualifier supports replication, then the Planner needs to support it as well. However, if the Qualifier has any restrictions or limitations then this can also affect the Planner. For example, what if the Qualifier supports table replication but does not support fragment replication? Because the Planner must read and interpret the Qualifier's output, the Planner is necessarily affected by the Qualifier. Therefore, the reusability of this component will depend on the modifications made to the Qualifier.

19.1.3.5 The Dem Subsystem This subsystem is responsible for reading the plan created by the Planner and carrying it out. Although the Dem is dependent on the Planner for reasons similar to those we discussed in the previous section, it is not coupled too tightly to the Planner or the Lem—in part, because the plan is merely read (followed) and the example Dem implementation does not perform any optimization activities. Similarly, although the Dem tells the Lem subsystems what to do, the coupling is loose in the extension implementation. Obviously, this situation can change drastically in a DDBE project where we focus on optimization or execution control.

19.1.3.6 The Lem Subsystem The Lem is responsible for carrying out the pieces of the global statement at a particular Lem instance (a local database at a particular site). The global statement will be broken into pieces by the Planner subsystem and delegated to the Lem by the Dem subsystem. The pieces of this global statement will typically be of the same type. In other words, a global query will usually result in one or more local queries; a global INSERT will usually result in one or more local INSERTS; and so on. The Lem can implement these operations in any way that it needs to, but typically, we would expect the Lem to leverage the facilities implemented by a local database management system (LDBMS) and accessed via the ADO.NET, OLEDB, and ODBC facilities. Although this is the technique used within the starter kit implementation, new projects can also choose to implement the operations in radically different ways. The Lem is essentially a data processor (DP), which means we can implement it in any of the ways we discussed in Chapter 1. In particular, we can use any of the alternatives we discussed in Section 1.3 and summarized in Figure 1.6.

19.2   DNET-SKIT DESIGN OVERVIEW

In this section, we will highlight some of the design details for each subsystem, and, in particular, we will identify the primary interfaces being used. This section will serve as a high-level roadmap for the code contained in the starter kit—the low-level documentation is provided with the code (and generated from it using XML Documentation Comments). From this high-level vantage point, we can consider the code to be divided into two major categories: the framework and the extension. Within the framework, we will look at three subareas, while the extension will contain seven subareas. Although namespaces within the Microsoft .NET Framework-based platform do not need to be tied to assemblies in a one-to-one fashion, we chose to do so for the starter kit. Even though the platform allows multiple namespaces within the same assembly and multiple assemblies within the same namespace, we did not do this in the starter kit. Instead, we have a separate namespace for each of the ten subareas, and each namespace corresponds to a single assembly within the starter kit.

19.2.1   DNET-SKIT Framework Design Overview

The framework contains no subsystems, but it does contain the assemblies that are used by one or more of the subsystems in the starter kit. In particular, there are three subareas within the framework, each of which is implemented using a separate namespace. The assembly name for each of these subareas is named using the namespace value.

The three subareas in the framework are the following:

- The framework interfaces area
- The framework exceptions area
- The framework parameters area

19.2.1.1   The Framework Interfaces Area   The framework interfaces area defines the abstract factory interface and abstract product interface for each of the six subsystems in the starter kit. There are no interfaces defined for the Ddbms Client subsystem, because it is not a service provider. The namespace for this area ("Srdbsoft.Ddbe.DnetSkit.Framework.Interface") which is also the name of the assembly that contains the compiled code for these interfaces. The interfaces are listed in Table 19.1, without the namespace details. All of these interfaces are in the same namespace.

If changes need to be made to the interfaces in this area, we have two options. We can choose to modify this assembly directly or we can choose to use a new assembly instead. If we choose to modify the assembly, we can either modify the existing interfaces or create new ones. Similarly, if we choose to modify the existing interfaces we can choose to modify the existing methods or we can create new ones. Obviously, whenever we change things directly, there is a potential for breaking other code. Therefore, we should take great care when modifying things in this area. Whenever possible, we should consider augmenting rather than modifying (adding but not modifying or deleting) these interfaces. We can also use inheritance to extend the interfaces in a more portable fashion. Ultimately, we can even choose to abandon the interfaces here completely. All of these choices are valid, but they have very different maintenance and reusability impacts.

19.2.1.2   The Framework Exceptions Area   Even though we should always try to use meaningful exception classes to represent all the possible, expected problems that our DDBE project might encounter, we also want to be able to create reusable code that is easy to use for prototype and proof-of-concept implementation projects. One way to achieve this is to use a common superclass for our exceptions. This makes it easier to wrap the derived classes and handle the exceptions by sacrificing some of the ability to ensure more detailed exception handling within the code. Because we can use different programming languages in this platform, the restrictions and rules for exception handling can vary somewhat. However, as a rule, exceptions in this platform are not the same as exceptions in Java. In particular, Java requires exceptions to be declared as "throws" clauses while this is not required for many Microsoft .NET Framework-compatible languages. Regardless, we like the idea of using clear exception class names in the starter kit. Because the naming convention in the popular programming languages for this platform (and, in particular, in Visual C#) is to avoid Hungarian notation, we did not use the same naming convention that we used for the J2EE SKIT. Instead, each class representing an exception has a name that ends with a common suffix (the word "Extension"). The classes in this area use a shared namespace ("Srdbsoft.Ddbe.DnetSkit.Framework.Interface.Exceptions"), which is also used as the assembly name. Note that the name looks like it is a subset of the previous namespace. This is intentional but somewhat misleading. From a development and deployment perspective, these assemblies and namespaces are independent of each other. However, they are, of course, conceptually connected to each other and therefore we feel that the naming is appropriate. Table 19.2 lists the unqualified names for all the base-class names for the exceptions in this area.

19.2.1.3   The Framework Parameters Area   We define a separate namespace and assembly for all the interfaces and classes used to represent the parameter types in the starter kit. These interfaces are used to represent the parameters that we pass between the subsystems in the starter kit extension. Most of these interfaces are actually implemented by classes within specific subsystems. The namespace for this area

TABLE 19.2   Subsystem-Specific Exception Base-Class Summary

Subsystem	Unqualified Exception Base-Class Name
DdbmsClient	DdbmsClientException
Ddbms	DdbmsException
Parser	ParserException
Qualifier	QualifierException
Planner	PlannerException
Dem	DemException
Lem	LemException

("Srdbsoft.Ddbe.DnetSkit.Framework.Interface.Parameters.") is obvious and intuitive. Once again, this is also the name for the assembly that contains the compiled code for these interfaces and classes. While we will not list all the interface and class names here, we will highlight the names of the most visible interfaces. This is done in part for parallelism with the J2EE-SKIT, and also to demonstrate the naming convention followed for the DNET-SKIT. Interface names begin with an uppercase "I" and another uppercase letter. After that, the names use mixed case (not camel case), with common acronyms listed in Pascal case. For example, an acronym like "SQL" is written as "Sql" in the construct name.

IParsedSql   This interface is used as output by the Parser subsystem and as input by the Qualifier subsystem. It provides access to the Parser output for the rest of the distributed database environment in general and especially the Qualifier subsystem. We must be careful when we modify or extend this interface. In particular, we should never expose any of the implementation details. Therefore, we should ensure that this interface only provides read-only access to the contents. Otherwise, we introduce implementation dependencies that make it very difficult to use a different implementation for the subsystems in other projects. In other words, if we are not careful we can damage our reusability.

IQualifiedSql   This interface is used as output by the Qualifier subsystem and as input by the Planner subsystem. Like the previous example, this interface should be used to provide one subsystem with read-only access to the output generated by another subsystem. Once again, we are concerned about hiding implementation details and providing read-only access. We are also a little more concerned about supporting multiple implementation alternatives for this interface because the Qualifier subsystem is often modified or reimplemented for different projects.

IDet   This interface is used as output by the Planner subsystem and as input by the Dem subsystem. Although this is also a read-only, implementation-independent interface, we do have some design details exposed though this interface—namely, the fact that this interface is intended to represent a tree. This will place some limitations and restrictions on the implementation alternatives for the Planner subsystem, but we can always modify the framework if necessary.

IQueryResults   This interface is used as output by Dem subsystem, and as input by the Ddbms subsystem. This same interface is also used to represent the output of the Lem subsystem—therefore, the interface is not read-only. It includes methods for population (but not modification) to make it easier to share a common interface (and perhaps implementation) between the different subsystems. There are also .NET classes and interfaces that we could use to either replace this interface or implement the class that supports this interface, for example, the "System.Data.DataSet" class.

19.2.2   DNET-SKIT Extension Design Overview

As we discussed in Section 19.1.2, the starter kit implementations use a simple subsystem interaction strategy. In this strategy, most of the subsystems are service providers to the other subsystems in the framework but the Ddbms subsystem is the primary service consumer for these services. The Ddbms is the only subsystem that needs to connect to the Parser, Qualifier, Planner, and Dem subsystems. Although this strategy is somewhat simplistic, it should be useful for many typical DDBE project scenarios. The Lem subsystem is a special case. It is not directly called from the Ddbms subsystem; the Dem subsystem is its primary service consumer in most DDBE projects. However, it is also the subsystem most likely to change its interaction between projects. Suppose we are experimenting with different execution control strategies in a new DDBE project. Compare this with another DDBE project that focuses on query optimization. When we compare these two DDBE project scenarios with the interactions outlined in Section 19.2.1, it is easy to see that the Lem communication and interaction can vary greatly.

Even though these new interactions are not necessarily represented in the framework, they are also not forbidden by the framework. We can simply create new interfaces and use them in the specific subsystem implementations as necessary. Since all of these details are contained within the extension, they have little or no impact on any other projects based on the framework and original starter kit extension. Aside from the caveat we just mentioned for the Lem, almost all extension implementations will implement the same interfaces—namely, the interfaces defined in the framework and identified in this chapter. Even when our DDBE project chooses to implement the code behind one of these interfaces using a different class name, a different namespace, or different implementation details, the interfaces will not necessarily need to change. In particular, the abstract factory interface should only need to change in rare cases where we implement a radically different server object or Remote-Code Execution strategy.

In the starter kit extension, each subsystem is implemented as a separate assembly and deployed as a managed component stored as an EXE file. This deployment includes a simple graphical user interface (GUI), with minimal status reporting and user interaction. While this is not the recommended deployment or implementation for a production level distributed database environment, we feel that this approach is useful for the types of DDBE projects we want to create. We would never implement services in a real, production-level distributed database environment using GUI applications that require user interaction to begin their interactions with other subsystems. However, in prototype, experimental, and academic projects, it is useful to be able to control the components, perhaps even setting break points within the code to study how certain algorithms are processing things.

For each of the service-provider subsystems, we provide a brief summary, listing the fully qualified names for the abstract factory interface, the concrete factory class, the abstract product interface, the concrete class, and the name of the assembly used to deploy this subsystem.

19.2.2.1 The Ddbms Subsystem In Table 19.3, we list the type names used by the Ddbms subsystem. This subsystem is implemented using "wellknown" server object activation for the concrete factory object, which is accessed via the abstract factory interface. This interface has a single method defined within it ("CreateDdbms()"). This method creates a concrete product instance and returns it to the caller via the abstract product interface. Because both the concrete factory and the concrete product extend (inherit from) the "MarshalByRefObject" class, they actually return a proxy object and execute their methods on the server rather than in the caller's Application Domain (and physical machine in the case of a remote client and server). The abstract

TABLE 19.3   Type Names for Ddbms Subsystem

Type	Name
Abstract Factory	Srdbsoft.Ddbe.DnetSkit.Framework.Interface.IDdbmsFactory
Concrete Factory	Srdbsoft.Ddbe.DnetSkit.Framework.Extension.DdbmsServer.DdbmsFactory
Abstract Product	Srdbsoft.Ddbe.DnetSkit.Framework.Interface.IDdbms
Concrete Product	Srdbsoft.Ddbe.DnetSkit.Framework.Extension.DdbmsServer.Ddbms
Assembly Name	Srdbsoft.Ddbe.DnetSkit.Framework.Extension.DdbmsServer.exe

product interface contains methods for executing SQL query and SQL DML operations against the distributed database environment that the project using this subsystem implements.

> Namespaces and assemblies in this platform follow an informal set of naming conventions. While these are more suggestions or conventions than strict rules, we tried to adhere to them within the starter kit. For further details, search for "Guidelines for Names" in the online help within Visual Studio or on the Web. We can add the text, ".NET Framework Developer's Guide" to narrow our search if we are using the Web rather than the online help. Notice that this convention is somewhat similar, but actually quite different from the naming convention used by packages in Java.

19.2.2.2   The Parser Subsystem   In Table 19.4, we list the type names used by the Parser subsystem. This subsystem is implemented using "wellknown" server object activation for the concrete factory object, which is accessed via the abstract factory interface. This interface has a single method defined within it ("CreateParser()"). This method creates a concrete product instance and returns it to the caller via the abstract product interface. Because both the concrete factory and the concrete product extend (inherit from) the "MarshalByRefObject" class, they actually return a proxy object and execute their methods on the server rather than in the caller's Application Domain (and physical machine in the case of a remote client and server). The abstract product interface contains methods for parsing an SQL statement. The Ddbms subsystem will use this subsystem to validate an SQL statement and add semantic information. The Parser only needs to handle a single SQL statement at a time. The syntax supported will be a subset of the ANSI-92 syntax for SELECT, INSERT, UPDATE, and DELETE.

TABLE 19.4   Type Names for Parser Subsystem

Type	Name
Abstract Factory	Srdbsoft.Ddbe.DnetSkit.Framework.Interface.IParserFactory
Concrete Factory	Srdbsoft.Ddbe.DnetSkit.Framework.Extension.ParserServer.ParserFactory
Abstract Product	Srdbsoft.Ddbe.DnetSkit.Framework.Interface.IParser
Concrete Product	Srdbsoft.Ddbe.DnetSkit.Framework.Extension.ParserServer.Parser
Assembly Name	Srdbsoft.Ddbe.DnetSkit.Framework.Extension.ParserServer.exe

There will not be much, if any, support for functions or complex subclauses (subqueries, aggregate queries, order by clauses, having clauses, etc.), and there is no support for vendor-specific syntax or features. Arguably, this subsystem could also be deployed as a simple "wellknown" object because it is Stateless, but the abstract factory method pattern was used for architectural consistency also to help minimize the threading issues from multiple clients.

19.2.2.3 The Qualifier Subsystem   In Table 19.5, we list the type names used by the Qualifier subsystem. This subsystem is implemented using "wellknown" server object activation for the concrete factory object, which is accessed via the abstract factory interface. This interface has a single method defined within it ("CreateQualifier()"). This method creates a concrete product instance and returns it to the caller via the abstract product interface. Because both the concrete factory and the concrete product extend (inherit from) the "MarshalByRefObject" class, they actually return a proxy object and execute their methods on the server rather than in the caller's Application Domain (and physical machine in the case of a remote client and server). The abstract product interface contains methods for qualifying the results returned from the Parser subsystem. Because this subsystem will often be implemented using a GDD, it makes sense to leave this as a factory method implementation—this way we can deploy it wherever the qualification database is stored (regardless of whether the GDD is implemented traditionally or actually using some other alternative such as a GCS or GIS).

19.2.2.4 The Planner Subsystem   In Table 19.6, we list the type names used by the Planner subsystem. This subsystem is implemented using "wellknown" server object activation for the concrete factory object, which is accessed via the abstract factory interface. This interface has a single method defined within it ("CreatePlanner()"). This method creates a concrete product instance and returns it to the caller via the

TABLE 19.5   Type Names for Qualifier Subsystem

Type	Name
Abstract Factory	Srdbsoft.Ddbe.DnetSkit.Framework.Interface.IQualifierFactory
Concrete Factory	Srdbsoft.Ddbe.DnetSkit.Framework.Extension.QualifierServer. QualifierFactory
Abstract Product	Srdbsoft.Ddbe.DnetSkit.Framework.Interface.IQualifier
Concrete Product	Srdbsoft.Ddbe.DnetSkit.Framework.Extension.QualifierServer.Qualifier
Assembly Name	Srdbsoft.Ddbe.DnetSkit.Framework.Extension.QualifierServer.exe

TABLE 19.6   Type Names for Planner Subsystem

Type	Name
Abstract Factory	Srdbsoft.Ddbe.DnetSkit.Framework.Interface.IPlannerFactory
Concrete Factory	Srdbsoft.Ddbe.DnetSkit.Framework.Extension.PlannerServer.PlannerFactory
Abstract Product	Srdbsoft.Ddbe.DnetSkit.Framework.Interface.IPlanner
Concrete Product	Srdbsoft.Ddbe.DnetSkit.Framework.Extension.PlannerServer.Planner
Assembly Name	Srdbsoft.Ddbe.DnetSkit.Framework.Extension.PlannerServer.exe

abstract product interface. Because both the concrete factory and the concrete product extend (inherit from) the "MarshalByRefObject" class, they actually return a proxy object and execute their methods on the server rather than in the caller's Application Domain (and physical machine in the case of a remote client and server). The abstract product interface contains methods for creating an execution plan based on the results returned from the Qualifier subsystem. This subsystem is probably shared across several projects, unless they happen to focus on a specific planning area such as execution control or optimization. Therefore, the standard deployment strategy is appropriate for most projects.

19.2.2.5 The Dem Subsystem In Table 19.7, we list the type names used by the Dem subsystem. This subsystem is implemented using "wellknown" server object activation for the concrete factory object, which is accessed via the abstract factory interface. This interface has a single method defined within it ("CreateDem()"). This method creates a concrete product instance and returns it to the caller via the abstract product interface. Because both the concrete factory and the concrete product extend (inherit from) the "MarshalByRefObject" class, they actually return a proxy object and execute their methods on the server rather than in the caller's Application Domain (and physical machine in the case of a remote client and server). The abstract product interface contains methods for executing the execution plan returned from the Planner subsystem. There are probably several methods in this interface, at least to support the separation of queries from commands. This subsystem is highly dependent on the Planner and Lem subsystems. It can be reused or reimplemented on a per-project basis.

19.2.2.6 The Lem Subsystem In Table 19.8, we list the type names used by the Lem subsystem. This subsystem is implemented using "wellknown" server object activation for the concrete factory object, which is accessed via the abstract factory interface. This interface has a single method defined within it ("CreateLem()") This method creates a

TABLE 19.7 Type Names for Dem Subsystem

Type	Name
Abstract Factory	Srdbsoft.Ddbe.DnetSkit.Framework.Interface.IDemFactory
Concrete Factory	Srdbsoft.Ddbe.DnetSkit.Framework.Extension.DemServer.DemFactory
Abstract Product	Srdbsoft.Ddbe.DnetSkit.Framework.Interface.IDem
Concrete Product	Srdbsoft.Ddbe.DnetSkit.Framework.Extension.DemServer.Dem
Assembly Name	Srdbsoft.Ddbe.DnetSkit.Framework.Extension.DemServer.exe

TABLE 19.8 Suggested Type Names for Lem Subsystem

Type	Name
Abstract Factory	Srdbsoft.Ddbe.DnetSkit.Framework.Interface.ILemFactory
Concrete Factory	Srdbsoft.Ddbe.DnetSkit.Framework.Extension.LemServer.LemFactory
Abstract Product	Srdbsoft.Ddbe.DnetSkit.Framework.Interface.ILem
Concrete Product	Srdbsoft.Ddbe.DnetSkit.Framework.Extension.LemServer.Lem
Assembly Name	Srdbsoft.Ddbe.DnetSkit.Framework.Extension.LemServer.exe

concrete product instance and returns it to the caller via the abstract product interface. Because both the concrete factory and the concrete product extend (inherit from) the "MarshalByRefObject" class, they actually return a proxy object and execute their methods on the server rather than in the caller's Application Domain (and physical machine in the case of a remote client and server). The abstract product interface contains methods for executing the pieces of the execution plan as determined by the Dem subsystem. Typically, it should have one method for executing queries and one or more methods for executing DML statements. We can choose to implement separate methods for each type of DML, or we can choose to implement a single method to handle all DML statement execution.

We can define other methods that are specific to our DDBE project as well. For example, we might define different methods for different Lem implementations when they use different execution control strategies. Consider how the interface might need to be different when implementing a "master–slave" control strategy versus a "triangular" control strategy (see Section 1.7 of Chapter 1 for an example of these strategies). We can also choose to define our methods differently depending on the types of parameters we want to use. Suppose we choose to pass the local SQL commands and queries into the Lem subsystem as strings. If this were the case, then our method would have a String (the SQL statement) as a parameter. Similarly, if we decided to use a more relational algebra-flavored approach, we could still use a String parameter (here it would contain a relational algebra statement instead of an SQL statement). This is not the only possible approach, however. For example, we might choose to use several parameters representing the individual "pieces" required for the specific relational algebra operation, instead of a single String parameter. This would mean that an SQL SELECT statement would be translated into a relational algebra command using several specific arguments. In this scenario, we might define our method parameters to represent a list of columns to be projected, a list of tables to be joined, a list of the join conditions to be applied, and a list of non-join conditions to be selected. We might choose from several other approaches as well (perhaps a tree structure containing those operators and operations, etc.).

Therefore, it is likely that this subsystem will be redesigned and reimplemented in many DDBE projects. In those cases, we might use a completely different abstract product interface. However, this should really only affect the Dem subsystem implementation in most scenarios—the Dem abstract interfaces are probably not affected.

19.3 SUMMARY

Our DNET-SKIT consists of many classes and interfaces, which are in turn factored into several different assemblies. A subset of these classes and interfaces form a framework representing the fundamental subsystems within a typical DDBE project. The framework provides an overall infrastructure and implements some of the foundations for building a DDBE project. Although the framework can also be directly modified, we intend the framework to be extended through inheritance rather than reimplemented whenever it is not able to satisfy the needs of a particular set of project requirements. The other assemblies that are not part of the framework are part of an example extension that is also included within the starter kit. While we would expect these interfaces and classes to be usable as they are or extended through inheritance to satisfy the requirements for some projects, this will not be true for all projects. We would expect some projects to completely ignore the extension and simply implement all of their subsystem code directly when this is the case. The code implemented within the SKIT extension or any other project-specific extensions can then serve as a basis for new implementations, or merely as examples, in addition to fulfilling their own project-specific requirements.

In general, all executable content deployed within the platform is based on assemblies. In our starter kit, we chose to bundle the assemblies as separate EXE and DLL files. These files, combined with the configuration file for each subsystem, are then ready to be installed on a new system. As we discussed in Chapter 18, there are several options for deployment within the platform. The starter kit is compatible with most of these approaches, albeit with some additional steps required in some cases. All of the subsystems implemented in the starter kit use the Abstract Factory design pattern. The starter kit as a whole makes use of a few other design patterns as well in order to deploy the subsystems using "wellknown" server activation and .NET Remoting for our Remote-Code Execution Requirements. There are other deployment alternatives possible, as well as other Remote-Code Execution alternatives available within the platform, but these are not implemented within the starter kit. That said, many of these alternatives are compatible with the starter kit and can be used with only minor modifications. We feel that the other alternatives are more complicated and require more substantial implementation or design changes as well as additional deployment configuration. Because the starter kit is extendable, and because we have all the source code for it, we can always attempt to expand the framework or one of its extensions to address these other alternatives. That, however, is left as an exercise for the reader.

The DNET-SKIT includes further details, recipes, and suggestions for building, deploying, and executing our DDBE projects based on the framework provided—but these details cannot cover all the specific details for all possible platform installations. Instead, these documents provide an example of how we can compile, deploy, and execute the SKIT extension in a typical installation. There are also recipes for modifying the deployment details once we have successfully built and deployed the example extension within an environment. Although these recipes might not be identical to the steps required for a particular installation, they should provide sufficient details to enable us to translate the steps into the appropriate actions based on the installation-specific configuration details. Once we have succeeded in deploying the example, it should be reasonably simple to create a new project that modifies or extends the starter kit, and then to redeploy the resulting code.

19.4 GLOSSARY

Assembly The fundament unit of work for any deployment considerations in the Microsoft .NET Framework. Although assemblies can consist of multiple files, we usually bundle all the modules into a single file written in the Portable Executable (PE) format and save it as either a DLL or an EXE.

Base Class Library (BCL) The set of application–programming interfaces (APIs) used to connect managed components to the underlying services and subsystems provided by the Microsoft .NET Framework-based platform.

Client-Activated Server Object   A remote object whose lifetime is controlled by the client. This means that it is created and destroyed on the server by the code executing on the client in order to support .NET Remoting.

Component   A deployable bundle that provides a reasonably cohesive set of functionality.

Component or Subsystem (COS)   A term that refers to a component or subsystem, ignoring any differences between the two concepts.

Deployment   Any features, issues, concepts, or considerations related to how a COS instance is installed on a particular machine at a particular site.

Global Assembly Cache (GAC)   The machinewide container for shared assemblies.

Managed Component   A piece of software that is designed, implemented, and deployed in such a way that it can execute inside the Microsoft .NET Framework-based platform, with the CLR managing its runtime environment.

Marshalling   The collection of techniques capable of converting parameters into a data stream, usually to support RMI, RPC, or Messaging—the opposite of unmarshalling.

Platform   A set of software that provides a well-defined set of operations, facilities, and functionality that serves as the foundation for components, subsystems, and other software that runs on top of the platform.

Remoting   The collection of techniques used to perform any remote functions including remote execution and messaging.

Service   A logical collection (specification/design) of well-defined, cohesively related functionality or a software instance (physical collection) that implements this functionality.

Service Consumer   A component or subsystem that uses a set of functionality implemented by some other component or subsystem (consumes a service implemented by some service provider).

Service Provider   A component or subsystem that implements a set of functionality and makes it available to other components and subsystems (provides a service to be used by some service consumer).

Singlecall   A mode used for wellknown server activated objects, indicating that each method call will receive a new instance of the server object. This also implies that the server object is Stateless since it is recreated (without any parameters passed to its constructor) just before each method invocation.

Singleton   A mode used for wellknown server activated objects, indicating that all clients and all method calls will share a single instance of the server object. This also implies that the server object is Stateful since it is not disposed of or recreated in between method invocations.

Subsystem   A collection of components and/or subsystems that is part of a larger system but also a system in its own right.

Unmanaged Component   The opposite of a managed component—a piece of software that does not use the CLR to manage its runtime environment and therefore does not run inside the Microsoft .NET Framework-based platform, although it can still coexist and interact with managed components that do run that way.

Unmarshalling The collection of techniques capable of converting a data stream into one or more parameters, usually to support RMI, RPC, or Messaging—the opposite of marshalling.

Wellknown Server Activated Object A remote object whose lifetime is controlled by the server. This means that it is created and destroyed on the server (by the code that is also executing on the server) in order to support .NET Remoting. It can have one of two possible modes: singleton or singlecall.

XML A markup language that uses tagging to indicate semantic details or logical structure for a set of data content.

REFERENCE

[Gamma95] Gamma, E., Helm, R., Johnson, R., and Vlissides, J., *Design Patterns Elements of Reusable Object-Oriented Software* Addison-Wesley, Reading, MA, 1995.

EXERCISES

Complete the following programming exercises.

19.1 Download the DNET-SKIT and compile, deploy, and execute the example extension.

19.2 After consulting the vendor-specific documentation and the recipes supplied with the DNET-SKIT, modify the deployment details for the example extension to use a different database vendor for the Lem databases.

19.3 After consulting the vendor-specific documentation and the recipes supplied with the DNET-SKIT, modify the example extension and deploy the Ddbms subsystem on a different machine. Next, move one of the Lem subsystems to another machine.

19.4 Section 4.5.1 discussed query execution strategies, including a triangular control strategy, as shown in Figures 4.18 (b) and (c). Create a new DDBE project based on the DNET-SKIT that implements this triangular strategy for query execution—this does not need to be based on query optimization details, but can be either hard-coded to use a particular pattern or controlled by deployment-specific settings (settings specified in the GDD or in the deployment descriptors).

INDEX

Note: Page numbers in **bold** refer to definition of the term.

Distributed Database Management Systems by Saeed K. Rahimi and Frank S. Haug
Copyright © 2010 the IEEE Computer Society